SCALE 1:37 million

S0-BSH-664

© Thomas Nelson and Sons Ltd D 007 i

Map Labels

Zanzibar

Aldabra Is.

Comoro Islands

Madagascar

2876

Mozambique Channel

INDIAN OCEAN

L. Malawi

East

Valley

Rukwa

Mweru

Lualaba

Zambezi

Luangwa

Kariba Lake

Kafue Dam

Victoria Falls

Cuando

Cubango

Cuanza

Cunene

Okavango Swamps

L. Ngami

Limpopo

Kalahari

Vaal

High Veld

Orange

Drakensberg Mts

Karroo

C. Agulhas

C. of Good Hope

Namib Desert

Edge of Continental Shelf

Tropic of Capricorn

Zenithal Equal Area Projection

OCEAN

Ascension

St Helena

SCALE

0   500   1000   1500   Kms
0   500   1000 Miles

20°

40°

20°

0°

0°

Legend

feet	
	high mountain
10,000	mountain
6000	
3000	upland
1500	high plain
600	low plain
0	depression

AFRICA
IN THE NINETEENTH
AND TWENTIETH CENTURIES

Editors

Joseph C. Anene M.A., PH.D.

Professor of History,
Head of Department of History,
University of Ibadan

Godfrey N. Brown M.A., D.PHIL.

Professor of Education,
University of Ibadan

AFRICA
IN THE NINETEENTH
AND TWENTIETH CENTURIES

A Handbook for Teachers and Students

EDITED BY
JOSEPH C. ANENE
AND
GODFREY N. BROWN

With a Foreword by K. O. DIKE, M.A., PH.D., *Vice-Chancellor, University of Ibadan*

IBADAN UNIVERSITY PRESS
AND NELSON

THOMAS NELSON AND SONS LTD
36 Park Street London W1
P.O. Box 2187 Accra
P.O. Box 336 Apapa Lagos
P.O. Box 25012 Nairobi
P.O. Box 21149 Dar es Salaam
77 Coffee Street San Fernando Trinidad

THOMAS NELSON (AUSTRALIA) LTD
597 Little Collins Street Melbourne C1

THOMAS NELSON AND SONS (SOUTH AFRICA) (PROPRIETARY) LTD
P.O. Box 7331 Johannesburg

THOMAS NELSON AND SONS (CANADA) LTD
81 Curlew Drive Don Mills Ontario

THOMAS NELSON AND SONS
Copewood and Davis Streets Camden New Jersey 0813

———

17 511259 2

Printed in Great Britain by
Thomas Nelson (Printers) Ltd, London and Edinburgh

FOREWORD
by K. Onwuka Dike

THIS book epitomises a number of significant developments in Africa at the present time. It reflects the twentieth-century renascence of African culture. Too often in the past Africans have been more familiar with the history and mores of 'metropolitan' European countries than they have with the histories of their own peoples. This book helps to restore the African historical birthright. At the same time, however, it recognises the extent and the nature of the expatriate contribution which, of course, has been especially pronounced in the nineteenth and twentieth centuries. The overall coverage that is given to the whole continent of Africa in this book may also be considered as an expression of the widely prevalent concern to promote African unity. Divested of its political overtones, this in essence is a concern to foster good neighbourliness. By making known the histories of many of the varied peoples of Africa this book may extend the limits of this process of fraternisation. It represents an attempt to make available to those who are particularly interested the new orientation and some of the findings of the research that has been undertaken in African history of recent years.

Inevitably, in attempting so much, certain limitations have had to be accepted. The observant reader of this book will detect differences of emphasis and of degree of factual content between its various chapters. Whether difference of emphasis is desirable or not is a matter of opinion, but differences of factual substantiation are a matter of fact or, less tautologically, frequently an expression of the uneven incidence of historical study on the continent. There are, too, omissions—especially in respect of the Interlacustrine peoples of Central Africa and of the Spanish and Portuguese colonies—and there are some topics which in equity might have merited a more extensive treatment than they receive. Had the Editors been prepared to see the years roll by in the preparation of this book, they could undoubtedly have produced a better book. But it would not have been a more useful one. Anybody who is familiar with the secondary schools and universities of Africa today will know that this book helps to meet a clamant need. That is why it has been produced, from start to finish, in a matter of months. Given these circumstances most readers will probably agree that its utility and interest far outweigh its shortcomings.

In conclusion, it seems to me that this book is of more than African appeal. I very much hope that it will commend itself to readers outside Africa. In the past African universities have largely depended on books written in other continents. *Africa in the Nineteenth and Twentieth Centuries* will, I trust, be seen as one acceptable pledge of our universities' determination to repay this debt in kind.

Ibadan, July 1965

EDITORS' INTRODUCTION

BOOKS on history are inevitably by-products *of* history. Of few books could this be more obviously true than this. Along with its companion volume, *A Thousand Years of West African History* edited by J. F. A. Ajayi and I. Espie, it has come into being to meet the urgent needs of educators in West Africa, although it is hoped that it will commend itself to students of Africa elsewhere.

Since the end of the Second World War, Gambia, Ghana, Nigeria and Sierra Leone have all been concerned to give their educational provision a more African outlook. The West African Examinations Council, which was established in 1950 to conduct external examinations for the schools of the four countries in association with the Cambridge Examinations Syndicate, introduced a school certificate paper entitled 'The Development of Tropical Africa'. This seemed a forward move at the time, but the development of a more scholarly approach to African history showed that the syllabus for this paper still reflected a European viewpoint on African history and was in fact largely concerned with European activities in Africa.

In 1964 the West African Examinations Council introduced two entirely new papers (effective from 1966) in African history—'History of West Africa A.D. 1000 to the Present Day' and 'History of Africa in the Nineteenth and Twentieth Centuries'—to replace the old Tropical Africa syllabus. Rarely can history syllabuses for school examinations have undergone so radical a transformation. The new syllabuses made new demands upon teachers not only with respect to teaching new content but also in the reinterpretation of already known material. They did so at a time when teaching materials for the new syllabuses had still not been produced. (In developing countries textbooks rarely appear before the examination syllabuses which themselves often continue unrevised because no suitable textbooks are available to make revision appear practical.) It was obvious that with the exception of graduates of the West African universities who had specialised in African history, many teachers would be confronted with a formidable challenge in teaching the new syllabuses effectively.

The West African Examinations Council consequently requested the Institute of Education and the Department of History of the University of Ibadan to mount a Workshop on the Teaching of African History. With the support of a generous grant from the Carnegie Corporation this was held at Ibadan in March 1965. It was attended by teams of carefully selected educators nominated by the eight Ministries of Education of Commonwealth West African countries. Both Ministries and teams accepted the responsibility of subsequently holding continuation workshops for teachers in their own areas.

The bulk of the chapters in this book, as in its companion volume, consists of the papers that specialists in the field of African history delivered at the Ibadan Workshop. It is hoped that their publication will help to shorten the considerable period, sometimes put at twenty or thirty years, that often elapses between the data and reinterpretation of historical research being made available to schools.

The circumstances of the genesis of this volume account for its nature. It has been produced as a matter of great urgency and to meet the needs of teachers embarking on the new syllabus on Africa in the nineteenth and twentieth centuries. It reverses the normal procedure whereby handbooks for teachers consist largely of methodological considerations and little subject content. In the present educational situation in Africa the content of African history has first to be acquired before a satisfactory teaching methodology can be perfected: the best teachers always remain students; this is especially true in respect of African histoy at the present time. Finally this book concentrates its emphasis on African history in the nineteenth and twentieth centuries. This is regrettable, though given the circumstances of its origin unavoidable. This concentration on recent history has to some extent been offset by chapters on the archaeology and art of Africa and by the selection of plates to be found at the end of the volume. Those who are anxious to learn of the considerable research that has been done in the history of pre-colonial West Africa are referred to the companion volume on West African history.

J. C. ANENE

G. N. BROWN

LIST OF CONTRIBUTORS

J. F. ADE AJAYI B.A., PH.D. (LOND.) is Professor of History in the University of Ibadan and Dean of the Faculty of Arts. He is the author of *Milestones in Nigerian History*, Ibadan U.P., 1962; *Christian Missions in Nigeria 1841–1891: the Making of a New Elite*, Longmans, 1965; and, with R. S. Smith, *Yoruba Warfare in the Nineteenth Century*, C.U.P. in association with the Institute of African Studies, University of Ibadan, 1964. He is a member of the Editorial Board of the *Journal of African History*.

I. A. AKINJOGBIN B.A. (DUNELM.), PH.D. (LOND.) is Lecturer in History in the University of Ife. He was a Research Fellow in the Yoruba Historical Research Scheme from 1957–60 and thereafter undertook research in Dahomey. He has contributed to the *Proceedings of the Nigerian Institute of Social and Economic Research*; the *Journal of the Historical Society of Nigeria*; and *Odu*.

M. A. AL-HAJJ M.A. (LOND.) is Lecturer in Arabic and Islamic Studies in the Institute of African Studies, University of Ife. He was formerly Academic Secretary in the University of Khartoum. He has contributed to *Odu*, the Journal of the Institute of African Studies, University of Ife.

JOSEPH C. ANENE M.A., PH.D., DIP.ED. (LOND.), Joint Editor of this volume, has been on the staff of the University of Ibadan since 1956 and is now Professor and Head of the Department of History. He was formerly Mathematics Master in Christ the King College, Onitsha. He contributed a chapter on 'King Jaja of Opobo' to *Eminent Nigerians of the Nineteenth Century*, C.U.P., 1960; and is the author of *Southern Nigeria in Transition, 1885–1906*, C.U.P., 1965.

E. A. AYANDELE B.A., PH.D. (LOND.) is Lecturer in History in the University of Ibadan. He has contributed articles to the *Journal of the Historical Society of Nigeria*.

GODFREY N. BROWN M.A., D.PHIL. (OXON.), Joint Editor of this volume, is Professor of Education in the University of Ibadan. He has been successively an officer in the British Intelligence Corps, a Social Affairs Officer at U.N. Headquarters in New York, a master in English grammar schools and a lecturer in the University College of Ghana. He is the author of a two-volume textbook, *An Active History of Ghana*, Allen & Unwin, 1961, and Joint Editor of the *West African Journal of Education*.

J. E. FLINT M.A. (CANTAB.), PH.D. (LOND.) is Reader in History in the University of London, King's College. During 1963–4 he was visiting Professor and Head of the Department of History in the University of Nigeria Nsukka. He is the author of *Sir George Goldie and the Making of Nigeria*, O.U.P., 1960. He has also contributed chapters to *The History of East Africa*, Vol. I, ed. R. Oliver and G. Mathew, O.U.P., 1964; and edited *Mary Kingsley, West African Studies* and *Mary Kingsley, Travels in West Africa*, F. Cass, 1964–5.

J. R. GRAY M.A. (CANTAB.), PH.D. (LOND.) is Reader in African History in the University of London. Previously he was a Research Fellow of the School of Oriental and African Studies after having been a Lecturer in African History in the University of Khartoum. He has published *The Two Nations. Race Relations in the Rhodesias and Nyasaland 1918–1953*, O.U.P., 1960; and *A History of the Southern Sudan, 1839–1889*, O.U.P., 1961.

JOHN O. HUNWICK B.A. (LOND.) is Senior Lecturer and Acting Head of the Department of Arabic and Islamic Studies in the University of Ibadan. He is in charge of the Centre of Arabic Documentation in the University's Institute of African Studies and Editor of the Centre's Research Bulletin. His publications include articles on aspects of Islam in the Songhay empire and on Islamic learning in West Africa.

COLIN LEGUM is Commonwealth Correspondent of *The Observer*. His published books include *Must We Lose Africa?*, W. H. Allen, 1954; *Bandung, Cairo and Accra*, The African Bureau, London, 1958; *Congo Disaster*, Penguin, 1961; *Pan-Africanism: A Short Guide*, Pall Mall, 1962; and with Mrs Margaret Legum, *South Africa: Crisis for the West*, Pall Mall, 1964.

BETHWELL A. OGOT is Senior Lecturer in History and Chairman of the Department of History in the University College, Nairobi. He is also Secretary-General of the East African Institute of Social and Cultural Affairs. He was formerly a Tutorial Fellow of Makerere

College, Kampala, and a teacher at Alliance High School, Kikuyu, Kenya. He has contributed to *African Studies*, University of Witwatersrand.

J. D. OMER-COOPER M.A. (CANTAB.), M.A. (RHODES) is Senior Lecturer in History in the University of Ibadan and Professor-elect of History in the University of Zambia. He is the author of *The Mfecane, A Nineteenth Century Revolution in Bantu Africa*, Longmans, 1965.

KEN W. J. POST M.A. (CANTAB.) is Lecturer in Political Science at the Centre for West African Studies in the University of Birmingham. He was Visiting Assistant Professor at the University of California, Berkeley, during 1963–64 and was previously on the staff of the University of Ibadan. He is the author of *The Nigerian Federal Election of 1959*, O.U.P., 1963; and *The New States of West Africa*, Penguin, 1964.

SVEN RUBENSON B.PHIL., L.PHIL. (LUND) is Associate Professor of History and Head of the Department of History, Haille Sellassie I University, Addis Abeba. He has been active as a missionary and educator in Ethiopia since 1947. His publications include *Wichale XVII*, Addis Abeba, 1964; and articles and reviews in the *Journal of African History* and the *Journal of Ethiopian Studies*.

THURSTAN C. SHAW M.A. (OXON.), F.S.A. is Research Professor of Archaeology in the Institute of African Studies of the University of Ibadan. He was formerly Reader in Education in the University of Cambridge. His archaeological career began in 1937 with his appointment as Curator of Achimota College Anthropology Museum. His work in Ghana culminated in his book *Excavation at Dawu*, Nelson, 1961. More recently he has worked in Nigeria, both in the Eastern Region, where he discovered the Igbo bronzes at Igbo-Ukwu, and in the Western Region where he has undertaken important excavations at Akure.

W. E. F. WARD C.M.G., B.LITT., M.A. (OXON.) was on the educational advisory staff of the British Colonial Office from 1944 to 1963. He was Director of Education in Mauritius from 1940 to 1945 and from 1924 to 1940 he was on the staff of Achimota College, Ghana. He is the author of *A History of Ghana*, Allen & Unwin, 2nd edition, 1958; *Educating Young Nations*, Allen & Unwin, 1959; *A History of Africa* (for schools), Vols. I and II, Allen & Unwin, 1960 and 1963; *Government in West Africa*, Allen & Unwin, 1965; and *Fraser of Trinity and Achimota*, Ghana Universities Press, 1965.

J. B. WEBSTER M.A. (BRIT. COL.), PH.D. (LOND.) is Lecturer in History in the University of Ibadan. Previously he had eleven years' experience of History teaching in secondary schools. He is the author of *The African Churches Among the Yoruba*, O.U.P., 1964.

DENNIS WILLIAMS is Lecturer in African Art in the Instute of African Studies of the University of Ife. He was a Lecturer in the Central School of Art, Holborn, from 1950 to 1957, during which time he also took tutorials at the Slade School of Art, University College, London. Subsequently he was a Lecturer in the School of Art in Khartoum and published a novel based on the Meroitic culture of the Sudan entitled *Other Leopards*, Hutchinson, 1963. He has also contributed to *Africa*, the Journal of the International African Institute.

ALFRED JOHN WILLS M.A. (OXON.) is Assistant Master in King Edward VI School, Norwich. From 1951 to 1958 he was an Education Officer in Northern Rhodesia (Zambia). He is the author of *A History of Central Africa*, O.U.P., 1963.

ACKNOWLEDGEMENTS

THE EDITORS wish to thank the contributors to this volume for their co-operation and readiness to treat its publication as a matter of first priority. They acknowledge with gratitude the assistance of the Steering Committee of the Ibadan Workshop on the Teaching of African History in its compilation. The Members of this Committee were Professor A. Ryder, Mr I. Espie, Mr J. D. Omer-Cooper and the Editors. The Secretary of the Committee was Miss Cynthia Adams who also acted as Secretary of the Workshop. The success of the whole endeavour owed much to her enthusiasm and industry. We also record our warm thanks to the Carnegie Corporation of New York for its grant which made the whole stimulating exercise in international co-operation possible. Finally, the Authors and Editors would like to thank the following for permission to use copyright material: Miss Ruth First and Penguin Books, for Figures 23*a* and *b*, from *South West Africa*; Professor J. Greenberg and Indiana University Press for Figure 7, from *Languages of Africa*; G. W. Kingsnorth and Cambridge University Press, for Figure 8, from *Africa South of the Sahara*; Musée de l'Homme, Paris, for Plate VI; Messrs Oliver & Mathew, editors, and the Clarendon Press, Oxford, for Figures 9 and 25, from *History of Africa*; Professor Sven Rubenson for Plates XII–XVI; the Institute of African Studies, the University of Ibadan for Plate I.

CONTENTS

PART IV: WEST AFRICA

PART V: SOUTH AFRICA

PART VI: EAST AFRICA

PART VII: EPILOGUE

PLATES AND MAPS

The maps of Africa Physical (A) and Africa Vegetation (B)
are printed respectively on front and back endpapers.

LIST OF FIGURES

1 The Place of African History in Education in Africa

GODFREY N. BROWN

PROFESSIONAL historians are apt either to ignore or to exaggerate the relative importance of history to other aspects of life. Whether this makes them better or worse historians might be discussed at length. But for the teacher of history in a school the situation is very different. He is part of a team concerned with the highly complex process of education and, unless he knows where his subject fits into the overall scheme and what his educational purposes are, he is unlikely to make his most effective contribution.

Accordingly, it is the object of this chapter to examine the nature of African history against the purposes that school education in history can be expected to fulfil in Africa. From the outset, however, it must be emphasised that such an examination is necessarily tentative since the study of African history in schools is a very recent development and since most African states are in the process of transforming their educational provision to make it accord better with their newly won independence. In such circumstances it would be as foolhardy to seek to give more than some general guidance as it would be unhelpful to refuse to make the attempt.

The underlying theme of this chapter is that in the very process of introducing new content into the history taught in African schools there is the opportunity for a radical departure from traditional views of both the subject itself and of the methodologies of teaching it. The attempt will be made to show that teachers in Africa should take a much broader view of history than has usually been the case and that this in its turn offers increased opportunities for worthwhile education.

THE NATURE OF AFRICAN HISTORY

To argue again the case for African history as an academic study is unnecessary. Only those who have either no first-hand experience of contemporary Africa or have made no attempt to study the continent's history can support such statements as 'Africa has no history' or 'African history is nothing more than the story of European activities in Africa'. This book itself and the bibliographies that it contains, demonstrate the ignorance and prejudice in such assertions. Yet, African history, no less than the histories of other peoples, has its own distinctive character and it is important to see this in perspective. African history is part of the human story: it is not synonymous with it.

Assets

The greatest asset of the study of African history in African educational institutions is that it is a first-pronoun subject: it is concerned with learning about people *like us* (admittedly a matter of degree). This is particularly important in a continent that is emerging from a period of colonial rule during which the history of aliens was endowed with unwarranted prestige. Even in the most altruistic society there is likely to be a stratum of self-regard just as even very selfish people are rarely concerned with self-welfare to the exclusion of everybody else. Most societies have manifested this aspect of the human condition in the form of curiosity about their own forebears and the origins of their institutions. To deprive African students of the opportunity of trying to satisfy this curiosity is to treat them as educational foundlings.

Certainly the artistic and aesthetic achievements of people *like us* in Africa have been considerable. Some account of the contribution made by African art will be found in subsequent chapters. Here it must suffice to mention such names as Meroë, Kush, Aksum, Kilwa, Zimbabwe, Nok, Benin, Asante to emphasise that an outline history of African art can itself be a good deal more life-enhancing than the study of 'the register of the wars, follies and misfortunes of mankind' which was Gibbon's description of history. Obviously the whole field of the African contribution to culture will be greatly enlarged in the future with the discoveries made by research. Achievements were not limited to the plastic arts but embraced music and dance as well.

In many ways, too, African history is rich in social significance. Whereas it is too early to undertake more than a very sketchy social history of Africa and perhaps this may never be possible in the sense that attaches to the concept in Europe, there is much material for sociological history. No matter how 'pure' historians may shudder at the expression, such history has considerable educational importance. The historical study of such topics as the extended family, the cohesiveness of tribal society, the multiple facets of culture contacts (the impact of Islam, commerce, Christianity, applied science, the problems of plural societies, etc.) if seen in terms not of abstractions but *of people* can be of great educational value. Incidentally such study can also be of value in Teacher Education. It is sometimes insufficiently appreciated that such concepts as 'education for life by life' were not the inventions of Ovide Decroly or John Dewey but essentially the underlying assumptions of indigenous African educational practices.

Allied with the sociological richness of African history is its ethnogeographical interest. The people of Africa comprise hundreds of tribes speaking something like eight hundred distinct languages, embracing a whole spectrum of religions; there is greater variety of peoples on the continent than is to be found in Europe, America or Oceania—greater even, in some respects, than in Asia. In addition there are several million people of European origin and perhaps two million people of Asian origin. Much of African history consists of the movements of its peoples and of their contacts with peoples from other parts of the world. Very often such movements are unintelligible unless the geographical background (e.g., the continent's arid regions; the incidence of the trade winds) is understood. It need not be emphasised that the educational advantages of viewing the continent's population and environmental resources together are very considerable in a continent that is seeking to speed its economic development.

Challenges

The greatest challenges of African historical study and teaching arise out of the lack of adequate aids to learning. Nevertheless the shortage is in reality less than is commonly supposed. As more sources of historical material are located and in particular as records are translated (especially from Arabic) African history will certainly become more meaningful. So, of course, will textbooks for schools. At present these are in desperately short supply and such books as there are have often been produced by people who lack familiarity with the African classroom. However the situation is improving and the next ten years are likely to see a radical transformation of the scene.

It is true, of course, that some aids to education in history are likely to remain in short supply. No African city, with the possible exceptions of some in Egypt and Ethiopia, can boast such visible architectural history as Athens, Rome or London. But in another way Africa is well endowed: in the lives of its people. It takes an effort of information and imagination to project oneself into the London or the Rome of several centuries ago; in Africa it often requires little more than the exercise of thoughtful imagination. In Africa the centuries co-exist in a way that is no longer true of more developed regions; one passes from the twentieth century to a much earlier century in the course of a comparatively short journey. Too much teaching of history ignores the illuminating examples that are still to be found locally. Obviously the study of local 'telescoped' history must be undertaken with considerable care but it should not be ignored. History may be a matter of words and sherds carefully dusted in libraries and museums in Europe; in Africa it is a living environment.

Indeed the shortage of written documentation which is likely to be characteristic of some areas of African history and which is a curse for the historian can be a blessing for the history teacher. In saying that African history is handicapped by lack of material what is very often meant is that it cannot be studied in the same way as European history has been studied. For this African teachers should probably be profoundly thankful. In too many history syllabuses in Europe the growth of an enquiring, critical capacity for thinking historically has been choked by the multiplicity of documents, details and dates that seem to proliferate like weeds. This has often resulted in a failure to be sufficiently selective in teaching history. The teacher has been reluctant to omit any part of an overfull syllabus for fear of mistaking as weeds what examinations might subsequently show to be prize plants. This has meant that history has seemed to many students to involve much work, involving a good deal of dull memorisation, and to provide little personal satisfaction in terms of understanding and achievement for the work involved. Consequently those whose main interests were in other fields have often gained little value from the study of history.

In Africa it may well be that African history can enlist their enthusiasm too. Linguists who are interested in African languages can be encouraged to collect and examine oral traditions; linguists who are involved in learning European languages such as French or Spanish have opportunities for studying the history of those countries in Africa where they are the official languages; and linguistic study itself can be a tool of considerable value to the historian of the peoples of Africa. Physicists can be interested in carbon dating; botanists can discuss the history that we can derive from plants in such studies as palaeobotany and ethnobotany; zoologists and geologists can consider such questions as the significance of the rock paintings of cattle found in the Sahara; physiologists and geneticists can study the incidence of sickle cell anaemia or gene frequency; and other scientific studies might also be called into contribution. Professor Ivor Wilks has even demonstrated that mathematics also has its uses as an aid to historical study in the statistical analysis of the lists of office-holders handed down from one generation to the next by oral tradition.[1] It is conceivable that a dearth of written historical records might help African educators to avoid the emergence of 'two cultures', one humanistic, the other scientific, that has been experienced in Europe. Writers of textbooks on African history would do well to exploit the opportunities that liaison with the scientists can provide.

Lacunae

At the same time as one recognises the great educational possibilities of teaching African history one must acknowledge that there are likely to be significant omissions involved in the study. Perhaps the most noteworthy of these is the lack of a history of science and technology such as is found in Europe and America. It would be wrong to consider that this is a situation peculiar to Africa; it is a situation that has characterised the history of many people whose educational patterns have emphasised communal virtues and the acceptance of wisdom handed down from one generation to another. In regard to scientific and mechanical achievement indeed it is European rather than African civilisation that is exceptional[2] and the Revolution of

Industrial Science has been brought about by European in-quisitiveness and acquisitiveness. Nevertheless, there is no gain-saying that progress for the people of Africa at the present time must involve the utilisation of science and that African education must take cognisance of this. It is therefore regrettable that the content, as distinguished from the methods, of African history provides little assistance in helping students to appreciate what is involved in the application of science to the problems of the continent.

Other lacunae in the study of African history for the educator can be briefly indicated since they are of less importance and are already implicit in what has been said previously. Thus, generally speaking, African history is not well endowed with regard to architectural or pictorial art (though the very important achieve-ments of Egypt and Ethiopia must not be forgotten); it lacks a history of literature on the European or Asian scale though research will undoubtedly do much to make good this deficiency both by collecting written documents in Arabic, Hausa and Swahili and by recording oral literature in a somewhat similar way to that by which the corpus of Homer must have been compiled. Finally, there is a deficiency of material on social history (especially with regard to first person accounts of day-to-day life) and of economic history (especially in statistical records).

The essential nature of African history thus presents the teacher with peculiar opportunities and problems not only in exploiting its potentialities, and tackling its challenges but also in the recognition of its limitations.

Africa and the non-European World

On widening the scope of our enquiry and considering the nature of historical education in the world at large, however, the 'peculiarities' of African history can be seen in better perspective. Against this background they emerge as a striking instance of a failure by Western historians to appreciate the culture and achievements of the non-European world. In reacting against this, there is the danger that historians of Africa may themselves partially perpetuate it by neglecting non-African and non-European history. According to their particular interests they may be very conscious that the culture and achievements of say the Asante, the Fulani, the Kikuyu or the Bantu have been sadly misrepresented in much European-orientated history. At the same time, however, they may not recognise that 'at the end of the fourteenth century an impartial observer could have defined Europe, without paradox, as a peninsula of Asia, peopled by strange and restless nations but naturally susceptible to the civilising influences which reached it gradually, sometimes after much delay, from the continent, in other words from the East.'[3]

In reacting against the view that Africa can be regarded as 'an extension of Europe' from the fifteenth and sixteenth centuries, it is salutary to be reminded that Europe no less than Africa has been the subject of considerable influences from without. 'European' is itself a portmanteau term to which peoples from all over the world have made contributions in much the same way as they have enriched the English language. The African child who delights in crying 'European' in his vernacular tongue when he espies a pink skin should at least be helped to understand what the word means. Europe derived its iron and wheat from Asia in prehistoric times, something of its culture and its science from the Middle East and North Africa in the 'Middle Ages' of the Western world; it has been subjected to considerable aesthetic influences from the Far East, and contributions to its political philosophy, its science, its industrial management techniques have been made by the American continent in the modern period just as, recently, African art has greatly influenced European artists. Such instances of cultural borrowings by no means exhaust the list. Almost everywhere in the modern world, whatever the colour of one's skin, a whole range of pigmentations has been incorporated in one's culture.

Africa is the last of the world's continents to be freed from European colonialism and there is perhaps a danger that the continent's history teachers may be so preoccupied with African affairs that they fail to see that the injustice that has frequently been done to their own continent in history textbooks has also been done to peoples of the greater areas of the world's surface. Particularly poignant in this connection is the way that Asian history is often neglected in East Africa despite the many Asians who live there, and the way that the history of Latin America and the Caribbean is often neglected in West Africa despite the many people living across the Southern Atlantic whose forebears originated in West Africa. As teachers in Africa move the emphasis of their teaching from a European to an African world they need to be aware that a similar process has gone on in America, North and then South and is still in process on the Indian continent and in South East Asia.

Such knowledge should help teachers to adjust their teaching to the contemporary context but there can be no doubt that it adds to their difficulties. It means that they are faced not only with the very proper requirement that in independent Africa they should move the centre of their history-teaching to their own country and continent but that simultaneously they should recognise that there is no centre in human history or perhaps, more accurately, that there are as many centres as there are distinguishable peoples on the earth's surface. At one and the same time they need to study the histories of their own people, with all the difficulties that are implicit in this task in the pioneering stage, and also to study the histories of other peoples which, in many cases, are similarly deficient in material for the teaching situation.

Summary

From this examination it will be seen that although the advantages, the problems and the lacunae of African history are all to some extent peculiar to the subject, they must nevertheless be viewed against the present world situation in which the history of non-Caucasian peoples has been largely neglected. It is likely that the concept of ethnohistory so much employed in African history, calling into contribution the sciences as well as the humanities, may be pregnant with considerable educational significance. But before considering this, it seems best to consider a question that itself has a history dating back to antiquity: 'Why teach history?'

THE PURPOSE OF HISTORICAL EDUCATION

Drawing upon experience both in Africa and in schools in other parts of the world helps to clarify the purposes in teaching history. There is a growing concensus of agreement on what is involved in the subject and in the objectives that it has. To this growth, improved communications, and the work of such bodies as the International Institute of Intellectual Co-operation of the League of Nations, and Unesco have made their contributions.

It is now generally agreed that history is not taught to impart universally recognised foundations of knowledge to the same extent as is true of some other subjects of the curriculum: teachers and pupils can choose the content of their subject, which period or topics they wish to study, in a way that is not possible in mathematics, science or English language. At the same time—and this is largely the justification for greater emphasis being given to the teaching of African history—it is generally agreed that pupils are more interested in themselves and their people and their environment seen in the context of history than in studying history that is apparently unrelated to their present condition in the modern world.

Secondly, it is usually agreed that history is not taught in schools with the object of producing historians. At the same time it is not taught with the object of *not* producing historians. It is hoped that one of the results of the history taught in school will be that certain pupils will wish to develop their critical, imaginative and literary abilities to the extent that is necessary to earn the description of 'historian' but in the nature of things such pupils are likely to be but a small minority. This is as it should be in Africa where education is called upon to produce people who can forward economic development more directly than most historians can claim to do. The teacher of history does well to remember that he may spend a life-time teaching very well and yet perhaps never produce a professional historian.

Thirdly, most reputable historians in the 'Western World' would be likely to counsel the exercise of considerable caution in using history-teaching for a moral purpose. They would argue that the teaching of history should not aim to produce more moral people, better patriots or supporters of a particular political party. However, such would not be the view of teachers in the U.S.S.R. where the Communist Party 'is the guarantor of the correct understanding of history' and where teachers of history are obliged to be members of the Party, or in Czechoslovakia where 'a communistic outlook is taught to young children not so much as a matter of catechism or dogma but through historically interpretive studies'.[4]

Historically speaking it would perhaps be true to say that history-teaching may be subjected to a more urgent moral purpose in countries which are undergoing rapid development.

Thus there was no lack of nationalistic histories in France, Germany and England in the nineteenth century and American history was consciously used in the U.S.A. in the early twentieth century as part of the 'melting-pot' procedure whereby very heterogenous immigrants were transformed into American citizens. It would be unrealistic to expect teachers in Africa, where rapid development is being made on all fronts, not to be subjected to pressures to slant their history-teaching according to certain political or moral considerations. They may well be urged to concern themselves less with historical truth than with nation-building.

On the other hand, it is possible that such pressures and exhortations may be resisted. African historians have already shown themselves no less jealous of their reputation for scholarship than their counterparts overseas. Many teachers have lived through an era in which the dangers of political indoctrination through education have been exemplified and are aware of them. Many would argue that education in history involves the attempt to distinguish fact and opinion and that thus it cultivates a critical habit of mind that is the best means of withstanding propaganda. True as this is, it is an argument that may not withstand those who maintain that an element of propaganda is necessary in the urgent task of nation-building and development that faces Africa at the present time. There is undoubtedly sometimes a confliction of principles that in the last analysis can only be resolved by the exercise of the teacher's judgement or conscience.

Educationally it seems desirable that such occasions should be reduced to a minimum. Often this can best be done by recognising that nation-building is more appropriate to a course of citizenship than to a course of history. It may well be that the same teacher may be concerned with both courses—possibly this is to be welcomed—but he should always try to keep their differing purposes distinct.[5]

What then should be the purpose of history-teaching in Africa at the present time?

It shares with other subjects of the curriculum the underlying purpose of enlarging the capacity of its students. In the case of history this enlargement is given a special emphasis. Just as mathematics increases the human capacity for dealing with concepts of number, and the study of languages does the same thing in respect of words, so does history afford the opportunity for students to increase their capacity for dealing with questions involving people. In such questions one needs to employ thought: to weigh the 'pro' and the 'con' of every possible interpretation of human data. Such level-headedness is usually an asset in life since it acts as a check on precipitate ill-considered action. People who have acquired the historical habit of weighing evidence are probably less likely to show unreasonable prejudice concerning people different from themselves or to advocate mass crimes of violence. That this is so, however, is not simply because history involves the exercise of thought in the sense of logical analysis but because it also involves the exercise of imagination as well.

As Croce and Collingwood so frequently stressed, it is necessary in studying history to be able to project oneself not only into the shoes of other people at other times but into their skins as well. Such an exercise of sympathetic understanding is perhaps particularly required in respect of African history in the nineteenth and twentieth centuries since much of the documentation for this period, produced by European officials, itself made little attempt to employ it. But this is only a signal illustration of what is an immensely complicated process, involving seeing things that were happening in the past as though they were happening in the present. Viewed in this light, it is true to say that history is not so much the study of the past, as the study of the past as though it were the present, because, in this sense, nothing ever happened in the past: the historical observer must always view events as though they were happening and he were present.

In the *essentials* of historical understanding it may well be that Africans have a better time-sense than the Europeans. Traditionally Africans have attached less importance to chronological time (cf., say, the Kano and the Anglo-Saxon Chronicles) and past and present have been less clearly differentiated (e.g. the omnipresent respect accorded ancestors in traditional societies) than has been the case in Europe. It is perhaps true to say that Africans have been more concerned with the human content of time than with mere chronology. Nevertheless, of course, chronology is important in the study of history just as an appreciation of 'Western time' is of great value in forwarding development schemes in Africa today. The study of history, if properly handled should be able to make a considerable contribution to the development of a very well-developed time-sense involving both human content and chronology. The concept of the study of history as being the study of the evolving present is obviously helpful in this respect.

But of course this is not sufficient. History must be concerned with what is *significant* in the evolving present. A French educationist has expressed this as follows: 'Origins and trends (in history) are significant to us because we now know the course of history. Neither the course nor its direction, or, consequently, its term, were given when historical events or facts occurred: thus these facts were not then significant. In other words the historical origins of the present, in so far as they are most important, would not be completely elucidated, for they would only be reconstituted in their totality if the past had been expressed by contemporaries as a function of an undetermined future which was, of course, unforeseeable.'[6] This of course could be illustrated a myriad times but one example must suffice. It seems likely that the Ethiopian who was asked why he was fighting the Italian at Adwa on the first Sunday of March 1896 would have said something about answering the summons of the King of Kings against the foreign menace. What he most certainly would not have said was that he was striking a blow in the cause of African nationalism—yet, seen in historical perspective, that in effect was what the Ethiopian victory amounted to. Thus what determines what is significant in historical study is subsequent events, the consequences of the happening in question, and the 'climate of opinion' in which an historical interpretation is made. That is why each generation has to rewrite its own history. In so doing it must of course distinguish carefully between the actual causes of an event and the significance that has subsequently been attached to it. This is one of the reasons why the present generation of historians in independent Africa is confronted with such an enormous task.

Finally, there is the language element involved in the study of history. In countries where the student's mother tongue is used as the medium of instruction this element need not unduly concern the teacher who may need to do little more than ensure that his classes acquire the vocabulary required for historical study. In Africa, however, the bulk of learning and teaching at the post-primary level is done in a language other than the student's mother tongue and problems of communication are much more important. Subjects of sentences become inextricably bound up with subjects of kings and the teacher must do the best he can to help. Unless the student can communicate fairly effectively, historical study becomes largely meaningless and the teacher cannot begin to evaluate his own performances. For this reason, in Africa particularly, historical study is the ally of language learning.

Summary

From this necessarily rather summary account, it is hoped that the underlying purposes of historical education may have been clarified. History-teaching should seek to enlarge a student's capacity to deal with problems of people by the exercise of thought in the assessment of evidence and in reaching conclusions, by the exercise of the informed imagination that enables one to put oneself in another person's place, or to associate oneself with a group of people and to appreciate and to communicate what is significant in the events involving such a person or group, once again by the employment of thought, informed imagination and of a time-sense. Surely this is just the sort of competency that is badly needed in the world; the study of history reveals how little it is usually to be found.

CONCLUSION

From the foregoing discussion of the nature of African history and the purposes of history-teaching, certain broad conclusions will be evident.

In the nineteenth century it was commonly political and civil history that was retailed in school textbooks and syllabuses. With the more scientific study of the subject this was supplemented by social and economic history. The result was a more intelligible study but often this was accompanied by the necessity of covering more material than hitherto. That this was so can be seen by glancing back at School Certificate examination papers set in England during the past forty years. As a result, the increased intelligibility of the history studied in schools did not by any means always result in increased understanding on the part of the students involved. The frequent complaints that history examiners made that students tended to reproduce all they knew, rather than answer the questions set, provided corroborative evidence.

Today the nature of African history, seen against the background of the neglect of non-European history, and the purposes of historical education together combine to pose a problem and provide a solution. At first sight it might appear that according justice to non-European history might overburden the teacher and his classes with even more material which, as a result, would be even less educationally sound than the overweighted syllabuses used hitherto. Such a situation, however, would obviously fail to satisfy the purposes of historical education. The acquisition of encyclopaedic knowledge about the people of the world far from enlarging the pupil's capacity to deal with the problems of people might well have a narrowing effect. It is not usually the 'know-all' who is most helpful in dealing with such problems but rather the man who is possessed of an open mind and a sympathetic attitude.

In this apparent dilemma the nature of African history can make a significant contribution. Broadly speaking we have seen that it partakes in considerable measure of the nature of ethnic history, or of *cultural* history—with 'culture' being understood in the anthropological sense of the term. Educationally we have seen that this concept has a great deal to offer, whereas traditional 'European' history has demonstrably been a very imperfect educational instrument especially with regard to those students who had neither the desire nor the ability to become professional historians.

In this situation therefore there is much to be said for the cultural approach being applied not only to African history but to non-African history as well. This could help to resolve the difficulties of excessive memorisation of detail and make a real contribution to forwarding the purposes of historical education: the enlargement of human sympathy and understanding. In such a situation the task of the teacher of history in our schools becomes clarified: he is there much less to study African and European history according to European example than to study history, both African and non-African, by methods particularly appropriate to African history and the world situation.

This, of course, is not so heretical a reorientation as at first sight it might seem to be. Textbooks have already started to appear in Europe and America that claim to be world histories. The influential portait studies of history made by G. M. Young were obviously moving in the direction of cultural history. But it is difficult for the European or American teacher of history to forsake the politico-civil, socio-economic approach to the subject that is the legacy of the teaching that he himself has received. On the other hand, the African teacher of history who possesses the more empirical, open approach that must perforce characterise the study of African history at this stage of the development of the subject, and who is ready to view what he teaches in the light of the purposes for which he teaches it, rejecting that which fails to fulfil this criterion, may himself make a new educational contribution of considerable value.

'Out of Africa there is always something new', as Pliny said nearly 2,000 years ago.

NOTES

1   See I. Wilks, 'The Growth of the Akwapim State: A Study in the Control of Evidence', *The Historian in Tropical Africa*, ed. J. Vansina, R. Mauny and L. V. Thomas, O.U.P., 1964.
2   Exceptional but not unique. Thus it has recently been shown that *inter alia* China possessed the rotary fan and rotary winnowing machine fourteen centuries before Europe; the wheelbarrow nine centuries earlier; iron-chain suspension bridges ten to thirteen centuries earlier; gunpowder five to six centuries earlier; the magnetic compass (with lodestone spoon) eleven centuries earlier; and printing, using movable type, four centuries earlier (J. R. Needham, *Science and Civilisation*, Vol. 1, p. 242, C.U.P., 1954).
3   G. Fradier, *East and West*, p. 19, Unesco, Paris, 1959.
4   E. King, 'The Concept of Ideology in Communist Education', *Communist Education*, ed. E. J. King, pp. 13–14, Methuen, 1963.
5   For discussion of the problems of teaching very recent history see pp. 334–6.
6   R. Cousinet, *L'Enseignement de l'Histoire et l'Education Nouvelle*, p. 41, Les Presses d'Ile de France.

SELECT BIBLIOGRAPHY

P. D. Curtin, *African History*, Macmillan, N.Y., Collier Macmillan, London, 1964.
J. Vansina, R. Mauny and L. V. Thomas, *The Historian in Tropical Africa*, O.U.P., 1964.
E. H. Dance, *History the Betrayer, A Study of Bias*, Hutchinson, 1964.
G. Fradier, *East and West*, Unesco, Paris, 1959.
W. H. Walsh, *Introduction to Philosophy of History*, Hutchinson, 1951.
R. G. Collingwood, *The Idea of History*, O.U.P., 1946.
H. Meyerhoff, *The Philosophy of History in Our Time*, Doubleday, 1959.
3

2 Teaching History in Africa[1]

GODFREY N. BROWN

EDUCATIONAL theories too often inhabit cloud-cuckoo-land. The purpose of this chapter, therefore, is to consider the rather theoretical discussion of the previous chapter in terms of the classroom situation in Africa at the present time: in respect of, first, the content of syllabuses and, secondly, the methodology of their presentation.

CONTENT

The scheme of treatment of the first part is unorthodox. Starting with School Certificate work, primary school and pre-School Certificate work are then considered and post-School Certificate work is treated separately. The priority accorded to the work for the School Certificate is in accordance with the realities of the situation in Africa where social pressures mean that obtaining a certificate becomes the focal point of endeavour of most secondary school pupils. The educator, who recognises that this, is so is not capitulating to the situation but simply placing himself in a better position to deal with the problems associated with it. Moreover, since the School Certificate is an *external* examination, its requirements must be predicated in any secondary school history course designed to be as effective as possible.

School Certificate History

Despite the external nature of the examination, the teacher of School Certificate history has rather more freedom in determining what he will teach than is commonly supposed.

First he must decide which of the possible School Certificate syllabuses to adopt. This, of course, will depend on local circumstances: the interests and ambitions of his classes, his own interests and competence, the availability of textbooks and teaching aids. Generally speaking, however, School Certificate history should be viewed as a cohesive part of the whole secondary school course. The teacher should not attempt to gear School Certificate history to the history which will be studied subsequently (usually only by a minority of students) but to conceive of the work of the four- or five- or six-year course leading up to School Certificate as a whole. Such an approach helps to avoid students' compartmentalising the subject into trivial and forgotten material which was covered in the lower part of the school, and the unrelated material, much more important (but still largely unappreciated?) that was needed for School Certificate.

Secondly, the teacher should exploit the rubric of a School Certificate history paper to the full in the interests—in both senses of the term—of his candidates. The rubric and constitution of most examination papers, the division into alternative sections leaves much more room for allowing teacher and taught to follow up individual interests than is often realised. Too often when teachers look at past papers they look more for 'chestnuts' than for opportunities for breaking fresh ground; much more variety of work is possible within the limitations of preparation for School Certificate history than is usually recognised.

Thirdly, any teacher who wishes to bring about change in the School Certificate course should seek to influence policy-makers through professional teacher organisations or national societies of historians. Exceptionally, he may also exercise the option that some examining authorities make available of submitting his own syllabus and having a special paper set for the candidates he teaches. Few teachers however are likely to wish to undertake the extra correspondence and work that this involves.

Another important choice that is open to the teacher of School Certificate history concerns the utilisation of the time at his disposal. In most schools this is likely to be a minimum of two periods a week and a maximum of four. Teachers need to resist the temptation to spend either too much time on School Certificate history or too little. Where schools are embarking on African history for the first time they may be inclined to allocate three years to covering the new syllabus; where schools have four periods a week given to history in the School Certificate forms, they may be inclined to think that the whole syllabus can be covered in one year. Generally speaking it will usually be found that the School Certificate syllabus can best be covered in two years.[2] To spend longer on it is likely to exhaust the class rather than the subject matter; to spend less is to give students a very imperfect understanding of what is involved in historical study and to set a premium on the parroting of answers in the School Certificate.

Schools which are fortunate enough to have four periods a week given over to history would be advised to devote one period a week or one period a fortnight to the study of current affairs and contemporary history. Such study can add an extra dimension to the student's concept of history and start to encourage him to look behind the rather facile accounts of contemporary problems that appear in the newspapers to their underlying historical causes. Bringing such an outlook to bear upon human problems results not only in better qualities of citizenship but also of historical thought.

Primary School History

Secondary school history teachers too frequently are unaware of the history that is taught in primary schools. If they do try to find out they often do so by enquiring about the content of primary school history syllabuses rather than by attempting to assess the qualities that primary school history teachers seek to encourage in their pupils. It is the latter from which their own teaching could most benefit.

In most African countries primary teachers are class-teachers and not subject-teachers. They are concerned to give an overall education to their pupils—and primary schooling, it must not be forgotten, is the only full-time education that is available to the majority of children in Africa. This means that primary school teachers seek to equip their pupils with the tools of learning, literacy and numeracy, which they can utilise when their formal education is ended, together with the encouragement of certain desirable social habits—the elements of citizenship.

It is in this second aspect of the work of the primary school that history is mainly concerned. Sometimes 'History' appears on the time-table; at other times it is treated as part of 'Social Studies'. No matter what guise it adopts, however, it usually is concerned fundamentally to (*a*) get primary school children interested in other people; (*b*) assist them to understand other people; and (*c*) seek to show them the need for helping other people. In the primary school, history justifies its place by reason of its social utility.

It means, of course, that the subject is seen as a much broader concept than is usually the case. In Independent Africa it seems likely that this broader social orientation will particularly commend itself.[3] Quite possibly, too, this may take the form of African Studies appearing on the time-table, not as witnessing to an exclusive preoccupation with things African but as an indication that social phenomena are now being seen from an African viewpoint. This could mean the incorporation of the tradition of indigenous African education whereby the accumulated wisdom of the past and advice on behavioural problems was made available to the younger generation by means of easily appreciated folklore and stories from local history. Such an approach arises naturally from the children's own background and interests, and provides admirable opportunities for the integration of local culture, history and geography.

The fact that such stories often involve a supernatural element might seem to invalidate their use as an introduction to history. Against this, on the other hand, the educator would argue that, quite apart from the literary value of such stories which often is considerable, it is precisely this element that enables pupils to begin an essential historical activity in the critical examination of evidence. Moreover such an exercise built around the question 'Do you think that the story we've discussed is true?' seems particularly appropriate for young children. It involves thinking about correspondence to life experience rather than the cohesiveness of abstract explanation in terms of cause and effect, and it seems especially suitable to the child's level of maturation at this stage of development.

If such trends in African primary education progress, as seems likely, the pupil entering the secondary school will be equipped less with a corpus of historical knowledge than with an attitude of enquiry and interest in questions involving people. If the history teacher in the secondary school is to fulfil the purposes of historical study that were discussed previously, he will seek to foster this attitude rather than to discourage it.

Pre-School Certificate History

The history teacher in English-speaking Africa usually has greater freedom to determine the content of his subject in lower forms of the academic secondary school than at any other stage of the educational process. He is freed from the Ministry constraints of primary education and the limitations imposed by external examinations. The history staff can make their own decisions concerning syllabuses in the junior and middle forms of the secondary school.

There are a number of considerations that should guide them. Lower school history should not simply repeat material covered in the primary school nor should it constitute a traumatic change from primary school study. It should be sufficiently broad and flexible to allow students to follow up individual interests: young people are not necessarily interested in wars and politics even if these have fascination for their teacher. And of course it should provide a background for understanding School Certificate history and engender an interest in the essentials of historical study.

Many varied syllabuses satisfy such desiderata. One teacher might embark on a course of *Social Studies* in the first and second forms with the course dividing into history, geography and citizenship in the third form. Another might employ a *concentric* syllabus starting with the study of local history over a given time span and widening the radius to include peoples farther afield. Yet another might use a *comparative* syllabus devoting one year to African history, one to European history and one to Asian history. Or again one might have a syllabus based on *lines of development* working upwards from the study first of relatively simple progress in such matters as housing, transport and means of production (though here to be really effective the comparative approach should not be ignored) to the complex developments represented in such themes as the growth of towns, the history of democracy, the attempts to ensure international peace and so on. Alternatively, it would be possible to divide the history course into 'patches' or 'eras' allocating a certain amount of time, say, to the study of India and China, at the time of Gautama Buddha and Confucius, to the Eastern Mediterranean at the time of Christ, to the Islamic world in the seventh century, to Africa at the time of Mansa Musa and so on.

An enormous variety of syllabuses is thus possible and, of course, one can combine elements of all these approaches: using for instance a chronological treatment with a term, here and there devoted to lines of development, or 'patches' or to local history.

Sets of study books[4] or plays[5] can be used in all the approaches outlined, from time to time, to create variety of treatment and stimulate project work and the development of individual interests.

The provision of good courses in history at the pre-School Certificate level can thus provide opportunities for much educational experiment and wide diversity in school syllabuses. Yet it would probably be unwise to set no limits to the possibilities of even well-devised courses. Where resources of textbooks and teaching aids are in short supply, it is obviously better to concentrate educational effort on providing a widely acceptable, educationally sound syllabus that has regard both to prevailing circumstances and African aspirations for the future than allowing resources and efforts to be dispersed over a whole range of courses.

The West African Examinations Council has embarked on a policy whereby secondary schools in Gambia, Sierra Leone, Ghana and Nigeria will have a choice of three history papers in the School Certificate: 'The History of West Africa from 1000 A.D. to the Present Day'; 'The History of Africa in the Nineteenth and Twentieth Centuries'; and a paper on 'Modern World History'. It may well be that other countries in Africa will adopt similar schemes for their external examinations in history. There is much to commend the West African example: a regional African paper, a continental African paper and a paper in World History, are all admirably equipped to provide historical education to students who are either terminating their studies or taking them further.

The case for other countries in Africa adopting the West African scheme, or something very similar, is strengthened by the great concern that is everywhere expressed to promote African unity. Without a certain amount of common education, particularly with regard to the history of the peoples of the continent, it seems unlikely that this cause will be greatly furthered. The history taught in schools in Europe in the past has too frequently contributed to the strengthening of national prejudices rather than their elimination; teachers in Africa should try to avoid this.

Were there to be a generally accepted scheme of syllabuses for teaching history throughout English-speaking Africa at least, it would then become much easier to devise courses for the lower forms of secondary schools. Taking the present West African syllabuses as a pattern, such courses would need to incorporate at least three features: the history of the student's own country, the history of the rest of Africa and some acquaintance with the history of significant developments in the rest of the world. Such a course would permit of great flexibility to allow for the individual interests of its students and at the same time provide an excellent introduction to any of the three history papers that may be taken in the West African School Certificate. (The School Certificate course proper would involve a much more thoroughgoing study of content than would have been possible in the lower school.) If secondary school teachers throughout the continent were to adopt some such scheme they would help to give their students an historical background of considerable value to African progress at the present time.

The School-University bridge

In Britain this section would be headed *The Sixth Form*. This is not possible in Africa; since achieving independence a number of countries have modified the traditional sixth form pattern. Thus it seems best to speak of the school-university bridge rather than the sixth form. Everywhere the essential common feature of immediate post-School Certificate education is bridging the transition between secondary school learning and university study. Here it is assumed that the bridge is of two years' duration since this is still generally true of Commonwealth Africa. Where the bridge is of only one year's duration, teachers will need to modify suggestions made accordingly.

The 'Bridge' history teacher is fortunate. Unlike many pre-School Certificate classes, students at this level should be studying the subject because they *want* to; many may be intending to study history for their degrees; there is much less need to consider the non-historically oriented than is the case in younger pupils. 'Bridge' students are themselves beginning to explore the world of ideas; they are beginning to experience concern for causes; they want to put the world to rights and they are starting to develop individual intellectual interests and enthusiasms. All of this is a great aid to the history teacher. His task is to build upon it: to temper ideas with logic, to complement idealism with objectivity, to encourage individual enthusiasms and interests with sympathy and guidance—and to help students to pass the examinations at the end of the course.

With regard to examinations at this level, it is unnecessary to repeat what has previously been said with respect to School Certificate history except to say that these remarks still apply to Higher School Certificate and Advanced level G.C.E. examinations. Indeed they are even more applicable because more time is usually available for historical study at this level and because these examinations themselves usually comprise two or three papers thereby opening up a much greater range of choice for the history teacher than is possible at the School Certificate level.

To begin with, the 'Bridge' classes must have a good introduction to historical study at this level. This might possibly last a term and might well not include anything drawn from the syllabus. In fact this introductory term might be devoted in some measure to helping a class to decide which syllabus it wishes to follow. Probably this can best be done by arranging a course that comprises two integrated parts: an introduction to the *span* of history, and an introduction to the *nature* of history.

With regard to the first of these parts, there are a number of paperbacks that will be found useful: books such as *A Short History of the World* by H. G. Wells and *A Short History of Africa* by Roland Oliver and J. D. Fage (both published by Penguin Books) are obvious examples. Sometimes it may be necessary to go back and read again some of the textbooks that have been used in the lower part of the school, using them now not as individual books but as a series to stimulate speculation. In this exercise they would be used differently from previously. They would be used to get students thinking about such questions as: 'Which do you consider to have been the most creative period in (*a*) African (*b*) European, (*c*) Asian history?' Such questions would involve reading a number of books (especially easily readable books) and reading them quickly. It has been found from experience that African university students read very slowly. In 'Bridge' study, students need to learn to read with care but they also need to acquire the facility for 'skimming and dipping'. Their teachers may start by prescribing chapters but as quickly as possible they should be prescribing a book or books.

Regarding the nature of history there must be some discussion of what history is and why we study it. There must also be some study of historiography which must be given consideration from time to time throughout the course. In many ways this can be the most difficult part of 'Bridge' teaching. Such books as R. G. Collingwood's, *An Autobiography* (Penguin Books); W. H. Wash's, *Introduction to the Philosophy of History* (Hutchinson); and D. F. McCall's, *Africa in Time Perspective* (Boston and Ghana University Presses), will be found helpful but they will need to be digested and then simplified by the teacher. Historiographical considerations can be illustrated by contrasting interpretations of historical events, and these the conscientious teacher might cull for himself and have duplicated for discussion in class.

Despite the difficulties, however, consideration of the nature and methods of history-writing at this level are well worth while since they help to disabuse students of the idea that they are in for another dose of 'O' level stuff. The boy who did so well in the fifth form as a textbook shadow and got 'B+' time and again and who submits his first school history essay somewhat complacently may get a salutary lesson if he receives it back with a 'D' mark and a liberal sprinkling of question marks in red ink. He may or he may not. It depends upon his character whether he will be stimulated or cast into depair. Teaching at this level involves a much more personal relationship than any that has gone before in the educational process. The teacher must assess with sympathy and care just how much time should be devoted to the red ink question marks in class discussion.

At the end of the period of introductory study the teacher can ask his class which of the various examination syllabuses they wish to take. He can be quite frank about the matter, declaring his own interest and competence in the subjects and periods concerned, and pointing out the resources that the school possesses in the way of books. (The fact that in Africa most students will probably have to buy their own books may make the choice more real.) He can also stress the desirability that at least one syllabus should provide some historical education *in depth*, such as is usually to be found in the 'special subject' papers taken at Advanced level in the G.C.E. From work done on the introductory course, students themselves should have seen the dangers of superficial treatment that are frequently to be found in 'outline' courses. Inevitably the choice of history syllabuses open to students is more apparent than real but it does help to establish a worth-while relationship in history-teaching at this level: students are working on matters that interest them and the teacher is there to help and guide them. Of course, exceptionally, a class may make a surprising choice and a teacher may have to declare it impossible. But he should do this only with the greatest reluctance. Even though it does mean more work, the teacher might well welcome an opportunity to teach a subject about which he does not know a great deal because it makes his job more interesting. No teacher of 'Bridge' history need ever complain that he is confined to an academic treadmill, repeating year after year the same old stuff.

METHODOLOGY

It is obviously not possible in the space available to deal with the host of possible ways of teaching history but fortunately there are a number of easily available books that give assistance on the methodology of history-teaching and these will be found in the bibliography on pages 39–40. Here the attempt will be made to discuss issues that are particularly relevant to the African context.

Historical education is complicated over a large area of Africa by the co-existence in education of at least two languages: the African language and the second 'official' language. In most countries of the continent history is studied in the second language rather than in the mother tongue, yet this fact is commonly overlooked. The presumption of much of the history taught in Africa is that it is studied in just the same way as it is studied in Britain and France. It cannot be. Although the *ends* of historical education may be the same, regard must be paid to the *means* and in particular to the implications of learning in a second language. Although this is a subject which is only just beginning to be fully explored there are some general lines of approach that the history teacher may find useful.

Perhaps the best advice is to co-operate as closely as possible with those who teach English (provided of course they themselves have an appreciation of recent developments in second-language teaching). In such co-operation there are many opportunities for improving both English and history. The pupil can improve his structural command of the language and his ability to marshall historical evidence simultaneously. Reading a historically significant novel can be of value to both subjects. Incidentally such co-operation can be taken further; an historical essay can be marked by the history teacher from the point of view of content and by the English teacher from the point of view of language.

In history lessons it is very important that students learn actively to *use* English. In modern language study less emphasis is today placed on the formal study of grammar and more on the use of language. This means that it is much better that a class history textbook should be 'too easy' than 'too hard'. It is wrong to think that complex ideas necessarily require complicated language. A well chosen vocabulary of common words can frequently convey meanings of considerable complexity more effectively than a jargon of abstractions. Just about half of all material written in English is composed of the three hundred commonest words.

The matter of meaning, of course, is a complex subject but Professor C. C. Fries in *The Structure of English* has introduced a distinction of value to the history teacher. He has shown that total meaning consists of linguistic meaning (the lexical and structural meaning) and also of social (or socio-cultural) meaning. This may perhaps be illustrated by examining the sentence: 'The Moroccan army crossed the Saharan desert in 1591.' Linguistically this means that a named army crossed a named desert at a given date. To the historian, however, the social meaning involved is very different from that of an army crossing the Sahara today when they would presumably use troop-transport aircraft. It is this social meaning that prevents language-learning descending into mere verbalism and it is this meaning with which the history teacher, along with other members of the school staff, must be especially concerned. Gradually he assists his students with regard to good language usage as well as with social meaning of such historically significant concepts as liberty, justice, equality, democracy, tyranny, despotism, totalitarianism and so on.

The teacher of history in Africa should not be discouraged by the language situation; in all countries history-teaching relies on the basic skills of reading, speaking and writing.

Reading

In reading history books students should be encouraged to cultivate flexible reading rates: intensive study for copies of historical documents; moderately intensive study for narrative history; skimming and scanning for historical reference purposes.

The textbook should be used as variously as possible: as a source for assignments—notes, essays, time-lines, historical graphs, character sketches, dialogues, classroom plays, etc.; its maps and pictures (frequently misunderstood by pupils in Africa) can be subjected to interpretation; its new words can become the basis of a glossary made at the back of the history notebook; its chapter arrangement can be used for improving reading skill (the class is instructed to read the title carefully, to examine any illustrated material, to read sub-headings and a few sentences in each paragraph and finally the conclusion—and then go back and read more carefully); it can be used as an introduction to a lesson or as a revision of it; its text can be compared with other books and any differing interpretations can form the basis for good historical discussion. Cross references in a history textbook can be very useful. Where they are not given the teacher should make his own. Classes can then be referred to other pages which they have previously read or to which they will come later. Above all the textbook must be used as a tool towards greater historical understanding. But students should be helped to appreciate that it is a very imperfect tool. Indeed it bears about as much relation to what happened as does the programme of the school play, staged many years before present students entered the school, does to the actual production.

Whenever possible the textbook should be supplemented with other material: pictures, newspapers, poetry, old photographs, film-strips, and so on, can all be called into contribution. Novels such as Peter Abrahams's, *Tell Freedom* (on South Africa) and such biographical novels as Joseph Abruquah's, *The Catechist* (on Ghana) and Dilim Okafor-Omali's, *A Nigerian Villager in Two Worlds*, and many of the volumes in Heinemann's *African Writers* series (all available as paperbacks) can be especially valuable in helping students to appreciate events of recent history in terms of people. Nor should poetry be neglected. The teacher will find *The Poetry of History* edited by D. J. Peters and B. E. Towers a useful book to possess.

Oral work

Question and answer is part of both the historical and the educational processes. In the latter the questions are often 'false': the teacher asks the questions but he already knows the answers.

Ideally, of course, the questions should come from those who are learning. In respect of African history at the present time this ideal can often correspond with reality. Teachers and taught alike are both learning. The educational and historical processes are fused and as a result can be more meaningful. The teacher who in answer to a question replies: 'I don't know; let's see if we can find out' is educating by example and profiting from the challenge that teaching African history has to offer.

By the skilful use of dramatisation in the classroom it is possible to exploit the challenge of the linguistic situation. There can be few better ways of teaching a language than by getting pupils to take part in a play that is written in good simple English. In the classroom 'I' and 'You' replace the 'He' and 'They' of the textbook, and this means that opportunities for expression, for really using the language, present themselves in a way that never happens when a descriptive passage from a book is being read aloud. The books tell us that Africa's first bishop, Samuel Crowther, was 'humble and devout' but the meaning of this is much more effectively brought home to a class through a little scene with Crowther in the classroom being told that he is to be recommended for a bishopric, and saying haltingly: 'I am not worthy. See the European missionaries who have been labouring for the cause of Africa so many years. Why should they be left and I be asked to take up such an office? No sir, I am their servant in the field and I can't accept it.' The classroom play is a living means of learning history and improving spoken English simultaneously.

But the teacher who launches into dramatisation without giving his classes any preparatory work will often be very disappointed by the result. Miming is a good introduction and the silent trade which used to be carried on in both East and West Africa provides a splendid opportunity for employing it in the classroom. The next stage can be the set speech (perhaps delivered by the teacher) and its effect on a crowd (the class). Many schools in West Africa have nicely re-enacted a fighting speech by Thomas Buxton on the question of abolishing slavery.

The classroom play is a more ambitious undertaking and requires more of the teacher who must be able to spot a colourful and significant event which can be turned into a small drama. He must try to put it into the mouths of his pupil actors in simple

English either by having his dialogue duplicated or having his class copy it down from the blackboard. So far as is possible, everybody in the class should take part in some capacity or other, often this can be done by using a chorus.

The next step in the use of spoken language in history is the dramatic exercise. The class constitutes the *dramatis personae* of an historical problem, e.g. Spanish 'experts' arguing whether or not to support Columbus' proposed voyage to India. The teacher can help to provide the arguments but the pupils actually use them. The next stage is for the pupils to provide their own arguments. The teacher is there just to set the situation and the problem. All these dramatic efforts help to promote the capacity for seeing 'the other person's viewpoint' which is a particularly valuable feature of the study of history.

With older classes, of course, more sophisticated debates and discussions can be held. They can sometimes take the form of mock trials. During the Workshop on the Teaching of African History held at Ibadan in 1965 the International School, Ibadan, staged a very successful mock trial of John Bull, British Imperialist, an exercise that was both enjoyable and significant in terms of the 'research' that had gone into it.

The effectiveness of classroom drama in history-teaching depends upon the enthusiasm and the guidance of the teacher, and this depends on how well the teacher can identify himself with his class. For him, it is a double dramatic process: identifying himself with the citizens of tomorrow who are identifying themselves with the citizens of yesterday. It is not easy but can be a stimulating and satisfying approach to history-teaching (see Plates III and IV).

Written work

Written work in school history can conveniently be broken down into three main divisions: notes; continuous prose (including essays); and one-word answers. The last of these is likely to become more important as examining bodies introduce tests involving one-word answers but it seems certain that the need to write continuous prose will continue to be a requirement of external examinations in history.

Objective tests

Objective tests are tests that can be shown statistically to be much less subject to error in marking than essay tests. They can also ensure much greater coverage of a syllabus than the more orthodox type of examination. Although guessing may enter into the results obtained, skilfully designed tests reduce this element to the minimum. Such tests, moreover, need not be limited to examination of factual material alone but can also demand the ordering of material in sequence, the deduction of general principles and the interpretation of evidence. Objective tests can constitute a rigorous enquiry into a person's ability to think historically.

Because of their objectivity such tests can be marked by machines and this, of course, commends itself to examining bodies which have to deal with large numbers of scripts. It should also commend itself to teachers since if they employ such tests they can get their pupils either to mark their own answers or mark those of one another. By employing a battery of say half a dozen questions, administered orally, the teacher can see how much has been learned, familiarise himself with the great difficulties involved in 'item' (or question) writing and enable his class to be introduced to the essentials of objective testing procedure.

Notes

All too often notes are either the work of the teacher and merely dictated to, or copied by, the class, or else they are the work of the pupil who has been left to fend for himself. The older school of history teachers often tend to adopt the former process; the younger school, having frequently been taught by training colleges and handbooks that this is wrong, adopt the latter. Many would subscribe to the assertion: 'note-taking is bad; note-making is good' without appreciating that this approach was essentially elaborated for children using their mother tongue as the medium of education. The situation is otherwise in Africa.

Those who teach in African schools should disabuse themselves of the idea that noting is an *either-or* procedure; it does not involve the agency of either the teacher or the pupil; it involves them *both*. Not until the sixth form should classes be left to make notes completely unaided by the teacher; nor with the possible exception of occasional 'examples' in the lower forms should notes be the exclusive work of the teacher. Throughout the school the personal contributions made by pupils to the noting procedure should increase as they grow older.

The essence of noting is that it is concerned with recording *essentials*, with the meaning behind the words employed. This is an immensely sophisticated procedure which not a few university graduates using their mother tongue have failed to grasp. How much more therefore should pupils in African schools be assisted with the task.

The first step in noting is *understanding*: again and again the teacher must ask for paraphrases in the pupils own words of difficult sentences and concepts by asking such questions as 'What do we mean when we say X?'; 'Was there anything in the pages that you have just read that you didn't understand?' He must be constantly on the watch for pupils who think they understand when they do not: e.g. those who think that *aliens* are synonymous with Europeans; those who write 'circular princes' for secular princes. Historical terminology must be thoroughly understood: the *Scramble* for Africa did not mean that the Berlin Conference (1884–5) broke up with the delegates dashing for the boats. Paraphrase is not something that should be limited to the English lesson. It can make a significant contribution in history. It is frequently worthwhile to get a first or second form to paraphrase one or two paragraphs from their textbooks. Possibly first of all they should be asked to read the passage and underline faintly in pencil the words they do not understand for discussion in class. In junior forms students' notebooks should less resemble the orthodox history exercise book with its headings and its 'Causes of X' all neatly docketed *a*, *b* and *c*, than an English exercise book which is abreast of the times. But it must be more than this: it must be an individual creation brought about by encouraging its owner to stick in appropriate pictures, make drawings, diagrams and time-lines; something of which the author feels proud. Much of the content should be comprehension exercises which the teacher has marked. At the back of the book it is often advisable to have a 'Guide to Historical Study' in which teachers and pupils working together define the meanings of words that are used: e.g. A.D.; B.C.; oral tradition; privilege (the most commonly misspelt word in African school history?); denomination; feudalism, etc., etc.

The second step in noting is *selection*. Here one moves on from

4

paraphrase to précis; and once again exercises are involved-execution. The class can be told to summarise a paragraph in a sentence and then say four paragraphs in four sentences. Possibly first of all they should be asked to read the passage and to underline those parts which they believe to be particularly important as a basis for class discussion. When reading study assignments are set, the teacher can often help students to undertake selection by indicating topics that are particularly significant or questions for which answers are sought. A quick five-minute written *quiz* on the topics or an oral discussion of the questions can then introduce the next lesson. This kind of work can lead on to the teacher's *précis-quiz*. The teacher himself makes a brief summary of the reading assignment and then proceeds to dictate it to the class to copy down. But this is no ordinary dictation exercise; significant words have been replaced with sounds for which the class is expected to substitute what has been omitted: e.g. 'It is believed that the Sabeans came from *Bing* (Arabia) and crossed the *Bong* (Red) Sea and settled in the *Bang* (Ethiopian) Highlands some time during the *Bung* (first) millennium B.C.' Learning takes place within a meaningful historical framework. At the end of the exercise pupils can exchange their exercise books and mark the quiz. Junior forms can derive great fun and considerable educational benefit from such exercises.

More formal noting can develop from the procedures outlined above. After a reading assignment it is useful to recapitulate what has been studied by means of a blackboard summary. To this the teacher and the class alike contribute by means of question and answer, making a great deal of use of abbreviations (e.g. *B*'s for Boers; *Br* for British and *Ba* for Bantu) and telegraphese (e.g. the omission of all but the essential words). Towards the end of the lesson the class can then copy down the notes completing all abbreviations and putting the whole into good sequential English. The blackboard summary in fact can be utilised a good deal in helping classes with their notes. A further development is to rub out all but the headings and the sub-headings of the summary and leave the class to copy these down and complete the notes for preparation or homework. Another alternative is to have a skeleton note consisting of a series of questions to which the class find out the answers. And of course blackboard summaries may consist of diagrams, graphs and time-lines and maps.

In noting, the good teacher has many possibilities for combining oral work, reading and writing and he should try to ring the changes as much as possible. There are, however, some warnings that he should heed: it is almost invariably unwise for any class, apart from possibly the sixth, to be expected to make notes while the teacher is talking; 'long notes' should be discouraged—the teacher can sometimes specify the maximum number of words to be used; dogmatism in notes should be avoided and question marks in parenthesis liberally employed, and where alternative interpretations exist these should be indicated.

Finally, the fourth step in noting is often ignored. It is *utilisation*. Students need to *use* their notes as much as possible not simply as a source of revision for an examination. Just as they needed to be helped to make a note from a paragraph so they will often require help in making a paragraph from a note. For example, there is the need to be given the opportunity to interpret a note in terms of people (e.g. imagine you were Yusuf bin Hassan. Explain why you took to piracy on the East African coast in the seventeenth century); to compose a dialogue between people (e.g. in a market-place in Gobir in 1803 before the *Jihād* or Holy War of Usuman dan Fodio). They can be encouraged to give small spoken reports derived from the notes they have made (e.g. explain why it took Wilberforce so long to bring about the ending of the slave trade). Once again there are many possibilities. In the context of English as a second language the elaboration of notes should not be neglected.

Continuous prose exercises

Too often students' essays on historical subjects are regarded as though they were the individual creations of those who wrote them. This is a very superficial view. Any experienced School Certificate examiner knows that he is not just marking the individual candidate's performance but the work of his teacher as well. An essay on an historical subject represents the joint endeavour of teacher and taught more subtly but no less surely than notes.

Although study based on the School Certificate syllabus should not take more than two years before the examination, careful preparation for writing essay-type answers should start in the first form. Here simple passages of descriptive work can be set: e.g. I want you to imagine that you are a merchant in Cairo in the year 1324 and you see Mansa Musa's pilgrim train passing on its way to Mecca. Write a paragraph describing it. Gradually the difficulty of exercises can be increased: e.g. I want you to write out an answer to this question, 'Why is the duiker the symbol of the Bangmanwato tribe?' Such exercises need not always be marked by the teacher though sometimes this must be done. At other times it suffices to go round the class while passages are being written, helping where necessary, and then to have three or four pupils read aloud their accounts. Slowly assignments can be increased in length and the analytical, rather than the descriptive, approach fostered.

In working on the School Certificate syllabus essay questions need to be set and marked. This is a very time-consuming process and the history teacher who has to mark thirty mock S.C. answers will probably find that the task takes him three or four hours. Fortunately he need not face such an assignment too frequently. During the first term of the School Certificate course it will probably suffice to get students preparing skeleton plans of essay answers. Each paragraph can be represented by a sub-heading and the substance of the paragraph noted under it. The teacher can launch the exercise by emphasising the importance of planning answers and by giving suggestions for sub-headings. To give more practice and variety, different questions can be set for the different groups into which the class is divided. Later the writing out in full of the concluding paragraph can be added to the exercise. These conclusions can then be read aloud by their authors and can often form the basis of a worth-while discussion. Still later questions can be set for 'prep' and last of all essays can be tackled 'under examination conditions' within a given time limit in the classroom.

Although the rate at which this whole process is developed will depend upon the progress that is made by the class, some such scheme seems essential. It contributes to the confidence of the candidate when he is confronted by the School Certificate paper and also, properly handled by the teacher, it can generate a good deal of enthusiasm in the class: 'Our friend has said in his essay that "the Industrial Revolution was the real villain of the Scramble for Africa". What do you think he means? . . . How many of you agree with him? . . . Why (not)?' Or: 'Imagine that you are examiners, what sort of mark would you give to an essay that ended in this way—. . .? . . . Why?' (If the example is poor, use an anonymous specimen, preferably from another class; if the example is good use a named specimen from the class!)

If this approach is adopted it can be carried over to 'Bridge' work. Here, however, the teacher must be prepared to be much more searching in his marking. Comments such as 'Why do you say this?', 'What about the alternative interpretation?' must be much more frequent. Students need not be encouraged to give their references in footnotes but it is useful for them to list the books they have used at the end of their essays.

The Social Factor

History is concerned with people; so are schools. History-teaching and school organisation should supplement each other. History should not just be something that is pigeon-holed into certain periods for certain classes; it should spill over into the life of the school just as education should spill over into the lives of those who have left school. The best means of ensuring that it does so is to have enthusiastic teachers who enjoy the subject and who are prepared to experiment in teaching it. They will find the History Room and a school society concerned with history very valuable aids in their work.

The History Room

It is fortunate that all the secondary schools that have been built in Africa over the past half century have been equipped with a History Room.

Teachers who have seen the rather elaborate plans and pictures of History Rooms that are to be found in manuals designed for teachers in developed countries may be surprised by this statement but it is nonetheless true. *Any* classroom is potentially a History Room. What brings about the transformation is not the equipment that the room contains but the use to which the room is put. If it is used for history-teaching and for scarcely any other subject then to the corporate mind of the school it will be 'the History Room'. In the last resort, then, whether a school possesses such a room depends upon its organisation. Students must go to history, in the shape of Mr X's room, rather than expect history, in the shape of Mr X, to come to them. Such an arrangement, of course, need not preclude the use of the room both as a form room and the headquarters of the school history society.

Given a classroom with a good blackboard, it can gradually be transformed. Hardboard can be fixed to wall surfaces for the display of maps, charts and posters. The visual aspect of history must not be neglected.

Where resources are limited it may not be possible for every pupil to have his own historical atlas though certainly classes should be encouraged to bring their geographical atlases to history lessons where they can very frequently be of the greatest use. Each History Room, however, should possess one or two historical atlases[6] which the teacher and the class can use for reference purposes. In addition a small collection of historical wall maps[7] can be acquired. In this connection teachers will find blank cellograph wall maps,[8] which can carry the markings of chinagraph coloured pencils, especially helpful. Many a lesson can be made much more meaningful by the teacher preparing a cellograph map from an historical atlas—a simple exercise that need only take five or ten minutes and then using it during the class.

Fortunately something like ninety per cent of the posters that are produced in Africa are suitable for use in the History Room, even if only their backs are used! In groups a class can produce sections of an historical display and then stick their sections to a commercially produced poster—and the teacher has a useful aid for next year's class. An historical frieze can be made by the class divided up into pairs—one pupil the artist, one the scribe—with an 'editor' advising and sticking the joint contributions together. There can be a time-line that goes round the room above or below the windows divided into centuries with each epoch illustrated by appropriate visual material. Hardboard on the walls is one of first priorities for a History Room.

Probably the next priority should be the provision of sensible classroom furniture: tables and chairs, *not* desks with seats attached. If possible the chairs should be of the stackable variety and the tables light and collapsible so that on occasions (e.g. when theatre-in-the-round is required for classroom plays) they will not take up too much room. Such tables should have flat tops (a plastic surface is a splendid refinement) and be of a standard height so that they can be pushed together to provide a large working area. Such furniture can often be made by a local carpenter quite cheaply.

If possible the History Room should also accommodate a small library. Desirable as this may be, however, lack of finance may make it impossible. Such books as can be bought have to be placed in the School Library and it is not possible to have libraries in classrooms. In such circumstances the history teacher is apt to lose touch with what is in the library and consequently cannot give much guidance to his classes on supplementary reading. The second-former who has been told 'to look it up in the library' is apt to be discouraged by the enormity of the undertaking. More specific guidance is necessary. In this respect it is helpful for the history teacher to let the School Librarian know the titles of books he considers particularly suitable for use by his classes, for inclusion in the library, and to keep an index. (He might perhaps take the dust covers off history books on their arrival. From these covers a small card index of the history books in the library can be built up and kept in the History Room. Pasting 'quotes' from the covers on cards might be one of the tasks of the History Society's 'Librarian'. The teacher will find such an index very useful in distributing assignments to his classes: 'I want you X to look up Basil Davidson's *Black Mother* (Gollancz) and give us a five-minute talk on Antera Duke's Diary', etc.

Where only a small sum of money can be spent on the History Room Library this should be invested in small sets of books: collections of documents and writings such as Norah Latham, *The Heritage of West Africa* (Hulton) and Zoë Marsh, *East Africa Through Contemporary Records* (Cambridge) project books, classroom plays, etc. When such sets are in use it may only be possible for there to be one book between five or six pupils. Work in such groups is still possible provided the classroom furniture is arranged accordingly. Moreover, it is sometimes possible to use a nearby classroom left empty by a class going to Physical Education or to the laboratory, say, for the accommodation of perhaps two or three groups. When a class is really interested in a project there should be few discipline difficulties.

Once the teacher has the facilities outlined above, he can embark on the acquisition of such equipment as radio, film-strips and projector, a daylight screen, a tape-recorder, an overhead projector, a film projector, television and so on, about which he will find no lack of advice in the many publications that are devoted to audio-visual aids. All such equipment can be put to worth-while use in the History Room but it should not be considered as a first priority. Teachers should first concentrate on: (a) blackboard and textbooks; (b) hardboard surfaces and display material; (c) suitable furniture; (d) supplementary material.

A School Society

'Containing' history in the average school curriculum is rather like trying to cram the requirements for a lifetime into a weekend case. One is obliged to make other arrangements. The wise history teacher encourages out-of-school interests in his pupils.

These interests can often be canalised in the activities of a school society which, of course, is not confined by syllabus requirements. Nor need it be restricted to any given subject. Indeed an extracurricular society can help compensate for the subject compartmentalism often found in secondary schools. It can, for instance, deal with geography, local culture, history and current affairs. It might be known as the Social Studies Society or the African Studies Club, or schools in West Africa might prefer to have a Blyden Society, schools in South and Central Africa their Luthuli Society or other appropriately named clubs.

Such societies can organise visits to sites of historical interest and to museums, arranging assignments for its members so that everybody who takes part in the visit has a particular job to do (for instance sketching a certain brick formation at Zimbabwe or an architectural feature in one of the Gold Coast forts). A society can arrange for talks by those who have some particular knowledge; it can help to provide teaching aids for history-teaching in the school, models, maps and wall charts; it can write and produce an historical play; it can stage a mock election or a mock trial. It can help with archaeological work; it can collect oral traditions; it can make an anthology of local myths and folklore; it can collect local arts and crafts and arrange for their display in the school; it can compile a scrapbook of local history, calling into contribution remembrances of older people, newspaper cuttings and such photographs and pictures as can be obtained; and it can stage festivals of traditional music and dances. It might even undertake the production of its own book. For a period of three years the boys of the Local History Society of the Secondary School, Methodist College, Uzuakoli in Eastern Nigeria undertook such a project so effectively that their book was published.[9] In Europe a school history society may be something of a luxury; in Africa it can be a vital part of school life, helping to compensate for the economy that has to be exercised in running schools and helping to exploit the peculiar advantages involved in the study of African history. At the present time in Africa, the history teacher needs to derive enjoyment from educational opportunities and satisfaction from sharing his enjoyment with his students. (See Plates I and II.)

NOTES

1 The author acknowledges with gratitude the information that he has received from many Ministries of Education in Africa concerning their schemes of history-teaching.

2 In Britain only one year has been authoritatively recommended, W. H. Burston and C. W. Green, *Handbook for History Teachers*, pp. 134–5, Methuen, 1962. In Africa, however, language difficulties, shortages of books and teaching aids and the innovatory syllabuses, especially in African history, make two years desirable.

3 One of the most carefully compiled schemes is that of Zambia. Teachers in other parts of the continent may care to consult Judith M. Temple, *Social Studies for Zambia*, Books I–IV, Lutterworth.

4 For example *History Bookshelves* and *Museums Bookshelves*, ed. C. B. Firth, Ginn; *Then and There* series, ed. M. E. Reeves and P. Hodgson, Longmans.

5 For example Alan Hill and Susan Ault, *History in Action* (4 books), Heineman; Godfrey N. Brown, *An Active History of Ghana* (2 books), Allen & Unwin. For fifth- and sixth-formers J. H. Bowles, *Dramatic Decisions 1776–1945*, Macmillan, will be found useful.

6 For example J. D. Fage, *An Atlas of African History*, Arnold, 1964; R. R. Sellman, *A Historical Atlas 1789–1962*, Arnold, 1963; *Muir's New School Atlas of Universal History*, George Philip, 21st edition, 1961; *Philip's Intermediate Historical Atlas*, George Philip, 21st edition, 1961.

7 The coloured maps contained in this book are published by Nelson.

8 An excellent series is published by Philip & Tacy.

9 *Uzuakoli; A Short History*, ed. A. J. Fox, O.U.P., 1964.

SELECT BIBLIOGRAPHY

K. D. Ghose, *Creative Teaching of History*, Bombay.
R. E. Crookall, *A Handbook for History Teachers in West Africa*, Evans, 1960.
W. H. Burston and C. W. Green, *Handbook for History Teachers*, Methuen, 1962.
M. V. C. Jeffreys, *History in Schools: The Study of Development*, Pitman, 1939.

H. Johnson, *Teaching of History*, Macmillan, New York, 1940.
P. Carpenter, *History Teaching: The Era Approach*, C.U.P., 1964.
J. Hemming, *The Teaching of Social Studies in Secondary Schools*, Longmans, 1956.
J. Dray and D. Jordan, *A Handbook of Social Studies*, Methuen, 1950.
E. Milliken and R. E. Crookall, *Historical Model Making for African Schools*, University of London Press, 1962.

3 The Teacher and Archaeology in Africa South of the Sahara

THURSTAN SHAW

STRICTLY speaking, history is the account of what happened in the past made up from the writings of people who lived at or soon after the period being described. In a wider sense, history is the story of what happened at any time in the past, whether anyone wrote down anything about it or not.

Now in all parts of the world, human beings have lived and loved, worked and fought, sought food and shelter, made tools and weapons and had children and brought them up, before they knew the art of writing. Therefore there was no one to write down their history, or the story of how they lived or obtained their livelihood or travelled about. Yet we are all interested in our ancestors and wish to know what sort of people they were and what were their achievements. This story of our preliterate forebears is immensely important, too, in the story of the emergence of Man from prehuman ancestors in the course of evolution, and this in turn contributes considerably to the understanding of modern man.

If no one wrote anything down about the ancient people, how can we know anything about them? There is a limit to the accuracy and time-depth of even the most carefully preserved oral traditions; and in some cases even these are entirely absent. Will not anything we say about these times, then, be pure speculation? At one time this was the case—and all sorts of conjectures and theories, myths and legends, were told concerning man's pre-literate period, including those contained in parts of the Old Testament of the Bible. Some of these guesses may have been 'inspired guesses' and not far from the truth, but they remain guesses as far as their factual content is concerned, even if, as in the case of the Bible, some of them were made the vehicles for what can still be regarded as spiritual truths.

However, in the course of the last hundred years or so there has been developed the science of archaeology, which is able to discover large parts of the story of man's unwritten past by studying the material objects he has left behind him. Of course it cannot be pretended that scientific archaeology can give as complete an account of a period of the past as can a written history, but it can reconstruct large parts of the story with far greater accuracy than mere speculation. The work of archaeological research is continuing, so that gaps are continually being filled and greater accuracy being achieved.

Archaeologists work rather like a detective who collects his data from a large number of different clues and then, putting them all together, reasons out certain deductions and conclusions from them, e.g. 'the murderer must have been a left-handed man'. The archaeologist works in just the same kind of way, using both common-sense observation and a whole battery of scientific laboratory techniques. Just as the detective may not be able to name the murderer but is able to narrow down the hunt to left-handed men, so archaeology may be unable to name a king or a chief or a people in the past but it can nevertheless give a lot of information about them: how they were dressed, how they got their food, how they made things, what sort of homes they lived in, how they buried their dead, what sort of trade or warfare they engaged in and how long ago they lived.

STRATIFICATION

One of the most important pieces of archaeological evidence derives from the *position in the ground* in which objects are found. It is obvious that if there has been no subsequent disturbance of the ground, something found *deeper* than a second thing must have got there or been put there *before* the second thing, perhaps a very long time before. This is the same principle as is used in geology, that of *stratification*, namely that the deeper layers are older than the upper layers (except in certain well-defined circumstances). We can, for instance, imagine a band of hunters living in a cave or under a rock-shelter. It is here that the game they have hunted is cooked and eaten and the refuse thrown away, as with the fruit, nuts and roots which they may also have collected; here that tools and weapons are made and waste materials left; here that common objects of everyday use are dropped and lost. In this way material accumulates in and around the cave, and embedded in it are some of the domestic articles characteristic of this hunting people. Then perhaps the climate changes slightly (as we know has happened several times in the past) as a result of which the game moves away, the hunters follow and the cave is left unoccupied. No longer is anything of human manufacture dropped in the cave, but dust and leaves blow in, pieces of stone fall off the roof and so a 'sterile' layer containing no 'artifacts' (anything made by man) is formed above the layer of the hunters' refuse. After a long time, perhaps a thousand years, a different set of people come along and use the cave as a ready-made habitation. These people practise agriculture and have completely different tools and weapons, pots and pans, clothes and ornaments from those of the previous hunters. Nevertheless, from living in the cave, these people lay down a layer of earth which contains *their* characteristic artifacts, in just the same way as the hunters had done. Later on these agriculturalists learnt to build houses, so they abandoned their cave and a sterile layer again started forming over their remains. Thus if we dig a trench through the cave deposits, the section through them would be something like this:

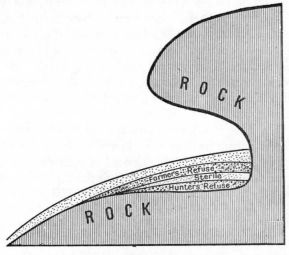

Fig. 1

If we dig and find a section like this, it does not require great powers of deduction to interpret the evidence as showing that the hunting people first occupied the cave, that then there was a gap of no occupation, followed by the advent of quite different farming people.

EXCAVATION

It sometimes happens that in their excavations, say of a richly furnished royal tomb, archaeologists find rare and precious objects or works of art of great beauty, but this is not what they are *primarily* looking for. Excavation is not a treasure-hunt, even if 'treasures' may be discovered in this way incidentally. What scientific archaeologists are seeking to obtain in their excavations is knowledge, information and data which will enable them to fill out the picture of the past more accurately. For this, a certain mark in the soil or a piece of charcoal may be more important than a ceremonial gold dagger. This is why, in their digging, archaeologists go so slowly and carefully, looking at every little piece of soil for evidence, measuring accurately the position of things found, keeping a photographic record, drawing plans, submitting many of their finds to laboratory experts for specialist reports—very much in the manner of the police detective trying to reconstruct a crime One of the most important specialist services used by the archaeologist and which helps him to date his deposits is that of radiocarbon analysis. This is a method whereby the proportion of the radioactive isotope of carbon (C 14) to ordinary carbon (C 12) is measured in such a way as to indicate the approximate age of the sample analysed. Any organic material can furnish a sample for radiocarbon dating, but charcoal is the best and commonest.

Inevitably there is a large element of chance in what survives to the present from among the objects made and used by the peoples of the past. If a people disposed of their dead by exposing them in trees or just throwing them into the bush we might have no idea of their physical form, whereas we might have a very good idea of this if they practised embalming and mummifying. If a people lived exclusively in tents we might have very little idea of their homes, whereas we might obtain a good idea of this if they built stone houses. Different climatic and soil conditions, too, affect the extent to which objects are preserved or destroyed. Objects of stone and pottery are almost indestructible, but objects of wood, leather, bone, basketry and textiles require specially favourable conditions for their preservation. Of metals, gold is almost indestructible, iron often rusts away to an unrecognisable lump, while copper, bronze and brass may or may not be well preserved. Much of the skill of the archaeologist consists in conserving the fragmentary remains of badly preserved objects, and digging in such a way that they are not damaged.

The first discovery of an archaeological find or of an archaeological site is very commonly made accidentally by an ordinary person and not by an archaeologist at all; in digging a well or the foundations of a house, in building a road or a railway, in mining operations or in farming. Anywhere where the ground is being dug into there is the chance of an archaeological find. Whenever one is made, it is important that the person digging should stop and not dig around to see how much more he can find, but report it to an archaeologist, so that with his special techniques he can extract the maximum amount of *information* from the find. If it is impossible to wait for the arrival of an archaeologist, careful notes should be made of the depth and position in which objects are found, and if possible photographs of the spot should be taken.

ARCHAEOLOGY IN AFRICA

In most of Africa south of the Sahara there are few written records before A.D. 1000, and in many areas there are none until a later date than this. What, then, is archaeology able to tell of Africa before written records? Regrettably, at the moment, the picture is very imperfect, and has many gaps in it, because it must be remembered that archaeological research in Tropical Africa has only been going on for a comparatively short time, on a limited scale and it has been very unevenly distributed.

It is now generally accepted that all the modern races of the world today belong to a single biological species, to which is given the name *Homo sapiens* ('thinking man'), and that in the course of evolution Homo sapiens emerged from more ape-like forms. It is not believed that Man evolved from apes or monkeys, but that apes and men have a common ancestry. This evolution appears to have taken place in Africa, at least most of the evidence for it so far comes from eastern and southern Africa. The point in time when this divergence began is well over a million years ago, and seems to have been connected with a drying out of the climate, which compelled forest-dwelling creatures to go partly to the more open country between the forest galleries which survived along the water-courses. These *Australopithecines*, or 'southern apes', as they are called, had taken to an upright gait instead of one on all fours, and had bigger brains and smaller snouts than apes; their hands were free to use tools. These developments represented important steps along the path of evolution towards true Man. These early ape-men had very crude stone tools, sometimes just a pebble with a few chips knocked off it to make a sharp cutting edge, and they appear to have diversified their food from the mainly vegetarian diet of the forest by beginning to eat meat as well. It is inevitable that the earliest and crudest stone tools should only be slight improvements upon naturally broken pieces of rock, and so they may be hard to recognise.

STONE

The form of 'ape-men' intermediate between the Australopithecines and Homo sapiens is called by the scientists *Pithecanthropus* ('ape-man'), but most of the fossil examples known come from Asia, although some interesting recent finds from Morocco appear to belong to this group. Pithecanthropus had a larger brain than Australopithecus and more nearly resembled Homo sapiens, although still not having as big a brain as he has.

All this period belongs to the Earlier Stone Age, and as time went on artifacts made of chipped stone acquired regular and recognisable shapes and forms. Most distinctive are those known as 'handaxes'. The early ones were lumpy pieces of stone trimmed to give a rough beak or point or a cutting edge down the sides, the later ones were much better made so as to be flatter and hava a blade-like point, or to be oval in shape and have a cutting edge all round. 'Cleavers' also appear—similar pieces of stone but trimmed in such a way as to give a straight cutting or chopping edge across the top. These handaxe people seem to have lived, by hunting and gathering, over the greater part of Africa, but to have kept outside the wetter, forested zones, except perhaps in some cases in the drier periods. This period of the Earlier Stone Age was immensely long, and development took place very slowly.

During the Stone Age there were changes in the climate which affected the whole earth. At times the North Polar ice-sheet spread far down into Europe, Asia and America, and during the height of these glacial stages so much of the world's water was locked up in the form of ice that sea-levels were lower over the whole world, sometimes making land-bridges for the movements of men and animals across places which are now covered by sea. In tropical latitudes there were 'pluvial' periods of increased rainfall, which made lake-levels rise, in place of glacial periods, but not necessarily at exactly the same times. It is possible to see evidence of these changes in the geological record of the earth's surface, and the finding of the handiwork of different kinds of Stone Age peoples in terraces of gravel or old lake-beds helps to date the different stages in relation to these climatic changes.

Succeeding the Earlier Stone Age a number of different cultures are known in different parts of Africa, apparently differentiated according to environment, whether forested or more open, and according to the raw materials available. We are now dealing with the period of about 50,000 years ago, and by this time Man in Africa probably had the use of fire. So the slow development goes on; on into the Middle Stone Age, with improved stone-working techniques and probably the introduction of the throwing spear, tipped with well-chipped stone points. Points appear with tangs, small projections to assist with fitting the point into the shaft, and projecting shoulders are left on the point to make rudimentary barbs; it is possible that this form of point indicates the introduction of the bow. These earliest kinds of tanged points have been found in North Africa and the Sahara, and others are known from the Congo area.

Further improvements in hafting techniques were later made, with the result that the stone implements become very small in size, since, as arrow-points and barbs and perhaps composite knives, they were slotted into shafts in which grooves were cut with tiny chisel-like tools. These very small implements are often called 'microliths' ('small stones'). Microlithic industries have been found in a large number of places in Africa, and a considerable number of regional variants are known. In Sudan and Kenya the later stages of these microlith-using people seem to have had pottery at an early date, in fact it may be the earliest in the world. It has been suggested that this was not later than about 7000 B.C., and that pottery may be an African invention, later transmitted to the peoples to the north after the beginnings of the earliest agriculture.

5

Probably rather more than 10,000 years ago, in the hill country flanking the northern side of the 'Fertile Crescent'—in parts of modern Iran, northern Iraq, Anatolia and the Syria/Jordan area—some of the hunting and gathering peoples of the time seem to have begun using for food the grains of certain wild grasses, which, after suitable grinding and preparation, were found to be good to eat. Later, some of the grass seeds were kept and planted near a living place, instead of people simply going out and foraging among the wild products. So the domestication of cereals began and the practice of agriculture was invented. The domestication of animals was an associated process, perhaps as a result of wild animals hanging round the now more permanent human settlements to obtain scraps or to try to eat crops or stubble; such 'lures' were seen to be an easier way of hunting, and an easier way still of ensuring a meat supply if you did not immediately kill all your captured animals but let them breed in captivity. The first domesticated animal seems to have been the sheep, followed by goat and pig and then cattle. The dog came after, at first probably for food rather than as a hunting companion. All this revolutionised the human way of life, making possible a greater permanence of settlement in one place, an accumulation of food resources, and with these an increase of leisure-time, the beginning of specialisation of jobs, and the release of some members of the community from the task of food production. This revolution in the human way of life is sometimes referred to as the 'Neolithic' (New Stone Age) Revolution, for it came in the last part of the Stone Age. In many cases, stone axes were now made, not simply by chipping, but by rubbing, grinding and polishing them to shape and to obtain a sharp cutting edge; this method made possible the use of tougher kinds of rocks which were less likely to chip or shatter in use.

The area of the present Sahara Desert was much less arid 10,000 to 5,000 years ago than at present, and supported a Mediterranean type of vegetation. In the later part of this period there lived in it a large population of peoples with a 'neolithic' type of equipment, which included pottery and ground stone axes; they were probably largely pastoralists, although the great number and variety of beautifully flaked stone arrowheads found, as well as bone harpoons, suggest that hunting and fishing also played an important part in the economy. Finds of the different regional variants of this 'Sahara Neolithic' are mostly confined to the north of 15° North latitude, but an interesting discovery of material of this kind has recently been made in northern Ghana, indicating that at least one group of these people migrated a long way to the south of their previous habitat, probably when the latter became too dry to support their former way of life there. The progressive desiccation of the Sahara must have had an important effect on folk movements during the second and third millennia B.C., and these must have had repercussions in western and central Africa.

Ground stone axes are found throughout the whole of West Africa including the forest area, but they are also known in smaller numbers in eastern and southern Africa. They are often believed by the present inhabitants to be thunderbolts hurled by the god of thunder or a sky-god, and as such to have magical properties.

From the third millennium B.C. onwards, desiccation set in throughout the Sahara, progressively forcing out the Late Stone Age peoples and turning it, if not into a complete barrier to human passage, nevertheless into an increasingly effective filter. This was unfortunate for sub-Saharan Africa because, combined with the Sudd swamps of the upper Nile, it largely cut the rest of Africa off from the important developments which were taking place in Egypt, the Middle East and Western Pakistan. It is ironical too, that the very effectiveness and self-sufficiency of ancient Egyptian civilisation served further to bar the rest of Africa from the developments which took place in south-west Asia. These developments constituted a second revolution in the human way of living, growing out of and made possible by the accumulated results of the first, or 'neolithic', revolution. This second revolution has been called the 'Urban Revolution', because, as a result of accumulations of wealth, an assured food supply and an increasing division of labour, people were able to live together in larger and larger numbers and the first permanent cities appeared. This process both fostered and was assisted by the discovery and development of metallurgy (at first copper, then its alloy with tin, bronze), as well as the art of writing, which is necessary before the scale of social and political organisation can advance beyond a certain point. It was in this phase of development also that the wheel was invented.

Now it has been claimed in the past by one school of thought that all human inventions stemmed from a single source and that they spread out from this source to the rest of the world by a process of diffusion. These 'diffusionists' claimed that nothing was ever invented twice. Another school of thought claimed that every human group passed through certain set stages in a process of cultural evolution, as a result of which many different groups followed a natural and logical course, each step of progress leading on to the discovery of the next, even if at different times. The holders of this view were called the 'evolutionists'. It was possible for these two opposing theories to hold the field at the same time because of lack of evidence to settle the argument. It can now be seen that the truth lies somewhere between the two, with diffusion playing the major role. There has been more than one independent invention of some things, for example agriculture in the Old World and the New, but the number of such instances is limited. If, therefore, for geographical or historical reasons, an area becomes cut off from fertilising contact with other parts of the world where discoveries and inventions are taking place, it may lag behind and some time may elapse before that area catches up with the new developments. Because of the barrier of the Atlantic Ocean, America had to wait more than five thousand years to receive the benefits of the inventions made in the Old World, just as the Old also had to wait a long time to receive the benefit of many useful crops domesticated in the New.

This kind of isolation, then, is the reason why there was no Copper or Bronze Age in Africa outside the brilliant civilisation of ancient Egypt, why there was no writing until the advent of the Arabic script, why there was no wheel until the nineteenth century in many places—not because of any inferiority of inventiveness on the part of the peoples living in sub-Saharan Africa, but because they were cut off at the critical moment, by a geographical and climatological accident, from the centres from which these ideas were diffusing to most of Europe and Asia. Wheels were known in Britain two thousand years ago only because contact was established with the Mediterranean world which had them; no one in Britain ever invented a wheel.

IRON

So it comes about that the next most important development in Africa was the coming of iron. Iron has considerable advantages over copper or bronze as a metal for tools and weapons, although its metallurgy is quite different and, in some ways, more difficult. Iron is harder and tougher than bronze but, above all, it is much cheaper and more easily available, because iron ores in one form or another are widespread. The art of smelting iron was discovered in Asia Minor, to the south of the Black Sea, in the area of the ancient Hittite Empire, during the second millennium B.C., and the Hittites may have intentionally kept the secret to themselves for some time. Ultimately, however, it spread to the Assyrians, and it was the superiority of their iron weapons that largely accounted for their conquest of the Bronze Age civilisation of Egypt, where iron did not come into common use until about 600 B.C., much later than farther north and east. Nubia was established as an African kingdom, with a capital at Meroë and strong connections with Egypt and the Mediterranean world, from the fifth century B.C. to the third century A.D., and was a great centre of iron manufacture, as the piles of iron slag at Meroë testify. It seems that this was the diffusion centre from which a knowledge of iron-working spread into most of Africa. It is also possible that iron-working may have been introduced into West Africa from the North African city of Carthage, which iron-using Phoenicians established in the ninth century B.C. It seems likely that Carthaginian traders and their intermediaries succeeded in tapping the gold resources of West Africa, and it is possible that as a result of this contact, a knowledge of iron-working may have been diffused in the opposite direction.

At any rate there is evidence for a knowledge of iron in West Africa by the third century B.C., and perhaps earlier, in the Nok culture, named after the village of that name in northern Nigeria. The distinctive feature of this culture is the production of terracotta (baked clay) figures and figurines of a distinctive artistic style and of great beauty. Human heads are the commonest (see Plate X), probably broken off from complete statues, but animals, such as monkeys and elephants, also occur. The human figures vary from two-thirds of life size to complete diminutive figures not more than 8 cm. high. They were probably cult objects placed on shrines in connection with the worship of ancestors or certain deities. The majority have been found in alluvial deposits being worked for tin, in which are also found iron objects and the pipes for carrying the forced draught from bellows into iron-smelting furnaces. Stone axes and microliths are also found in these deposits, so the time represented may be the period of transition and overlap of the use of stone and iron; or the stone implements may be older material also washed into the deposits by the flooding rivers. Finds of the Nok culture are known from a wide arc of country west, south-west and south of the Jos Plateau.

It seems that a knowledge of iron-working spread fairly rapidly over some parts of Africa, much more slowly to others, and not at all in some cases. It is believed that it reached central Africa early in the first millennium A.D., but when Europeans first came to the most southerly part of the continent they found Bushmen and Hottentot people there who had no iron and were still using stone and bone tools and weapons.

It is very likely that the change from food-gathering to food-production in Africa south of the Sahara was associated with the spread of iron. Unfortunately we do not as yet know as much about the beginnings of agriculture in Africa as we should like. As elsewhere, doubtless the change was a gradual one, and food production, while making possible more permanent settlement and ultimate urbanisation, does not preclude the continued practice of hunting and of gathering wild products, as in many food-producing African societies today. One anthropologist has claimed an independent invention of agriculture, as long ago perhaps as the fifth millennium B.C., in the upper Niger area; however, the evidence is largely botanical and the botanists are not agreed. There is a claim for a West African domestication of one kind of rice and it does seem likely that yams were indigenously cultivated, although we do not know whether this was before or after the introduction from Asia of the banana and the Asian yam some two thousand years ago. Maize, cassava and sweet potatoes were only introduced to Africa after the discovery of America. The evidence on this question of the beginnings of agriculture and vegeculture in Africa is not strictly archaeological, but comes from anthropology, botany and linguistics. There is linguistic evidence to suggest that the Bantu-speaking peoples had a centre of dispersal in the area south and east of the middle Benue River, and it is possible that this great movement of African peoples—still going on at the time of the advent of Europeans in the nineteenth century—was associated with a population increase resulting from food production and a much more efficient mastery of the environment through the use of iron tools and weapons.

As has already been pointed out, there are many gaps in African archaeology today, and one of the periods we very much need to know more about is the first millennium A.D., when the spread of iron-using was going on in so many areas. Some valuable evidence has been found, predominantly in the southern province of Zambia, concerning the early Iron Age people there, in what is known as the Kalomo culture.

CENTRAL AND SOUTHERN AFRICA

Rhodesia provides a good example of the use of archaeological methods, and the way in which firm knowledge can only come after prolonged and patient work. Zimbabwe has been the focus of antiquarian interest and speculation ever since Europeans first set eyes on its magnificent stone ruins. Their mental outlook for a long time prevented them from believing in anything but a foreign origin, and a great antiquity was assigned to them. Here were King Solomon's Mines, this was the land of Ophir, here also was the hand of the Phoenicians! All very romantic, and all speculation. For a time also a scandal occurred, until it was stopped, in the form of an adventurers' company digging into the ruins to obtain gold ornaments as an easy form of gold-mining. When the first serious archaeological investigation in 1905, confirmed by more up-to-date methods in 1929, cast doubt on the high antiquity and foreign origin of Zimbabwe, many people were still too emotionally conditioned to accept the evidence. An African origin and a mediaeval date seemed, to their way of thinking, so much less romantic, when in fact, in some ways, it is very much more so. More prolonged and systematic work during the last twenty years, not only at Zimbabwe itself but at the many other sites in Rhodesia as well, together with the help in dating derived from the new radiocarbon technique, has revolutionised our knowledge and our levels of certainty about Zimbabwe. It is clear now that there was at Zimbabwe and at other sites in Rhodesia, a 'pre-ruin' iron-using culture from at least the second century A.D. onwards, characterised by a family of pottery which is known also from many sites in central and eastern Africa, and is associated with the earliest use of iron. An occupation of the Acropolis at Zimbabwe by this culture is carbon-dated to around

A.D. 330. It is followed by four successive stages of occupation, marked by changes in the pottery and associated objects. There was still no stone-building by the second stage, carbon-dated to the eleventh century, but by the mid-fifteenth century, in stage three, there was simple stone-building on the Acropolis, the Great Enclosure and some of the valley ruins. It is the succeeding period, that of the empire of the Monomotapa, up to the end of the eighteenth century, which saw the erection of the buildings of coursed masonry such as the Conical Tower and the best part of the Girdle Wall. Confirmation is also provided that Zimbabwe was built by indigenous peoples, even if they had received an infusion from another African stock from the Abyssinian area, as the traditions of some modern Shona-speaking groups in the area maintain.

There seems little doubt that Zimbabwe, although only the most impressive of a large number of stone ruins in Rhodesia, owed its importance and its wealth to being the entrepôt for a trade in gold, ancient workings for which have been found in a wide arc of country to the north and west. The outlet for this trade in gold was doubtless the ancient port of Sofala on the Indian Ocean, where, soon after their arrival, the Portuguese came to hear about the magnificence of the powerful kingdom in the interior which had fortresses of stone and was the source o gold.

Another archaeological discovery is that of Mapungubwe, some two hundred miles to the south of Zimbabwe and just south of the Limpopo River in the Transvaal. Here were discovered and excavated in the 1930s a series of royal burials richly furnished with gold objects. Unlike Zimbabwe, Mapungubwe had not been devastated by the depredations of earlier treasure-seekers. It clearly has some relationship with Zimbabwe, but whether actually as part of the same kingdom, or as a vassal or a rival state, is not yet clear.

EAST AFRICA

Mention of the port of Sofala reminds us of the archaeological work that has been carried out in recent years, throwing light upon the trade that was carried on across the Indian Ocean to and from the East African coast from the seventh century A.D. onwards, and of the trading cities that grew up all along that coast (and of which Sofala appears to have been the most southerly), long before the advent of the Portuguese. Arab and Islamic influence and stimulus were strong, but many of these cities seem to have been predominantly African. Their ruins are being investigated, and finds of coins, pottery and porcelain imported from China, are being used to build up the chronological sequence.

WEST AFRICA

The great mediaeval empires of the Western Sudan—Ghana, Mali and Songhay—are mostly known through written Arabic sources, but undoubtedly in time archaeological techniques will throw more light upon them. Excavations have been carried out at Kumbi Saleh, believed to be one of the capitals of ancient Ghana, but more work needs to be done in this area. There are interesting circles of dressed standing stones in the middle Gambia valley, whose age, purpose and origins are not yet satisfactorily explained, and an archaeological investigation of them is taking place at the moment of writing.

To the south of Lake Chad there are traditions of a race of 'giants', referred to as the 'So' or 'Sao', who preceded the Kanuri inhabitants and who were non-Moslems. Enormous pots, probably originally used for grain or water-storage, but also used for burials, are known from these people. Their mounds and occupation sites have been excavated, revealing a fascinating array of modelled clay objects and a number cast in bronze. The excavator recognises three Sao periods, beginning in the eleventh century A.D.

The mention of the Sao bronzes introduces an interesting archaeological problem. There seems to be an ancient tradition of casting objects in bronze by the lost-wax method which is widespread in West Africa. It has many regional variants in the forest belt from the Ivory Coast to Cameroon, but also, in addition to the bronzes from the Lake Chad area just mentioned, bronze objects apparently of some antiquity have been found in mounds in the middle Niger area. The lost-wax method of casting has a high antiquity in the Middle East and ancient Egypt, and is the method whereby a model of the desired object is first made in wax or latex and then invested with clay, but leaving a rod of wax reaching the outside. When the whole object is heated in a fire, the wax runs out of the baked clay, leaving inside a space into which molten metal is poured through the hole left in the clay where the projecting rod of wax was. When the metal has cooled and solidified, the clay is broken off to reveal the object desired modelled in bronze.

It is always believed that the oldest bronzes in West Africa are the naturalistic heads from Ife, since there is a Benin tradition dated to the fourteenth or fifteenth century telling of a bronze smith being sent from Ife to teach the art in Benin. Accordingly the earliest Ife work is placed in the eleventh century A.D. In spite of some intensive archaeological work at Ife, there is as yet no direct archaeological evidence on the dating, and some estimates place these works of art from Ife at an earlier date. It seems most likely that the introduction of this craft into West Africa followed the greater opening up of the trans-Saharan trade routes by the Arabs. We speak of 'bronzes', but many of these objects are not alloys of copper with tin; some have more lead in them, some are brass and some are almost pure copper. Work to determine their composition is at present going on and may ultimately throw some light on their origins.

This illustrates how much archaeological research still needs to be done in Africa, to fill the many gaps in our knowledge. It will take much long and patient work to fill in these gaps and obtain sufficient pieces of the jig-saw puzzle to achieve a reasonably complete picture; and it will require adequately supported research in *all* the countries of Africa.

SUGGESTIONS FOR PRACTICAL WORK

1 Try to show the class at least one example of a genuine archaeological object: a piece of worked stone, a piece of iron slag, an old piece of pottery or a piece of pottery that has been dug up.

2 Get hold of some quartz (as close-grained as possible), or chert, or flint, or similar stone and try hitting it near its edges with another stone suitable for use as a hammer-stone to try to strike off flakes and make sharp cutting edges, as was done in the Stone Age when metal was unknown.

3 Walk through a town or village looking at all that can be seen, inside and outside buildings, to answer the question: 'What would survive, and what state would it be in, if the place was abandoned today and vegetation and the weather allowed to do their work unhindered for a thousand years before an archaeologist of the future came to investigate it?'

4 To show the principle of stratification: prepare a number of samples of soils of different colours and consistencies—small lumps of angular rock, red earth, sand, charcoal, brown earth, small pebbles. Put a suitable quantity of one into a transparent container to form a layer (a small glass or plastic aquarium is best,

failing this a wide-mouthed bottle will do); then put in another layer of a contrasting soil—and then similarly all the other samples. Which layer is 'oldest' (put in first)? Which 'most recent' (put in last)? Half the class could see it done, half be made to deduce the answers from only seeing the results in the container.

5 A 'mock excavation' can be carried out in the school grounds. One section of the class to dig a pit, cook a meal in it on an open hearth, leave the blackened hearth-stones, etc. in place, break one of the pots used and leave it there, scatter refuse from the meal about the hearth, including at least one labelled tin; fill in the pit. Next day, or next week, the other section of the class to excavate the pit, using only trowels or small hoes gently, and sieving the material. What do their finds indicate? (1) Some people lit a fire and did some cooking. (2) They broke their cooking pot. (3) They were eating x, y and z (deductions from refuse). (4) How long ago was this? (deductions from state of remains). (5) Possible reasons for abandonment of cooking place. (6) Who were the people? etc., etc. A brief report of deductions made should be written and presented to the other section of the class, who can check their accuracy. Any *un*justified inferences? Any justifiable ones not spotted? Any ambiguous ones? (This will stress the often uncertain nature of archaeological evidence unless confirmed from more than one site, e.g. what sort of people consumed the contents of the tin, Africans or Europeans?)

SELECT BIBLIOGRAPHY

A. J. Arkell, *A History of the Sudan from the Earliest Times to 1821*, Athlone Press, London, 1961.

Grahame Clark, *World Prehistory*, C.U.P., 1961.

J. Desmond Clark, *The Prehistory of Southern Africa*, Penguin Books, 1959.

Sonia Cole, *The Prehistory of East Africa*, Weidenfeld & Nicolson, 1964.

J. Hawkes and L. Woolley, 'Prehistory and the Beginnings of Civilisation', *History of Mankind, Cultural and Scientific Development*, Vol. 1, Allen & Unwin, 1963.

C. McBurney, *The Stone Age of Northern Africa*, Penguin Books, 1960.

R. Mauny, *Tableau Géographique de l'Ouest Africain au Moyen Age*, Mém. Inst. Franç. Afr. Noire, no. 61, Dakar, 1961.

R. Summers, *Zimbabwe: a Rhodesian Mystery*, Nelson, 1963.

Many journals contain archaeological material concerning Africa; the following may be mentioned:

Bulletin de l'Institut Français d'Afrique Noire; series B, Dakar.
Bulletin of the South African Archaeological Society, Cape Town.
Journal of African History, London.
Journal of the Historical Society of Nigeria, Ibadan.
Journal of the Royal Anthropological Institute, London.
Kush, Khartoum.
Man, London.
Notes Africaines, Dakar.
Nyasaland Journal, Blantyre.
Transactions of the Historical Society of Ghana, Legon.
Uganda Journal, Kampala.

A series of conference proceedings containing archaeological material on Africa:

Panafrican Congress on Prehistory
    First, Nairobi, 1947: *Proceedings*, Blackwell, 1952.
    Second, Algiers, 1952: *Actes*, Arts & Métiers Graphiques, 1955.
    Third, Livingstone, 1955: *Proceedings*, Chatto & Windus, 1957.
    Fourth, Leopoldville, 1959: *Actes*, Tervuren, Musée Royale de l'Afrique
        Centrale, 1962.
    Fifth, Tenerife, 1963.

4 An Outline History of Tropical African Art

DENIS WILLIAMS

TO the present day the study of African art has been conducted largely on an iconographical[1] level, since hitherto so very little has been known about the history of the peoples who produced it. Today, however, the efforts of the historian of Africa have placed a new responsibility on the student of African art: it now becomes necessary to read this art, like any other, as an historical phenomenon. Though it is early yet to conceive of a history of African art in the sense in which histories have been written, say, of European or Egyptian art, certain general features are beginning to emerge. It is these which will be treated of in the present outline. We must bear in mind though that apart from the historical there are also iconographical and aesthetic levels of interpretation, and that it is all these together which constitute the field of interest of the historian of African art. In an outline such as this, however, it will be necessary to confine our attention to historical data. That is to say, we shall attempt to say no more than that such and such an idiom in art occurred at such and such a time among a given people or group of peoples, and questions as to why a particular idiom appeared, or why having done so it should be subject to evolution as expressed in style, must remain unanswered here.

What are the data? How are they to be read? African art is expressed in such a welter of media and a variety of idioms that it will be necessary, initially, to break the data down into smaller categories, each of which will be autonomous and intelligible within its own frame of reference. In each category it will be found that the field of reference is not coterminous with present geographical and political units. Thus a field in which we examine the use of stone as a medium of expression will have a spatial reference to almost the entire continent and a depth in time extending in parts to the Neolithic, with an upper extension into our own times. A field in which we examine the use of iron as a medium of expression will again have a spatial reference to most parts of the continent, but a time-depth extending at its deepest to the Meroitic culture of the Sudan of *c.* 300 B.C., with an upper limit at about the end of the first quarter of the twentieth century in Yoruba, Dahomey, Bambara and Congolese iron sculpture and artifacts. Lost-wax brass-casting would have a spatial reference primarily to a belt along the Guinea Coast extending from the Cameroons in the east to Liberia in the west, and this refers to a time-depth, in the present state of our knowledge, of perhaps no more than a thousand years or so, with an upper extension in certain cult-arts of the present day. Wood-carving, the most widely employed of all expression media of Tropical Africa, would probaby refer us to the very earliest periods of sculpture, but here data are lacking, little material of historical significance having come down to us. In view of this we need to seek evidence for its practice in more permanent media whose earliest extant forms might afford us a glimpse, such as Roman does of Greek painting, of earlier states of the carving which we know today.

IRON

It is a peculiarity of the cultures of Tropical Africa that the Iron Age preceded the Bronze Age, but we must be careful in the use of this latter term, for a true Bronze Age, an age in which this alloy came to be universally used in the manufacture of every type of utilitarian and decorative object, can hardly be said to have taken place in Tropical Africa. Bronze, or more precisely speaking, brass, has always been a luxury material in Tropical Africa and has always been relatively scarce; it was hardly ever purely utilitarian, being employed chiefly by king and priest. For the Western Sudan an Age of Copper has been proposed as following on the Neolithic (or New Stone Age). In such an Age of Copper tools and weapons would have been fashioned by hammering rather than by casting, the casting of copper being by no means a simple matter.

At the site of the city of Meroë, about 120 miles to the north of Khartoum in the Sudan, can still be seen the slag heaps of an iron industry which was flourishing there perhaps as early as the third century before Christ. The suspected scope of this industry has led one writer to refer to Meroë as 'the Birmingham of ancient Africa'. It is certain that by the opening of the Christian era iron was commonly used there for fashioning tools and weapons, and for all manner of day-to-day domestic appliances such as door hinges and so on. In its later stages the technology of this industry might have been influenced by the Romans in Egypt in the same way as were Meroitic architectural techniques and sculpture in the round (see Plate V). Excavated at the Palace of Amun is an almost life-size plaster figure of a woman which, though African in subject-matter and treatment, is conceived in the Greco-Roman sculptural tradition. Two pieces of iron armature from this figure (Khartoum Museum 538) are interesting for a glimpse which they provide of the industry. They are (a) 38 cm., and (b) 30 cm. long respectively, wrought-iron rods 1·6 cm. thick incised with oblique V-shaped cuts for gripping the plaster. Most interesting is the fact that for about 8 cm. at one end one of the rods has been tapped for threads (Fig. 2a). This indicates the use of a harder metal for the die, probably steel. Although this industry appears to have been advanced, however, there have occurred at Meroë no instances of the *casting* of iron (a necessity in the manufacture of true steel), and this lack of knowledge of steel metallurgy is a characteristic of all the iron industries of Tropical Africa.

From Meroë the knowledge of iron-smelting and working appears to have spread slowly southwards through Uganda into East and Central Africa and finally into Southern Africa. The path of this diffusion has been determined by linguistic means. The earliest metal-using peoples of Rhodesia have provisionally been dated at *c.* A.D. 90. A later mining people were working Rhodesian iron before A.D. 400. They lacked hard steel tools. The spread of the knowledge of iron-working seems also to have taken a westward course, and to have reached the peoples of the Western Sudan, or some of them at any rate, as early as the opening years of the first millennium A.D. But though iron industries in the Western Sudan, in West Africa and in the Congo are considered generally to have derived from Meroë, we cannot rule out the possibility of another and independent route of diffusion from North Africa, perhaps as early as the closing centuries of the first millennium B.C. In any case the bowl bellows associated with these industries throughout Tropical Africa is of a type used in Egypt as early as the Seventeenth Dynasty, and is of Mesopotamian origin.

It has been possible, from fragments in the Khartoum Museum (K.M. 4953) to make a hypothetical reconstruction of the Meroitic iron-smelting furnace. This appears to have been of more or less cylindrical shape with a number of holes around the base in which

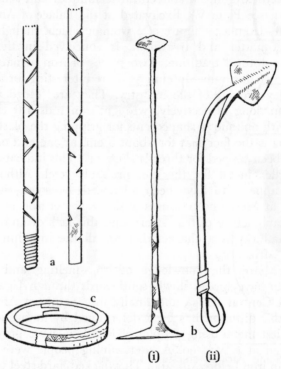

Fig. 2   (a) Iron armature from a Meroitic plaster figure; (b) two examples of African iron currency: (i) Sierra Leone, (ii) Congo; (c) copper bracelet from the Upper Niger, c. A.D. 1000.

clay pipes were inserted to create a forced draught. Fragments of these clay pipes have survived and are identical in design and manufacture with those still in use today by African smiths. Furnaces of Meroitic type occur throughout Tropical Africa, using either a forced or a natural draught, and varying in height. The Meroitic furnace seems to be the prototype of the traditional furnaces of Tropical Africa (Fig. 3e).

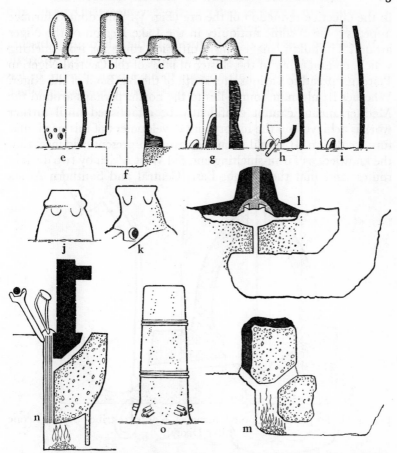

Fig. 3 Some African smelting furnaces: (*a–d*) Egyptian (cuprous metals); (*e*) Meroitic (reconstructed Williams); (*f*) Uganda (Roscoe); (*g*) Togo (Rattray); (*h*) Dahomey (Foa); (*i*) Songhai (Barth); (*j*) Congo (Baumann); (*k*) Congo (Maquet); (*l*) Yoruba (Williams); (*m*) Nupe (Wilcox); (*n*) Nupe (Nadel); (*o*) Mandingo (described Mungo Park).

In certain parts of the Western Sudan and West Africa, however, a different type of furnace design appears. This is a domed furnace (a furnace in which the combustion area is dome-shaped rather than cylindrical) usually of natural draught with in some cases—as among the Yoruba of Nigeria, the Koranko of Sierra Leone, the Fulani of Futa Jallon, and others—an underground chamber and drain-hole for draining off slag, a necessary process in the effective reduction of the ore (Fig. 4). This domed furnace appears to be of some antiquity in the Lake Region of the Niger around Timbuktu, suggesting a diffusion route for iron-smelting which, commencing in the cluster of lakes of the Central Nigerian Plateau, spread to various sites south of the Big Bend of the Niger. Whether its ultimate source lies to the north, perhaps around the Mediterranean, cannot confidently be established until further work is achieved on the history and development of this particular furnace design. It would seem, however, on present evidence, that the knowledge of iron-smelting entered West Africa by two distinct routes, and that the Congo, East, Central and Southern Africa

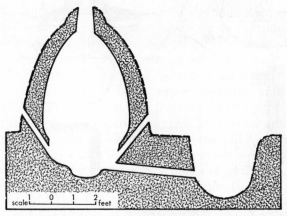

Fig. 4   Example of a domed furnace, Koranko tribe, Sierra Leone (after Dixey).

were unaffected by the route represented by the distribution of the domed furnace (Figs. 3l, 4).

It is now considered that by c. A.D. 500, the peoples of the Congo had acquired the knowledge of iron-smelting, and the same date has been advanced for the Forest Cultures of the West Coast. But iron-smelting had earlier been known in the Nok Culture of Northern Nigeria, which has been dated to c. 300 B.C.– c. A.D. 200. The common use of this metal would have revolutionised certain activities in these societies, affecting the formation of larger social groups with more powerful means of defence, a more productive agriculture, and a wider range of expression in the arts, notably wood-carving, for instance, the undated Esie stone figures of Western Nigeria were made by an iron-using people as is evidenced by representations on them of iron weapons. The double appellative of Ogun among the Yoruba—God of Iron and God of War—possibly refers to two historical stages, the latter characterised by the revolution occasioned by the adoption of iron weapons. Iron sculpture, not surprisingly, came to be associated with the cult of Ogun among the Yoruba, and with Gu, the equivalent deity among the Fon of Dahomey (see Plate VI). Among the Bushongo of the Congo it was associated with the Blacksmith-King Miele as early as the opening decades of the sixteenth century, and iron figurines claimed to be from his hand have survived. The more impressive of African iron sculptures have found their way into the history of art by means of their influence on European artists of the School of Paris in the twentieth century, but it is a medium of expression which, resulting from the importation of large quantities of cheap European iron in modern times, has quite died out. The traditional iron-smelting furnaces began to close down during the first quarter of the present century, and it is today extremely difficult to trace the remains of these very important 'documents' of the iron industry. Blacksmiths now fashion only agricultural implements, during the dry season.

Concerning iron as a source of wealth and power we may note the pear-shaped lump of this metal still preserved in the Palace Compound of the Oni of Ife, and recorded by Frobenius in 1910. Similar lumps, measuring some forty inches high, might have been held by the king as reserve wealth for the forging of emergency weapons in times of war. From the store-houses of the Assyrian King Sargon II (722–705 B.C.) were recovered a similar hoard of reserve iron forged into bars held for just this purpose. At Ife, Frobenius was unable to decide whether this great lump had been forged (beaten) or cast (made to run into shape from a liquid state). It now seems certain that they were forged and not cast, cast-iron being traditionally unknown in African metallurgy.

Iron, finally, played a role in traditional African cultures in its use as native currency; an indication, until almost the present day, of its past value and importance.

COPPER, BRASS, BRONZE

The most famous objects in all African art have been fashioned in brass, and around them centre some of its great mysteries. Despite general use of the term *bronze* to describe this category of work, very few African works of art are known to be true bronzes, an alloy of roughly one part of tin to ten parts of copper. Though tin has traditionally been mined in Nigeria, and copper as early as the eighth or ninth century in the Congo, it is doubtful whether the metallurgy of bronze was ever understood in these regions or, for that matter, the metallurgy of brass, an alloy of copper and zinc. It is reported, though, of the early mining peoples of Rhodesia that they were making a bronze alloy before A.D. 400. For West Africa it seems certain that all brass employed in the lost-wax[2] industries was imported. Our earliest objects in this category have been excavated in the Western Sudan from graves bordering the Lake Region of the Upper Niger, and from sites bordering Lake Chad. The Upper Niger objects are small, decorative articles of very rudimentary design beaten from copper, probably made before the techniques of casting were mastered. Isolated objects of bronze have been identified in the Sao culture of the Chad region. Dates suggested for these cultures are around the eleventh century, though it seems that brass was already being imported into ancient Ghana as early as the ninth century. Around this date copper was also being forged into jewellery and small ingots by the inhabitants of the Congo. The importation of copper (copper, brass and bronze are not distinguished between in the Arab records) into the Western Sudan has been described by several mediaeval writers, Arab and European. This copper was mined at sites in the Sahara and traded south for slaves and gold. The most important of these mines was at Takedda where copper was described by Ibn Battuta (1354) as a currency for purchasing these commodities. It was thence taken to Zaghay north-east of Bornu, to Bornu, and to Songhay. According to an eye-witness stationed at Tuat in the Sahara in 1447, another source of copper was Romania, in Europe. This was exported to Alexandria and sent thence to the Sudan. Routes and dates by which the metal and possibly also its techniques of working spread into the Guinea forest are not yet clearly determined, though a seventeenth-century writer (Barbot) mentions a coastal trade from the Ivory Coast with Arabs (?) in the interior, and three north-south routes have been traced which served an indigenous trade along the Niger basin before it was influenced by European commerce. These latter routes carried various items of European manufacture from North Africa to the coast. This North African trade with the Upper Niger Region (by silent barter) was described as late as the eighteenth century, comprising such everyday European commodities as scissors, etc.

In considering the links between these early brass industries of the Western Sudan and the possible subsequent growth of schools of brass-casting in the Guinea forest, we might note the evidence, meagre as yet, of the incidence and distribution of the copper bracelet in these cultures. From the earliest times copper bracelets were used as money in the Western Sudan and exchanged for gold by traders from the Mediterranean. Arab writers have reported the use of this form of currency in the Fezzan, Ghana, Tekrur and Kanem, and as late as the fifteenth century these bracelets were still being imported from the Magrib. To the present day smiths in Northern Nigeria pour their molten brass into grooved clay moulds in the form described by Ibn Battuta in the fourteenth century—into bars of a span and a half long— before then bending them into bracelets (see Plate VII). The method is also described of the Bida smiths in modern times by a writer who observed that the metal they used was always imported, since they had never mined copper. 'Main products of the Nupe brass industry are sword hilts and daggers (blades are mostly old, of German manufacture, and have been traded for centuries to Nigeria and Nupe across the desert from North Africa), horse trappings, bowls, jugs, trays, ladles and receptacles of various kinds.'[3] The brass bracelet still made today by the Northern Nigerian smith is perhaps the type to which the Portuguese *manilla* (finally withdrawn as a currency in Nigeria only in 1948) succeeded in the fifteenth century. Copper-brass bracelets have been found at various excavated sites south of the Sahara, e.g. at Kumbi Saleh, Lobi, Rao, Wukari (Jukun), Benin, and at various places along the Lower Niger. Of interest in establishing the direction of their diffusion is the fact that certain of these bracelets are hinged, i.e. made up from two or more sections meeting in a 'gate' whereby they are fastened together sometimes by a pin, sometimes by a mortice-and-tenon joint. They often occur in two or more tiers. An early bracelet of this kind was excavated at Killi in the Lake Region of the Upper Niger bearing two hinges (Fig. 2c) and dated to before A.D. 1050. At around this date, as we have seen, smiths in the region, as also in the Congo, were still forging small objects from beaten copper; the technique of casting brass had apparently not yet appeared, though it was soon to come; we find cast-bronze bracelets in the Sao culture south of Lake Chad around the eleventh century. These hinged bracelets occur today in the Guinea forest, though it is unlikely that they were cast there in periods before the tenth century. Very possibly the copper trade described by Ibn Battuta as reaching as far to the west as the borders of Lake Chad, and which was conducted in this bracelet currency, was also the bearer of design ideas from sources outside the Forest Regions.

East of the Niger we have an instance of this mobility of brass objects over great distances in traditional times. The so-called 'Ibo' brass bell, or 'Ibibio' bell, is of a distinctive design, with a characteristic rounded shoulder and a suspension ring built up from coils of wax; they are decorated with flat spirals, bosses, loops, strings, etc., and cast by the lost-wax method, top end upwards (see Plate VIII). In 1923 an observer in the Cameroons described these bells being cast there by the Eyāp tribe, not for their own use but for sale to neighbouring tribes. These bells are common nowadays over a wide area of Eastern Nigeria and are considered typical of the region, but they were in all probability manufactured in the Cameroons and used as trade goods or currency. Their design ideas appear on brasses throughout the region.

GOLD

We cannot close this brief study of the place of metals in African art without a glance at the oldest, possibly, of all metals used in African art—gold. The connection of the brass industries of the Forest Cultures with the Mediterranean, which we have just described, must be seen against the background of the gold trade with which it was closely linked, and which might be said to have brought it into being; art following upon trade and wealth as ever in the history of man.

We have seen that brass from the Sahara and the Mediterranean was traded south for slaves and gold. From the remotest antiquity this gold trade has linked the Mediterranean first with its hinterland, and then with the states of the Western Sudan and the forests. Herodotus mentions the trade in gold by silent barter with the Carthaginians on the Atlantic coast of 'Lybia', and some authors suggest that Carthaginian explorers may have carried this trade as far south as the mouth of the Niger. We do not know. It is not until the coming of the Arabs in the eighth century that we have written records of the existence of this trade in the Western Sudan, and it is recorded thereafter throughout mediaeval times to the eighteenth century, providing the wealth of such great Sudanic empires as those of Ghana and Mali.

The history of this gold trade is important in its effect upon the design of objects produced in the Forest Cultures, for one effect of this culture-contact would possibly have been the transmission of metal-working techniques, notably the lost-wax method of brass-casting. It must be emphasised that equipment associated with lost-wax brass-casting as practised in the Forest Cultures, such as bellows types, crucibles, clay pipes, etc., are all of known Mesopotamian origin of the third millennium B.C., and used in Egypt as early as the Eighteenth Dynasty. The route by which this technique and its associated equipment entered the Forest Regions would therefore have been either westwards from the Nile, or southwards from the Mediterranean. But considering the date at which brass-casting seems to have reached the Western Sudan, and subsequently the forests, we must view a Nilotic source as unlikely. Bronze objects found at sites in the ancient Sudan, in Nubia for instance, are known to have been imported from Egyptian workshops; the working of bronze, though known in ancient Meroë, does not appear to have been highly developed there. We must remember that from around the opening of the Christian era Meroë was sliding into the long decay which terminated with its destruction, around A.D. 324, by the Aksumites. In A.D. 54–68 two centurions sent by the Emperor Nero to see whether the Sudan was worth conquering returned to Rome with the report that the country was too poor to be worth the trouble of conquest. After the sack of Meroë c. 324, Ezana, the King of Axum, boasted, among other things, that he had carried off all their food and copper, and destroyed the statues in their temples. The scene of culture subsequently shifted to the Meroitic successor states of the north, bordering upon Egypt, and it is from such cultures that we have recovered bronze objects of Mediterranean design manufactured in Egyptian workshops and exported into the Sudan. Two brass copies of such objects found in old graves in modern Ghana provide evidence for the brass-gold trade and its significance in the introduction of casting techniques, for no doubt exists that these copies were of local manufacture, from imported objects. It seems very likely that the lost-wax technique of brass-casting followed upon the brass-gold trade of the Western Sudan at a period after the eighth century and before the tenth, as the caravan trade acquired momentum.

One area of this influence seems to be in the delicate filigree gold work of the Baule-Asante smiths, and in the Asante kuduo, a brass vessel of marked Islamic design but made by Asante smiths. Attention has been drawn by one writer to the similarity between the small lost-wax brass figurines made by the Habe for weighing gold and those of the Baule-Asante. Finally, for evidence of trans-Saharan connections with the Mediterranean, let us note that in 1929 several gold figurines, undoubtedly of a style originating in the Western Sudan or in the Forest Regions, were found in Tripoli. Thus for gold, for brass, and even perhaps for part of the iron industry of West Africa, we might, as a guide to future research, need to look for sources of technological influence around the Lake Region of the Upper Niger and possibly further afield, to the Mediterranean and even beyond. It must be said at once, however, that these technological influences, though accounting perhaps for the rise of metal industries in these regions, exactly as they did in Europe, for example, do not explain the heights of art achieved in their use by African smiths. In every case the particular genius of expression is of this continent and its very soil; the finest creations of African bronze-casting are the equal of any produced in five thousand years of the craft, in the entire history of the world's art (see Plate IX).

CARVINGS AND TERRACOTTA

Wood-, stone- and ivory-carving are media of expression of the greatest importance in the study of African art, but these cannot for the present be the subject of historical study, the data still being comparatively meagre. The same applies too for terracotta, an art of the greatest antiquity and the utmost beauty, as examples from Nok, Ife and Benin show (see Plate X). No technique, however, physical or art-historical, has as yet been developed by means of which we can confidently examine these works chronologically.

ARCHITECTURE

No history of architecture has so far been attempted either for Africa as a whole or for particular African cultures, though for particular cultures where there are architectural remains of an historical nature it is possible to arrive at general conclusions as to the growth of architectural thought and the influences at work. Such architectural remains exist in Ethiopia reaching back to c. 500 B.C. Briefly, a development can be traced here from the earliest buildings erected under South Arabian influence, covering more than two thousand years, to the castles and churches of Gonder, which owe much in form and technique to the contemporary architecture of Portugal. In the course of this long history the Ethiopians of Aksum developed an architecture covering the first thousand years of the Christian era, and characterised by giant monolithic stelae and magnificent churches of originality and great beauty. These buildings are technically remarkable for their method of dry-wall construction, in which blocks of stone were so accurately dressed that huge edifices were erected without the use of mortar. Along with the growth of these buildings a very beautiful ecclesiastical art was developed, similar in use to the sacred art of the European Middle Ages. These building techniques finally flowered in the magnificent rock-cut churches of Lalibela, a later Ethiopian culture, which lasted from c A.D. 1000–c. A.D. 1270, and was succeeded by the 'Portuguese' styles of the sixteenth century at Gonder (see Plates XV and XVI).

No less brilliant in architectural achievement though in quite a different idiom, was the architecture of classical Meroë. Here, on the Nile, a great architectural system arose owing much initially to Egypt with, in its later stages, Hellenistic and Roman influences brought about by trade. In due course, however, during the first century B.C. or so, the people of Meroë developed a very individual style of building in brick and plaster (see Plate XI). The outer walls of palaces were white-washed and decorated with glowing mural paintings while the inner walls were similarly embellished with paintings heightened with gold-leaf ornament. Walls were extremely thick, strengthened by a core of sun-dried brick. The Meroitic building brick was itself very large (13 in. by 7 in. by 3 in.), and very hard. The plan of the Meroitic Palace was grid-like and geometric, with curiously elongated rooms, passages and galleries (Fig. 5).

At the other end of the continent, in Rhodesia, are the ruins of Zimbabwe, about a hundred acres of buildings erected by Africans possibly in mediaeval times. These buildings are com-

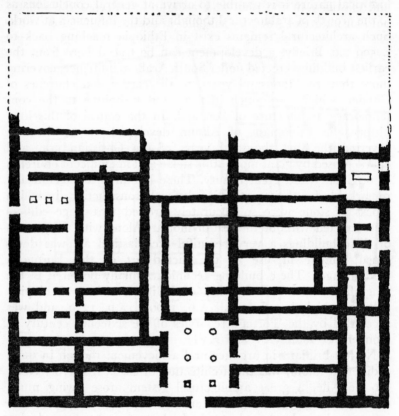

Fig. 5   Sketch plan of a Meroitic Palace, c. 45–12 B.C. (after a drawing by the contributor).

parable in architectural achievement with other examples from the great periods in African architecture: from Axum, Lalibela, Meroë; and in terms of sheer labour and skill recall the pyramids of Egypt.

'Mediaeval', too, is the court architecture of Benin and Yoruba. The first Englishman to visit Benin in 1553 described the great hall of the Oba's Palace, its earth walls, and what has come to be known as its 'impluvium' roof, a roof which surrounds a closed courtyard on all four sides thus letting in light and air without the need of windows. These courtyards were connected with each other by archways and passages, which resulted in a great fluidity and elasticity in the plan and accurately reflected the indoor-outdoor nature of African social life, in contrast to the closed units

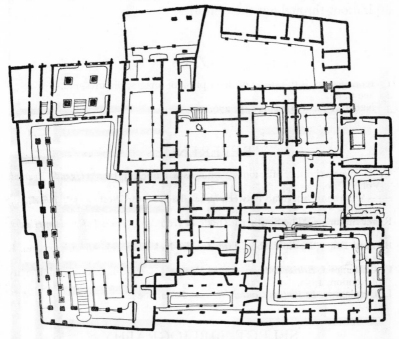

Fig. 6   Sketch plan of a Yoruba Palace (after a scale drawing by Anthony Harrison and Denis Williams).

which characterise the architecture of colder countries. The galleries were traditionally supported by carved veranda posts bordering the courtyard, a peculiarly African and very arresting convention. At one stage in the history of Benin the veranda posts were covered with bronze plaques representing historical scenes. These bronze plaques are now considered among the masterpieces of Benin art, and reveal to us a great deal of the life, customs and dress of the people. It is interesting to compare the organic, very 'human' plan of such a palace (Fig. 6) with the plan of the typical Meroitic Palace, which is formal and abstract (Fig. 5).

When, finally, a history of African architecture comes to be written we should expect it to be very illuminating of the lives and times of the people it housed and of their various intellectual responses and adaptations to their environment. For architecture, like every other aspect of art, is an exact index of the state of a culture at any given moment, and a valuable reflection of human aspirations throughout the centuries.

NOTES

1   Iconography is th : study or description of images, pictures, etc.
2   See p. 69.
3   Nadel, *A Black Byzantium*, p. 270.

REFERENCES

G. A. Wainwright, 'Diffusion of -uma as a name for Iron', *Uganda Journal*, Vol. 18, no. 2, 1954.
—— 'Pharaonic Survivals between Lake Chad and the West Coast', *J.E.A.*, 35, 1949.
Roger Summers, 'The Southern Rhodesia Iron Age', *Journal of African History*, Vol. 2, no. I
Bernard Fagg, 'Radio-carbon dates for the Nok Culture', *Africa*, xxxv, no. I, 1965.
C. C. Ifemesia, *British Enterprise on the Niger, 1830–1869*, Ph.D. thesis, University of London, 1959.
L. Desplagnes, *Le Plateau Central Nigerien*, Paris, 1904.

SELECT BIBLIOGRAPHY

Margaret Shinnie, *Ancient African Kingdoms*, Arnold, 1965.
E. Leuzinger, *Africa, The Art of the Negro Peoples*, Methuen, 1960.
A. R. Wilcox, *The Rock Art of South Africa*, Nelson, 1963.
Denise Paulner, *African Sculpture*, Elek Books, 1962.
W. Fagg, *Nigerian Images*, Lund Humphreys, 1964.
W. Fagg and M. Plass, *African Sculpture*, Studio Vista, 1964.
U. Beier, *Art in Nigeria*, Cambridge, 1960.
—— *African Mud Sculpture*, Cambridge, 1965.
W. Stevenson Smith, *The Art and Architecture of Ancient Egypt*, Penguin Books, 1958.

5 A Survey of the Cultural and Political Regions of Africa at the Beginning of the Nineteenth Century

J. F. A. AJAYI

INTRODUCTION

IN a brief survey of the history of Africa such as is attempted here, it is not possible to go into detail about the history of every country, state or ethnic group. Our purpose is to highlight the main factors that are significant for understanding the history of the continent as a whole. We must, however, avoid the temptation to concentrate attention only on those aspects of European activities such as abolition, exploration, missionary expansion and colonial rule which can be studied easily on a Pan-African level. These are no substitutes for the history of African Peoples. It is true that culturally and politically, Africa is very complex. But we must make the effort to find the main lines of development, to simplify and synthesise, without distorting the picture unduly. It is possible to consider the African past in terms of some broad regions: the Magrib, the Nile valley and Ethiopia, East and Central Africa, South Africa, the Congo basin, the Sudan and the Forest Areas of West Africa.

These regions are geographical. This serves to remind us that in history we must not neglect the importance of geography. We need to emphasise the extent to which our culture, our way of life, our social and political institutions are influenced by our geographical environment. Life in the desert breeds a nomadic existence; nomadic existence affects attitudes towards the rules of inheritance as well as political and economic organisation. While grasslands encourage movement and the creation of larger states, forests, swamps and mountains restrict movement and encourage political organisation on a smaller scale. Religious beliefs reflect the problems we have to deal with; danger of floods and too much rain in one place, danger of drought and too little rain another. It therefore makes sense that any attempt to divide Africa into regions that reflect historical development must take account of geographical features. In this connection, relief maps and rainfall and vegetation maps of Africa are valuable aids to historical study (see maps A and B).

Any cultural and political survey of Africa should take account of other factors besides geography. In the past, it has been customary to classify African peoples in terms of racial stocks. Many books in use still talk of Pygmies, Bushmen, Hottentots, Hamites, Negroes, Bantus and Arabs as the main races in Africa. But race is a very unsatisfactory factor of classification because it is so imprecise. For one thing, Bantu and Hamitic are linguistic, not racial terms. The people who speak Hamitic and Bantu languages are racially mixed. Somebody looking like a Negro may be from Senegal or the Sudan or East Africa. He may even be from New Guinea or the United States of America. When classifying people in terms of related cultures and historical connection, language is a far more reliable guide than race. A common origin is often to be presumed for people speaking closely related languages. But not always, since it sometimes happens that a people learn another language and forget their own. American Negroes provide a good example: culturally they are classified as Americans not Africans since they speak American-English. Even if related languages do not indicate a common origin, they point at least to some close historical connection and the sharing of certain ideas and institutions in common. We should, therefore, look at a map of the main language families of Africa, e.g. as classified by Joseph H. Greenberg (Fig. 7).

Against the background provided by the geographical and the linguistic maps this chapter will survey briefly the main regions referred to earlier. Its aim is to draw attention to the broad outlines of historical development and in this way provide a background for the history of Africa in the nineteenth and twentieth centuries.

THE SUDAN BELT

Let us begin with the Sudan belt, stretching from the Senegal across Africa to the Nile Valley and the Red Sea. It is a country varying from open parkland to grassland, thinning northwards

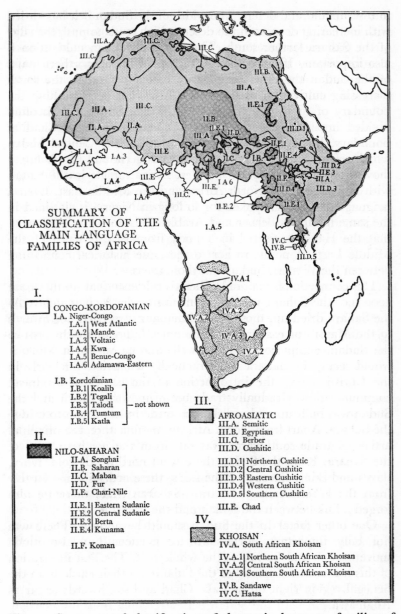

SUMMARY OF
CLASSIFICATION OF THE
MAIN LANGUAGE
FAMILIES OF AFRICA

I.

CONGO-KORDOFANIAN
I.A. Niger-Congo
I.A.1 West Atlantic
I.A.2 Mande
I.A.3 Voltaic
I.A.4 Kwa
I.A.5 Benue-Congo
I.A.6 Adamawa-Eastern

I.B. Kordofanian
I.B.1 Koalib
I.B.2 Tegali
I.B.3 Talodi   — not shown
I.B.4 Tumtum
I.B.5 Katla

II.

NILO-SAHARAN
II.A. Songhai
II.B. Saharan
II.C. Maban
II.D. Fur
II.E. Chari-Nile

II.E.1 Eastern Sudanic
II.E.2 Central Sudanic
II.E.3 Berta
II.E.4 Kunama

II.F. Koman

III.

AFROASIATIC
III.A. Semitic
III.B. Egyptian
III.C. Berber
III.D. Cushitic

III.D.1 Northern Cushitic
III.D.2 Central Cushitic
III.D.3 Eastern Cushitic
III.D.4 Western Cushitic
III.D.5 Southern Cushitic

III.E. Chad

IV.

KHOISAN
IV.A. South African Khoisan
IV.A.1 Northern South African Khoisan
IV.A.2 Central South African Khoisan
IV.A.3 Southern South African Khoisan

IV.B. Sandawe
IV.C. Hatsa

Fig. 7   Summary of classification of the main language families of
Africa.

into scrubland and desert. The width of the Sudan belt has varied with increasing dryness in the desert which tends to push the edge of the Sahara farther south. The factor of human cultivation is also important. If cultivation is disrupted in the northern parts of the Sudan the desert can easily creep in, and in the south increasing cultivation of the Forest Areas has been pushing the boundary of the Sudan farther south. The Sudan belt is often divided into Eastern and Western Sudan with Lake Chad as boundary, but occasionally writers speak of the Central Sudan which refers to the Sudan of Northern Nigeria and Chad. Fig. 7 shows how languages based in West Africa mingle in the Sudan with languages from North Africa and the Middle East. Even a language like Hausa spoken for so long in Nigeria is classified in the same family as Berber and Arabic. This does not itself mean that the Hausa migrated in a body from North Africa or the Middle East. It points rather to the close historical connection between the Western Sudan and those areas.

This connection is very old. There is evidence that up till about 4000 B.C. the Sahara was by no means as dry as it is today. As the Sahara dried up, most of the inhabitants receded northwards to the Magrib or eastwards to the Nile Valley or southwards to the Sudan, except round a few wells and oases. For a while, it would seem, the Sahara was practically a barrier. But early in the Christian era, the introduction of the camel reintroduced communication. Gradually trade between North Africa and the Sudan was built up and well-known trade routes began to bridge the Sahara. Apart from North African manufacture, the principal article of trade southwards was salt from the northern edge of the Sahara. From the Sudan there went northwards gold, ivory, slaves and skins. Except for the skins, these articles came largely from the Forest Areas. The trans-Saharan trade therefore also forged a link between the Sudan and the Forest Areas.

One other factor in the Sudan should be noticed. There was not only important north-south connections but also much movement to and fro across the whole belt. The best illustration of this has been the spread of the Fulani and their cattle from the Senegal region right on to Lake Chad and southwards as far as Adamawa.

This element of human mobility, coupled with the stimulus of trade, has encouraged the growth of trading cities and conquering dynasties and empires in the Sudan. With the trade came also Islam which provided a written language and a class of literate officials which an imperial state could use in administration. Further, Islam helped to loosen ethnic ties and increasingly provided a bond of union in the larger states. While the rulers of ancient Ghana remained pagan, they began to employ Muslim judges and scribes. The rulers of Mali became Muslim but they had to contend against the ties of the traditional religion. Later on, the court of the rulers of Songhay was dominated much more by Islam. Increasingly the rules of succession and the laws were being modified under the influence of Islam. But these states and others like Tekrur were not Islamic states. Islam was the religion of the rulers, the traders and scholars of the main cities. The bulk of the rural population remained tied to the traditional religions, laws and customs. Important areas in the Western Sudan like the Mossi-Yatenga kingdoms remained impervious to the spread of Islam. With the Moroccan defeat of the Songhay rulers in 1591, Islam suffered a reverse. Pagan dynasties established the Bambara states of Segu and Kaarta and the Fulani state of Futa Toro, Fouta Djallon and others. Islam and Islamic influences remained powerful but, increasingly in the eighteenth century, there was a growing feeling of frustration among Muslims, and a strong desire to revive Islam and return to the great days of Askia Muhammad Toure of the Songhay empire, which were regarded as a Golden Age of Islam in West Africa. It was this feeling of frustration that prepared the way for the wave of Islamic revolutions throughout the Sudan belt in the nineteenth century.

FOREST AREAS OF WEST AFRICA

To the south of the Sudan belt and closely connected with it are the Forest Areas of West Africa. As we have seen, as Man masters the forest and cultivates it intensely, it thins out and recedes and the Sudan creeps southwards. It is important to notice that partly through cultivation, partly also through the direction of the rain-bearing trade winds, the Sudan belt reaches nearly down to the coast of Dahomey and Eastern Ghana, thus cutting the forest areas into two. This may not always have been so.

Generally speaking, the forest was an area of small groups with strong ethnic ties and great reverence for the ancestors and Mother Earth. The languages of the area are related though mutually

7

unintelligible, each having grown over a period of time, some 4,000 years, in relative isolation. Even in places like the Ibo country where the same language is spoken over a wide area (though with different dialects) often no large kingdom or organised state emerged. Political, social and religious power remained diffused among the elders, age-grade associations and secret societies. Such secret societies could become very powerful and widespread thus providing a strong integrative factor.

There were exceptions to this. The Yoruba, for example, developed an urban type of society and a monarchical form of government in the different towns. But even then, there were several kingdoms. Only Old Oyo on the edge of the Sudan belt developed a cavalry force and built up an empire of considerable size, but Old Oyo could not unite the several Yoruba kingdoms in the Forest Area. A Yoruba dynasty planted among the Edo built up Benin into a large city and through trade and conquest, spread Edo influence over a wide region.

The Forest Areas had been subject to the influence of trade not only northwards with the Sudan but also, since the fifteenth century, with the Europeans along the coast. To begin with, this trade was in a variety of goods like gold, ivory, pepper, soap, ostrich feathers, gum, etc., but, increasingly, attention came to be concentrated on slaves. This trade produced along the coast a number of small city-states exploiting the trade and playing the role of middle-men. It is often said that by supplying ammunition, this trade encouraged the growth of larger states in the interior of the forest belt. More probably what happened was that the people in the hinterland had to organise themselves to ensure that they did not become raiding grounds for the slaves required on the coast. East of the Niger, the Aro organised the slave trade going down to the coast. To the west, Benin and Old Oyo did the same. Farther west still, Dahomey developed on the interior plateau, and came down to the coast to dominate the trading states. In Ghana, a number of states developed, Denkyira and Akim, then Akwamu, and finally Asante which came to dominate the whole of Ghana and parts of what is now Ivory Coast and Togo. At the beginning of the nineteenth century Asante's power was still expanding and it threatened to engulf all the coastal states. By contrast, Old Oyo had declined and the nineteenth century was to see its collapse.

THE CONGO BASIN

The forest zone of West Africa extends eastwards beyond the Cameroon Mountains into the northern part of the Congo basin. Linguistic studies have established that the Bantu family of languages which covers the bulk of Africa from the Cameroon Mountains to the Indian Ocean, southwards to South Africa, is a branch of these West African languages. So close is the link that it is now generally believed that the Bantu-speaking peoples must have spread from the Benue-Cross river region from about 1000 B.C. and reached the coast of South Africa by the fifteenth century. Within this Bantu-speaking area, the Congo basin and Angola region is one of the areas where the ethnic and cultural map is most complicated, an area about whose history so little is as yet known that it is not easy to speak of the main outlines. In the Forest Areas Bantu languages dominate, leaving only a few pockets of Pygmies, who preceded the Bantu in the region. The forest has remained thicker than in West Africa and therefore the different ethnic groups have developed in greater isolation.

To the south, the forest thins out into a Savannah belt. Here, there is a record of greater mobility of people and the rise and fall of a number of states. It is an area rich in minerals, particularly copper and gold in the Katanga region. This gave rise to far-ranging trade, conquering dynasties and kingdoms. But the influence of each kingdom tended to penetrate less deeply into the fabric of the different ethnic groups than did the empires of the Sudan. There was nothing comparable to the extensive influence of Islam and Islamic culture in the Sudan or of its judges and officials possessed of a written language.

The best known of these states was near the mouth of the Congo, founded by a dynasty from the region of the Gabon. The kingdom of the Kongo was founded in the fifteenth century at the end of which it welcomed Portuguese traders and missionaries. The rulers became Christian and went into partnership with the Portuguese. This partnership soon broke down and by the seventeenth century the kingdom had disintegrated.

Among the Baluba of Katanga, there are traditions of an earlier kingdom whose existence has been confirmed by the archaeological evidence of a large cemetery near Lake Kisale. By the sixteenth century this kingdom had disappeared and the Baluba were ruled by a people called the Songye. Later the Luba threw off Songye rule and founded what is called the Second Luba empire. It was a member of the ruling dynasty of this empire who, in the seventeenth century, founded a large empire among the Lunda to their west under the title of Mwata Yamvo. The empire of the Mwata Yamvos soon outshone the Second Luba empire. With Katanga copper as a basic item of trade and cowries from the Portuguese along the coast, the Lunda established trading connections between the Atlantic and Indian oceans. Lunda social and political ideas are to be found among several ethnic groups like the Bemba, the Lozi and others. But by the end of the eighteenth century, the empire of the Mwata Yamvos had declined; a new kingdom of the Cazembe farther east on the Luapula River, gained prominence and was trading not only to the west but also south-eastwards to the Zambezi and the Indian Ocean.

The Portuguese remained on the coast of Angola which, for sailing vessels, was the nearest part of Africa to their colony of Brazil. For about 100 miles inland, they established their rule of ruthless exploitation, designed to furnish large numbers of slaves as cheaply as possible for the Brazilian market. The administration was weak and corrupt but it had succeeded in subduing the coastal peoples, dividing the different ethnic groups one against the other, disrupting their political and social development and thus placing them at the mercy of the Portuguese officials, settlers and traders and their mulatto agents, who roamed the interior to gather slaves.

One final point should be noticed. With the exception of a few people on the plateau in the interior of Angola, notably the Ovimbundu, the Bantu-speaking peoples of the Congo basin were basically farmers as were the people of West Africa until the Fulani spread cattle-rearing from the Sudan belt. This was in marked contrast to the Bantu of South and East Africa whose lives were dominated much more by cattle; cattle was the basic element of wealth and the index of status. Without cattle there was no bride-price and no wives. Tax or tribute, war indemnities and so on were all paid for in cattle.

SOUTH AFRICA

The life of the Bantu on the South African plateau thus revolved round their herds of cattle. It was a cardinal aspect of South African life that rainfall was low and irregular, especially to the west. This kept the units of society small and encouraged trekking and a semi-nomadic life in search of pasture if there was prolonged drought. There were chiefs in the different clans and emphasis was given to the rituals that might induce rainfall. Age-grade associations were also important.

In addition to the Bantu there were the Hottentots and the so-called Bushmen, people who spoke languages distinguished for their click-sound. The Bushmen were nomadic hunters with only small-scale ethnic organisations. The Hottentots were more sedentary; they farmed, but like the Bantu they were essentially cattle-rearers. When the Dutch colonised Cape Town in 1652, it was with the Hottentots and the Bushmen that they first came in contact.

The basic interest of the Dutch East India Company in the area was the provision of a station where ships going to the Far East could stop to collect fresh supplies of water, vegetables and meat. It had believed that soldiers guarding their fort could get the water and grow the vegetables and then trade in friendship with the Hottentots for the meat. But when the soldiers refused to become farmers, the Company began to send out a few settlers. Soon the settlers found cattle-rearing more profitable than crop-farming. And as they took to rearing cattle they became rivals of the Hottentots whom they soon began to dominate. After a while the Company stopped assisted immigration from Europe, but encouraged the importation of slaves. Instead of staying close to Cape Town and planting vegetables as the Company had expected the Dutch became Boers (i.e. farmers) each living on large isolated farms, sustained by a fanatical form of Calvinism, each a patriach in his household full of slaves. They were conservative, yet anarchist in their distrust of organised government. Younger members of each family were encouraged to move along the ridge of the plateau into the interior in search of better pasture and large farms. In this way, the small colony spread out thinly on the ground till by the end of the eighteenth century they encountered the more populous Bantu at the Great Fish River.

The opening years of the nineteenth century saw far-reaching changes in Bantu society. Shaka the Zulu revolutionised Bantu warfare, and instead of merely taking the cattle and women of those he conquered, he conscripted all the captured young men into the relevant age-grades of the Zulu people. These age-grades became a centre for assimilating the conquered into Zulu national culture and ideas, as well as into regiments of the Zulu army. His ideas and methods broke up many small ethnic groups, caused far-ranging migrations and gave rise to larger kingdoms such as that of the Basuto, the Ndebele (Matebele) and the Tswana (Bechuanaland). The temporary dislocation in Bantu Society encouraged the migration of Boer farmers into Natal, the Orange Free State and across the Vaal. The stage was thus set for the three-cornered struggle for the control of South Africa between the Bantu states, Boer farmers and the British government which had seized Cape Town from the Dutch during the Napoleonic Wars.

EAST AND CENTRAL AFRICA

In East and Central Africa, the importance of geography must be stressed. There are not the regular geographical zones of West Africa, coastal swamps followed by thick forests thinning out into grassland, nor the even distribution of population. The prevailing vegetation is open orchard country and the fertility of the soil varies considerably. Behind the rich coastal plains, there are large areas of thorn bush which, without being desert, are very difficult to inhabit. These are broken by highlands around which the soil becomes more fertile. Beyond is the rift valley, and the great lakes round which again the country becomes very attractive and fertile. Thus, while on the whole, it will be true to say that the population is thinner than in West Africa, and more fluid, with fewer organised states, cities and markets and therefore less recorded history, there are important exceptions.

An important exception is the strategic region between the lakes, the inter-lacustrine region between Lake Victoria Nyanza and Lakes Albert and Edward. This was a veritable cultural and, presumably also, commercial crossroads of East Africa. There is evidence of contact with the peoples of Ethiopia and the Horn country. There are also traditions of migrations of Nilotic people from the Nile Valley, but the population is Bantu-speaking. It is an area of well-organised kingdoms with a stratified society reflecting waves of conquest. In all the kingdoms, there is a ruling aristocracy of cattle-owners, called the Hima in Bunyoro, Buganda, Ankole and Karagwe, and Tutsi in Rwanda and Burundi. In some areas, the Hima integrated with the mass of the people and, especially in Buganda, there had developed, since the seventeenth century, a bureaucratic system of government independent of the Hima. There is a great deal of controversy as to the origin of this pastoral aristocracy and of their ideas of government. But there is no dispute about the fact that the basic culture of the inter-lacustrine region in terms not only of language but also music, arts and crafts are those of the Bantu-speaking peoples.

Another important exception to the general East African picture is the region south of the Zambezi, the area of the Great Zimbabwe and other ruins. There, archaeological evidence has shown that the kingdom that built the earlier portions of the Great Zimbabwe flourished from about the eleventh to the fifteenth century. The people built in stone and imported expensive luxury goods from the Far East. They mined gold, iron, copper and salt. Later the centre of the kingdom shifted northwards where it was known to the Portuguese in the sixteenth century as the empire of the Monomotapa (i.e. Mwene Mutapa). Access to the rich mines of what is now Rhodesia as well as to the copper belt and the coastal trade stimulated the growth of large and organised states in the region.

There is much speculation about the origin of those who built the Monomotapa empire. They were almost certainly Bantu-speaking. It should be emphasised also that there were several dynasties and kingdoms in the area. The power of the Monomotapa fluctuated. Contact with the Portuguese and the attempted conversion to Christianity merely further weakened it. With its decline, there were conquests from outside, and vassals of the empire rose to power. It was one of these vassals, the Changamire dynasty, that established itself in the eighteenth century on the Zimbabwe site and rebuilt the ruins. This new kingdom lasted a century and was destroyed in 1830 by the Ngoni, a breakaway movement from Shaka, led by Zwangendaba through Central Africa across the Zambezi to the Lake Region of East Africa.

The coastal trade was probably older than either the inter-lacustrine kingdoms or the empire of the Monomotapa. It is reckoned that the migration of Bantu-speaking peoples reached the Tanganyika coast early in the Christian era, and soon after that Arabs began to trade down the coast. Later, especially with the rise of Islam and the persecution of schismatic sects, refugee

Arabs began to settle there. By the tenth century traders from the Far East were also taking part in the trade across the Indian Ocean. From this interaction of peoples there grew up the Swahili culture, which may give East Africa a common indigenous language. All along the coast from Mogadishu to Mozambique, the traders and refugees built city-states of impressive quality. The states were disunited but prosperous. They minted their own coins, imported stoneware from Siam and porcelain from China. A good deal of the inspiration came from the Arabs, but it is a mistake to regard these coastal towns as Arab. Arab and Bantu fused into Swahili. The style of architecture was often new. Many of the art motifs were Bantu and would have offended the strict Muslims of Arabia.

The other major influence on the coast was the Portuguese who intruded into the Indian Ocean at the end of the fifteenth century. They soon secured control of the Indian Ocean and sought to exclude the Swahili and other traders from the coast. They tried to convert the Monomotapa rulers to Christianity and to use this to gain access to the gold mines. They established themselves at the mouth of the Zambezi but only weakened the Monomotapa empire at a time when it faced competition from other rival states. Similarly by seeking to monopolise the gold and ivory trade of East Africa without intending to return any goods from the Far East, the Portuguese weakened the coastal states. Yet Portugal was never strong enough to rule them. By the seventeenth century Portugal had declined. Arabs from the Arabian mainland, especially from Oman, developed the ambition of uniting all the coastal states under one dominion. An Omani ruler succeeded in this in the nineteenth century.

For the rest, the Bantu-speaking peoples of East Africa remained largely in segmentary clans. Even in a place like Nyamwezi, where over a wide area the same language and culture prevailed, there was little political unity. A change began with the Ngoni invasion of the nineteenth century which brought Shaka's ideas of state formation into East Africa. This, coupled with the impact of Arab traders who gave new impetus to the slave trade and made life unsafe for the smaller unorganised peoples, encouraged the Yao, Nyamwezi and others to organise themselves like the Ngoni and arm themselves with Arab imported guns and ammunition.

THE NILE VALLEY AND ETHIOPIA

We come now to consider briefly the Nile Valley. The River Nile traverses several geographical, political and cultural zones on its journey northwards as the White Nile from Lake Victoria Nyanza, and the Blue Nile from the Ethiopian mountains. The linguistic map shows that the Upper Nile region is most complex. It was an area where several cultures met: Kushitic, Sudanic and Nilotic principally with some Semitic languages. But it was rather isolated, cut off from Egypt by the intervening cataracts and difficult to penetrate because of the sudd[1] on the Upper Nile. For the rest, from the Horn country, along the Red Sea, to Egypt and the Magrib, there are principally two main language families: Hamitic languages like Gallinya of Ethiopia, Beja of Eritrea, Ancient Egyptian, Berber of the Magrib and Tuareg of the Sahara; or Semitic languages like Amharic of Ethiopia and Arabic. It should be repeated that it is a mistake to regard Hamitic as a racial stock of 'white' Africans who brought civilisation to the other African races. Hamitic languages are spoken by some of the most backward peoples in Africa today. Such languages spread among people of different racial stocks throughout North Africa except the more remote parts of the Upper Nile Valley and the Sahara. Arabic and South Arabian languages first crossed the Red Sea into Aksum. The Arab conquest of North Africa later spread Arabic south, up the Nile Valley, and west into the Magrib. The linguists now believe that Hamitic (including Berber, Ancient Egyptian, Kushitic), and Semitic languages in fact belong to the same family of Middle Eastern or West Asiatic languages. Greenberg calls them 'Afro-Asiatic'.

In spite of the vast area covered, the Nile Valley has shown more unity historically than some of the areas we have discussed. When Christianity came to Egypt, it spread southwards up the Nile Valley into Nubia. Although Ethiopia was largely Christianised by Syrian missionaries who entered by way of the Red Sea, the Ethiopian Church took on the characteristics of the Egyptian (Coptic) Orthodox Church and remained a branch of the Coptic Church down to 1951. When Islam overwhelmed Egypt, Christianity survived on sufferance as the religion of poor people. Islam and Arabic similarly spread up the Nile Valley and the Red Sea coast. By the fifteenth century only Ethiopia remained

Christian. Early in the sixteenth century, a Muslim Jihād was proclaimed in the Horn of Africa and Ethiopia was overrun, but the timely arrival of Portuguese Catholic soldiers helped to save it from forcible conversion.

It is true that even with Egypt historical development did not always move along the Nile Valley. The best rulers of Egypt had, however, always been very Nile-Valley conscious, because they knew that without the Nile Egypt was nothing but desert. The Pharaohs developed mathematics largely in order to watch the tides and control irrigation. They explored and traded down the Nile into Nubia and Kush. In turn, a dynasty from the Sudanic kingdom of Kush came to rule in Egypt in the eighth century B.C. This dynasty was displaced from Egypt a century later by the Assyrians, but Kush remained until the fourth century A.D. an important cultural and commercial centre linking the Nile Valley with Dafur and Wadai to the west. From the third century B.C. onwards when the capital shifted from Napata to Meroë, Kush became well known not only for its trade but also its iron culture, and Kush was probably an important centre for spreading the useful knowledge of iron to other parts of Africa. From the time that Alexander conquered Egypt, her successive rulers saw Egypt not as a separate entity but only as part of Hellenistic, Arab, Persian or Turkish empires. At such times when the Nile was neglected, Egypt suffered. The area of land under cultivation shrank, her population declined. This was the position at the end of the eighteenth century when Napoleon tried to revive Egypt. When the English made Napoleon's position there untenable, an Albanian adventurer, Muhammad Ali, inherited his ambition. Muhammad Ali began to explore down the Nile again.

Ethiopia survived as a Christian country behind her mountains, but the same mountains made it a difficult country to unite and govern. The Muslim Jihād of the sixteenth century had weakened the monarchy. The Portuguese soldiers were followed by Jesuit missionaries who attempted the conversion of the country to Catholicism as a price for their services. They were unsuccessful but the religious and political unity of the country had been undermined. Moreover, this internal weakness encouraged the infiltration of pagan and Muslim Gallinyas into the country. The upshot of all this was the growing power of formerly appointed provincial governors who made themselves hereditary and began to act independently of the emperor. The decline in the power of Muslim Egypt and the Ottoman empire removed one of the greatest driving forces of Ethiopian unity. By the end of the eighteenth century Ethiopia had disintegrated. The new ambition of Egypt in the Nile Valley was later to help revive Ethiopian nationalism in the second half of the nineteenth century.

THE MAGRIB

The Magrib is a comparatively small area, much more homogeneous than any of the other regions we have discussed. The basic population consisted of the Berbers whose language is Hamitic. There were, however, various ethnic groups, and because Berber was not a written language, the different dialects were often not mutually intelligible. In particular, there were great differences between the more sedentary and cosmopolitan Berbers of the coastal plains and those of the mountains who showed stronger ethnic attachments and were either nomadic or semi-nomadic.

Because of the excellent harbours in the Magrib, and because of their strategic position for traffic on the Mediterranean Sea, the coastal plains have often been subject to foreign invasion. First, the Phoenicians built Carthage near the present city of Tunis and showed that the Tunisian plains could supply southern Europe with corn and olive oil. The Romans conquered Carthage and brought much more of North Africa into the Roman Empire. With Rome Christianity came to the Magrib. The Berbers resisted official Catholicism but expressed their ethnic protest against Rome by embracing the more unorthodox sects. After Rome came the Vandals, the Germanic tribe that ended the last days of imperial Rome. In the seventh century A.D. came the Arab conquest and the spread of Islam and it was these that really began the unification of the Magrib.

At first, the Berbers resisted Islam as they had done Christianity, but they soon began to embrace it, particularly the more heterodox sects, as a way of fighting the Arabs. When in the tenth century roaming bands of Arabs began to conquer and colonise the Magrib the more fanatical Berbers migrated to join the nomadic ones of the desert. Out of these grew such movements as the Almoravids of the eleventh century and the Almohads of the twelfth and thirteenth centuries. These movements were a unifying factor in the Magrib, and it was out of the provincial administration of the Almohads that the Eastern, Central and Western Magrib began to emerge as Tunisia, Algeria and Morocco respectively. Gradually, Arabic began to displace Berber as the written, and even now as the spoken language. On the plains and in the cities, Arabs and Berbers became fused, but relatively pure Berbers survived in the mountains and in the Sahara desert.

A good deal of the history of the Magrib concerned the struggle for the control of the Mediterranean Sea. The initiative for a long time lay with the Magrib. The Almoravids and the Almohads conquered and ruled Spain. With the Crusades, Christian Europe tried to fight back with little success. From the end of the fifteenth century, however, the tide began to turn. The Christians drove the Muslims out of Spain and became progressively stronger on the sea. The rise of the Ottoman Turks and their conquest of Tunisia and Algeria, but not Morocco, for a while stabilised the position. With the decline in the power of Turkey, however, and the increasing technology of Europe the initiative passed to the Europeans. By the beginning of the nineteenth century, the Europeans were ready to launch the offensive.

NOTE

1 A vast extent of permanent, fifteen-foot-high papyrus swamp which obscured and obstructed the channel of the main river.

QUESTIONS FOR FURTHER STUDY AND DISCUSSION

1 Discuss the value of the study of languages to the study of history. Why is language a better classifying factor than race?

2 Discuss the historical importance of the cattle complex in the life of the Bantu-speaking peoples of South and East Africa.

3 Discuss the historical significance of the idea of the unity of the Nile Valley.

4 Discuss the influence of geography on the history of the Western Sudan.

5 In what ways has the environment of the Forest Areas affected the beliefs and institutions of their different peoples?

6 What do we mean by the Hamitic Hypothesis? Examine the arguments for and against this interpretation of African history.

SELECT BIBLIOGRAPHY

R. Oliver (ed.), *Dawn of African History*, O.U.P., 1961. A collection of short broadcast talks.

J. D. Fage, *An Atlas of African History*, Arnold, 1963.

R. Oliver and J. D. Fage, *A Short History of Africa*, Penguin Books, 1962. A useful general survey, but care should be exercised with regard to the Hamitic hypothesis and the concept of the all-pervading Sudanic type of state.

B. Davidson, *Old Africa Rediscovered*, Gollancz, 1959. *The African Past*, Longmans, 1964.

G. P. Murdock, *Africa: its Peoples and their Culture History*, New York, McGraw-Hill, 1959.

J. H. Greenberg, *Languages of Africa*, Indiana U.P., 1963.

6 Slavery and the Slave Trade

J. C. ANENE

BRYAN EDWARDS in his *History of the West Indies* expressed the view that 'a good mind may honestly derive some degree of consolation in considering that all such of the wretched victims as the slaves in Africa were, by being sold to the whites, removed to a situation infinitely more desirable, even in their native Africa'.[1] The author went on to argue that in Africa the slaves could not look forward to any security either for their own persons or for their property. This sweeping hypothesis is indeed typical of the arguments of those who are at pains to justify or mitigate the horror which accompanied the most iniquitous of transactions in human history. These arguments are for the most part based on a misconception of traditional African socio-economic life. It is therefore necessary to consider the institution of slavery in a few African societies before domestic slavery slid grimly into a wholesale traffic in human beings for sale and export. It will also be helpful to bear in mind that slavery was in no way peculiar to African communities.

The retention of captives taken in battle was a recognised practice among every people before the beginning of written history. The ancient records of the Assyrians, the Egyptians, the Phoenicians, the Hebrews, the Persians, the Indians and the Chinese are all full of references to slaves and the types of labour on which they were usually employed. With the Greeks and the Romans, the institution of slavery reached new heights. The economy came to be dependent upon slave labour. The Greek colonies in the Mediterranean were founded by Greek pirates who descended on the towns and sold the population into slavery. Ninety per cent of the population of Greece consisted of slaves, and according to the Greek philosopher, Aristotle, 'certain peoples are naturally free, others are naturally slaves. For these latter slavery is both just and expedient.' The Greek leisured class also naturally found slavery convenient. The population of the Roman empire comprised more slaves than freemen. The slaves drawn from Britain, Europe, Asia and Africa occupied positions as tillers of the soil, labourers, servants, court jesters, cooks, hair dressers, musicians and gladiators. Other European groups brutally enslaved not only their weaker neighbours but their own lower classes as well. The transformation from slavery to serfdom and then to freedom was already in process of completion by the end of the medieaval period. In China and in Muslim countries the institution of slavery persisted well into modern times. What is, therefore, indeed remarkable about slavery in Africa is that it was from Africa alone that large sections of the population were, until recent times, deported as slaves to other parts of the world.

DOMESTIC SLAVERY IN AFRICA

It is obviously unwise to generalise about the institution of slavery in Africa. There is evidence that some African groups had no place for slaves in their social system. For instance, the nomadic Masai and similar groups were interested only in capturing cattle and in getting rid of the cattle-owners who dared to oppose them. They captured no slaves. At first when the social and economic organisation of African communities was very simple, the institution of slavery did not have a recognised place in the social system. No social distinctions would exist between individuals and there was no room for the employment of slave labour. The idea of slavery might still be perfectly clear as members of the community would readily sell the members of their own group who committed certain crimes or the members of other groups captured in war. It is perhaps reasonable to assume that the more sedentary the people became the more likely were they to require the assistance of slaves (usually, at first, captives of war) for the continuous labour involved in agriculture. In such a society, the local social and economic system would not necessarily depend upon, but was certainly interwoven with, what came to be called domestic slavery. There was another status in most African societies often confused with domestic slavery. This was a condition of voluntary servitude. In an age when any un-protected man and woman exposed himself to the loss of personal freedom, submission to the protection of a powerful man amounted to an insurance against slavery. In discussing slavery in African society a basic distinction must be made between slaves who were captured from other groups in war and those who voluntarily gave themselves up in order to enter into a master-servant relationship with a protector. Closely associated with this category were pawns for debts. These were people who gave themselves into the bondage of creditors for unpaid debts either incurred by themselves or by a relative. Johnson in his *History of the Yorubas* clearly distinguishes between the 'Iwofa' system which he considers a part and parcel of the Yoruba social system and 'slavery' which he claims is an extraneous institution. As regards the first Johnson says, 'It has been compared to slavery by those ignorant of the legal conditions ruling the system; but an Iwofa is a free man, his social status remains the same, his civil and political rights are intact, and he is only subject to his master in the same universal sense that a borrower is servant to the lender.' A rare type of slavery was one connected with donating captives or local criminals to the gods. The victim was virtually ostracised. He had little social contact with the group but was not otherwise ill-treated. There was, of course, the horrible possibility that the slave belonging to a god might be no more than a reserve offering to be sacrificed to the god at the appropriate time.

The manner in which domestic slaves were treated varied from society to society. Captives of war from other groups could be sold, could be sacrificed, and could be eaten. Those who were absorbed into the economic life of a family did not have a very bad time. They worked for their masters but also were given their own pieces of land. They often became so linked with the families of their masters that there was hardly any difference in the manner of their living and that of their masters. In some cases they could marry free-born women, but the prejudice against slaves was so strong as to make such marriages very rare.

In some societies the personal services of a man bonded for debt counted towards the liquidation of the debt and therefore of the slave status. It is reasonable to assume that in many cases a well-behaved and energetic pawn could abruptly end his servitude by marrying the daughter of his creditor, or, if a bondswoman, by marrying her creditor. With more sophisticated communities, particularly with those which had become Islamised, slavery formed the very basis of the social and economic system. All labour not performed by individuals themselves was left to slave labour. The tilling of the soil, household chores, the care of the harem and so forth, were recognised assignments for slaves. In some cases, wealth and property consisted almost entirely in slaves. In some North African and Sudan states eunuchs were acquired as reliable harem-keepers, courtiers and guards of the palace. In spite of the fact that some eunuchs attained positions of eminence, we cannot but shudder in retrospect at the horror involved in this type of slavery. In these countries the Koran expressly permitted the faithful to possess slaves. The economic structure came to depend heavily on a system of slavery. Slaves became a matter of necessity. The more land a Muslim aristocrat possessed the more slaves he required to cultivate it. The larger the household, the greater were his requirements in terms of harem attendants, concubines and servants. Where trade was developed, the slaves were employed as beasts of burden and even as currency. The last two services were also performed by slaves in non-Muslim African communities.

Nowhere were slaves more completely integrated into the family of the owner than among the coast communities of Nigeria. Generally the owner put the slaves into the house of one of his wives. These women became the 'mothers' of the slaves and treated them as if they were their own sons. The slaves naturally still laboured under some disabilities. The remarkable 'house'[2] system which evolved meant that slaves and freemen together belonged to closely knit trading corporations in which the slaves had opportunities to acquire wealth, demonstrate their energy and intelligence and consequently to improve their social status. In many of these communities, slaves not only rose to become heads of 'houses' but in some cases attained supreme authority in the affairs of communities. Many dynasties traced their origin to people who were first acquired as slaves.

TRADE IN AFRICAN SLAVES

It has been shown that slavery although extensively practised in African communities until recent times was not an institution devised by Africans alone. What is remarkable as far as Africa is concerned is the situation dramatically expressed as follows: 'It is one of the harsh and unpalatable facts of history that the principal—almost the only—industry of tropical Africa for many centuries was the trade in slaves carried on mainly by the Christian peoples of Western Europe and by Muslim Arabs.[3] The sale of Africans began long before Christ and Muhammad, and their

8

followers sought profit from the traffic. There is evidence that in Ancient Egypt, African slaves were acquired not only for domestic work but also for the construction of such colossal projects as the Pyramids. The Egyptian hieroglyphics have also revealed that Pygmy slaves were employed during the dynastic period to act as court jesters. It is clear therefore that the sale of African slaves must have begun at a very early date. The first Africans to be sold out of Africa must have been the Nubians who lived south of Egypt. From Egypt they were sold to Europe and the Middle East; hence the constant reference in the literature of Greece and Rome to 'Ethiopian' slaves. During the Carthaginian period in North Africa, vast numbers of slaves were employed in the cultivation of estates, and labour requirements stimulated trade in slaves between North Africa and the Sudan. The extent of the Negro slave trade is not clear but detailed studies of cemeteries have yielded many skulls of a negroid character. The Carthaginian armies included many Negroes. Carthaginian demands for slaves from the Sudan were to initiate the tragic traffic which lasted till the end of the nineteenth century. The best-known centre for the Carthaginian traffic was the Fezzan which linked the territories north and south of the Sahara. The North African littoral was progressively littered with slave markets to supply the domestic needs of Greece and Rome.

Another important source for the early slave trade was East Africa. The majority of slaves from there found their way to Asia. In Turkey, Arabia and Persia they became a substantial element in the population. A guide book for navigation and trade written about A.D. 80 by a Greek seaman mentions slaves as one of the exports of East Africa. It is clear that the Arabs, Persians and Indians who found their way to the coast were already indulging in the slave trade. Early Chinese books describe how Africans were enticed by food and were then caught and carried off for slaves. The extent to which the north-eastern and eastern portions of Africa must have been exploited for slavery is demonstrated in the stories of slave revolts which have been preserved. The ruler of Bagdad had apparently initiated the policy of enrolling Zinj slaves in his army. When the slaves realised their large number they chose a leader called 'Lord of the Blacks' and revolted. There was also a time when tens of thousands of African slaves captured and sacked Basra and for fourteen years dominated the Euphrates basin. African slaves were also being exported in large numbers into India. In the Muslim kingdom the African slaves were drafted into the army by the ruler who was reputed to have possessed over eight thousand of them. The slave trade created a considerable Negro population in Bengal, Gujarat and the Deccan. From among these Africans arose army leaders who usurped the throne and inaugurated remarkable Negro regimes. In 976, the arrival of a Negro slave caused a great sensation at the court of the Chinese emperor. African slaves were subsequently absorbed into the countries of the Far East.

The Arab incursions into the Magrib and the Sahara inevitably stimulated the outflow of slaves from West Africa. Arab merchants were soon attracted to the Fezzan by the slave trade. Then there were marauding Arabs overwhelming Berber and Negro groups and carrying away as slaves those whom they did not slay. The later spread of Islam in no way abated the horror of the slave trade. The Muslim preacher was also a trader, and the slave was the inevitable article of trade. The links between West Africa, the Mediterranean and the Middle East were multiplied and sustained by caravans which dominated the Saharan trade. Slaves were the greatest inducement for camel-men to risk the hazards of the trans-Saharan journey. In these cases, enormous quantities of slaves were required. The mediaeval kingdoms of West Africa derived great wealth from the export of not only gold but slaves. The capital of Old Ghana, Kumbi, was noted for its slave market, which was no doubt kept well supplied by raids on the peoples living to the south. The name Demdem was given by the Arabs to the slaves which they purchased in the Ghana slave markets. When the empire of Ghana was overthrown by the Almoravids, Kumbi was sacked and many of its inhabitants were carried off to be sold as slaves in North Africa. We know from Ibn Battuta that the Mali aristocracy kept a large number of slaves. Their educated female slaves fetched a high price. On his pilgrimage to Mecca in 1324, Mansa Musa of the Mali empire crossed the African continent with a convoy of five hundred slaves carrying gold articles. Other pilgrims combined trade in slaves with their religious objectives, and took along slaves to barter for the goods of the Middle East. There is ample evidence that the rulers of the Hausa states were extensive dealers in slaves. The early expansion of Bornu-Kanem towards the region south-east of Lake

Chad was actuated by a desire to acquire new areas from which to capture Negro slaves for the export trade to Egypt and North Africa.

The arrival of Europeans on the West Coast of Africa opened a new phase in the African slave trade. When the Portuguese first began to feel their way along the western shores of the African continent they were encouraged by the hope that they might find the land of gold. In one of these early expeditions before the middle of the fifteenth century, a whole cargo of captives was sent back to Lisbon where the captives were sold into slavery. The Portuguese soon learnt how lucrative it could be to enslave and sell Africans. It is useful to bear in mind that when the Portuguese made their way to West Africa, they encountered a settled population of farmers who wore cotton garments dyed with indigo, and ornaments of gold and ivory. These people were eager to exchange gold for European product including beads, brass pots, hatchets and knives. Portuguese exploration of the African coast continued during the second half of the fifteenth century. In 1475 Portuguese ships crossed the Equator, and shortly after Captain Diogo Cão came to the mouth of the Congo River. Four years later Bartolomew Diaz rounded the Cape of Good Hope. Two years before the end of the century, Vasco da Gama went beyond the Cape and, after sailing up the East African coast, crossed the Indian Ocean to Calicut in India. The key points of Portuguese contact with West Africa were the Cape Verde islands and the neighbouring mainland lying along the coast between Senegal and Sierra Leone. In the Gold Coast Portugal constructed a number of forts, the earliest of which was Elmina Castle. A factory was set up at Gwato, south of Benin. Benin City was visited in 1485 by the Portuguese who discovered in the first instance that trade in ivory and pepper could be established. The key position which was destined to dominate Portuguese slave-trading activities was the island of São Tomé. It quickly rose in importance as the entrepôt for the slave trade between Guinea and the Congo and the New World.

The establishment in the New World of European plantations for the large-scale production of sugar, cotton and tobacco necessitated the search for cheap and abundant labour. The local Indians were being wiped out through subjection to arduous plantation labour and it was out of solicitude for these Indians

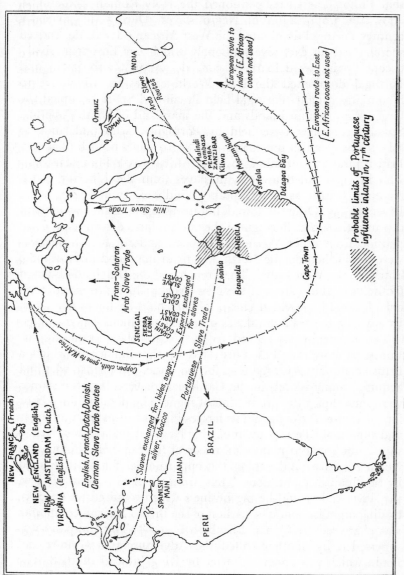

Fig. 8   Slaving and other trade routes.

that Bishop Las Casas petitioned the Holy Roman Emperor to allow the importation of Negro slaves. During the sixteenth century Portugal dominated the West African slave trade. Indeed she claimed an exclusive monopoly which her European rivals, except Spain, were loath to concede. At first also Spain and Portugal dominated the New World estates for which Negro labour was sought. Portugal held Brazil and Spain occupied the larger West Indian islands and the mainland of South America. Spanish contracts were held by Portuguese who undertook to ship to the Spanish possessions the Negro slaves needed. The first British pirate to intrude into West Africa was William Hawkins who in 1530 sailed away with slaves from the Liberian coast. Another British sailor, Captain Windham, visited the Benin River in 1553. Others followed, but it was not until the seventeenth century that the Portuguese began to face determined competition from other Western European nations. British colonies were established on the North American mainland and on some islands in the West Indies. The French and the Dutch all obtained footholds in those areas of the New World which promised incalculable wealth provided cheap labour could be made available. In any case the traffic in slaves promised enormous returns.

The importance attached to the Negro slave trade by the European Powers is best illustrated by the manner in which a British company was organised for the trade. The British who had acquired many islands in the Caribbean realised that the islands were suitable for the production of sugar. The demand for labour for the care of the cane and its harvesting for processing into sugar and rum could be met by importing Negroes. Britain, too, had to supply the tobacco plantation needs of the Southern Colonies of North America, and exploit the opportunities for profit offered by the Spanish plantations. Thus, from the British point of view, the slave trade could be big business which required an effective trading organisation. The earliest of the British African companies was chartered by Queen Elizabeth in 1588. The company was superseded by another called the Adventurers to Guinea and Benin which was given a charter by King James I in 1618. The company built Fort James on a small island in the Gambia River. Yet a bigger company which founded trading posts at Sierra Leone and the Gold Coast came into being after 1660. The slave trade was organised as a commercial enterprise. Liverpool and

Bristol grew rich on the slave trade and the trade was often referred to as 'the great support of our people'. Liverpool boasted of being 'the principal slaving port not only in England, but in Europe'.

The other Western European Powers were, of course, not to be outdone by the British. The Dutch founded a company for the West African trade and set up forts, particularly on the Gold Coast, in order to challenge the position of other rivals. The Portuguese, the French, the Dutch, Danes, Germans, Swedes, Spaniards and the British were all involved in the traffic in Negroes. They built ships designed to carry the largest number of slaves in the minimum of deck-space. Although the Europeans established forts on the coast, they did not themselves send expeditions into the interior for the capture of the Negroes. The activities of Portugal in Angola was an exception which will be considered separately. Local African potentates obtained the slaves and transacted sales with the European slavers on the coast. For instance, in Nigeria, the states of Lagos, Bonny and many others were ruled by chiefs who themselves made fortunes out of the slave transactions. The slaves were therefore produced by an interminable chain of middlemen which ramified into all parts of the hinterland. West Africa was also a favourite haunt for European pirates who were not averse to organising local raids of their own. Sierra Leone, for instance, was a pirate's anchorage. On the whole the Europeans were content that war-like African rulers should make war against their weaker neighbours in order to maintain the flow of slaves to the 'factories' established along the West African coast. At one time or another, Britain had fourteen, Holland fifteen, France three, and Portugal and Denmark four each.

THE CONGO, ANGOLA AND SOUTH AFRICA

The major field of Portuguese slavery activities was the Congo and Angola region. Here the Portuguese were freer from the competition which practically destroyed their former ascendancy in the more northern areas of the West Coast. Slaving was indirect in the Congo, but in Angola from the start the main concern of the Portuguese was slaving. Luanda became the greatest slave port in Africa. Forts were established by Portugal in the hinterland to provide centres of military strength which protected the slave caravans on their way to the coast. The interior forts were intended also to overawe African chiefs who might be disposed to interfere with the slave trade. Irregular taxes (usually paid in slaves) were imposed on African chiefs in order to compel them to raid their neighbours for slaves. The exploitation of Angola and the Congo for slaves produced the era of the notorious *pombeiros*, half-caste Portuguese who ranged through the country-side acquiring slaves which they marched down to the coast. It was not uncommon for the *pombeiros* and the Portuguese captains of the interior forts to stir up a local war in order to make captives available for slavery. The prosperity of Portuguese Brazil was inseparably bound up with slaving in Angola. The Portuguese Crown approved the devastations that went on in Angola and in the Congo as long as Brazil received the appropriate number of slaves needed in the plantations. Indeed, the Portuguese Governor of Angola augmented his income by manipulating slaving licences granted to contractors, and the so-called Portuguese wars of conquests were no more than military expeditions which ransacked the hinterland in order to stimulate the flow of slaves to the ports of Luanda and Benguela *en route* to Brazil. Thus, the Governor was usually the principal dealer in slaves, the only real article of trade in Angola. There were contractors working for him or for a corporation of investors, who purchased licences permitting them to export an appointed number of Negroes in a certain period of time. These contractors often used the services of the *pombeiros* to scour the interior.

The Dutch occupation of South Africa from about the middle of the seventeenth century necessitated the importation of Negro, and also Indian, slaves to provide labour. The slaves did the hard work in the vineyards, grain-lands and vegetable gardens owned by the settlers. Throughout the seventeenth and eighteenth centuries regular shiploads of slaves from West Africa, India, Ceylon and the Malay Archipelago were brought into South Africa. Other sources for slave labour in South Africa were the Bushmen and the Hottentots. The Bushmen were thinly scattered over practically the whole plateau of the immediate interior of the Cape. They relied for their subsistence on game and wild vegetables. The Dutch settlers found excuses for raiding Bushmen settlements and capturing women and children who were, to use the common euphemistic term, 'apprenticed' among the Boer farmers. They were held in virtual slavery. The Hottentots were not a large people and they had little internal cohesion. As pastoralists the tendency was for sections of a tribe to split off to seek new pastures. The Dutch settlers wanted Hottentot grazing-land, their cattle and their labour. The result was the gradual enslavement of Hottentots through the usual process of apprenticeship to Dutch farmers.

ABOLITION MEASURES

After nearly three centuries of callous indifferences to Negro suffering the conscience of religious and humanitarian groups in Western Europe and in America was roused against the iniquitous traffic. The Quakers petitioned the British Parliament against it. There were many individuals who were resolved to dedicate their lives to uprooting the evil of slavery. They included Thomas Clarkson, Granville Sharp, Wesley and Wilberforce. In the British Parliament, members sympathetic to the cause of the Negro, formed an Abolition Committee which attempted to mobilise opinion against the slave trade both inside and outside Parliament. The growing influence of the Abolition Committee was reflected in a speech by Pitt, the British Prime Minister: 'How can we hesitate a moment to abolish this commerce in human flesh which has so long disgraced our country and which our example will contribute to abolish in every corner of the globe?' The businessmen who had a vested interest in the Negro slave trade were more interested in their property than in the sufferings inflicted on the Negro, so it was not until 1807 that the British Parliament declared the slave trade illegal for British subjects. Much remained to be done before the Atlantic slave trade could be ended. French, American, Spanish and Portuguese slavers still hovered around to seize the trade which British subjects were being compelled to abandon.

From 1807 onwards, the British government stationed on the West Coast a unit of the navy known as the 'Preventive Squadron'. Although the squadron was usually able to rescue about three thousand slaves a year, it was clear that as long as large numbers of slaves were in demand in the New World and as long as the other Western European Powers were indifferent, slavers would resort to all kinds of stratagems to continue to make even greater profits than when the slave trade was an open one. It should also be remembered that many African coast chieftains who had become accustomed to the ready profit of the slave trade were reluctant to abandon the sale of their own people. Without the promise of adequate compensation it was unlikely that the Niger Coast chiefs of Bonny, Brass, Calabar and so forth, would have agreed to sign the 'slave treaties' with the British officers of the

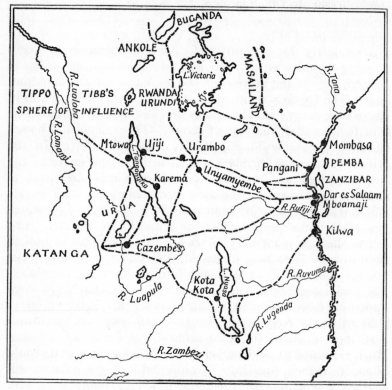

Fig. 9   The caravan routes of East Africa.

Preventive Navy. Portugal, Spain, France and then the United States gradually began to co-operate with the British government. The abolition of slavery in the United States and the virtual blockade of Brazil more or less marked the end of the Atlantic slave trade.

The extinction of the Atlantic slave trade left two regions of Africa almost completely unaffected. If anything, the export of slaves in the direction of East and North Africa was intensified.

The East African trade had always been in the hands of the Arabs who had settled in the coast towns of East Africa. A few of the Arabs may have made their way inland, but for the most part they relied on Africans to fetch their own fellow-Africans for sale. The position was dramatically transformed when in 1840, the Arab ruler of Oman, Seyyid Said, decided to transfer his court from Muscat to Zanzibar in order to inaugurate a systematic exploitation of the resources of East Africa. One of the most important items of these resources was the African slave. In the first place, the expansion of clove and other plantations begun by Sultan Said intensified the demand for African slaves. There were, too, the inexhaustible markets for slaves in the Middle East and Arabia. Under Said's protection and assisted with Indian finance, more and more Arabs organised caravans which penetrated almost every portion of East Africa. Arab activities reached the great lakes of Central Africa and beyond. In a number of places, the Arabs established 'colonies' as centres for the collection of ivory and slaves. In the upper regions of the Congo River, Arab adventurers completely mastered the poorly organised Bantu, raided their villages and seized the men and women required as slaves.

The Nile and the Saharan trade routes provided other avenues for the export of Negroes to North Africa and the Mediterranean. The wars precipitated by the Fulani Jihād in Hausaland and in Adamawa provided opportunities for the capture of 'pagans' for the slave trade. Bornu continually raided the regions south of Lake Chad for slaves. In Kano, Katsina and so forth there were open slave markets. Slaves were the main, if not the exclusive, articles of trade along the Bornu-Fezzan and the Wadai-Benghazi routes during the nineteenth century. The trans-Saharan trade in slaves had unique features which were more hideous than the sea-borne trade to America. Many of the slaves were young women and eunuchs. The long march across the desert and the heavy mortality it involved has no parallel in the tale of Negro suffering. The depredations of Arab slavers and the horrors of the Saharan trade were not brought to an end until well after the close of the nineteenth century.

EFFECTS OF THE SLAVE TRADE

The effect of the long centuries of traffic in African slaves on the Africans and their societies can never be fully assessed. Of the suffering to which the victims were subjected there can be no doubt. Those who saw the slaves being marched across the Sahara have left vivid pictures of the hideous suffering involved in slavery. The British Vice-Consul at Benghazi saw slaves who 'were emaciated to mere skeletons, their long, thin legs and arms and the unnatural size and prominence of their knees and elbows, hands and feet, giving them a most repulsive and shocking appearance'. An even greater number of these slaves succumbed to the thirst and agony of the Saharan route or to the whips of the slavers which were in constant use. The accounts of the gruesome details of the Saharan slave trade left by Saharan travellers such as Richardson, Denham and Barth are still available. The Atlantic slave trade, too, had its own horrors for the African slave. After the long march to the coast, the slaves chained together were herded in barracoons until they could be sold. The sickening conditions aboard ship and the notorious Atlantic sea-passage defy description. Through disease, suicide or suffocation, a considerable proportion of the slaves never reached their destination. The suffering inflicted on African communities by the raids is clearly revealed in the account left by the missionary, George Grenfell, who travelled along the Congo River in 1884. He saw hundreds of canoes carrying homeless families in flight before a band of Arab raiders. He noticed the smoking ruins of numbers of African towns, and people sleeping in their canoes because they feared night attacks on their villages.

There can be no doubt that the slave trade depopulated vast areas of Africa. It has been calculated that the European slave trade in the Atlantic was responsible for the removal from Africa of at least twelve million Africans; this without reckoning those who perished in the process. The small population of East and Central Africa, areas subjected to the slaving from antiquity, must be accounted for by the prodigious number of slaves who were captured and exported. Speke, the explorer, observed that the desolation of the shores of Lake Tanganyika struck him with much surprise. A former beautiful country had been despoiled of its men and cattled for distant markets. The journals of Dr Livingstone tell the same story.

The slave trade was primarily responsible for the disruption of a number of African states. The kingdom of the Kongo encountered by the Portuguese in the fifteenth century had the foundations of an organised state. The rulers were willing, and later even anxious, to have in their midst not only Portuguese missionaries, but also Portuguese teachers, mechanics, printers and builders. One Mani-Kongo after another was converted and baptised with thousands of Kongolese. Churches and schools had gone up. Then what happened? In spite of appeals by the African rulers for assistance in the peaceful modernisation of the Kongo, the Portuguese turned their attention to the slave trade, undermined the authority of the Mani-Kongo among his subordinate chiefs, and the Kongo state collapsed and became nothing more than a haunt for slaves shipped across the Atlantic to Brazil. There were, no doubt, other African groups who were subjected in the same way to the corrosive effects of the slave trade.

Benin, Dahomey and Asante, to mention but a few, afford examples of African states which, through the prevalence of the slave trade, diverted their energies from the peaceful development of politics, arts and culture to preoccupation with slaving wars and wanton destruction. It has been suggested, rather unwisely by some writers, that these states came into existence or expanded as a result of the slave trade. Benin, for instance, was in existence before the Portuguese initiated the sea-borne slave trade. Early Portuguese accounts of Benin spoke of the orderliness and peace of the kingdom. Then Benin took to the slave trade. She required slaves for export and for human sacrifice, and by the end of the nineteenth century, she had earned herself the doubtful reputation of being the 'City of Blood'. The annual incursions of the state of Dahomey into Yorubaland and into the territories of her neighbours were undertaken to amass the slaves required for export and for sacrificial rites. The disintegration of the Yoruba empire was not unconnected with the constant raiding for slaves which was one of the objectives of the groups involved in the civil wars which dominated the nineteenth century. The constant state of hostility which characterised the relations between Buganda in Central Africa, and her neighbours points inexorably to the corrosive virus of the slave trade.

The anarchic state of affairs resulting from slaving was probably worse among poorly organised African communities. The absence of political integration exposed these communities to the ravages of their more powerful neighbours or of Arab adventurers. There were many regions in Africa to which broken communities fled. For instance, the thickly forested area to the east of the Cross River basin became the home of splinter and often undefinable groups fleeing from the Benue spring-board of Fulani slaving raids. The inaccessible heights of the Cameroon and Adamawa mountains offered refuge to formerly peaceful 'pagans' whom the Adamawa Fulani raided for slaves. In Central Africa, many small groups of Bantu clung to the swampy islands of Lake Victoria to escape the Arabs and the Baganda. Instances of communities fragmented and driven from their original homes are too innumerable to be listed here. It is hardly surprising that many of these fugitive communities remained highly suspicious of outsiders well into the twentieth century.

A remarkable by-product of the slave trade was the foundation of Freetown and Liberia, both in West Africa. The establishment of Freetown was a practical measure undertaken by British philanthropists to settle emancipated slaves at Sierra Leone. The first slaves to be landed there were collected in London. There were reinforcements from Canada and the Caribbean, and soon there were 1,200 citizens in Freetown, destined to become the capital of Sierra Leone. Liberia was the brain-child of the American Colonisation Society. In 1822 parties of liberated slaves arrived to begin the foundation of the capital town of a new country called Liberia. The first 'African' President of the new state proclaimed its independence and Liberia began its precarious career as an African state. The beginnings were anything but auspicious. The liberated slaves of Freetown and Monrovia had great contempt for the indigenous Africans whom the immigrants regarded as 'bush-niggers'. The integration of the 'civilised' Negroes and the 'bush-niggers' has not quite been completed even today.

On the whole, however, the long period of slavery almost completely undermined all elements of civilising growth in Africa. The achievements of mediaeval times in many areas were obliterated by the wholesale traffic in human beings, and were forgotten. The Europeans who traversed Tropical Africa in the nineteenth century found themselves amidst chaos and stagnation. They imagined that desolation was part and parcel of African history from time immemorial. As for the Africans themselves, they came to be regarded as mere instruments to serve the ends of white men. A recent analysis of the South African situation recalls that the settlers who acquired the Africans as slaves began to look upon them as uncivilised, heathen and inferior beings. Here was the beginning of deep-rooted contemptuous prejudices which are likely to die hard. Apparently slavery is the proper condition of the black race. Who can say that this assumption has been completely eradicated from the European and the Asian consciousness?

NOTES

1 Edwards, *History of the West Indies*, Vol. II, p. 99. Stockdale, 1794.
2 For detailed understanding of the 'house' system see K.O. Dike, *Trade and Politics in the Niger Delta*, pp. 34–7, O.U.P., 1956.
3 H. W. Jones, *Africa in Perspective*, p. 89, London, 1958.

QUESTIONS FOR FURTHER STUDY AND DISCUSSION

1 Comment on the statement that the institution of slavery in Africa has been much misunderstood by outside writers.
2 Discuss the view that many African communities benefited from the slave trade. Or 'The slave trade stained and ruined much of the fabric of African society while permitting nothing better to replace it'. With what evidence would you support or reject this judgment by Basil Davidson on the African slave trade?
3 Describe briefly the origins and growth of the trans-Saharan slave trade.
4 Why did the trade in African slaves last as long as it did?

SELECT BIBLIOGRAPHY

F. D. Lugard, *The Dual Mandate in British Tropical Africa*, Chapters IV, XVII, XVIII, XIX and XX, 2nd edition, Blackwood, 1923 (reprinted F. Cass, 1965).
James Duffy, *Portuguese Africa*, Harvard University Press, 1959.
W. L. Mathieson, *British Slavery and Its Abolition, 1823–38*, Longmans, 1926
Cambridge History of the British Empire, Vol. I, under 'West Indies' and 'West Africa'.
J. Simmons, *Livingstone and Africa*, English U.P., 1955.
A. Adu Boahen, *Britain, the Sahara, and the Western Sudan*, Clarendon Press, 1964.
E. W. Bovill, *The Golden Trade of the Moors*, O.U.P., 1958.

7 Chartered Companies and the Scramble for Africa

J. E. FLINT

BEFORE the 1880s there was little sign of any great interest on the part of European powers in the possibility of colonising Tropical Africa. Outside the tropical areas, at the extremities of the continent where a milder climate permitted Europeans to settle permanently, Britain had taken over Cape Colony from the Dutch after the Napoleonic Wars, and France had begun in 1830 the long struggle to subdue Algeria, but in the rest of Africa European settlement or political rule seemed insignificant; such European possessions as there were, often legacies of slave-trading days, were mere coastal enclaves of uncertain title, like the British and Dutch forts on the Gold Coast, or the French posts at St Louis and Gorée in Senegal, or the vast claims, but sketchy administration, maintained by the Portuguese in Mozambique and Angola. Between 1787 and the 1880s, it is true, there were some advances in European political control. The Sierra Leone Colony, founded by the private initiative of British humanitarians in 1787 as a settlement of free Negroes, was taken over by the British government in 1807 as a naval base for the operations of the anti-slave-trade naval patrols and as a place for landing slaves liberated from captured slave ships at sea. After decades of vacillation in policy the British finally declared the coastal areas of the Gold Coast a colony in 1874, having annexed Lagos in 1861. The French did something to secure a firmer hold on Senegal, and began to advance towards the Niger under the energetic administration of Faidherbe between 1854 and 1865, and throughout the century they were expanding the area of their effective control in Algeria. In South Africa the British, though regarding Cape Colony as more a naval base on the route to India than a field for expansion of settlement, had followed up the 'great trek' of their disgruntled Boer subjects by annexing Natal in 1845, although in the 1850s they agreed to the independence of the Boer Republics of the Orange Free State and Transvaal created by further trekking. Taken as a whole, and viewed against the vast map of Continental Africa, all of these moves made little impression on the pattern of authority (see Maps C and D).

Several factors kept European interference at a minimum in the years before 1880. In Tropical Africa, Europeans, lacking the immunities against tropical disease built up by Africans, faced fantastic death rates in all their activities before 1857, when quinine first began to be used extensively. Moreover, they had richer and more attractive areas to engage their attention; Britain in particular was colonising Australia and New Zealand, expanding settlement in the Canadian west, and preoccupied with Indian questions after the Indian Mutiny of 1857. Russia had a vast field for colonisation in her Asian territories to the east, whilst the United States absorbed her energies in the colonisation of an ever-moving western frontier. Other European powers had internal problems so acute that they prevented all thought of a planned or sustained colonial activity. Germany and Italy did not exist as united nation-states until 1870, and both areas were troubled by revolutionary movements and Europeans wars. France suffered revolution in 1830, 1848 and 1870, and her constitution was not finally stabilised until 1879. Even the United States was torn in two by the issue of slavery erupting into civil war, and only became a stable unit after the victory of the north in 1865. Before 1870 new forces were wrecking traditions of the European race; democracy, nationalism, liberalism and socialism had produced an unstable ferment.

Of the major powers only Britain came through the nineteenth century without revolution or major political instability. At the same time Britain had a lead in industrial development, in finance and in shipping. This gave Britain a unique and peculiar position. Her commerce was supremely competitive, and did not need the protection of colonial tariff preferences, and before 1880 it seemed that the other powers were in no position to retaliate by establishing colonies of their own as protected areas for their exports. Gradually after 1832 Britain became a free-trading country, dismantling her own tariffs both at home and in her colonies. As colonies ceased to be protected markets for British trade, economists began to challenge their very existence. Why should the taxpayer be burdened with possessions which served no useful purpose to Britain?

9

THE PRELUDE

This did not mean that the British had no ambitions in Africa. Indeed, before the Scramble, the British were in a sense more ambitious than they could ever be after the partition had begun. Before 1870 the free traders could dream of the day when Africa would be completely dominated by Britain, but this would not be through colonies, but by the gradual penetration, decade by decade, of British trade and British missionaries. Much breath has been wasted in trying to assess which was a more important British motive at this time—humanitarian desire to suppress the slave trade or economic motives in the search for tropical produce and tropical markets. In reality the British trader and the British missionary were but two arms of a single culture, the arrogant, self-satisfied, supremely confident, competitive, and at times nobly inspired culture of Victorian England. The doctrine of 'legitimate commerce' was in fact an adaptation to African conditions of the free-trade policy. The slave trade might be a sin and the work of the Devil to the missionary, to the economist it was a wasteful and unnatural system of production, less efficient than wage labour, and one which hindered the proper economic development of African produce which could be utilised in British industry. The best way to eradicate the slave trade was not by force or colonisation, but by the competition of a superior commerce and culture —'Christianity' and 'Commerce' would bring 'Civilisation', and by 'Civilisation' the Victorians meant, of course, British culture.

Translated into political terms, the policy of 'legitimate commerce' was basically opposed to colonial activity, except in extreme circumstances. Between 1852 and 1861 the British intervened in Lagos on the ground that they were replacing a ruler who supported the slave trade with a dynasty that favoured legitimate commerce.[1] But such policies were uncharacteristic; wherever possible the British attempted to find congenial local political regimes and work through them, building up their strength through military advice and supplies, to create states which could give added security to commerce and have power to suppress slave-trading. Abeokuta was singled out in this way because of its welcome to missionaries. The states of the Oil Rivers received similar treatment as a result of the immense legitimate trade in palm oil which their African middlemen brought down to the coast for the Liverpool traders. At times it was hoped to use Asante and Nupe as powers which would tap the supposedly vast trade of the Muslim Sudan. The classic case, however, was in East Africa, where Britain gradually built up a position of diplomatic dominance in the court of the Sultan of Zanzibar. The Sultan was encouraged to create a trading empire in East Africa, with settlements along the coast from Somaliland to the northern border of Portuguese Mozambique, so as gradually to develop 'legitimate trade' as compensation for a step-by-step reduction in the slave trade of his Arab subjects. This 'persuasion' was not only 'friendly'; in 1873 he was threatened with naval blockade if he would not abolish the seaborne trans-shipment of slaves. When he capitulated, British aid was redoubled, a British officer came to train the Zanzibar army, and large gifts of modern arms and ammunition were made.

In North Africa, Egypt was an even more spectacular example of such policies, although here France and Britain jointly participated. Both assisted the Khedive in his bid for independence from Turkish control, military officers were seconded for service in the Egyptian army, the French successfully constructed the Suez Canal, and large financial loans were floated in Paris and London to enable the Khedive to live in considerable style and to expand Egyptian authority into the Sudan along the Nile. Throughout this period there was no attempt to secure any direct colonial authority in Egypt. The basic objectives of British and French policy were secured without the need for such responsibility or expense.

The British scarcely realised that this policy of commercial and cultural penetration without political rule depended on two conditions: first, the African states needed to be able to withstand the strains created by European commercial, financial and cultural impact; secondly, Britain needed to be free from outside intervention if she were to pursue the policy without political control of African states. If such states fell under the control of other European powers the policy collapsed.

In fact, the Scramble for Africa represented just this collapse of the traditional British policy, and the Scramble began with signs that the two conditions outlined above were ceasing to operate.

In those parts of Africa most subject to European financial penetration there were signs of internal collapse from 1870. In

North Africa, Turkish control, already weakened by Egyptian independence, began to disintegrate all along the coast, and local rulers, whilst declaring independence, proved financially incapable of maintaining it. In 1869 France, Italy and Britain assumed direct control of Tunisian finances, but in 1876 came a much more serious crisis in Egypt, where the Khedive found that Egyptian finances were no longer sufficient to meet interest payments on the huge debts of the state. France and Britain were therefore given financial control, with significant powers over state expenditure. Meanwhile Britain had begun to take steps designed to give her greater control over the Suez Canal which was vital for her communications with her Indian empire; she purchased the Khedive's shares in the Suez Canal Company, and at the Berlin Congress of 1878 she acquired Cyprus from Turkey as a base to survey the Mediterranean end of the canal. However, this by no means meant that the British were ready to make imperialist moves into Africa. When similar stresses began to assert themselves in Zanzibar and the Sultan in 1879 tried to pass over the administration of the mainland territories to a company headed by Sir William Mackinnon, chairman of the British India Steamship Company, the British Foreign Secretary, Lord Salisbury, wrecked the scheme, fearing that it would implicate the government in unwanted responsibilities.[2]

Much more serious, however, than the cracks developing in some African states, was the appearance of other European powers on the African scene to challenge Britain's policy of informal influence. After 1870 Europe achieved a new stability. In that year the Prussians crushed the French armies and overthrew Napoleon III's regime; in the throes of victory the German Reich was proclaimed. In the same war Italy seized Rome and completed her unification. Germany, under Chancellor Bismarck, became the centre of the European diplomatic system. But Britain had little to fear from Germany, and even less from Italy, in her African policies, or so it seemed, for Bismarck was opposed to German colonisation, and had rejected the suggestion that Germany should seize France's colonies after the victory of 1870. Nor at first was there much to fear from France; defeated and demoralised by the losses of Alsace and Lorraine in 1870, France was beset by warring ideological groups. But then, in 1879, France suddenly achieved stability as the republicans got control

of the presidency and ousted bonapartists and monarchists from
the centres of power. Almost immediately France began to assert
herself in Africa.

Germany welcomed this development. Chancellor Bismarck
felt that colonial activity could only weaken France, and it might
divert her energies from plans of revenge against Germany. Thus,
at the Berlin Conference of 1878 he played the role of 'honest
broker', not only urging Britain to annex Cyprus, but pressing the
French to take Tunis where they were worried by the presence of
20,000 Italian settlers in a country which bordered Algeria. In
1881 a French force occupied the country, and Italy remained
powerless in the face of Bismarck's tacit support of the French
move.

The French were also active elsewhere from 1879. In Senegal
they began building the railway from Dakar to St Louis, and in
1880 planned to extend the line to the Niger, sending out surveying
parties which provoked the first military push designed to link
the headwaters of the Senegal and Niger rivers.

Neither the Tunisian intervention nor the advance in Senegal
were sufficient to precipitate a scramble, for they were well
removed from British areas of influence. The real beginnings of
the process of partition are to be seen in the development of two
quite distinct situations, each of which was to have far-reaching
repercussions, the one on the Congo, the other in Egypt.

THE CONGO AND EGYPT

The Congo, like the Niger, was an area of informal British
predominance; earlier in the century there had been official
expeditions up the river, and later its trade had been developed
by merchants from Liverpool and Manchester. Baptist missionaries had also become active. Farther north, on the Ogowe and
Gabun rivers, French traders and missionaries were well established. In 1876, events began to take a new and surprising turn
with the intervention of King Leopold of the Belgians. An
ambitious and clever man, bored by the strict limits of his constitutional position in Belgium under the parliamentary regime,
he had conceived the idea of carving out a personal empire for
himself in Africa. The project was at first disguised as an international 'philanthropic' scheme of co-operation through a newly
formed International African Association. Exploring missions

were sent to the Congo basin (several approaching it from the East African coast, which alarmed Zanzibar) of which the most important were those led by H. M. Stanley. By 1880 it was becoming increasingly clear that the 'international' aspect of these moves was a sham, and that King Leopold was assuming a distinct political role for himself. The French were first to realise this, partly from information given to them by the explorer, de Brazza, who had himself been approached by Leopold for his services. The Minister of Education in the French government at this time was Jules Ferry, a convinced imperialist who believed that France could only rebuild by securing tropical raw materials and protected markets for her backward industries. Using Ministry of Education funds, Ferry dispatched de Brazza to the northern banks of the Congo ostensibly on a 'scientific' mission. In reality de Brazza concluded a series of protectorate treaties with African rulers, which by 1882 secured the north bank of the Congo to France and laid the basis for the colony of Gabun. De Brazza's activities only served to intensify treaty-making by Stanley on behalf of King Leopold. This in turn alarmed the British, anxious for the position of their traders and the Baptist missionaries. By 1882, the Congo question began to have wider implications; the British consul in the Oil Rivers expressed fears that the French would use the Gabun Colony to expand into the Cameroons and Iboland to control the sources of supply of the lucrative palm-oil trade; at the same time British traders on the Niger, now led by Goldie, began sending home alarming reports of French competition and attempts to make treaties on the Niger.

As the British began to decide what to do in face of the Congo and Niger situations, events in Egypt were moving to a climax. The financial control of British and French officials imposed in 1876 naturally irked the Khedive Ismā'īl, and in April 1879 he dismissed them. Britain and France in reply arranged for the Sultan of Turkey (nominally the Khedive's suzerain) to dismiss Ismā'īl, and replace him as Khedive with his son Tawfīq. This action was the origin of the modern nationalist movement in Egypt among the army officers, who found a leader in Colonel Ahmad Urābi (Arab Pasha), rose in revolt against foreign influence, and succeeded in gaining control of the country by 1882. Both Britain and France had large issues at stake: both had big financial investments in Egypt which the nationalists might now repudiate (indeed Egypt was not in a position to pay the interest on her loans); both had invested in the Suez Canal, and the canal was for Britain an essential strategic link with the Indian empire and her Australian, New Zealand and Far Eastern trade and colonies. In May 1882 France and Britain agreed on a joint military intervention, the object of which would be to depose the nationalists under Urābi and restore the pliant Khedive Tawfīq.

At the critical moment, however, there was a change of government in France, and it was the British alone who in June 1882 bombarded Alexandria and landed a force of troops which defeated Colonel Urābi's forces in September at al-Tal al Kabīr (Tel el Kebir). The British had no idea of establishing a colony, or even a protectorate. The Liberal Prime Minister, Gladstone, believed that the troops could be used to 'restore the Khedive's authority', and then withdraw. The French were assured that the occupation was strictly temporary and that the troops would be withdrawn very soon. But what did the phrase 'restore the Khedive's authority' really mean? Fundamentally it meant that Egypt should be able to pay her debts and honour the interest payments. This was not something which could be achieved by a few months' military occupation, for existing Egyptian revenues were insufficient. Production would have to be increased; this in turn entailed land reform to liberate the Egyptian peasant from debt and semi-serfdom; the revenue system had to be purged of corruption—in short 'restoring the Khedive's authority' implied a generation of financial, political and social reform! The British, therefore, whilst continuing to claim that the occupation was 'purely temporary', continued to stay in Egypt.

To the French this seemed like sheer hypocrisy, and as months, and then years, passed, the British occupation engendered a deep resentment among French politicians. The Egyptian occupation created a basic distrust of British motives in Africa among Frenchmen which was to last for the rest of the century, and is a basic factor in understanding the Anglo-French rivalry during the partition. The French felt that by their financial investments in Egypt, by the work of their officials there, by the fact that the Suez Canal had been conceived and executed by the Frenchman, de Lesseps, France was entitled to a special and predominant position in Egypt, of which she had been robbed by a ruthless British opportunism. This resentment intensified the feeling of politicians like Jules Ferry that France, in need of colonial markets that could be reserved for French industry by protective tariffs, must act quickly in other parts of Africa if she were not to be forestalled by Britain.

The Egyptian occupation also led, indirectly, to German intervention in the politics of Africa. It was not that Bismarck opposed the British occupation of Egypt; on the contrary he looked upon it with something like glee; he had been pressing the British to do just this since 1878. Bismarck's motive for feeling this way was entirely diplomatic. Germany, now the dominant power in Europe, had secured alliances with Austria in 1879 and with Russia in 1881, and Italy joined this system in 1882. Of the great European powers only France and Britain remained aloof. The only danger to Germany was a French war of revenge for the humiliation of her defeat in 1870, but she could not attack Germany without allies. Ideologically, Britain and France should have been natural allies; they were both liberal parliamentary regimes with a common interest in the security of the English Channel and the Low Countries. It was their colonial rivalries which divided them and therefore isolated each internationally. The British occupation of Egypt was thus a heaven-sent opportunity to Bismarck to try to intensify this rivalry.

In detail, however, there were even more opportunities for Bismarck in the Egyptian situation. Between 1876 and 1879 an international debt commission had been set up as a result of the Egyptian financial crisis. By maintaining the fiction that the occupation was temporary and that the Khedive was still the ruler of Egypt, Britain ensured that this international supervision would continue. France would naturally oppose her vote on the commission to British policies. Britain was thus dependent on the votes of Germany and her allies if she were to succeed in her policies in Egypt. Naturally Bismarck expected that the British government would realise its dependence on Germany and give concessions in return, even perhaps to the extent of ceding the North Sea island of Heligoland or joining in formal alliance with Germany and thus completely isolating France.

The Liberal government in Britain, however, refused to see things in this cold and rational light, but imagined that they could go on much as before. Much thought was given to the situation in the Oil Rivers and Niger, where it was realised that something would have to be done to protect British traders, but the British Consul's idea of a colony was firmly rejected. In principle it was agreed by the Cabinet to set up some kind of protectorate under the Foreign Office, whereby local kings would cede to Britain their right to have any foreign relations, thus making a French protectorate impossible. Once decided there were months of delay in finding £5,000 to equip the treaty-making consul with 'presents'. In face of the Congo threat, the British adopted an even more indirect approach; here it was decided to oppose the designs of King Leopold and those of the French by resurrecting the ancient claims of Portugal. In the Anglo-Portuguese treaty of February 1884, Britain recognised Portuguese claims to the mouth of the Congo River, in return for which Portugal agreed to free access for British traders and missionaries. It was the old policy of commercial and cultural penetration—Portugal could pay for the administration! It was hardly to be expected that either France or King Leopold would accept such a device.

THE ROLE OF GERMANY

With German support the British might have carried the Anglo-Portuguese treaty through. But British reactions to Bismarck's demand that she should recognise her dependence on Germany in Egypt served only to infuriate the German Chancellor. Throughout 1883, the Germans had been sounding Britain about her claims to Angra Pequena in South West Africa, where a German merchant, Herr Lüderitz, had ambitions to form a chartered company. Bismarck at this stage had no wish to entangle Germany in colonial adventures; instead he hoped that the British would oblige by 'protecting' Lüderitz. The Germans were met first with evasion, but after further pressure, the German government was given the extraordinary reply in November that although Britain had no claims whatsoever over Angra Pequena, and had no intention of establishing any authority in that region, any German claim would infringe the 'legitimate rights' of Britain. This was an openly arrogant claim to preserve the old informal commercial and cultural British supremacy—opposed to colonisation herself, Britain would not allow others to colonise. As Bismarck commented, it was tantamount to a 'Monroe doctrine for Africa'.

This rebuff resulted in a revolutionary change in German policy which was to have profound results on the future course of the partition. Bismarck decided to establish German colonies in Africa. This decision had nothing to do with any change in Bismarck's view of colonies; he still regarded them as useless encumbrances and had no intention of establishing a Colonial Office or setting up official German administrations in these colonies; instead the German merchants on the spot, like Lüderitz in South West Africa, would be given administrative powers on the model of the old British East India Company. The motive behind the new policy was diplomatic,[3] and the policy was directed exclusively against Britain; the new colonies would all border upon existing British areas of predominance. Bismarck could foresee two possible results, either of which would suit his purposes; the British might realise that the move was designed to convince them of Britain's dependence on Germany, and react accordingly; or, by following an anti-British line Bismarck might achieve the near-impossible and gradually win over the French, who now had a colonially minded ministry with Jules Ferry as Premier.

Once made, the German decision was implemented with characteristic swiftness and efficiency. In April 1884, Bismarck announced that Angra Pequena had become a German protectorate. On the same day he proposed to Jules Ferry that France and Germany should work together against the British. Ferry cautiously agreed, and the two powers then proceeded publicly to denounce the Anglo-Portuguese Congo treaty. In June 1884, the British began to 'see reason' and, recognising their isolation, accepted the German protectorate at Angra Pequena and abandoned the Anglo-Portuguese treaty. But these concessions were now too late, for Bismarck was intent on the more ambitious scheme of developing Franco-German co-operation to see where it would lead. In the same month, Bismarck used the German vote at the London Conference on Egyptian finances to wreck the British schemes for reform. In July, Dr Nachtigal, a specially appointed 'Commissioner' for West Africa whose travels had been assisted by unsuspecting British officials, proceeded to annex Togoland, near the British settlements on the Gold Coast, and the Cameroons. The annexation of the Cameroons was particularly annoying to the British, for they had planned to make it the headquarters of their Oil Rivers Protectorate. In the following month, the Germans extended the Angra Pequena Protectorate to cover all the coast between Portuguese Angola and Cape Colony, renaming it German South West Africa. Finally, in October 1884, the fruits of Germany's overtures to France were revealed when the two powers 'invited' Britain to attend a conference in Berlin to discuss ways of establishing international control over the Congo and Niger rivers, and means of defining future acquisitions on the coasts of Africa.

WEST AFRICA

The Berlin West African Conference which began in November 1884 thus had its origins in an attempt to destroy British informal influence on the Niger and Congo, the two most important avenues of access to the interior of Tropical Africa. The British were well aware of this, but there was little they could do with regard to the Congo, for they had already abandoned the treaty with Portugal. This left the field wide open for both the French and the King of the Belgians, and Leopold now showed consummate diplomatic craft. He first succeeded, by careful use of propaganda and personal influence, in persuading the United States and its delegate that his plans were really a crusade against the slave trade. At the same time he was winning over important British trading and humanitarian interests into the belief that his regime would be far more liberal and free-trading than either the French or Portuguese could ever be. But his stroke of genius lay in encouraging among the French delegates the idea that his proposed personal colony would fail, through lack of financial support. He then proceeded to negotiate a secret agreement with France whereby Leopold's Congo Free State would revert to France in case of bankruptcy. France thus came forward to support Leopold, and the conference agreed to recognise the Congo Free State as the authority administering the Congo. Most of the powers would soon regret the decision, for the 'liberal' regime was not very long in turning itself into a ruthless, monopolistic organisation in which human life was considered less valuable than rubber.

If the British were checkmated in the Congo, they salvaged their position on the Niger. Here Goldie, who had united the British traders in 1879, fought a bitter commercial war against French competition. On the eve of the Berlin Conference he had bankrupted the French traders, and bought up their interests. At the same time his agents began making treaties with Africans on the river purporting to grant political and administrative rights to the company. Goldie himself went with the British delegation to Berlin as an unofficial adviser. By the time the Congo question was settled and the Niger came up for discussion the friendship between Germany and France was breaking down, for the French politicians were afraid that their electorate would turn against policies which appeared pro-German. As a result the conference declared Britain to be the power responsible for administering rules for the Navigation of the Niger, which it proceeded to draw up, but with no kind of international commission to enforce such rules they remained a dead letter. The British government was still reluctant to saddle itself with the expense of administration on the Niger, hence, in 1886 Goldie's company was granted a charter of administration as the Royal Niger Company. It thereafter proceeded to use its administrative powers to establish a complete monopoly of trade. The Oil Rivers, where several British firms were in competition, remained a separate protectorate under the consular administration of the Foreign Office.

Meanwhile the French had not been inactive in West Africa. During 1885 they established themselves on the Ivory Coast and the coasts of Dahomey (Porto Novo and Cotonu), and continued their campaigns in the Senegal hinterland. Thus, by the end of 1885 the whole western coastline of Africa, from the Cape of Good Hope to Senegal, was claimed by European powers, with the single exception of the Republic of Liberia.

EAST AFRICA

Meanwhile, the British position in East Africa, where they had worked for so long through the Arab empire of Zanzibar, also collapsed in 1885, and again through German activity. After the German intervention in the Cameroons some of the younger members of the British Cabinet (including Joseph Chamberlain) had wished to uphold certain treaties made by Harry Johnston, then a young naturalist working near Mt Kilimanjaro, so as to forestall any possible German moves in East Africa, but Prime Minister Gladstone intervened to veto the idea of a colony near 'the mountain . . . with an unrememberable name'. In November and December 1884, whilst the Berlin Conference was actually in session, Karl Peters and his associates entered Tanganyika and claimed to have made treaties inland. In March 1885, on the day after the Berlin Conference ended, Peters and his friends were granted German protection and the right to set up an administration in East Africa. They proceded to form the German East Africa Company to do so.

The British were in no position to resist Germany in East Africa, even though this meant the end of their policy of development through Zanzibar. The Egyptian situation had become desperate, for the Egyptian Sudan had risen under the Mahdist religious revival and the popular British hero, General Gordon, had been killed at Khartoum in January 1885, for which the government, and Gladstone in particular, were unfairly blamed.[4] In March, there was a crisis between Russia and Britain over Afghanistan which came to the brink of war—Britain could not afford to antagonise Germany at such a juncture. Consequently, the Germans were allowed to round off their inland treaties in Tanganyika, establish themselves farther up the coast at Witu, and force the Sultan of Zanzibar under threat of naval bombardment to accept what had been done. Gladstone publicly announced that his government wished 'God speed' to German colonisation. A joint British, French and German Commission 'delimited' the Sultan's possessions on the mainland just as Germany wished.

Indeed, when it came, the British attempt to salvage what was left of their position in East Africa was made expressly with German approval. The initiative, as on the Niger, came from private interests, prompted by the consular officials in Zanzibar. The essence of the plan was to revive the Sultan's concession scheme of 1879 to rule what became Kenya by a chartered company headed by the shipping magnate, Sir William Mackinnon. Though Mackinnon's association began making treaties in Kenya in 1886 they could not yet obtain official support; in fact the British government, anxious not to offend Germany, went so far as to inform Bismarck in advance of the Association's plans. But Bismarck had no reason to exploit such confidences; his colonial intervention had achieved the purpose at least of convincing the British of their need for German support and intensifying Franco-British hostility. Bismarck in fact was by now becoming somewhat alarmed by his own colonial enthusiasts in Germany, for though he had succeeded in passing administrative costs on to chartered companies in South West and East

Africa, the merchants in Togo and the Cameroons had refused the burden, and official regimes, which lost money, had to be established. In the autumn of 1886 therefore, Bismarck tried to bring the East African business to a close, and Britain and Germany agreed to divide the mainland along a line from the Umba River to Lake Victoria, retaining Witu as a German enclave inside the British sphere. Despite this agreement, Mackinnon still had many months to wait for his charter. The British government had yet to be convinced that there were serious enough interests in East Africa to warrant official sanction of this kind. It was far from clear what British interests were left, for the islands of Zanzibar and Pemba with their clove trade remained outside German control under the Sultan's rule, whilst the trade in the interior of Africa by British Indian subjects had been mostly in the area now controlled by Germany. Kenya had nothing to offer in the way of trade, and its strategic value was doubtful.[5]

Doubtful, that is, assuming that the British occupation of Egypt was about to come to an end. In 1887, Lord Salisbury, the new Conservative Prime Minister, actually attempted to withdraw from Egypt. His plan was for Turkey to resume control, on condition that British troops would be allowed to reoccupy the country and defend the Suez Canal in case of war. The Sultan actually signed an agreement to this effect, but when the French saw the re-entry clause they, with help from Russia, succeeded in persuading Turkey to refuse ratification of the agreement. Lord Salisbury now came to the conclusion that British withdrawal from Egypt on terms which would guarantee British interests was not feasible in the foreseeable future. The best would have to be made of the occupation.

THE NILE VALLEY

Once this decision was made at the end of 1887, Egypt's geographical interests now became British interests, and the Nile waterway became of paramount importance to Britain for Egypt was a country of several million people living in a desert by irrigating the land with the Nile floodwaters. Any power with the technical knowledge which gained a foothold on the upper Nile, whether in the Sudan, Ethiopia or Uganda, could, by damming the waters, literally destroy Egypt. Control of the Nile therefore became a central plank in the policy of the British from 1888.

The immediate danger lay in Uganda, where the Nile flowed out from Lake Victoria. The Mahdists in the Sudan could conveniently be left alone for the time being, for they had proved themselves capable of resisting European-officered troops, and at the same time did not have the technical skill to interfere with the water supply. More to be feared was a European advance from the East African coast. Thus Mackinnon, who had tried unsuccessfully to obtain a charter throughout 1886 and 1887, now had one hurriedly thrust upon his Imperial British East Africa Company in 1888! Immediately, the British and German East African companies began a race for the Nile sources. At first rivalry concentrated on Equatoria, a province of the old Egyptian Sudan where a German officer of the Egyptian government, Emin Pasha, still held out against the Mahdists. A British relief expedition was financed by public subscription[6] and succeeded in withdrawing Emin before his German compatriots reached him, and the Mahdists occupied Equatoria. Uganda now became the centre for competition; both companies sent expeditions to Buganda, but the Germans were first to make a treaty with the Kabaka.

Lord Salisbury was unwilling to await events in Africa, and determined to settle the Uganda question in Britain's favour by direct negotiation. As bait he offered Germany the small British island of Heligoland in the North Sea in return for which he demanded German recognition of Uganda as British, German withdrawal from the enclave of Witu in Kenya, and German recognition of a British protectorate over the Sultan of Zanzibar's island possessions. It may seem odd to Africans that Germany should have accepted joyfully the exchange of a small rocky island in Europe for hundreds of square miles of African land. But Heligoland was of supreme importance to Germany for it commanded the approaches from the North Sea to the Kiel Canal, begun in 1887, allowing the German navy to communicate between the Baltic and the North Sea through German territory. The bargain was agreed to in the Anglo-German (Heligoland) Treaty of 1890.

The sole remaining danger to the Nile from the eastern approaches lay with Italy, already established in Eritrea. In 1889 the Italians concluded a treaty with Emperor Minilik of Ethiopia, which they claimed gave Italy a protectorate over his country.[7]

If substantiated this claim would have given Italy control of the Blue Nile; in 1891, therefore, Britain agreed to recognise Italy's extravagant claims, but the boundary of the 'protectorate' was so drawn as to exclude her access to the Nile itself, and Italy bound herself not to alter the flow of water on the Nile by building any dams on its tributaries.

ANGLO-FRENCH RIVALRY

The Heligoland Treaty of 1890 seemed to exclude France from East Africa, and this did not go unnoticed in France. Moreover, the treaty recognised a British protectorate over Zanzibar despite an Anglo-French agreement in 1862 to 'maintain the Sultan's independence'. The French used this to extract a British recognition of a French protectorate over Madagascar and to try to limit British expansion in West Africa. The Heligoland Treaty had also settled boundaries between British colonies and German Togoland and Cameroons, and in the latter case hinted at a future Anglo-German partition of the Lake Chad area. The French had exaggerated fears that the Royal Niger Company might advance from Lake Chad right across to the Nile and forever prevent the joining together of French Algeria, Senegal and the Gabun. Thus France readily agreed in the Anglo-French Declaration of August 1890 that a line from Say on the Niger to Barruwa on Lake Chad, leaving the empire of Sokoto in the Niger Company's sphere, should form a frontier between French and British spheres of influence. It was a curious arrangement, for neither France nor the Niger Company had any real claims in the area, and at the same time it left the Niger Company's boundaries open on the eastern and western sides. In 1893, Sir George Goldie, largely by his personal efforts, obtained an agreement with Germany dividing the region south of Lake Chad; the German Cameroons was thus extended so far northwards that the Royal Niger Company was protected from French incursions on its eastern frontiers by German territory.

The western boundaries of Nigeria provided a focus for mounting Anglo-French rivalries after 1894. The French, after conquering Dahomey between 1892 and 1894, began pushing troops into Borgu, and the Niger Company's resources were inadequate to meet this challenge. In 1897 Lugard was put in charge of the newly formed West African Frontier Force, which was moved into

Borgu. By 1898 the situation threatened war, but the Niger crisis was settled in the Anglo-French agreement of June, which established the basis of Nigeria's present frontiers, besides resolving all outstanding Anglo-French frontier disputes in West Africa.

The Niger crisis was almost immediately followed by that of Fashoda, on the Nile. Having secured the approaches to the Nile from the east, the British hoped that Germany would expand from the Cameroons to cut off any French approach to the Nile from the west. Instead, in March 1894, Germany agreed with France to close off the eastern frontier of the Cameroons, leaving the Nile approaches from Gabun through Ubangi-Shari open. In May 1894, the British tried to overcome this by granting King Leopold a lease of the Bahr al Ghazal, thus placing the Congo Free State in the path of a French advance, but in August the French persuaded King Leopold to drop the scheme. The French now began to organise the expedition which would cross Africa from the west and establish itself on the Upper Nile. In March 1895, the British publicly declared that a French expedition to the Upper Nile would be regarded as 'an unfriendly act'. In March 1896, the Italians, attempting to assert their claim to Ethiopia, were decisively defeated by the Ethiopian army at Adwa; the French had supported Ethiopia, and the British now feared that the Nile lay open to their influence from both sides. Two weeks after the Italian defeat, Britain made the decision to conquer the Sudan from the Mahdists, and Lord Kitchener's army began slowly advancing southwards along the Nile. Shortly after Kitchener's victory over the Mahdi at Omdurman in September 1898, he found himself faced with a French force under Marchand which had occupied Fashoda on the Nile. For a time it looked as if Kitchener might attack Marchand, and war seemed close. But in November 1898, failing to secure diplomatic support, the French withdrew Marchand's force. In March 1899, France accepted her exclusion from the Nile valley in an agreement with Britain settling all remaining colonial disputes. The Anglo-French colonial conflict was over, and within five years France and Britain were in alliance against the growing military threat of Germany in Europe. The partition of Tropical Africa was over.

SOUTH AFRICA

So far we have concentrated on the partition of Tropical Africa;

the partition in Southern Africa was influenced much more by local factors, including the rivalries of British and Boer populations. Britain, since the 'Great Trek' northwards of the Boer population in the 1830s, had consistently refused to allow the Boer republics access to the sea, for fear they should try to gain the support or protectorate of other European powers. When the gold discoveries on the Rand in the 1880s began to shift the economic power of South Africa from the British Cape to the Boer Transvaal this became even more a cardinal principle of British policy.

The position was further complicated by the establishment of German South West Africa in 1884 and German East Africa in 1885, for there now seemed a real danger that the two German colonies might try to join together in a solid block of German territory, which might also give Germany a common frontier with the Transvaal Republic. Portugal also made claims to a solid belt of territory joining Angola and Mozambique, and German intervention stimulated Portuguese ambitions. It therefore seemed essential that Britain should secure the 'road to the north'.

Once again, as in East Africa and on the Niger, the British were able to make use of private interests; Cecil Rhodes, already a formidable politician in the Cape, controlled a huge slice of South Africa's gold and diamond industries. He believed there was more gold to be had north of the Transvaal, and dreamed imperialist dreams of an all-British route from Cairo to the Cape. His agents went north, seeking mineral concessions from Lobengula, king of the Matabele. In 1889, Rhodes's company was incorporated by Royal Charter as the British South Africa Company, with powers of administration, and soon afterwards white settlers moved into Mashonaland, an area tributary to Lobengula. Rhodes's company also undertook to subsidise the newly formed British protectorate of Nyasaland. During 1890, the Company engaged in bitter rivalry with the Portuguese in Mozambique until the boundaries were settled in the Anglo-Portuguese Convention of 1890–1, much in Rhodes's favour. In the next three years white settlement in 'Rhodesia' was extended, the South African railway system extended into the country, and resistance by Africans crushed. Rhodes became even more ambitious, and mounted a plot designed to unify all South Africa under the British flag. A revolution was planned in the Transvaal, whereby the disgruntled

'Uitlanders' would rise against the Boers, and Dr Jameson, the British South Africa Company's administrator, would invade the Transvaal and come to the rebels' assistance. But the rising failed to materialise, Jameson rode in to be captured by the Boers, and Rhodes's position in South African white politics collapsed.

Germany attempted to use the Jameson Raid fiasco to build a European League against Britain, with whom by now she was in naval rivalry, but France and Russia[8] would not co-operate and the German navy was not yet strong enough to give assistance to the Boers. In succeeding years the Boers were isolated by British diplomacy. By an Anglo-German agreement of August 1898, the Germans renounced interest in Delegoa Bay, the Mozambique port which was the Transvaal's outlet to the sea.[9] In 1899, Portugal agreed with Britain to close Delegoa Bay to the Transvaal in the event of war between the British and the Boers. The Boer War of 1899–1902 was the final act in the partition of Southern Africa, ending in complete British control of the Boer Republics of the Transvaal and Orange Free State.

CONCLUSION

By 1900, therefore, Europeans had seized political control almost everywhere in Africa.[10] It has been possible to tell this story almost without reference to the African peoples involved or their rulers, because their wishes hardly counted. The best policy for the shrewd African ruler was to make the best bargain he could, for African states were too small and disunited and their armies too ill-disciplined and ill-armed to provide effective resistance, except in exceptional cases like Ethiopia with its ancient unity or the well-organised Zulu and Asante nations. Worst of all, from the African point of view, Africans (except for a tiny intellectual minority in West Africa) lacked any sense of racial identity or unity; African states and peoples feared, distrusted and betrayed each other more than they opposed European control. In the last resort, however, the Europeans had overwhelming supremacy in weapons, or, as an English poet and opponent of imperialism cynically expressed it:

> Whatever happens we have got
> The Maxim gun and they have not.

Once accomplished, the partition altered the course of African history almost completely. Africa was forcibly jerked on to the stage of world history, carved up into new, and often artificial units, which nevertheless form the African nations of today. Her people were placed in situations in which they were made by circumstances to adopt new concepts to African conditions, to digest the European idea of the state, to adapt to capitalist economic organisation, rapid communications, scientific technology and even to adopt French or English in order to be able to communicate with fellow-Africans. Such changes amounted to a fundamental revolution in the economic, social and political life of Africa.

Yet the significance of the partition need not be exaggerated. By 1965, the European political control established by the partition has virtually disappeared in the face of African nationalism (see Map H). In most of Africa, therefore, European control lasted a mere sixty to eighty years, and in the ocean of history that is but a wave breaking on the shore.

NOTES

1 Though the reality was much more complicated than this.
2 It seems strange that a ruler should try to solve his problems by passing power over to Europeans in a chartered company, when such an expedient could result in colonial rule. However, the ruler would hardly be in a position to know this, and presumably hoped that a body of Europeans with vested interests in his state would serve to advocate its interests, especially against other foreign threats. The Asante, on the eve of the British invasion in 1895–6, made similar overtures to British and French businessmen for the formation of an Asante chartered company.
3 It has also been argued that Bismarck had an eye on coming elections for the German Reichstag, and hoped to secure support by raising an imperialist enthusiasm.
4 Unfairly, because Gordon had been sent to *withdraw* British forces from the Sudan, instead of which he took it upon himself to attempt to hold out against the Mahdists in Khartoum. The real blame on the government lay in sending such an unstable man to perform so delicate a task.
5 British naval officers had pointed out as early as 1823 that Mombasa had a good natural harbour, well placed for naval operations in the Indian Ocean. But the Admiralty and the British government pooh-poohed the importance of Mombasa as late as 1886.
6 The major subscribers to the fund were practically identical with the shareholders of the British East Africa Company.
7 The claim was false, for the Italians had cheated Minilik by writing the protectorate clause into the Italian language version of the treaty whilst omitting it from the Amharic translation.

8   Russia left the alliance with Germany after 1890, and thereafter France and Russia drew increasingly together in fear of growing German military and naval power.

9   In this same agreement there were secret clauses whereby, in the event of Portugal becoming bankrupt, which then seemed likely, Germany and Britain would offer a joint loan, and Germany would take over the Portuguese empire, except for Mozambique, as security.

10   Liberia and Ethiopia remained independent. In 1900 Morocco and Tripoli also were independent, but this was not to last. In Morocco, the French feared a foreign protectorate lying next to Algeria, whilst the British were afraid that a French protectorate would nullify the effect of the British fortress of Gibraltar, which controlled the entrance to the Mediterranean. The British therefore supported Spanish claims to Morocco. By 1904, however, the British and French were practically allies, and in that year France obtained British and Italian recognition of her 'preponderance' in Morocco, recognising in return British control of Egypt, and giving Italy a free hand in Tripoli. Germany at first opposed French preponderance in Morocco, but in 1911 recognised it in return for French transfer of territory from the Gabun to the German Cameroons. In 1912 the Sultan of Morocco was forced to accept a French protectorate, and later in the year a Spanish zone was set up. Italy invaded Tripoli in force in 1911, but met with fierce resistance, and it was not until the Fascist rule of Mussolini that the last embers of resistance were crushed. The political divisions of Africa in 1914 and 1924 are illustrated in maps F and G. The Fascists also invaded Ethiopia in 1935, and forced the Emperor to flee into exile in Britain, where he maintained a government in exile which reoccupied the empire after the defeat of Italy in the Second World War.

QUESTIONS FOR FURTHER STUDY AND DISCUSSION

1   Discuss the way in which King Leopold established the Congo Free State How far did Leopold's activities precipitate the Scramble for Africa?

2   Examine the use made of chartered companies in the partition of Africa.

3   Analyse in detail the motives which led Europeans to assume political control in any *one* African country of your choice.

4   Write a brief biography of any one important figure active in the Scramble for Africa stressing particularly his motives.

5   Analyse an example of an African state or people which resisted European control forcibly during this period, emphasising the strengths and weaknesses of African resistance.

SELECT BIBLIOGRAPHY

Cambridge History of the British Empire, Vol. III, Chapters 2–5, for Southern Africa; Vol. VIII, Chapters 20–2, in revised edition of 1963 *only*.

S. E. Crowe, *The Berlin West Africa Conference*, Longmans, 1942.

J. E. Flint, *Sir George Goldie and the Making of Nigeria*, O.U.P., 1960.

W. O. Henderson, *Studies in German Colonial History*, especially Chapters 1 and 2, reprinted F. Cass, 1960.

W. L. Langer, *The Diplomacy of Imperialism*, especially Chapter 3, also Chapters 4, 8 and 9, A. Knopf, New York, 1951.

R. Oliver, *Sir Harry Johnston and the Scramble for Africa*, Longmans, 1957.

R. Oliver and G. Mathew, *History of East Africa*, Vol. I, Chapters 10–12, O.U.P., 1964.

M. Perham, *Lugard, Vol. 1—The Years of Adventure*, Collins, 1956.

S. H. Roberts, *History of French Colonial Policy*, Chapters 8–10, reprinted by F. Cass, 1963.

R. Robinson and J. Gallagher *et al.*, *Africa and the Victorians*, Macmillan, 1961.

H. R. Rudin, *Germany in the Cameroons, 1884–1914*, Cape, 1938.

R. Slade, *King Leopold's Congo*, O.U.P., 1962.

M. E. Townsend, *The Rise and Fall of Germany's Colonial Empire*, Macmillan, New York, 1930.

8 External Influence on African Society

E. A. AYANDELE

FROM the dawn of African history to the present day there has been mutually beneficial contact between Africa and the outside world. In the commercial realm, for instance, legitimate and illegitimate trade flowed between Mediterranean Europe and Africa north of the tropical forest, through the network of the trans-Saharan trade routes. In the matter of food for human consumption North Africa was of some service to the outside world. By their high level of agricultural production Egypt and the Magrib became respectively suppliers of wheat and olives to the Mediterranean world for many centuries.

ISLAM AND CHRISTIANITY

Two monotheistic creeds which were to have profound effects on African society came from the Middle East; Christianity from Palestine and Islam from the Arabian Peninsula. In territorial, political and statistical terms it was the latter that came to gain priority over the former. For according to the latest provisional statistics there are seventy-five million Muslims to twenty-four million Christians in Africa today, and of the Muslim figure sixty-five million are to be found in the northern third of the continent. Although the Cross preceded the Crescent in the Magrib and the Nile Valley for many centuries, it was not long before Islam, born in the seventh century A.D., effaced Christianity in the Magrib, extirpated it in the Christian kingdoms of Alwa and Maqurra in modern Sudan, and reduced drastically the number and influence of the Christian adherents in Egypt. It was only in Ethiopia that Christianity not only held its own but became the state religion of the country.

The reasons why the Cross receded before the Crescent in so dramatic a fashion cannot be treated in detail in this chapter. But they deserve some attention, in view of the fact that Islam has for centuries maintained its statistical lead in a way astonishing to

Christian missions, and the latter have attempted to explain away the bewildering success of Islam in a prejudiced way. They have often been inclined to believe that Islam must have been forced upon unwilling African peoples by fire and sword. No one can deny that in the past, at one stage or another, the Islamic frontier expanded through Jihāds. It was largely by conquest that the whole of Mediterranean Africa and the Sudanic state of Ghana became Islamised by the eleventh century, a method revived in the nineteenth century with effect throughout western and central Sudan. However, in the intervening centuries, in the areas just mentioned, Islam was propagated in a peaceful and unobtrusive manner, through the agencies of malams and traders.

It would, in fact, be misleading to see Islamic expansion solely, or even primarily, in terms of force. There were many reasons why Islam was irresistibly attractive to Africans. In the early centuries Islam conferred definite privileges, such as full citizenship and exemption from certain taxes, on the faithful. The unbeliever in a Muslim state had to pay more taxes than the believer. Islam also encouraged literacy and scholarship, the former on a fairly extensive scale. African Muslims who had academic interests were beneficiaries of the universities of Cairo, Kairwan, Timbuktu, Katsina and Jaghbub. But it was perhaps in their human relationships that the Muslim missionaries gained the support of Africans at the expense of Christian missionaries. In the main, Muslim missionaries professed and practised the brotherhood and equality of all the faithful in matters of shelter, clothing and diet. Looked upon by their votaries as fellow-Africans they claimed no biological superiority over their adherents. Furthermore Muslim teachers had a practical solution to each of the many problems confronting potential converts. Take for instance the malam's solution to African belief in the existence of witchcraft and malevolent forces. The malam gave his wards concrete materials which the latter were made to believe possessed extraordinary potency that could neutralise all evil powers. In most cases, too, Muslim missionaries sought to convert the rulers and, through the latter, households and families, rather than individuals. Significant too, in African eyes, was the fact that Muslim missionaries waged no war upon the basic institutions of polygamy and slavery, but rather encouraged them. The communal aspect of traditional life was little disturbed by

Muslim missionaries, whilst the latter not only abjured their followers to refrain from alcohol but they themselves also remained abstemious.

By contrast the Christian missionary, a late arrival in many parts of the African continent, was an alien—a fact that often made African chiefs suspicious of his intentions. Even when he was a liberated African, as in West Africa, he was still considered by the chiefs as a 'white man'. Moreover, in the nineteenth century, he came to Africa with preconceived ideas of the superiority of his race, his religion and the customs and institutions of his country. We have no space in this chapter for an analysis of the social consequences of his teaching, but it is essential to compare his attitude to Africans with that of his Muslim counterpart already mentioned. His attitude was largely patronising. Everything about him bore the air of superiority and separateness. His diet was different, his clothing was different, his house sometimes may have seemed to many African chiefs more of a threatening fort than a building intended for peace-loving strangers. He encouraged his wards to imitate himself in all respects and gave them the impression that the less African they were the more Christian they became. Moreover the Christian missionary lectured the chiefs about the barbarity of their ways and ridiculed polygamy, tattooing, slavery, bride-price and wakes as 'unchristian'. His coming into the interior about the same time as the trader and administrator was unfortunate for the missionary. Africans were often inclined to doubt the genuineness of his propaganda. They could not see their way to making any distinction between him and other white men. In their opinion all white men were birds of the same feather, and they saw them flocking together on many occasions. The Christian missionary preached equality of all men before God but in the church he was frequently the imperious master; he emphasised the spiritual danger of faithful converts laying up for themselves treasures in this world, but at the same time the missionary's 'brothers', traders, concentrated on earthly prosperity, often at the Africans' expense; the missionary preached against the sinfulness of drunkenness, but the Africans saw themselves being compelled to exchange their oil and elephant's teeth mostly for exciting spirits. While the Africans believed in the reality of witchcraft the missionary admonished him to stop being superstitious, gave him nothing concrete to remove his fear and urged him to trust in the efficacy of abstract prayer to an unseen God. In a matter of a generation or two the missionary began to doubt the quality of his wards whom he denounced as 'nominal' Christians. Comparing his lack of success with the success achieved by his Muslim counterpart the missionary attempted to explain away his failure in racial terms. Christianity, he began to argue, could only be comprehended by the higher species of mankind, because it comprised deep and difficult metaphysical truths and imposed a severe demand on the African's moral strength and resolution. Islam, the missionary argued, offered a short but simple credo and demanded a much less high moral code; therefore Africans preferred it to Christianity.

By the middle of the nineteenth century when Christian missions began to revive their activities in many parts of the continent, Islam had already become supreme in the northern third of the continent. It had become the state religion of all the countries north of 12 degrees N. latitude; the society had become leavened by the Muslim faith. Literary activities, morality, jurisprudence and every aspect of human activity in these states were permeated by Islam. Even in matters of foreign policy their attitude towards the Christian infidels, who began to threaten their sovereignty and territorial integrity, had already taken a definite shape. The cause of Islam became a vital ingredient in the nationalist movements which the occupation of this extensive area by infidel powers awakened. These states felt that they had no need of Christian missionaries. And, although under the protection of infidel colonial administrations, Christian missions operated in these states, the Muslims refused to be converted or to change their way of life. In 1965, after the withdrawal of the colonial administrations, Islam continues to be the basis of human life in the states north of 12 degrees N. latitude.

The southern two-thirds of the continent was at the middle of the nineteenth century, and is still in 1965, predominantly 'pagan'. This area has been influenced considerably by the activities of Christian missions, Protestant and Catholic alike. It is important to emphasise that the political and social effects of missionary activity have not been on the same scale or of the same complexion in all parts of the continent. The political effects may be divided into three, viz. (1) missionaries viewed by Africans as heralds of European imperialism, (2) missionaries as tribunes of the oppressed in colonial Africa and (3) the nationalistic consequences of missionary activity.

(1) *Missionaries viewed by Africans as heralds of European imperialism*

In many parts of Africa where the Cross preceded the Flag, missionaries found themselves in a very difficult situation. West Africa, particularly Yorubaland, the only place where missionaries were allowed to operate on a big scale in the pre-colonial period, provides the best illustration. In the interior, missionaries were only tolerated. They knew that in any trial of strength they would be overwhelmed; it was, therefore, impossible for them to be authoritarian and they did their best to respect the wishes of the chiefs, whose protection was indispensable to their enterprise. In fact they bribed the rulers with appropriate European goods such as umbrellas, looking glasses, biscuits, velvet cloth and chairs. Nevertheless missionaries were not completely at the mercy of the chiefs in the interior as one might imagine. This was so because missionaries were an asset to rulers in many ways. The chiefs coveted the superior talents of the missionaries in architecture, their chairs, their magic of reading and writing. But the greatest usefulness of missionaries lay in the part it was believed they could play in the intra-tribal politics of the country. It is essential to emphasise the fact that in the middle of the nineteenth century missionaries found chiefs at loggerheads one with the other whether in the small kingdoms of Badagry, Lagos or Old Calabar, or in the interior among the tribal groups of Egbas, Ibadans, Ijebus and Oyos. In Badagry, the Wawu, chief of English Town and traditionally only fourth in rank among the Badagrian chiefs, was already claiming a constitutional status that traditionally belonged to Chief Akran, chief of Portuguese Town. And British traders were already encouraging Wawu's claims. In Lagos the dynastic struggle between Akitoye and Kosoko was already brewing. In the interior the Egbas, who were surrounded by enemies—Ibadan, Ijebu and Dahomey—invited missionaries in order to fulfil the Egbas' political aspirations. They expected that the missionaries would supply them with weapons of precision, bestow upon them economic prosperity and drive away their enemies.

It is clear then that, in these circumstances, missionaries could not escape being involved in local politics. The missionaries reduced the various economic and political issues which concerned the combatants to a purely ethical denominator. In the case of Badagry the Wawu was represented as a good man and supporter of legitimate trade; in Lagos Akitoye, too, was held out to the world as a fanatical hater of the slave trade; the Egbas were portrayed as the best people on the continent of Africa who eschewed war, the slave trade and slavery, and as Providence's instrument for the spread of the gospel in Africa; their sufferings at the hands of their neighbours were painted in a lurid manner.

The motive of the missionaries must be properly grasped. They were not primarily interested in politics, but in the spread of the Christian faith. When, therefore, they called upon the consul and the man-of-war to offer them and their wards protection they believed that they did so in the interest of their enterprise; when they asked that anti-missionary chiefs in Badagry should be expelled, or that Kosoko should be deposed and Akitoye reinstated on the Lagos throne, or that the Egbas should be given military help against the powerful state of Dahomey, the missionaries believed that the result would conduce to the growth of God's kingdom and the benefits of the peoples among whom they were working.

So long as the missionaries confined their activities to siding with one faction against the other, they ran into no trouble But the moment it occurred to the chiefs that the missionaries were nursing political ambitions of their own, inimical to the interest of the country as a whole, hostilities began to build up against the missionaries. After all, no one in Yorubaland, however friendly they were with the missionaries and the British officials, wished foreigners to occupy any part of Yoruba soil. This was why the British occupation of Lagos alienated all the chiefs from the British. The Egbas began to regret that they had ever patronised the missionaries, whilst people like the king of Dahomey, the Awujale of Ijebu-Ode and Jaja of Opobo believed that they had been justified in their suspicion of, and hostility to, missionary propaganda. In short, missionaries came to be regarded as political disturbers and heralds of European imperialism.

In Central, Eastern and Southern Africa the phenomenon of African chiefs regarding missionaries as forerunners of European imperialism was not absent. Like the Efiks and Yorubas of West Africa the chiefs did not suspect at the beginning that missionary propaganda might prepare the way for the loss of their lands and sovereignty to Europeans. Take, for instance, the pathetic case of Mzilikazi of Matabeleland and Robert Moffat, a London Missionary Society missionary. Both of them became friends but later the former regretted their friendship on the grounds that traders and settlers came to seize his lands and sovereignty through Robert Moffat's exertions. It is not surprising then that Mzilikazi's son, Lobengula, described the process of British infiltration into his country to a missionary in 1889 in these words. 'Did you ever see a chameleon catch a fly? The chameleon gets behind the fly and remains motionless for some time, then he advances very slowly and gently, first putting forward one leg and then another. At last, when well within reach, he darts out his tongue and the fly disappears. England is the chameleon and I am the fly.' In Buganda, in East Africa, the Kabakas thought they could use missionaries for their own political ends. But as a result, during the Scramble, the British Protestant missionaries consciously worked to see that the country became part of the British empire, whilst the French Catholic missionaries also exerted themselves to see that the territory was annexed by any power but the British. What was more, the chiefs and their supporters became divided into pro-British and pro-French factions. Even the Muslims came to be involved in the 'religious wars', and the Arabs had a vague idea of wishing to see the same territory become part of the Sultan of Zanzibar's dominions. It was largely through the efforts of missionaries that Uganda and Kenya became a part of the British empire. In the same manner, the Scottish missionaries in Nyasaland (Malawi) made the assimilation of this territory to the British empire possible and stultified the efforts of Portugal to annex the area to Mozambique.

(2) *Missionaries as tribunes of the oppressed in Colonial Africa*

In many parts of Africa where colonial regimes exploited Africans in one way or another missionaries became spokesmen of African interests and rights. For instance, in South Africa for more than twenty years in the first half of the nineteenth century, Dr John Philip, an L.M.S. missionary, protested against the inhuman treatment of the natives by Afrikaners. He was instrumental in the passing of the famous 50th Ordinance of 1828, which recognised the equality of all races before the law. Also he protested against the dispossession of the Hottentots of their land, and called for the halting of the territorial expansion of Afri- kanerdom in South Africa. In East Africa, in the third decade of this century, missionaries organised opposition against adminis- trative measures which were likely to reduce Africans to a condition of servitude under the white settlers. They protested against the scheme of the British government to settle ex-soldiers in Kenya, a scheme which would further dispossess Africans of their lands and compel them to sell their labour to the settlers at a cheap price. Their opposition to Governor Northey's circular of 1921[1] is particularly worthy of attention. In the Congo, Protestant missionaries played a major role in the activities of the Congo Reform Association founded in Britain by E. D. Morel in 1904. Through their agitation Leopold's Congo became the Belgian Congo and the atrocities of greedy money-makers were minimised to a certain extent. In Nigeria it was the Protestant missionaries who agitated against the demoralising effects of the liquor traffic in Southern Nigeria, and they succeeded in bringing about the institution of a Royal Commission of Enquiry which studied the problem.

(3) *The nationalistic consequences of missionary activity*

If missionaries contributed to European occupation of many parts of Africa, the credit for the awakening of national conscious- ness, which terminated colonial rule, should to a great extent be given to them. This is not to say that Christian missions con- sciously encouraged the awakening and development of a nationalism that ultimately became a secular manifestation. Even the largely ecclesiastical independence which Henry Venn's scheme of appointing African clergy and bishops in Nigeria was designed to encourage did not receive the approval of most of the Church Missionary Society missionaries in Africa. Nevertheless, the propaganda of Protestant missions produced effects they had not anticipated. By teaching their wards the art of reading and writing, by allowing them to have an unrestricted access to the Bible, Africans began to interpret the Bible in a way that encour- aged an independent, nationalistic spirit. Take, for instance, the doctrine of the brotherhood of men and equality of all races in the Bible, which Africans began to ask their spiritual masters to practise in West Africa, when Europeans began to exercise a control and exhibit an exclusive attitude that could not be justified by the Scriptures. This was why in the Belgian Congo, in South Africa and in areas where there were white settlers, Protestant missionaries became unpopular and came to be regarded as fomenters of political agitation. It was in West Africa that the political effects of Christian missionary propaganda produced the greatest effects. Here, more than in any other part of Africa, partly because of the treachery of the climate, partly because of the death-producing mosquito, and partly because of the conscious liberal policy of many of the Christian missions, native agency came to be encouraged most. Education was also encouraged here more than anywhere else in Africa. The consequence was that a class of educated Africans came into existence. These educated Africans became familiar with the British parliamentary system of government, a system discernible in the organisation of the Congregational churches. Even the Anglican missions had something to offer to nationalist-inclined Africans. The church councils, school boards, and a host of other committees on which Africans were represented by members of their own race were to have nationalistic implications. In the view of the educated Africans, the Church, through these committees, provided an excellent opportunity to demonstrate their capacity to organise, administer and rule. Gradually they began to show eagerness in the assumption of financial responsibility for their churches, not because they wanted thereby to improve their spirituality, but because they wanted to control their affairs themselves. They looked forward to the day when they would control the Church and the spread of Christianity throughout Africa without any assistance from Europe or America. They hoped that this would logically result in the control of the administration of their countries too. They looked into the Bible for portions that would seem to justify their nationalistic thinking. The verse that became most popular was Psalm 68, verse 31, 'Ethiopia shall soon stretch forth her hands unto God'. This they interpreted to mean that Ethiopia would at some future date become the cynosure of the world, the territory from which the rest of the world would learn of wonderful human achievements. They equated Ethiopia with Africa and the Ethiopians with the Negro race. This was the origin of West African Ethiopianism. It is essential to emphasise that Ethiopianism not only manifested itself earlier in West Africa than anywhere else in Africa, but that it had a complexion essentially its own, different from the Ethiopianism of South Africa and Central Africa with which people are more familiar. The educated Africans assumed that the European missionaries would willingly co-operate with them in their aspirations for independence in church and state. The consecration of Samuel Ajayi Crowther as Bishop of the Niger territories and the complete Africanisation of the Niger Mission before 1880 excited the hopes of Africans.

But in the eighties their hopes in Christian missions began to wither away. European missionaries were introduced into the Niger Mission and the African Bishop himself lost his administrative authority. Africans who felt that the time had come for them to stand on their own and make Christianity reflect the African environment broke away from mission churches and founded their own churches in Nigeria and the Cameroons.

In South Africa, Central Africa and the Belgian Congo, where Christian missions were slow in promoting Native Agency, the interests of white settlers or European mining or trading companies made the effects of missionary enterprise in these territories different from those in West Africa. In South Africa where the Dutch Reformed Church overtly sanctioned the apartheid policy of the state, where Africans lost their best lands and became mere servants to the white people, the African 'separatist' church became the only institution through which they could ventilate their feelings and grievances without any restriction. It became the only institution in which they could organise, prove their ability to rule and even evolve a theology of their own. In the church they found solace in a way the Negroes in the United States found solace in their churches during those times when they were denied political rights and fundamental liberties. This is probably why it is among the Bantu that Christianity, statistically, has been most successful in Africa. Some of the 'separatist churches' have synthesised indigenous religion and Christianity. In others political grievances are reflected in the racialist interpretation they have given to some parts of the Bible in favour of Africans. It is not surprising that some of the churches preached the doctrine that Christ was black in colour, had appeared in Zululand in the first decades of this century and would come again to rescue Africans from their white masters. In the past Ethiopianism was associated with African violence and conspiracy against the whites and many extremist Ethiopians did not eschew violence. The Ethiopian movement became a bugbear to the South African government. Ethiopians were believed to have had a hand in the 1906 Bambatta Rebellion in Natal. One might also mention the extremist, blindly foolhardy Israelite movement led by Enoch Ngijima in Bullhoek, South Africa. This man claimed he had dreamed that the British and Afrikaner whites of South Africa would be crushed by the Africans. His followers came to believe in his supernatural powers when he defied government orders to pull down the huts, which had been built by his followers on Crown land which they had not asked permission to use. When in 1921 the government sent soldiers against Enoch Ngijima he admonished his followers to expose themselves to the white man's bullets, under the fatal belief that the bullets would turn into water.

In Central and Eastern Africa there were the Chilembwe Rebellion of 1915 and the Thuku Rising of 1921–2. The former was led by an African minister who had come under the influence of one Joseph Booth, an Englishman who identified himself with African interests in Nyasaland (Malawi). John Chilembwe had been trained in the United States, where he saw for himself the prejudices under which the Negroes there were living. On his return to Nyasaland he founded his own mission, the Provident Industrial Mission, and in 1915 he organised a rebellion against the white settlers. In Kenya, Harry Thuku, a junior civil servant, incarnated the grievances of Africans in Kenya against the white settlers, and he encouraged agitation against them. In the Belgian Congo where the administration encouraged Catholicism on the grounds that this brand of Christianity produced docile Africans, and where the political effects of the Protestant missions' teaching were deprecated, Simon Kimbagu, a Protestant, led in 1921 an anti-white movement. Even today the shrine of Kimbagu is frequented by the Congolese and the movement that has arisen after him is still regarded as an obstacle to their progress by the alien Christian missions.

The African national consciousness awakened by missionary activities had a cultural aspect. African converts did not share the belief of many of their teachers that until they, the converts, became Europeanised they could not become genuine Christians. In places like West Africa many converts began to discard their
11

European names for African ones, began to wear traditional clothing and synthesised indigenous freemasonry and Christianity. It is in this cultural sense that the retention and encouragement of polygamy by many of the African churches should be viewed. They believe that Christianity is not necessarily debased by a church that countenances polygamy, and they believe that for the moral well-being of Africa traditional, organised polygamy is preferable to the disorganised monogamy which has arisen from missionary teaching. In Kenya there was the sect known as *Watu wa Mungu* (People of God), founded in 1929 by the Kikuyu Christians in protest against the opposition of the Church of Scotland Mission to the custom of clitoridectomy. They have also integrated belief in the cult of ancestors into their doctrine: ancestors holding the same place in their thinking as the saints hold in Catholicism.

COMMERCE AND ECONOMIC DEVELOPMENT

In a sense, then, missionary activities had the effect of denationalising African converts. But we must take care lest we put the role of missionaries in the disintegration of tribal society out of focus. Missionaries should not be held as being primarily responsible for a phenomenon brought about by the white man's activity in all its manifestations. The commercial and industrial effects of the white man on the Bantu in South Africa reveal clearly the potency of other agencies in the detribalisation of traditional society. The missionaries' responsibility should be confined to the effects of their doctrine, which encouraged individualism in a society largely communal, a society in which the thinking, behaviour and beliefs of the individual were regulated to fit into the communal pattern in the interest of the solidarity, orderliness and happiness of the community as a whole. The individual was a unit in an organic whole.

Broadly speaking the intrusion of Europe into Africa created three kinds of economic pattern, First, there is the relatively liberal West African pattern, which provides a parallel to the liberal policies of colonial administrations, particularly the British, and of the Christian missions. In the absence of white settlement, and with the Africans left in possession of their lands, the plantation system of production, with its disadvantages for Africans, was ruled out in this part of Africa. True, this meant a denial to the territory of European capital investment outside the mining sector of the area's economy, but the inhabitants rejoice that they gained by producing with their own resources, in however unscientific a way, cash crops and sylvan products such as cocoa, oil palm, palm kernels, cotton, ground-nuts, beniseed, timber and rubber. Moreover, they produce all these materials on a scale which competes successfully with labour-worked plantations. The result has satisfied the inhabitants to a great extent; their purchasing capacity has progressively improved and an increasing number have been able to afford a standard of life that compares with that of the average wage-earner in Europe. Manufactured articles of all descriptions and better forms of housing have raised the standard of living far higher than that of the traditional society. Particularly gratifying to West Africans is the fact that they own their land and are in no way compelled to provide cheap labour for white traders or miners. In the former German territories like Tanganyika, the Cameroons and Togoland, which were mandated to the British and French after the First World War, the West African pattern of economy came to be encouraged by the mandatory powers.

The second type of economic pattern evolved in the former French North Africa and British Kenya. In these places where there were white settlers, the latter depended mainly on an agrarian economy produced in a scientific way. Side by side with them, except in Kenya and Algeria where Africans were deprived of their best lands, were African cultivators who were denied the resources of scientific farming. In Kenya and Algeria Africans became labourers on European farms, on low wages out of which they were expected to pay taxes. In the former French North Africa the French, more than the British in West Africa, diversified the economy by establishing industries such as flour mills, breweries, textile mills, chemical, machine and metallurgical industries. But one feature of the commercial and industrial activities of Europeans in all Africa is the fact that, until the attainment of independence by many African states, Africans were not participants in capital investment and large concerns such as commercial firms, banking and shipping. At this point the words of an educated Nigerian sum up the state of affairs: 'You exploit the country with foreign capital and you say you have developed its resources; when capital has deducted its principal and interest, and the shipping its profits, precious little is left for the country, and it is that little that is the local wealth . . . to a poor country like our own where the money comes from abroad, and both the principal and interest will have to go out, I see no advantage, I see impoverishment.'

The third kind of economic pattern has been the worst for Africans. It is best represented in South Africa, although the old Belgian Congo, Southern Rhodesia, Northern Rhodesia (Zambia), Nyasaland (Malawi) and the French Congo may to a limited extent be included in this category. Mining interests in South Africa have made the investment here the highest in Africa; industrialisation has also advanced considerably, whilst agricultural economy still attracts a large number of African labourers. The chief characteristic of the South African economy is that not only have Africans been deprived of their best lands but legislation have been designed to force them to become labourers on low wages. In short, Africans are no more than an instrument for the furtherance of the interests of the white settlers in the Republic, and of the big concerns owned by Americans and British.

Perhaps it is not altogether inappropriate to conclude this chapter with the social effects of the white man's activity in South Africa where the Christian missions have recorded their greatest statistical success. It has been estimated that one out of two Bantu is a Christian convert. Industrialisation, mining and the white man's farming, have also been responsible for the high degree of urbanisation in the Republic. It has been computed that one out of three Bantu has left the tribal society for the artificial agglomerations of the towns, and another one-third reside on European farms. The remaining third remain in the so-called Reserves. In the urban areas, where most of the workers stay for a long period of time before returning to the tribal society, there is no cohesion similar to the traditional one. Nor are there any sanctions that can compel an adoption of a uniform code of behaviour or morality. More than in the traditional village, individualism is the order of the day; avidity for European clothes and manufactured goods is greatest in these towns; native industries are being killed; sodomy and prostitution have continued to increase; tribal life has been rocked to its foundations. In the Reserves the periodical migrations of the men to seek work in the towns have weakened parental control over children;

labour migration has led to a shortage of young men and an increase in the number of unmarried women; sexual morality has relaxed and illegitimacy is on the increase. Generally, in the Republic, polygamy is going out of fashion but is being replaced by concubinage; women no longer decorate themselves with tatooing and scarification, but with European cosmetics.

The disintegration caused by external influences in African society reveal a dilemma for Africans. They are becoming more and more hybridised. The rapidity with which the traditional is being lost or severely modified, and with which the new is being apparently adopted, leave very little time for Africans to fully understand the new forms of European customs and institutions they are adopting. They do not have the time, or do not take the trouble, to make a judicious selection of what is best in the European for a grafting upon what is best in the old Africa.

NOTE

1 According to Governor Northey's circular, District Officers were to discourage the Africans of Kenya from growing 'cash crops' in the Reserves. The chief spokesman for the Africans was Dr J. H. Oldham, who had been a missionary in India, and who became secretary of the International Missionary Council in 1921. For the missions' role as tribunes of African interest in East Africa, cf. R. Oliver, *The Missionary Factor in East Africa*, Longmans, 1952, pp. 248ff.

QUESTIONS FOR FURTHER STUDY AND DISCUSSION

1 What were the political consequences of missionary enterprise in West Africa in the nineteenth century?

2 Describe the significance of the independent church movement in Africa south of the Sahara in the twentieth century.

3 Compare the effects of European intervention on the economic life of the indigenous inhabitants of eastern and western Africa.

4 Write short notes on the following: (a) Dr John Philip; (b) David Livingstone; (c) the Mahdi; (d) Apolo Kivebulaya; (e) Samuel Ajayi Crowther.

SELECT BIBLIOGRAPHY

C. P. Groves, *The Planting of Christianity in Africa*, Vols. II, III and IV Lutterworth Press, 1955 and 1958.

R. Oliver, *The Missionary Factor in East Africa*, Longmans, 1952.

Shepperson and Price, *Independent African*, Edinburgh U.P., 1958.

M. J. Bane, *Catholic Pioneers in West Africa*, Clonmore & Reynolds Ltd, Dublin, 1956.

J. S. Trimingham, *Islam in the Sudan*, O.U.P., 1949.

—— *A History of Islam in West Africa*, O.U.P., 1962.

—— *Islam in East Africa*, O.U.P., 1964.

Sir A. W. Pim, *Financial and Economic History of the African Tropical Territories*, O.U.P., 1940.

Westermann, *Africa and Christianity*, O.U.P., 1937.

B. G. M. Sundkler, *Bantu Prophets in South Africa*, O.U.P., 1961.

C. G. K. Baeta, *Prophetism in Ghana*, S.C.M. Press, London, 1962.

R. L. Buell, *The Native Problem in Africa*, Vols. I and II, Macmillan, New York, 1928.

G. H. T. Kimble, *Tropical Africa* (2 vols.), Anchor, New York, 1960.

A. McPhee, *The Economic Revolution in British West Africa*, Routledge, 1926.

K. O. Dike, *Trade and Politics in the Niger Delta*, O.U.P., 1956.

G. D. Kittler, *The White Fathers*, W. H. Allen, 1957.

D. C. Gordon, *North Africa's French Legacy, 1954–62*, Harvard U.P., 1962.

9 The Emergence of a New Elite in Africa

J. F. A. AJAYI
and J. B. WEBSTER

IT is necessary to distinguish the new elite of Africa from the old and to specify that we are here concerned with the emergence of only the new elite. Some traditional communities in Africa were stratified and it is possible to speak of a ruling class possessing special status and political, military, economic or religious power. Others were not stratified: political, military, economic or religious functions were diffused throughout a very wide sector of the community. In either case, we can still speak of an old elite, people who enjoyed status and whose characteristics inspired others to wish to be like them. In some communities, the elite were the ruling class; traditional rulers, people wealthy in cattle, land, farms, wives and children. In Muslim communities, apart from the shaikhs, amirs and imams, there was the ulema class learned in the Qur'ān, law and traditions, the grammar and philology of Arabic, and other Islamic sciences. In yet other communities, the elite were the elders distinguished for their wide knowledge of traditional lore. In still others, they were the priests and doctors respected for their ability to cure diseases and control the fortunes of men and the forces of nature.

European (including American) activities in Africa introduced new values, new ways of acquiring status and imitability. The class of people who were attracted to these new ideas and who have imbibed them most became the elite that has been so crucial in the development and modernisation of contemporary Africa. In the rise of this new class, the very presence of Europeans, European trade and other aspects of the European impact have been significant, but the most important single factor has been education, particularly secondary and higher education. In turn, the development of education has to a large extent been dependent on missionary activities. It is these and other factors that affected the emergence of a class of western-educated elite in different parts of Africa that will be briefly discussed in this chapter.

EUROPEAN ACTIVITIES IN THE PRE-COLONIAL PERIOD

To understand the distribution of this class of new elite in different parts of Africa and some of their characteristic attitudes, it is important to examine the impact of European activities in two stages, the pre-colonial period and the colonial period. This is because the attitudes of Europeans towards the emergence of a new elite differed widely from place to place, and from time to time, particularly between the pre-colonial and the colonial periods.

In the nineteenth century, before the colonial period, the areas of intense European activities were the coastal parts of West Africa, South Africa and the North African states. Broadly speaking, since few people imagined that general European rule was imminent, there was a basic assumption that European interests had to be pursued and protected in partnership with the local people, preferably those of them in whom the new European values associated with the slogan 'Christianity, Commerce and Civilisation' had been inculcated. Hence the ready co-operation between missionaries and the anti-slavery movement, explorers, traders and government officials.

The missionaries operated on the assumption that if the nineteenth-century effort to introduce Christianity into Africa were to be any more permanent than earlier attempts, it had to be accompanied by a thorough-going modernisation of traditional African society. By this, they meant stopping the overseas slave trade and eventually the internal slave trade, encouraging in its place new commerce and a cash economy, introducing some of the new technology of Europe, and above all creating a class of people who could initiate and carry on such revolutionary changes. Long term hopes apart, the high rates of mortality and repatriation of Europeans through illness stressed the urgent need to train African missionaries, schoolmasters and other agents to assist and eventually to replace Europeans. For such reasons, the missionaries put a liberal policy of education very high in their order of priorities.

Sierra Leone and Liberia provided unique opportunities for practising these ideas. Apart from the settlers from Britain, Nova

Scotia and Jamaica in Sierra Leone, and the different states of America in Liberia, there were also Africans captured from different parts of West Africa and set free to make a new home in these colonies. These liberated Africans had to be integrated into the European or American culture of the other settlers. Though their traditional laws and customs survived, their predicament away from their own ethnic groups and their gratitude to their liberators made them unusually responsive to new ideas. In turn the missionaries hoped that these colonies would become the 'nursery bed' from which 'civilisation' would be transplanted to the rest of West Africa. Particularly in Sierra Leone, education was taken so seriously that it has been said that in the 1850s the proportion of children going to school to those of school age in the colony was higher than in Britain.

Besides Sierra Leone and Liberia, the old centres of European trade in Senegal, Ghana and Southern Nigeria also offered some opportunities since there was a growing demand by the local people themselves for some formal education for commercial purposes. From these coastal areas missionary work began gradually to penetrate inland. However, nowhere in the interior offered such opportunities as the Yoruba country, torn by war, many of the victims of which had found their way to Sierra Leone and were anxious to return. In a few places like Abeokuta, there was an appreciable demand for education and modernisation as part of the process of reconstruction and nation-building.

Similarly South Africa offered some opportunities. The replacement of Dutch rule by that of a British government, subject to some pressure from missionary circles, in the first half of the century, opened up opportunities for missionaries of all countries. A good deal of emphasis is usually put on the work of English missionaries there in the struggle for racial equality in the Cape Province. But perhaps even more significant was the work of French, American and other missionaries in the new Bantu states formed after Shaka's revolution. Rulers like Moshesh of the Basuto and Khama of the Bamangwato began to ask for education in their task of nation-building.

There were few attempts at missionary work in East Africa before 1875, and little of significance was achieved. The North African states attracted more attention. The memory of the Christianity that Islam had displaced, memories too of the long conflict between the Cross and Crescent induced many missions to seek to establish themselves in that region. To some extent the states themselves were anxious to modernise and therefore not unwilling to welcome Europeans, including a few missionaries. In Egypt there was positive encouragement and a tradition of Western education became established particularly in training new recruits for the Army. Elsewhere, except among European and Jewish settlers, missionary success was very limited. Algeria, however, quickly entered the colonial period and Christianity enjoyed many privileges at the expense of Islam, Churches at the expense of Mosques, with the inevitable result that a few Berber-Arabs began to acquire Western education and Western values.

REACTION AGAINST THE NINETEENTH CENTURY TRADITION

As a result of this early nineteenth-century policy of liberal education, small groups of educated Africans began to emerge in West, South and North Africa. By 1890, for example, there were a large number of primary schools, eight or more secondary schools and one university institution in West Africa. Besides these, a number of people had also been educated abroad in Europe or America. Thus, at the time of the partition, countries like Sierra Leone, Ghana and Nigeria had more people with secondary and post-secondary education than some other African countries were to have later at the time of independence.

This was because, on the whole, colonial administration did not favour a liberal policy of education. Beginning from the 1880s the ideas of racists who believed in the inherent inferiority of Africans, intellectually, morally and spiritually began to be popularised. These ideas fanned up the tide of European nationalism. The partition of Africa was interpreted not as a search for new economic opportunities but as a fulfilment of the divine mission of the 'superior' races to rule the 'inferior' peoples more or less permanently. Since such rule needed to be bolstered up by creating respect for the ruling people among the ruled, a liberal education could not be pursued. Education had to be directed to teach the student that he was inferior. This could be done either by teaching him that his master's culture was beyond his reach, or by telling him he could eventually become like his master provided he first divested himself of his traditional culture and self-respect.

A determined effort was made at the beginning of the colonial era to reverse the policy of the early nineteenth century. Missionaries in South Africa, always under fierce attack, could no longer depend upon humanitarian support as in the earlier days of Dr John Philip. Bishop Colenso was excommunicated for his liberal views. In West Africa promotion of Africans to the Senior Civil Service practically ceased. The percentage of Africans in the Nigerian service dropped to its lowest level ever in 1920. Europeanisation became the firm though unproclaimed policy. African doctors were no longer engaged as government medical officers even though Edinburgh University carried out a long battle with the colonial office on their behalf. The two Black Bishops in the Anglican Communion, Crowther of the Niger and Ferguson of Liberia, and the African superintendents of other missions were replaced by Europeans. The top ranks of the mission churches were to remain white for the next sixty years. Fourah Bay declined and was almost closed down for lack of moral and financial support.

The situation in French and Portuguese Africa was similar. After the high tide of French liberalism in 1848 when African citizens of the empire were given equality of rights with French citizens, including the right to elect a deputy to the French Assembly, French policy often abandoned assimilation for the principle of association which laid less emphasis upon a new African elite. In the Portuguese territories the number of *assimilados* ceased to grow after the unsuccessful efforts of the liberal Bandeira government (1836–40) to make all Africans citizens of Portugal. And, in any case, the mere proclamation of equality neither produced the schools, finances or economic development upon which such equality could be built.

However, these efforts during the colonial period to reverse early nineteenth century practice were never totally successful. The four communes[1]—the cradle of the Senegalese elite—fought a long battle to preserve their citizenship status. The colony areas of Sierra Leone, Ghana and Nigeria like the Senegalese communes struggled to retain their privileges. The educated elements in these colonies, though small, were vocal and equipped with lawyers and newspapers. They wielded enough influence to perpetuate their class. Their young men continued to attend Fourah Bay College, Freetown, and to seek education overseas.

Colonial policy might slow down but could not stop the growth of this class.

Not only did the whole process of education begin later in East and Central Africa but more important it began at a time when Europeans, obsessed by current theories of European superiority and African inferiority, doubted the wisdom of efforts to create an African elite. Even apart from settlers with a vested interest in preventing the growth of an African educated class, an important factor was the absence in East Africa of the early nineteenth century tradition of liberalism.

COLONIAL POLICIES

Within this general reaction against the tradition of liberal education, there were important variations in the colonial policies of the different European countries which affected to some extent the emergence of a new elite in different parts of Africa. These variations concerned colonial policy towards education and missionary activities generally and the role provided for an African educated elite in the colonial administrations.

French and Portuguese colonial policies were similar. Both sought to create a highly polished elite, a few shining stars, thoroughly conditioned by French or Portuguese culture. They therefore encouraged state financing of education in the colonies and they encouraged a picked few to study in the 'metropolitan' countries. They made some provision for the employment of such *evolués* and *assimilados* in the colonial administrations. But they were also concerned that such an elite should not politically disturb the unassimilated mass of the people. They therefore preferred the *evolué* and *assimilado* to live and work in France or Portugal. Also for that reason they carefully controlled the activities of missionaries, often insisting that only mission societies originating from the metropolitan country and sharing its colonial ideals should be allowed to operate.

Belgian policy stood in marked contrast to the French and Portuguese. In French and Portuguese colonies the masses remained illiterate, a middle class hardly existed and much energy was spent on a top quality elite; in the Congo the Belgians created the most technologically advanced colony in Africa based upon a solid lower middle class employed in the skilled and semi-skilled trades. Belgian policy frowned upon the development of an elite, and although missions of all kinds were permitted to operate their policy was strictly controlled to conform to official goals. Overseas travel and education were discouraged. Thus no class of elite could develop in the Congo, though there were a few outstanding individuals working exclusively within church and, later, trade union organisations.

In contrast to the other European powers, the British had no consistent policy for an educated class. On the one hand missionaries were given a freer hand and more assistance in British Africa than elsewhere on the continent. As a result there emerged in British colonies the largest group of educated people in Tropical Africa. On the other hand the British refused to employ the elite in the administration and professional services of their colonies. Lord Lugard's theory of indirect rule which dominated the thinking of British administrations up until the Second World War envisioned an evolution of traditional African political systems built upon the principle of hereditary chieftaincy. It provided no place for a western-educated elite. Successors to Lugard wavered between two extremes. Some sought to find a place for the new elite within the indirect rule system. Traditional government, however, had little need for the skills the western-educated possessed. Others sought to restrict the growth of the elite. But the reluctance of the colonial office to interfere with the missionaries, the main agents in the production of the elite, frustrated such efforts. This contradictory policy of the British produced the paradox that Nigeria, the show place of indirect rule, developed one of the largest western-educated classes.

However, we must not exaggerate the importance of colonial theories whether of indirect rule, assimilation or association. The French who sought an elite as a fulfilment of their policy of assimilation and spent much money seeking its development were less successful than the British who frowned upon an elite as an embarrassment to the indirect rule system. More fundamental was the colonial power's attitude to missionary activity. France, through suspicion of missionaries, and unwillingness to extend state aid to mission schools, turned her back upon the most potent agencies for creating an *evolué* class of educated and acculturated Africans. The British, by welcoming missionary assistance, produced the elite which France needed, but for which Britain had little use. France sought to produce her elite by state finance. In her wealthier West Coast colonies the results were significant. In the poorer Equatorial African territories a few individuals but hardly a class emerged. In marked contrast was the development in Togoland and the Cameroons where missions were protected by the mandate which France held from the League of Nations. In the Cameroons the state was educating 1,000 in 1913 and 12,000 in 1953 while the missions in the same years were educating 43,000 and 113,000, a situation the reverse of elsewhere in the French empire. Thus, where France was compelled to tolerate the missions, as in the mandated territories, the size and quality of the elite resembled those of the neighbouring British rather than the neighbouring French colonies.

SETTLERS AND ECONOMIC DEVELOPMENT

The correlation between mission activity and the emergence of an elite was, however, a phenomenon of non-Muslim, non-settler areas, and confined to the West African coast and Uganda. The widely varying colonial policies towards missionary activity has not been the crucial factor in the settler colonies of East and Central Africa.

Permitting missionary activity did not in itself guarantee the emergence of an elite. Both Britain and Belgium allowed missions originating anywhere in the world to operate in their colonies. The Berlin Act compelled Belgium to afford all missions protection. But by a concordat with the Vatican in 1906 Catholic missions controlled by Belgian nationals, were made the educational arms of the Congo government. Since the state paid the mission piper it called the curriculum tune. The result was not 'education' in its accepted meaning but rather what would be better called 'training'. The Protestant missions were not assisted and, as elsewhere, the cost of secondary education in quality and quantity proved difficult if not impossible without state aid. The Congo, therefore, with the largest mission establishment at work in Tropical Africa did not produce an elite before its independence.

In her settler colonies Britain failed almost as woefully as the Belgians to create an African elite. The contrast with West Africa is indeed dramatic. While Southern Nigeria possessed thirty secondary schools in 1937, there was no fully developed secondary school for Africans in Kenya. British policy followed settler ideas and available revenue was swallowed up by state education of settler children. The major concern of the colonial administration was how to control rather than how to aid African education, especially after 1930 when the Kikuyu began their independent schools. Settlers were critical of any liberalism in missionary education and state aid was extended or withheld to promote settler goals. As in the Congo, missions found it difficult to carry the expense of secondary schools unaided. Thus, regardless of conflicting aims and policies, the results as far as the emergence of an African elite was concerned were negligible in settler colonies whether the controlling power was British, Belgian or Portuguese.

The rate and extent of economic development of a colony was a determining factor in the size of the educated elite which developed, and which the colony could support. This factor became even more important where the colonial power excluded the elite from senior posts in the administration. The people of Dahomey pursued education with the same vigour as Western Nigeria. Although the French employed Dahomians extensively in the administration all over French West Africa, Dahomey was poor compared to its Nigerian neighbour. Dahomey could not support an elite comparable to Western Nigeria even though in Nigeria the elite was excluded from the senior civil service. In Western Nigeria an expanding wealthy class was demanding the services of doctors, lawyers and graduate teachers.

In West Africa the level and pace of economic development would seem to have been the major determining factor in the size of the educated class. Ghana possessed the largest elite, followed by Western Nigeria with Sierra Leone and Eastern Nigeria trailing. The poorer French coastal colonies all fell further behind. In addition Sierra Leone and Liberia, in the nineteenth century the proud possessors of large elites, could not compete with Nigeria and Ghana once modern economic development had begun in the latter countries.

In East and Central Africa, however, the level of economic development was not indicative of the size of the elite. If anything, the reverse might be postulated, that the greater the economic development of a settler colony the smaller the African elite. Katanga had no African educated elite; the Rhodesias almost none; Kenya, Tanganyika and Nyasaland very little. Rapid economic development contributed to the growth of the settlers who *were* the elite in colonial Africa. The African population became a proletariat, too poor to produce or support a professional elite.

Settlers tended to operate in two ways. In the early days, when they were few, government services were stocked by expatriate officers while Africans slowly began to rise from unskilled to skilled occupations. As the settler element grew, it tended to replace expatriates at the top in government and economy, and displace Africans at the bottom. Thus the African middle class out of which an elite might have emerged was consistently destroyed and forced back into the proletariat. In South Africa the railway and postal services were in the early 1920s almost exclusively manned by Africans. By the 1940s all Africans had been displaced by whites. The economic depression of the 1930s hastened this process. Politically influential settlers brought pressure to bear on the government to solve European unemployment. The easiest way of doing this was by giving African jobs to Europeans.

Furthermore, growing settler monopoly of civil service positions made it increasingly difficult for a colonial governor to pursue anything but pro-settler policies. His advisers were settlers and those who carried out his orders were settlers. This partly explains why, although settlers could not frame colonial policy, it could only be carried out in their own way. This also explains why settler views were so important with regard to the policy pursued towards missionary activities noted earlier. Since an African middle class threatened the lower settler ranks and an African elite threatened the higher, all were united against African advancement. Settlers found very convenient the views of those who advocated the theories of racial superiority, so popular at the time they were settling in East and Central Africa. Elsewhere in the world these views were challenged and ultimately discredited. British and French policy in their last twenty years of rule in West Africa reflected this change and speeded up programmes to produce a capable elite. The settlers of East and Central Africa clung tenaciously to their earlier beliefs and held up any significant change of policy until overtaken by African nationalism and shocked by the Mau Mau revolt.

RACIAL BIAS

It is difficult to estimate the overall influence of racial attitudes upon policy. Although no colonial power was entirely free from racial prejudice, the French and Portuguese were least disturbed by it, the Belgians and British most. Settlers were more prejudiced than expatriates, and the larger the settler element the greater the discrimination. The largest settler populations in Africa were in Algeria and the Union of South Africa. Racial thinking dominated both, even though one was French the other English-Dutch.

In South Africa racial bias has been the major factor in the retardation of the elite. Most of the other prerequisites existed for the growth of the largest and most sophisticated educated class in Africa. Missionary activity on liberal nineteenth-century lines had begun early and on a massive scale. The discovery of gold and subsequent industrialisation promoted an African middle class, with an income, to produce and support a growing elite. By the time the Union was set up and settlers were free to frame domestic policy, the process had gone too far to be reversed. The government, therefore, sought first to provide a kind of education which would no longer create an elite, and second so to circumscribe the elite which had emerged that it would be unable to perform the functions of leadership which the term 'elite' suggests. In pursuance of the first objective, the initial institution of higher learning set up for Africans, Fort Hare, emphasised 'training' in the Belgian manner rather than 'education' after the fashion of Fourah Bay. In 1936 the Union's philosophy of education was that: 'the education of a white child prepares him for life in a dominant society, the education of the black for a subordinate society'. The settlers set their faces against an African elite. The only elite in the Union was to be the white population. The increasing use of authoritarian laws and police-state methods on the African people in the last twenty years is an indication that the educational policy has not proved entirely successful, and that an African elite continues to grow in power, influence and number in the Republic of South Africa.

MUSLIM AFRICA

In Muslim Africa, special problems arose from the attempts by Christian colonial powers to create an elite in their own image. Britain had less difficulty from this since it was not her policy deliberately to foster the growth of an educated elite. France, on the other hand, ruled by far the largest area of Muslim Africa and her assimilationist policy was repugnant to Muslims proud of their religion, language and culture. French citizenship at one time or another required a Muslim to become a Catholic, marry only one wife, give up his personal status under Muslim law and accept the doctrine of the inherent superiority of French culture. It is not surprising that few Muslims sought citizenship under such conditions.

British policy had peculiar difficulties in the Sudan belt where pockets of non-Muslim peoples survived in Muslim countries. Because they wished to rely on a traditional elite, they did not create a vigorous system of state education beyond a few schools intended primarily to train members of the traditional elite. Yet, because Muslims did not respond well to missionaries, the British sometimes departed from their usual open policy and kept missionaries out. But, at the same time, they encouraged missionaries to concentrate their attention on turning the non-Muslim pockets into Christian enclaves. Thus, while relying politically on a traditional elite, they were raising a Christian elite of professionals and officials. This complicated administration, especially on the attainment of self-government. In countries like Upper Volta where the economy was too poor to bear an adequate state system of education, a similar situation could arise under the French, but the best examples are in British territories, Northern Nigeria and the Republic of the Sudan, except that in the latter country the position was even more complicated.

At least in the Western Sudan the Muslim and Christian elites shared a common second language. British policy in what used to be called Anglo-Egyptian Sudan was less consistent. Because of Egyptian influence, the Northern Sudan more quickly combined Islam and Arabic learning with western scientific thought. Gordon College at Khartoum set the pace, and the largest western-educated elite of Sudanese Africa grew up there within a setting of Islam. Meanwhile, in the non-Muslim southern areas, the British encouraged missionary activities and rigidly excluded Muslim influence. Makerere College in Uganda rather than Gordon College was the formative influence in the growth of the southern Sudanese elite. The result was an elite, Christian, fluent in English, with no appreciation of Islamic culture or ability in Arabic which upon independence became the official language of the Republic of Sudan. The clash between the two incompatible elites has given rise to serious unrest and civil strife in the Southern Sudan and contributed to the instability of the central government.

Today, the smallest elites in Africa outside the settler areas are to be found in the Muslim states of the Western and Central Sudan. In contrast, Muslim North Africa possesses one of the largest western-educated classes in Africa. In the nineteenth century North Africa had faced the problem of missionary societies and colonial governments offering science and technology at the price of conversion to Christianity. In close proximity to Europe, Muslims were conscious of the disparity which the Industrial Revolution had created between Europe and Africa. This disparity produced a ferment and unrest throughout the entire Muslim world. Some sought a remedy in a return to the pure and stringent ideals of primitive Islam. Others worked to show that Islam was not incompatible with science, technology or even European philosophic thought. Muhammad Ali's experiments with technical schools in Egypt in the first half of the nineteenth century and his demonstration of the power of science in Muslim hands had considerable significance for the Muslim world. The significance was pressed home with the collapse not only of the North African states but also of the Turkish empire as a whole.

Those seeking to harmonise western techniques with Islam worked both within orthodoxy and outside it. Heterodox groups such as the Ahmadiyya, Ansar-u-Deen and Nawair-u-Deen brought a whole range of western and Christian techniques to the service of Islam. Important impetus was given to the movement by the wave of nationalism following the First World War and the revolution of the Young Turks in 1919 when a thorough reformation of Islam was carried out. The ideas emanating from Egypt and Turkey profoundly influenced the Magrib, and schools imitating those of the Christian missions without accepting the supremacy of Christian ideals, produced the elite of the present day. Egypt, having begun the process earlier and having been independent for over forty years, outstripped the rest of North Africa in the size of its educated elite.

Unfortunately these ideas did not spread quickly to the Sudan, for the nineteenth century witnessed the progressive elimination of the ancient ties of the Sudan with the Magrib, first in the replacement of the caravans by the trade with Europeans on the

Niger-Senegal, and later by the colonial boundaries. In the nine-teenth century the Sahara became a barrier, rather than a high-way of intercourse. In the twentieth century Sudanese Muslims faced the European challenge cut off from the spiritual and intellectual assistance of that part of the world whose language they spoke and whose thought processes they understood best. Recently, the development of air travel has once again begun to bridge the gap.

NOTE

1 The four Senegalese towns recognised under the law of 1848 as municipalities like other municipalities in France: St Louis, Gorée, Dakar and Rufisque.

QUESTIONS FOR FURTHER STUDY AND DISCUSSION

1 Examine the nature of pre-colonial missionary education in West Africa and discuss its significance for African history.

2 Compare French and British policy towards education in their different colonial territories in West Africa.

3 Examine the factors within Islamic states favouring the emergence of a western-type African elite.

SELECT BIBLIOGRAPHY

'African Education South of the Sahara' (Journal of Negro Education Yearbook, No. 30), 1961.

J. F. A. Ajayi, *Christian Missions in Nigeria 1841–1891: The Making of a New Elite*, Longmans, 1965.

G. N. Brown, 'British Education Policy in West and Central Africa', *Journal of Modern African Studies*, Vol. 2, no. 3, 1964.

C. P. Groves, *The Planting of Christianity in Africa*, Vols. III and IV, Lutterworth Press, 1955 and 1958.

Lord Hailey, *An African Survey*, O.U.P., 1957.

F. H. Hilliard, *A Short History of Education in British West Africa*, Nelson, 1957.

T. Hodgkin, *Nationalism in Colonial Africa*, Muller, 1956.

Guy Hunter, *The New Societies of Tropical Africa*, O.U.P., 1962.

F. Parker, *African Development and Education in Southern Rhodesia*, Columbus, Ohio, 1960.

10 The Nile Valley: Egypt and the Sudan in the Nineteenth Century

MUHAMMAD A. AL-HAJJ

FROM its most remote source near Lake Tanganyika down to the Mediterranean, the Nile covers a distance of 4,160 miles and passes through a number of countries: Tanzania, Kenya, Uganda, Sudan and Egypt. The importance of this great river, however, is especially linked with the last two countries. Without the Nile, the northern Sudan and the whole of Egypt would be a desert; with the Nile, this region developed a remarkable civilisation which stretches back to 5000 B.C.

Egypt came under the suzerainty of the Ottoman Turks in 1517 after Sultan Selīm had defeated the Mamlūks at the battle of Cairo. The Mamlūks were a caste of slaves of varied races who had established a dynasty in Egypt in 1249 and ruled the country as overlords. Their defeat at the hands of Sultan Selīm had no major effect on their long established authority. They remained the effective power though henceforward every Sultan sent his viceroy as the legitimate ruler.

The story of the Nile valley in the nineteenth century begins with Napoleon's expedition to Egypt in 1798 and ends with the Anglo-Egyptian occupation of the Sudan in 1898. When Napoleon Bonaparte landed in Egypt he crushed the Mamlūks at the battle of the Pyramids. Soon, however, Britain intervened and Nelson destroyed the French navy in the Mediterranean. Napoleon, cut off from his supplies and reinforcements, deserted his army and sailed off to France in August 1799. His troops, left behind, could not hold out long against the joint forces of the Ottoman Sultan and the British. By 1801, the French were compelled to withdraw from Egypt.

Napoleon's occupation, though sudden and short-lived, was in fact an important event in the modern history of Egypt. It had demonstrated the rivalry between Britain and France in their attempts to gain spheres of influence in the Middle East. Napoleon, it is true, proclaimed that he had come as a friend of the Egyptian people to save them from the maladministration of the Mamlūks. He adopted Arab dress and issued proclamations in praise of Islam and the Muslim way of life. His real motive, however, had been to weaken British hegemony in the Orient through the control of the overland route to India. But the British acted swiftly and foiled his plans at an early stage.

The coming of the French was also significant for the Egyptian people. It had shaken the Mamlūks' power; it had illustrated the weakness of the Ottoman empire; it had opened the gates of Egypt to the inflow of western ideas and institutions. 'Our countries must change', said Shaĩkh Hasan b. Muhammad al-Attār (c. 1766–1835), 'and we must adopt from Europe all the sciences which do not exist here.'

MUHAMMAD ALI

Following the French withdrawal, the history of Egypt for the first half of the nineteenth century was virtually the story of one man, Muhammad Ali Pasha. Muhammad Ali, an Albanian by origin, came to Egypt as a young officer in the Turkish army which the Sultan sent to help drive the French out of the country. During the turmoil which followed the French withdrawal, he emerged as the only man capable of restoring peace and order. He worked his way to this position by cautious strategy calculated to win the support of the Egyptian people. The French agent Drovetti, who watched with interest the movements of Muhammad Ali at the time, despatched a report to Paris in which he said:

The measures of the enterprising Albanian leader, make me think he hopes to become Pasha of Cairo without fighting and without incurring the displeasure of the Sultan. Every act reveals a Machiavellian mind, and I really begin to think he has a stronger head than most Turks have. He seems to aim at obtaining power through the favour of the Shaikhs and the people, so as to reduce the Porte to the necessity of giving him freely the position which he will have seized.[1]

Drovetti guessed right. Four years after the departure of the French, Muhammad Ali was acknowledged the undisputed Pasha of Egypt. During these four years Egypt was reduced to anarchy. The Mamlūks fought each other. The Turkish army was divided into racial factions; Kurds fought Albanians, and the Janissaries fought both. The Egyptian people, on the other hand, were opposed to all these alien factions. Muhammad Ali gave evidence of his genius when he recognised the importance of the mass of the people in this struggle and associated himself with their aspirations.

The Egyptian people, led by the religious Shaikhs, staged violent demonstrations against the Turks. Almost simultaneously, the Albanian regiment, which came directly under the command of Muhammad Ali, besieged the residence of the Viceroy and demanded arrears of pay. On 13 May 1805, Shaikh al-Sharqāwi, Rector of al-Azhar, and Umar Makram, the head of the religious nobility, jointly declared the Sultan's viceroy deposed and installed in his place Muhammad Ali as the popular choice. Meanwhile the demonstrations continued until the Sultan was compelled to withdraw his representative and confirm the appointment of Muhammad Ali as Pasha of Egypt. Thus, Muhammad Ali achieved his ambition by associating himself with the people's revolt. It should be borne in mind, however, that he was not concerned with Egyptian nationalism except in so far as it could serve his rise to power. His main concern was to make Egypt a modern state on the European model and then to take her out of the Ottoman empire in the interests of himself and his family. All his achievements were related to this overall plan.

The most urgent task that confronted Muhammad Ali was the need to secure enough revenue to support his plans for the modernisation of Egypt. To achieve this, he imposed state control over the means of production by appointing himself the chief proprietor in the fields of agriculture, commerce and industry. He took possession of the cultivable land and endeavoured to extract from it the maximum possible yield. He repaired the canals, developed the methods of irrigation and introduced cultivation of the long-staple cotton which forms the principal source of revenue in the country today. He reorganised the methods of taxation by abolishing the Mamlūk's system whereby the tax-farmers squeezed as much as they could out of the *fallāhīn* (peasants) for themselves against a fixed sum that was sent to the government. Under the new system, the state officials collected the whole land-produce, supervised its sale, deducted the rents and taxes for the government and then paid the *fallāh* his share.

Thus Muhammad Ali was able to receive regular revenues for the state and at the same time improve the lot of the *fallāh*.

Muhammad Ali stimulated the development of foreign trade by introducing a new currency and stabilising the rate of exchange. It was unfortunate, however, that external trade was handicapped by his system of tariffs imposed for the protection of his new industries. He spent enormous sums on local industries such as textiles and glass manufacture, but these enterprises proved unsuccessful despite the efforts of his foreign technicians and managers. The mechanisation of these industries needed skilled labour which Egypt at the time could not provide. On the whole, however, there was a marked increase in the volume of imported goods, in contrast with the Mamlūks' period when trade with the 'infidel' was frowned on as unlawful in the *Sharīa*.

As revenue increased, Muhammad Ali set out to create a strong and well-equipped army capable of overcoming the bands of mercenaries used by the Mamlūks and the Ottoman Sultan. He tried at first to build an army, on the model of the Janissaries, out of black slaves imported from the Sudan. But, out of 20,000 slaves sent down the Nile from the Sudan to Egypt, only 3,000 survived the hazards of the journey and the change of climate. He was compelled, therefore, to give up his dream of a black army and so he turned to the *fallāhīn* whom he regarded at first as only capable of tilling the soil. The *fallāhīn*, on the other hand, resisted conscription with such bitterness that some of them mutilated themselves to avoid service. Nevertheless, Muhammad Ali managed successfully to drive them into his army by the use of the whip (*kurbāj*). By 1826, he possessed an army of 90,000 men trained by French instructors and equipped with the most up-to-date European weapons.

The military campaigns of Muhammad Ali started as early as 1811. His first expedition was directed against the Wahhābis of central Arabia, a fanatic Muslim sect which conquered Mecca and Medina and hindered the annual pilgrimage. The Sultan, who was officially the custodian of the Holy Places, requested Muhammad Ali to fight the war against the Wahhābis. Muhammad Ali agreed, but he was wise enough not to send his troops on this mission before he had dealt with the Mamlūks at home. On the eve of the departure of the expedition, Muhammad Ali held a reception in the Citadel to which he invited the most powerful

Mamlūk chiefs and other notables. When the reception was over, he gave the signal to his bodyguard to execute all the Mamlūks among the guests. Three hundred Mamlūks were instantly beheaded. Then followed a general persecution of the Mamlūks throughout the country; their property was confiscated and their leaders were executed. Only a few managed to escape along the Nile into the Sudan. This ruthless annihilation of the Mamlūks, bloody as it was, was a great service to Egypt because their continued existence would have made it impossible for Muhammad Ali to introduce most of his reforms successfully.

The Wahhābis put up a strong resistance. The war dragged on until 1818 when they were finally defeated and their capital, Dar'īyan, was taken. In 1820 Muhammad Ali embarked on his second campaign which led to the conquest of the Sudan. At the time when Muhammad Ali had risen to power, the Fūnj Sultanate of Sinnār had been in the last stages of complete disintegration. Many tribes in the region between Dongola and Sinnār had broken away from the Fūnj authority and were constantly engaged in intertribal warfare among themselves. The time was therefore opportune for Muhammad Ali to invade the Sudan and add it to his dominions.

The ambition of building an empire, however, was not the only reason that made the Pasha covet the Sudan. He hoped to obtain enough slaves for conscription into a black army that would be loyal to him personally;[2] secondly, reports about the Sudan indicated that the country was rich in gold; thirdly, the Pasha wanted to harass the remnants of the Mamlūks who had fled into the Sudan; lastly, the conquest of the Sudan would enable Egypt to have complete control over the Red Sea. By controlling this sea, Muhammad Ali believed he would automatically become the guardian of the Holy Places.

The actual invasion began in 1820. Two expeditions were sent along the Nile, one directed against Sinnār, and the other against Kordofān and Dār Fūr. Muhammad Ali appointed his son, Ismā'īl, to command the first force, and his son-in-law, Muhammad Bey Khusraw al-Daftardar, to command the second. Ismā'īl met no resistance until he reached Dongola. When he marched farther south, however, he encountered the Shāiqīya, a warlike tribe which had broken away from the Fūnj authority some 150 years before. The Shāiqīya fought with great courage but they were

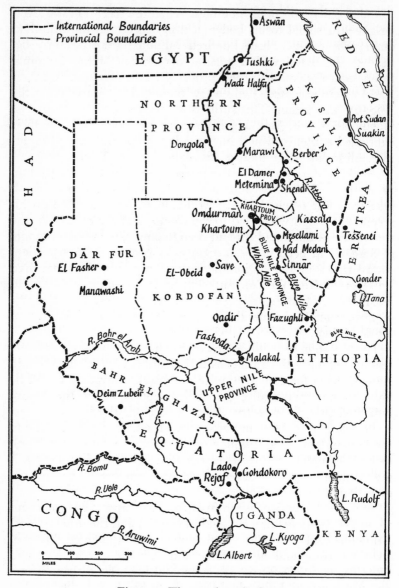

Fig. 10 The modern Sudan.

defeated in the end by the invading army. Instead of exterminating the Shāiqīya after their defeat, Ismā'īl took steps to enlist them as irregular cavalry in his force. This indeed was a wise decision because the Shāiqīya proved to be useful allies to the new regime. Ismā'īl advanced southwards until he entered Sinnār (June 1821). The Fūnj Sultan, Bādī, met him outside the town and surrendered his crown.

The force under the command of the Daftardar marched through the desert until it reached Kordofān which at the time was under the suzerainty of Dār Fūr. The Governor, Maqdūm Musallam, left his capital, El-Obeid, and met the Egyptian forces at Bāra. The Daftardar defeated the Governor and entered El-Obeid in triumph. The conquest of Dār Fūr, however, was abandoned following new instructions from Muhammad Ali. The Sultan of Dār Fūr, on the other hand, made no attempt to regain Kordofān.

With the conquest of Sinnār and Kordofān completed, the main parts of the northern Sudan came under Egyptian control. The Egyptians, however, were disillusioned and the whole venture seemed to some rather futile. The non-Muslim[3] Negroes who could be enslaved were farther south in a swampy region difficult to traverse. The rumours about the fabulous wealth of the country proved false; Sinnār was nothing more than a village of scattered huts, and the few gold mines in the Red Sea region were already exhausted. Additionally, the climate was very trying to the Egyptians who were not accustomed to heavy rains.

In the face of such poverty, the Egyptians decided to make their conquest worthwhile by taxing the Sudanese heavily. Assessments were unrealistically high and the methods used in collection were most inhuman. It was not long before the Sudanese rose in revolt against this gross injustice. The violence of this protest was in sharp contrast with their failure to show any signs of major resistance at the time of the invasion. This can be explained by the fact that at the time of the invasion the Sudanese believed the Egyptian propaganda that the Egyptians were entering the Sudan as agents of the Ottoman Sultan, the head of the Muslim community by virtue of his office as Caliph, a title the Sultan assumed in 1517. The Egyptian force was accompanied by three clerics (ulamā') whose duty was to persuade the Sudanese not to resist the agents of the Caliph.

When the Sudanese discovered the real motives for the invasion, they reacted violently; they resisted the payment of taxes, and attacked isolated detachments of Egyptian troops and killed them. In October 1822, the Commander-in-Chief of the Egyptian troops in the Sudan, Muhammad Ali's son, Ismā'īl, arrived at Shendi and demanded from the chief of the Ja'liyīn, Mak Nimr, that 30,000 *riyāls* (dollars) and 6,000 slaves be handed over within twenty-four hours. When Mak Nimr tried to explain that this demand was unreasonable and impossible to meet in the specified time, Ismā'īl lost his temper and struck him with his pipe across the face. That night, while Ismā'īl and his bodyguard slept, the Ja'liyīn piled forage around their tents and set fire to them. Ismā'īl and all those who had come with him were burned to death.

When the Daftardar heard the news at El-Obeid, he immediately set out for Shendi to avenge Ismā'īl's death. On his arrival, he vented his anger on the Ja'liyīn by the most ruthless massacre ever known to the tribe. Mak Nimr, however, fled to the Ethiopian marshes where he established himself in a mountainous region inaccessible to the Egyptians. The revolt of the Ja'liyīn encouraged other tribes to resist tax payments, but they were treated in a harsh manner and likewise pacified. Thus, the Daftardar managed to suppress the Sudanese revolt. In fact this tribal resistance was an uprising of despair, spasmodic and without aim or leadership. The Sudanese were to wait for sixty years before they could rise again under a national leader, Muhammad Ahmad al-Mahdi.

It is convenient to return to Egypt at this juncture to describe the relations between Muhammad Ali and the Ottoman Sultan. Although in practice Egypt was virtually autonomous, theoretically she remained part of the Ottoman empire. Muhammad Ali continued to pay annual tribute to the Sultan together with bribes in the form of presents and gifts. He obediently sent his troops to fight the Wahhābis at the request of the Sultan. When the Greeks rose in rebellion against the Ottoman administration, the Sultan again requested Muhammad Ali to come to his aid, promising him Syria as reward. Muhammad Ali sent his son Ibrahim against the Greeks, and the rebellion was suppressed. But the Sultan was unwilling to fulfil his promise of reward because he became increasingly anxious about the growing power of his viceroy. Muhammad Ali decided to seize Syria by force. His son, Ibrahim, marched into Syria and defeated the Sultan's forces in a number of pitched battles. Then he advanced northward and was almost at the gates of Constantinople when a threat from Russia forced him to retreat. A peace treaty concluded in April 1833 gave Syria to Muhammad Ali.

Meanwhile, the Sultan had been relieved of his anxiety by the intervention of the European powers who were equally alarmed by the growing power of Egypt. The Great Powers joined hands to help the 'sick man of Europe' gain a new lease of life. Britain in particular led the battle against Muhammad Ali. In 1839, Britain occupied Aden to counteract Egypt's control of the Red Sea. Then she signed a commercial treaty with the Sultan giving her the right to trade in the Ottoman empire against a tariff of only three per cent. Muhammad Ali refused to accept this concession and demanded commercial independence. The Sultan declared him a rebel, and sent his forces against Syria. The Ottoman forces were severely defeated. The Sultan's position became more critical when, shortly afterwards, his fleet defected and joined Muhammad Ali.

At this juncture the Quadruple Alliance was concluded between Britain, Russia, Prussia and Austria in July 1840 through the successful diplomacy of Lord Palmerston. The Great Powers joined hands to defend the integrity of the Ottoman empire and to force Muhammad Ali to relinquish Syria. In November, the Allied fleet, under Sir Charles Napier, assembled off the Syrian coast, bombarded Acre and forced the Egyptians to evacuate the country. Then the fleet appeared before Alexandria and forced Muhammad Ali to agree to relinquish Syria and return the Ottoman fleet to the Sultan. This initial agreement was later formalised by the Treaty of London. The treaty gave Muhammad Ali the hereditary right to rule Egypt, but he was called on to return Syria to the Sultan. The Egyptian army was to be reduced to 18,000 men and appointments to the higher rank were to be made by the Sultan. Further, Muhammad Ali was to pay a fixed annual tribute to the Sultan.

The Treaty of London (1841) arrested the military ambitions of Muhammad Ali but gave him, under international guarantee, the hereditary right to govern Egypt. Thus, the Albanian adventurer successfully established a dynasty which continued to rule Egypt until 1952 when the army *coup d'etat* forced the late King

Farūq to abdicate. At the time of the treaty, however, Muhammad Ali was already an old man of seventy-two. He died a few years later, in 1849.

Muhammad Ali laid the foundations of modern Egypt by introducing western technology and adopting western methods of economic and social reforms. His profound admiration for European civilisation was in direct contrast with the traditional contempt which the Mamlūks had for foreign ideas and institutions. But it would be a mistake to regard him as 'the father' of modern Egyptian nationalism. It is true that he rose to power at the turn of the century by associating himself with the revolt of the Egyptian people against foreign rule. His regime, however, was based on Turkish superiority and he himself remained to the end of his life an alien autocrat. But these considerations should not alter the fact that he was the architect of modern Egypt.

We may conclude this story of his life by some remarks he made about the massacre of the Mamlūks a few years after the episode:

> I do not love this period of my life . . . and what would the world profit by the recital of this interminable issue of combat and misery, cunning and bloodshed to which circumstances imperatively compelled me? My history shall not commence till the period when, free from all restraint, I can arouse this land from the sleep of ages.[4]

MUHAMMAD ALI'S SUCCESSORS

Abbās (1849–54), to whom the succession went after the death of Muhammad Ali, was a fanatic traditionalist with profound contempt for European civilisation. He closed the secular schools built by Muhammad Ali, dismissed the European advisors and reduced the army to a few thousands. He reigned for five years, and was then murdered by his own bodyguard.

Sa'īd (1854–63), who succeeded Abbās, was educated in Europe where he developed a profound admiration for western civilisation. During his reign, all restrictions against private enterprise were lifted; the ownership of land was restored to private hands; local industries and monopolies were abolished; imported goods entered the markets untaxed. Consequently, foreigners flocked to Egypt where they enjoyed wide privileges. Trade flourished and yielded enormous profits to the foreigners, though the position of the *fallāḥīn* hardly changed. Sa'īd's greatest contribution to the development of Egypt, however, was that he granted to Ferdinand de Lesseps the concession to build the Suez Canal. Work on the canal started in 1859 but Sa'īd did not live to see its completion.

Ismā'īl (1863–80) is a controversial figure in the modern history of Egypt. On the one hand, he could be regarded as the real executor of the policies and ambitions of his great ancestor in regard to the modernisation of Egypt. On the other hand, his passion for spending money threw his country into financial difficulties which culminated in the British occupation of 1882.

He endeavoured successfully to obtain from the Porte a number of firmans which secure the autonomy of Egypt. In the first place he succeeded in securing for his family the right to rule by direct succession, with inheritance passing from father to son. Secondly, the Porte bestowed on him the title of Khedive (ruler) which in effect implied that the Viceroy was elevated to the status of a sovereign in his own right. Thirdly, he obtained the right to have complete independence in all internal affairs: administrative, legislative and judicial.

Ismā'īl contributed immensely to the economic and educational development of Egypt. He developed the system of irrigation by the establishment of new canals. He encouraged trade by building new docks and harbours and extending the railway lines. He showed great interest in the development of national education; during his reign the number of state-supported schools rose from 185 to 4,817.

Ismā'īl's financial policies, however, were not based on sound economic planning. He depended on foreign loans which he could not repay and the result was state bankruptcy. His personal extravagance was displayed at the opening ceremonies of the Suez Canal in 1869. It is believed he spent more than one million pounds on entertainment to celebrate this grand event.

During the early period of his reign, Ismā'īl had no difficulty in getting loans. European bankers at the time regarded Egypt as one of the most promising fields for investment. The economic system was based on free enterprise, and the terms of transactions which Ismā'īl accepted were excessively profitable to the financiers. It was soon discovered, however, that there was no prospect of repayment, and so the creditors began to ask for their 'pound of flesh'. Britain and France intervened to protect the interests of their citizens. In 1878, they appointed a commission of two men, one British and the other French, to regulate Egyptian fiscal policy in a way that would make it possible for Egypt to repay her outstanding debts. It was not long, however, before the commissioners clashed with Ismā'īl, and he dismissed them. The European powers reacted by putting pressure on the Sultan to declare Ismā'īl deposed. The Sultan, thereupon, deposed him and appointed Tawfīq, Ismā'īl's oldest son, as his successor in June 1879. Under the pliant Tawfīq, Egypt was in fact ruled by the commissioners.

THE REVOLT OF AHMAD URABI

These events precipitated an army revolt under the leadership of Colonel Ahmad Urābi (Arabi). The revolt was not simply the adventure of an ambitious military man as some historians have claimed. It was in fact the expression of a 'broad-based' national movement against foreign domination. The army took the initiative because it was in the army that the grievances of the Egyptian people were most felt: the *fallāhīn* constituted the rank and file, while the higher ranks were reserved for foreigners, Turks, Circassians and Albanians. Furthermore, the language used in the service was Turkish.

Ahmad Urābi drew his support not only from the rank and file in the army but also from civilians in the towns and villages. As the son of a *fallāh*, he could claim to speak for the inarticulate Egyptian people in general and, in this respect, he was the first leader of this type in the history of modern Egypt. From then on, any person who aspired to gain political leadership had to speak for the *fallāhīn* in the villages of Egypt.

On 20 May 1880, Urābi and Colonel Abdul-'Āl presented a petition to the Khedive for a redress of grievances regarding pay and promotion for the rank and file of the Egyptian army. The Khedive summoned his Council of Ministers which decided that the two colonels should be arrested and tried by court martial. When the two colonels heard the news, they defiantly offered themselves for arrest. They were arrested, but before the court martial could decide their fate, a regiment of their soldiers arrived and carried them off in triumph.

Strengthened by this victory, Urābi put forward more demands, including constitutional reform, and the control of the national budget by the Chamber of Notables. The last demand was directed against Anglo-French control of the fiscal policy of Egypt. Britain and France objected strongly, and sent a joint note stating that the only authority they recognised was the Khedive. The Khedive, on the other hand, was powerless in the face of the immense popularity which Urābi enjoyed. Urābi was therefore appointed Minister of War, and another nationalist, Sāmī al-Barūdi, was appointed Prime Minister.

It was clear by then that the nationalists were in control. Britain and France intervened and arranged for a demonstration by their fleets before Alexandria. This action provoked the people of Alexandria, and during the violent disturbances the British Consul was injured, and a number of Europeans were killed. Then Urābi started fortifying Alexandria to prepare himself for the next show of power. The British, on the other hand, became anxious about the security of the Europeans in Egypt. Since France had recalled her fleet from Alexandria to deal with the revolt in Tunis, Britain had to act alone. On 11 July 1882, the British navy bombarded Alexandria. On 13 September, General Wolseley defeated Urābi's forces at the battle of al-Tal al-Kabīr. Two days later, Urābi himself was captured in Cairo. He was exiled to Ceylon where he remained until 1901 when he was allowed to return to Cairo.

BRITISH OCCUPATION

The British announced that their occupation of Egypt was only a temporary measure intended to put the finances of the country in order. They remained, however, for half a century. This was inevitable because, in the first place, Britain became more aware of the need to control the Suez Canal in order to secure her sea-route to India. Secondly, once she had assumed the responsibility for regulating the finances of Egypt, she was confronted by the formidable task of improving the material welfare of the inhabitants. Thus, Britain's imperial interests supported by the requirements of the country necessitated the extension of the period of occupation

Egypt, during this period (1882–1936), was in fact part of the British empire. The British Consul-General was virtually the ruler though, in theory, he possessed no more legal authority than any other Consul-General in Egypt. Under Sir Evelyn Baring (later the Earl of Cromer) as Consul-General from 1883 to 1907, the Khedive and his alternating ministeries were no more than puppets.

It must be acknowledged, however, that Egypt owes much to the reforms of Cromer's administration. His regime managed successfully to improve the lots of the *fallāhīn* who had laboured for many centuries under gross social injustive. Hitherto, it had been the general practice among Egyptian civil servants to practise flogging and other tortures in the collection of taxes. This practice was made unlawful and those found guilty of it were severely punished. Again, the *fallāhīn* had been required to clean out the canals before the annual flood of the Nile; a demand which constituted in effect forced labour. This practice was also abolished. In addition to these social reforms, the finances of the country were regulated, and the state revenue was substantially increased. The Aswan Dam, which was built between 1898 and 1902, promoted the cultivation of cotton—the crop which formed the backbone of the country's revenue.

It was unfortunate, however, that Cromer had far less interest in the questions of education than in economics. In the years between 1882 and 1908, the sums provided for education were less than half the costs of the Aswan Dam. This reluctance to promote education was explained by his successor, Lord Lloyd, when he said that Britain had no intention of imposing her culture on the indigenous culture. The foreign culture in Egypt, therefore, remained French which had been adopted by the upper classes since the expedition of Napoleon.

The story of the Egyptian national movement which culminated in the revolution of 1919, is outside the scope of this paper. Before the turn of the century, however, there were indications of resistance against alien rule. Khedive Abbās II (Hilmi) who came to the throne after the death of his father, Tawfīq, in 1892, made courageous attempts to free himself from the tutelage of Lord Cromer. But he suffered a series of humiliations which made him give up any interference in government affairs and confine himself to the administration of his estates. In 1894, Mustafa Kāmil, a middle-class lawyer who had studied in France, founded the 'Fatherland party' (al-Hizb al-Watanī) and sought to influence public opinion in Egypt and in Europe. But neither the Khedive nor Mustafa Kāmil found real popular support before the turn of the century. It was not until 1906 that the Egyptian people were aroused by an incident which shocked the whole nation. On 13 June 1906 some British officers were at a pigeon shoot in the village of Dinshawāi (Denshawi) and, in the course of their sport, a woman was shot and died. The angry villagers attacked the officers and killed one of them. On 28 June, Cromer had four of the accused villagers publicly hanged, and seventeen flogged and then sent to prison. This high-handed act aroused indignation not only in Egypt, but in Europe as well. In May 1907 Cromer retired, but the national movement was already at a high pitch. In December, Mustafa Kāmil convoked a national congress which was attended by 1,017 representatives from all over the country. The call, 'Egypt for the Egyptians' began.

THE EGYPTIAN REGIME IN THE SUDAN, 1821–81

The sixty years of Egyptian rule are still associated in the minds of the Sudanese with the memory of heavy taxation and the tortures applied in its collection. From the outset, the Egyptian Viceroy was determined that the Sudan should pay its way since it could not give the occupying country any substantial benefits. His representatives, therefore, tried after their different fashions to obtain the costs of their administration from taxation. The demands on the inhabitants became heavier when many civil servants in the Sudan spared no effort to enrich themselves during their tenures of office. Muhammad Ali and his successors frowned at these malpractices, but failed to curb the excesses of their representatives. The difficulty of transport and the size of the country made constant supervision from Egypt hard to undertake. Muhammad Ali, it is true, sent investigating officers to report on the behaviour of the civil servants in the Sudan, and on the strength of such reports, those suspected of corruption were relieved of their posts and their property confiscated. Nevertheless, corruption was never completely eradicated throughout the period of Egyptian rule.

It should be acknowledged, however, that it was during the time of the Egyptian rule that the foundations of the modern Sudan were laid. The administrative structure survived the tumultuous years of the *Mahdiyya* to be adopted *in toto* by the Anglo-Egyptian Condominium (1898–1956). The provincial boundaries and capitals that exist today go back to Egyptian times. The ranks in the army bear names adopted from Turko-Egyptian military tradition. The cultural and religious links which bind the Sudan to Egypt today have their origins in the period of Egyptian rule. Finally, the fervent call for the 'unity of the Nile valley', which finds support among a sizeable section of the Sudanese, looks back to the time when Egypt and the Sudan were one political unit.

THE MAHDIST REVOLT IN THE SUDAN

Mahdism as a popular belief is well known in Islam. During times of political upheaval or the degeneration of the religion, Muslims look forward to a saviour, similar to the expected Messiah of the Jews, who will come and 'fill the world with equity and justice after it has been filled with tyranny and oppression'. In 1881, Muhammad Ahmad b. Abdallāh assumed the office of the expected Mahdi and took upon himself the duty of restoring the faith and reorganising the state by force of arms. He defeated the government forces in a series of battles which culminated in the fall of Khartoum and the death of General Gordon in 1885.

The Mahdi's revolt was successful because it was not confined to one class or territorial group but spread throughout the country among people who had specific grievances against the Egyptian administration. There were three principal causes of discontent among the Sudanese people. First, the devastation of Shendi by the Daftarder in 1822 created bitter ill-feeling and inspired a general desire for revenge. Secondly, the inequitable system of taxation and the barbarous methods adopted in its collection had become an unbearable burden. Thirdly, the attempts of Khedive Ismā'īl to suppress the slave trade struck at an important source of wealth in the economy of the country.

On the other hand, conditions in Egypt at the time hindered the government from taking a decisive step to crush the Mahdists at the outset. Urābi's revolt and the British occupation turned the attention of the Egyptian government away from the Sudan to more immediate problems at home. Britain at first refused to be involved in the affairs of the Sudan. Gladstone was determined to limit the responsibilities of the British government to the internal problems of Egypt.

Thus, it was not long before the Mahdists controlled the greater part of the country. In January 1884 the Egyptian government, under pressure from Britain, decided to withdraw its troops from the Sudan and abandon the country to the Mahdists. General Gordon was sent to supervise the evacuation. In the meantime, the Mahdi marched from El-Obeid on his way to attack the capital, Khartoum. He arrived and besieged the town, but General Gordon refused to surrender. On 25 January 1885, the Mahdists attacked Khartoum and, in a couple of hours, the town fell to them. Gordon himself was killed on the staircase of his palace. Thus ended the Egyptian regime in the Sudan.

THE MAHDIST STATE, 1885–98

A few months after the fall of Khartoum, the Mahdi died at Omdurman after a short illness. His right-hand man, the Khalīfa Abdullāhi, succeeded him as the head of the Mahdist state. The Khalīfa's regime (1885–98) is frequently presented as an extreme example of tyranny and oppression. This is not altogether true. The reputation of the regime suffered greatly from the hostile propaganda that followed Gordon's death.[5] Public opinion in Britain, and elsewhere, regarded General Gordon as a martyr who died in an attempt to suppress the slave trade. The Khalīfa's faults were, therefore, exaggerated and his achievements ignored.

The Khalīfa's regime should be judged in the light of the circumstances that surrounded it. The Mahdi died shortly after the success of the revolt, and to the Khalīfa fell the more difficult task of the restoration of order and the consolidation of the new state. In the midst of internal anarchy and constant threat of external aggression, the Khalīfa succeeded in creating a workable administration and maintaining the independence of the Sudan for twelve years. In 1898, however, his regime was brought to an end by Anglo-Egyptian forces under the command of Kitchener.

NOTES

1   Quoted by H. Dodwell, *The Founder of Modern Egypt*, p. 20, 1931.
2   In his early correspondence after the conquest, Muhammad Ali urges his lieutenants to supply him with slaves at all cost! 'You are aware that the end of all our effort and this expense is to procure Negroes. Please show zeal in carrying out our wishes in this capital matter.'
3   According to the Shari'a law, Muslims are not to be enslaved.
4   Puckler-Muskau, *Egypt under Mehemet Ali*, Vol. I, p. 317; quoted by Dodwell, op. cit., p. 38.

5 A number of books which came into circulation before the re-conquest should be read with caution, e.g. F. R. Wingate, *Mahdism and the Egyptian Sudan* (1891); Fr. J. Ohrwalder, *Ten Years, Captivity in the Mahdi's Camp* (1892); R. C. Slatin, *Fire and Sword in the Sudan* (1896).

QUESTIONS FOR FURTHER STUDY AND DISCUSSION

1 Consider the contributions of Muhammad Ali to Modern Egypt.

2 Consider the causes, course and consequence of the Mahdist revolt against the Turko-Egyptian administration.

3 Describe the revolt of 'Urābi and the British occupation of Egypt.

4 Describe the course of Sudanese-Egyptian relations in the twentieth century.

SELECT BIBLIOGRAPHY

J. M. Ahmed, *The Intellectual Origins of Egyptian Nationalism*, O.U.P., 1960.

L. A. Fabunmi, *The Sudan in Anglo-Egyptian Relations*, Longmans, 1960.

Richard Hill, *Egypt in the Sudan, 1821–1881*, O.U.P., 1959.

P. M. Holt, *The Mahdist State in the Sudan, 1881–1898*, Clarendon Press, 1958.

—— *A Modern History of the Sudan*, Weidenfeld & Nicolson, 1961.

H. E. Hurst, *The Nile*, Constable, 1952, revised edition 1957.

A. B. Theobold, *The Mahdiya*, Longmans, 1959.

11   The Magrib in the Nineteenth Century

E. A. AYANDELE

BROADLY speaking, two administrative and political systems were to be found in the Magrib in the opening years of the nineteenth century. On the one hand was the independent Magrib el Aksa (Morocco), under the Sherifian dynasty of the Alawites or Filali, a dynasty founded in 1649 and still on the Moroccan throne. On the other, were the semi-independent administrations of the Regencies of Algeria, Tunisia and Libya, under the effete suzerainty of the Sultan of Turkey.

The political and administrative state of affairs at the beginning of the nineteenth century was as follows: Starting from the west to east is Morocco, a country in which the monarchy has for centuries been of the greatest significance. The monarchy came to be the institution on which Berber sentiments of nationality and solidarity focused, curiously enough through Islam. Before the Islamic invasion of the eighth century the Berber inhabitants of the Magrib had no form or emblem of unity. But when the majority of them had embraced Islam, they came to have a mystical reverence for the Prophet Muḥammad and all his descendants. By genealogical connection with the Prophet and the inheritance of *baraka,* the celestial unction which the Prophet was believed to possess in inexhaustible abundance, the Filali Sultan came to be venerated by the Moroccans. His person was sacred; he was the first of all Muslims, 'Lord of the Believers', the great Imam, Commander of the Faithful and the vicegerent of God on earth, whose faults should be excused and attributed to a divine inspiration which ordinary mortals were incapable of understanding.

The significance of the divinity that hedged the Sultan was that it provided him with the spiritual qualification with which he commanded the obedience of the entire Berber-Arab population of the country in specified circumstances. For politically the Berbers, particularly those of the Sanhaja, Masmuda and Zenata groups living in the Blad es Siba, the country of disobedience, were traditionally unsubmissive. They eschewed centralisation in any form and would not transfer their loyalty to any unit larger than the clan, except when the entire race was threatened by external aggressors. The Blad es Maknes Berbers, that is Berbers living in the country of submission, coterminous with the plains and coastal areas, however accepted the administrative and political overlordship of the Sultan as well.

In these circumstances the extent of the power of a Sultan depended on his ability and military power. And indeed only three monarchs in Moroccan history before 1800 ever succeeded

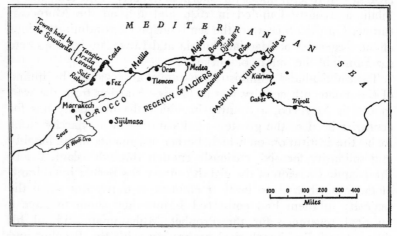

Fig. 11 The Magrib under Turkey.

in welding the various tribes into one. No nineteenth century Sultan succeeded in achieving this. Thus it is not surprising that Morocco's domestic history throughout the century saw the rebellion of one locality after another.

The situation in the rest of the Magrib was not happier and was perhaps less stable than in Morocco, in the absence of a monarchy of the Sherifian concept. Algeria was administered from Turkey, in whose orbit the territory had fallen since 1518. The Turkish administration was headed by the Dey, appointed by the Porte from among the soldiers quartered in the nine garrison towns in the country. He was expected to be advised by the Diwan or Council, composed principally of thirty Yiah Bashees (Colonels).

As in Turkish Egypt, the relations between the Diwan and the Dey were anything but cordial. An everlasting struggle for power by colonels seemed to characterise the Turkish administration. The Regency was divided into three administrative provinces: Western, Titan and Eastern, with headquarters respectively at Oran, Medea and Constantine. Outside the administrative and garrison towns, Turkish ascendancy in Algeria existed more in theory than in practice. The Berber tribal groups, fanatical lovers of their independence, were allowed to rule themselves and many of them found refuge in the physically difficult Aures, Kabylia and other mountains. Whatever influence the Turkish officials, who are said to have numbered in all about 20,000, had over the country was owed to their tactics of aiding the stronger factions among the Berbers against the weaker factions in the eternal inter-clan warfare characteristic of the people.

Tunisia, like Algeria, had been a beylik of the Ottoman administration since the end of the sixteenth century. But in 1705 Husain ibn 'Ali Agha, a jannisary of Cretan origin, usurped the supreme authority and founded the Husseinic dynasty which ruled over the country until 1957. Unlike the Algerian Deys, the Husseinic dynasty was hereditary and had some root in the sentiment of the Berbers. For in the eighteenth century the Husseinic Deys acquired Berber blood and established genealogical connection with the Hafsid dynasty, the purely Berber dynasty which had ruled Tunisia from the thirteenth to the fifteenth century. The Husseinic dynasty attempted to enforce the authority of the central administration against the centrifugal forces of tribal life.

Libya was in 1800 being administered by Yusuf, the most powerful member of the Karamanli dynasty which had established itself independent of the Turks in 1711. This dynasty of Coloughis remained on the throne till 1835. And yet it was during Yusuf's reign, 1795–1832, that revolt followed revolt in a country where the ethnic and social structure gave rise to localised parochialism.

However, internal political weakness and the fissiparous tendencies in the Magrib notwithstanding, all the governments were sovereign *vis-à-vis* the European powers. For centuries the 'Barbary corsairs' and European countries had indulged in mutually beneficial piracy on the Mediterranean waters and the former had established their superiority over the Europeans. They captured Europeans as slaves, a situation that contrasted with that in the Atlantic seaboard of West Africa; they compelled European slaves to erect their palaces, till their land and row their galleys. The European powers recognised the sovereignty of the Magrib governments. This sovereignty was more than just paper recognition.

ALGERIA

The sovereignty being exercised over their nationals by the Magrib rulers was unpalatable to the European and American powers. From 1800 onwards they began to undermine the sovereignty of the rulers either by refusing to pay 'exactions', or by bombarding their coast, or by supporting rival candidates to the thrones. This undermining of the sovereignty of the Magrib rulers by the European powers was a manifestation of European economic imperialism in Mediterranean Africa, a factor of decisive importance in North African history throughout the nineteenth century. It manifested itself on a major scale in the French attack on Algeria in 1830, an event that marked a turning point in North African history. Traditionally, particularly in the economic sphere, Algeria and France were on friendly terms. Their friendship foundered over the joint economic interests of two influential Jews and some Frenchmen in Algeria, and over the insulting behaviour of Deval, the French consul, a man of questionable character. As in Morocco and other parts of the Magrib, the Jews were financiers and traders of considerable importance in Algeria. Towards the end of the eighteenth century two Jews, Bacri and Busnach, had attempted to monopolise all Algeria's export trade. The Dey of Algeria was involved in this business in a manner which is still obscure, but it is clear that he felt himself cheated over a debt he owed to the two Jews. Tension was already high before the celebrated meeting which took place between Deval and the Dey in April 1827. The latter struck the French consul with his fly-whisk because, according to the Dey, Deval had said in an insulting manner that the Dey could not expect the French government to reply to his letters, and then added derogatory remarks about Islam.

The fly-whisk incident was no more than an occasion for the French attack and occupation of Algeria, for worse treatment had been meted out to Europeans continually for three centuries.

Nor can the French declaration that the invasion was undertaken to suppress 'piracy' be taken seriously, for 'piracy' had already been suppressed by many bombardments of Algiers before 1830 and the naval superiority of the Europeans. More to the point was the fact that Charles X, the last of the Restoration Bourbons, wished to turn the Algerian issue to advantage to revive the prestige of France. He sent a fleet that blockaded Algiers for there years although General Bourmont's victory of July 1830 over Hussein was too late to influence the elections which overthrew him.

The French invasion of Algeria had many motives. There was an imperialistic intention. This intention was not declared by the French immediately, for fear of British reaction. Therefore Polignac, the French Prime Minister, wished Muhammad Ali of Egypt to occupy Tripoli and Tunis and punish Algeria. In this enterprise the French were to aid the Egyptian Pasha with a naval fleet and financial encouragement. But Britain persuaded Muhammad Ali to refrain from such an adventure and advised the Sultan of Turkey to punish the Pasha, should he venture westwards. Later, when Polignac advised a show of strength, he indicated that he had been dreaming of a scheme 'to establish the influence of France on the African shores of the Mediterranean and right into the heart of Asia'. The Minister of War, General Gerard, justified the conquest of Algeria by the 'need to open up a vast outlet for our surplus population and for our manufactured products in exchange for other products, foreign to our soil and to our climate'. Louis Phillippe, who came to power only a few weeks after the expedition landed near Algiers, declared that it was France's intention to found 'an important colony' in Algeria.

The Berbers reacted sharply and swiftly against the French, who had expected that the Berbers would see in them, the French, liberators from the alien rule of the Turks. But the Berbers looked upon the French as infidels on whom a Jihād must be proclaimed. The man around whom Berber nationalism and resistance to the French invasion revolved was Abdel Kader. The almost universal support given to this man in Algeria from 1832 to 1847, and the continuation of resistance to the French by the Berbers after his surrender to them, were a clear testimony to the fact that, in a sense, Algeria was a living political entity before the advent of the French. The view often expressed by French writers that the

Algerian nation was exclusively the creation of the French is not substantiated by facts.

Abdel Kader is one of the few African personalities of the nineteenth century whose qualities and career have attracted the attention of foreign biographers. The latter portray the Algerian Sultan as a patriot, a soldier, a religious leader, a statesman, an administrator, a learned man and a diplomat—all rolled into one. It is essential to note that the resistance he organised against the French forced the latter to sign two treaties with him in 1834 and 1837. When it became convenient for the French to break these treaties they did so. Morocco was punished for giving aid to the Algerian Sultan, whilst French military power compelled Tunisia to be 'neutral'. At last French forces became overwhelming and they discovered the Sultan's military tactics of burying granaries underneath the ground; in the face of fire and sword he was deserted, except by a small band of faithful followers. In 1847 he voluntarily surrendered himself to the French, after the French had given a solemn undertaking that they would take him to a Muslim country, a pledge they did not honour.

Punishment of the most brutal kind was meted out to the Berbers. Animals and land were seized, fines were imposed, many people were executed, others were deported and many were transferred to France as hostages. War was waged on plantations and on trees; several thousand olive trees were destroyed, hundred of villages were burned down and friendly tribes had their throats cut. On the whole, the French occupation of Algeria proved to be a lucrative venture. The Berbers were made to pay the cost of subjugating them and the French made a net gain of seven million francs on the operation.

The French invasion of Algeria was a turning point in the history of the Algerian Berbers and it struck terror into the rulers of the other parts of the Magrib. Infidels began to settle in the best parts of their country from which they themselves had either been forcibly removed or bought out by questionable means. The consequences to the natives of this influx of Europeans into Algeria were tremendous and far-reaching. The Berbers were systematically deprived of their lands, to the tune of eight to nine million hectares, the equivalent of four-fifths of the area available for cultivation in the Tell and on the High Plateaux. French laws began to replace traditional laws and the Berbers were not taken into partnership in the administration of a territory which was believed by the French to be an integral part of France.

The Algerian Berbers' reaction to the repressive policy of Frenchification was one of sullen resignation to their fate. Their past was being uprooted, their present was miserable and their future bleak. They had no love for French rule; they despaired; disaffection began to seethe among them. The eloquent silence of the masses was misconstrued by the French as evidence of satis-faction with their rule, and in later days when the effendiya (educated Africans) launched the nationalist movement the French argued that these nationalists did not represent the wishes and aspirations of the apparently apathetic majority. They needed the events of 1954 to 1962 to show them the explosive cumulative bitterness of the Algerian masses to their rule.

The French invasion and occupation of Algeria had effects on North Africa as a whole and on the Magrib in particular. The rest of the Magrib read the writing on the wall. It became clear that the occupation of the rest of Mediterranean Africa by the European powers was only a matter of time. European imperialism had evidently come to stay. What postponed the evil day for many of the North African states was the mutual jealousy arising out of the conflicting interests of the various European powers who had a stake in the appropriation of this part of the continent. For many decades the interest of one power cancelled out that of the other, until they agreed among themselves on how to share the spoils. But it is important to note that many of the African rulers discerned the conflict of interests of the European powers and did their best to play one power against the other, thereby postponing an inevitable doom; Morocco and Tunisia are excellent illustrations of this.

MOROCCO

In Morocco the imperial interests of Britain, France and Spain converged. For Britain Morocco was of the highest strategic value. The northern coast, and especially that part of it forming the southern shore of the straits of Gibraltar, guarded the entrance to the Mediterranean. British interests in Greece, the rise of Muham-mad Ali and French activities in other parts of Mediterranean Africa enhanced the importance of Morocco to the British. British trade with Morocco was also substantial. To France, too, Morocco was of first-class interest, particularly after the Algerian invasion. France feared that Morocco might become the springboard for attacks on Algeria by 'rebels', or a means of fomenting rebellion by leaders of the Moroccan tarīqas (religious brotherhoods). Moreover, France feared that any other European power who occupied Morocco might easily elbow her out of the Sahara and restrict her programme of expansion in the interior. Spain's interest in Morocco, of course, dated back to the fifteenth century. To all these powers Morocco was potentially a promising territory for financial investment. The rivalries of all three became the strength of the Sultan of Morocco, ensuring the country's independence until the French and British concluded the agreement of 1904 which gave to the former a free hand to annex the territory.

Sultan Abdel Rahman's (1822–59) weakness and domestic problems were exploited to the full by the European powers. In 1828 the British blockaded Tangier; the following year the Austrians bombarded Arzila and Tittawin. For the moral and military help the Moroccans were giving to Abdel Kader, the French bombarded Mogador and Tangier. The Moroccan army was defeated in the battle of Isly in 1845 and Morocco withdrew all support from the Algerian Berbers.

The Battle of Isly strained Franco-Moroccan relations. In 1851 the French bombarded the port of Sale. In 1859, on the accession of Sidi Mohammed IV, Spain declared war on the Sultan, after a dispute over the Spanish fortification of Melilla. With an army estimated at 30,000, Spain took Tetuan and was only prevented from advancing into the heart of Morocco by British intervention. A convention was signed in 1860 by which more territory around Melilla was ceded to Spain and the latter was given the right to punish any Berber attackers on Melilla with impunity; Morocco was also asked to pay an indemnity of four million pounds. This sum was obtained from the territory's customs receipts until the 'eighties. A 'most-favoured nation' convention was also signed, according to which no trading privileges were to be granted to other powers unless they were granted to Spain as well. The commercial privileges forced on Morocco by Spain opened the way to France and Britain to extract similar demands.

Although in 1865 Moroccan goods were allowed to go to French Algeria customs-free, France remained the greatest danger to

Morocco. During the 1871 rebellion of Berbers against the French in Algeria, French forces pursued some of the rebels into Morocco.

The successor to the Sherifian throne in 1873, El Hassan III, was a dignified, well-respected strong man who attempted to restore order and unity in the country. He was a moderniser who carried out some administrative and judicial reforms. He appealed to Pan-Islamism and renewed diplomatic relations with the Sultan of Constantinople. But he could not put his house in order; the situation was beyond repair. European influence was strongly entrenched in Morocco and could not be removed as easily as he wished. All he could do was to play one power against another. He was fortunate in reigning at a time when the French were otherwise occupied. There was reconstruction to be effected in France; Egypt and Tunisia demanded greater immediate attention, and it was not until the 'nineties that France could concentrate on the Moroccan affair in a forceful fashion. In these years, too, Anglo-Moroccan relations improved, and in return for commercial concessions Morocco looked toward Britain to safeguard Morocco's interests against the intrigues of other powers. Britain was given monopoly of the trade in merino wool and the opportunity to exploit Moroccan iron and phosphates. Morocco also imported largely from Britain. Nonetheless, Spain's commercial interests increased during the period, and Germany and Belgium entered the commerce of the territory in the last decade of the century.

Throughout his reign Hassan had to deal with internal problems. It took him ten years to consolidate his kingdom and to obtain undisputed possession of the territory. The main consequence of his constant involvement in the pacification of his country was that he did not have the time to carry out administrative, economic and military reforms, such as those carried out by Muhammad Ali for the modernisation of Egypt. He tried to introduce an army trained by Europeans, but Arab aversion to professional soldiery led to the failure of the scheme. Many who received arms from him deserted to the dissident tribes and fought against him.

It may be asked why, in spite of his strong character, Hassan did not obtain the co-operation of his people. In the latter's view all the nineteenth century Sultans had committed a heinous crime by associating themselves with Europeans. For instance, Abdel Rahman had betrayed the interests of the country by not supporting Abdel Kader at all hazards. The masses came to believe that their Sultans were selling their country to rapacious infidels. Hence in 1878 and 1887 there were Berber demonstrations against Hassan when foreign men-of-war in the ports demonstrated, ostensibly to protect their nationals. What could this be, asked the Berbers, but a combined design on their independence?

In 1894 Hassan died and was succeeded by Abdel Aziz, the opposite of his immediate predecessor. He was an impotent, timid and idealistic ruler. Nor was he a powerful religious dignitary. His chief mistake, however, was that he allowed himself, like Sa'īd and Ismā'īl of Egypt and Muhammad es Sadek of Tunisia, to be unduly fascinated by European gadgets. He spent a great deal of money on lawn-mowers, cameras, cigarette-lighters, musical boxes, silk dresses and ostrich-feathered Parisian hats. His court came to be known as the court of amusements and he earned the name of 'the mad sultan', believed to have been bewitched by foreigners. The significance of his extravagance was that he was soon compelled to do what other rulers in North Africa had done: borrow. This frequently became the pretext on which European powers occupied territory. In 1900 the establishment of French rule over Morocco was only a question of time.

TUNISIA

The Husseinic Dey of Tunisia's first reaction to the French attack on Algeria was one of delight, partly because the Dey of Algiers was his traditional enemy and partly because he felt that by allying with France the latter would allow him to annex Constantine, the eastern part of Algeria. In fact at one time it seemed that the French toyed with the idea of handing over the administration of Algeria to a Husseinic prince. More and more Tunisia and France drew together, as the British, who deprecated growing French influence in Tunisia, began to put pressure on the Sultan of Turkey to reassert his claims over Tunisia. During the reign of Ahmed Dey, 1835–55, French influence in Tunisia increased considerably. In 1842 the Dey was successfully persuaded to abolish the slave trade. In 1846 he went to Paris on a state visit and was received with great pomp. The conversations he held with French officials dealt with the necessity for reforms in his country. The French government asked him to abolish the disabilities under which the Jews were suffering and to grant concessions to Roman Catholic schools in Tunisia. The Dey acceded to all these requests in an attempt to please the French, whose support he felt he needed for the maintenance of his independence against the Turkish threat.

Ahmed Dey also decided to turn moderniser in order to prevent annexation of his country by European powers on a pretext of his country's 'backwardness'. Therefore, like Muhammad Ali of Egypt, the Dey attempted to modernise the army and the navy and he spent not less than two-thirds of the country's revenue on defence alone. Like Ali of Egypt, too, aware of the political implications of borrowing, he kept Tunisia solvent and was cautious in yielding to European pressure for social and constitutional reforms. At his death in 1855 he left in the treasury 120 million francs.

His successor Muhammad es Sadek, 'the Magnificent', was comparable to Ismā'īl Pasha of Egypt. He dissipated the Tunisian revenue on beautiful Georgian, Turkish and Circassian slave girls, leaving only a small surplus to be swallowed up by French engineers in bringing pure water to Tunis over the aqueduct of Adrian. On 24 October 1855, Muhammad es Sadek signed his first convention with France concerning the construction of electric telegraph communications in Tunisia. By 1862 the Treasury was empty, and in May 1863 a substantial loan was negotiated in Paris from Messrs Oppenheim and Erlanger. The terms imposed by this loan were so onerous that the Dey only received in cash one-seventh of the sum. By 1869 the financial condition of the country had become so desperate that an international commission was established to consolidate the debt and arrange for its servicing. On this commission, British French and Italian interests were represented though the greater part of the debt was in the hands of the French creditors.

In the meantime European commercial and financial interests were scoring one success after another. The British held a concession for an important railway from the city of Tunis to Goletta. After 1870 the Italians joined in the scramble for opportunities and soon began to outbid their British and French rivals. In 1870 the Dey granted an Italian agricultural company an

14

estate at Jedeida, while a French citizen, the Comte de Saucy, was put in possession of the fruitful domain of Sidi Tabet. The latter concession was destined to provide one of the excuses for the French occupation of Tunisia in 1881.

The Dey's position in Tunisia became very weak as a result of his prodigality. The man who acted as Prime Minister from 1837 to 1873, Mustapha Khazinda, was behind the foreign loans; he was not only corrupt but he also encouraged the Dey to rule despotically. Such rule was against European interests. For only a narrow sea separates this territory from Sicily, and Europeans feared that a despotic ruler in Tunisia identified with Constantinople could easily make Tunisia become a part of the Eastern Question. If this were to happen, it was feared, the balance of sea-power would be overturned by any power that had Tunisia on its side. For many years, therefore, the Europeans were incessant in pressing the Dey to liberalise the constitution of his country. In 1857 and 1861 the Dey made abortive attempts at constitutional reforms.

By 1871 the Dey began to find French relations irksome and to feel that Tunisia was being milked by the French like a cow. Against the wishes of the French, therefore, the Dey decided to cultivate the goodwill of the Sultan of Constantinople. To this end an imperial firman was issued by the Sublime Porte, declaring Muhammad es Sadek Pasha vizir of Tunisia and conferring upon him 'the right of hereditary succession', renouncing the annual tributes Tunisia had been obliged to pay for centuries and binding Tunisia to give positive support to Turkey should she be involved in war with any other power. Furthermore the Dey alienated the French by flatly refusing to entertain Ferdinand de Lesseps' suggestion of an 'inland sea', presumably a canal, in Tunisia. Finally, in 1880 the Dey refused the French harbour concessions at Goletta.

France was enraged by these events and began to look for pretexts to justify the occupation she had been entertaining for a long time. Up till 1878 it was British opposition that had prevented France from declaring her suzerainty over Tunisia. In this year, however, the British gave the French a blank cheque in Tunisia, in return for French recognition of British occupation of Cyprus. At the Congress of Berlin in which Britain gave the French a free hand, Bismarck was also favourably disposed towards a French occupation of Tunisia, hoping thereby to draw France's attention away from Alsace Lorraine which had been annexed by Germany in 1870.

The only remaining formidable opponent of France over Tunisia was Italy. Tunisian friendliness towards Italy, which Tunisia entertained as a counterpoise to the dangerous imperialist aspirations of the French, made the French decide to occupy Tunisia in 1880. In this year the Dey was asked to sign a Protectorate treaty, a proposal which he spurned. A pretext for military action was found in a raid on the Algerian frontier by the Krumirs in March 1881. There was nothing unusual about these raids. Indeed it is said that there had been over 2,000 of them between 1870 and 1881. In 1879, the French also alleged, the Krumirs had provided the Berber rebels in the Aures with ammunition. Moreover, the French liked to believe that the Pan-Islamic movement in North Africa (including the Colonel Urābi 'rebellion' in Egypt, the Mahdi movement in the Sudan, the massacre of Flatters, a French colonel, in the desert, and the insurrections of South Oran) was most active in Tunisia and that although it was directed against the Christian powers of Europe in general, it was 'specially' directed against France. This Muslim fanaticism, the French contended, endangered the lives of French nationals in Tunisia and demanded intervention.

After a 'military promenade' the Dey surrendered in May and signed the Treaty of Bardo which established what amounted to a French Protectorate over Tunisia. By the articles of this treaty, France was to control Tunisian foreign policy. By the Treaty of Marza, signed in 1883, the French established control over the internal affairs of the country as well, including finance and the judiciary.

The French occupation of Tunisia was similar to the British occupation of Egypt in many ways. The relationship between the Dey and the Resident-General was similar to that between the Consul-General and the Khedive in Egypt. The civil controllers in Tunisia, who supervised the qadis and shaikhs in the interior, were the counterparts of British muffatash in Egypt. There was, however, a basic difference. The Dey appointed his ministers who had limited functions, while side by side were departments under the Resident-General. In Egypt the Consul-General appointed ministers.

But the treaties of Bardo and Marza are not a true guide to the power actually wielded by the French. Tunisian independence was really a fiction. The resultant protectorate was one in which the Deylical authority was gradually usurped by the French administrators. Armed opposition to the presence of the French continued into the last years of the nineteenth century, by which time the Ottoman Sultan finally relinquished his sovereignty over Tunisia.

LIBYA

In comparison with other parts of the Magrib, Libya was much less subject to the threat of European imperialism in the nineteenth century, but this came all the same—from Turkey. In 1835, after intrigues against the Karamanli dynasty by the French and British, Turkey reoccupied Libya. But this second occupation of the country by Turkey, like the first, was not accompanied by well-organised administration. Thus a tarīqa, or religious brotherhood, came to exercise the greatest influence in the interior of Libya.

In Islamic history religious brotherhoods have been of considerable influence, assuming varying complexions in different parts of the world at varying points of time. Although essentially religious and spiritual in their purpose, tarīqas often took on a political complexion particularly when threatened by the infidels. In Morocco, for instance, the tarīqa's zawiyas, or lodges, were among the focal points of Moroccan patriotism and resistance to the Spanish and Portuguese in the fifteenth and sixteenth centuries. In Arabia in the nineteenth century the Wahābbis rebelled against Constantinople and for a time founded their own state. And in the last years of the nineteenth century until 1932, the Sanusiya, the Libyan brotherhood, was anti-French and anti-Italian.

The tarīqa's zawiyas, besides being centres of religious activities, often served as well as schools, infirmaries and charitable institutions, and might be compared with the monasteries of Mediaeval Europe. But it is the political implications of the religious brotherhoods that concern us in this chapter. For many important religious and political figures in Islamic Africa were influenced by one of the brotherhoods. Usuman dan Fodio of the Nigerian Fulani jihād, for instance, was a member of the Quadariya brotherhood and the Mahdi of the Sudan was influenced by the Sammaniya.

The Sanusiya tarīqa was named after the founder, Sayyid Muhammad bin 'Ali al-Sanusi, the Grand Sanusi. He was born in Algeria about 1787 into a distinguished family of sherifs. After a long period of contemplation and learning, the Grand Sanusi established his Order at Mount Abu Qubais Mekka in 1837. In 1841 he left the Hijaz for North Africa, with his disciples. In 1842 he reached Libya and the following year he established the Mother Lodge of the Order at al-Baida on the central Cyrenaican plateau. In 1856 he made Jaghbub, one hundred and sixty kilometres from the coast, his headquarters. This place became the centre of the Order and the seat of an Islamic University, second in Africa only to Al-Azhar. It was chosen because it had certain political advantages. In this oasis the Grand Sanusi gathered over three hundred learned men. Under his personal supervision and that of his disciples, far from worldly distractions, the Grand Sanusi was able to train the future leaders of the Order. In 1859 he was succeeded by his eldest son, al-Sayyid Muhammad al-Mahdi, after a period of Regency administration. It was under al-Mahdi that the Order extended into the Sahara and the Sudan. In 1895 he moved its headquarters to Kufra. The choice of this place was due partly to its strategic location with regard to Libyan oases and routes, partly because of the rise of the Mahdi in the Sudan, and partly because of the military and political activities of the French nearer the coast.

It must be emphasised that the Sanusiya Order, particularly in its early years, was predominantly a missionary organisation. It aimed not only at reviving Islam and infusing it with spirit, but at bringing Islam within the reach of people who had not known it. And until the last years of the century the Sanusi refused to be drawn into the vortex of European conflict with Muslim states. Hence, although the Sanusiya co-operated with the Turks in the administration of Libya, the Sanusi family and the Brothers of the Order disapproved of their way of life. They resisted Turkish demands for assistance in the war against Russia (1876–8); they refused the aid asked for by Urābi in Egypt in 1882; and by the Sudanese, in 1883, against the British. Sayyid al-Mahdi likewise rejected diplomatic overtures by the Italians and Germans. It was not until the French invaded its Saharan territories and destroyed its religious houses, and when later the Italians, also without provocation, did the same in Cyrenaica, that the Order resisted European imperialism with arms.

But within Libya itself the Grand Sanusi and his successors could not escape exercising political authority over the peoples. The almost mass acceptance of the Order by the Bedouins was due mainly to political and religious reasons. By virtue of the baraka which the Grand Sanusi was believed to possess in great profusion, he became a centripetal force welding the factious tribal groups together, as did the Sherifian Sultans of Morocco. The Grand Sanusi and his band of followers were mainly foreigners. They therefore stood outside the tribal system, and were not involved in the traditional loyalties and feuds inherent in Bedouin society. For the missionary organisation of the Sanusiya was separate from the tribal system, and, by centring it in the distant oasis of Jaghbub, the Grand Sanusi prevented it from becoming identified with any one tribe or section of the country, as it might have become had it been centred in Cyrenaica, where the tarīqa was strongest. Also many of his immediate lieutenants, the shaikhs, came from outside: the Dardafi and Ismaili families came from Tripolitania, the Ghumari family from Morocco, the 'Ammur, Bu Jibali and Khattab families from Algeria and so on.

Moreover the tribal groups in the country were made to believe that the Order belonged to them. To this end the distribution of the lodges was based on tribal sections. These lodges came to be regarded as tribal institutions. But each lodge also came to be a cult centre. The tribes of Cyrenaica became, through the Order, linked from above in a common, if loose, organisation under a single sacred head. National sentiment became strong, particularly in face of outside interference by the Turks, and later by the Italians, against whom all the tribes had common hostility. Thus a loose federation of tribes was turned into a nation.

The tarīqa succeeded in establishing peace among traditionally warring tribes. It established peace between the Tibu and the Bedouin Arabs in the north and the Tibu and Uled Sliman in the south, thus rendering the Tripoli-Fezzan-Wadai trans-Saharan route safe. Hussein Bey, an Egyptian Oxford graduate who travelled along the route in 1923, met some Bedouins who told him that in the days of al-Mahdi, a woman could walk from Berea in Cyrenaica to Wadai unmolested. 'There can be no doubt', he wrote, 'that the influence of the Senussi brotherhood upon the lives of the people of that region is good. The ikhwan (teachers) of the Senussi are not only teachers of the people both in the field of religion and of general knowledge, but judges and intermediaries both between man and man, and between tribe and tribe. . . . The importance of these aspects of the Senussi rule in maintaining the tranquillity and well-being of the people of the Libyan desert can scarcely be over-estimated.'

Economically the Order took part in the cultivation of land. Like the Christian Church in mediaeval times the tariqa was endowed with lands. The Sanusi were not mendicants, but they tilled their estates, controlled the trade of their territory and collected gifts. By 1911 the total lands of the Order were more than 200,000 hectares, somewhere in the neighbourhood of half a million acres. Moreover, the zawiyas of the Order, usually built along the trans-Saharan route, served as hotels for pilgrims and traders. Many of the shaikhs of these lodges, Dr Boahen says, promoted 'great caravans themselves and gave every stimulus to the trade'.

The ideology of nationality and the feeling of oneness, which the Sanusiya tariqa infused into the inhabitants of Libya, assumed a military complexion at the turn of the century when the French attacked the Order, and when the Italians occupied Libya in 1911. The brunt of the defence fell on the Head of the Order, Sayyid Ahmad ash-Sharif. When, later, the Head of the Order, after long-drawn negotiations with the Italian and British governments, concluded in 1920 the Treaty of ar-Rajma, he naturally became the head of the state, recognised by his people as their spokesman and ruler, and acknowledged by the two European powers concerned as such. After the Italians had destroyed the zawiyas they discovered that the Libyans were deeply attached to the tariqa, and in an attempt to appease the people the Italian administration rebuilt some of them. The importance of the Sanusiya tariqa until modern times is clear from the fact that Libya has become a monarchy under a descendant of the Grand Sanusi, Mohammed Idris, now King Idris I of Libya.

QUESTIONS FOR FURTHER STUDY
AND DISCUSSION

1 Describe and assess the achievements of: (*a*) Abdel Kader of Algeria; (*b*) Muhammad Ali of Egypt.

2 Why did France attack Algeria in 1830 and with what consequences for North Africa?

3 Why has the Monarchy been the central institution in Moroccan history?

4 Account for the decline of the trans-Saharan trade routes in the nineteenth century.

SELECT BIBLIOGRAPHY

N. Barbour (ed.), *A Survey of North West Africa*, O.U.P., 1959.

W. Blunt, *Desert Hawk: Abdel Kader and the French Conquest of Algeria*, Methuen, 1947.

Evans Pritchard, *The Sanusi of Cyrenaica*, O.U.P., 1949.

S. H. Roberts, *History of French Colonial Policy* (first published in 1929 by P. S. King), Frank Cass, 1963.

Charles-Andre Julien, *L'Afrique du Nord en Marche*, Julliard, Paris, 1952.

F. H. Mellor, *Morocco Awakes*, Methuen, 1939.

J. Soames, *The Coast of Barbary*, Cape, 1938.

Encyclopaedia of Islam, Luzac & Co. Ltd.

12 Nationalist Movements in North Africa and the Achievement of Independence in the Twentieth Century

E. A. AYANDELE

ALTHOUGH for over a century Egypt has been the spearhead of nationalism in North Africa, nationalistic manifestations appeared there latest, in the opening decades of the nineteenth century. The Berbers of the Magrib had been for centuries an intensely fierce people, aware of their racial and national identity. This was why they had refused to embrace the Roman Catholic faith during the period of Roman rule, until a Berber brand of Christianity, Donatism, was evolved. This was also why they would accept only Islam. For three centuries, from the eighth to the eleventh century, the Berber Muslims organised a racial and national resistance against Arabisation and the political designs of the Arab invaders, through the Kharijite movement.

And yet throughout the nineteenth century Egypt was the centre of nationalism in Mediterranean Africa, a primacy which she retained by being the first to achieve independence and by becoming, until a few years ago, the sanctuary and inspiration of nationalist leaders from the rest of North Africa. This unique position enjoyed by Egypt has been due to several factors among which may be mentioned her geographical situation and rapid economic development, the concentration of European interests in the territory and early manifestation of European technological development; all of which were much less in evidence in the rest of North Africa. Additional factors were the careers of Muhammad Ali and Ismā'īl Pasha, which led to the granting of a great measure of independence to Egypt, at a time when the rest of Mediterranean Africa, except Morocco, lost its independence.

The first vigorous exposition of Egyptian nationalism followed in the wake of the establishment of a parliamentary system of government by Khedive Ismā'īl in 1866, when he created the Assembly of Delegates. By 1879 the Assembly had begun to win the initiative. In no other part of Mediterranean Africa was any attempt at a parliamentary system of government made in the nineteenth century. In Tunisia the constitutional proposals of 1857 and 1861 remained mere paper declarations.

Other factors strengthened the nationalist movement in Egypt, sometimes with effects on other parts of North Africa. Of great importance was the intellectual ferment and rationalist modernisation programme, along Islamic lines, associated with Djamal al-Din al-Afghani and Muhammad Abdu of Egypt. It is to these two Muslim scholars that the origins of Pan-Islamism, in the modern sense, should be credited. The substance of their teaching, which found reception throughout all North Africa, was that Muslim countries should imitate European states in accepting the implications of the scientific revolution, and that this could be done without compromising any of the basic tenets of Islam. But Muslims should reject the boulevard civilisation of the infidels which they said was causing moral degeneration among Muslims all over the world. These teachings, and the idea that they could be implemented only within the framework of a parliamentary system of government, were echoed in the Salafiya movement in Morocco and infected the al-Hadirah group in Tunisia, the founders of the Ibn Khaldun Institute. An element in the teachings of these 'Modernists' was the necessity for Muslims to present a united front against the infidels. The Pan-Arab element was later on, in the third decade of this century, added to this stock of ideas by Shaikh Arslan, a rich man who, living in Geneva, guided the publication of *La Arab Natione*, which was circulated in North Africa, and established close working relations with many of the North African nationalists.

The significance of the return-to-pure-Islam doctrine, side by side with modernisation, lies in the fact that Islam throughout North Africa became the foundation upon which the nationalists had to build their ideology. All the nationalists, including Frenchified *evolués* of the Ferhat Abbas type, rejected the idea of a secular state. This was very important. The cause of Islam became the slogan with which nationalists rallied the masses to their support against the religious, cultural and political threats of the European infidels.

In fact, throughout North Africa specific acts of the colonial powers were given religious interpretations. In Egypt there was the declaration of the Himaya, Protectorate, over the country at the outbreak of the First World War. This word for Protectorate was seen in Quranic terms. According to the Quran it was Christians who ought to be 'protected' by the faithful, but the British 'unbelievers' now arrogated to themselves the right to 'protect' the believers! In Morocco there was the notorious Berber Dahir of 1930 by which the French deliberately sought to de-Islamise the judiciary among the Berbers, under the illusion that the latter had never wanted to embrace Islam, but had been forced to profess it by the Arab elements of the Moroccan population. Of course the French discovered that they had only stirred the hornet's nest, to the advantage of the effendiya (educated Africans) who capitalised on the Muslim ardour of the Berbers that had been aroused. In Tunisia the nationalist movement was up to 1914 almost religious in its complexion, whilst in Algeria a religious body, the Society of the Reforming Ulema, founded in 1931, became an arm of the nationalist movement.

EGYPT

The nationalist movement in Egypt gathered momentum as a result of several factors; there was the Urābi movement against the alien Turks and the intruding Europeans. It is worth noting that this pure Egyptian, Colonel Urābi, was the first nationalist leader of note to express the view that republicanism was the best form of constitution for Egypt. Then, from the Egyptian viewpoint, there was the unnecessary and unjustifiable occupation of their country by Britain, and the prolonged stay by the British became extremely irritating to the nationalists; the latter also deplored the way the British bolstered up the alien Turkish and Circassian elements and the corrupt Khedival authority in the administration of the country. The Egyptians who had seen the fallāh Colonel Urābi purge these oppressors, 'devoid of the morality essential to governing' (Milner), from the army and administration, regarded their reinstatement by the British as an act of disservice to Egypt.

As a consequence of the British retaining these aliens in power there developed a progressively widening gap between the Khedive and the alien elements on the one hand, and the radical effendiya, mostly Egyptian by blood, on the other. It was this irreconcilable difference, social, mental and political, that led ultimately to the abolition of the monarchy in Egypt. The difference was reflected in the political parties that emerged in the first decade of this century. The aristocrats, landowners, were mainly represented in the Umma Party, the 'constitutionalists', who took office under the British up to 1914.

Their main demand was that the Khedive, who was in a sense associated with them, should rule constitutionally. On the whole, they had confidence in Britain and wished to co-operate with the British in preparing Egypt for gradual independence, and many of them, until alienated by Cromer, were friendly towards the British. The radical effendiya were led by people like Mustafa Kāmīl, Muhammad Farid and Said Zaghlul, who were all mainly of *fallāh* origin. They did not believe that the British deserved tender handling. Through the Press and legislature they spared no language in venting their bitterness towards the British administration, whose catalogue of crimes included the use of English as the official language, British monopoly of the higher positions in the civil service, the Dinshawāi incident of 1906,[1] the rape of Egypt through the foreign-owned Suez Canal Company, the robbery of the Sudan from Egypt and the assimilation of the country to the British empire at the outbreak of the First World War. In fact the war exasperated the Egyptians. Their country became a military base; they were conscripted as carriers for the British army; their food and camels were commandeered; foodstuff became curtailed by the martial law under which they were governed throughout the war period.

The Egyptians resorted to violence after the war. After a Commission of Enquiry under Lord Alfred Milner, the British decided to grant a measure of independence to Egypt. In the declaration of independence made unilaterally by Britain in 1922, the nationalists having broken off negotiations on the British terms, Britain reserved for herself, pending treaty negotiations, defence and foreign policy, defence of the Suez Canal, protection of minority communities and their interests, and a share in the administration of the Sudan.

Egypt then became virtually independent in 1922. Anglo-Egyptian relations remained strained until, gradually, over the years, Egypt became a full sovereign state. In 1956 one of the principal grievances of the Egyptian nationalists was removed by the nationalisation of the Suez Canal by Colonel Abdel Nasser.

BRITISH AND FRENCH ATTITUDES COMPARED

Compared to French North Africa the nationalist movement in Egypt had an easy time. In the French areas, where nationalist articulations had begun before the outbreak of the First World War, the effendiya nationalists were already having a very hard time. A comparison of British and French attitudes may be attempted at this point. The British attitude to the effendiya nationalists was on the whole realistic and to a certain extent positive; that of the French unrealistic and negative. During the earlier stages in Egypt, the British did not regard the nationalist movement as a healthy manifestation, and looked upon the effendiya as a band of half-baked, westernised, hybridised and disgruntled agitators. British officials in Egypt believed that Ismā'īl had been guilty of hastily launching excessive democracy. The antidote for the irrational and irresponsible nationalism of the 'Fallāhīn Assembly', as an Englishman called this Assembly, was thought to be a Legislative Council which would be pre-dominantly nominated and filled with landowners of Turkish descent. But the British did not discard entirely the elective principle and the effendiya continued to be elected into the General Assembly. Nationalist demands were voiced in the Assembly, which by 1913 came to be dominated by the effendiya. Realistically the British accepted the consequences of the process they had initiated in 1883 by the creation of the Assembly. And, although the nationalists were treated with undisguised contempt and disdain, the extremists were either exiled or imprisoned, and the Press controlled, yet there was no attempt to drive Egyptian nationalism underground. The consequence of all this was that self-government was handed over to the Egyptians with the minimum of bloodshed, and with the minimum of bitterness between the Egyptian people on the one hand, and the British on the other.

The French attitude to the effendiya nationalists was different. Nationalist articulations were considered illegitimate and illogical in the context of the so-called policy of assimilation which the French said they were implementing in their North African territories. In the French view the true effendiya was the man who discarded Arabic, threw by the board African customs and institutions, and appropriated with gusto the French language, French education, customs and modes of thinking. The more French he was, that is the less African he was, the more 'civilised' he was thought to be, meaning by this that he was in a condition to be accepted into the French community on terms of equality. To nurse African feelings meant being anti-French, opposed to civilisation and progress. It is noteworthy that the first generation of effendiya in French North Africa, generally speaking, were prepared to accept this interpretation of civilisation, so long as the French were prepared to accept them as equals. But when they discovered that the French would not do so (the colons would not recognise them as Frenchmen of any sort), they became disenchanted with this bogus assimilation policy. The French view of the effendiya can be well imagined. As the French press once referred to them, they were no more than 'a small clique of gangsters with doubtful primary school certificates who try to pretend that they are Ghandhis and Zaghlouls'. Until about ten years ago, when the nationalist movement became subterranean dynamite, the French believed that African nationalism could be exorcised by a policy of repression. It was commonplace to describe the effendiya as communist-inspired agitators. Consequently the French answer to the nationalists consisted of imprisonment, exile to the edge of the Sahara, gagging of the press and suppression of liberties.

TUNISIA

In Tunisia it was not until 1932, three years after the appearance of a radical lawyer, Habib Rugayba (the name was Frenchified as Bourguiba), in the nationalist movement, that the Destour party (which had replaced an earlier party in 1920, but which had been driven into disarray by the repressive French administration), acquired a renewed vigour. In 1934, under Bourguiba, the party was given a shake-up and a new orientation. Opposed to the Destour party dominated by the upper-class, the 'old crocodiles', the Neo-Destour party, as Bourguiba's party came to be known, was associated with the people. Its organisation remains perhaps the most efficient political machine in Africa, and resembles Communist party organisation in many ways. The smallest units were local cells; these were then grouped into regional federations, composed of the regional federations' elected representatives to the National Congress, from which, in turn, the board of twelve party directors known as the Political Bureau was elected. By 1960 there were not less than 2,000 local cells and a membership of about 350,000 in the Neo-Destour party. Because of the country-wide nature of the organisation nationalism became deeply rooted in the masses. The exiling or imprisonment of the leaders only made them martyrs in the eyes of the people.

Habib Bourguiba, the man who epitomised Tunisian nationalism until the achievement of independence, is still popular with the masses and might perhaps be considered the most realistic of all nationalists of his day. He is the exponent of a philosophy now known as 'Bourguibism', which a scholar has defined as 'a willingness to shape policies to fit existing circumstances without losing sight of ultimate goals, and to compromise in order to achieve a meaningful, immediate objective rather than refusing to make any concessions and thus accomplishing nothing'. He finds no place for a dogmatism that cannot yield practical results, whether in religion or politics. In the struggle for independence from French rule his watchword was gradualism. Having assessed the military capacity of France, the absence of the higher principles of morality and 'justice' from international politics and the relative weakness of Tunisia, he judged that discretion was the better part of valour; therefore he eschewed violence against France in any form. He believed that pressure, constantly brought to bear on France, would ultimately, if slowly, lead Tunisia to her ultimate goal—full sovereignty. But this was to be achieved by stages; first, a decent voice for Tunisia in the Protectorate administration, then internal autonomy and then complete independence. The clearest vindication of his political philosophy was shown by the attenuated independence which he negotiated for Tunisia in 1955, against the wishes of the Arab League and the extremists within the Neo-Destour party. He believed that to expect France to grant full independence in that year was a wild dream; and to attempt to force France to grant it would end in the spilling of Tunisian blood and further postpone the achievement of the desired goal. But if the attainable were accepted by the Tunisians and cordial relations with France were maintained, then the desired goal would be reached not long afterwards. For history was on the side of the nationalist movement, and events in other parts of North Africa would convince France of the advisability of granting full independence to Tunisia. Within a year he was proved right and on 20 March 1956 Tunisia became an independent state. On the economic plane, Bourguibism recognises the economic importance of the colons and French entrepreneurs, whose services should be retained. Even in military affairs, Bourguiba believed Tunisia was weak; therefore for some time to come, France must continue to protect the territory. Although the French administration forced him into exile for several years and flung him into jail a number of times, he believed that Tunisia could achieve independence only in co-operation with France, and without bitterness. Even after independence the French were not to be alienated since Tunisia would long continue to need French technical and financial assistance. Bourguiba believes that it is contrary to reason to have enemies in politics.

The social aspect of Bourguibism is Fabian to some extent, and in certain respects the dogma of Islam has been sacrificed before the altar of modernisation. For instance, women are no longer veiled and they are allowed to take part in politics, so that all human resources in the country may be utilised. And he has abolished polygamy in his Islamic state. In foreign policy Bourguibism means enmity to none and friendship with all foreign countries. But Bourguiba has no place for Communism in his programme, nor is he Pan-Arabist to the extent of hating and discriminating against the Jews. The spirit of give-and-take that pervades his thinking and philosophy is reflected in the complexion of the Neo-Destour party. The party is all-embracing; it has room for political conservatives and radicals, for the large landowners and trade unionists, for the ulemas and for secular-minded elements. The party has committed itself to no specific programme, except that of independence and modernisation.

During the Second World War, when France was occupied by the Germans and the nationalists might have co-operated with the Axis, the nationalists in Tunisia and Morocco supported the French Committee of National Liberation in the hope that after the war the French would requite their gestures with a grant of their legitimate aspirations. This hope was doomed to disappointment. In 1944 Bourguiba asked for self-government, but had to withdraw to Egypt before he could be apprehended. The contact he established in the next few years with other North African leaders like Ferhat Abbas and Alal al Fassi, and his extensive travels to Syria, Iraq, Saudi Arabia and the United States, had the effect of making world opinion aware of the Tunisian question.

The French did not remain absolutely intransigent; they began, gradually, to relax control. In 1945 a Legislative Assembly in which the French settlers and Tunisians were equally represented was established. This was an unsatisfactory concession to nationalist Tunisians who successfully boycotted elections to the new Legislature. Strikes and demonstrations forced the French to grant concession after concession until 1954 when the pragmatic French statesman, Mendès-France, decided to preside over the gradual liquidation of the French empire. He entered into negotiations with the Tunisian people among whom 20,000 French soldiers were kept busy, a people whose nationalist spirit could not be suppressed by martial law. Indeed they were already being driven to the wall. It was becoming clear to them that the French would listen to no language except force. The interior of North Africa was an ideal ground for guerilla warfare. And in 1954 the Tunisians were not alone in their decision to resort to violence against the French administration. Equally, the effendiya in Morocco and Algeria, with the support of the masses, were being driven into exasperation, and were resorting to the mountain regions to wage a relentless warfare against the French.

MOROCCO

In Morocco, which the French had occupied in 1912, the birth of a nationalist movement of the effendiya type synchronised with the Abdel Karim resistance movement against the Spaniards in the Rif area from 1924 to 1926. In the latter year, two effendiya, Ahmed Balafrej and Alal al Fassi, formed two organisations which soon fused into the Moroccan League, the nucleus of the Istiqlal party. Within the first few years of its existence the Moroccan League became nation-wide, with branches in most towns and in some country districts. By 1932 the movement had found sufficient numbers of supporters in France to be able to publish there a French review, *Maghreb*, edited by Balafrej. Their contact with France added to their political concepts the newer notions of trade unionism and socialism.

The first measure which inflamed Moroccan nationalist ardour

15

was the Berber Dahir, which has been mentioned. This did for the Moroccan effendiya what Dinshawāi had done for the Egyptian nationalists. Hitherto nationalism had been confined to a few intellectuals, students and a sprinkling of urban merchants, mainly in Fez, Meknès and Casablanca. The Dahir attracted the sympathies of the masses. Ironically then, France, through the Dahir, 'played a fundamental role in the birth of Moroccan nationalism'. French policy after 1930 was that of relentless suppression of nationalists until 1937 when the Moroccan League was proscribed.

But although the nationalist movement went underground, nationalist sentiments were openly fostered by Sultan Mohammed V. Sidi Mohammed, a moderniser and a well-educated ruler possessing practical sense, who must be recognised as unique among the North African potentates. He was the exact opposite of the Egyptian Khedives and Kings, rulers who were predominantly reactionary and luxury-loving, and who failed to identify themselves with the aspirations of the fallāhīn and effendiya. In fact the Egyptian court often allied with the British against the nationalists. It is nothing to wonder at, then, that in 1952 an army composed of Egyptian personnel liquidated the monarchy and declared a republic. Five years later the short-sighted, luxurious, conservative occupier of the Husseinic throne in Tunisia was removed, and Tunisia, too, became a republic.

In Morocco, on the other hand, the monarchy took an active part in the nationalist movement. In the eyes of the effendiya, Sidi Mohammed began badly as an apparently docile instrument of the French. In fact he had been selected in 1927 by the French administration as Sultan because he looked pensive and controllable and never gave the picture of someone who would ever strike an emphatic line in politics. And, from 1927 until the outbreak of the Second World War he co-operated with the French and did the bidding of the Resident-General. During these years he did not associate himself with the nationalist movement. However, all that Mohammed V was doing was biding his time until he would be able to strike decisively. This he came to do in a fashion that delighted the effendiya and the masses, thereby enhancing the value of the monarchy to the Moroccan peoples.

Mohammed V had studied Moroccan history, knew his country's weaknesses and attempted to remedy these by a thorough modernisation of his state. This objective, he realised, could be achieved only through schools which would combine the best of European education with the best of traditional education. To this end, he advocated Islamic education for children in their formative years so that their moral fibre might be developed and strengthened. Upon this Islamic education, was to be grafted the knowledge and techniques of western education. His eldest son, Moulay Hassan, now the Sultan, obtained a degree in French law; his daughter discarded the veil and came out of seclusion. His children took part in sport and wore European-type clothing. At the same time he never outraged the principles of the Muslim faith, and in public he performed punctiliously the many religious functions demanded of an Imam.

By 1952 the differences which had begun to occur between the Sultan and the French administration during the Second World War became more pronounced. In the French view, the Sultan was guilty because he had made speeches on the desirability of Morocco's sovereignty; he held views identical with those of the nationalists, who had formed the Istiqlal party in 1943; he had refused to sign decrees offensive to the nationalists and designed to strengthen French control of Morocco; he had been acclaimed by Abdel Karim, the nationalist of the Rif area; he had appealed several times to Paris above the Resident-Generals' heads; he had refused to denounce the nationalists. In 1952 he demanded independence for his country. In 1953 the French, having organised pro-French tariqas and pashas against Mohammed V and having encouraged Thami el Ghouai, an over-mighty subject, to insult the Sultan, deposed Mohammed V. General Guillaume, the Resident-General, had presented him with demands amounting to an ultimatum. Sidi Mohammed was asked to sign all those decrees which he had been refusing to sign for years. Another member of the Alawite, Moulay Arafa, 'an old man who can neither read nor write, nor yet do simple arithmetic, nor speak French', was 'installed' as the Sultan, after Sidi Mohammed had been whisked off to Corsica in his pyjamas.

By 'deposing' Mohammed V the French removed the one restraining influence on the nationalist movement. The lower ranks of the Istiqlal party, many of them in the employ of the administration (unknown to the French), believed that negotiation with France would no longer achieve anything. Mohammed in exile became stronger than Mohammed V on the Sherifian throne, since many Moroccans believed that he had been immortalised and had become part of the moon, and that 'God has now placed him in the moon to watch over us'. An excellent condition for violence had been created.

ALGERIA

In all French North Africa a nationalist movement of the effendiya type appeared latest in Algeria. This was because there, more than in any other territory, the so-called policy of assimilation was strongly established. French power was built up by a very large number of colons, numbering over a million in 1960. They controlled the economy and administration of the country. In the French view, therefore, the Arab-Berbers could not nurse the hope of one day becoming independent in the way the Tunisians and Moroccans could do within their Protectorate system. The French felt that their hands were in no way tied in Algeria. They committed themselves to a thorough policy of Frenchification and integration of Algeria with France.

The real founder of the modern Algerian nationalist movement was Hadj Messali, for many years a worker in the Renault factory in Paris. He was associated with the formation of L'Etoile Nord Africaine, a social organisation for North African workers, which was soon turned by Messali into a political organisation with an essentially revolutionary, proletarian, nationalist and Muslim character. Its aims were the extreme opposite of those of the Frenchified effendiya like Ferhat Abbas and the doctors, lawyers and businessmen, who were often inclined to be rather complacent 'yes men' and sat as Muslim councillors in the local assemblies in Algeria. Unlike the latter, who until the forties stood for the specious policy of assimilation, Messali and his followers declared that nothing short of an independent Berber-Arab controlled Algeria would satisfy them. It is not surprising, then, that the Messalists were ruthlessly oppressed in the twenties and thirties by the police. In 1937, having discovered that the French Communist party, with which the E.N.A. had been associated, would after all place French interests above those of Algeria, Messali broke away from them and in the same year founded the Parti Populaire Algérien (P.P.A.). Two years later the new organisation was banned, the leaders having been exiled or flung into jail. In 1941, Messali was sentenced to sixteen years with hard labour by the Vichy regime.

In 1943, having been chastened by experience, Ferhat Abbas rejected the so-called assemblies, and issued a *Manifeste au Peuple Algérien* (Manifesto to the Algerian People) in which he demanded a separate Algerian constitution, equal political rights regardless of race or religion, large-scale land reforms and measures of social improvement, the recognition of Arabic as an official language side by side with French, freedom of the Press, the right to form political parties and trade unions, and free and compulsory education.

Wishing to enlist greater support from the nationalists during the war, General de Gaulle decided to placate them by removing the disabilities under which Muslims had suffered in the past. He announced in Constantine in December 1943 that Muslims could become French citizens without losing their personal legal status as Muslims. Voting rights were also to be accorded to the majority of Muslims who were not French citizens, but these would have to vote as a separate college. The proportion of Muslims in local assemblies would be increased though they would remain in a minority. These reforms were embodied in the Ordinance of 7 March 1944, and the new system of representation came into effect in 1945. Three-fifths of the members of the assemblies were to be elected by French citizens, the other two-fifths by Muslims who were not French citizens. The inadequacy of the proposals from the Muslim viewpoint is clear from the fact that the Muslims, most of whom refused French citizenship, constituted seven-eighths of the population. Moreover, liberal though the de Gaulle proposals seemed to the French, they could no longer satisfy the nationalists who were already completely disillusioned with the bogus policy of assimilation which the proposals attempted to foster. Indeed the proposals had the effect of bringing together the three groups of nationalists—Abbas' 'Friends of the Manifesto', the Reformist Ulema and the Messalists —and in March 1944 they formed a loose alliance called *Amis du Manifeste et de la Liberté* (Friends of the Manifesto and Liberty). They declared that it was their aim 'to make familiar the idea of an Algerian nation, and spread the desire for the constitution in Algeria of a new autonomous republic federated to a renewed anti-colonial, anti-imperialist, French republic'.

In May 1945 a bloody insurrection broke out near Sétif, an area inhabited by militant Berber-speaking Kabyles. Altogether about one hundred Europeans were killed. The French retaliated on a massive scale. The French army, assisted by armed civilian commandos and supported by aircraft and gunfire from warships off the coast, put the insurrection down with the utmost ruthlessness. Officially fifteen hundred Muslims were slaughtered, unofficially six thousand. Four thousand others were arrested, and of these nine were executed.

The insurrection had the effect of dividing the nationalists into two parties. On the one hand were Ferhat Abbas and his followers who, perhaps scared by the physical display of 1945, began to recant their radicalism and to advocate a policy not dissimilar to the de Gaulle reform proposals already mentioned. Immediately he was absolved from complicity in organising the insurrection (he was himself a native of Sétif), Abbas published an *Appeal to Moslem and French Youth* in which he unfolded the idea of a multi-racial Algeria in which the colons would abandon their 'colonial complex' and their 'pride as conquerors', and in which the Muslims would abjure their 'mediaeval theocratic concepts' and the outmoded idea of Muslim nationalism. Later his new party, Union Démocratique du Manifeste Algérien (U.D.M.A.), began to win the elections into the second Constituent Assembly, as a result of rigging by the French administration.

There remained Messali and his followers who saw themselves being increasingly pushed towards extremism. Shortly after the Sétif insurrection the Messalists founded the Mouvement pour le Triomphe des Libertés Démocratiques (Movement for the Triumph of Democratic Liberty). When it became clear to the colons that the Messalists, if given a free hand, would go on capturing almost all the seats reserved for Muslims in the Algerian Assembly, as they actually had done in 1947, they began to urge the Governor-General that it was his patriotic duty to 'arrange' elections. M. Chataigneau, who was held responsible for the Messalist victory of 1947, was recalled by Paris, in response to pressure from the settlers. In 1951 and 1953 the administration ran the elections in such a way as to produce the desired result. Henceforth the beni oui oui (yes men) were 'elected' to represent the Muslim community in the Algerian Assembly, Municipal Councils, the 'Conseils Generaux' of the three Algerian Departments and the National Assembly in Paris. The masses, of course, did not recognise these hand-picked men as their authentic representatives. The consequence of all this was that the Muslim community came to lose all confidence in the French administration and began to doubt the wisdom of peaceful political action. This parody of democracy induced in the minds of the majority of politically-conscious Muslims a total loss of confidence in the methods of leaders like Ferhat Abbas. It was becoming clear that the time for talking had passed; the era of sabotage and violence must be introduced.

But until 1954 the French seemed capable of containing extremism. Sporadic acts of sabotage occurred here and there and in 1950 a huge 'plot' was revealed and a lot of ammunition was discovered; the Messalists were either exiled or imprisoned. In 1952 Messali himself was sent to France. It appeared to the French that the mischief-makers had been removed from the country. They were soon to learn that the calm they imagined was prevailing in Algeria was deceptive.

INDEPENDENCE

Violence became characteristic of the nationalist movements in all the three territories of French North Africa in 1954. In order of achievement of independence Morocco came first, followed almost immediately by Tunisia, and then ultimately by Algeria.

Confronted with rebellion in the three territories and with the humiliation suffered by the French army in Indo-China, the French government could not avoid granting concessions to Morocco in a matter of a year or two. The type of violence organised against the French in Morocco was not what they had expected. The French police were literally confounded, for it was almost impossible to apprehend the assailants who enjoyed the sympathy of the population. The French 'eyes and ears', that is Moroccan informants of the French police, were the first victims; then the farms and the shops of the colons went up in flames; then came an economic boycott; then there followed bomb attempts on the puppet Sultan. It was certainly more than the French could cope with. Ben Arafa was deposed and Mohammed V was reinstated; negotiations for full independence were completed in February 1956.

In Tunisia the guerilla fighters known as *fellaghas*, about 13,000 strong, kept the French administration busy; it was only to be expected that the first instalment of independence which had been granted in 1955 would be followed by full independence, now that less sophisticated Morocco had achieved that goal.

In Algeria the fiercest war in colonial Africa occurred. It was organised by the National Liberation Front which had been formed in Cairo and which began warfare in November 1954. For eight years the war of attrition dragged on. It was bloody. Perhaps over half a million Berber-Arab Algerians were killed; the French army lost not less than twenty thousand men; half a million French soldiers were kept busy. It is estimated that in one year alone, 1958, the French spent about £1,000 million pounds on the war. In 1962 General de Gaulle, having discovered that his hurried, comprehensive economic and social legislation could not win the Algerian Berber-Arabs to see the advantages of integration with France, dealt the 'Algeria is France' theory a deadly blow. A firm believer in the virtue of plebiscites, he agreed with F.L.N. leaders that the Algerians should be given the opportunity to express their constitutional wishes in a referendum. The people, as was expected, voted in favour of independence against the open rebellion of the extremist colons. In 1962 Algeria became a sovereign state.

Independent Morocco, Tunisia and Algeria have discovered that the task of nation-building is a formidable one. Although political independence has been won from France by 'blood and iron', the French presence remains, and will have to remain, for many years to come. In the economic field the French cannot be dislodged suddenly without dislocating the economy of the territories; the three territories have also learned that socially the French language and educational system have to be retained, but modified, until national educational systems evolve; in technological matters French assistance is needed and appreciated. As in many independent African states it will be a long time before all forms of domination disappear.

NOTE

1 Dinshawāi is a small village in Egypt. In an incident in which one of a band of British pigeon-hunters was killed by enraged villagers, many Egyptians were executed. The Egyptians believed that the British administration was unjustly

severe. Dinshawāi came to mean to Egyptians what Peterloo means to English Trade Unionists.

QUESTIONS FOR FURTHER STUDY AND DISCUSSION

1 What part did Islam play in the nationalist movements in North Africa?
2 Why did national feeling grow in Egypt between 1875 and 1922?
3 Describe the role played by two significant nationalist leaders in North Africa in the twentieth century.
4 How would you explain the violence of the nationalist movement in Algeria?

SELECT BIBLIOGRAPHY

'Alāl al-Fāsi, *The Independence Movements in Arab North Africa*, American Council of Learned Societies, Washington D.C., 1954.
R. Landau, *Moroccan Drama, 1900–1955*, Hale, 1955.
John Marlowe, *Anglo-Egyptian Relations 1800–1953*, Cresset Press, 1954.
Lorna Hahn, *North Africa: Nationalism to Nationhood*, Public Affairs Press, Washington D.C., 1960.
Majid Khadduri, *Modern Libya*, John Hopkins Press, Baltimore, 1963.
D. E. Ashford, *Political Change in Morocco*, Princeton, 1961.
J. M. Landau, *Parliaments and Parties in Egypt*, Israel Publishing House, Tel-Aviv, 1953.
M. K. Clark, *Algeria in Turmoil*, Thames & Hudson, 1960.
K. Wheelock, *Nasser's New Egypt*, Stevens, 1960.
G. Mansell, *Tragedy in Algeria*, Institute of Race Relations, O.U.P., 1961.
Jaques Baulin, *The Arab Role in Africa*, Penguin Books, 1962.
N. A. Ziadeh, *Origins of Nationalism in Tunisia*, American University of Beirut Faculty of Arts and Sciences Oriental series, no. 37, 1962.
Pierre Fontaine, *Abd El-Krim*, Les septs couleurs, Paris, 1958.
P. I. Vatikiotis, *The Egyptian Army in Politics*, Indiana U.P., 1961.

13 Modern Ethiopia

S. RUBENSON

ETHIOPIA has a long history with a comparatively large amount of continuity. In one and the same area, the same ethnic group has been the chief bearer of spiritual, material and political culture throughout some twenty centuries. The Ethiopian church and monarchy of today are the direct descendants of those institutions in the Aksumite empire; the alphabet used now is but a slight modification of the one used at Aksum. A strong and living heritage from the past (see Plates XIII–XVI) has thus gone into the making of modern Ethiopia and played a role in giving Ethiopia a different history from that of the rest of Africa, also during the last one and a half centuries.

In spite of the strong continuity of Ethiopian history and the well-known difficulty of establishing valid epochs in history, it is possible to say that the creation of modern Ethiopia began with the reign of Emperor Tewodros 1855–68. The first half of the nineteenth century, however, foreshadowed the coming developments in some respects. The penetration of Europeans into the interior of Africa was directed also towards Ethiopia. This led to the breaking of an isolation which had lasted for two centuries. Explorers and missionaries, both Roman Catholic and Protestant, flocked to Ethiopia. France and Great Britain established consulates at Massawa in the eighteen-forties. Regional rulers were approached with offers of friendship, trade and arms. The first formal treaty between any Ethiopian ruler and a European power was signed in 1841 by King Sahle Sillase of Shewa in central Ethiopia and Captain Cornwallis Harris for Queen Victoria. Another treaty with Great Britain was signed in 1849 by Ras (Duke) Ali for the Imperial government but without the knowledge of the Emperor at Gonder. The French government was also active and made a treaty with Sahle Sillase in 1843. These agreements, however, led to no immediate practical results, and are important only as evidence of European interest in Ethiopia and not *vice versa*.

In the same way there was no concerted Ethiopian reaction to the first appearance of Turkish-Egyptian troops in the Ethiopian borderlands after Muhammad Ali's conquest of the Sudan. Such problems were left to the governors along the undefined boundaries in the west and north. The reason for this was the disunity and general weakness of the Ethiopian monarchy at that time. The period from 1759 to 1855 is in traditional Ethiopian history called *Zemene Mesafint* the age of the dukes (or judges). The state was in fact no more than a conglomeration of regional kingdoms and dukedoms. The Emperor had gradually become a shadow king with almost no income and no power. Even the unity of the Ethiopian church was on the verge of being lost. By 1850 there was little to indicate that the Ethiopians would, in spite of their long common history and common heritage, be in a position to cope with the pressing problems of the new era, and in particular the onslaught of Egyptian and European imperialism. But at the crucial moment when the survival of Ethiopia demanded action, Tewodros and his successors Yohannis and Minilik accepted the challenge and in so doing created the framework of modern Ethiopia.

TEWODROS II, 1855–68

Tewodros II was born about 1820 in the area between Lake Tana and the Sudan border. He belonged to the governing class but had no rightful claim to the throne, which was reserved for members of the Solomonian dynasty. Over a number of years he increased his power and influence, and in 1852–5 he defeated the princes of three of the four main provinces, Gojam, Begemdir and Tigre. Then he deposed the last puppet emperor at Gonder and declared himself the sovereign of all Ethiopia. The same year he also occupied Shewa. His aim was to build a unified modern national state with a centralised administration, with paid governors rather than feudal lords in the provinces, and with a trained and well-equipped standing army under his own command. But because of the resistance of the nobility and the church, both great landowners, he failed in his attempts to create a financial basis for his reforms. His modern ideas were rejected, and rebellion followed upon rebellion throughout his reign.

With regard to foreign relations Tewodros was acutely aware of both possibilities and dangers. He was very willing to allow consular representatives to reside in Ethiopia but would give them

- - - - - - Ethiopian–Italian boundary according to the Wichale treaty 1889
———·——· Ethiopian–Italian boundary agreed upon 1900–1908
———·——· Ethiopian–Italian boundary of 1897 "The 180 mile line"
———·——· Ethiopian–Italian boundary of 1897 "The Minilik line"
—·—·—·— Boundaries between British and Italian spheres of influence
according to treaties of 1891 and 1894

Fig. 12 The making of modern Ethiopia, 1850–1960.

no judicial rights in his country. Moreover, these matters should be reciprocal. He wrote to both Queen Victoria and Napoleon III in 1862 to tell them that he intended to send embassies to their capitals. He also sought their moral support in the war with Egypt which he expected would break out at this time. Foreigners, especially teachers and artisans of all kinds, were welcome. The majority of these were employed by the Emperor himself in building roads and manufacturing arms. He even had them establish a cannon foundry near his capital Debre Tabor and succeeded in manufacturing his own cannon. When his approaches to France and Great Britain did not meet with the response he had expected, he became disappointed. He began to suspect that Britain was actually siding with Egypt. Misunderstandings and intrigues followed, and the British consul in Ethiopia was arrested together with a number of missionaries and other foreigners. This led ultimately to the British expedition to Ethiopia in 1868. But long before the Indian-British army had even landed at Zula on the Red Sea coast, the Emperor had lost control of most of his provinces. His once large and 'invincible' army had dwindled to less than 10,000 men. The British therefore met with no resistance on their way to Meqdela, the Emperor's main fortress and state prison. Only when they arrived below the fortress did Tewodros attack with his last faithful followers. It was a short and very unequal combat. The British with their superior arms mowed down the Ethiopians by the hundreds, while losing only some twenty wounded themselves. Tewodros released the European captives, but rather than surrender himself he committed suicide on 16 April 1868. The British immediately left Ethiopia, as they had promised to do. The events connected with Meqdela are only an episode as far as Ethiopian history goes. What really caused Tewodros' fall was the internal conflicts in the country. He left behind an Ethiopia almost as disunited as the one into which he had been born. But although he had failed in his work to unify the country, he had given birth to the concept of a strong, united and progressive Ethiopia, and this idea survived his fall.

TEKLE GIYORGIS, 1868–71

At the death of Tewodros there were three main contenders for supreme power: Minilik of Shewa, Gobaze of Wag and Lasta, and Kasa of Tigre. Of these Minilik had revealed his ambitions by beginning to style himself King of Kings even before Tewodros's death. In fact, however, Minilik contented himself with consolidating his power in Shewa and waiting to see the outcome of the struggle in the north. Gobaze occupied the old capital, Gonder, which had been destroyed by Tewodros and proclaimed himself Emperor under the name of Tekle Giyorgis. Kasa alone made no immediate claims. But when attacked by Gobaze in 1871 he won a decisive victory at Adwa on 11 July and the way to the throne lay open to him.

YOHANNIS IV, 1871–89

In January 1872 Kasa was crowned at Aksum as Yohannis IV. He is in some Ethiopian traditions called the monk and the soldier, the first probably due to his vigorous ecclesiastical policies or personal austerity, the second because of the battles he fought against the enemies of his country. It was during the reign of Yohannis that Ethiopia's struggle for survival as an independent state really began. The first to attack was Khedive Ismā'īl's Egypt. Ethiopia's boundaries were not clearly defined at the time. On the contrary, the Ethiopian state had usually been surrounded by a number of semi-dependent tribes, whose autonomy had varied with the power of the Ethiopian rulers. As the armies and administrators of the Egyptian government moved into these borderlands, the question of territorial boundaries took on new importance. In 1865 Khedive Ismā'īl had taken over Massawa from the earlier weak representatives of the Ottoman Empire and some penetration inland from the north had also begun. This led in 1872 to a sudden attack and occupation of the Bogos province in the mid-highlands of central Eritrea by a small Egyptian army under the command of the governor of Massawa, a Swiss adventurer named Munzinger. Yohannis, who as governor of Tigre had befriended the British in 1868, made an attempt to solve the conflict by appealing to Queen Victoria and the British government to interfere and arbitrate. The response was half-hearted and in 1875 a regular war broke out between Egypt and Ethiopia.

In September that year four different expeditions were directed towards Ethiopia. The easternmost was sent to Brava on the coast of the Indian Ocean but was turned back because of the protests of the Sultan of Zanzibar to the British government. The second was directed from Zeyla towards Harer, which was successfully occupied by Rauf Pasha and remained under Egyptian rule for almost ten years. The third under Munzinger's command was a combined military and political mission. Starting from Tajurah it was to receive the submission of the Afar (Danakil) tribes and then press on to Shewa to incite Minilik to attack Yohannis from the south. This expedition was, however, attacked and almost annihilated by the Afar, and so Munzinger never reached Shewa. The fourth and direct attack on Yohannis had Massawa as its base. A small but well-equipped Egyptian army marched inland as far as Gundet near the Mereb river without meeting any resistance. There they were met by an Ethiopian army under the Emperor's command, and in a battle on 16 November they were completely annihilated. Yohannis did not follow up this victory but offered Ismā'īl peace in a letter which concluded: 'My brother, you are not greater than your forefathers and we are not less than ours. What is the purpose of dismantling the frontiers of this kingdom? It is not good. It is better that our respective positions remain unchanged'. But a new and larger Egyptian army under the command of Ratib Pasha, the commander-in-chief of Egypt's armed forces, was already at Massawa. When it started to march inland, Yohannis mobilised again, and troops from as far south as Gojam joined the army. In a three days' battle at Gura, 7–9 March 1876, the Egyptians were again defeated. They evacuated the northern highlands except Bogos, and opened peace negotiations, which were to last until 1884.

Yohannis felt that he had nothing more to fear from the Egyptians and turned his attention towards the internal affairs of his state. He had been received and acknowledged as Emperor at Gonder already in 1873 and had done much to bring central Ethiopia under his control before the war with Egypt broke out. Now he made Debre Tabor his residence town for a few years while consolidating his rule over the southern provinces. A peaceful agreement was reached with Minilik in March 1878. The latter agreed to drop his title King of Kings and pay tribute to Yohannis. In return the Emperor confirmed him as King of Shewa and crowned him. Three years later Yohannis crowned the Ras of Gojam king as well, and there are indications that he intended to appoint kings also for Begemdir and Tigre. This shows that Yohannis was prepared to accept a far less unified and centralised state than the one Tewodros had attempted to create. On the other hand, Yohannis' claim to be the supreme ruler of all Ethiopia was accepted everywhere, and therefore his policy actually brought unification closer than before. In an attempt to prevent conflict in the future a marriage was arranged between

Yohannis's son Araya Sillase and Minilik's daughter Zewditu, but this failed because of the death of the young prince in 1888. In the interest of conformity and unity in religious matters a council was called in 1878 to denounce certain sects within the Ethiopian Orthodox Church as well as any mission groups working in the country. Muslims and pagans were ordered to accept Christianity within three and five years respectively. Although these policies were very imperfectly implemented, the Orthodox Church gained adherents in new areas and a stronger position generally speaking.

In the years 1876 to 1883 there had been no hostilities between Egypt and Ethiopia beyond some raiding across the *de facto* borders. But neither Yohannis nor the British, who had become increasingly involved in Egyptian affairs, were happy about the situation. Yohannis wanted to have Bogos back and obtain free access to the sea either through Massawa or some other of the Red Sea ports occupied by Egypt. Several peace missions had been sent to Ethiopia including one under Charles Gordon in 1879. But since they were not authorised to give back any territory, they all failed. Gordon did his utmost to gain favourable terms for his master the Khedive, but he alsoadmitted privately: 'Now Johannes will not give me his help for nothing when I persist in keeping what we have stolen and . . . I have abused them (the Ethiopians); for they (like us) want an eye for an eye, and twenty shillings for one pound.' But by 1884 the successes of the Mahdists in the Sudan made it imperative for the Egyptian government to come to terms with Yohannis in order to receive his help and permssion to evacuate Egyptian garrisons on the Ethiopian-Sudanesei border through Ethiopia home to Egypt. This was achieved through the treaty of Adwa, 3 June 1884, between Ethiopia, Egypt and Great Britain. By Article 1 Ethiopia was guaranteed 'free transit through Massowah to and from Abyssinia for all goods, including arms and ammunition under British protection'; by Article 2 Bogos was restored to Ethiopia. The terms of this agreement were favourable to Ethiopia, but its political consequences were all but disastrous. Ethiopia had in fact traded one weak enemy for two strong. Yohannis must have been fully aware of the fact that his help in evacuating the Egyptian garrisons would bring him face to face with the Mahdists in the west. What he could not have foreseen was the arrival of a new expansionist neighbour in the north, the Italians.

The first step towards the establishment of an Italian colony on the Red Sea had been taken in 1869, when the Italian missionary Sapeto had bought Aseb from the local sultan for 6,000 Maria Theresa thalers. For ten years there was little activity at Aseb but around 1880 it became the base for Italian exploration and commercial and diplomatic activity. In 1882 its status was changed into that of an official Italian colony. The Italian government offered treaties of friendship and commerce to both Yohannis and Minilik, and the latter signed the Ankober treaty in 1883, which guaranteed him free access to the outside world through Aseb. With Yohannis no agreement was reached, probably because he had such good hopes of solving his own problems through a treaty with the Egyptians and British. But although he succeeded in this, he soon found himself betrayed by the British. He had been told that he could have the use, but not the possession of, Massawa since it belonged to the Ottoman empire. Six months later the British government implicitly invited the Italians to Massawa without informing Yohannis and without obtaining any guarantees that they would abide by the Adwa treaty. On 5 February 1885 the Italians occupied Massawa. This British step was at least partly dictated by their concern that the French might increase their influence in the Red Sea. The result was that the French increased their Obok colony of 1862 by occupying Tajurah and Jibouti. Yohannis was very disturbed and grew increasingly so when he saw the Italians push inland occupying villages and areas which the Egyptians had just left. Ethiopian trade was interfered with. All the small ports were occupied by the Italians and duties had to be paid at Massawa. Yohannis protested and, when this did not help, his general, Ras Alula, attacked and annihilated a small Italian force at Dogali in January 1887. The British made some half-hearted attempts to mediate, but only managed to upset Yohannis still more by revealing that they had accepted that the Italian demands for territory, including Bogos, were justified. Yohannis's reply to Queen Victoria was, '. . . when they (the Italians) wanted to begin the quarrel, they stopped the traders and came to the places in my country called Sehati and Wia and fortified them. . . . To make me look like the offender when I am not, does not that appear to be an order that I should give them the land which Jesus Christ gave to me. Reconciliation is possible when they are in their country and I in mine, but now, sleeping

16

with our swords in hand and keeping our horses bridled, are not we and our armies as good as in combat already?' In spite of this both sides hesitated. The Italians wanted to incite Minilik to rebel against Yohannis first but were not very successful in their attempts to do this. The Mahdists had invaded western Ethiopia and sacked Gonder. Yohannis marched against them first and lost his life in the battle of Metemma on 9 March 1889.

MINILIK II, 1889–1913

Minilik was by this time the most experienced political leader in the country and had a large army of his own. He proclaimed himself King of Kings, once again, without meeting any very serious opposition. His first act as Emperor was to sign the treaty of Wichale (Uccialli) with the Italians on 2 May 1889. Throughout the years from 1885, and particularly after the battle at Dogali, the Italians had tried to detach Minilik from Yohannis. But although the relations between them had deteriorated during the last two years of Yohannis's life, Minilik had agreed to remain neutral in the conflict only on condition that the Italians promised not to annex any Ethiopian territory, which was of course exactly what the Italians were doing. In the Wichale treaty, however, Minilik gave up the territory north of a line from the coast just south of Massawa to Kassala, including Asmera and Keren on the Italian side. This was organised as the Italian colony of Eritrea from 1 January 1890, and it became the base for two major invasions into Ethiopia in 1895 and 1935. But of this Minilik could know nothing in 1889. He thought that he had satisfied all Italian demands and appreciated the state of 'perpetual peace and constant friendship' promised him by a European power, since it gave him international recognition and a free hand to deal with his other problems. As soon as the treaty had been ratified the Italian government, however, claimed that Article 17 of the treaty made Ethiopia an Italian protectorate. Since the equally authoritative Amharic text said something else, Minilik protested to the European governments and in 1893 abrogated the whole treaty on the basis that the Italian government had attempted to cheat him, which was certainly true at least of their negotiator in Ethiopia, Count Antonelli. The Italians were not prepared for this loss of face and invaded Ethiopia in 1895 to force Minilik to accept their 'protection'. Minilik mobilised a united Ethiopia against the invader and after initial Ethiopian successes at Amba Alagi and Meqele the armies met at Adwa. The Italians had placed their hopes in Ethiopian disunity, in better arms and superior military skill. But Minilik had consolidated Ethiopian unity and managed to import vast numbers of firearms. At Adwa the majority of his and his generals' 80,000 to 100,000 men were armed with firearms. The Italian commander, General Baratieri, had less than 20,000 men at his immediate disposal but hoped to balance the Ethiopians' superior numbers by making a surprise attack from carefully selected positions in the early morning of 1 March 1896. But the Ethiopians were alerted and in a long day of heavy fighting they crushed the Italian brigades one by one. The Italian losses amounted to more than 6,000 dead, about 1,500 wounded and at least 3,000 prisoners of war. The Ethiopians lost an estimated 7,000 killed and probably as many wounded, but there were no prisoners of war, and the battlefield remained Ethiopian.

The victory of Adwa is not only the cherished symbol of the Ethiopian love of freedom, and determination to fight for it, it is also the most important single event in the modern history of Ethiopia. It decided the outcome of a war, and at the same time —and more important—the outcome of a long and determined struggle for international recognition, for the very right to exist as an independent state. In the peace treaty Italy admitted that the Wichale treaty was void and that Ethiopia was an absolutely sovereign and independent state.

On the other hand Minilik did not continue the war to regain Eritrea, but even allowed the Italians the natural boundary of the Mereb. As far as Minilik was concerned, the war had been a defensive operation. His aims were to secure independence and put a limit to Italian colonial expansion at Ethiopia's expense, and this he succeeded in doing for forty years. The battle of Adwa changed the attitude of the powers in Europe almost overnight. Diplomatic missions flocked to Addis Abeba to compete for Minilik's favour. The French wanted to make sure that Jibouti would become Ethiopia's main port and hoped that they might with Minilik's help outwit the British in the Upper Nile valley. The British wanted to have the boundary of their Somaliland Protectorate settled and some assurance that Minilik was not going to support the Khalifa in the Sudan. Treaties were signed with both in the beginning of 1897, defining the boundaries of Ethiopia in the north-east. An Ethiopian army, with some French officers attached to it, pushed forward as far as the White Nile but returned before Marchand had arrived at Fashoda. And although the relations between Minilik and the Khalīfa had improved, the Emperor stayed out of the conflict in the Sudan. After the British conquest of the Sudan, the western boundary of Ethiopia was settled in 1902, and this was followed by a treaty defining the boundary with Kenya in 1907. On the Somali coast of the Indian Ocean, Italy had established some protectorates in the eighteen-nineties. A secret agreement as to the boundary was reached in 1897, but the frontier was defined differently in the text and on the attached map. A new Ethiopian-Italian treaty was signed in 1908 but, if anything, it increased the confusion, and even in 1934 the boundary had not been demarcated.

The establishing of frontiers through treaties with foreign powers is only part of the story. There was also the actual conquest or peaceful incorporation into the Ethiopian state of the areas which fell within the boundaries. In actual fact the expansion mostly came first, and it was only when the foreign powers saw that the Ethiopians were already in possession that they agreed to boundaries which often represented a loss of territory which they had expected to include in their colonies. Minilik's expansion started for strategic reasons under the pressure of the Egyptian threat to encircle Ethiopia in 1875–6, and with brief intervals the development continued until 1908. In 1891 Minilik wrote a circular letter to the European powers and claimed roughly all land between 5 and 15 degrees north and from the White Nile to the Indian Ocean as Ethiopian territory. He also declared that he had 'no intention of being an indifferent spectator' if far-off countries came to occupy these areas, and in fact he and his generals had already been busy for more than a decade making his claims good by actually establishing Ethiopian authority and administration, however vague, throughout the areas concerned. In doing this Minilik used peaceful means wherever possible, but broke down all opposition by his superior armies wherever local kings or chiefs resisted. Thus many of the western Gallas, subjects of the King of Leka and Sultan Abba Jifar of Jimma, submitted peacefully in 1881–3 and continued to be governed by their former rulers, while Kefa farther to the south-west was almost completely devastated before it was forced to surrender in 1897. In the east Harer was occupied in 1887 and the main thrusts to the south took place in 1894–9. The forms of government introduced in the new areas varied, depending on earlier systems and on the amount of military force that had been used in the occupation. Where garrisons were regarded as necessary to maintain peace and order they were left behind and a kind of serfdom was introduced for their upkeep. Although Minilik was tolerant in comparison with his predecessors and raised Gallas in his service to high positions, the general rule was that the Amharic language and Orthodox Christianity were gradually introduced wherever representatives of Minilik's government established themselves.

While Minilik ruled the provinces, either through the more or less hereditary chiefs of the areas or through his own generals, he kept the reins of the central government in his own hands as long as he could. His cousin Ras Mekwennin and the Swiss Alfred Ilg were his chief advisers, particularly in foreign affairs, during the first decades of his reign. In 1907, when his health began to decline, the Emperor appointed Ethiopia's first council of ministers to take care of central government and administration. This was not as radical an innovation as it might seem, however, for almost every minister in fact carried some old title which had been used about the court for centuries and filled the functions of an established courtier within the new framework. But in many other fields Minilik's reign was a period of rapid change. The new capital Addis Abeba was founded in 1887. A few years later Ilg received a concession to build a railway from Jibouti to Addis Abeba and work started, although it was held up for long periods because of foreign intrigues. The telegraph was also introduced and roads and bridges were constructed. Farming and mining concessions were granted to foreigners but on a fairly small scale. The volume of trade grew and so did state income. In 1909 Minilik issued his new currency, the first Ethiopian coins for about 1,000 years.

During the last years of his life Minilik was paralysed and much of the internal stability that he had created was lost. Intrigues, foreign as well as internal, were rife. The British, French and Italians had already in the Tripartite treaty of 1906 resolved their differences and agreed on how to partition Ethiopia if the occasion should arise. But the arrival of Germany on the scene caused new concern. The Emperor's grandson Yasu was proclaimed heir in

1908, but he was then only a twelve-year-old boy, and there were other candidates as well.

YASU, 1913-16

When Minilik died in 1913 Yasu became Emperor. He was not capable of uniting the factions. On the contrary, the differences between them deepened. Yasu, whose father Ras Mikael had once been a Muslim, showed particular favour to Muslims and was gradually accused of having become a Muslim himself. When the First World War broke out, German and Turkish activity in Ethiopia increased. Yasu showed his preference for the Central Powers and this in all probability contributed to his fall in September 1916.

ZEWDITU AND TAFARI MEKWENNIN, 1916-30

Yasu was succeeded by Minilik's daughter, Zewditu, as Empress, with Ras Tafari, son of Ras Mekwennin, as Regent and heir to the throne. The purpose of this arrangement was obviously to divide the power between certain reactionary or at least conservative elements who rallied round the Empress and the Coptic Arch-bishop Matewos, and Ras Tafari and his progressive associates. Matters pertaining to internal government remained largely in the hands of the former until 1926, when both Minilik's old Minister of War, Habte Giyorgis, and the Archbishop died.

The realm of foreign relations became Ras Tafari's special con-cern. In 1923 he brought Ethiopia into the League of Nations. The following year he made a tour of several European countries to learn from them, and to secure financial aid for his plans to develop Ethiopia, and better terms for Ethiopian export and import through Jibouti. When Great Britain and Italy agreed in 1925 without consulting Ras Tafari to support each other's plans for building a dam at Lake Tana and a railway from Eritrea to Italian Somaliland respectively, the Regent protested not only to the governments concerned but also to the League of Nations. To the members of the League he wrote: '. . . on our admission to the League of Nations we were told that all nations were to be on a footing of equality within the League, and that their independence was to be universally respected. . . . We were not told that certain members of the League might make a separate agreement to impose their views on another member even if the latter considered

those views incompatible with its national interests. . . . Throughout their history they (the Ethiopians) have seldom met with
foreigners who did not desire to possess themselves of Abyssinian
territory and to destroy their independence. . . . Nor must it be
forgotten that we have only recently been introduced to modern
civilisation and that our history, glorious though it be, has not
prepared us for ready adjustment to conditions which are quite
often beyond the range of our experience. . . . With our well-known
eagerness for progress—given time and the friendly advice of
countries whose geographical position has enabled them to out-
distance us in the race—we shall be able to secure gradual but
continual improvements which will make Abyssinia great in the
future as she has been throughout the past.'

With one eye on the past and the other on the future Ras Tafari
had selected the priorities for his country: a universally respected
independence and equality with other nations first, and a gradual
but continual improvement of internal conditions second. It was
in line with both of these aims that Ras Tafari in 1928 signed a
treaty of friendship and arbitration with Italy, and a convention
providing for road construction and Ethiopian-Italian economic
co-operation with regard to import and export through Aseb and
road transport. Foreign investment was encouraged by the granting of concessions and monopolies to various nationalities: Greeks,
Swiss, Italians, Belgians and French.

Their activities included coffee and cotton plantations and
timber business. But road construction moved slowly, and the
railway had got no farther than Addis Abeba. Most of the movement of both goods and persons was by donkeys, mules and horses.
Domestic slavery was still widespread in the country. The Regent
was both by inclination and commitment to the League of Nations
bound to attempt to abolish it, but although laws with severe
punishments for selling or buying slaves restricted such transactions, it was much more difficult to do anything about slaves who
had been integrated into the households and would have nowhere
to go even if they were freed.

One of Ras Tafari's early interests was education. With the
exception of one school founded by Minilik all modern education
was in the hands of missionaries, and their contribution in this field
particularly in Eritrea, at Harer and in western Ethiopia has been
considerable. In spite of opposition Ras Tafari encouraged the

missionaries to expand their work and added private schools and a hospital of his own in the capital. Promising young men were sent abroad for further education to be ready to fill the posts in government and administration, when the Regent would take over full power.

HAILE SELLASSIE I (FROM 1930)

In 1928 Ras Tafari had received the title of King, and when the Empress died in 1930 he was crowned King of Kings with the throne name Haile Sellassie I. As head of state he soon showed that he had further plans for modernisation. One year after his coronation he gave Ethiopia its first modern constitution, which provided for two deliberative chambers, one appointed by the Emperor and the other elected by the chiefs and dignitaries. The idea behind this step was undoubtedly to prepare the people to deal with state affairs within a modern framework, and it did not have any immediate political effect. As the share in power and government of the earlier class of governors and counsellors decreased, the Emperor appointed foreign advisers, mainly from minor European countries such as Belgium, Sweden and Switzerland, and countrymen returning from education abroad to work for the country.

All this activity was interrupted by Mussolini's decision to conquer Ethiopia and wipe out the 'scar of Adwa'. The decision was certainly taken as early as 1933, but it was a border incident at Walwal in Ogaden in November–December 1934 that was used by Mussolini as a pretext for stepping up his war preparations. There were attempts to arbitrate, and the Emperor hoped that these would succeed or that the League of Nations would intervene. Ethiopia was not prepared for war. In the forty years that had passed since the battle of Adwa, Ethiopia had from a military point of view lost ground tremendously in comparison with her adversary. The Emperor was aware of this, but had decided to put his faith in what Minilik's Ethiopia had lacked: the recognition of Ethiopia's independence by European powers, including Italy's treaty obligations of 1928 and Ethiopia's membership of the League of Nations. When the Italian armies crossed her frontiers on 2 October 1935, Ethiopia had barely started her mobilisation and had little to fight with. The Emperor appealed to the League for action. Although almost all the members admitted that this was

the most flagrant aggression possible, no really effective sanctions
against Italy could be agreed upon. The members of the League
were obsessed with fear that war might break out in Europe and
sacrificed Ethiopia, not, however, without forebodings The war
was one in which the Ethiopians had to endure everything, not
excluding the spraying of poison gas from planes over retreating
armies and peaceful villages alike. Mussolini wanted to win the
war and win it fast. The decisive battle was fought at May Chew
on 31 March 1936, with the Emperor in command of the
Ethiopian army, which was heavily defeated. One month later
Haile Sellassie I left his capital to go to Geneva to make a last
personal appeal. His address to the League of Nations on 30 June
1936 is one of the historical speeches of our time:

> I, Haile Sellassie I, Emperor of Ethiopia, am here today to claim
> that justice which is due to my people and the assistance
> promised to it eight months ago when fifty nations asserted that
> an aggression had been committed. . . . I assert that the problem
> submitted to the Assembly today is a much wider one than the
> removal of sanctions. It is not merely a settlement of Italian
> aggression. It is collective. It is the very existence of the League
> of Nations. It is the confidence that each state is to place in
> international treaties, it is the value of promises made to small
> States, that their integrity and their independence be respected
> and ensured. It is the principle of the equality of states on the
> one hand, or, on the other, the inevitability that they will be
> forced to accept the bonds of vassalship. In a word, it is inter-
> national morality that is at stake. Apart from the Kingdom of
> the Lord there is not on this earth any nation which is superior
> to any other. . . . God and history will remember your judge-
> ment. . . . Are the States going to set up the terrible precedent
> of bowing before force? Representatives of the world, I have
> come to Geneva to discharge in your midst the most painful of
> the duties of a Head of State. What reply shall I take back to
> my people?

These were prophetic words but the warning went unheeded.
The sanctions were lifted, and one by one the European governments accepted the claim of the Italians to be the lawful rulers of
Ethiopia. But in Ethiopia the war continued in guerilla operations
by small patriot forces, and some areas were held throughout the

five years of the Italian occupation. When Italy entered the Second World War, the plans for Ethiopia's liberation immediately began to take shape. The Emperor left his exile in England and went to Khartoum to head a small force through Gojam to Addis Abeba. Larger British forces entered Eritrea from Kassala and Italian Somaliland from Kenya. Except at Keren they met very little resistance, and after four months' campaign the Italian viceroy surrendered at Amba Alagi just north of May Chew. On 5 May 1941 the Emperor made his triumphal entry into Addis Abeba, five years to the day after Marshal Badoglio had occupied it in 1936.

Although some of the British officers at first showed some desire to govern the country themselves, the Emperor set up a government and took control of most of the country. British officers remained as advisers and as administrators in part of the Ogaden and in the old Italian colonies. At the peace conference Ethiopia claimed both of the colonies, but it was only in 1952 that Eritrea was returned to her under a federal agreement which was followed in 1962 by the integration of Eritrea into the mother country. The case for claiming former Italian Somaliland was weaker than that for Eritrea, and when it found no international support Ethiopia accepted and even sponsored the creation of an independent Somalia which was born on 1 July 1960, incorporating British Somaliland as well. Only French Somaliland remains as a European colony in the Horn of Africa.

Ever since the Second World War ended Ethiopia has played an active role in international affairs. In spite of, or, probably because of, his experience with the League of Nations, the Emperor has been a staunch supporter of the United Nations, and Ethiopian forces were made available both in Korea and the Congo. When the United Nations Economic Commission for Africa was established in 1958 it received its permanent headquarters in Addis Ababa. In May 1963 again Ethiopia became the host for the summit meeting of all African heads of state at which the Organisation of African Unity was born.

With regard to internal conditions in the country there has been slow but steady progress. The constitution was revised in 1955 to provide for the direct election by the people of the Chamber of Deputies, and in 1957 the first general elections took place. There is a growing interest in political affairs and a growing feeling of urgency with regard to economic and social reforms. Education is expanding. A University College was founded in 1951 and integrated with a number of mainly professional colleges into Haile Sellassie I University ten years later. Road construction, which is essential for any economic development in the country, has been speeded up. The urbanisation process has just begun. A few new factories—shoes and textiles, cement and other building materials —have been opened, and hydro-electric power plants constructed. Coffee is increasingly cultivated as a cash crop, and sugar and cotton plantations have been started. But only a small minority have as yet felt the impact of change. Ethiopia's established institutions, the church and the monarchy, and its long history and rich traditions ensure that change is gradual but continual, as the present Emperor promised forty years ago.

QUESTIONS FOR FURTHER STUDY AND DISCUSSION

1 Describe the breaking of Ethiopia's isolation in the first half of the nineteenth century and consider its consequences for modern Ethiopia.

2 Consider the significance of the battle of Adwa (1896).

3 Describe the contributions to the development of Ethiopian history of the following: Tewodros II, Yohannis IV, Minilik II, and Haile Sellassie I.

SELECT BIBLIOGRAPHY

A. H. M. Jones and Elizabeth Monroe, *A History of Ethiopia*, O.U.P., 1955.

Richard Pankhurst, *Journeys in Ethiopia*, O.U.P., 1964.

Edward Ullendorff, *The Ethiopians: An Introduction to Country and Peoples*, O.U.P., 1960.

David Mathew, *Ethiopia: The Study of a Polity*, Eyre & Spottiswood, 1947.

Ernest Work, *Ethiopia: A Pawn in European Diplomacy*, New Concord, Ohio, 1935.

Richard Pankhurst, 'Fire-arms in Ethiopian History', *Ethiopia Observer*, Vol. VI, No. 2.

Sven Rubenson, 'Some Aspects of the Survival of Ethiopian Independence', *University College Review*, 1961, Department of History, Haile Sellassie I University.

Sven Rubenson, *Wichale XVII. The Attempt to establish a protectorate over Ethiopia*, Institute of Ethiopian Studies, Haile Sellassie I University, 1961.

Abyssinia and Italy, Royal Institute of International Affairs, O.U.P., 1935.

Arnold J. Toynbee, *Survey of International Affairs, 1935*, Vol. II, O.U.P., 1936.

Leonard Mosley, *Haile Sellassie: The Conquering Lion*, Weidenfeld and Nicolson, 1964.

Christine Sandford, *The Lion of Judah Hath Prevailed*, Dent, 1955.

Margery Perham, *The Government of Ethiopia*, Faber, 1947.

Ernest W. Luther, *Ethiopia Today*, Stanford U.P., 1958.

14 Peoples of the Windward Coast

J. C. ANENE

THE area bounded by Senegal on the west and the Ivory Coast on the east is for convenience divided into the upper windward and the lower windward coast. Unlike the lower windward coast the region of the upper windward coast has no mountain ranges to separate the coast from the interior. A low-lying area, with many creeks and navigable rivers, its coast peoples had close links with those of the interior. The peoples who inhabit this coast are called Senegambians since the majority live in Senegal and Gambia. Some, however, inhabit Portuguese Guinea and 'French' Guinea. The two most important groups are the Serer and the Wolof.

THE SERER

The Serer consisted at first of politically unco-ordinated groups. There were small chieftaincies. Then Mandinka immigrants settled among them and took over some chieftaincies. The new rulers of Mende origin were Muslims when they took over the Serer states, but they soon became pagans. The two most important Serer states were Sine and Saloum; the authority of the latter state at one time extended to the Gambia River. The other Serer states generally paid allegiance to either Sine or Saloum.

The social structure of Serer society consisted of seven castes, the most important of which was the warrior's caste made up of soldiers, judges and tax collectors. Then there were castes of freemen. Below these was the caste of artisans: blacksmiths, leather-workers, weavers, wood-carvers, praise-singers and musicians. The lowest social rank comprised domestic and trade slaves. The social and political structure of the Serer rested on traditional religious practice which enabled the people to resist Islamic proselytisation. Sine and Saloum continued to be described as pagan states up to the end of the nineteenth century.

THE WOLOF

To the north of Serer lies the country of the Wolof. The Wolof were probably pushed down to the area south of the Senegal River

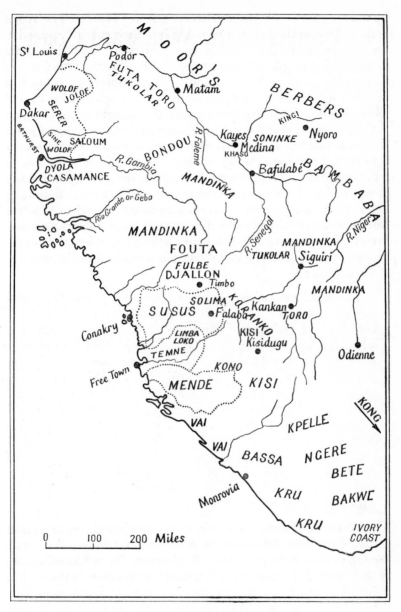

Fig. 13   The Windward Coast peoples.

by the pressure of the Moors, Berbers and the Tukolor. The Wolof apparently absorbed diverse elements into their culture, and today the people have little that is not shared in some degree by neighbouring peoples. The adoption of Islam by the Wolof was at first a slow process. In the middle of the nineteenth century a people's movement developed, and this was accelerated by the increasing domination of France over the Senegal.

Originally all Wolof states owed allegiance to the ruler of Jolof. The Wolof developed an elaborate system of government in which a noble class dominated the country, and selected rulers whose functions were to safeguard the integrity of the state by leadership in war and to bring prosperity to the people. Wolof rulers and the lesser chiefs had to prove themselves to be strong and rich, otherwise they ran the risk of being displaced. It was for this reason that Wolof rulers often surrounded themselves with warriors and praise-singers. A description of Wolof chiefs is contained in the writings of Cadamosto:

> The Kingdom (of Senega) is not hereditary, but commonly three or four lords (of which there are many in the country) choose a king to their own liking (yet always of noble parentage) who reigns as long as he pleases them. They often dethrone their Kings by force; and the Kings many times render themselves so powerful, as to stand on their defence . . . This king has no certain revenue, but the lords of the country, to court his favour, make him presents every year of horses . . . and other beasts such as cows and goats, also . . . millet, and such like things. This King likewise lives by robberies, and forcing some of his subjects and those of neighbouring provinces into slavery, part whereof he employs in cultivating the lands assigned him, and sells the rest to the Azanaghi, and Arabian merchants who trade here with horses and other things . . .

The Wolof were, even more rigidly than the Serer, organised into castes. The castes of the freeborn ranged from the royal lineages at the top to that of the peasants at the bottom. Slaves formed a class of their own. All organised and settled communities in this region followed a similar pattern of domestic slavery. There were two categories of slaves owned by the Wolof. The first comprised those slaves who were either captured in war or acquired by purchase. These were not considered to be an integral part of the household, and could be sold. The second category of slaves consisted of those born in the household. They were practically treated as children of the family. The stigma attaching to slave status must not be over-emphasised, because, as in many Muslim communities, slaves among the Wolof sometimes rose to the position of royal advisers. In this capacity they wielded tremendous influence. The majority of slaves, however, were tied to the soil which they tilled for their owners.

The Wolof had always allowed Tukolor clerics to settle among them. In the nineteenth century, they faced not only the pressure of French imperialism but also the growing influence of a Tukolor cleric called MāBā who gathered around him forces of resistance to the French by exhortation to a jihād. The old religious founda-tions of the Wolof rulers were wrecked and Islam made rapid progress. French occupation meant the dismemberment of the Wolof states and this process was complete after 1886.

THE TUKOLOR AND THE MANDINKA

The Tukolor occupied the middle Senegal. They originally con-trolled a territory far to the north of the Senegal until the pressure of the Berbers forced them back to the Senegal valley. The Tukolor, led by their ruling dynasty, accepted Islam with enthusiasm. They were in fact the first Negro converts to Islam in the Western Sudan. Tukolor clerics were largely instrumental in spreading Islam to the Wolof and neighbouring peoples. It is worth noting that the famous jihāds of West Africa were led by clerics who originated from Tukolor, for instance Al-Hājj 'Umar and Usuman dan Fodio.[1]

From the Gambia to what is today the state of Guinea, Mandinka peoples predominate. The pattern of political organisa-tion in all Mandinka states was the same. The village units were under the authority of the elders. Superimposed over these elders was the king who was venerated by the members of the state. It would be misleading to suggest that the Mandinka king was an autocrat, since he was constrained to rule in close consultation with the elders of the village units. The king did not possess the admini-strative paraphernalia with which to control such matters as local justice, the collection of trade duties and the distribution of land. This type of Mandinka state organisation was found in the com-munities to the east of the Gambia River.

THE FULBE[2] JIHĀDS

There were two areas in which Fulbe infiltration ultimately led to local jihāds during the eighteenth and nineteenth centuries. The first was Fouta Toro where the clerical class, the Torodbe, founded a clerical state by 1776. Political control was extended from here over the various groups of Wolof and Mandinka. The state was a feudal theocratic elective state under an al-mami. The latter distributed both land and political authority to the leaders of the jihād. The clerical class largely displaced the indigenous rulers, became the new nobility and formed an electoral college which chose the head of state. The state had no capital, and each elected head resided in his own village. In the middle of the nineteenth century the great influence of Al-Hājj 'Umar strengthened the resistance against French penetration, but after the death of the Muslim leader the state fell into anarchy. The French military governor, Faidherbe, won over many of the dismembered provinces of the state to accept French protection. They were annexed to Senegal.

The Fouta Djallon comprises a vast plateau broken here and there by deep valleys. The original Negroes, the Susus, were excellent farmers but Fulbe elements were gradually superimposed on them. The Fulbe were accompanied by clerics who, towards the end of the eighteenth century, inaugurated a jihād. Fouta Djallon became a religious republic under an elective ruler. The new state was in the nineteenth century really a federation of small feudal states. The central authority was very weak. The other Fulbe state was Bondou which was organised in the manner already described. Lack of unity among the Fulbe states facilitated French conquest in spite of the rallying cry of Islam.

SIERRA LEONE TRIBES

In Sierra Leone the number of peoples is such as to defy accurate classification. Along the coast the inhabitants belong to groups known as the Atlantic sub-family. They include the Bulom and the Sherbro. These are confined to the coast by the pressure of immigrant groups from the plateau behind. To the south-east of Sierra Leone the Mende migrated into the forest zone. They were themselves also under pressure from other tribes to the north. The Mende came as settlers and hunters. They were later organised into war-chiefdoms. Walled towns were established and young men were conscripted as war-boys to fight the chiefs' battles. Slave-raiding became an important economic occupation and provided an additional inducement for the wars between neighbouring chiefs. Large confederacies were built up as a result of war, but do not seem to have been very stable. One Mende war chief during the nineteenth century was Kai Lundo who, through hard fighting, became the overlord of an empire which stretched from Guinea to Liberia.

The north of Sierra Leone is a land of many peoples. These include Mandinka tribes, the Susus, the Limbas, the Konos and the Temnes. The Temnes conquered the land and enslaved the Susus, Limbas and the Lokos. They created a strong state which derived much of its prosperity from the slave trade with Euro-peans. In the nineteenth century however the Susus were con-verted to Islam. They revolted against the Temnes and set up their own state on the Scarcies rivers. In fact they became the overlords of the Temnes. Muslim kings ruled in the area until the establish-ment of European rule.

The coast belt of what is today Liberia and the Ivory coast is low-lying and is honey-combed with lagoons and mangrove swamps. This is the home of many groups belonging to the Atlantic sub-family. The best known of these are the Kru. The Kru and their neighbours, the Vai, the Bassa and the Bakwe, lacked a complex type of integration. Authority was in the hands of elders representing family segments which claimed a common ancestry. During the nineteenth century the Kru fondness for life at sea stood them in good stead. They were employed in vessels operating along the coast of West Africa and were also recruited for contract labour in Spanish Fernando Po.

Tribes who inhabit the country behind the coast are Mende elements. Little is known about these groups except that they were a Negroid race and spoke related dialects. They specialised in agriculture, trade and handicraft manufactures. Behind them were Muslim Mandinka elements who traded and spread Islam into the upper Ivory Coast region. These traders settled at first in villages along the trade routes and brought a measure of prosperity to the pagan people among whom they settled. During the nineteenth century the Muslim groups made various attempts to gain political control, and small states were formed. The most important of these

17

states was that of Kong. Under a Muslim leader, called Shaiku, Kong became the centre of a feudal state which extended its authority to the borders of the forest in the south. When the French explorer, Binger, visited Kong in 1888, he found a town of 15,000 inhabitants. There were mosques, and the houses of the ruling classes were adorned with terraces. The activities of the adventurer, Samori, disturbed the peace and prosperity of the northern region of Ivory Coast. Samori's troops invaded the area in 1895, massacred the clerics and razed Kong to the ground. French protection could not avert this disaster.

FRENCH 'COLONISATION'

Thus during the nineteenth century the portion of West Africa considered in this chapter was subjected to two great forces: militant Islam from the north and European expansion from the south. The results of the local jihāds in Fouta Toro and Fouta Djallon having been examined, the consequences of European action in the second half of the century must now be considered. European expansion invariably began with the occupation of the coast. So it was with the French who had a settlement at the mouth of the Senegal River. It was a wretched settlement which dragged out a wearisome existence until Governor Faidherbe arrived in 1854 when a handful of languishing trading posts was soon transformed into the beginnings of the town of St Louis. In 1857 Dakar was founded. The indigenous chiefs of the immediate hinterland were forced by treaty or conquest to surrender their territory to what became the colony of Senegal.

Faidherbe's ambition went beyond the coastal region. To control the hinterland trade the French had to expand inland and encounter the hostility of the Muslim states which emerged from the local jihāds. Behind these states was the powerful Tukolar leader, Al-Hājj 'Umar who controlled an empire that stretched from the Senegal to the Niger. Faidherbe organised a formidable army, and in a series of campaigns destroyed the petty Fulbe states of Fouta Toro and drove 'Umar eastwards. By the 1860 treaty with 'Umar, the French gained full control of the Senegal River. In addition to a compact block of territory in the Senegal, the French had nuclear posts along the coast of what became Guinea and the Ivory Coast. The Guinea base was secured in the rear by a military expedition organised from Conakry against

Fouta Djallon. The holy Muslim city of Timbo was captured and the Muslim 'republics' dismembered. Then from the Senegal and Guinea bases the French began their advance towards the Niger basin.

The son of 'Umar, Ahmad, had attempted to rebuild his father's empire, so once again the French advance had to take the form of military expeditions. Between 1880 and 1883 the French waged campaigns against Ahmad. Bamako was occupied in 1883, and there followed the establishment of military posts from Medina on the Senegal to Bamako on the Niger. French inland advance from the Ivory Coast was retarded by impenetrable forests and the absence of centrally organised African groups in the immediate hinterland. Two states in the north of the Ivory Coast, Kong and Odienne, became French allies against Samori who had consolidated the inland tribes and made himself the most formidable African opponent of French colonial expansion. In the closing years of the nineteenth century Samori was defeated by the French. The dream of linking French coastal possessions with one another and, through Timbuktu, with Southern Algeria became a reality. The French venture was in the main an imperialistic one based on military conquest: a *peace or powder* policy! Disorganisation and anarchy naturally followed the military campaigns right across the Sudanese belt of territory. Much of this whole region remained under French military control up to the end of the century.

BRITISH COLONIES AND PROTECTORATES

The British had for centuries owned a trading station which ultimately became Bathurst, the capital of Gambia. Britain regarded the valley of the Gambia River as hers by right of discovery, exploration and 'possession for three hundred years'. The claim was a hollow one, and indeed as late as 1881 the British Governor of Bathurst wrote of the river above Yarbu-Tenda as a region where one 'sought in vain for homestead or hamlet, for clearing or cultivation or other sign of human occupancy of the land, but met with instead the sadness of what it is no hyperbole to call the "abomination of desolation" which reigned over the scene'. When however the French began, from the Senegal base, to burn villages up to within three miles of the Gambia River and chase the village chiefs across the river itself, Britain decided to make effective her claim to the Gambia River. As a result of negotiations between Britain and France, the former withdrew her claims to the watershed of the Gambia River but retained the navigable portion of the river. A boundary agreement signed in 1889 restricted British Gambia to a narrow strip on each bank of the river as far as Yarbu-Tenda.

Another British possession which the spectacular hinterland penetration of the French reduced to a comparatively small enclave was Sierra Leone. British enterprise had begun with the foundation of Free Town in 1787 by a British philanthropic organisation to settle freed slaves. Negro immigrants arrived from Britain, Canada and the West Indies, and included also African slaves rescued on the high seas by the British navy. After extremely hazardous beginnings, the settlement took root and the British government made it a colony in 1808. The boundaries of the colony comprehended Freetown and the Peninsula, Sherbro Island and Turner's Peninsula. The remainder of the coast up to the Mano River, which forms the boundary with Liberia, was acquired from the local chiefs. For nearly three-quarters of the century British authority was confined to these regions. In the hinterland the indigenous groups, the Mende, the Temne, the Kono and so forth, continued to live their traditional lives. Chiefs fought one another to capture slaves either for labour and prestige, or for sale to the Sofa traders from the north. These activities were inconsistent with the prosperity and peace of Freetown. Indeed, the Mende brought one of their many wars down to the Sherbro in 1880. From this time the British authorities in Freetown sought through treaties and arbitration to restore peace and trade to the hinterland, and recalcitrant chiefs were arrested and deported. The presence of a large number of the dreaded Sofas facilitated Britain's task in securing treaties of protection. These Sofas were slavers and mercenaries who were willing to fight for any chief who could employ them and their passage invariably left behind a trail of devastation.

Following a boundary agreement with France in 1895, Britain proclaimed the Sierra Leone hinterland a Protectorate. The chiefs were loath to abandon their traditional pattern of life, but no resistance was necessary when British authority was only represented by Travelling Commissioners and the occasional appearance of Frontier Policemen. The introduction of the Hut Tax in

1896 sparked off rebellion and British colonial troops had to do some pretty severe fighting, especially in the Temne country. Then again in 1899 the behaviour of the tax collectors and policemen precipitated the Mende war. Creoles and Europeans in the Mende country were butchered in cold blood. The rebellion was soon suppressed, and the British authorities came to the conclusion that more effective rule should be imposed on the hinterland regions.

LIBERIA

The beginnings of Monrovia were similar to those of Freetown. The enterprise here was initiated by American philanthropists and others who either sincerely wished to found a proper home for American Negroes or were merely anxious to rid the United States of the inconveniently large number of freed Negroes in their midst. In 1822 the first contingent was landed in what became Monrovia by the American Colonisation Society. Through the purchase of land from the indigenous owners the coastal region was soon consolidated. From 1822 to 1847 Monrovia was managed by the Colonisation Society which appointed agents to act as governors. In the latter year the Monrovian Negroes assembled in a convention and proclaimed their colony a free and independent republic. The relations between the new republic and the neighbouring Kru people were uneasy. In the hinterland the Bassa, Gola, Kisi and Mende groups were left to their own devices. Although Monrovian explorers traversed the hinterland and signed treaties with chiefs here and there, the lack of resources, including a Frontier Force, made it impossible for the republic to prevent the French from truncating the hinterland. The peoples of what was left of the hinterland continued to live very much as they had before the foundation of Monrovia, indulging in raids and inter-village warfare. International agreements carved out an area which became Liberia, but the task of subduing the hinterland groups was one which Monrovia could not undertake during the nineteenth century.

The disturbances which overwhelmed this portion of West Africa, from the Senegal to the Ivory Coast, whether stemming from the Tukolar jihāds or from the activities of Europeans, left their mark on the indigenous African peoples. Many tribes and chiefdoms were broken up. African traditional society was disrupted. In the end, the imposition of a new system of rule by the

Europeans or by the westernised Negroes produced a new social and political order.

NOTES

1 See p. 294.
2 The Fulbe are called Fulani in many parts of West Africa. See p. 307.

QUESTIONS FOR FURTHER STUDY AND DISCUSSION

1 Describe the political institutions of any two groups in the area covered in this chapter.

2 How would you account for the great influence of the Tukolar before the imposition of European rule?

3 'A rather doubtful monument of an over-optimistic adventure in philanthropy.' Consider this verdict on the foundation and early history of Freetown.

4 Describe the relations between the British authorities in Freetown and the hinterland groups between 1880 and 1900.

5 Why was French expansion bound to cause the disruption of the indigenous political order?

6 During the nineteenth century, Liberia was a mere geographical expression. Why was this bound to be so?

SELECT BIBLIOGRAPHY

J. Spencer Trimingham, *The History of Islam in West Africa*, Chapters 4 and 5, O.U.P., 1962.

C. P. Murdock, *Africa: Its Peoples and Their Culture History*, Parts 3, 4, 7 and 11, McGraw Hill, New York, 1959.

T. J. Alldridge, *A Transformed Colony*, Seeley, 1910.

S. H. Roberts, *History of French Colonial Policy (1870–1925)*, Vol. 1, London, 1925; reissued F. Cass, 1963.

R. Earle Anderson, *Liberia*, University of Northern Carolina Press, 1952.

15 Asante and Fante in the Nineteenth Century

GODFREY N. BROWN

ALTHOUGH it is invidious to focus attention on the history of the Asante and Fante and largely to ignore the history of the other peoples of Ghana, this can to some extent be justified. Both Asante and Fante belong to the Akan group of peoples; together and with their allies in the nineteenth century they constituted the majority of the people living within what are now the frontiers of Ghana. Moreover, the history of their relationship epitomises two significant themes in the modern history of Africa: resistance to European-type development in the case of the Asante and adaptation to this type of development in the case of the Fante.

The place of origin of the Akan peoples is a matter of historical speculation, but it is now generally agreed that they moved into what is now Ghana at some period during the eleventh, twelfth and thirteenth centuries. In all probability they reached the coast about the time that the Ga-Adangme and Ewe peoples were moving into south-east Ghana from the Togo-Dahomey area. There was certainly some intermixing between the Akan and the Guan whom they found in their areas of settlement.

The growth of both Asante and Fante occurred largely in the eighteenth century but it was made possible by earlier developments, notably the expansion of trade. In the case of the Fante, trade was carried on with inland towns and possibly by canoe with the Benin region as well as with Europeans in the trade forts; in the case of Asante there was considerable trade with Jenne and other towns on the bend of the Niger as well as with the coast. With trade, of course, went the firearms that contributed to the expansion of both peoples. In respect of Asante, to these factors must be added the statecraft exhibited by such rulers as Osei Tutu in the first years of the eighteenth century and Opoku Ware whose reign as Asantehene was probably from 1720 to 1750. To Osei Tutu is attributed the foundation of Kumasi which was to astonish Bowdich by its wealth and admirable sanitation in 1817. Much less is known about the rulers of the Fante, and of Abora, described in 1752 as 'the first town in Fante'.

By the beginning of the nineteenth century the Asante Confederacy covered a large area embracing the whole of the present-day Asante Region and much of Brong-Ahafo and part of the Western and Eastern Regions together with considerable territory in the Ivory Coast, Togo and Dahomey. The Fante Confederacy on the other hand, covered much of what is now the Central Region of Ghana. Within the Fante area the people of Elmina acknowledged the authority of the Asantehene, and the Dutch occupants of its castle paid him an annual sum as they had done since the battle of Feyiase (1701) when the Asante had acquired the 'note' for the fort from the Denkyira.

The Asante form of government was exceedingly complex and flexible involving something of divine right (with those in authority occupying a special relationship with the omnipresent ancestor world); something of feudalism (with a hierarchy of chiefs owing varying degrees of allegiance and obligation); something of 'indirect rule' (with tributary chiefs empowered to rule their own peoples, sometimes 'under the immediate care of' a 'resident' from the Asantehene); something of a system of checks and balances (particularly in the see-saw relationship between the nuclear Kumasi chiefs and the chiefs of outlying provinces); plus an admixture of democratic practice (e.g. the Asantehene and his chiefs might be 'destooled' for sacrilege, repeatedly rejecting sage counsel or excessive cruelty). Government was carried on through a three-tier organisation: the Asantehene; the Council (to tender advice especially on external relations); and an Assembly of Chiefs and Captains (with a much more restricted role than that of the Council). And government had at its command a remarkably well-ordered army. Finally, pervading the whole social structure of Asante, there was the Golden Stool, the 'soul of the people', brought down from the heavens by a miracle. Truly the Asante Confederacy was unique. It was not surprising, though it was tragic, that expatriates from Victorian Britain failed to understand it and represented it as 'that stronghold of Satan' (Maclean).

Less is known about the government of the Fante Confederacy; in all probability because it was much less well organised. The Fante appear to have lacked the mystique of government and the unity that had been so highly developed amongst the Asante, and

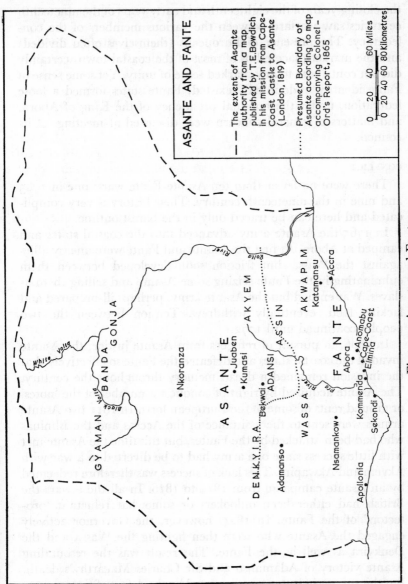

Fig. 14 Asante and Fante.

ASANTE AND FANTE

— — — The extent of Asante authority from a map published by T. E. Bowdich in his mission from Cape-Coast Castle to Asante (London, 1819)

· · · · · · · Presumed Boundary of Asante according to map accompanying Colonel Ord's Report, 1865

0   20   40   60 Miles

0 20 40 60 80 Kilometres

the closing years of the eighteenth and early years of the nineteenth centuries saw warfare between the various members of the confederacy. The presence of Europeans (themselves often divided) and the market-place ethos of most of the coastal towns certainly did not contribute to any marked sense of unity. Yet some sense of Fante identity undoubtedly existed; Fante states formed a loose federation, under the nominal presidency of the King of Abora, and matters of general concern were discussed at meetings of its council.

CONFLICT

There were no fewer than ten Asante-Fante wars: one in 1765 and nine in the nineteenth century. Their history is very complicated and here can be traced only in the barest outline.

In 1765 the Asante army advanced into the coastal states and camped at Abora. At first the Asante and Fante were uneasy allies against the Wassa but friction soon developed between them culminating in the Fante seizing some Asante and selling them as slaves. War ensued but the Asante army, perhaps ill-prepared and lacking food, eventually withdrew. Tension between the two peoples continued until 1772.

In 1806, in pursuit of refugees from Asante justice, the Asante invaded the coastal states and defeated the Fante so effectively that the invasion remained a dread memory throughout the century. The Asante acquired by right of conquest a number of the 'notes' or ground rents of some of the European forts. In 1811 two Asante armies were sent to the assistance of the Accras and the Elminas who had been attacked by the Fantes, but this time the Asante met with little success since one army had to be diverted to a war with Akyem and Akwapim. This lack of success was therefore redeemed by an Asante campaign from 1814 to 1816. In all these wars the British had either been onlookers or somewhat reluctant 'protectors' of the Fante. In 1824, however, the Governor actively engaged the Asante who were then fighting the Wassa and the Denkyira as well as the Fante. The result was the resounding Asante victory of Adamanso and Sir Charles Macarthy's death. But this success in its turn was reversed by the defeat of Katamansu, largely owing to the employment of congreve rockets by the British. And so this phase of conflict was brought to a close with a treaty negotiated in 1831 by Governor Maclean who used the good offices of the Asante Princess, Akiawa. By this treaty, *inter alia*, the Fante, Denkyira and Assin were freed from allegiance to the Asantehene, and trade routes were to be kept open.

Despite a number of incidents, active warfare between Asante and the people of the coast did not break out again until 1863 when the British again failed to hand over a refugee from Asante justice. The conflict was indecisive but the Asante appear to have had the better of it and retired across the Pra at the onset of the rainy season. Fante hostility to Elmina led to another invasion in 1869 which was combined with a war with the Krepe, and although peace negotiations were started peace was not achieved. With the cession by the Dutch of Elmina Castle to the British in 1872—an action which the Asantehene considered an affront to his long-established rights—war was renewed and the Fante again defeated. The British thereupon determined to take much more drastic action than hitherto. Sir Garnet Wolseley was sent out. He conducted a hasty campaign, invaded Asante and destroyed Kumasi. By the Treaty of Fomena (1874) the Asantehene agreed *inter alia* to pay an indemnity of 50,000 ounces of gold, to renounce all claims to the allegiance of Denkyira, Assin, Akyem, Adansi and 'the other allies of Her Majesty formerly subject to the Kingdom of Ashantee'; to give up all claims to Elmina and all payments in respect of the forts; and to promote freedom of trade.

In the contest between the two Akan peoples, British participation became increasingly marked: the Asante from fighting the Fante in 1806 were fighting Anglo-Fante forces in 1824 and thereafter, and the whole process neared its climax in 1901 when the British occupied Kumasi and sent the Asantehene, Prempe I, and members of the royal family into exile. The different attitude adopted towards the British by the Fante resulted in a similar outcome; gradually British jurisdiction increased. The Bond of 1844 between Maclean and the Fante chiefs was to achieve an exaggerated significance in Ghanaian history, but it certainly seems to have meant that, in the coastal states, reference of crimes involving killing to British courts became general. British power became paramount when the coastal area was transformed into the Gold Coast Colony in 1874. Finally, in 1902 the frontiers of the colony were defined, Asante became a crown colony and the Northern Territories Protectorate was created. Thus baldly stated, it might seem that British policy in the nineteenth century was single-mindedly devoted to the introduction of colonial rule in Ghana but the reality was very different: its hesitations, its flirtation with the idea of complete withdrawal, its reluctance to do anything and its vacillations of intent were in fact a signal illustration of 'muddling through'.

CAUSES OF CONFLICT

Amongst the numerous reasons for Asante-Fante conflict, economic and cultural factors merit especial consideration.

Economically much of the conflict arose out of trade rivalry. The Asante wished to trade directly with the forts on the coast; the Fante wished to act as middlemen. In such circumstances occasions for conflict were numerous: complaints about the maltreatment of traders and commercial malpractices were common. In 1817, for instance, the Asantehene informed the Governor of Cape Coast 'the Ashantees send gold to purchase merchandise, and the Fantees mix bad with it'. It was owing to trade and especially the importation of firearms that Asante attached so much importance to the possession of Elmina. A great number of the diplomatic negotiations of the century were concerned to keep 'the paths open' so that trade might flow freely.

The economic pattern, too, largely contributed to the link between the Fante and the British. The latter might well have feared an Asante monopoly of trade and have supported the Fante for this reason, but a more direct motive for their policy was their realisation that they were largely dependent on the coastal peoples for their very existence. Through these people they obtained wood and water, fish and vegetables. The Fante supplied them with labour and with concubines who contributed to the mulatto population of the Coast. Inevitably mutual interests drew the British and the Fante together, although there was, of course, considerable friction from time to time.

Thus was created the cultural cause of the conflict between the Asante and the Fante. The Asante refused to compromise the integrity of their institutions and were prepared to fight for them. The immediate cause of many of the wars was an affront to Asante practices and institutions. The Fante, on the other hand, showed much greater readiness to accept the process of acculturation. An instance of this was their willingness to submit disputes to the arbitration of George Maclean from 1830 to 1844 at a time when there was no legal basis for the exercise of his jurisdiction nor means available to enforce it.

The differing attitudes of the two peoples is clearly illustrated by their treatment of Christian missions. In Asante the Wesleyans were permitted to establish a station in Kumasi in 1843 but they were clearly only there on sufferance and their work fell into desuetude. In 1876 they were told: 'The Bible is not a book for us . . . we will never embrace your religion.' They made more progress during the last few years of the century but in 1900, in the course of the Yaa Asantewa war (occasioned by the folly of the Governor, Sir Frederic Hodgson, in demanding the Golden Stool), most of their churches were destroyed. Other missions had to wait until the twentieth century before they could start work in Asante.

In Fante, largely owing to the existence of the trade forts, the missions had made more progress by the end of the eighteenth century than they had in Asante a hundred years later. A few Fante had been converted to Christianity in the 1750s and some converts such as Jacobus Capiten and Philip Quaque had gone on to become missionaries in their turn. The Wesleyans arrived in Cape Coast in 1833 after they had received a request for a case of Bibles. Thereafter, particularly in the second half of the century, they came to enjoy considerable influence amongst the Fante largely owing to the work of Thomas Birch Freeman. Other missions, too, were established in their midst.

One result of the different attitudes of the Asante and the Fante to the missions is shown on a map produced by the Gold Coast Education Department in 1902.[1] This locates over thirty schools in Fante; in Asante there is only one (government) school.

Despite such differences, however, the Asante and Fante possessed much in common: speaking dialects of Twi, recognising common lineage patterns and similar laws of inheritance. Their social associations were similar: often being dedicated to religion, hunting or war. At the same time it seems likely that the different circumstances of the two peoples led to some differences even in traditional institutions. Thus the Asante prohibited the warrior companies (Asafo) from drumming when there was no war or other emergency. In Fante, on the other hand, rivalries between Asafo within a town, even in normal times, sometimes resulted in bloodshed. 'Beyond the Colony such outbreaks would be almost impossible,' wrote A. B. Ellis in 1887, 'but the Colonial

Government while destroying the power of the chiefs has left the company organisation intact.'[2]

CONCLUSION

In 1903 the Ghanaian scholar J. E. Casely Hayford pointed out in his *Gold Coast Native Institutions* that since the Fante and the Asante derived from the same stock their differences in character arose 'from their respective local environments', and today it is difficult to gainsay this conclusion. Retrospection, however, does afford an opportunity of appreciating both the Asante and Fante achievements.

The Asante were remarkably successful in retaining their cohesion as a people. Dr Adu Boahen has observed that it is a fitting testimony to the unifying force of the Golden Stool that Asante today consists almost solely of the states which are said to have been represented when the stool made its first appearance. Moreover, Asante has managed to keep much of its traditional culture as can be seen in the work of its Kente weavers and its goldsmiths. Ghana today is undoubtedly enriched by the traditions and achievements of Asante civilisation.[3]

The Fante achievement has been no less considerable. It spearheaded the rise of a non-traditional elite but at the same time, in the Fante Confederation formed in 1867, it demonstrated how both the educated and the traditional rulers might work together for the common good. Thus its Mankessim Constitution of 1871, amongst other provisions, declared that a chief and an educated man should be chosen from each district to sit as members of a Representative Assembly of the Confederation to serve for a three-year period of office; that this Assembly should elect members of the Executive Council for the same period; and that this Council should carry on many of the functions of government, ensuring that taxes were paid, good roads were built and schools provided so that compulsory education might be introduced. The reaction of the British administrator to the deputation who brought him the Mankessim Constitution was to have its members arrested on the charge of treason. The Secretary of State acted more sanely and ordered their release, but the Constitution was not given the serious consideration that it merited.

Finally, it must be emphasised that some educated Fante like J. Mensah Sarbah and Casely Hayford were far from being slavish adherents of things European. The latter, in particular, was ardently concerned to promote both Asante-Fante unity and African culture. Indeed, his remarkably prescient novel, *Ethiopia Unbound, Studies in Race Emancipation*, published in 1911, contained almost all the ideas and ideology of modern African thought. Nor was its vision limited to Africa: 'the kind of history that I would teach would be universal history with particular reference to the part that Ethiopia has played in the world'.

NOTE

1 This map is reproduced in D. Kimble, *A Political History of Ghana*, facing p. 75, O.U.P., 1963.
2 Asafo were prohibited in Asante at the end of the nineteenth century. In Fante and elsewhere they remained and often performed work that would now be called community development. The annual deer-catching competition of the Efutu that is still held at Winneba is perhaps the best-known test of the manliness of the Asafo.
3 For eloquent visual testimony of this see A. A. Y. Kyerematen, *Panoply of Ghana*, Longmans, 1964.

QUESTIONS FOR FURTHER STUDY AND DISCUSSION

1 What traditional practices do the Asante and the Fante have in common?
2 Did the presence of (a) the British and (b) the Dutch on the coast serve to conciliate the Asante and the Fante or to aggravate their differences?
3 Would it have been possible to have carried out the proposals of the Mankessim Constitution in the nineteenth century?
4 In what circumstances did (a) the Golden Stool 'reappear' in 1921, and (b) Prempe I return to Asante?

SELECT BIBLIOGRAPHY

W. E. F. Ward, *A History of Ghana*, George Allen & Unwin, revised 2nd edition, 1963.
J. D. Fage, *Ghana: A Historical Interpretation*, University of Wisconsin Press, 1959.
A. Boahen, 'Asante and Fante: 1000 to 1800' and 'Asante, Fante and British, 1800–1880', *A Thousand Years of West African History*, Ibadan U.P./Nelson, 1965.
D. Kimble, *A Political History of Ghana*, O.U.P., 1963.
G. E. Metcalfe, *Great Britain and Ghana, Documents of Ghana History, 1807–1957*. Nelson, 1964.

I. Wilks, *The Northern Factor in Ashanti History*, Institute of African Studies, University College of Ghana, 1961.

Freda Wolfson, *Pageant of Ghana*, O.U.P., 1958.

A. W. Lawrence, *Trade Castles and Forts of West Africa*, Cape, 1963.

J. H. Nketia, *Drumming in Akan Communities of Ghana*, University of Ghana, Nelson, 1963.

Articles by I. Wilks, Margaret Priestley and W. Tordoff in *The Journal of African History* should also be consulted.

16 Dahomey and Yoruba in the Nineteenth Century

I. AKINJOGBIN

FOR most of the nineteenth century the kingdom of Dahomey covered only approximately the southern third of the present republic of Dahomey. It had a frightening reputation, particularly in the latter half of the century, when the mere mention of the name aroused fear, passion or admiration in the countries immediately surrounding it. Europeans too had a fantastic impression of the kingdom. To some it was the kingdom of the Amazons, where women fought much more efficiently than men. To others it was simply a barbaric outpost in jungle Africa, where the slave trade reigned supreme and European civilisation was resisted.

The Dahomean authorities themselves did little to give their kingdom a better image in the outside world. They mercilessly massacred their war prisoners and delighted in razing to the ground a once crowded city. They delayed every European visitor, put him in something like honourable confinement and made him an unwilling spectator of human sacrifice.

The behaviour of the kings of Dahomey (and the impression which they created outside their territories) became known in the nineteenth century through their relations with the Yoruba. This chapter examines briefly the history behind Dahomey's adoption of the policies that gave it such a bad reputation, traces its operation in the nineteenth century and discusses its consequences.

DAHOMEY AND YORUBA

The relations between Dahomey and Yoruba go far back into history. Oral traditions of the Yoruba, the Aja and the Ewe peoples witness to the fact that long before Dahomey had a political identity there had been strong cultural contact between the Aja peoples under the leadership of Allada and the Yoruba peoples under the leadership of Ife. This cultural contact was so strong that by the early seventeenth century the Yoruba language was the *lingua franca* of both the Aja and the Ewe. Nor did the contact abate

18

after that period, for recent studies show that the majority of the religious beliefs of Dahomey derived from the Yoruba country. But although we have evidence for this cultural contact we are yet uncertain as to whether it was shared from a common source or was imposed by force or persuasion on the Aja.

However, from about the last quarter of the seventeenth century, the relationship between the Oyo (a section of the Yoruba) and the

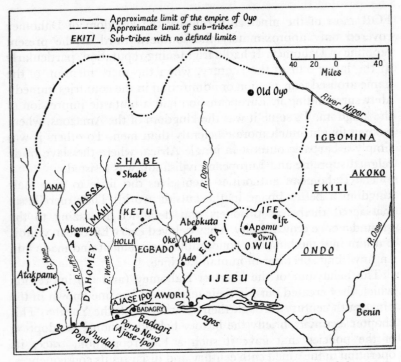

Fig. 15   Yoruba and Dahomey at the beginning of the
nineteenth century.

Aja started to change to that of master and vassal. Twice between 1680 and 1700 the Oyo army invaded Allada (Ardra) the capital of the Aja family of states. The first invasion occurred between 1680 and 1682, and by the time of the second invasion in 1698 Allada would seem to have become a vassal state of the Alafin of Oyo.

By the time that Oyo was overrunning Allada, events within the Aja family of states, notably the introduction of the trans-Atlantic slave trade with its effects on pre-existing social and economic organisations, had started to weaken their traditional political organisation. From about the middle of the seventeenth century there were constant rebellions against Allada, the hitherto accepted leader of the Aja states. These rebellions often resulted in civil wars and further fragmentation, all of which clearly demonstrated that the traditional concept of organisation was no longer adequate for the existing situation. But Oyo overlordship concerned itself mainly with the regular collection of tributes and not with internal administrative reforms, so that it did not stop disintegration within the Aja country. Clearly then, at the beginning of the eighteenth century, there was a power vacuum within the Aja family of states.

This gave Dahomey the chance to establish its political identity. Before the beginning of the eighteenth century, Dahomey had been only one of the states within the Aja family and by no means one of the most important. Its king had always been crowned at Allada. But partly as a result of adversity, which arose because of constant raids from its southern neighbours, particularly Whydah, Popo and Allada, Dahomey was forced to organise itself on a strong military basis which by the beginning of the eighteenth century was powerful enough to resist aggression from its southern neighbours and fill the political vacuum that was being created in Aja.

In 1724, on the invitation of a contestant to the Allada throne who lost, but was unwilling to abide by the traditional methods, Agaja, the King of Dahomey, invaded and destroyed Allada, thus destroying the basis of the traditional concept of government. It therefore became incumbent upon Dahomey to bring the rest of the Aja states under a new form of authority. In 1727 Whydah was conquered and by 1730 the Dahomean Revolution had been accomplished.

No sooner had Dahomey attempted to fill the vacuum in the Aja states than it fell foul of the Oyo authorities. For two reasons, the Oyo could not stand passively by and watch Dahomey's expansion. First there was, as we have seen, the tributary relationship between Allada and Oyo; and, naturally, Oyo would not tamely submit to its rights being abrogated. Secondly, the Aja family of states were organised on patterns similar to the Yoruba family of states. The conquest of Allada therefore meant the overthrow of the old principles familiar to the Oyo and it was a revolutionary move which must be checked if it were not to spread confusion. So the Oyo authorities invaded Dahomey four times between 1726 and 1730, ravaging the area and breaking the powers of resistance of the nascent kingdom of Dahomey

At the same time that the Oyo were showing their unmistakable dislike for the political implications of Agaja's conquests, the Europeans were reaching the conclusion that he would not be such a ready slave dealer as they had expected. They noticed that he forbade his subjects to trade in slaves, burned the European slaving houses and sought contact with Europeans other than the slave traders. They therefore developed a hostile attitude to him and decided to side with his enemies. The result was that although the Europeans and the Oyo never came to an agreement for a concerted action against Dahomey, each side put pressures on Agaja simultaneously and forced him to do their will. In 1730 Agaja agreed formally to Dahomey being a tributary state of Oyo and that a small part of the old Allada kingdom should be carved out into a new kingdom of Porto Novo (Ajase-Ipo).

Furthermore, he agreed with the Europeans that he would protect those within his territory and not oppose the slave trade in the way he had hitherto done. But he also gained a few important concessions. He was left as master over the internal affairs of his kingdom and was allowed to retain his army—something not commonly granted to many tributary states of the Oyo empire. In the same way, it was left to Agaja and his successors on the throne of Dahomey to determine the positive policy that was to be taken about the slave trade in the future. In a way the relations between Dahomey and Yoruba in the nineteenth century were governed by the way this very important treaty of 1730 worked out during the rest of the eighteenth century.

Politically for the rest of the century, Dahomey remained a tributary state within the Oyo empire. The attempt made towards the end of the reign of Agaja and the beginning of the reign of Tegbesu (between 1738 and 1748) to throw off the Oyo yoke seems to have resulted in very heavy punishment for Dahomey. After 1748 Dahomey did not again neglect to pay the annual tribute for the rest of the eighteenth century. Indeed from 1740 onwards until the end of the century the court of Dahomey increasingly imbibed both cultural and religious ideas from the Yoruba. But Dahomey was not completely happy with the situation. Gaha, the famous (or infamous) Bashorun of Oyo, must have kept a very strict control over Dahomey as he did over all the rest of the Oyo empire. Alafin Abiodun, who was more conscious of his imperial rights than any of his immediate predecessors, and who knew how to exploit them to the full, maintained the control over Dahomey by diplomatic threats. It was made quite plain to Dahomey that although it was allowed to keep its army in the 1730 treaty, Oyo regarded the Dahomean army as an agent that must be used mainly for Oyo interests, and expected to be consulted and its permission obtained before any military operations were independently undertaken by Dahomey. What may have irked Dahomey more than anything else were the petty restrictions which further emphasised that the prestige of its kings was very limited. For instance Oyo periodically passed laws prohibiting the kings of Dahomey from using for their garments certain materials, regarded as only fit for the sovereign. The Alafin also regarded themselves as heirs to all the most important chiefs within Dahomey and would not tolerate any attempt to cheat them of this right.

The record of the Oyo rule over Dahomey was however not all oppression; indeed it could be plausibly argued that Dahomey gained more than she lost. For example, Oyo shielded Dahomey from its estranged neighbours and therefore prevented its destruction when it was weak. Moreover, by preventing Dahomey from dissipating its energy in useless expansionist wars, Oyo gave Dahomey a period of peace at home during which the latter consolidated its internal organisation. Dahomey was even able to borrow administrative ideas from Oyo. But the Dahomeans did not always remember these. The net result left the Dahomeans completely dissatisfied with the Oyo rule and nurtured in them an inveterate hatred for the Yoruba. They watched assiduously for an opportunity to throw off the hateful yoke of the Oyo oppressors.

While the Dahomeans were nursing their resentment against the Yoruba people, they were not feeling particularly happy about their economic situation at home. The slave trade which became the basis of their economy from about 1740 onwards only made the country superficially prosperous for a few years. From about the middle of the eighteenth century the true implications of a slave economy started to manifest themselves, though the Dahomean kings did not fully appreciate the situation. The slave trade depended on external forces for its regular supply and demand. If the forces of supply or demand were not favourable, Dahomey's economy would suffer greatly. From the middle of the eighteenth century onwards both the supply and demand conditions were unfavourable to Dahomey. The Oyo who were the largest suppliers decided to export their slaves through Porto Novo, the port of the kingdom of Ajase-Ipo, a tributary state of Oyo, and the supply of slaves that should have gone to Dahomey from Oyo dwindled drastically. On the demand side, from the mid-eighteenth century onwards, the European wars of that period not only restricted the number of ships that could be used in trade (since many of them were requisitioned for war purposes), they also made sailing on the seas hazardous because of seizures by combatants of enemy ships as prizes. European traders were therefore unwilling to risk their capital and they often did not venture out while the wars lasted. The greatest blow came in 1807 when the British government abolished the slave trade and gradually persuaded other European powers to do the same, thus seriously reducing demand. The result of both the Oyo policy and European actions was an economic depression in Dahomey which started around 1750 and continued for another century.

By the end of the eighteenth century, therefore, political subjugation and economic depression had combined to cause a widespread dissatisfaction among the Dahomeans against their rulers. A Frenchman who visited Dahomey around that time rightly forecast that there would soon be a revolution. The first concrete sign of dissatisfaction came in 1797 when Agonglo was murdered and an unsuccessful attempt was made to change the dynasty. For the next twenty years conditions did not improve in Dahomey despite all the efforts made by Adandozan, Agonglo's young son and successor (1797–1818).

In 1818, therefore, the clamour in Dahomey was still for political independence and economic improvement. On this crest of popular demand Gezo rose to power. With his organising ability and the backing of da Souza, the richest Portuguese mulatto slave trader at Whydah, Gezo overthrew Adandozan in 1818 to become king of Dahomey. For a few years afterwards he seems to have been engaged in overcoming the internal opposition to himself, notably from the women's army corps which remained loyal to the deposed king. By 1821 the internal opposition appears to have been dealt with and he was then ready to tackle the two problems of political independence and economic improvement.

Attempts to achieve these two national Dahomean objectives inevitably brought conflict with the Yoruba. To achieve political independence Gezo had to fight the Oyo. To achieve economic viability he had to find new raiding grounds if he were to continue the slave trade, or, if agricultural products became fashionable, he had to secure an area climatically suitable for the growth of whatever products the Europeans demanded. Whichever economic product might eventually be needed, the country lying eastwards and south-eastwards, in the direction of Egbado and the Egba kingdoms, would provide the objects of Dahomey's ambition.

The political situation in the Yoruba country at the end of the eighteenth century and the beginning of the nineteenth helped Dahomey to realise its ambitions and solve its problems. From about 1796 trouble had started within the Oyo empire which caused the administration to collapse and left Oyo without a king for a fair, though unspecified, length of time. The lack of central authority in Oyo and the insecurity to life and prosperity consequent upon this, compelled the ordinary Oyo citizens to flee and seek safety in other Yoruba kingdoms and encouraged the ruling classes to reduce little areas to order under their own authority. The collapse of such a strong empire as Oyo, which occupied more than half of the total land area of the Yoruba country, was bound to have far-reaching effects on the rest of this country.

In 1821, before such consequences were completely worked out, another civil war, the Owu war, which was far more serious in its consequences for the Yoruba country, broke out and continued until about 1828. Although the underlying reasons for the war are not adequately explained by available sources, it was sparked off by a quarrel between two traders at Apomu over a few cowries' worth of guinea pepper. According to the Oyo version, Amororo, the Olowu, attacked a number of Ife towns and villages at the instigation of Adegun, the Onikoyi, and Toyeje of Ogbomosho, the Kankanfo, ostensibly to protect the Oyo from being taken captive and sold into slavery. Such an attack, however, was against the constitutional arrangements in the Yoruba country, and Olowu Amororo ought to have known this. The most probable explanation for his action may therefore be that there was a feeling among the people who ought to have been the jealous guardians of the

Yoruba constitution that the old constitution was no longer adequate.

The result of Amororo's action was unmistakably disastrous. It threw the whole of the Yoruba country into a series of civil wars. Ife invited Ijebu to join it in defending the traditional constitution which the latter promptly did, particularly because many Ijebu traders allegedly suffered in the Owu attack. Also joining the Ife against the Owu were a large number of the Oyo population who were the more willing because they no longer had a permanent abode and naturally wanted to secure one for themselves. The reigning Oni ordered, with his traditional authortiy, that Owu city must be completely destroyed, and must never again be inhabited, thus giving it as prey to the allied armies.

For five years, a siege was laid against the city of Owu. At first the Owu people resisted bravely, but the longer the siege lasted the more famished they became. Finally they submitted under great distress and were largely put to the sword. The survivors were pursued from one Owu town to another. First to Erunmu, then to Ogbere until all the large Owu towns were completely destroyed and the flourishing Owu kingdom reduced largely to farmlands.

It is not clear whether Adegun, the Onikoyi, and Toyeje of Ogbomosho, who originally instigated Amororo's attack, came to his aid. The chances were that they did not because they too had to face the consequences of Afonja's declaration of allegiance to the Fulani Crusade; a declaration that came openly in 1824, three years after the siege of Owu had started.

The end of the Owu war in about 1825 did not see the beginning of peace in the Yoruba country. The Egba kingdom which had become independent of Oyo towards the end of the eighteenth century was attacked and its towns destroyed one after another. By 1828 the old Egba kingdom had almost ceased to exist.

The old constitution having thus been clearly shown to be no longer effective, alternative arrangements to ensure peace and prosperity were needed. Unfortunately the events of 1821 to 1828 appear to have been an unpremeditated revolution. Each of the most powerful leaders therefore sought to make effective arrangements in their new towns. In Ibadan, where the Oyo elements eventually dominated the situation, a military aristocracy was established. In Ijaye, another Oyo centre, military absolutism was established under Kurunmi. The remnants of the Egba settled at Abeokuta where they eventually had a syncretic kind of constitution with little pieces of the old and little pieces of the new, held together by the notion of the British monarchical system which the Egba repatriates had brought from Sierra Leone. Ife, of course, tenaciously held on to the view that the old ways were best, and in this it was backed by Ijebu. Most of the political history of the Yoruba country for the rest of the nineteenth century, with its disastrous wars, centred largely on which of the four constitutions was to rule the whole of the Yoruba country. None eventually succeeded in doing so, though Ibadan and its military aristocracy came nearest to it.

The first effect which the Yoruba Revolution of 1821–8 had on the relations between Dahomey and Yoruba was that it made it easy for Gezo, king of Dahomey (1818–28) successfully to declare independence from the Oyo. He thus achieved the first objective which had been expected of him when he ascended the throne. He still had to solve the economic problem which had been confronting his kingdom since the mid-eighteenth century, and this was to prove more difficult. For after the Yoruba Revolution, Abeokuta, the capital of the new Egba kingdom, was established in about 1830 in precisely the area towards which Dahomey would have liked to expand. The real bone of contention between these two kingdoms was which of them would control Ajase-Ipo (with its port at Porto Novo) and Egbado, the two kingdoms lying between Dahomey and the new Egba. Both had been controlled by Oyo during its hegemony. The fall of the Oyo empire created a political vacuum in the area and there was need for a new master. Ajase-Ipo would appear to have been annexed by Dahomey soon after 1822 without much resistance. And Dahomey may have hoped that from its base at Ajase-Iop it would easily swallow the whole of Egbado.

ABEOKUTA

With the establishment of Abeokuta, however, a new rival for the same area emerged. The Egba and the Egbado were culturally related and both were for a time together under the rule of the Alafin. However, they had not always agreed on vital issues and the destruction of the old kingdom of the Egba and their resettlement in Abeokuta brought them nearer to the Egbado than hitherto. If therefore their new home were to be secure, they would have to make sure that they controlled the Egbado people, who were in any case not very strong. Moreover, the Egba needed a port of their own, the route to which it was vital for them to control since, in the economic and political context of the early nineteenth century, possession of European firearms, obtained most easily from the coast, was essential to survival. Badagri appeared an easier place to attempt to control than Lagos and the route to Badagri from Abeokuta passed through the Egbado country. For economic and political reasons therefore both Dahomey and Egba wanted the Egbado kingdom. The Dahomeans under Gezo moved first. In the mid-1830s Gezo's army attacked Refurefu, apparently a big and flourishing Egbado town, and completely destroyed it. Its inhabitants who were not murdered were taken to Dahomey and resettled in a royal plantation, renamed Lefulefu, after the name of the destroyed town. So thoroughly was this destruction carried out that no one has yet been able precisely to identify the site of the old Refurefu.

The Egba did not come to the aid of Refurefu probably mainly because they had not yet gained sufficient confidence. Certain of their leaders thought they should press on with territorial conquests while others thought they should consolidate each gain before venturing farther. For a time the cautious party gained the upper hand. However, after the Egba conquest of Otta in 1842, a detachment of Egba soldiers was sent to besiege Ado, an Egbado town where the first open clash between the Egba and the Dahomeans occurred. About 1844 Gezo decided to relieve Ado on the pretext that it was part of the Ajase-Ipo (Porto Novo) kingdom which had by then come under Dahomey. The relief force was allegedly led by Gezo himself, but Dahomey had the worst of it. A few important items of the royal insignia of Dahomey, such as the royal umbrella, the royal stool and the royal war charms were seized by the Egba and Gezo himself narrowly escaped capture. From then on, Dahomey decided, rather imprudently, on the total destruction of Abeokuta under the pretext that it wanted to recover the royal emblems captured at Ado.

The first Dahomean attack on Abeokuta occurred on 3 March 1851. A large army of about 16,000 men and women (so-called Amazons, generally called 'our mothers' in Dahomey) marched on the town from the direction of the Aro gate where the town walls were in a very good state of repair. As in 1844 the Dahomean army had the worst of the engagement; more than three thousand of them were killed, a great many more were wounded and hundreds were taken captive. Thus, humiliated a second time, Gezo was never again to face Abeokuta before his death in 1858.

His son and successor, Gelele, swore at his father's death that he would avenge the insult at Abeokuta. After an abortive attempt in 1863, he finally attacked Abeokuta on 15 March 1864 with a force estimated at 10,000 strong. But this army of invasion was punished even more heavily than before. It has been estimated to have lost about 4,500, almost half of its strength, whilst the Egba lost only fifty men, a clear indication of the superiority of the Egba over Dahomey. Indeed, this engagement not only put an end to any effective invasion of Abeokuta, it also almost broke the strength of the Dahomean army. This Dahomean failure to subjugate Abeokuta meant that it never got control of the rich areas of the Yoruba hinterland as Gezo had hoped. To that extent the economic problem which had been facing Dahomey remained unsolved. Fortunately for Dahomey, however, Abeokuta never grew powerful enough to threaten Dahomey's political existence by carrying the war into its territory.

The Egba were able to ward off the Dahomean menace for many reasons. Among the most important was the help which the British government, through the representatives of the Church Missionary agents at Abeokuta, and the Lagos administration, gave them. In 1851, field-pieces were provided for the Egba army. Trained army officers were sent to Abeokuta to advise on the repairs needed for the defences and to train a few Sierra Leonian repatriates to mount and fire the field pieces that had been provided. Even in 1863, when relations between Abeokuta and the Lagos administration were not at their best, the Lagos administration was instructed by the British Government to allow the Egba to import as many firearms as would be needed to ward off the menace.

Help was also given by the Ishaga people. On the approach of the Dahomean army in 1851, the Ishaga declared themselves friends of the Dahomeans whom they 'advised' on how best to take Abeokuta. They asked the Dahomeans not to attack at night and told them that the Aro gate was the weakest point in the Abeokuta defence. These two pieces of advice were calculated to mislead the

Dahomeans and, by following them, Dahomey lost all the advantages of surprise, its most effective weapon, and attacked Abeokuta at its strongest point.

A great deal of the credit must go however to the Egba themselves. On two out of the three occasions, between 1844 and 1864, they fought and conquered the Dahomeans on their own, or with very little help. In 1851, when the menace was most dangerous, the discovery by the Egba soldiers that they were fighting against women greatly restored their morale and self-confidence and made them determine on total victory. On that occasion also, the Egba women performed as they had never done before. They kept their men regularly refreshed with food and drink at the battle front.

Another important factor created by the general political situation within the Yoruba country helped to bring about the Egba victory over the Dahomeans. On the three occasions between 1844 and 1864 when the Dahomeans had attacked Abeokuta, the Egba army had not been engaged in any other major war, and no major war had been going on in the rest of the Yoruba country. The result was that most, if not all, of the Egba able-bodied males were available for the defence of their town on only one front.

The three consecutive defeats which the Dahomeans suffered at the hands of the Egba may also suggest that the Dahomean army was not as strong as it was reputed to be. Even the number of the soldiers may have been exaggerated.

KETU

Egba and Egbado were not the only Yoruba kingdoms which the Dahomeans attacked during the nineteenth century. Ketu was also attacked with much greater success than Abeokuta. The full story of the relations between Dahomey and Ketu need, however, still to be traced in detail (though the outlines are already known).

Between Ketu and Dahomey there does not seem to have been much political conflict until the last half of the nineteenth century. Indeed for much of the eighteenth century, the impression created by the documents is that of amity between the two states. In any case, while Oyo remained strong and effective, it was unlikely that Dahomey would have attempted an attack on a respectable Yoruba kingdom.

Conditions changed towards the end of the reign of Abiodun. Oyo grew progressively weaker. Dahomey's economic problem which had started around the middle of the eighteenth century remained unsolved. The traditional slave-raiding grounds on which Dahomey depended for its prosperity seemed to have been denuded of their population. New raiding grounds had to be found since the Dahomean authorities were convinced that only an increase in the export of slaves could solve their economic problems. Kpengla the energetic king of Dahomey between 1774 and 1789 thought that the time was opportune to make Ketu the new Dahomean slave-raiding ground. In 1788 he attacked Iwoye, a town within the kingdom of Ketu; he was only partly successful though not discouraged. The following year he mounted a formidable expedition against Ketu city itself but his army was beaten off, apparently with great losses. Kpengla died immediately after the return of the army to Abomey, allegedly of smallpox. For almost one hundred years after that Dahomey made no other attempt on Ketu.

However, between 1883 and 1896, Gelele, king of Dahomey, attacked it twice. The first attack of 1883 occurred when the bulk of Ketu soldiers had gone to protect their farms against Ibadan raiders. Dahomey thought it was the most favourable opportunity to attack Ketu, and accordingly encircled the city in the early hours of one morning, having travelled all night to conceal their movements. The inhabitants were taken unawares and, though they fought bravely, the town was taken. The Dahomean army collected booty and withdrew before the arrival of the main Ketu army who, on their arrival, repaired the defences of the town and took every precaution to prevent another surprise attack.

In 1886 the Dahomean army again appeared in front of Ketu, but this time the town was fully prepared. The Dahomeans, in their usual style, attempted to take Ketu by storm but were repulsed from the walls with very heavy losses. They therefore laid siege to the town which finally surrendered because of the acute starvation of the besieged.

It is significant to note that on these two occasions Dahomey took no steps to occupy Ketu effectively. Had it done so it really would have offered no advantage, because at that time the slave trade had already stopped, and Ketu is climatically as poor as Dahomey for agriculture.

In explaining why Ketu fell, attention probably ought to be drawn to the isolation in which Ketu increasingly found itself, particularly after the civil wars started in the Yoruba country in 1821. Moreover, although the age had shown the necessity of firearms and the importance of seaports in procuring them, Ketu remained completely shut off inland, and was therefore unable to secure as much ammunition as either Dahomey or Abeokuta. Since Ketu had not befriended any of the power centres in the Yoruba country, it was unlikely that any of them would have come to its aid. Even if some freebooters had wanted to come, they probably would have found greater opportunities elsewhere For the period of the Dahomean attacks on Ketu was the era of the Kiriji war, in which practically all the rest of the Yoruba country was involved.

CONCLUSION

Thus the reputation of Dahomey as a menace to the Yoruba country was more widespread than real. It would be more accurate to say that throughout the whole of the eighteenth century the Yoruba of the Oyo empire were a menace to Dahomey. In the nineteenth century, whenever the Dahomean army met a properly constituted Yoruba army in a planned battle, the Dahomean forces, more often than not, had the worst of it. Only against the isolated, kingdom of Ketu were Dahomean arms successful.

Nor is it accurate to say that the Dahomeans were simply a bloodthirsty nation. They were fighting for political survival and economic self-sufficiency which made them seek independence from Oyo and brought them into conflict with the Egba, the Egbado and the Ketu. They succeeded in retaining their independence for most of the nineteenth century, but, although they were victorious twice against Ketu, they were never able to take Abeokuta, a failure which rendered their economic gains in most of the Egbado area insecure.

QUESTIONS FOR FURTHER STUDY AND DISCUSSION

1 Describe how Dahomey came under the rule of Oyo in the eighteenth century.

2 What were the consequences of the Owu war for Yoruba country?

3 Give an account of the economic condition of Dahomey at the beginning of the nineteenth century.

4 State the origins of the conflict between Abeokuta and Dahomey, and explain why Abeokuta won.

SELECT BIBLIOGRAPHY

S.O. Biobaku, *The Egba and their Neighbours, 1842–1887*, Clarendon Press, 1957.

C. W. Newbury, *The Western Slave Coast and its Rulers*, Clarendon Press, 1961.

G. Parrinder, *The Story of Ketu*, Ibadan U.P., 1956.

F. E. Forbes, *Dahomey and the Dahomians*, Longmans, 1851.

R. F. Burton, *A Mission to Gelele*, 2 vols., Tinsley Brothers, 2nd edition, 1864.

S. Johnson, *A History of the Yorubas*, Lagos, C.M.S. Bookshop, 1921.

A. Akindele and C. Agessy, *Contribution à l'étude de l'histoire de l'ancien royaume de Porto Novo*, I.F.A.N. Memoires no. 25, I.F.A.N., Dakar, 1953.

A. Dalzel, *A History of Dahomey*, printed for the author by T. Spillsbury, 1793.

M. Herskovits, *Dahomey*, Augustin, New York, 1938.

Ellis, *The Ewe Speaking Peoples*, Chapman & Hall, 1890.

J. Adams, *Sketches taken during ten years voyages to Africa*, Hurst, Robinson and Co., 1822.

17 The Peoples of Benin, the Niger Delta, Congo and Angola in the Nineteenth Century

J. C. ANENE

BENIN, one of the most remarkable of the states of the Guinea forest, was the centre of an empire the size and orderliness of which attracted the attention of the Portuguese who visited the Guinea coast towards the end of the fifteenth century. These visitors were impressed by the size of the metropolis itself with its great streets and rows of neat houses. They also noted the palace courtyards and galleries. The brass figures and the carvings which abounded witnessed to the artistic genius of the Benin people. The precise boundaries of the Benin empire remain a matter of speculation, but it seems likely that at the zenith of the power of Benin, the empire stretched from the Niger to Lagos and from the Kukuruku country to the Niger Delta and beyond. The period 1500 to 1800 spans three centuries during which a series of events occurred which in one way or another adversely affected the tranquillity and integrity of the Benin empire. These events included the rise of the Yoruba empire centred on Oyo, the slave trade and a series of civil wars precipitated by disputes about the succession among the princes of the ruling house. In the circumstances, it is not surprising that at the opening of the nineteenth century the decline of Benin was in an advanced stage.

However, the Oba still remained at the centre of the remarkable political system evolved by the people of Benin. In theory he held absolute power. In practice the title holders, who formed a complicated hierarchy, wielded more or less extensive influence according to the personality of the Oba. There were also juju priests who alone could perform the religious ceremonies essential to the Oba's welfare. The people of Benin City came into two categories: the nobility and the common people. The nobility from whom all the officers of state were appointed were organised into three societies: the Iwebo society was charged with the Oba's

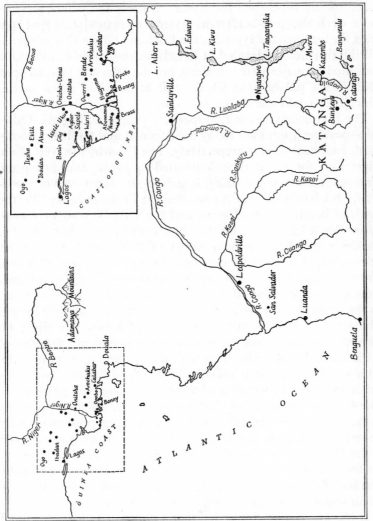

Fig. 16   The Basins of the Niger and the Congo.

19

regalia; the Iweguae society took care of the Oba's private apartments and provided the personal attendants of the king, and the Ibiwe society supervised the harem. Outside the palace societies there were also title-holders who were important state functionaries, for instance the Iyashere, the Ebohon and the Ologboshere.[1] All the title-holders formed in practice a council which the Oba consulted on major state questions, but the Oba also held an open court in the palace to which the title-holders had access and in which they could voice their opinions.

The Bini belong to the Edo-speaking peoples of Nigeria. Other Edo-speaking groups are today the Afenmai and the Ishan, to the north and east of Benin respectively. The Ibo who live west of the Niger were for a long time dominated by Benin, and during the nineteenth century the ruling houses in the Ibo towns of Issele-Uku, Onicha-Olona and Agbor claimed Benin ancestry. To the south of Benin live the Itsekiri and the Urhobo who were once under Benin hegemony. By the nineteenth century, however, the Itsekiri were virtually independent of Benin, and the Urhobo acknowledgment of Benin overlordship became more and more a matter of convenience. The area where Benin authority remained more or less firmly rooted was among the Ishan and the Afenmai. In the Ishan country the administrative unit was under the Enogie whose title was conferred by the king of Benin. Usually each administrative unit had a protector in the person of a member of the Benin palace nobility. This person acted as a link between the Oba and the provincial Enogie. At the death of an Enogie his eldest son and heir would send a message to announce the death. The Oba would in return send a white cloth to signify his assent to the burial. The heir of the late Enogie then sent presents (usually slaves) to the Oba to beg for the staff of office which was the token of the Oba's recognition of the Enogie's heir's right to succeed to his father's office. The continuance of the ceremony provides the best test of the extent to which Benin maintained her hold over the Ishan and the Afenmai during the nineteenth century.

It was also during this period that a number of Obas attempted to hold down some Yoruba groups to the west of the empire. The fortunes of Benin arms in this area do not reveal a clear picture, and it seems likely that only peripheral towns in Owo district and in Ekiti country remained for any length of time under Benin overlordship. On the whole much depended on the personality of the Oba and the exigencies of internal Benin politics. It is therefore necessary to consider briefly the careers of the Obas who reigned in Benin during the period under review.

The Oba who succeeded to the throne of Benin at the opening of the nineteenth century was Obanosa. Because of the unusually long reign of his father, he was practically an old man when he became Oba in 1804. There is a story in Benin that this man got tired of waiting for his father's death and took to sending his grey hair periodically to the old Oba in order to suggest that it was about time he succeeded to the throne. Even then the new king had to struggle with rivals when the old king at last died. A thousand people, according to Benin tradition, lost their lives in the struggle for the succession. The new king reigned for only thirteen years, and his two sons plunged Benin into a bloody civil war. One of the contestants finally hanged himself after setting fire to the palace. The next Oba, Osemwede, reigned long and rather successfully. He was popular among the Ishan people and was fully supported in his campaigns against Akure and Ekiti who were forced to accept the Oba as emperor and to pay tribute to him. The empire of Benin during the nineteenth century probably attained its widest extent under Osemwede's reign which lasted from 1816 to 1848.

The succession to the throne of Adolo in 1848 was accompanied by the now regular corrosion of civil war. The Oba's brother retired to his mother's town in the Ishan country and from there organised expeditions which did much to disturb the peace of the empire. In the meantime the outlying portions of the empire exploited the divisions in Benin to declare their independence or passed under the control of other powers. Thus, for instance, the new power of Ibadan was able to extend its hold to Ilesha and to Ekiti towns formerly under Benin. In time Adolo proved himself a good-hearted Oba. He encouraged commerce, built new towns for his many slaves and reigned for forty years. He was succeeded after a period of turmoil by the last independent king of Benin, Ovonramwen, called Overammi in British records. The new Oba ascended the throne in 1888 and shortly afterwards the British established the Protectorate of the Oil Rivers. In 1892 one of the British Vice-Consuls, Gallwey, visited Benin City and met the Oba. The Vice-Consul reported that he had successfully persuaded the Oba of Benin to accept British protection and to open his empire to trade. Gallwey's observation that there were many fetish restrictions on trade in Benin prepared the ground for the overthrow of that kingdom.

There is no way of verifying the allegation that the Oba forbade his subjects to trade. Considerable quantities of European goods certainly percolated into Benin, and there was no specific religious taboo against external trade. The Oba was undoubtedly suspicious of the activities of white men on the coast. He was also vaguely aware that somehow the presence of white men in his kingdom would upset religious practices cherished in Benin for centuries. The white men who now condemned slaving and banished local coast rulers could not countenance the mass slaughter of slaves for religious observations and funeral rites. In the meantime, the British agents and traders who were operating in the neighbourhood of the Benin River were fed with stories of dark happenings in Benin by Itsekiri middlemen traders who were anxious to exploit the economic resources of the Benin empire.

The British Protectorate officials began in 1895 to nurse plans for the overthrow of the kingdom of Benin. The Consul-General, Ralph Moor, confessed in a private letter to his predecessor that if he ever got into Benin he would, to use his own words, 'act like soapy sponge'. Once he got in the Oba would not find it easy to get rid of him. In the following year the Acting Consul-General, J. R. Phillips, decided that the time had come to deal with Benin. He asked the British government for permission to visit Benin City and depose the Oba. This permission was not given, not because the British government wished to respect the independence of Benin but because troops were not available to accomplish, without a hitch, the Acting Consul-General's objectives. Phillips at last decided to pay a friendly visit to Benin. Although he was advised by the Oba of Benin that the time was not the right one for receiving foreigners, the British agent insisted on going. The Itsekiri leaders who knew that the Oba of Benin was 'making country custom' pleaded with Phillips to postpone his trip. It was no use.

On 4 January 1897 the British party was ambushed on its way to Benin City. It is not easy to give a coherent account of the events in Benin City itself which culminated in the massacre of British agents. Oba Ovonranwen who was crowned in 1888 did not by any means succeed to an empire still possessed of its ancient power and glory. The Ishans were in revolt. The Fulani incursions from Nupe had almost dismembered the Afenmai part of the empire. Internally the Oba had apparently lost the firm control which the ruler traditionally had over his titled councillors. According to one witness at the trial of the Oba later in 1897, the Oba had been willing to receive the British mission but his chiefs overruled him. On the whole, the role of the Oba in the crisis which now engulfed his kingdom was not that of a master of his own house. To the British government the next step was clear. Benin City must be destroyed; the king and the fetish priests must be punished and removed in order 'to do away with a reign of terror and all its accompanying horrors'.

The king of Benin and his chiefs knew what was coming. Even then there is no evidence that Benin City was placed in a state of defence or that the Oba rallied the support of 'feudal levies' from his chiefs and provincial representatives. The one positive under-taking of the Oba was to slaughter, on the advice of his priests, many slaves in order to ward off the impending British attack on Benin. It was not long before Benin City was captured by them. It was only natural that the British representatives could hardly resist the temptation to paint what they saw there in the most lurid colours. According to Ralph Moor, 'the city presented the most appalling sight, particularly around the King's quarters . . . Sacrificial trees in the open spaces still held the corpses of the latest victims . . . One large open space, 200 to 300 yards in length, was strewn with human bones and bodies in all stages of decomposi-tion'. Moor concluded that he supposed that 'no worse state has ever existed in any country or at any time'. The Oba was soon brought to trial, was convicted and then deported to Calabar. The Benin empire came to an end.

THE COAST COMMUNITIES

Benin City and the empire overthrown by the British in 1897 lay beyond the mangrove swamps which characterise the Nigerian coast. The latter region includes the Niger Delta and is the home of the Itsekiri, the Urhobo, the Ijaw, the Kalabari, the Ibeno and the Efik peoples. The most striking feature of the coast is indeed the mangrove type of vegetation, most fully developed at the mouths of the many rivers and creeks which form an almost continuous network from the Benin River to the Cross River. The land is low-lying, for the most part only a few feet above sea-level. Local traditions are agreed about the early foundations of settlements and kingdoms on the coast, and also about the infiltration of Ibos from the hinterland which substantially affected the ethnic character of the communities.

The slave trade had provided a lucrative source of wealth with the result that the coast settlements underwent remarkable political and social developments. City-states had emerged. The most important were Warri, Sapele (Itsekiri and Urhobo), Brass, Akassa, Twon, Nembe (Ijaw), Buguma, Abonnema, Bakana (Kalabari), Bonny (Ibeno) and Creek Town, Henshaw Town and Duke Town (Efik). No description of the political life of the coast peoples is intelligible without an analysis of the social structure known as the 'house' system. Each city-state comprised a number of 'houses'. Now each 'house' was more or less a trading association of freemen and slaves under a head or chief. There were usually four social classes in a 'house'—the chief, the sub-chiefs, the freemen and the slaves. The division into classes was not a rigid one, and a dynamic and successful slave could rise to become the head of a 'house'. Technically the heads of 'houses' formed a sort of advisory council over which presided the king of the city-state. Inter-house rivalry was a constant menace to stability, and if there were a weak king civil war invariably threatened. Among the Efik there was evolved a remarkable society known as the Ekpe society which enforced peace and order, safeguarded the interests and privileges of the nobility, and kept the women, slaves and masses of the population in subjection.

The abolition of the slave trade by Britain in 1808 transformed the economic life of the Delta and coast communities. Where before they had traded profitably in slaves, they had now to turn their attention to exploiting hinterland products such as palm produce, timber and ivory. It took some time before the coast chiefs became reconciled to the less dramatic and less profitable trade in legitimate goods, but the British naval vessels which operated from Fernando Pó kept close vigilance on the activities of the coastal communities. In time the chiefs were induced to negotiate treaties with the British naval commanders in which the chiefs promised to throw the weight of their authority on the side of humanitarianism. One of the British commanders, Edward Nicolls, declared it was his intention to make the coast area 'a glory and advantage to British commerce and the cause of Humanity'. During the early decades of the nineteenth century, the peoples of the coast were gradually adjusting themselves to the new state of affairs created by the abolition of the slave trade and the presence of British naval officials who began to interfere in the internal affairs of the city-states. British merchants who were developing the new trade in palm produce indulged in the belief that with the British navy behind them they could defy the authority of the coast chiefs. Their complaints which flooded the British Foreign Office usually emphasised what they called 'the wickedness and the slaving propensities of the local rulers'.

The history of Bonny during the middle years of the century throws abundant light on the fortunes of the Delta and coast peoples during the period. As already explained, the 'house' system which was the characteristic structure of the social, economic and political life of the people served a number of useful purposes. It was also a source of weakness. The strength and influence of a 'house' depended on the wealth derived from trade. It thus happened that the king of a city-state who owned his own 'house' had to compete in trade with subjects who also had their own houses. A poor king could not hope to command in a society apparently preoccupied with trade. William Dappa Pepple ascended the throne of Bonny in 1837 as Pepple V. At this time the royal 'house' was being outstripped in wealth by other 'houses', especially those of Manilla Pepple and Annie Pepple; these two 'houses' were under the control of dynamic ex-slaves who had risen to the headship of their 'houses'. The opposition which they led against the king stemmed directly from the manoeuvres of the latter to revive the fortunes of the royal 'house' through manipulating the trade of the hinterland markets. The growing weakness of the central authority produced far-reaching consequences. In the first place, the British merchants, supported by the British Consul, formed their own courts, apparently to supersede the local courts presided over by the king. In 1854 the British Consul, Beecroft, deported Pepple V of Bonny. A period of confusion thus began in Bonny affairs. After 1866 the situation further deteriorated, and the king who reigned between 1886 and 1888 hardly exercised any influence over his 'over-mighty' subjects who drifted into a civil war.

In Calabar, the same British Consul who deported Pepple of

Bonny arrogated to himself the right to preside over the selection of a successor to the throne. There were serious weaknesses in the local affairs of Calabar which did much to undermine the independence of the Calabar 'republics'. The Calabar rulers had, in addition to the slave members of the trading corporations or 'houses', plantations in the neighbourhood which were occupied and cultivated by Calabar-owned slaves. In the 1850s the plantation slaves organised themselves under their own leaders to protect their members against the arbitrary exactions of their masters. The slave society was aimed primarily at the Ekpe society which was the instrument at the disposal of the Calabar rulers for keeping their slave population in complete subjection. Now as soon as the slaves had organised their own secret society known as 'the Order of Blood', they not only defied the authority of the Ekpe society but threatened to invade Duke Town. Civil war was averted only by the intervention of the British Consul, merchants and missionaries.

The internal affairs of the Kalabari people were not unlike those which reduced the rulers and chiefs of Bonny to the status of being mere satellites of the British Consul. Up to 1879 the citizens of New Calabar had lived together under their king, Amachree. Here as elsewhere the divisive competitiveness inseparable from the 'house' system was bound to produce in New Calabar the political instability already noted in Bonny. Will Braid, the head of the Barboy 'house', became very prosperous through the energy of his boys' trading activities. Naturally King Amachree was apprehensive of the possibility of Braid becoming an 'over-mighty' subject. The king therefore sought to destroy the Braid 'house' by various devices, including arbitrary fines. Braid did not wish to precipitate a civil war. He quietly evacuated his 'house' and occupied a new site on the main New Calabar route to the hinterland market. The king's dispute with Braid thus led to the splitting up of the city-state. The king and his followers settled at Buguma. Another wealthy chief, Bob Manuel, founded his own settlement at Abonnema, while Braid consolidated his position at Bakana. A kind of guerilla war persisted for some time between the various Kalabari factions, and canoes and goods as well as men and women were seized in this undeclared civil war.

JAJA OF OPOBO

The history of the coast was dominated during the 1870s and 1880s by one man who rose to greatness from the debris of the civil war in Bonny. This man was Jaja of Opobo. Jaja began his career as a slave who was sold in an Ibo market to a 'house' in Bonny. In time he rose to head the 'house' in which he had began as a slave. During the civil war which broke out in Bonny in 1866, Jaja's 'house' was not having things its own way. Jaja, therefore, secretly planned the evacuation of the chiefs attached to his 'house'. A site in the territory of the Andoni people north-east of Bonny was chosen. Here Jaja founded the kingdom of Opobo. He not only established a port but also built plantation settlements in the immediate hinterland. Opobo's commercial expansion radiated in three directions. To the north Jaja's men began to dominate the oil market of Ohambele. The oil producers from Bende and the Oworri districts in Iboland brought their oil to the Ohambele market. Jaja cemented his friendship with this important market by taking a wife from among its people. To the north-east Jaja established trading settlements on the creeks which discharge into the Opobo River. Here he was brought into contact with the Ibibio people and it took a number of military expeditions to guarantee the security of Jaja's trade in the area. Jaja's eastern frontier at the Qua-Eboe River was both commercial and political. The turbulent Annang groups were subdued and they acknowledged Jaja as their king in 1881.

Jaja acquired a pervasive influence throughout the coast. When Bonny and New Calabar threatened to destroy Okrika, it was Jaja's intervention which ultimately restored peace in the area. But it was precisely at this time that the British government had decided to establish its authority on the Nigerian Coast. The British Consul, Hewett, was instructed to obtain treaties of 'protection' from all the local chiefs who ruled the coast states from the Benin River to the Cameroons. In 1885 a British Protectorate was proclaimed over the Oil Rivers, and the independence of the coast city-states was shortly to come to a formal end. The only serious effort to resist the new political order was made by Jaja of Opobo. He subjected the British representative to searching questions and asked for a clarification of the word 'protectorate'. Jaja was told that the Queen of England did not want to take his country but was anxious to extend to the king of Opobo her 'gracious favour and protection'. Jaja was apparently satisfied, and he signed the treaty accepting British protection. He believed however that his 'empire' would remain intact. The other chiefs of the coast city-states had no misgivings about accepting the protection of Britain. The British Consul presented glittering articles which their cupidity could hardly resist and they willingly accepted a new relationship with Britain, the implications of which they hardly understood.

The local British representative was not at all happy about the independent posture which Jaja of Opobo continued to assume after the formal proclamation of the British Protectorate of the Oil Rivers. He deliberately precipitated a quarrel with Jaja which culminated in the deportation of the latter to the West Indies in 1887. The details of the disgraceful sequence of events do not concern us here. The fall of Jaja, however, meant the final over-throw of the independence of these states which had for many centuries played a spectacular part not only in the slave trade but in the development of the trade in palm produce. Before the end of the nineteenth century British authority was firmly established on the coast.

THE IBO AND THE IBIBIO

While the Ijaw and other coastal communities figured promi-nently in the all-important trading activities of the coast and the Niger Delta, the peoples of the hinterland supplied the main articles of trade, whether slaves or palm produce, which ensured the prosperity and existence of the coast city-states. The hinterland peoples comprised two major linguistic groups known as the Ibo and the Ibibio. It is not known for certain when these peoples first occupied their present home, but is is reasonable to assume that the Ibibio arrived first and were later pushed to the south-eastern corner of Nigeria by the more numerous Ibo groups who moved in later. As pointed out already, it is probable that these immi-grants had also forced Ijaw-speaking peoples to move into the inhospitable regions of the Niger Delta and its neighbourhood. During the nineteenth century there is not much to tell about the Ibo and the Ibibio. They were not integrated into kingdoms seeking conquests. They produced no hierarchy of rulers whose lives and careers could provide material for dramatic stories.

Nonetheless, the manner in which they organised their political life, and the remarkable role that one Ibo group called the Aro came to play during the century under review deserve detailed consideration.

The physical environment of Ibo country is one dominated to a large extent by thick forest. On the one hand, the thick vegetation provided excellent defence against large-scale invasion from outside; on the other hand, its very inaccessibility did not aid mobility and easy intercourse among people who were primarily agriculturists. The Ibo (probably because of the reasons indicated here) never came under a single pyramidal system. They lived in small communities, often described as village 'democracies'. The political unit was the village-group consisting of lineage segments bound together by the belief in the common descent of all the segments from one ancestor. These localised lineage groups were structurally equal units. The study of political authority among the Ibo is not concerned with formal institutions. The groups were concerned primarily with their corporate existence and therefore also with the formulation of rules and standards of social behaviour. The supernatural world was a pervasive reality and for this reason religion, law, justice and politics were inextricably bound up. No Ibo community was complete without a shrine of the god of the land. There was indeed a hierarchy of gods. Law and custom were believed to have been handed down from the spiritual world, from time immemorial, from ancestor to ancestor.

The nearest one can get to what may be regarded as an organ of government was the council of elders who were 'fathers' of component family segments. These elders were fundamentally the representatives and mouth-pieces of the community's ancestors. The council of elders was not a legislative body in the ordinary sense of the word. The meetings of the elders were neither formal nor frequent. When they prescribed any laws as deterrents against bad behaviour they were supposed to be reaffirming the wishes of the ancestors in order to preserve the solidarity of the village community. Judicial proceedings were also informal and were intended to restore solidarity. Misbehaviour on the part of a village member was expected to evoke the displeasure of the spirit world against the culprit and his family, and because of this belief a police force formed no part of judicial control among the Ibo. The institution of age-groups, however, played an important part in the performance of services carried out in other societies by the executive organs of government. The senior grade was concerned with peace and war and provided the leadership needed by the community to meet the exigencies of external danger. The junior age-grade of young men was charged with social services, such as sanitation and related matters. There were lower grades for music, recreation and for other agencies of socialisation. Generally speaking, the Ibo communities were democracies in the sense that the government of the communities was the concern of all. The manner in which these democracies operated was subtle and complex.

Ibibio social and political organisation shared many of the characteristics evolved by the Ibo and had successfully amalgamated some lineage groups to form clans. The clan, however, did not represent a political organisation or a central authority. Thus, neither among the Ibo nor among the Ibibio was there any subjection to one political authority. The pervasive influence of seligion among the Ibo and Ibibio provided a basis for the important role of priests who mediated between God and Man. More important still were the Aro who controlled the Aro oracle, the notorious Long Juju at Arochuku. The Long Juju shrine was the court of appeal to which serious internal and inter-group disputes were referred.

ARO HEGEMONY

What was the nature of the hegemony enjoyed over the Ibo and Ibibio by the Aro up to the end of the nineteenth century? The Aro territory and Arochuku are located on the eastern periphery of the Ibo country. The Aro were an Ibo group which incorporated Ibibio elements. They were both priests and clever traders. In both capacities they travelled and traded extensively in Ibo and Ibibio land. Various Aro settlements were established and through these the Aro dominated the local markets. They specialised in the buying and selling of slaves, and it was indeed through them that the coast communities received slaves and other commodities for their vital export trade. Trade routes in the hinterland which the Aro dominated radiated in all directions, but Aro domination did not amount to a comprehensive political control. As oracle agents and traders they wielded tremendous influence, they deployed mercenaries in Ibo and Ibibio inter-village wars in order to facilitate the capture of slaves for export, but the Aro did not during the nineteenth century, or earlier, evolve a centralised organisation with which to build and sustain an empire. When the British intruded into the country towards the end of the nineteenth century they believed that there was an Aro empire, and grossly exaggerated the role of the Aro in Ibo and Ibibio village affairs. The result was that at the first opportunity the local British representatives mounted a colossal military expedition which destroyed the Long Juju shrine and subsequently subdued one Ibo and Ibibio village group after another.

NIGERIA-CAMEROONS BORDERLAND

The territory which lies east of the Cross River and stretches in a south-easterly direction to the Congo has been described as the borderland of the Bantu and Semi-Bantu-speaking peoples. It was also a sort of refuge for heterogeneous groups fleeing from more powerful neighbours. The rise of the Fulani Adamawa empire at the beginning of the nineteenth century intensified the influx of odd Semi-Bantu and Bantu intrusive elements to produce a situation in which diverse groups speaking languages which are not mutually intelligible lived side by side. Some groups originally Semi-Bantu speaking had in their migrations adopted Bantu, and *vice versa*. Thus, because of the extreme intermingling which must have begun before the nineteenth century, the complexity of linguistic pattern and the diversity of origin of the people are perhaps without parallel in any African territory. During the nineteenth century there is little to tell of them beyond the fact that they did their best to escape the raiding expeditions organised by the Fulani from the Benue and from the direction of southern Adamawa. Many of these hinterland groups provided the articles of trade, human beings, and then ivory and palm produce, which coast towns like Calabar and Douala relied upon for their prosperity. The fragmentary communities themselves lived in a state of perpetual fear. The legacy of the slave trade, of enmity and strife left its unmistakable mark. One of the groups north of Calabar informed the missionaries that 'Inside or outside, speaking, eating, or sleeping, we must have our guns always ready for use . . . we . . . know not the moment we may be attacked'.

THE CONGO BASIN

Following the coastline southwards, after the Guinea Coast, we come to the Congo River which with its many tributaries dominates the last region to be considered in this chapter. The inhabitants of the region include Pygmies and Bantu. Groups belonging to the latter were responsible for the creation of remarkable states some of which survived till the end of the nineteenth century. The Pygmies were the oldest inhabitants of the land and were probably driven into the heart of the Congo by incoming Bantu-speaking peoples. During the nineteenth century the Pygmies lived in isolated groups in the thickly-forested portions of the Congo. They obtained their livelihood by hunting wild animals with poisoned arrows. They also gathered edible fruits and roots with which to supplement the flesh provided by the victims of their hunting expeditions. The nomadic nature of the Pygmy life did not allow the formulation of extensive permanent settlements. A few Pygmy groups which came into close contact with the Bantu took easily to agriculture and, indeed, considerable inter-marriage took place. The Europeans who explored the Congo River during the last three decades of the nineteenth century were all agreed that the Pygmies they encountered were short, primitive and very distrustful peoples.

There were also forest-dwelling Bantu in the centre of the Congo basin and in the upper regions of the Upper Congo. The Bantu here lived in small isolated agricultural villages, each independent of its neighbour. The villages were under petty chiefs who constantly quarrelled among themselves. Because of the resultant political confusion and disunity the people could not withstand the ambitions and devastations of Arab slavers who invaded the area in the second half of the nineteenth century. The Bantu of Manyema illustrate the fate of many fragmented Bantu forest dwellers. Into the region moved lawless Arab and half-caste Arab adventurers who imposed their authority on the Bantu. They seized slaves and ivory by force and in the process massacred a large section of the native population. The career of Tippo Tibz deserves special attention. George Grenfell, the Baptist missionary who made his way up the Congo River in 1884, noted the smoking ruins of many Bantu villages and homeless families fleeing from Arab raiders. When King Leopold of the Belgians acquired control of this portion of the Congo he authorised military campaigns against the Arabs between 1892 and 1895. The end of the disturbances, which the Arab raids provoked, and the return of peace and security to the forest Bantu prepared the ground for the emergence of the Orientale province of the Congo state.

CONGO STATES

South of the forest region of the Congo basin is a belt of tall grass and woods. Here lived Bantu groups which evolved celebrated kingdoms. These included the Kongo kingdom, west of the River Cuango, the Bushongo kingdom, between the Rivers Kasai and Sankuru, and the Luba kingdom of the Katanga. The ancient kingdom of the Kongo was already well established by the end of the fifteenth century when the Portuguese first arrived at the mouth of the River Congo. It is not known for certain whether the kingdom was the creation of conquering groups from outside or whether the Bantu Mbundu peoples themselves amalgamated to form a remarkable state in this part of Africa. The kingship system of the Bakongo was similar to that found in scattered areas of central Africa. The king of the Kongo (or the Mani-Kongo) was paramount chief of a federation comprising six provinces governed by lesser chiefs. The early Portuguese contact with the rulers of the Kongo kingdom began very auspiciously. One king after another was converted, and there appeared the possibility that the Kongo might become a 'Europeanised' state in the heart of Africa. This, however, was not to be. The Portuguese turned their attention to the slave trade. Portuguese residents of the Kongo penetrated all parts of the kingdom and incited wars among the Mani-Kongo's petty chiefs. These proceedings gradually paralysed the central authority. The eighteenth century was a period of succession wars and anarchy. In the nineteenth century the kingdom, thanks largely to Portuguese slaving and the depredations of the Jagas, shrank to a small territory around the original capital, Mbanza Kongo. The prestige of its ruler had gone. The cohesion of the many groups who had enjoyed peace and security in the kingdom was dissolved. Nothing was left except the ruins of churches and monasteries in the capital.

Between the rivers Kasai and Sankuru, on the fringes of the forests, lies a region which nursed the emergence of another remarkable kingdom, usually known as the Bushongo kingdom, because the descendants of the small Bushongo group became the kings of the state. The most famous of the rulers was Shamba Bolongongo who introduced his people to new crops, such as maize and groundnuts. He encouraged trade and his people carried on trading in all directions. The high standard of material culture attained by the Bushongo is reflected in the fragments of pottery discovered by archaeologists. During the nineteenth century this state witnessed a long period of peace, prosperity and flourishing trade. The system whereby the able-bodied men were concentrated in the capital meant that it was always easy to mobilise an army stronger than the levies of the peripheral chiefdoms. The stability of the kingdom was maintained until the arrival of Europeans in the 1880s when the territory fell into the sphere of influence of Leopold of the Belgians. The sequel was the overthrow of the Bushongo kingdom just after the turn of the century.

The last Congo region which deserves special mention is that of the Katanga with its copper deposits. The mines had been exploited by the Baluba for many centuries, and these remarkable people were not only advanced in mining techniques, they were also excellent traders. Many historians have speculated on the possibility that the founders of practically all the Congo kingdoms came originally from the Luba country. One group consolidated an empire to the east and south of the Congo-Zambezi watershed. Their ruler styled himself the 'Lord of wealth'. One of his descendants was Kazembe V who was ruling the region of the Luapula valley at the beginning of the nineteenth century. Two Portuguese half-castes who reached Kazembe's capital between 1802 and 1811 noted that 'the Kazembe is powerful in his capital and rules over a great many people . . . The trade . . . consists of ivory, slaves, greenstones and copper bars'.

Even more remarkable was the empire inaugurated in Katanga by an adventurer who came originally from Nyamwezi. This ruler, known as Msiri, gained control of the whole region from the Lualaba to Lake Mwaru and the Luapula, and from the Luvua to the Congo-Zambezi watershed. Msiri had his capital at Bunkeya and was the strong ruler of a centralised state. The capital was a strategic point for the trade which flowed to Uganda, the Zambezi, Angola and the Congo basin. Ivory, salt, copper, iron ore and slaves were the chief ingredients of the long-ranging trade. They provided the fire-arms with which the empire was held together. The ruler's harem included the daughters of the peripheral governors whose loyalty was thereby guaranteed. The capital was visited by German and Portuguese agents as well as by missionaries during the 1880s.

The missionaries of the Garenganza Evangelical Mission, founded to follow up the work Dr Livingstone had begun, were attracted to Katanga by Msiri's fame. The ruler received the missionaries warmly at his court because he believed that the presence of the Europeans could help to undermine the growing influence of the Arabs. The empire built up by the Arab adventurer farther north and the fact that the Arabs were the main suppliers of guns should be borne in mind in order to understand the attitude of Msiri towards the first Europeans who settled at his court. The efforts of the missionaries at conversion did not produce any dramatic results but a small group of slave children formed the nucleus of missionary endeavour. Apart from this, little could be done to cope with the evils of military devastation involved in the capture of slaves and widespread polygamy. The ruler was the principal culprit. The region was shortly drawn into the vortex of European imperialistic designs. The British South African Company had its eyes on the mineral riches of the region; the Belgian king, on the other hand, was not willing to see the most promising part of his 'estate' grabbed by the British company. The Belgians despatched a military expedition in 1891.

Msiri refused to accept the Congo state flag and declared, 'I am the master here and so long as I live the kingdom of Garenganja shall have no other.' However, he allowed the Belgians to establish a state post some distance from his capital. The end of the kingdom was near. Groups whom Msiri had held down were quick to see that the presence of the Belgians foreshadowed the overthrow of Msiri. The latter was now an old man who could hardly cope with the new situation but he continued to resist until he was treacherously murdered by a Belgian captain. The Congo state's flag was hoisted and the next ruler of Katanga was a nominee of the Belgians. The little chiefdoms which Msiri had held together now considered themselves free from the control of the capital Bunkeya. By the end of the century the old order had broken down completely.

ANGOLA

When the Portuguese moved southward from the Congo their principal aim was to extend an area for the acquisition of slaves for the plantations in the New World. This explains the character of the relationship which developed between the Portuguese and the indigenous groups. The story of Portuguese activities in Angola up to the nineteenth century is a chronology of military expeditions and 'dedicated commerce in black humanity'. This resulted not only the disruption of the indigenous order but the fact that the Portuguese depredations left Angola one of the most sparsely populated regions of Africa. The first Angolan people encountered by the Portuguese were the Kimbundu whose chief was known as the Ngola (the name Angola was derived from the chief's designation). The territory occupied by the Kimbundu was known as the Dongo country which was at first a province in the Mani-Kongo's empire. Under the Ngola, the Dongo continued to owe some sort of allegiance to the Kongo until the Portuguese began their work. Portuguese settlements grew up on the coast at Luanda and Benguela and from here a number of fortified posts radiated into the interior.

The Portuguese found allies in the nomadic bands of Yakas who dominated the regions to the north and south of Donga. They harried the villages and sold their captives to the Portuguese. The Yakas or Jagas have been described as a tall, fierce, murderous people who ate human flesh. The origin of the Jaga is a matter of controversy. Some writers believe they were related to the Masai of East Africa. Others have suggested that they may have sprung from a Chagga group which moved westwards from Kilimanjaro. A third hypothesis connects the Jaga with the Bechuana. It is also not known why Jaga men and women preferred plunder to growing food and raising cattle. One of the most celebrated of the Jaga rulers was the redoubtable woman, Queen Nzinga. It is ironic that Portugal, a nation who prided herself on the work of her missionaries in the Congo and its neighbourhood, should have used the fierce Jaga as auxiliaries in her military campaigns. In due course some Jaga groups settled on the Cuango; others retired north of the Congo and lived in the area now inhabited by the Bateke. The remaining Jaga bands were scattered by the Portuguese when they had no further use for them.

The story of Angola in the nineteenth century is concerned exclusively with the Portuguese military occupation of the country and the slave trade, and it is not a pleasant story. It was not until 1858 that a decree was promulgated in Portugal to set free in twenty years Africans who were held in slavery. The legal abolition of slavery enabled Angola during the second half of the nineteenth century to sever 'the major link with a discredited past'. Even the Portuguese themselves began to realise that the military subjection of the Angolan peoples and an economy based on slaving could hold little promise for the future. Portugal's gifts to Angola were slaving, which took the Africans away from their country and degraded those that remained, and Portuguese wastrels, exiles and criminals who sought profit, adventure and refuge in Angola. A new page was not turned in the history of Angola until 1891 when Tovar de Albuquerque arrived to clean up the debris of many centuries of Portuguese 'colonisation'. Angola has since been drawn into the complexities of the modern age in Africa, with Portugal still indulging in the illusion that she has an imperial mission there.

CONCLUSION

The peoples considered in this chapter illustrate the variety which characterised the political organisation of indigenous African society. There is no doubt too that they had much in common. The long period of slave-raiding had left its mark on all. Whether they were centrally organised (as in Benin) or fragmented (as the Ibos), they had evolved peculiar organisations which sustained their continued existence and attempted to safeguard group solidarity. But in the area between the Cross River and the Congo it is difficult to talk of group solidarity during the nineteenth century. In the Congo and in Angola, Portuguese greed had produced chaos. By the end of the nineteenth century a new political order symbolising European rule had more or less overwhelmed them all.

NOTES

1   These title holders performed functions approximating to those of prime minister, minister of external affairs and commander-in-chief.

QUESTIONS FOR FURTHER STUDY AND DISCUSSION

1 Examine the factors which contributed to the decline and fall of the Benin empire.

2 Analyse the value and the weaknesses of the 'house' system among the Niger coast communities during the nineteenth century.

3 'Among the Ibo and Ibibio peoples the absence of political integration did not symbolise anarchy.' Discuss.

4 Did the Aro of Eastern Nigeria found an empire?

5 'The Congo region contained many centres of effective political power before the imposition of European rule.' Consider this statement.

6 'The history of Angola is the history of Portuguese greed and spoliation.' Discuss.

SELECT BIBLIOGRAPHY

A. G. Leonard, *The Lower Niger and Its Tribes*, Macmillan, 1906.
K. O. Dike, *Trade and Politics in the Niger Delta*, O.U.P., 1956.
G. I. Jones, *The Trading States of the Oil Rivers*, O.U.P., 1963.
C. Partridge, *Cross River Natives*, Hutchinson, 1905.
C. K. Meek, *Law and Authority in a Nigerian Tribe*, O.U.P., 1937.
M. M. Green, *Ibo Village Affairs*, Sidgwick & Jackson, 1947.
J Egharevba, *A Short History of Benin*, Ibadan U.P., 3rd edition, 1960.
R. Oliver (ed.), *The Dawn of African History*, O.U.P., 1961.
J. Duffy, *Portuguese Africa*, Harvard U.P., 1959.

18   The Nineteenth-Century Jihāds[1]

J. O. HUNWICK

THE FALL of the Askia dynasty of Songhay in the 1590s before the impact of the Moroccan invasion led to a rapid break-up of the far-flung empire that had been built up by Sunni 'Ali[2] and extended and consolidated by the first Askia, Al-hājj Muhammad (ruled 1493–1528). At its height this empire is said to have included the eastern areas of the Mali empire, the area adjacent to the banks of the Niger from Jenne down to Kebbi, the desert areas north of Timbuktu to the Central Sahara and perhaps some areas of Hausaland. Within this area were united for a period such diverse peoples as Soninke, Fulani, Tuareg, Songhay, Bozo, Arabs and Hausa. The only unity the whole area possessed was that of a strong ruler with a well-organised system of provincial governors. Islam, though the religion of many, but by no means all (or even perhaps a majority) of the peoples was not sufficiently strongly established to provide an effective bond in the face of an attack on the centre from a major foreign power. In the event, the Moroccan pashas of Timbuktu were only able to establish their sovereignty over the riverain area between Gao and Timbuktu and with varying degrees of success over Jenne. The other areas which had been incorporated into the Songhay empire by conquest broke off and re-established their independence.

Songhay, then, was the last major empire of the mediaeval Western Sudan and no other comparable empire was to be seen until the jihād of Usuman dan Fodio established one based on Sokoto in the early years of the nineteenth century. With the political disintegration of the great mediaeval empires of the Western Sudan the fortunes of Islam in general fell, and the seventeenth and eighteenth centuries witnessed the proliferation of smaller states in which Islam was not generally the major force. In those areas where Islam had once been strong there was an increasing tendency to seek accommodation with local custom— even when directly opposed to the law of Islam. The days when the rulers sought the advice and counsel of their Muslim scholars and jurists was gone; instead the rulers, while formally declaring themselves Muslims, sought to accommodate local custom and practice and to produce some kind of synthesis between Islam and indigenous religious traditions and customs.

It is against this background that we must consider the three great jihād movements of the nineteenth century which all aimed at reforming the syncretist situation which had grown up, and at re-establishing Islam as the state religion and mode of government. In considering these movements, more attention will be paid to the jihād of Usuman dan Fodio than either that of Seku Ahmadu or Al-hājj 'Umar, partly because a good deal more is at present known about it and partly because it remains until this day a living tradition of reform and the basis of the administrative system which still exists in northern Nigeria in the form of the emirates and their native authorities. However, it is necessary to stress the tentative nature of conclusions drawn in this chapter about the jihād movements. Serious study of these movements has only just begun and many of the written documents in Arabic have not yet been properly studied. Fortunately a number of scholars are now engaged in studies of these movements, so that it may well be that in a few years' time our picture of the nineteenth century Islamic movements will have changed considerably.

At the outset it may not be out of place to review the concept of jihād in Islam before seeing how it was interpreted and put into practice in nineteenth-century West Africa. Jihād is a religious duty prescribed by the Qur'ān and endorsed by the Sunna, or received tradition of the sayings of the Prophet. It is, however, a 'collective duty' incumbent upon the Muslim community at large as opposed to an 'individual duty', such as the five daily prayers, the Ramadan fast and the pilgrimage to Mecca, required of every individual Muslim. That is to say, the duty is accomplished if some members of the community undertake it on behalf of the whole.

Muslim jurists divided the world into two parts, the 'Abode of Islam' and the 'Abode of War'—that is the territory not under Muslim rule. It is the duty of every Muslim to summon the unbelievers to embrace Islam; if they accept the invitation then they become members of the Muslim community and their territory becomes part of the Abode of Islam. If they refuse then they should be fought against; if they are defeated, those captured in war become slaves and their goods become booty which goes into the Muslim state treasury. The ordinary citizens of a land so conquered are allowed to continue following their old religion but come now under the status of 'protected persons'; such people are required to pay a *per capita* tax and a tax on their lands but are, in return, given military protection and not asked to join the Muslim army.

The jihād, then, is to be undertaken against the unbelievers, i.e. all those who do not declare themselves Muslims. This seems perfectly straightforward, but not half a century passed in the history of Islam before disputes arose as to who was a Muslim and certain extremist groups sought to denounce other Muslims as 'unbelievers' because they did not accept some of their stricter tenets.[3] This problem of who was a Muslim and who was not was the basis of the theological rationale of the nineteenth-century jihād movements, and an understanding of this problem is fundamental to our understanding and interpretation of the jihāds.

THE SOKOTO JIHĀD

By the middle of the eighteenth century Zamfara was the leading power of the Rima river system, having superseded Kebbi in the early years of the century. However, Zamfara itself was soon to be eclipsed by the rising power of Gobir. In the second half of the eighteenth century Gobir sacked Birnin Zamfara and established its own capital at Alkalawa, some twenty-five miles downstream from Birnin Zamfara. By the end of the eighteenth century, however, Gobir itself had grown weak and under Nafata (*c.* 1796–1802) there was disorder; Zamfara was in revolt and Katsina was raiding, and Kebbi's allegiance had become uncertain.

Within the area of north-western Hausaland were large groups of Fulani who had migrated over the centuries from the Futa Toro area of Senegal. Many had settled in towns and villages and intermarried with the Hausa population; others were semi-nomadic. Both these groups were mainly Muslim.

There were also purely nomadic pastoral Fulani who in the main were not Muslims. The two main concentrations of Fulani were one to the east of Birnin Kebbi—politically dependent on Kebbi and the second grouped round Birnin Konni. Between these two groups lay two other Fulani-speaking groups who were considered 'cousins' to the Fulani—the Toronkawa,[4] claiming some Arab blood and the Sullebawa who had some admixture of Mandingo blood.

It was to the Toronkawa that Usuman dan Fodio[5] belonged, tracing his descent from a certain Musa Jokolo, who had migrated from Fouta Toro in perhaps the fifteenth century. The ancestors of Dan Fodio, or the Shehu,[6] as he is commonly called, had settled in Konni originally. In the early eighteenth century they moved to Maratta and some time after the birth of the Shehu in 1754 had moved to Degel, to the north of the present Wurno and on the other side of the river. The Toronkawa were a strongly Muslim group, many of whose members were teachers and preachers; in fact they constituted something like a missionary tribe. The Shehu himself was a very erudite man, as were many of the members of his family, and had undertaken a deep study of Islamic law, theology and mysticism, all through the medium of the Arabic language which was, and is, the common medium of scholarship amongst all Muslim peoples.

The Muslims in Hausaland fall into two groups: those based primarily on the towns and those based outside the main centres who were nomadic or semi-nomadic. The former, who were largely Hausa or settled part-Hausa Fulani, were closely bound to the obligations of their settled society and had, through these circumstances, come to accommodate a great deal of non-Islamic practice into their expression of Islam; it was clearly in their better interests to keep the favour of the ruler. The latter, who were largely Fulani or Tuareg, lived a life independent of the towns, and particularly in the case of the Fulani, divorced from the pagan culture of their kin; they thus depended on Islam for their values, ambitions and their sense of security. In the final analysis it was the clash of outlook between these two groups that led to the jihād. During the course of the jihād campaigns and the establishment of Sokoto power no doubt many other and mixed motives were present, both among the leaders and among the rank and file who joined in the jihād, but there seems no reason to doubt that the Shehu himself was absolutely sincere to his ideals of reviving Islam and setting up an Islamic system of government and social order along lines which he considered to be orthodox. In order to appreciate this we must, therefore, first examine the career of the Shehu up to the time of his declaration of jihād and see how far the movement fits into a more general pattern of Islamic reform in the Western Sudan.

In his early years the Shehu studied the Islamic sciences under his father and his uncles, and while still continuing his studies began to preach in Degel around 1774–5 at the early age of twenty. Soon afterwards he began to go on preaching tours, one of which took him to Kebbi; he also spent five years in Zamfara, teaching and preaching. During the 1780s he also had some contacts with the rulers and visited Bawa the Sultan of Gobir to explain to him the doctrines of Islam; this certainly increased his prestige among the people, though he did not allow himself to become tied to court circles which would have inhibited his freedom to preach and exhort as he wished.

By the late 1780s the Shehu had built up a considerable following and there were already signs of strain in his relationship with the rulers. In 1788–9 the Sultan of Gobir plotted to kill him but failed. He then tried to buy his goodwill, but instead the Shehu seized the opportunity to obtain some concessions from Bawa, chief among which were the right to preach freely and the promise that those who responded to his preaching would not be subjected to pressure. At this point it is not clear whether the Shehu had the idea of a jihād clearly in his mind. However, he continued his preaching tours and the building up of his following who came to be known as his jamā'a (community), that is those who were convinced by his preaching and prepared to accept his spiritual leadership. The Shehu not only gained new adherents during his preaching tours but students also came to reside at Degel; the Shehu also spread his teachings through widely distributed pamphlets in Arabic and poems in Hausa.

The Shehu, in addition to being a scholar and teacher, was also a mystic, belonging to the brotherhood called the Qādiriyya, named after its founder Abd Al-Qādir, a twelfth-century saint of Baghdad. At the mystic age of forty[7] he claimed that he received a vision instructing him to 'unsheath the sword of truth'. The effect of this was that by 1795 he began to preach that the preparation of arms is a sunna—a recommended practice, sanctioned by the Prophet's usage.

The new Sultan of Gobir, Nafata, who came to power in about 1796 tried to arrest the situation of potential conflict by seeking to restrict the Shehu's powers and curb the activities of his Jamā'a.

He proclaimed that nobody except Dan Fodio (among the jamā'a) should be allowed to preach; that there should be no more conversions to Islam and that those who had not been born Muslims should recant. Finally he forbade men to wear turbans and women to wear veils. The last privation was no doubt aimed at demoralizing the jamā'a, since the wearing of turban and veils was considered a sunna and seems to have been the distinctive dress of the jamā'a and a unifying symbol of the group.

By the turn of the nineteenth century, however, the Shehu's power had grown to the extent that he had groups of supporters scattered throughout Gobir, Zamfara and Kebbi who were willing to come to his support at a time of trouble. It was this widespread allegiance to him and his ideals which was to be crucial when the final clash with authority came in 1804.

In 1802 Nafata was succeeded by his son Yunfa who proved to be even more harsh in his attitude towards the jamā'a and he soon decided on a trial of strength. At the turn of the year 1804 Yunfa came into conflict with Abd al-Salam, a non-Fulani supporter of the Shehu, and attacked him and his followers. Members of the Shehu's jamā'a came to his aid and Yunfa planned a reprisal on them but asked the Shehu and his family to move away from Degel so as not to become involved. The Shehu refused but instead ordered his jamā'a to emigrate from the land of Gobir to Gudu which was outside Gobir territory.

The decision to emigrate—to perform the hijra—was full of significance and could only lead to open hostility. This brings us back again to the Islamic doctrine which lay behind the jihād and the interpretation which the Shehu gave to it. The basic doctrine which the Shehu explained and elaborated upon in numerous pamphlets and books is as follows: a Muslim should not willingly dwell in a land of unbelief, but if he has the means at his disposal should emigrate from it to the Abode of Islam. Those Muslims dwelling in the Abode of Islam should wage the jihād against those in the Abode of War (the unbelievers). This is the more urgent if the unbelievers are making a pretence of Islam which may lead others astray or are claiming their actions to be in the name of Islam while in fact they contradict the law of Islam. Furthermore, Muslims should come to the aid of other Muslims who are being attacked or oppressed by unbelievers. These ideas are not new to Muslim thought nor were they new in the Western Sudan, for al-Maghīlī, the late fifteenth-century preacher and scholar, had reiterated them in a series of replies to questions put to him by Askia Al-hajj Muhammad of Gao round about the year 1500. The Shehu was deeply read in Islamic law and had carefully studied the replies of Al-Maghīlī which provided the only authority from a Sudanese context.

The doctrine itself begs the much more difficult question of who is a believer, and in the situation of the early nineteenth-century Hausaland this was not a simple matter to decide—indeed it led to a great deal of rather inconclusive argument with Al-Kānemī when the jihād later extended to Bornu. The extremist view that the commission of 'grave sins' made a man an unbeliever had been preached in and around Hausaland by a certain Jibril ibn 'Umar who had been one of the Shehu's teachers. The Shehu, however, was more moderate and did not accept this view of Jibril. The Shehu sought to argue that Gobir was infidel territory on three main counts: (1) the ruler, by his action, had shown himself not to be a Muslim, and a land is to be considered a land of Islam or a land of unbelief according to the religion of its ruler; (2) the unbelief of the Sultan of Gobir was shown by the way in which he followed certain un-Islamic practices such as the veneration of rocks and trees, consultation with magicians and soothsayers, the imposition of illegal taxes, the banning of the wearing of the veil by women, etc.; (3) the ruler had shown himself not to be a Muslim by the fact that he had attacked and persecuted Muslims.

The call to emigrate then went out to the Shehu's jamā'a and from all over the country they began to move towards him. The 'cold-war' which had been in existence between the Gobir rulers and the jamā'a for nearly fifteen years now led to open hostilities through the attack of Yunfa who, by his action, had identified himself with the unbelievers. There seems little doubt that the Shehu's followers did sincerely regard their opponents as unbelievers and that the preaching of the Shehu and his writings on this subject were effective.

During the first few months after the hijra there was a lull, during which time the only military action was the capture of Matankari and Konni by the Shehu's forces. Then in June 1804 came the first major engagement with Gobir forces at Tabkin Kwotto some twenty miles to the south-west of Gudu. Although the Gobir army was superior in numbers, with a hundred heavy cavalry, the superior morale and determination of the Shehu's forces, who were fighting for their own survival as a group and for their faith, won the day and Yunfa's army was routed. The effect of this victory on the Shehu's support was considerable. The Sullebawa now came to the side of the Shehu and the Kebbi Fulani came into active alliance. From now on, the Shehu's cause came to be more closely identified with the Fulani and this may well have cost him the support of some of the Hausa, especially since his need to feed his army inevitably led to pressure on the peasants. The character of the jihād had already changed. At the very first the army had consisted largely of members of the Shehu's jamā'a, pious men and scholars; the pastoral Fulani who had now entered into the forces were no doubt less actively interested in the ideals for which the Shehu was fighting and were more in the nature of mercenary troops for whom the campaigns were a source of material enrichment. It is clear that as time went on the Shehu found it increasingly difficult to keep a check on these elements and he wrote a number of pamphlets and booklets in which he explained, for example, the correct way in which to divide the booty in accordance with Islamic law.

At the beginning of the dry season of 1804–5 the Shehu's forces moved up into the dry-season pasture lands near the Gobir capital, Alkalawa. It was here that the Gobir forces with Tuareg support put in their counter-attack at Tsuntsua in December 1804, defeating the Shehu and killing at least two thousand of his followers. The Shehu's forces were not, however, dispersed and, recovering from the defeat, moved down into Zamfara territory in early 1805 in search of food and a more friendly environment. From Sabon Gari, where they camped, a successful expedition was sent against Kebbi led by the Shehu's brother Abdullāh and the army commander Ali Jedo. The Shehu's son, Muhammad Bello, also headed an expedition against Gobir. The capture of Birnin Kebbi and the defeat of the Kebbawa in April 1805 made possible the move in September 1805 to Gwandu which was to become a permanent base for the jihād.

From there contact was established with the Muslim leaders in Katsina, Kano, Daura and Zamfara who met with Muhammad Bello in the dry season of 1805–6 and swore oaths of allegiance to the Shehu. From Gwandu the campaigns continued to Yauri, Borgu, Dendi and Bauchi. After the harvest of 1805, in October, a major expedition was launched against the Gobir capital Alkalawa. An army was sent from Gwandu under Muhammad Bello and Ali Jedo, another came up from Zamfara while a third approached from Katsina led by 'Umar Dallaji who was the first emir of Katsina. Surrounded on all sides, the walled town of Alkalawa fell to the Shehu's combined forces in October 1808 and the Sultan of Gobir was killed. The fall of Alkalawa was the turning point in the military history of the jihād and resistance to the Shehu was swiftly undermined as news of the defeat spread.

While the initial phase of the jihād was over in Hausaland, the conflict had now spread to Bornu. Local Fulani Muslim groups had already been engaged in conflict with pagans in Gombe and Bauchi and it is probable that there had been conflicts between them and the Bornu authorities. Two leaders arose, Buba Yero in Gombe and Bi Abdur in Hadejia on the western borders of Bornu, and Fulani began to emigrate to these leaders. When the rulers of Katsina, Kano and Daura had appealed to the Mai of Bornu for aid against the Shehu, the Mai had sent troops which were, however, blockaded and defeated by the Ardo Lerlima, through whose territory they had to pass. Prior to this there had been no conflict between the jihād leaders and Bornu. Now, however, the Sokoto leaders began to become increasingly involved in Bornu, though no definitive conquest ever came about. The Mai had written to ask about the reasons for the jihād, and in his reply Muhammad Bello had asked him not to aid the Hausa rulers, whom he condemned as unbelievers, against the Muslim armies of the Shehu. The Fulani Muslim leaders in Bornu also corresponded with Bello and mentioned the un-Islamic practices which were current among the Muslims of Bornu. There arose a protracted but inconclusive correspondence between Bello and Al-Kānemī, who was himself a scholar of some standing, in which Bello sought to prove that Bornu was a pagan land because of the pagan customs which were tolerated there. Al-Kānemī defended his state against this charge with skill,[8] but Bello was able to fall back on the charge that Bornu had proved itself pagan by coming to the aid of the 'pagan' rulers of some of the Hausa states. To this Al-Kānemī did not reply in detail. The paper war was as inconclusive as the armed struggle, for while the Bornu capital Birnin N'Gazaragamu was three times captured, it was also three times recaptured by Al-Kānemī's forces and after 1810 there was no serious attempt to bring

Bornu into direct military submission to Sokoto, though raids continued.

In 1812 the Shehu, who had in 1809 moved to Sifawa, about twenty miles south of Sokoto, divided the administration of the nascent empire between his brother Abdullāhi and his son Muhammad Bello. The latter, whose territories included Zamfara, Katsina, Kano, Daura, Bauchi and Katagum, based himself at Sokoto which he had established in 1809 while Abdullāhi, who was to control Nupe, Dendi, Borgu, Ilorin and Liptako, stayed at Bodinga, two miles from Sifawa until the Shehu's death in 1817 when he moved to Gwandu.

The Shehu himself had never taken an active part in the military campaigns. He was already fifty years old when the jihād began and was, by nature, a scholar and teacher, rather than a warrior or administrator. He was given the title *Amīr al-mu'minīn* (Commander of the Believers), the supreme title of the Muslim leader of a wide area, by general consent, at the outset. From then on his main role was to advise and counsel his army commanders and administrators on how to undertake the jihād according to the strict dictates of the Islamic law, and how to administer their provinces in the same way. It has sometimes been asserted that the Shehu was an Islamic primitivist and that he wished to restore the kind of situation there had been during the life of the Prophet and the first four caliphs. This is certainly a misconception of his thinking, for while he looked always to the sayings and deeds of the Prophet and his immediate followers as inspiring examples for emulation, he nevertheless looked more to the later law-books, written centuries after the Prophet's death, to see how the scholars had interpreted the divine law and what rules they had laid down for the working of the judiciary, the collection of taxes, the administration of markets, the organisation of the treasury and so on. He thus accepted in full the later organisational development of the Islamic state as part of the essence of the religion; he also accepted the idea of the sūfi (mystic) brotherhoods with their accompanying litanies and cult of saints, through whom intercession with God might be sought.

The administration of the new empire was established in a somewhat haphazard fashion. When expeditions were sent out to specific areas the commander was given a flag of authority by the Shehu. Once these flag-bearers had successfully carried out their campaigns and established their power they were confirmed in this and made lieutenants or emirs. In some cases local Muslim leaders came to Sokoto to receive a flag and the Shehu's authority to carry on the jihād in his name in their own areas. All these flag-bearers but one (Yaqub in Bauchi) were Fulani, but this is perhaps not surprising since the main military strength of the jihād came from the Konni and Kebbi Fulani leaders and the leaders of the Sullebawa and Alibawa who were able to call upon large resources of warriors. The history of the jihād after the death of the Shehu and the accession to power of his son Bello as successor in 1817 is the history of the individual emirates rather than that of Sokoto. Although Sokoto maintained an overall hegemony most of the emirates were, in practice, semi-autonomous, tribute-paying subordinates under the shadow of the caliphal authority of the Sultan of Sokoto.

THE JIHĀD OF SEKU AHMADU

The Masina area to the south of the lacustrine region of the Niger which lies upstream from Timbuktu is crossed by several branches of the Niger. Within the area at the beginning of the nineteenth century resided a number of different peoples including the Muslim Fulani and Soninke, side by side with the pagan Bambara and Bozo and some pagan pastoral Fulani. It was an area of direct confrontation between Muslims and non-Muslims and therefore a potential area of disturbance. The ruling clan of Masina was the Fulani Dyālo who were rivalled by another clan, the Sangare, to which Seku Ahmadu belonged.

Seku Ahmadu, who was born in 1775, received a traditional Muslim religious education and early in his life began to travel. In 1805 he had been in Hausaland, at the time when Dan Fodio was embarking upon his jihād; this no doubt provided him with the inspiration to challenge the leaders of his own area and later to proclaim his own jihād. On his return he settled in a small village near Jenne but was expelled from there by the arma, the rulers of the town descended from the Moroccans who conquered the Songhay empire in 1591. He then settled in Sebera and taught there, gathering around him a group of ardent disciples, as Dan Fodio had done at Degel. One day one of his students killed the son of the ruler (ardo) of Masina who sought to revenge his death and called upon the Bambara ruler of Segu, to which he was a tributary, to assist him against Seku Ahmadu. This brought the tension to a head, for the ruler of Segu was a pagan and the fact that a Muslim ruler (the ardo of Masina) had called upon a pagan to aid him against a Muslim (Seku Ahmadu) would be sufficient for him to be branded as a pagan. This is closely paralleled by the views of Dan Fodio on Al-Kānemī's aid to the Hausa rulers against him.

Seku Ahmadu had already sent two of his brothers to Sokoto in 1817 and they returned the following year with flags and letters of investiture to carry on the jihād in Masina. Seku Ahmadu therefore proclaimed his jihād with this moral support but, having obtained it, continued his struggles completely independent of Sokoto. The people of Jenne, a long-standing city of Islam, sought his protection but when he sent representatives to rule in his name they were killed by the arma; Seku Ahmadu then besieged the town and captured it. He established a new capital at Hamdallahi (1819) and during the following years until his death in 1844 built up an empire which embraced the whole of the river region between Jenne and Timbuktu and some areas to the east and west.

The empire of Seku Ahmadu was remarkable, not for its territorial extent, which was not enormous by Sudanic standards, nor its longevity—for it was largely broken up by Al-hājj 'Umar in 1862. Rather it was remarkable for its well-organised administration and the firmly Islamic stamp which it bore. This Islamic character created an atmosphere of zealousness which helped to make the later jihād of Al-hājj 'Umar more acceptable. Executive, legislative and judicial power in the state [9] was vested in a Grand Council which consisted of forty learned men with a further sixty assistant arbitrators. At the head of this body was a Privy Council of three, consisting of Seku Ahmadu and two members of the Grand Council. The age of the councillors was to be about the mystical age of forty. In cases of conflict within the Grand Council, forty were chosen at random from the sixty arbitrators and their decision was final; no decision was ever to be taken that was not in accord with Islamic law. He also appointed an emir and a qādī to each province and organised a state treasury, taxes being raised by harvest tithes, war booty, fines and confiscations and legacies.

Before his death he nominated his son Ahmadu as successor and he ruled until his death in 1852. Ahmadu himself nominated his son as successor but it was during his reign that the great conqueror Al-hājj 'Umar invaded. Although Ahmadu III allied himself with the Bambara of Segu and the Kunta Arabs he was defeated by Al-hājj 'Umar who entered Hamdallahi in 1862 and put Ahmadu III to death.

THE JIHĀD OF AL-HĀJJ 'UMAR

The man who largely broke up Seku Ahmadu's empire, Al-hājj 'Umar had, in 1838, been his guest for a short while as he travelled westwards on his long drawn out return from a pilgrimage to Mecca. Born in 1794 in Fouta Toro, 'Umar ibn Sa'id Tal set out on a pilgrimage in the 1820s. It was during his stay in Mecca that he was initiated into the newly formed Tijāniyya mystic brotherhood by a certain Sidi Muhammad Ghali who was a deputy of the founder of the order Ahmad al-Tijānī (died 1815). Al-hājj 'Umar became a zealous adherent of the brotherhood and was himself made a deputy (Khalifa) and attained the highest rank within the order. On his return from the pilgrimage he stopped for a time in Bornu with Al-Kānemī and then passed on to Sokoto where he spent several years with Muhammad Bello and married one of his daughters. He also assisted him in the campaigns he was still fighting and thus acquired a considerable booty of slaves.

There seems little doubt that the successful jihād of Usuman dan Fodio encouraged Al-hājj 'Umar to think in terms of raising the jihād in his own territory. The Tijānī brotherhood was of an exclusivist nature and held as a doctrine its own moral superiority over other mystic brotherhoods and the superiority of the brotherhoods in general over other Muslims who were not attached to any. Under these circumstances Al-hājj 'Umar could not tolerate living side by side with pagans or those he considered to be pagans, nor could he even treat other Muslims on terms of equality.

Al-hājj 'Umar's jihād shows many parallels with that of Dan Fodio and, like the latter's jihād, some conscious modelling on the pattern of the Prophet Muhammad's struggles with the unbelievers of Mecca and his emigration (hijra) to Medina. In 1839 he settled in Fouta Djallon with a following of disciples and for the next nine years prepared himself for his jihād by gathering together an army of disciples (talaba), all instructed in the Tijānī doctrines and litanies; he also began to purchase firearms from the Atlantic Coast.[10] In 1848 he 'emigrated' (or made the hijra) from Fouta Djallon to Dinguiray accompanied by his disciples who were then named Muhadyiriina like the Muhājirīn, the emigrants who

21

followed Muhammad on his hijra from Mecca to Medina. Those who came to his support at Dinguiray were named Lansaaru like Al-Ansār who supported the Prophet in Medina.

In 1862, after spending forty days of mediation, Al-hājj 'Umar received the call to 'sweep the country' and launched his jihād. He tried to gain control of his native land, Fouta Toro, but was repulsed, though his own people, the Tukolor, became his strongest supporters. In 1854 he entered Nyoro but by now the French were a force to be reckoned with in the area, and three years later in 1857 they relieved the town of Medina which Al-hājj 'Umar had been blockading. He now turned his attention to the Bambara kingdom of Segu and captured the town in 1861. He pushed on to attack the Fulani state of Masina, accusing the Muslims there of being hypocrites or naafige (from the Arabic Munāfiq), which was applied to the Muslims of doubtful loyalty in Medina in the days of the Prophet). He tried to impose his Tijānī doctrines on a largely Qādirī population and this proved his undoing. It provoked a strong reaction among the Fulani Muslims who were aided by the Kunta Arabs who were the most strongly Qādirī group in West Africa, and in the struggle Al-hājj 'Umar lost his life (1864). His attack on Segu could scarcely be called legitimate as he was attacking another group of Muslims, and he therefore sought to justify it. His main argument was that the ruler of Masina, Ahmadu III, had allied himself with the pagan ruler of Segu and that thereby he should be adjudged an infidel himself. This was the same kind of argument that Dan Fodio had used against Al-Kānemī who had sought to come to the aid of the Hausa sultans who were to be considered pagans. It is interesting that his second successor, Al-Tijānī, was prepared to call upon the pagan Dogan to aid him in reasserting his authority over Masina in 1874.

Before his death Al-hājj 'Umar designated his son Ahmad as successor, but he had not the authority of his father and the various provinces of the empire were ruled in mutual independence by their governors. The break-up of the empire was brought about by the French who began to move into the interior of the border as from 1878, and the rising empire of the Mandinka conqueror Samori.

CONCLUSION

The three great jihād movements of nineteenth-century West

Africa are certainly linked together in their sources of inspiration, and it is quite possible that the earliest, that of Dan Fodio, was itself partly inspired by early eighteenth-century jihād movements in Fouta Toro and Fouta Djallon, but as yet no direct link can be shown. That of Dan Fodio differs from the other two in that Dan Fodio was not the military leader of the movement but the scholarly guiding hand in the background. He was concerned that the jihād be organised according to the strict dictates of Islamic law and that the empire thus set up should follow the same principles. Seku Ahmadu and Al-hājj 'Umar, on the other hand, were themselves men of action and their jihāds show a much less weighty intellectual approach. Again Dan Fodio had within his family and community the necessary scholars to carry on in the same fashion after his death, whereas this does not seem to have been the case with the other two. He was able to lay the foundations of an administrative system which was solid enough to last down to the end of the nineteenth century and which, in a very real sense, persists until today. The coming of the British to Hausaland at the turn of the twentieth century did not destroy the system which had sufficient vitality to become the basis on which to rest a policy of indirect rule The wave of deeper Islamisation which that jihād set in motion proved to be solid and lasting, and the tide of Islamic influence it sent out is still today surging through Nigeria with undiminished vigour.

NOTES

1   The author is much indebted to Dr D. M. Last for permission to make use of material drawn from his Ph.D. thesis, 'Sokoto in the nineteenth century with special reference to the Vizierate', Ibadan, 1964, at present being prepared for publication. This chapter should be read in conjunction with the author's *Islam in West Africa A.D. 1000–1800* in the companion volume of this book.

2   See note on the spelling of Muslim names and note on Fulani, Fulbe, etc. on pp. 306–7.

3   For example the Kharijites, who held that a Muslim who commits 'grave sin', such as adultery or wine-drinking, ceases to be a Muslim. Those who did not share this view (the vast majority of the early Muslims) were considered to be 'unbelievers'.

4   Toronkawa is the Hausa form; in Fulani the same people are called Torodbe.

5   This is the Hausa form of his name. In Arabic he usually referred to himself as 'Uthman ibn Fudi.

6   Shehu is a Hausa form of the Arabic shaikh which means 'chief' or 'senior'. The form seku is also used in the far western areas of the Sudan.

7   Forty is considered by Muslims to be a mystic age because it was at the age of forty that the Prophet Muhammad received the first revelation of the Qur'an.

8   See Chapter 16, p. 286 in the companion volume of this book for the opening stage of Al-Kānemī's correspondence.

9   Called, significantly diina from the Arabic din, religion.

10   In this he certainly differed from the Fulani leaders in Hausaland who appear to have made no use of firearms, though their use was known. This would not be for doctrinal reasons, but rather, perhaps, because a strategy based largely on camel and horse cavalry would have little place for firearms.

NOTE ON MUSLIM NAMES

Probably the most common Muslim personal names in use are Muhammad (after the Prophet), Ahmad (also a name of the Prophet), Abū Bakr, 'Umar, 'Uthmān and 'Alī (after the first four caliphs of Islam), and names compounded with 'Abd (servant, slave) such as 'Abd al-Rahmān (servant of the Merciful), Abdullāh (servant of God) and 'Abd al-Karīm (servant of the Generous). In Arab practice it is usual to denote one's descent from father and often grandfather and great-grandfather by indicating that one is son of so-and-so; thus Muhammad ibn 'Umar ibn 'Alī (Muhammad, son of 'Alī, son of 'Umar). The word ibn (son) is often abbreviated to the letter b. Sometimes men are best known simply as son of somebody, e.g. Ibn Battūta, Ibn Khaldūn.

A man may also be known by what is called his nisba which relates him to a particular tribe, country or town. Thus Al-Kānemī, the man from Kānem, Al-Bakrī, the man of the tribe of Bakr, Al-Maghīlī, the man of the tribe of Maghīla. Sometimes a nickname may be added to the personal name or even used in preference. Thus Ahmad Bābā, Ahmad nicknamed Bābā, Muhammad Bello, Muhammad nicknamed Bello, 'Uthmān ibn Fūdī, who was actually 'Uthmān son of Muhammad, nicknamed Fūdī. This is the Arabic form of his name which we commonly find in written documents, but he is also known by the Hausa form of his name Usuman Dan (son) Fodio or simply Dan Fodio.

Finally a man may have an honorific added to his name. The commonest is al-hājj, the pilgrim, often locally pronounced alhaji or alaji, e.g. Al-hājj Muhammad, Al-hājj 'Umar. Other common honorifics include al-imām (the leader of prayer), Al-faqīh (the jurist) and Al-shaikh (the leader or elder). Thus 'Uthmān b. Fūdī is commonly called Al-shaikh or, in Hausa usage, the Shehu. The same word is also pronounced as Seku in the more westernly areas of the Sudan belt—thus Seku Touré, Seku Ahmad.

The writing of Arabic names in Latin characters is a problem and in order to transliterate accurately one has to make use of a system of dots under certain letters to distinguish sounds which the Latin alphabet cannot represent and bars above the vowels a, i and u when these are to be pronounced as long vowels. The dots under letters can be left out for all practical purposes for the general reader but the bars above vowels may be usefully retained as an aid to correct stress.

NOTE ON FULANI, FULBE, ETC.

A number of names have been used by various writers to describe their people and their language. The word Fulani is actually the Hausa plural form (sing.

Ba Fillaci) indicating the people. In their own language they call themselves Pulo in the singular and Fulbe in the plural; hence the French term peuls or peulhs. In Arabic they are known as Fellāta (sing. Fellāti (masc.) and Fellātiyya (fem.)). Their language is correctly Fulfulde.

QUESTIONS FOR FURTHER STUDY AND DISCUSSION

1 In what sense can the jihād of Usuman dan Fodio be described as a reformist movement?

2 Discuss the theories on which the jihād of Usuman dan Fodio was based as revealed in the correspondence between Muhammad Bello and Al-Kānemī.

3 What features had the three great jihāds of nineteenth-century West Africa in common? What were the main differences between them?

SELECT BIBLIOGRAPHY

J. S. Trimingham, *Islam in West Africa*, Clarendon Press, 1959.
—— *A History of Islam in West Africa*, O.U.P., 1962.
V. Monteil, *L'Islam Noir*, Editions du Seuil, Paris, 1964.
I. Wilks, *The Northern Factor in Ashanti History*, Institute of African Studies, University of Ghana, 1961.
Abdullah b. Muhammad, *Tazyin al-Waraqat*, Ibadan U.P., 1963.
H. F. C. Smith, 'A Neglected Theme of West African History: the Islamic Revolutions of the nineteenth century', *Journal of the Historical Society of Nigeria*, Vol. II, No. 2, pp. 169–85.
F. H. El-Masri, 'The Life of Shehu Usuman dan Fodio before the jihād', *Journal of the Historical Society of Nigeria*, Vol. III, No. 2, pp. 329–31.
J. O. Hunwick, 'Ahmad Baba and the Moroccan invasion of the Sudan (1591)', *Journal of the Historical Society of Nigeria*, Vol. II, No. 3, pp. 311–28.
—— 'A new source for the biography of Ahmad Baba al-Tinbukti (1556–1627)', *Bulletin of School of Oriental and African Studies*, Vol. XXVII, Part 3.
M. Hiskett, 'Kitab al-Farq: a work on the Habe Kingdoms attributed to Uthman b. Fudi', *Bulletin of the School of Oriental and African Studies*, Vol. XXIII, Part 3, pp. 558–79.
—— 'Material relating to the state of learning among the Fulani before their jihād', *Bulletin of the School of Oriental and African Studies*, Vol. XIX, Part 3, pp. 550–78.
—— 'An Islamic Tradition of reform in the Western Sudan from the sixteenth to the eighteenth century', *Bulletin of the School of Oriental and African Studies*, Vol. XXV, Part 3, pp. 577–96.
—— and A. D. H. Bivar, 'The Arabic Literature of Nigeria to 1804: a provisional account', *Bulletin of the School of Oriental and African Studies*, Vol. XXV, Part 1, pp. 104–48.

19 Colonial Rule in West Africa

W. E. F. WARD

THERE are difficulties in understanding the history of colonial rule. One difficulty is that the very word 'colonial'—especially in the nouns 'colonialism' and 'neo-colonialism'—rouses strong emotions. Another is the tendency to over-simplify the policy of the colonial powers, such as Britain and France: to regard the French and British governments as groups of determined and far-sighted planners, and assume that everything that happened in Africa was the result of a deliberate policy decision in London or Paris. The truth is very different, and far less simple. A third difficulty is that although all the countries of West Africa emerged from the colonial period within a few years of each other, they entered it at very different times. The colonial period began for Sierra Leone Colony in 1787; for the protectorate in 1896; it began for the Gold Coast Colony in 1874; for Asante in 1902; for Lagos in 1861 and for the Oil Rivers in 1885; for Dahomey in 1892 and the Ivory Coast in 1893.

WHAT WAS THE COLONIAL SYSTEM?

The colonial system came into being because a number of people in western Europe, holding certain ideas in matters of religion, social policy, politics and economics, came into contact with African peoples holding different ideas and living under a different system. To understand colonialism it is necessary to appreciate what were the prevailing ideas in western Europe, and what were the circumstances which brought Europeans and Africans into contact.

Britain and France were commercial countries, and their traders had for centuries been trying to sell their goods all over the world. They believed that trade was a good thing both for buyer and seller, and they had learned from the British writer Adam Smith (1723–90) that governments should not try and direct or control trade. Every man, they thought, was the best judge of his own interests, and he should be left free to act as he thought best for himself. If he did make a mistake, he would learn by experience not to make that mistake again; and other people, too, would learn by his bitter experience. This extreme doctrine was in full force when the British founded Freetown, and for long afterwards. Gradually it was seen that it led to horrible absurdities, but all through the nineteenth century the idea lingered in Britain that government interference in economic matters should be kept to a minimum. That was one reason why, in Africa as well as in England, education was left so entirely in the hands of the churches: and also, why governments were so slow in trying to do anything to control international trade and world market prices.

Western Europe was experiencing the industrial revolution. In Britain (and the United States) especially, people were beginning to think more and more as if technology were the most important part of civilisation; the widening field of knowledge and the emphasis given to applied science meant inevitably that less regard than formerly was paid to the arts and humanities. Western society was individualistic and competitive: a man was expected to make his own way in the world and of course his family would be expected to benefit as a result. But there was nothing in western Europe like the African extended family with its close network of obligations.

Christianity, as expressed in the practice of the Christian Churches, also contributed to the colonial system. At the very beginning of the colonial period Christians decided that the slave trade was evil, and in one country after another, groups of Christians persuaded their national government to prohibit it. (Denmark in 1792 and Britain in 1807 were the first.) But it was harder to stop the trade than it had been to start it. After more than fifty years of naval patrolling, Britain decided that she could not stop the trade completely without annexing the island of Lagos which she did in 1861. Christian missionaries also found certain African practices (e.g. sacrifices) distasteful and they thought they should be stopped by force.

All this is almost equally true of Britain and of France, though Britain was ahead of France in the industrial revolution, and, on the other hand, France was more inclined than Britain to centralise its government, and tried to exercise more control from Paris than the British ever tried to exercise from London.

On the economic plane the policies of France and Britain were for the most part similar. Economic development in French and

British colonies was geared to the needs of the colonial powers. Colonies were expected to absorb manufactured goods and to produce raw materials. Consequently agricultural production especially of export crops was encouraged and little or no thought was given to the development of industries except for mining industries financed by British or French companies. One result of this policy was that the Industrial Revolution in West Africa had to wait until the Colonial Period had ended or was about to end. Neither economic development nor the widespread improvement of social services received sustained attention in French or British West Africa until about thirty years before France and Britain relinquished control.

The colonial system was not invented complete as a system of government; it developed step by step, as Europeans holding these ideas faced the task of living and working in a continent which seemed different in every way from their own. Africa after three hundred years of the slave trade was different from what it had been earlier. The first Portuguese captains to visit Benin and the Congo were impressed with the civilisation they found there; and it may be that only the trans-Atlantic slave trade prevented a fruitful three centuries of intercourse between Europe and West Africa. (Though we should remember that West Africa suffered another severe blow when the Turks conquered the North Africa shore and Morocco destroyed the Songhay power.) Europeans on the West Coast in the nineteenth century had to take Africa as they found it. It is probable that some sort of colonial system was inevitable, though it is possible to imagine several improvements in the colonial system which actually came into being.

HOW DID THE COLONIAL SYSTEM BEGIN?

Freetown was established, even before the British government decided to prohibit the slave trade, as a settlement for freed slaves. For the first few years these were Negroes who had been living in England; a judgment of the English courts in 1772 had established that no man could be a slave in England. After 1807 the population of the colony was greatly increased by the settlement of Africans taken from slave ships by British cruisers on the high seas. It is interesting to note that it was not at first intended as a colony but as an independent state under the name 'Province of Freedom'. The Province of Freedom was unlucky; it had a misunderstanding with its landlord King Jimmy, and he destroyed it. It had to be refounded as a Company's colony in 1791, and as a Crown colony in 1808: as a colony because the settlers needed strong backing, and as a Crown colony because the Company could no longer afford to keep it going.

Here we see how one step leads to another. The first settlers are reinforced by the Nova Scotians and the Maroons: by sending them to Africa, someone in Britain (Granville Sharp, or Clarkson, or the Company), has incurred a responsibility, and you cannot drop people in Africa and leave them to their fate. Then the misunderstandings begin; the settlers and their governors make treaties with their landlords, which they interpret in the light of their European ideas, not understanding that Africans have a different understanding of the relationship between landlord and stranger. So in the end the British government has reluctantly to assume direct responsibility: the more so as Freetown harbour is the best harbour on the whole coast, the only possible naval base for the anti-slavery patrol, and the place to which captured slave ships must be brought and where the international commission must sit to judge them.

A somewhat similar gradual process can be seen at work on the Gold Coast. In the days of the Company there had been a similar misunderstanding of the relationship between landlord and stranger. The long settlements of the Europeans at Elmina and Cape Coast and the other forts brought about responsibilities; after the Asante invasion of 1806 the Fante people looked to the Europeans to protect them against the Asante. The short experiment of direct colonial rule from 1821 to 1828 was a failure, and the British government wished to abandon the Gold Coast altogether. But the traders refused to go, and the Fante did not want them to go; and as a compromise the government agreed to subsidise a Company government. There followed the work of George Maclean, and after that events moved swiftly: resumption of Crown control in 1843, the Bond of 1844, the Poll Tax assembly of 1852, and then the great opportunity which the British government missed: the Fante Confederation. After Wolseley's defeat of the Asante in 1874 the government in London had to find some way of avoiding a repetition of the misfortunes of the last twenty years. It rejected the idea of using the Fante Confederation, and so was forced to make what it called the 'very evil choice' between annexing the country up to the Pra River and abandoning the Gold Coast altogether. It seems pretty clear that the government would have preferred to abandon the country altogether, but felt that this was not practical politics And so the annexation, which was described in April as 'too ghastly a scheme to contemplate', was proclaimed in July.

When we move eastward to Nigeria, we have Professor Dike to show us how trade and politics intermingled in the Niger Delta. Here there was a valuable trade, and it was natural that Africans and Europeans alike should have wanted to make as much profit out of it as they could. The Europeans naturally wanted to buy direct from the producers so as to keep down the price of the oil by competition; the African coastal chiefs just as naturally were determined to keep the handling of the oil in their own hands so as to make a middleman's profit.

Meanwhile other forces were at work As soon as the true mouth of the Niger was discovered the missionaries wanted to use it as a road to the interior of Africa The government too, full of the hope that the interior might be healthier than the delta country, had its scheme for planting a commercial settlement at Lokoja, but the experiment was a disaster. Travellers and missionaries like Mary Kingsley and Mary Slessor were at work, describing life in Nigeria as they saw it, and trying to remedy some of the evils it contained. There is a pathetic passage in Chinua Achebe's novel, *Things Fall Apart*, describing how a group of women coming home from the farm in the evening hear the wail of an infant that has been exposed by its mother to die in the bush. The British people were, and still are, very ignorant of African life and the ideas which lie behind it; but it was a genuinely kindly feeling which led them to think it their duty to stop the human suffering contained in such practices as human sacrifice and the exposure of twins. Similarly, the British public was horrified when it read Barth's descriptions of the trans-Saharan slave trade as he saw it, with masses of skeletons heaped up near the oases in the desert.

Thus there were other forces at work leading towards colonial rule, besides the obvious cause of imperialistic international rivalry. We shall make a mistake if we label the Africans and Europeans of those days as simply nationalists or colonialists. They were human beings, with imperfect knowledge, trying to under-stand each other and to do their best in difficult situations. There is a Twi proverb in Ghana which comes to mind over such negotiations as theirs: 'Minim sa anka' ka akyi'—'After it is all over we say, "If only I had known!".'

But of course imperialism existed as well. There was the colourful career of Sir George Goldie, with his Royal Niger Company: a man with much the same outlook as Cecil Rhodes' in South Africa. 'Open up the country, push the trade, hoist the flag; philanthropy is good, especially if it pays five per cent dividends.' And all the half-formed and contradictory policies of British governments were resolved when Bismarck (much against his own will) decided that Germany must enter the race and obtain a 'place in the sun'. It was in 1884 that the enterprising German empire-builder Karl Peters made his first treaties in Tanganyika and convinced Bismarck that his work there must be followed up. In 1884 Bismarck summoned a conference of the Powers to Berlin, which resulted in the treaty called the Berlin Act. Under this Act any European country which could show that it had a predominant interest in any African region would be accepted by the others as the administering power in that region; but it had to make its administration a reality. The British government would gladly have allowed France and Germany to divide eastern Nigeria between them; but again the missionary and commercial interests combined to protest, and the government gave way. Goldie, the business man, and Hewett, the British Consul on the spot, persuaded the British government to claim the Niger coast and the Lower Niger as a British sphere of influence. And it followed, of course, from the Act that spheres of influence had to be converted into protectorates.

Lugard forms the bridge between the old humanitarianism and the new imperialism. His career in Nyasaland and Uganda, before he came to Nigeria, had been devoted to putting down the Arab slave trade and stopping civil war between Catholics and Protestants among the Baganda. In Nigeria he was given the job of conquering the North, primarily with the purpose of stopping the slave trade across the desert.

It might be said that for Northern Nigeria the colonial period began with the Fulani conquest. What Usuman dan Fodio had started as a holy war developed into a war for power and dominion, and the upshot was that the greater part of Northern Nigeria was organised into a series of Fulani emirates, which systematically raided their pagan neighbours and exported large numbers of slaves across the desert. The three years' campaign which Lugard fought over the great spaces of the North against the Fulani emirs, who were not supported by their Hausa-speaking subjects, was part of the old humanitarian tradition that runs from Granville Sharp through Wilberforce and Livingstone. But Lugard's conquest of the North was also welcome to Chamberlain, the British Colonial Secretary, because he saw in it a means of forestalling the French advance from the west. Lugard's race against the French to plant boundary posts along Nigeria's western border was part of the new imperialistic world.

France was always less reluctant than Britain to plant her flag in Africa. In the 1830s she began the conquest of Algeria. Twenty years later, in 1854, Napoleon III (not without opposition) had transformed France from a republic into an empire; and General Faidherbe as Governor of Senegal began pushing inland from the coastal settlements. After the Franco-Prussian war of 1870–1 the new French republic showed surprising powers of recovery, and Bismarck was afraid that France might wish for a war of revenge. So he encouraged France to seek glory in Africa instead of in Europe. In 1881 France occupied Tunis, and the Fouta Djallon region of Guinea; one year earlier the French explorer Brazza had founded Brazzaville. After the Berlin Act, France expanded her African settlements rapidly; she annexed Dahomey in 1892 and the Ivory Coast the following year; and in 1902 she took a step which Britain never took: she organised all her West African territories into an empire with a Government General at Dakar.

PROBLEMS OF THE NEW COLONIAL GOVERNMENTS

By the beginning of this present century all West Africa (except Liberia) was living under a colonial regime, though the colonial powers had still to complete their task of establishing their authority firmly from end to end of their territories. The French had to fight in the Ivory Coast until 1910, the British in Nigeria at least until 1914. The colonial period lasted for about sixty years: two generations, a very short time. There may easily be old men living in Kano or Sokoto who can remember the days before Lugard came. But of course in some places, such as Freetown and the original Gold Coast Colony, the colonial period began much earlier.

The new rulers faced enormous difficulties. Africa was an unhealthy country; the causes of malaria, yellow fever and sleeping sickness were unknown. Dr Aggrey used to say that the malarial mosquito was West Africa's best friend, because it saved West Africa from European settlement. Hardly anything was known about the natural resources of the country, apart from the palm oil of Nigeria, the gold of the Gold Coast, and small quantities of cocoa, pepper and other tropical crops. Transport and communications were difficult; the rivers had sand-bars and rapids, the tsetse-fly made animal transport impossible in the Forest Region, and everything had to be carried from the coast by head-loads. (Benz and Daimler invented the modern type of internal-combustion engine in the same year as the Berlin Act, but it was another thirty years before Henry Ford invented the mass-production system.) Railways were badly needed, but were slow and expensive to construct. It took three years to build the first Gold Coast railway line the forty miles from Sekondi to Tarkwa, and nearly four years to build the first Nigerian line from Lagos as far as Ibadan. West Africa badly needed capital, but in those days there were no international agencies to help. All finance was private, and it was rare for British public money to be used.

Additionally there were hundreds of different languages and great differences in customs all contributing to the difficulty of lack of staff. There were not nearly enough European officers to provide all the senior posts that were needed even in the administration, much less to do all the technical work that was needed in health, education, forestry, public works and so on; nor were there more than a handful of Africans with any useful amount of education. The new colonial governments had everything to do at once, and very little resources to do anything with.

Before we discuss the policies they formed to meet these difficulties we may as well look ahead in time, and point out three great hindrances they met with in developing their African territories. First there came the 1914 war, which made both Britain and France take their attention away from Africa and concentrate all their resources on fighting Germany. After the war there were about ten years of recovery and development, and then came the economic depression from about 1929 to 1937: world market prices slumped and government revenues fell. As far as West Africa was concerned there followed a short period of prosperity when rearmament in Europe brought a large demand for tin, manganese and diamonds; and then in 1939 came the Second World War.

COLONIAL POLICY IN FRENCH AND BRITISH WEST AFRICA

Both France and Britain faced the same problems, but the French problem was even more difficult than the British. France had occupied by far the greater area, but much of it was desert or semi-desert, and distances were even greater than in British territory. The four British territories were separated from each other, and only one of them was of any great size and heavily populated; but, on the whole, they were more fertile, and had a much wider range of products and a much heavier population.

Just as France and Britain differed in the way in which they set about acquiring colonies in Africa, so they differed in the way in which, having acquired them, they set about administering them.

France was always conscious of her responsibility for bringing French civilisation to Africa. But this mission could not be accomplished without a great and deliberate effort. To open up the country, France planned a great system of railways to link the great highway of the River Niger with the seaports all round the coast: Dakar, Conakry, Abidjan, Cotonou. The system was ultimately to be completed by a railway across the Sahara, but the development of the internal-combustion engine made this enormously expensive piece of construction unnecessary. To this day we can see how Ouagadougou is connected by a roundabout railway line to Abidjan, instead of by Tamale and Kumasi to Takoradi or Tema.

The French believed in efficient administration, and to secure efficiency they considered that three things were necessary. There must be an adequate staff. The staff must understand the people and be understood by them: the administration must not be hindered by misunderstanding in its own ranks. Thirdly, the system must be uniform, so that wherever an officer was posted he would find things familiar.

From these assumptions certain consequences followed. The French made much more effort to staff their colonies adequately with Frenchmen than the British ever did with British officials. In colonial days a French teacher might find himself posted to Paris —or to Ouagadougou; he had to go where he was sent. In spite of France's great need of men in the armed forces, service in French

Africa was sometimes counted as the equivalent of compulsory military service. The centralised French system made it easier for officials of any kind to pass backwards and forwards between service in France and service in Africa.

The French had a simple answer to the problem of communication: French was to be the language of commerce and administration all over French Africa, and Africans learned French, and spoke it fluently and with a good accent.

A uniform administrative system meant that there could be no adaptation to local conditions. The French believed in direct administration. Three things struck me forcibly when I visited the Ivory Coast in 1929. One was that Africans who, if they had been Gold Coasters, would have been speaking poor English spoke decent or even good French. The next was that the cocoa farms I saw were in beautiful condition, well-weeded, clean, with shade trees at regular intervals: a great contrast to the average Gold Coast cocoa farm of those days. I asked the French how they managed it. They said it was simple: every cocoa farmer knew that if he did not keep his farm in good order he would be turned out, and there was a waiting list of people wanting to take over from him. The third thing that struck me was that the French treated the chiefs as mere subordinate government officials. A French district officer asked me in what condition I had found a certain bridge in his district. I could not give him a good report of it. 'I will have it repaired at once,' he said. I asked him how he could do that without going to see it and without indenting on the P.W.D. He explained that he would instruct the local chief to repair it, and a fortnight later he would send a corporal of police to see that the work had been done properly. If it had not been, the corporal would bring the chief into the headquarters and the D.O. would deal with him.

The British system was very different from this. The idea of Indirect Rule was not new. The system had been used by other Governors in West Africa but it was applied on a large scale under Lugard in Northern Nigeria. Here he used the system partly because it suited the country and partly because he had no choice in the matter: he had only a tiny handful of administrative officers to cover this huge country, and no prospect of ever getting enough to make direct government possible. But indirect rule had a tradition behind it: large parts of India were left to the rule of the

Indian princes, and Lugard had served in Uganda, where it would indeed have been difficult to take over the powers of the Kabaka of Buganda. One audacious official did indeed suggest doing so, but he received no sympathy from his seniors.

Indirect rule was a familiar system in Africa. The great African rulers of old, like Mansa Musa or Sunni 'Alī, had to rule their vast empires through the local chiefs, and the Asante, for example, used much the same system in governing their conquered provinces. It was a system well suited to Northern Nigeria, where distances were large, where there was a well-established system of government with laws and law-courts, and a financial administration based on Islamic law. But Lugard and the British were faced with a problem which did not face Mansa Musa or Sunni 'Alī. Those rulers did not try to change the system of government or introduce new ideas; all they had to do was to see that the provinces served them faithfully, paying their taxes and contributing their quota of armed men. The British had to make changes: to abolish slavery and the slave trade, to prohibit some of the brutal punishments such as mutilation sanctioned by the emirs' criminal courts, and to open up the country with large-scale commerce and thus introduce the native administrations to all the ideas of the modern world.

Lugard's scheme had two parts: the first part was to rule Africa through its natural rulers, the native administration; the second was to educate and develop those native administrations into efficient organs of modern local government. The British hoped that national feeling would grow up from below: that chiefs and their councillors would become accustomed to handling local affairs in a modern and efficient way, that they would then form some sort of regional councils to handle regional affairs, and that finally the regional councils would appoint representatives to a central legislature and executive. This neat scheme did not succeed; it is not the way in which national feeling and national governments come into being.

The first difficulty was that indirect rule had been devised to suit a region (the Hausa-Fulani part of Northern Nigeria) where there were large well-established native administrations already in existence. It needed a good deal of adaptation to regions with a different system, such as the clan system of the Ibo. The second difficulty was that outside the Hausa-speaking area (where many of Lugard's men learned to speak Hausa well) very few British officials learned enough of any African language to be able to dispense with an interpreter, and it was a long time before any serious anthropological study was done; so the system of indirect rule did not in fact get adapted. The British were so full of the idea that there must be a chief and his council in every district, that if they could not find chiefs they tended to try and appoint them. One important cause of the Aba riots of 1929–30 in Eastern Nigeria was that certain individuals tried to exert authority which the British had given them but which the people did not recognise. The third difficulty was that chiefs and their councils, naturally enough, took much more interest in matters they understood than in matters which were new and unfamiliar. A district commissioner in the Gold Coast had no difficulty in persuading chiefs and their councils to make lorry roads; for they could all see that lorries meant trade, and trade meant money. But he found it almost impossible to persuade them to set aside forest reserves, for they could not understand the reason for forest conservation: why waste good land on growing bush when it might grow cocoa? Consequently, the second part of Lugard's programme, the education of chiefs and councillors in modern ideas, needed long, patient and skilful effort; many British officers had not the patience and skill required, and for that matter they were moved far too often from one district to another. This part of the Lugard policy was not applied as strenuously as Lugard himself wished. The fourth difficulty was that there grew up in the big towns on the coast a group of educated men (Blyden, Sarbah, Casely Hayford and others) who saw that this process of developing traditional authorities into national governments was bound to be very slow, and who were unwilling to wait. In the 1860s the Fante Confederation in the Gold Coast had been drawn up by traditional authorities and by the educated Fante working together in complete agreement. In 1897, when the Gold Coast Aborigines' Rights Protection Society was founded, chiefs and educated men still worked together, and, in fact, the Society claimed to be able to speak for the whole body of Gold Coast chiefs. But in 1917, when Casely Hayford founded the National Conference (subsequently Congress) of British West Africa, disagreements began to appear; and when the Congress sent to London a petition asking for a sort of federal government for the four British West African countries, a group of Gold Coast members took the strong step of cabling to London

22

that the Congress had no authority to speak for the Gold Coast chiefs.

This split between chiefs and educated leaders was the turning-point in the history of indirect rule. From that moment it was certain that although indirect rule might perhaps lead to good local government, it would not lead to national government. The split was widened by the Gold Coast constitution of 1925, in which Sir Gordon Guggisberg set up provincial councils, and brought representatives of the provincial councils to sit on the Legislative Council in Accra. This Governor knew that it was not consti-tutionally possible for a chief to study a Bill and use his own discretion on it; he knew that he was the mouthpiece of his people, and must have time to consult them. But it was hoped that the programme of legislation would be so small that all Bills could be circulated to members of the Legislative Council in good time for the necessary consultations to take place. This, of course, did not meet the situation where an amendment to a Bill was moved during debate, nor did it face the certainty that as West Africa developed, the legislative programme would grow till the leisurely process of consultations became impossible.

Thus, for the first forty years of this century, French and British policies were very different. The French had a deliberate policy of drawing their territories closer together under the government of Dakar, and of drawing the whole of West Africa under Paris. Some educated African leaders (e.g. in the Four Communes of Senegal) were granted full French citizenship, and some of the territories elected deputies to the French Parliament in Paris. Thus some of the leaders of French-speaking Africa today, such as President Senghor and M. Houphouët-Boigny, learned the art of politics as parliamentarians in Europe.

Such an idea as inviting the Gold Coast and Nigeria to send Messrs Kobina Sekyi, Casely Hayford, Awolowo, Dr Azikiwe and the Sardauna of Sokoto to occupy five seats at Westminster would never have occurred to the unimaginative British. It is difficult to say how far there was a deliberate British policy. The British certainly clung to the idea of indirect rule; in 1944, for example, they carried through the Native Authority Ordinance and the Native Courts Ordinance in the Gold Coast, which linked local and central governments closely together; and four years later, when the Watson Commission was reporting on the Gold Coast riots, the government in London disagreed with the proposal that a more modern type of local government should be set up. It thought that the people would prefer to see the native authorities continue to develop. British officials tended to take it for granted that subsistence agriculture would continue to be the main occupation for a very long time to come, and Governors and Provincial Commissioners criticised educationists for not turning out people equipped with sound ideas on hygiene, nutrition and agriculture, who were content to stay on the land. Education departments in the 1920s set up trade schools and technical schools, but the example of Europeans in white-collar jobs was so strong that some of them had to be closed for lack of students. Thus education, to the disgust of professional educationists, remained almost exclusively bookish. When A. J. Fraser of Achimota visited Nigeria in 1927 to report on Nigerian education, he was very scathing in his comments: he said, 'It may be urged in excuse that our administration in Nigeria is yet young. It might be aged and decrepit judged by the pace at which its education moves.' And he once bitterly told the Gold Coast government that at its then rate of progress it would be 300 years before it got all its children into primary school.

On the other, the British did realise that nationalism was bound to develop, and that independence was bound to come, though it came faster than they expected. When I joined the British Colonial Service in 1924 the fashionable slogan was 'trusteeship': I was told that West Africa was not yet ready for self-government, but that it would be one day. Meanwhile Britain was in the position of a trustee, and I must look on my work as directed to helping Africa to take the government into its own hands and terminate the trusteeship. Later the slogan 'trusteeship' was replaced by that of 'partnership', but the underlying idea was the same. We were expected to work ourselves out of a job, though it cannot be claimed that all of us realised it, or that all of those who did realise it approved of the idea.

ENDING OF AN ERA

The French spent a great deal on economic development, administered the country directly and provided a limited outlet in the French Parliament for political ambition. The British believed in indirect rule: until the Colonial Development and Welfare Act of 1945 they spent little or nothing from British funds on economic development (leaving that to depend on private enterprise and on colonial revenues); but from an early date they set up legislative assemblies in which African members had an opportunity to discuss and criticise government proposals. Economic development went faster on the French side, but nationalism developed much sooner in British Africa.

The great weakness of the legislative councils was that the British did not trust the African members with responsibility. Until 1946 there was an official majority in all four legislative councils, and Africans never numbered more than one-third of the whole membership; moreover, many of the African members were nominated, not elected. The position which the colonial government took up was: 'This is what we propose to do, but we shall be glad to listen to your comments if you have any.' It was natural that the African members of the councils should regard themselves as an Opposition. Moreover, Africans always suspected the governments of wanting somehow to get hold of the land; their suspicions were not justified, but were understandable enough in view of the Gold Coast Lands Bill of 1897 and the Kenya Crown Lands Ordinance of 1902. The Lands Bill agitation brought about the formation of the Aborigines Society, and the Society's proposals in 1920 would have provided British West Africa with something like a federal legislature, in which half the members would have been elected, and which would have controlled revenue and expenditure, and hence policy.

The 1939 war and its social and economic consequences enormously stimulated the growth of national feeling; there was a great difference between the Gold Coast Youth Conference which Dr Danquah ran before the war and the Gold Coast Convention which he ran after it. After the war the British had clearly lost their struggle to maintain a steady and balanced development, in which economic progress, developments in education and health and other social services, and constitutional advances should all move together. The people were demanding two things above all: more education and more political self-government. In the last days of the war the Gold Coast education department carried out a survey of the existing schools, so as to be able to plan a great expansion of teacher training, but the figures obtained were already out of date before they were collated.

It was the same in constitutional matters. The Burns constitution of 1946 in the Gold Coast was greeted with enthusiasm everywhere, but the Watson commission of 1948 was clearly right in saying that it was already inadequate. Progress was quickened by the ten-year plans of social and economic development which the British financed through the Colonial Development and Welfare Acts of 1945 and later. These plans provided West Africa with schools, universities, hospitals, roads and airfields, geological surveys, and (most important of all) trained African staff, which Africa could not have provided from its own resources. If only this had been possible forty years earlier!

The Gold Coast riots of 1948 were the decisive event which made the British government realise that it had lost control of West Africa's constitutional advance. The riots were a tremendous shock to British confidence; if this sort of thing could happen in the Gold Coast, often regarded as 'a model colony', there seemed no future for the colonial government in any African territory. From that time onwards the Colonial Office set itself to equip the African territories as fast as it could for independence. One could wish that this sense of urgency, like the Colonial Development and Welfare Acts, had come about forty years earlier.

In granting constitutional advances, the British followed a definite pattern. The first step was to place one or two African unofficial members on the Governor's executive council; this happened in Ghana in 1942 and in Nigeria in 1943, and in Sierra Leone a year later. This gave Africans a chance to discuss proposals before they reached the legislature; but since the Africans were individuals, not members of any party, and like all other members of the executive council were sworn to secrecy, it did not really mean very much. The next step was to overturn the official majority in the legislative council and replace it not merely by a majority of unofficial members but by a majority of elected members. This step was taken in Nigeria and the Gold Coast in 1946, in Sierra Leone in 1951, in the Gambia in 1954.

When this stage had been reached something had to be done about the executive. The Governor's executive council contained African members, but it was a collection of individuals, responsible to the Governor, engaged in formulating official policy. It had no responsibility whatever to the Legislature, and the Governor was not even bound to take its advice This primitive council had now to be transformed into a cabinet. In 1951 the executive council was modified in Nigeria and the Gold Coast, and the next year in Sierra Leone. In Nigeria and the Gold Coast the members of the council were chosen from the members of the legislature (whether official or unofficial); the legislature could compel an individual African minister to resign, but not the council as a whole. The Sierra Leone council was modified even less than this. The executive council was fully transformed into a cabinet in 1954 in the Gold Coast, in 1957 in Nigeria, in 1958 in Sierra Leone, and in 1963 in the Gambia The *ex-officio* ministers were removed; all ministers were chosen by the Prime Minister from the members of the legislature who belonged to his party; the Prime Minister could dismiss any of his colleagues, and if the cabinet lost the confidence of the legislature the whole cabinet might have to resign.

There were other constitutional changes as well from time to time: an increase in the size of the legislature, the replacement of indirect election by direct, a federal system in Nigeria. But these were unimportant compared with the essential points of an elected majority in the legislature and a cabinet which is entirely drawn from the elected members of the legislature and is completely independent.

Nationalism developed differently in French West Africa. In 1946 France organised the whole French empire into a French Union. The Union consisted of Metropolitan France (France, Corsica and Algeria), the Overseas Department (such as French Guiana and the island of Réunion) and the Overseas Territories. French West Africa became one of the overseas territories. The Union had a council and an assembly, which included representatives from West Africa. All Africans became French citizens, but only some of them were given the right to vote; the right to vote was given to all Africans in 1956.

In 1958 France changed its constitution and the French Union became known as the French Community. Guinea voted to stay outside the Community and become completely independent; the other seven West African territories voted to remain within the Community. But by the end of 1960 all of them had asked for, and received, complete independence, though they are still in the French Community. The French Community is thus similar to the British Commonwealth; it is an association of states, most of them independent but some still dependent, which find it convenient for historical, sentimental, economic or other reasons to remain in association. Guinea, which chose to cut its links with the Community, is in much the same position as Burma, which chose to cut its links with the British Commonwealth.

NOTES

1 The author wishes to express gratitude to Dr T. N. Tamuno for his many constructive suggestions in the drafting of this chapter.

QUESTIONS FOR FURTHER STUDY AND DISCUSSION

1 Consider the contributions made by indirect rule to development.
2 Consider the contributions made by (a) Sir Gordon Guggisberg, (b) Lord Lugard to the history of Commonwealth West Africa.
3 Describe the nationalist movements in the period before 1939 in a West African country of your choice.

SELECT BIBLIOGRAPHY

D. Kimble, *A Political History of Ghana*, O.U.P., 1963.
F. M. Bourret, *Ghana: The Road to Independence*, O.U.P., 1960.
W. E. F. Ward, *History of Ghana*, Allen & Unwin, 2nd edition, 1958.
C. C. Reindorf, *The History of the Gold Coast and Ashanti*, Kegan Paul, 1951.
W. W. Claridge, *History of the Gold Coast and Ashanti*, Murray, 1915 (reissued F. Cass).
F. C. Fuller, *A Vanished Dynasty*, Murray, 1921.
R. S. Rattray, *Ashanti Law and Constitution*, O.U.P., 1929.
J. M. Gray, *A History of the Gambia*, C.U.P., 1940.
A. G. Burns, *History of Nigeria*, Allen & Unwin, 6th edition, 1963.
M. Crowder, *The Story of Nigeria*, Faber & Faber, 1962.
K. O. Dike, *Trade and Politics in the Niger Delta*, O.U.P., 1956.
G. I. Jones, *The Trading States of the Oil Rivers*, O.U.P., 1963.
A. P. Kup, *A History of Sierra Leone, 1400–1787*, C.U.P., 1961.
C. Fyfe, *A History of Sierra Leone*, O.U.P., 1962.
E. J. Yancy, *The Republic of Liberia*, Allen & Unwin, 1959.
W. E. F. Ward, *Government in West Africa*, Allen & Unwin, 1965.
V. Thompson and R. Adloff, *French West Africa*, Allen & Unwin, 1958.
—— *Emerging States of French Equatorial Africa*, O.U.P., 1960.

20 Nationalist Movements in West Africa

K. W. J. POST

ALTHOUGH Nationalism has passed into general usage in an African context, it is in fact a misleading term. As used in the classical European sense, related to, say, Ireland, Poland or Germany in the nineteenth century, it implies a unity of language and culture, and often a tradition of former political unity, existing prior to the attempt to free the people in question from foreign rule and to reunite them politically if (like the Poles and the Germans) they had become disunited in the meantime. In Africa, however, we are frequently told that one of the basic problems facing the new states after independence is to create a feeling of national unity, and the most cursory survey reveals their wide internal differences of language and culture, while in none of them was there an overall political unity in the pre-colonial period. African 'nationalist' movements, then, campaigned not in the name of an already-existing unity, but rather for the right to be free politically to try to create one. It is this distinctive quality which led Lord Hailey to suggest that 'Africanism' would be a better term to use than 'nationalism' in this particular context, and although this may be unacceptable because it seems to make Africa too much of a special case, nevertheless it is probably as well to remember that the descriptive phrase 'independence movements' may ideally be preferable to the one used in the title of this chapter. As we shall see, it is even difficult to speak of 'independence movements' in the context of French West Africa.

The use of the term 'independence movement', however, still implies the need to discuss the question, independence *from* what or whom, a nationalist movement *against* what or whom? These movements must be seen in terms of action, reaction and inter-action: action in the sense that we are dealing with a period of very rapid economic, social and political change; reaction in the sense that opposition to alien elements (i.e. colonial rule) is involved; and interaction in the sense that developments in one colonial territory affected those in another, and they were all affected by developments outside Africa itself. It is a complex situation, then, which must be reduced to some sort of order and set out with clarity in our teaching. How best may this be done?

Probably it is best to seek some fairly simple starting-point, one grasped easily enough to make further deductions from it readily understandable, and yet not constituting an over-simplification which distorts our whole picture when developed further. Such a starting-point could be the principle that any organisation to be effective needs a leadership to direct it and followers to put into effect the decisions of the leaders. This principle was of course true of the modern independence movements in West Africa: indeed, the significant point in their development came when potential leaders united with a large enough following to put effective pressure on the colonial governments. This situation came about roughly in the middle and late 1940s.

THE COLONIAL PERIOD

We are usually accustomed to view the period of colonial rule as something rigid, imposed from the outside, therefore alien and unacceptable to Africans. This is all no doubt true, but, from the point of view of the development of independence movements, it must also be remembered that the effect of this alien imposition was to set in train a process of rapid economic and social change within African society itself. The weakening of traditional authority, either by removing the chiefs' governmental powers (as often under the French) or by the British use of them in systems of 'indirect rule', and by the attack on old beliefs and their priests by the Christian missionaries; the introduction of cash-crop cultivation for the European market; the imposition of taxation; the importation of a much wider range of consumer goods; the laying-down of a communications network of railways and telegraphs and later of all-weather roads; the growth of old towns and the founding of new ones; the opening of government and mission schools; all these together had a profound effect on African society. Taken all in all, what we may say is that new opportunities to enhance their social position and thus their prestige were provided for a relatively small number of Africans. Just as Jaja of Opobo even before colonial rule was imposed was able to use his skill in the palm-oil trade to rise from slave to king, so the changes introduced by colonial rule gave chances to earn new wealth, to get the new education, to become eminent and influential as a trader or lawyer, contractor or teacher.

This is not to imply, however, that such opportunities were unlimited. For one thing, the number of Africans given access to the new opportunities was very small indeed, and they were very unevenly distributed; the coastal towns like Lagos, Accra, Freetown, Dakar and St Louis were especially favoured. In general terms, Christians were much better placed than Muslims, particularly in the field of education. Economic and social change had also generally gone much less far in French West Africa; a small educated elite may have been 'assimilated', but Frenchmen monopolised a wider range of economic activities than their British counterparts. Secondly, we must remember that colonialism meant alien rule which in turn inevitably meant frustration for any African who succeeded in taking advantage of new opportunities to advance himself. Thus, administratively, the local district commissioner or commandant, however new and callow, however stupid and ill-informed, ultimately could always impose his will upon an African, however senior and experienced. The youngest European officer could earn more than the most senior African clerk. Economically, though Africans might be active in trade, transport and contracting they knew always that the overall control of the economy rested with the expatriate trading companies and banks, and that their own personal positions depended upon the willingness of such institutions to grant them credit. Politically, for the period up to the end of the Second World War it was quite obvious that neither France nor Britain had any intention of giving power in any real sense to Africans.

The effect of all this was to create a group of potential leaders for an independence movement; 'leaders' because they had risen socially far enough to command respect among their own people, 'potential' because it was not until the 1940s (perhaps later in French West Africa) that they really began to show their interest in independence, as opposed to securing much more limited concessions from the colonial rulers. The leaders of the late nineteenth and early twentieth-century organisations, not concerned to recruit mass followings, made little effort to penetrate the hinterland behind the coastal towns. Their aim was to bargain with the colonial governments to secure better terms for themselves, rather than to force them to listen to radical demands because of the threat of mass action. At most, a mass meeting in one of the coastal towns was all they needed, not a permanent organisational network capable of mobilising activity in many different parts of the country.

Even before the Second World War, however, there were changes in British West Africa, both in the nature of the leaders and of their followers. By the late 1930s significantly named new organisations had begun to be formed: the Nigerian Youth Movement, Dr Danquah's Youth Conference in the Gold Coast, the West African Youth League of I. T. A. Wallace Johnson—all of them showing by the emphasis on youth in their titles the consciousness of a shift to a new generation of leaders. They also made efforts to recruit members on a wider basis, both geographically and socially, than before. Economic and social change had gone further and spread more widely, consequently a greater range of people were becoming aware of the colonial situation and its frustrations. Thus the late 1930s saw events of great significance in the Gold Coast and the Western Provinces of Nigeria, when the cocoa farmers, convinced that they were being cheated by the expatriate companies which monopolised the export of their produce, combined to hold back their harvest and refuse to sell it except at an increased price.

THE SECOND WORLD WAR

This was just on the eve of the Second World War. The effect of that cataclysm, in both French and British West Africa as in the rest of the colonial world, was greatly to strengthen the growth of independence movements. It had a catalytic effect, speeding up two processes, one of them the development of a new, more radical leadership, the other the emergence of a large group of potential followers for such leaders. Thus the potential leaders could not fail to be impressed by the lesson of Britain's defeat early in the war at the hands of both Germany and Japan, and the German occupation of France; suddenly their potential opponents must have seemed far less formidable. Much could be made, too, of the propaganda of the Allies during the war. Britain, the U.S.A. and the Free French claimed to be fighting for freedom, for the right of all peoples to choose the form of government under which they would live. Yet, when pressed, the British and Free French made it plain that this did not include colonial peoples, although they were being called upon to make great efforts to support the conduct of the Allied war effort.

The conduct of the war by the Allies had more tangible effects on the West African countries than merely to introduce them to new ideas. The production of arms and other war supplies greatly increased the demand for colonial raw materials, putting more money in the pockets of the producers, but at the same time working together with the shortage of consumer goods to produce inflation. At the same time the wages of urban workers remained low, failing to rise as rapidly as prices. The urban population was growing in numbers, as more people moved from the bush to the towns, hoping to get jobs in the new factories which were being built in small numbers to produce the unobtainable consumer goods. The new jobs were never as numerous as the people who came to look for them, and unemployment grew, despite another source of employment created by the influx of Allied servicemen. In British West Africa perhaps the most important contribution of these last was to help to destroy the myth of white superiority, carefully fostered by the insulation of Europeans from too much contact with Africans in the 'reservation' system. The tendency of servicemen to display natural human weaknesses, and the fact that some of them were even socialists or communists, opposed to the colonial system, made their contacts with West Africans educationally significant in more ways than one.

Lastly, it must not be forgotten that a considerable number of West Africans served in the Allied forces during the war (some 65,000 from the Gold Coast, for instance). The effect of this experience must have been great, since it gave them the chance to travel to other countries and to see their European counterparts at close quarters. Although the role of the ex-servicemen after they returned to civilian life is a matter for further research (like so many other aspects of this subject), some of them certainly were among the most militant members of the independence movements after the war, and all of them were an important source of new ideas.

In the immediate post-war period, then, a more militant leadership with a potential mass following appeared, at least in Senegal, Guinea, Ivory Coast, French Sudan (now Mali), Nigeria and the Gold Coast. Particularly in British West Africa, the potentiality existed for the putting of far more pressure upon the colonial administration than before. Moreover, the Second World War had also had an important effect upon Britain itself; the colonial power was now far more receptive to such pressure. The new Labour government had realised that some measure of colonial reform was necessary, and was gradually facing up to the fact that the devolution of political power to Africans must be begun, provided that African leaders basically sympathetic to the British point of view should inherit this power. There was a sense, then, in which the post-war British government—be it Labour or Conservative—was from the beginning anxious to respond to the demands of the independence movements.

'BRITISH' WEST AFRICA

It was at this point that differences between the countries of English-speaking West Africa began to be more significant than the similarities. From the mid-1940s they began increasingly to take different paths to independence Thus in the Gold Coast the decisive factor was the emergence. in July 1949 of a militant and radical independence movement—the Convention Peoples Party, led by Kwame Nkrumah—which replaced the U.G.C.C. and its moderate, more 'respectable' leaders. Having won the 1951 elections, the C.P.P. was able to increase its power as this was gradually handed over by the British, and to beat off the challenge presented by the National Liberation Movement and other opposition parties in the period 1954–7. By doing this, it left the British Government with no choice but to accept it as the only possible heir to complete political power when independence came in March 1957.

Nigeria presented a very different picture. Here the modern independence movement, the National Council of Nigeria and the Cameroons, led by Nnamdi Azikiwe, got off the ground earlier, in 1944, but was neither so militant in its demands nor so well organised as the C.P.P. The decisive factor in Nigeria seems to have been the early emergence (in 1948–51) of regional rivalries and of parties expressing them. As a result the period 1951–8 became a period of the adjustment of interests between three major parties, between the north and the two southern regions taken together, and between the majority and minority ethnic groups in each region; the first and second of these adjustments resulting in the adoption of a fully federalised constitution in 1954. These internal divisions enabled the Colonial Office to retain the initiative much more effectively than in Ghana, and also ensured that the federal government which emerged after the 1959 election and led Nigeria into independence in October 1960 represented an uneasy coalition of very disparate interests.

Sierra Leone and the Gambia presented a rather similar picture: the decisive factor in their progression to independence being internal divisions, and also their lack of economic and social development compared with the two larger territories. In Sierra Leone, rivalry between the Colony and the Protectorate delayed constitutional change in the period 1945–51. However, the difference in population between the two meant that any party which gained the support of the Protectorate, and kept it, would be the party which led the country to independence. The Sierra Leone Peoples Party, emerging in the election of 1951, was able to do this, weathering the storms of economic crisis, strikes, anti-chief riots and a split in its own ranks in the period 1955–8, and consolidating its position from then until independence in April 1961.

The Gambia was also distinguished politically by rivalry between the Colony and Protectorate, and it was not until the end of 1962 that there emerged the Progressive Peoples Party, emerged which was really able to control the majority of votes in the all-important hinterland. For the next three years the most important issue was to be whether or not the Gambia would actually become independent itself, or would enter into some sort of union with Senegal. This did not become immediately practicable, however, and in February 1965 the last of the British possessions in West Africa became independent.

'FRENCH' WEST AFRICA

The course of events in French West Africa after the Second World War followed a very different pattern. There, as mentioned earlier, it is somewhat difficult to talk of 'independence movements' at all, at any rate until the very end of the colonial period. Unlike British colonial theory, the French attitude to their overseas possessions did not envisage ultimate independence for them, but rather sought to find the best form of association between them and France itself. Moreover, this attitude was shared by almost all the African leaders: thus the Rassemblement Démocratique Africaine, formed in 1946 primarily on the initiative of Félix Houphouët-Boigny of the Ivory Coast, even in its most militantly anti-colonial mood still seems to have envisaged some close link with France, but a France itself radically changed and no longer devoted to colonial exploitation. These changes in France itself were to be achieved by the R.D.A.'s ally, the French Communist Party. By 1950, however, Houphouët-Boigny had decided that this alliance was too much of a liability, exposing his party to severe repression by the colonial administration. From 1950 onwards, therefore, he sought (successfully) to make his party respectable in the eyes of France, and to find a form of association with the colonial power, acceptable to both sides.

The R.D.A. was originally founded to provide one unified party for the whole of French West and Equatorial Africa, but, increasingly after 1951, the various territorial sections diverged. This was especially true after the Loi Cadre ('Outline Law') reforms of 1956–7 enabled governments with limited powers to be set up by African leaders in each individual territory. French West Africa had hitherto been treated as one federal unit; from 1957 onwards each territory developed along its own lines.

Differences in development also involved different views on future relations with France. Houphouët-Boigny envisaged close links between each individual territory and France, but Sékou Touré of Guinea, much more radical in his approach to politics, favoured collective bargaining between the African countries and France to strengthen the position of the former in this association. Compromise between the two views seemed impossible, but the whole picture was changed in May 1958 by the collapse of the French government and the coming to power of General De Gaulle. The General favoured the creation of a new unity, the Franco-African Community, and gave the African territories the chance to accept or reject this in the referendum of September 1958. Sékou Touré and his Guinean section of the R.D.A. decided to reject the community, regarding it as a disguise for continued French rule, and to take the complete independence which De Gaulle had made clear was the alternative to Community membership. Thus Guinea became independent on 1 October 1958, while all the other territories voted to become members of the Community. In fact, however, Guinea's choice of independence was the death-blow to attempts to preserve any integral unity between France and the

African countries. The example was contagious, and by late 1960 all the former French colonial territories had claimed and secured independence, making the Community a dead letter. Nevertheless, we can thus see that actual political independence became an issue very late in the colonial history of French West Africa.

TEACHING PROBLEMS AND SUGGESTIONS

The subject has now been discussed in the general terms o content and the specific terms of what points would seem to be essential to our (and our pupils') understanding of the development of the independence movements in West Africa.[1] We must now consider how to teach it. It is with some diffidence that a university teacher should proffer advice to those who teach in schools and teacher training colleges, since our job is far easier than theirs. This is particularly true of French-speaking Africa.

Moreover, what studies there are must often (and inevitably) suffer from bias. However open-minded the British or other expatriate writer, he is bound to view social change and its political effects in certain ways, to have a view of society and the political process which does not derive from African experience. Similarly, any African writer is likely to be committed to a view of the independence movement which may not take full account of the complexities of the colonial situation in its last years. Bias, too, is a menace to both teacher and pupils. In the former it is a problem because, remembering the colonial period well and possibly having been involved in the independence movement, the teacher is likely to show a much greater personal commitment than usual, while the pupils may not have participated in the events personally, but doubtless have absorbed some of the prejudices of their parents.

Perhaps the most difficult of our problems in teaching the history of these very recent events is our awareness of our responsibility to present governments—governments representing parties which developed as independence movements and often containing men especially active during this last phase of the colonial period. We have already mentioned the way in which emphasis is now laid upon the creation of a sense of national unity, which will transcend tribe and region. It is obvious that one of the most important single elements in creating this awareness, probably the most important, is education. There must inevitably, then, be great pressure of which we all have the responsibility to be aware.

Amidst all these pitfalls, what hope is there that this part of the syllabus can be taught in such a way as to give the pupil a reasonably intelligible and balanced picture of how his country came to attain independence, and how its recent history in this respect compares with that of similar countries? It can be done, but it will provide the severest test of the abilities of the teacher, who, having mastered his own bias and keeping that of his pupils in control, must seek to arouse their imagination sufficiently to transcend the lack of material, while at the same time teaching them much which we might normally regard as within the provinces of sociology and political science, rather than history. In this situation it would seem that much attention will have to be paid to creating one's own material, that is, to supplementing inadequate published material with local 'projects' of one sort or another. (Though obviously this will not be possible for the study of the French-speaking countries.) For one thing, the experience of the present writer and that of others working in similar fields would suggest that many more newspapers and pamphlets of the independence movement period have survived than might normally be expected, and people who have these stored away in cupboards and boxes might very well be prepared to give them to a local school. Similarly, there are many men and women to be found who, while no longer active themselves in politics, may have been very active in the immediate post-war period. Records made of their life-stories, and particularly of their experiences in the early days of the independence movements, would prove invaluable guides to an understanding of people's motives at this time. It may also be possible to persuade some of the more eminent people who were leaders at that time to come and give talks in the schools.

In understanding the social change which produced the leaders and their followers, much can probably be made of local projects, asking pupils to find out what social changes occurred in their area in the colonial period, what cash-crops were introduced, when roads were built, who built the first storey house, when the first bicycle was brought into the area, when the missionaries arrived and who they were, and many other questions. After all, people are in fact alive who know all these things, and it is possible to find them out. Similarly, it should be possible to discover when the first

23

branches of the modern political parties were established in a particular area, and by whom; with any luck that person will still be living in the area and available to give a talk to the class!

Once again, of course, there are problems here. Reference has already been made to the uneven nature of economic and social change in the colonial period, to the fact that some areas witnessed far greater changes than others. Some teachers will be fortunate in the location of their schools in this respect, others not so fortunate. However, to continue raising objections of this kind seems pointless at this stage. There is probably not one positive statement in this chapter concerning either the subject-matter discussed or the ways in which it be presented which cannot be challenged, or at best heavily qualified. All that can be done is to accept the challenge that this very stimulating topic presents.

NOTE

1 It is hoped that it will be fully understood that the selection of certain points as 'essential' is the author's own, and must not be regarded as absolutely finals Others may wish to vary the emphases. However the writer is convinced that some attention must be paid somewhere in any course to all the above comment. and interpretations.

QUESTIONS FOR FURTHER STUDY AND DISCUSSION

1 What were the effects of the Second World War on the development of the nationalist movements in Commonwealth West Africa?

2 Describe the attainment of independence by Sierra Leone and the Gambia.

3 Describe the main social and economic problems that have confronted your country since independence.

4 Write biographical sketches of the following showing their special contribution to the nationalist movements in their countries: Nnamdi Azikiwe, Kwame Nkrumah, Sékou Touré.

5 What similarities and what differences can you detect in the effects of the Second World War on the nationalist movements in French- and English-speaking West Africa?

6 What were the main differences between the nationalist movements in French- and English-speaking West Africa?

7 Compare and contrast the attainment of independence in Ghana and Nigeria, Ivory Coast and Guinea.

8 Consider the importance of the following: Léopold Senghor, Felix Houphouët-Boigny, the Loi Cadre, the 1958 referendum, Modibo Keita, the Brazzaville Conference.

SELECT BIBLIOGRAPHY

T. Hodgkin, *Nationalism in Colonial Africa*, Muller, 1956.

K. A. B. Jones-Quartey, *Biography of Dr Azikiwe*, Penguin Books, 1965.

K. W. J. Post, *The New States of West Africa*, Penguin Books, 1964.

I. Wallerstein, *Africa: The Politics of Independence*, Vintage, New York, 1960.

F. M. Bourret, *Ghana: The Road to Independence*, O.U.P., 1960.

J. S. Coleman, *Nigeria: Background to Nationalism*, University of California Press, 1958.

K. Ezera, *Constitutional Developments in Nigeria*, C.U.P., 1960.

K. Nkrumah, *Ghana: the Autobiography of Kwame Nkrumah*, Nelson, 1957.

R. Sklar, *Nigerian Political Parties*, Princeton U.P., 1963.

D. Austin, *Politics in Ghana, 1946–1960*, O.U.P., 1964.

M. Crowder, *Senegal: A Study in French Assimilation Policy*, O.U.P., 1962.

P. Neres, *French-Speaking West Africa*, O.U.P., 1962.

R. S. Morgenthau, *Parties of French-Speaking West Africa*, O.U.P., 1964.

21 South Africa at the Dawn of the Nineteenth Century

J. D. OMER-COOPER

SOUTH AFRICA can be described in geographical terms quite simply as the southern end of the African continental land mass; the southward prolongation of an immense plateau which stretches northward to the Sahara. Erosion has nibbled away at the plateau edges over thousands of years and this, together with changes in sea-level in geological times, has given rise to a coastal strip of variable width that runs round the edge of the interior table-land. The transition is marked by an escarpment, which varies in height and general character depending on the nature of the rock in different places and the extent to which it has been affected by the erosive action of wind and water. In the summer months rain-bearing winds sweep in from the Indian Ocean. The rains fall most heavily on the eastern coastal strip and on the mountains of the escarpment (which are there known as the Drakensberg). They diminish gradually as one moves westward until they die away almost to nothing in parts of the Kalahari desert. The cold Benguela current runs down the west coast causing the air from the Atlantic Ocean to shed its moisture before it reaches the land.

Winter from June to August is bitterly cold in most places, with severe frosts and snow on the mountains and highlands, but very little rain. Only in Natal and its vicinity does the warm water of the Indian Ocean moderate the winter climate to a pleasant mildness, but even there snowfalls are not unknown on the higher land. In accordance with the rainfall pattern, vegetation is generally most luxuriant on the east coast and grows more sparse as one moves westward; but even the most favoured areas are far from lush and drought is a recurrent problem. Much of the interior is strikingly stark and desolate except for a few months after the rains, and cannot support a very large agricultural population. In the immediate vicinity of the Cape itself, changes in the ocean currents allow winter winds to bring rain, producing a 'Mediterranean' climate with wet winters and dry summers. A series of short ranges known as the 'Cape series' prevents these conditions spreading far inland and this gives rise to the large semi-desert area of Karroo.

THE BUSHMEN

In the perspective of prehistory South Africa appears as a *cul de sac*; a last refuge of peoples and cultures which had disappeared from the rest of the continent. This continued as late as the beginning of the nineteenth century and, perhaps, in another sense

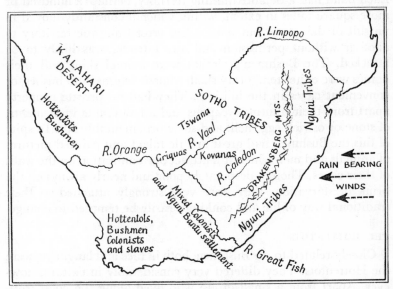

Fig. 17   The distribution of South African peoples at the beginning of the nineteenth century.

it is still true today. The earliest inhabitants of South Africa belonged to a distinct race of mankind which had once occupied central and much of east Africa as well. These were the Bushmen; a short people with a tawny yellow skin, very short stature possessing a number of other physical peculiarities and speaking languages containing distinctive clicking sounds which are unknown in any other human tongue except those of peoples who have been in contact with them.

Bushmen culture was of the simplest possible type. The men hunted wild animals and the women collected naturally growing herbs, fruits and tubers. They did not practise any kind of agriculture and they did not keep any domestic animals except hunting dogs. They could not afford to congregate together in very large communities and lived in bands of a few hundred at most, made up of fairly close relatives. Within the band, decisions were taken by discussion amongst the adult members. There was no chief or other formal system of government but everyone was equal, and every successful hunter shared some of his kill with the other members of the group. The feeling of internal unity was high. Each band had a definite hunting territory, perhaps a hundred or more square miles in extent, within which it constantly moved in pursuit of the game, but none could cross from one territory to another without permission and any intruder was likely to be attacked. The Bushmen's clothes were animal skins and their homes were either temporary shelters made of grass and bushes, or convenient caves in the hillsides. They had no private property apart from their hunting weapons and a few simple implements, of stone or ostrich egg shell, and some ornamental beads. In spite of this the Bushmen had great artistic talent and painted pictures of animals and men which still attract our admiration on the walls of their caves. Though desperately poor and nearly always on the brink of starvation, they were very strongly attached to their traditional way of life and could not easily be tempted to change.

THE HOTTENTOTS

Closely related to the Bushmen, both in race and language, were the Hottentots. They differed very considerably in culture, however. Apart from a small group who lived along the coast, subsisting by fishing and gathering shell-fish (the strandloopers whose kitchen rubbish dumps of sea shells can still be seen on South African beaches), the Hottentots were a pastoral people. Cattle and sheep were their mainstay, though they were also keen hunters and the women gathered wild foods to supplement their diet. Like the Bushmen they practised no agriculture. Because of their cattle they could live in larger communities than their cousins and were organised in tribes each made up of a number of related clans. One of these was always recognised as the senior and its head was chief of the tribe. But these chiefs had very little power and no special officers to help them carry out their duties or enforce their commands and the tribes were very unstable. The chiefs ruled purely by consent of the other clan heads and, if there was a serious disagreement, a tribe frequently broke up. Any clan head could always break away becoming an independent chief, and this inevitably happened whenever the population of a tribe grew large. The sparse vegetation of most of South Africa meant that a relatively few cattle required extensive grazing lands, so when herds grew too large to be grazed together separation was the obvious answer.

Like the Bushmen, each Hottentot group laid claim to an area of land as its tribal territory but, perhaps because they took their most important source of food supplies, the cattle, with them whenever they moved, the Hottentots tended to migrate over larger distances and to be less strongly attached to a particular territory. Their material standard of living was only slightly higher than that of the Bushmen. They had more assured food supplies and could use the skins of their animals as cloaks against the winter cold, but their houses were no more than simple shelters, often woven of grass, and light enough to be carried on the back of an ox when they changed camp. Like the Bushmen, they shared much of their food and other goods with one another, but cattle constituted a kind of private property, making some richer than others. This was perhaps why the Hottentots could be tempted more easily than the Bushmen to abandon their traditional way of life in return for material reward. The Hottentots were not so widespread in South Africa as the Bushmen. They were generally to be found near the coasts, in south-west Africa, at the Cape itself and up the east coast at least as far as the Transkei. Their relations with the Bushmen were often hostile. The Bushmen resented the intrusion of Hottentot cattle on their hunting grounds and retaliated by stealing the animals or killing the herdsmen, and the Hottentots in return tried to destroy the Bushman communities. But sometimes peaceful agreements were made and occasionally Bushman bands lived in association with Hottentot tribes acting as herdsmen and hunters.

THE BANTU

By the beginning of the nineteenth century both these peoples had long been replaced in most of South Africa by a third much more numerous folk, the Bantu. Bantu is a general name given to a vast group of peoples who speak several hundred different languages which can be shown to be related to one another. They are basically of Negro stock and probably originated somewhere in West Africa and spread out gradually over thousands of years to occupy most of East, Central and South Africa. During this process they intermarried with other peoples and developed a wide variety of cultures and political systems. One of the most remarkable of these was in modern Rhodesia. There the Bantu were in contact with Arab traders who had established a trading post at Sofala.[1] Gold from innumerable small diggings and other commodities were exchanged for Chinese porcelain and other imported goods and the Bantu developed a powerful kingdom generally known as the Monomatapa empire with its impressive buildings at Zimbabwe.[2]

The Bantu who settled in South Africa belonged to a branch of the Bantu peoples known as the Southern Bantu. They had much in common with the peoples of the Monomatapa empire and they shared a common culture with one another. When they first began to enter South Africa is not known with any degree of accuracy, but it was certainly several hundreds of years before the nineteenth century. They can be divided into a number of groups by reference to their languages. The east coast strip was the home of numerous tribes belonging to the Nguni-speaking group. Perhaps because the area was so fertile they had advanced farther southward than any other Bantu people in South Africa. By the eighteenth century they occupied the coastal area as far as the Great Fish River and were beginning to settle to the south-west of that river in the land known as the Zuurveld. The languages of the Nguni tribes were sufficiently similar for different peoples to understand one another though there were some important differences of vocabulary and dialect. As they had been in particularly close contact with the Bushmen and Hottentots the Nguni peoples used more of the click sounds in their languages than other South African Bantu.

The central plateau from the escarpment to the fringes of the Kalahari was occupied by a great group of peoples speaking Sotho languages. Some of the earliest of this group to enter South Africa were the tribes who are generally known as the Tswana (Bechuana). Their dialects differ slightly from the others, and they lived on the western part of the plateau near the Kalahari in the area now known as Bechuanaland. The rest of the Sotho group spread into the Transvaal and the northern parts of the modern Orange Free

State, and are sometimes divided into northern and southern Sotho. Though the Nguni and Sotho groups were separated by the Drakensberg mountains they were not kept completely apart. Some tribes crossed the escarpment, especially where it was less sharply marked as in northern Zululand and Swaziland. So there were some Nguni tribes living on the plateau in the Transvaal and some Sotho peoples on the edge of the coastal strip in Swaziland. The Sotho peoples had not advanced as far south as the Nguni and were still north of the Orange River at the beginning of the nineteenth century, though they were continually expanding and taking over more land from the Bushmen. West of the Kalahari a third group the Herero and the Ovambo were beginning to occupy South West Africa, but they had made much less progress than the other groups and most of the country was still occupied by the Namaqua Hottentots and the Bushmen.

All the South African Bantu, with the exception of the Herero whose way of life was very similar to the Hottentots, were mixed farmers. They kept cattle which were their most prized possession and the basis of their existence, but they also practised agriculture. Thus they were able to maintain much larger populations on the same area of land than either of the earlier peoples and to live as larger communities in more permanent dwellings with less need for frequent migration. Their houses were round huts sometimes built of mud with thatched roofs and attractive designs painted in coloured clay on the walls, sometimes simply woven of grass. Their pattern of settlement depended largely on water supplies made vital by the dry climate. Where there were many springs and streams, as on the east coast, the people lived in little family hamlets scattered widely over the country. Where water supplies were scarcer, the people had to congregate around them. Thus the Sotho tended to live in substantial villages and the Tswana on the edge of the Kalahari in towns of considerable size.

The Bantu were organised in tribes, each of which consisted of one central clan, though it might contain members from other clans as well. The chief came from the central clan and was the head of the community in every sense. He had the last word in all political matters and he was the final judge in all legal disputes. He was the link between the community and its ancestors, and took the lead in all important ceremonies, controlling the activities of the magicians who summoned rain and the witch doctors who detected persons guilty of black magic and communion with evil spirits. But in spite of this wide ranging authority the chief could not rule as a despot. He had a number of personal officers, called indunas, to help him enforce his commands. They were usually chosen from families with no claim to royalty so that they would not be tempted to seize the throne. The powers of these officers were limited however, and the administration of most of the territorial sub-divisions of the tribe was delegated to important members of the royal family. These were powerful men who could lay claim to the throne if the ruler became unpopular so it was impossible for him to govern in peace without their consent. Bantu rulers therefore governed in close consultation with the leading men in their tribe. In day-to-day affairs the chief worked with a small body of personal advisers; leading members of the royal family, who happened to be living at his homestead, indunas and personal friends, or men noted for their wisdom. On more important occasions all the district rulers would be assembled. In addition, amongst the Sotho tribes where the peoples lived in large settlements, public assemblies were held on specially important occasions and any adult member of the tribe could take part in discussing matters of policy. In theory chiefs could ignore the advice of all these bodies since there was no formal voting and it was the chief who announced the decision after discussion, but in practice a ruler who went against the wishes of the leading men and the people was asking for civil war. In each of the districts of the tribe the ruling sub-chief had his own indunas and councillors. In case of a dispute it was not difficult for him to make use of his local following in a bid for the throne, or to break away and form a new tribe. This type of break-away was very common, for in the healthy climate of South Africa the population increased very rapidly and as tribes grew too big for convenience they split into two or more. Very often the death of a chief was the occasion for such divisions. The succession was frequently disputed and the defeated aspirant often led his followers away to found a new tribe.

Except on such occasions, the Bantu tribes were internally peaceful and law-abiding. All serious disputes were handled in public courts where the chief or district sub-chief sat with his advisers and heard evidence, examining witnesses for both sides. Litigants who were dissatisfied with decisions in the district courts could appeal to that of the chief himself which served as a court of appeal for the whole tribe as well as a court of first instance for those living near by. Land was regarded as belonging to the community and its use was regulated by the chief or his local subordinates. There were no boundaries between the lands of different families, and cattle were allowed to graze freely in the general area allotted to a village or hamlet. It was the general custom, however, that anyone who had first cultivated a piece of land should have a right to plant his crops there in future even if he had not made use of it for a prolonged period. The chief could allow another tribe to graze their cattle on the tribal land, and for this a small tribute was generally paid in recognition of the chief's authority and the prior rights of the tribe which occupied the territory. Such agreements did not amount to outright sale. They were never intended to exclude members of the chief's own tribe from using their ancestral land, but merely to give others a temporary right to share the use of the soil.

The most important cultural institution of the Southern Bantu was the system of initiation to manhood. When a boy reached an age when he was mature enough to marry and take on the responsibilities of adult life, he went through the ceremony of circumcision followed by a prolonged period of living apart from the tribe, during which he would receive instruction in the customs of his people and the duties expected of an adult man. Thereafter he would be received back into the community with an elaborate ceremony and begin a new life as an adult. These ceremonies made a profound impression on the minds of the young men and imbued them with a respect for the traditional culture of the community. So important was the experience that men only counted the years of their lives after initiation, boyhood being considered too insignificant to be worth recording. In all tribes these initiation ceremonies created a sense of fellow-feeling amongst men who were initiated about the same time, but amongst the Sotho tribes this feeling was particularly strong. In their case, initiation ceremonies were conducted under the authority of chiefs or district heads. All the youths of appropriate age in a given area were initiated together in an initiation school, which was generally held when the chief or sub-chief had a son of age for initiation. After the ritual period was ended, the boys who had participated in an initiation school retained a sense of corporate identity. In times of war they fought as a group under the leadership of their age-mate prince, and at other times they assembled to perform special services for the ruler such as building him a new homestead.

Warfare between tribes was not uncommon. As population increased and grazing land became scarce, disputes often occurred between neighbours. When a chief died, squabbles over the succession often involved fighting and when, as so often, these troubles led to the division of the tribe the different sections might continue to nourish feelings of hostility for one another. In addition the herds of neighbouring tribes offered a constant temptation to a people who regarded cattle as the sign of social status. It was not unusual for the young bloods to prove their courage and improve their marriage chances by organising raids on their neighbours' cattle. Wars were aimed at capturing a few cattle or forcing a neighbouring tribe to abandon a grazing ground, not at destroying the enemy completely. Thus a war usually ended after a single battle when one side admitted defeat; non-combatants were usually respected and prisoners returned for a ransom. The Southern Bantu tribes had no standing armies and no special war chiefs.

THE IMMIGRANTS

In 1652 when the Dutch East India Company at last took action to establish a permanent post at the Cape, which had been used as a stopping point for ships travelling to and from the Indies for over a century, a new element was added to the pattern of South African peoples. At first the refreshment station was intended to be no more than a vegetable patch cultivated by the Company's personnel. But soon it was decided that farmers growing crops for their own profit would perform the task more efficiently than Company servants working for salaries. A small number of the Company's men were released from their service agreements and given land on which to set up as free burghers. The nucleus of the future South African white population had been created.

Soon afterwards the need to increase the defensive strength of the settlement against possible attack by other European powers led to a definite policy of increasing the white population by assisted immigration. The colony was extended from the tiny Cape peninsula to the mainland and a number of French Huguenots, refugees from religious persecution, were settled together with the predominantly Dutch settler population. They brought with them skill in viniculture and wine-making, and soon made wine one of the main products of the Cape and its immediate vicinity.

The white settlers were mostly of humble stock, but they brought with them the expectation of a material standard of living considerably above that of any of the indigenous South African peoples, the European conception of individual property rights, and the Calvinist religion with its stern moral code and its belief in the predestined division of mankind into the chosen and the damned. In the conditions prevailing at the Cape, successful farming required considerable labour. Attempts were made to

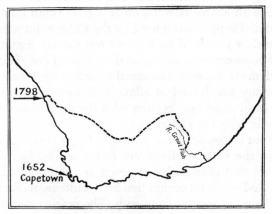

Fig. 18   The expanding colony area.

bring out whites as agricultural workers (Knecht), but it was difficult enough to persuade anyone to leave Europe to settle as a farmer at the extremity of the African continent, and it was almost impossible to recruit labourers. Most of the Knecht took any opportunity to leave their employers and set up on their own, and the settlers clamoured for slave labour. Some of the Company's officials were strongly opposed to allowing the Cape to become a slave-owning colony but eventually they were overruled, and after 1716 the free importation of slaves was permitted. This put an end to the growth of a white working class and added another element to the composition of South Africa's population. The slaves came mainly from West Africa, Madagascar and Mozambique, but there were also some Malays from modern Indonesia who formed the nucleus of a Malay, largely Muslim, population, in Cape Town and its close neighbourhood. In the area around the Cape itself where the 'Mediterranean' climate favours the growth of vines and wheat and where proximity to the port provided easy access to the market, a substantial population of white landowners developed. Some were men of considerable means with vineyards and corn-fields, large slave establishments and farmhouses beautified with traditional Dutch gables. Until well into the nineteenth century this area contained the bulk of South Africa's white population and served as a reservoir supplying population to the frontier areas where the most important historical developments took place.

The Company's intention was that its burghers would occupy themselves with arable farming on relatively small land holdings, while the meat supplies, required by the Cape population and the ships, would be obtained by barter from the Hottentots. But the Hottentot economy was not geared to the sale of their precious stock, and meat supplies remained irregular and unsatisfactory. The Company was forced to allow its subjects to keep cattle for themselves and sometimes even to relax the regulations prohibiting private trade with the Hottentots.

Apart from innkeepers and traders in Cape Town itself, the vast majority of the Cape whites were farmers. The introduction of slaves meant that manual labour even of a semi-skilled or skilled type was ruled out as an occupation for a white man. Farming near the Cape however was far from easy. The market for wheat, wine and other agricultural commodities at the Cape was distinctly limited, and early attempts to provide an export market for the Cape's wine and wheat failed because of their low quality and high cost of production. Successful farming, moreover, required con-siderable capital expenditure on slaves and equipment. An impe-cunious young man had to borrow heavily to set himself up, and in the poor and uncertain state of the market he was unlikely ever to free himself from the burden of debt. In contrast with this gloomy outlook there were possibilities of making a reasonable living as a stock raiser in the interior. Cattle were in demand for their meat and for hides which could be exported. They could walk to market and did not need expensive transport. Unlike crops they were not immediately perishable and could be kept from one year to another if market conditions so required. Moreover, the cost of living in the interior was much lower than at the Cape. The farmer might expect to derive much of his food from hunting and the produce of his cattle. He did not need the expensive clothes and other luxuries required by Cape Town society, and he was able to persuade Hottentots to enter his service instead of the much more expensive slaves. Small wonder that men began to cross the mountains into the hinterland, first as traders bartering with the Hottentots, later as cattle ranchers.

The general aridity of the South African climate means that the cattle-carrying capacity of grazing land is strictly limited. But the white cattle farmer needed a considerable herd if he were not only to provide for the food of his family and his servants but also to pay for his wagon and supplies of essential commodities, such as gunpowder and lead, without which his existence would be impossible. A farm of less than about 6,000 acres was economically unviable and in less favoured areas even this was not adequate. The company adopted a policy of allowing settlers to make use of cattle runs of about 6,000 acres in return for a nominal annual rent and many farmers made use of more than one such ranch.

With this development the colony began to expand with extraordinary rapidity, and this was accelerated because the extensive Karroo area in the hinterland of the Cape could not be permanently occupied for lack of water in the summer months. Farmers grazed their cattle there in the winter but staked out farms beyond its limits. The Company looked with some displeasure on the inflation of its once tiny colony and increased its attempts to keep the settlers within fixed boundaries, but the venality of the Company's officials defeated all attempts to stabilise the frontier.

RACE RELATIONS

This territorial expansion inevitably took place at the expense of the indigenous peoples. Shortly after the first establishment of the Cape settlement a minor war took place between the infant colony and a tribe of Hottentots who felt that their ancestral lands were being taken away. It ended with the Hottentots being forced to recognise that their land had gone forever. Thereafter there were no further serious conflicts between the colony and the Hottentots. The impact of an exchange economy and the attraction of European material goods provoked a drastic disintegration of Hottentot culture. This was increased by the effect of devastating smallpox epidemics introduced into the country by ships returning from India. Thus, as the colonists advanced, the Hottentots parted with their lands with hardly a struggle, and either entered the service of the settlers as farm labourers or retired farther into the interior. The Bushmen, on the other hand, were not so easily attracted by material goods nor did they have anything to trade with the farmers. They fought back with desperate courage, killing herdsmen with poisoned arrows, stealing and destroying stock on a large scale. In retaliation the white farmers organised themselves for defence. In each district one of the farmers was appointed the local commander, and in case of need he was entitled to summon the farmers within his area, with their horses and guns, to form a commando. When large-scale expeditions were planned the farmers of many districts would combine forces. Official commandos were supported by the government which paid for the ammunition used. This system remained the normal military organisation of the Boers down to the Great Boer War.

Against the Bushmen the commandos waged a war of extermination. They were literally hunted down like animals, but they fought back so fiercely that at one time they actually drove the frontiers of the colony back and brought the commando system to the verge of collapse. Expeditions against the Bushmen became so dangerous and unprofitable that farmers increasingly refused to turn out. Then for some time an alternative policy of winning the Bushmen over and weaning them away from their traditional culture by giving them gifts of cattle was tried. It brought a considerable measure of peace to the frontier until, as the colonial population increased, the Bushmen were too hopelessly outnumbered to offer further serious resistance.

When the Cape settlement was first established it was not the intention of the Company that it should develop along lines of racial separation. The Company was anxious to retain good relations with the indigenous peoples and believed that intermarriage would be one of the best ways of ensuring this. Thus the surgeon of the little colony was given promotion when he married a Christian Hottentot woman called Eva and a wedding party was held in the commander's house. The Dutch settlers tended to despise the Hottentots with their very simple material culture, but this was basically a matter of culture and religion rather than of race. Freed Negro slaves acquired burgher status and lived on familiar social terms with their white fellow farmers, and the children of mixed unions were readily accepted as members of white society. Later, however, this attitude began to change. In the very early days the settlers were predominantly males and relations with Hottentot women were very common, but in time the proportion of men to women in white society reverted to normal and there was then much greater resistance to the idea of such unions being regarded as legitimate, or their offspring being accepted into white society. The introduction of slaves on a large scale after 1716 and the elimination of a white working class produced a sharp stratification of society along lines of colour. All whites were farmers or held other positions of responsibility; all labourers were non-white. Inevitably, attitudes altered to justify the existing social structure. Moreover, as the farmers began to penetrate the hinterland, and live in isolation amongst the Hottentots, fear of losing contact with their own group led to an increased sense of racial solidarity. Most important of all, the white farmer in the interior found himself in a position of authority over a mixed group of servants: slaves, Hottentots and sometimes a few Bushmen. Many of these were not accustomed to the work which the farmer required of them or the kind of authority it was necessary for him to exercise. Yet the farmer was very isolated, his nearest white neighbour might be several miles distant. He often found it necessary to provide his herdsmen with guns to protect the cattle against wild animals or the Bushmen. He could only hope to enforce his commands if he and his servants accepted his position of authority without question. In such circumstances a myth of racial superiority appeared a necessity of survival. Finally, the struggle against the Bushmen had a generally brutalising effect and lowered the value of non-European lives in the eyes of whites who became accustomed to hunting them like vermin. Thus the original attitude of ignoring racial differences, except where they were accompanied by cultural and religious contrasts, was replaced by an ever-increasing race consciousness. Non-Europeans whether slaves or Hottentots came to be looked on more as 'living instruments' than as persons entitled to equal rights. It became unthinkable for a Hottentot to take his master to court and be treated on a basis of legal equality. Religion itself was interpreted to sanctify the *status quo*, and most simple farmers believed that discrimination between the races was the will of God even if this was not accepted by the official synods of the church.

24

As the frontiers of the colony expanded, some Hottentot groups retreated into the interior and, as the barriers of race discrimination began to rise, many of the descendants of white/Hottentot unions, who would otherwise have been absorbed into the settler group, migrated beyond the frontiers rather than submit to a position of inferiority. Towards the end of the eighteenth century a tribe of Hottentots known as the Korana, who had originally lived near the Cape but had found themselves driven farther and farther back, began to settle around the Orange River and then move on northwards, settling in small clan groups on both sides of the Vaal River up to and around its junction with the Harts. There they came in conflict with the southernmost of the Tswana tribes. Though armed only with bows and arrows, the Korana succeeded in defeating one of the Tswana tribes and killing its chief. Thereafter they met with relatively little resistance and took to a life of combined cattle-raising and brigandage. They became more formidable when joined by a notorious German outlaw from the Colony named Jan Bloem who brought them firearms and ammunition and became the leader of one of the clans.

In the wake of the Koranas, parties of mixed blood and some pure Hottentots began to congregate around the Orange River. One heterogeneous group settled on the north bank near the confluence of the Orange and the Vaal. There they were encountered by missionaries at the beginning of the nineteenth century. Under missionary influence they took the name of Griqua and adopted a modicum of settled government. This took the form of a compromise between Hottentot ideas of hereditary chieftaincy and Dutch republican institutions. But internal quarrels and the attempts of the missionaries to insist on modes of behaviour which many of their flock found unacceptably strict led to a division into three main Griqua communities, while others remained independent of any of these. The distinction between Griquas and Koranas was never very precise and, in spite of missionary attempts to prevent it, many Griquas indulged in predatory practices.

Though a thin sprinkling of settlers spread out rapidly over a wide extent of country north and west of the Cape, the main stream of expansion flowed up the east coast, along the line of greater rainfall. The settlers did not at first enter the fertile Zuurveld between the Sundays and Fish rivers because they feared the possibility of clashes with the Bantu who were beginning to occupy it. Instead, they went inland towards the Sneeuwberg and Bruintjies Hoogte, but Bushman resistance there was so fierce that the stream of migration turned back towards the coast and settlers began to establish themselves as cattle traders and farmers alongside the Bantu in the Zuurveld. The Company's government heard disturbing rumours about the behaviour of its subjects in the frontier areas, and in 1778 Governor Van Plettenberg made a tour of the colony, with a view to defining definite boundaries and bringing the whole situation under proper control. He found the Zuurveld occupied indiscriminately by white farmers and Bantu tribesmen; a situation which he felt was bound to encourage undesirable conduct on the part of the settlers and lead eventually to serious conflict with the Bantu. He determined to regularise the situation by establishing a definite border between the peoples. He met some chiefs on the Fish River and made an agreement with them that the river should be the frontier. Unfortunately these chiefs were not the rulers of the people living on the Zuurveld and, even if they had been, they would not have been justified according to Bantu custom in giving the grazing land of the people away. Thus the Bantu remained on the Zuurveld, but in the eyes of the government and the colonists they were illegally intruding on the territory of the colony. Trouble was not long in coming and in 1779 mutual charges of cattle theft led to violence. A Boer commando was assembled and succeeded in killing considerable numbers of Bantu, driving many to flight across the Great Fish River and capturing a large number of cattle. The effects of this raid were only temporary however. The Bantu soon returned to their homes, and their number increased as the pressure of rising population on the other side of the river caused further migration into the Zuurveld.

In 1786 the Company finally decided to open a new magistracy for the eastern frontier areas in the hope of introducing normal law and order. It was situated at Graaff Reinet from where it was hoped that the situation, both on the northern part of the frontier where the struggle with the Bushmen was continuing, and in the southern part where colonists were in contact with Bantu, could be kept under review. The first magistrate (Landdrost) soon proved unsatisfactory and was dismissed to be succeeded by his secretary, Maynier, an able and intelligent man of Huguenot descent, from the more settled part of the colony. Maynier soon found difficulty in carrying out what he believed to be his duty. He tried to ensure that Hottentot servants were not treated cruelly, and that relations between the colony and the Bantu on the Zuurveld should be determined by official policy, not the whims of the local farmers. Both these lines of action made him bitterly unpopular; he was felt to be subverting the proper relations between the races and undermining masters' authority over their servants. When he refused to give credence to all the complaints of cattle theft by the Bantu or to permit farmers to organise reprisal commandos without official sanction, he was accused of preferring heathens to Christians. Finally, a war with the Bantu broke out and after an inconclusive campaign had taken place, he agreed to make peace on conditions which allowed the Bantu to remain on the Zuurveld. The farmers broke into open revolt. Maynier was driven out and an independent republic of Graaff Reinet declared. So great was the sympathy for this move amongst the settler population that the burghers of the neighbouring magistracy of Swellendam immediately followed suit.

The Company's government was brought to an end by the British occupation before it could resolve the trouble. The first period of British rule at the Cape, 1795–1803, produced no fundamental change in the basic situation. The settlers continued to seek new land as their population increased. They also clung to their belief of racial superiority, and resented any interference by government in their treatment of Hottentot servants. Tension between them and the Bantu population of the Zuurveld persisted. A frontier rebellion against British authority and the attempt to suppress it by a force which included Hottentot troops led to a mass uprising of Hottentots and a war with the Bantu which devastated the eastern frontier districts. If the succeeding three years, 1803–6, when the Cape was governed by representatives of the Dutch Batavian Republic were a period of calm, it was only because all parties in the frontier area were too exhausted to wish to resume the struggle immediately. The problem remained unsolved to face the second British administration from 1806. But though the changes of government between 1795 and 1806 had little immediate effect on the South African situation they coincided with the beginnings of large-scale missionary activity in the colony. The Cape was being brought within the reach of the European missionary and philanthropic movement which was to

have important effects on the subsequent history of the sub-
continent.

CONCLUSION

By the beginning of the nineteenth century, the Bantu, expanding steadily southward, and the colonists, pushing north under the
influence of the land-hunger generated by their use of large
ranching areas, had come face to face with one another in the
Zuurveld. In the hinterland direct contact had not been fully
established, but the Bantu were feeling the effects of the advancing
frontier indirectly through contact with the Korana and Griquas.
The Cape settlers had developed a society highly stratified along
racial lines and a doctrine of white racial superiority. A pattern
had been set of conflict between the colonists and the frontier
tribes, accompanied by internal tensions in white-dominated
society, with the government attempting to preserve a measure of
justice and normal principles of law and order.

The Hottentots and Bushmen who had served as a buffer
between the two major races had been very largely eliminated.
They had either been absorbed into Bantu tribes or forced to enter
the service of the whites, where they intermarried with slaves and
persons of mixed descent to form what was essentially the working
class of the white community, though debarred on racial grounds
from social and economic opportunity. Others still clung to their
old way of life in remote and unfavourable parts of the sub-
continent, particularly South West Africa. Only the Griquas and
the Koranas remained a significant historical force east of the
Kalahari. The stage was set for the great conflicts and upheavals
which marked the next phase in South African history.

NOTES

1 See pp. 54, 441.
2 See pp. 53, 54.

QUESTIONS FOR FURTHER STUDY
AND DISCUSSION

1 Give an account of the most important cultural differences between the
Hottentots and Bushmen in the early nineteenth century.

2 What were the most striking features of southern Bantu social and political
organisation before the colonial period?

3 How far does the geography of South Africa help to explain the distribution of peoples at the beginning of the nineteenth century?

4 Either (a) describe and explain the development of race attitudes in the South African white community before the nineteenth century, or (b) explain the hostility of the frontier farmers to the government in Cape Town at the end of the eighteenth century.

SELECT BIBLIOGRAPHY

I. Schapera, *The Khoisan Peoples of South Africa*, Routledge, 1930.
—— *Government and Politics in Tribal Societies*, Watts, 1956.
—— *The Bantu-speaking Peoples of South Africa*, Routledge, 1946.
E. Walker, *A History of Southern Africa*, Longmans, 3rd edition, 1957.
S. D. Neumark, *Economic Influences on the South African Frontier, 1652–1836*, Stanford U.P., 1957.
I. D. MacCrone, *Race Attitudes in South Africa*, Witwatersrand U.P., Johannesburg, 1957.
J. S. Marais, *The Cape Coloured People*, Witwatersrand U.P., Johannesburg, 1957.

22 The Mfecane and the Great Trek

J. D. OMER-COOPER

BY the beginning of the nineteenth century two expanding societies, the Bantu and the white settlers, faced one another in South Africa. Within each of these societies population growth and land-hunger were generating internal tensions which would culminate in suddenly accelerated processes of change. Although this might seem less true of white society with its relatively small population within the total land-area of the colony, the methods of land-use employed by the Boers and their insistence on individual ownership meant that land-hunger was at least as great a problem to the handful of white farmers, in their vast territories, as to the much denser Bantu populations. In the colony, moreover, the internal stratification of society, and the attitude of the government to it and to the question of relations with the Bantu, were additional sources of tension while the political unity of the society favoured the rapid spread of ideas. It was amongst the Bantu, however, that the first explosion occurred and this contributed to the subsequent upheaval in white society. Much of the subsequent history of South Africa must be seen as the consequences of these two distinct but interrelated movements.

THE FRONTIER PROBLEM

By 1800 conflict between white settlers and the Xhosa people, the advance guard of the Nguni-speaking group of Bantu, had begun in the Zuurveld. Changing governments at the Cape had failed to resolve the problem since it arose from causes beyond ordinary political control. The Boer, anxious for the future of his sons, seeking no alternative for them but the life of cattle ranchers and aware that any substantial reduction in the size of farms would lead to ruin, pressed that the Bantu be driven from the Zuurveld and the frontier further extended to the Koonap or, if it might be, to the Kat. The Ndlambi and Gunukwebe branches of the Xhosa living on the Zuurveld knew that they would not be welcomed if they retired across the Great Fish River to lands fully occupied by other branches of their people and refused to move. In the absence of fences or other effective barriers between two peoples, both dependent on cattle raising and both possessing a proportion of rascals amongst their number, conflict could not be prevented for long.

In 1812 the British government attempted to rationalise the situation by establishing a clear division between white and Bantu. The Ndlambi and Gunukwebe tribesmen living on the Zuurveld (estimated at about 20,000) were forcibly evicted and driven across the Great Fish River, and a series of forts (including the important strategic settlement of Grahamstown) were built to guard this frontier. However, this produced intolerable tensions in the immediate hinterland of the boundary. The newly exiled inhabitants of the Zuurveld nursed the ambition to drive the colonists from what they regarded as their own land. A prophet named Makanna rose amongst them and proclaimed that their ancestral heroes would return to fight on their side. He attracted many followers away from the Gqika branch of the Xhosa who had always lived west of the Great Fish River and had no particular quarrel with the colony. In 1818, as the land sweltered under a fierce drought, the Ndlambis and the Gqikas came to blows over grazing lands. The Ndlambis were victorious at the bitterly fought battle of Amalinde and the colonial forces intervened on the Gqika side. The Ndlambis, inspired by the prophecies of Makanna, then poured into the colony. Thus the government's policy had resulted in the very conflict it was intended to avoid, but, at the conclusion of the war, yet another attempt at permanent segregation was made. The Xhosa were forced to surrender a strip of land between the Great Fish River and the Keiskamma to be converted into a buffer zone kept empty by military patrols. Such a no-man's land between two land-hungry peoples was hardly likely to be successful: pressure from both sides inevitably led to concessions and the neutral strip began to take the place of the Zuurveld as a source of contention.

The British government, however, had more fundamental ideas for dealing with the situation. It realised that the extensive land-holding pattern was responsible for the inflated size of the colony, the low degree of urbanisation and economic diversification, and the constant pressure for further expansion. An official of the

Batavian government had analysed the economic difficulties of the Cape along these lines as early as 1804 Particularly distressing was the fact that while there was constant pressure to expand the frontier, the population within it was too thin for adequate defence. The answer seemed to lie in a different farming pattern: farms of 100–200 acres instead of 6,000. This the government hoped to encourage by a number of measures: persuading farmers to acquire permanent property rights in their farms instead of temporary leases; making provision for the sub-division of farms among heirs; stopping further grants of Crown land and offering it for auction

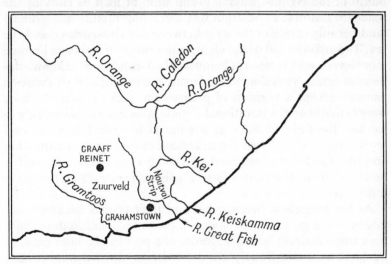

Fig. 19   The Eastern Frontier problem, 1812–35.

instead. The most important method, however, was to be the example to be provided by settling Englishmen on small farms on the Zuurveld. This would at the same time greatly ease the problems of defending the frontier area and create a solid block of loyal subjects in the most sensitive part of the colony. (It would also provide a partial solution to unemployment in England.) But, although the 1820 settlement brought about 5,000 English people to swell the Cape white population, the attempt to introduce a new type of farming was an almost complete failure. It ignored the economics of South African farming, and within a few years the settlers established on the Zuurveld had either abandoned the land for the towns, where they tended to drive out Dutch traders, or were demanding large farms and non-European labour.

While tension continued along the frontier and the pressure of land-hunger on both sides of it grew steadily more severe, a cataclysmic upheaval began far in the interior probably quite uninfluenced by events on the border between the races.

THE MFECANE

Zululand and Natal had possessed a considerable population of Bantu of the Nguni-speaking group from at least as early as the sixteenth century. Population was increasing rapidly and grazing land became scarce in the strip between the Drakensberg and the sea. Towards the end of the eighteenth century tribal wars became more severe, and, instead of being satisfied with formal acknowledgment of defeat, victorious chiefs began to try to make their defeated enemies accept a position of permanent subordination. As wars were so frequent, the traditional initiation ceremonies were likely to weaken the fighting force of a tribe at a critical moment and several tribes abandoned them. Instead of practising circumcision and ritual seclusion, they borrowed an idea from the neighbouring Sotho peoples. The youths formed age-regiments which fought as units whenever necessary.

As the struggle between tribes and their leaders became more intense three great figures emerged, each of whom began to build up a tribal empire: Sobhuza, leader of a people who later came to be known as the Swazi; Zwide, ruler of the Ndwandwe and Dingiswayo, the famous Mthethwa chief. As their power grew they inevitably came into collision. The Ndwandwe were victorious and Sobhuza led his men out of the area of conflict into central Swaziland. There they found many small Sotho-speaking tribes who were conquered one by one and their loyalty secured by Sobhuza's mild policy. When these tribes were conquered their young men were allowed to fight in the age-regiments and very soon they began to identify themselves with the conquerors. In this way the foundations of the present Swazi nation were laid.

In Zululand itself, Dingiswayo and Zwide continued to extend their power till about 1817 when they engaged in open conflict. Dingiswayo unwisely left the main body of his army and climbed a hill from which he could look down on the battle and, perhaps as the result of treachery or of ill-fortune, walked into an ambush, was captured and put to death. The Mthethwa were seized by panic and fled from the scene. Their dominant position in Zululand disappeared overnight. But by this time another figure had emerged to resist the triumphant Zwide.

Shaka was the son of Senzangakona, chief of a small tribe known as the Zulu. His mother's bad temper led to her being driven away from her husband's household and taking refuge with her own people. Shaka went with her and spent an unhappy childhood, bullied and mocked by his companions; memories of this humiliation were to give him a ferocious thirst for power. As a youth he joined Dingiswayo's forces and earned a reputation for reckless courage which gave him considerable influence with the great chief. He made use of this on the occasion of his father's death to get Mthethwa's aid to remove a brother from the chieftaincy of the Zulu and make himself the ruler of his father's people. He then began to build up his forces by training his followers in new methods of warfare. Instead of the traditional throwing spear he introduced the short-handled stabbing spear which could be retained throughout a battle and which enabled his warriors to manoeuvre and fight in close formation. He also introduced the idea of continuous military service and kept his age-regiments constantly under arms in special military towns. When he heard of Dingiswayo's death and the defeat of the Mthethwa, he began at once to increase his strength by conquering neighbouring tribes and putting their young men into his regiments. Thus when Zwide's forces attacked he was ready to receive them. The first Ndwandwe invasion was repulsed and when Zwide sent his whole army against the Zulu, Shaka defeated it by superior tactics. He wore them out by constantly retreating out of their reach, destroying all the crops and foodstores as he went, then, as they were retreating wearily homeward, he won a decisive battle on the Mhlatuze River (1818).

After this Shaka was supreme in Zululand, and every year his regiments went out on campaigns which increased his herds of cattle and widened his sphere of influence. He transformed the traditional Bantu attitude to warfare and introduced the conception of total war. Defeated tribes were incorporated into his kingdom and their young men drafted into the age-regiments which were commanded by able military indunas especially chosen by him. As his victorious armies extended their conquests even further, many tribes fled before them. Two sections of the defeated Ndwandwe escaped northwards after the battle on the Mhlatuze River: the Ngoni of Zwangendaba and the Shangana of Soshangane. They penetrated into the southern part of modern Mozambique and were joined there by a third group of refugees the Maseko and the Msene who had moved together under Ngwane and Nxaba. All these exiled peoples adopted the methods of their Zulu conquerors and employed them to conquer the Mozambique

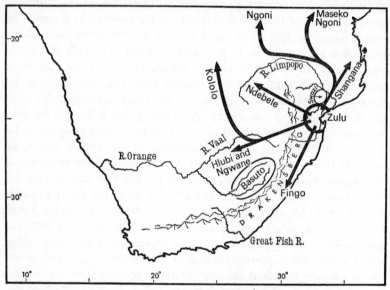

Fig. 20 The main movements of migration in the Mfecane.

tribes. In about 1831 a three-cornered struggle took place and Soshangane defeated both the other rival groups and drove them out of Mozambique, where he continued to build up a powerful kingdom on Zulu lines. Zwangendaba moved westward through the lands of the Monomatapa empire, bringing this venerable kingdom to a sanguinary end. When he reached the neighbour-hood of modern Bulawayo, he turned northwards and in 1835 his cohorts crossed the Zambezi. They continued their tremendous journey as far as southern Tanganyika where they broke up into sections which went on to form a number of kingdoms in modern Zambia, Malawi and Tanzania. The Maseko also pursued a northward course after their defeat by Soshangane; keeping to the east of Lake Nyasa they crossed the Ruvuma River and entered the Songea district of modern Tanganyika. The Msene, on the other hand, travelled westward along the same path as Zwangendaba and eventually met their destruction in the flood-plain of the upper Zambezi.

While these tribes fled northwards from Zululand, others were driven westward across the Drakensberg on to the plateau with its Sotho-speaking population. The Hlubi and the Ngwane entered the area between the Orange and the Vaal rivers and threw the Sotho population into chaos and confusion. The first major Sotho-speaking tribe encountered by the Hlubi were the Tlokwa. They were then ruled by a Queen Mma Ntatisi, who was acting as regent for her son, Sikonyela. The Tlokwa were driven from their homes with the loss of their cattle and their grain stores, and were forced into a predatory existence. They earned such a terrible reputation that the name 'Mantatees' came to be applied indiscriminately to any wandering and pillaging horde. Ultimately they settled around a strong mountain position near the north-east corner of modern Basutoland. Meanwhile, the two invading tribes from the east devastated a wide area and fought desperately with one another until the Ngwane finally destroyed their rivals. In 1828 the Ngwane moved out of the area of Trans-Orangia across the escarpment to seek richer raiding ground amongst the Tembu near the colonial frontier. There they were met and dispersed by British forces in mistake for the Zulu.

The havoc caused by the invasion of the plateau by the Hlubi and Ngwane, and the tribes which they drove to a life of banditry, produced fearful conditions amongst the Sotho population of the plateau. The area of the modern Orange Free State was virtually deserted, famine followed in the wake of war, and the country was infested by disorganised bands of leaderless men, the remnants of broken tribes who lived by banditry and even cannibalism. In these circumstances the southern Sotho produced two remarkable leaders; Sebetwane, chief of the Fokeng, led his tribe and others who joined them out of the area to the north-west. First they moved down on Dithakong where Moffat, of the London Missionary Society, had his station with the Tlapin. But after a brief experience of gunfire, from the Griquas who came to Moffat's aid, they turned north. Under the name of Kololo, they traversed the Tswana country, then crossed the Zambezi and moved up its banks to enter modern Barotseland where they founded a shortlived empire.

In southern Sotho country itself the chaotic conditions called forth the political genius and tactical skill of a young chief, Moshesh. He established himself first on the flat-topped hill of Butha-Buthe in north-eastern Basutoland and successfully beat off an attack by the Tlokwa, but a second attack and prolonged siege showed the inadequacy of his position and he moved his people to the larger, more defensible hilltop of Thaba Bosiu in central Basutoland. From this base he gradually built up an extensive kingdom, bringing the remnants of many tribes together under his authority. At the same time he drove off attacks from the Ngwane, the Ndebele and from the Griqua and Korana who were raiding cattle in the disturbed southern Sotho country. From these last enemies Moshesh learnt the value of horses and fire-arms, and his people began the process of converting themselves into a nation of mounted gunmen. In 1833 Moshesh invited missionaries of the Paris Evangelical Missionary Society to his kingdom and they commenced work with his people. Moshesh took care not to allow himself to fall under missionary authority and made skilful use of their help in his subsequent dealings with white peoples.

About 1821 one of Shaka's generals, Mzilikazi, defied his overlord's authority and fled over the escarpment into the Transvaal. He was accompanied by a section of the Zulu army which became known as the Ndebele. They established a first camp in the eastern Transvaal, then moved westward to the vicinity of modern Pretoria, then westward again into the territory of the Tswana tribes, establishing themselves in the Mosega basin (near modern Potchefstroom). Mzilikazi followed the Zulu custom of incorporating the young men of conquered tribes in his age-regiments and thus developed a formidable military power. In the course of almost incessant campaigns his regiments drastically reduced the population of wide areas in the Transvaal.

In Zululand itself, Shaka's military system centralised power in the hands of the King since the district rulers, having lost control of their fighting men, could no longer act as checks on royal authority. Moreover, although Shaka consulted the generals who had become the most powerful people in the state, they were commoners personally appointed by himself and could not easily resist his will. In 1824 a small party of British traders succeeded in landing at Port Natal and made contact with the Zulu king. He welcomed them for the hitherto unknown material goods which they brought him and for their fire-arms which he perceived would be of great value in certain military circumstances. He allowed them to make use of a wide area of Natal which had been almost entirely devastated by his regiments and to gather together the remnants of the Natal population, about 3,000 in number, over whom they ruled as chiefs.

As Shaka's reign progressed he became increasingly despotic and his people began to weary of the cruelties and hardships of his regime. His mother's death threw him into paroxysms of grief, and he forced his people to submit to almost intolerable deprivations during a period of mourning which he planned should end in a grand military campaign to destroy all the tribes between Natal and the colonial frontier and open direct contact with the British. For this purpose he sent an embassy to the Cape and, in 1828, set out on his campaign. But the embassy's return was delayed and one of the traders warned him that the British regarded the frontier tribes as under their protection. Shaka turned his forces back after ravaging Pondoland and sent them on a campaign to the north to attack Soshangane instead. The British had indeed equipped forces to help the frontier tribes against the threatened invasion. They failed to meet the Zulu but attacked and dispersed the Ngwane who chose that time to come down from the plains of Trans-Orangia. While the Zulu army was away on the northern expedition, two of Shaka's brothers conspired with his chief induna to assassinate him. Choosing a suitable occasion when his attention was diverted they stabbed him to death. Dingaan, one of the assassins, then succeeded in removing his rivals and made himself the new Zulu king. He intended at first to follow a policy of peace and to demolish Shaka's military system, partially at least, but a revolt by one of Shaka's generals, Nqeto, taught him the necessity to rule in the spirit of his predecessor.

The upheaval in Bantu society which Nguni speakers call the Mfecane (in Sotho 'lifaqane') did not end with the death of Shaka but continued into the period of the Boer's Great Trek. By about 1830 the distribution of Bantu population had been greatly altered. Wide areas in Natal, the present Orange Free State and the Transvaal were virtually deserted. In other areas like Basutoland a very concentrated population had developed. The coastal strip between the colonial frontier and Natal had escaped severe devastation, and its already crowded population was increased by refugees driven out of Natal who came to be known as Fingos.

THE GREAT TREK

In the Cape, land-hunger continued to increase and, as the frontier on the eastern coastal strip did not advance fast enough to cater for the expanding white population, the flood of migration turned inland. In 1824 the frontier was advanced as far as the Orange River opposite Philippolis, and farmers were beginning to take their herds across the river to graze them outside the colonial boundaries for part of the year at least. The government's attempts to introduce a new pattern of farming served to increase land prices and the introduction of the 1820 settlers increased economic competition within the colony. At the same time the government under pressure from the philanthropic movement came to adopt an attitude which proved most distressing to the settlers. At the commencement of the second British period (1806) the government at the Cape, representing a high Tory administration in the home country, sympathised with employers rather than employed. Missionaries were out of favour and the government tended to regard their Hottentot stations as schools of idleness, keeping useful labour off the market. Nevertheless, the government was determined to govern and to exercise legal control over labour relations. Thus in 1809 the position of Hottentots was defined in a series of regulations that were very favourable to the white farmers. Every Hottentot must have a fixed address and this meant that he must reside either with a white farmer or on one of the mission stations; he could not travel from one district to another without a pass from the local magistrate; failure to conform to these stipulations would make him liable to arrest on a charge of vagrancy. On the other hand, any farmer employing a Hottentot must enter into a formal labour contract with him, one copy of which must be deposited with a magistrate, and detailed regulations were laid down governing the right of masters to withhold pay from their servants. These regulations confirmed the existing position of the Hottentots whereby they were virtually forced to enter the service of white farmers. Restrictions on their freedom of movement made it difficult for them to change employers and sell their labour in the highest market, and still more difficult for them to withdraw their labour altogether by taking refuge in a mission settlement. In 1812 a further ordinance was issued giving farmers the right to apprentice Hottentot children for ten years if they had grown to the age of eight on their property. In theory this was intended to induce the white farmers to take an interest in the welfare of non-European children on his farm, but it helped to give him an almost complete hold over his employees.

Though biased in favour of the white employer class, the regulations nevertheless meant that disagreements between master and servant were subject to legal arbitration. In 1812 when the government was rejoicing the hearts of the settlers by driving the Bantu from the Zuurveld it was also acting in a manner far less pleasing. The governor, Lord Charles Somerset, stung by missionary accusations of the indifference of his administration to injustices inflicted on Hottentots, instructed the Circuit Court to investigate all such complaints with the utmost rigour. The Court concluded that the missionary accusations had been seriously exaggerated and many complaints turned out to be trivial or malicious, nevertheless a good deal of injustice was uncovered and two farmers were even convicted of murder. Many farmers had been forced to leave their families undefended to travel to court to answer charges brought by their servants, and this added to the main source of their annoyance—the dramatic statement of the principle that Hottentots and white men could be brought before the courts on the basis of equality before the law.

The furore raised by the Black Circuit had not died down three years later. A farmer named Bezuidenhout was summoned to appear on a charge of ill-treating a Hottentot servant, he refused and entrenched himself in a cave on his farm. When the magistrate went to arrest him with a posse of Hottentot police he opened fire and was shot dead. Some of his relatives were so inflamed that they tried to launch a rebellion of the frontier farmers. The uprising fizzled out without serious fighting and the ringleaders were captured. Seven of them were publicly hanged under very distressing circumstances at Slachters Nek. The government had demonstrated that it was not to be lightly defied.

The Black Circuit was however only a minor grievance compared with what was to follow. The philanthropic movement was gathering force for the final struggle over emancipation and the missionaries addressed a flood of complaints to a receptive public on behalf of their Hottentot protégés. Foremost in the movement was the London Missionary Society and the most important figure in the agitation its energetic general superintendent, Dr John Philip. Philip believed that non-Europeans whether Hottentots or Bantu were capable of development to the highest level attained by Europeans. The demoralising conditions of economic servitude in which they were kept in Cape society, however, denied them any possibility of progress. They must be given a measure of economic independence before their potentialities could be realised to the benefit of themselves and society. This could be done by allowing them to live on mission settlements where they should be given enough land to enable them to support themselves by farming, and where they might acquire education and practical skills. It could also be done by freeing the Hottentots from the restrictions on freedom of movement so that they could sell their labour in the highest market or withdraw it altogether by settling on a mission station. In 1826 he published his most important work *Researches in South Africa,* and though he was successfully sued for libel in the Cape the book had an immense effect in England. It skilfully combined an appeal to moral feelings against the near-slavery of the Hottentots with arguments based on current *laissez-faire* orthodoxy. Freed from serfdom the Hottentots would become much more effective consumers and help provide a greatly increased market for British goods. Deeply impressed, Parliament in Westminster decided that the Governor should be instructed to draw up legislation removing the odious restrictions on Hottentot freedom. But, in fact, Acting Governor Bourke, moving with the spirit of the times, had already done so. After consultation with the philanthropic Dutch official Stockenstroom he had framed the famous 50th Ordinance (1828). Parliament simply added a rider that none of its provisions could be altered without reference to the King-in-Council.

The 50th Ordinance removed all the restrictions to which Hottentots were subject and placed them and other free coloured persons on a basis of legal equality with whites. It struck directly at the economy of the frontier farmer for many Hottentots abandoned the land and flocked to town villages or mission stations. The wages of those who remained inevitably rose and the farmer's control over them was greatly diminished. Moreover, the Ordinance came into operation in a period when farm labour was difficult to find. The price of slaves, driven up by the limitation of supply which resulted from the stopping of the slave trade in 1807, had risen too high for slaves to be employed very extensively by frontier farmers operating on small capital. The immediate effect of the measure on the economy, however, is only a small part of the reason for its intense unpopularity. It amounted to a revolution in the legal ethos of society and constituted a direct affront to the Boer's sense of racial superiority, which seemed to endanger his whole way of life.

The movement of opinion reflected in the 50th Ordinance was primarily directed against the institution of slavery. After 1807 measure after measure was introduced to regulate the master's treatment of his slaves, progressively limiting his authority over them and clearly preparing the way for total emancipation. When this finally came in 1834 it had long been anticipated and did not in itself rouse very strong opposition. But arrangements for the payment of compensation were badly mishandled so that many slave-owners were cheated. More galling than financial loss, however, was the provision that, after a period of apprenticeship to their former masters, slaves would come under the provisions of the 50th Ordinance and enjoy legal equality with their erstwhile owners.

The enthusiasm of the missionaries and their philanthrophically-minded supporters in England for the cause of the indigenous peoples in South Africa extended to relations between the colony and the frontier tribes. It was pointed out that the settlers as well as the tribesmen must bear responsibility for frontier tensions. In particular the reprisals system, under which a local magistrate could call out a commando on the complaint of a farmer that his cattle had been stolen and proceed across the frontier to the nearest Bantu settlement to seize an appropriate number of cattle in compensation, was condemned for making the innocent suffer for the guilty and opening the way to gross abuses. With the prospect of finding farms for his sons diminishing; his control over labour considerably reduced; under a government of foreigners which insisted on English as the official language and which denied the principle of race superiority, and seemed more concerned with the non-Europeans within and without the colony than with the white settlers, the Boer frontier farmer felt increasingly discontented. In earlier year she would have rebelled, but Slachters Nek had shown that the government was not to be lightly opposed.

Meanwhile the events in the interior were beginning to become known in the colony. The English traders in Natal spread news of the deserted state of its delectable territory. Indeed they had hardly established themselves there before they began pressing for the area to be made a colony. The farmers who crossed the Orange River with their herds, the missionaries on their journeys to and from their stations, and the traders who penetrated into the Transvaal and visited Mzilikazi, spread information about conditions on the interior plateau. It became known that in the interior there were wide areas suitable for cattle-farming lying empty for the taking. The idea of emigrating out of the colony to establish a society of their own far from the hated British policy of racial equality began to gain strength amongst the frontiersmen.

In 1834 three spying parties (Commissie Trekke) were sent out to investigate the situation in the interior. One went to South West Africa, another penetrated into the Transvaal, where it escaped the notice of Mzilikazi's regiments, and the third visited Natal. When they returned the first party held out little hope of finding suitable land in the arid wastes of South West Africa, but the others were optimistic; especially the Natal party who were burning with enthusiasm.

The devastation of Natal by the Zulu regiments had driven thousands of refugees amongst the frontier tribes. Called Fingos by their hosts, they settled down in a subordinate relationship to the Xhosa, Tembu and Pondo. Their arrival aggravated the existing overcrowding in the frontier areas. Tension along the frontier had never died away and in the early 1830s it grew steadily greater. The system of reclaiming cattle often meant that innocent Bantu families lost their means of livelihood. Some were then forced to cattle theft in earnest and the frontier was always in turmoil. An even greater cause of tension was the situation in the erstwhile neutral strip between the Fish and Keiskamma rivers. The no-man's land agreement had soon proved unworkable and a number of Xhosa groups had been allowed to return to it, provided they remained of good behaviour. The threat of expulsion was held over their heads to force them to exert themselves in checking stock theft.

In January 1834 D'Urban arrived as Governor. The philanthropic movement was at its height and he was sent to carry through emancipation. He was also to devise a more just frontier administration and to abolish the reprisals system which was such a scourge to the frontier tribes. He held discussions with Philip and sent him to the frontier to meet the chiefs and prepare them for his own arrival. The chiefs greeted the news that a new frontier system was to be introduced with the greatest pleasure, and cattle thefts dropped sharply. Prospects seemed good. But the Governor, delayed by endless paper work connected with the emancipation, did not follow up the initial negotiations. The military authorities in Grahamstown were not in favour of the new system and resumed their patrols as soon as Philip left. Prolonged drought added to the tension, and the Xhosa began to suspect that the negotiations were a trick to keep them quiet while the government prepared to seize still more of their land for the settlers. A small fracas in which chiefly blood was shed brought matters to a head and in December 1834 the tribesmen burst into the colony.

Wide areas were devastated and many farms burnt to the ground before the colonial forces began to get the upper hand and strike back across the frontier. D'Urban who had come to the frontier at last was so horrified at what he saw that he described the Bantu as irredeemable savages. He decreed the annexation of the entire area between the Great Fish and the Kei rivers as Queen Adelaide Province. The Bantu were to be driven out of it for ever and it was to be given to white settlers. The Boers had found a Governor after their own heart and ideas of trekking out of the colony were set aside.

But the plan to drive the Bantu out of Queen Adelaide Province proved militarily impracticable. They fought desperately in remote and difficult areas, conducting a guerilla war and even raiding the colony whenever the attention of the troops was diverted. D'Urban was forced to modify his plans, and in the meanwhile the missionaries raised a howl of protest at his 'extermination policy'. Where was the policy of seizing Bantu land in the interest of finding a more defensible frontier ever to stop? Was it not to end until the Bantu had all been destroyed or turned into herdsmen to the whites? The moment was propitious for missionary protest and a parliamentary select committee on the fate of originesab in the British colonies was meeting in London. Thus

D'Urban's policy was rejected in favour of an idea advanced by the Dutch official Stockenstroom. Treaties would be made with frontier chiefs so that they would serve as government agents in maintaining law and order on the borders. Stockenstroom was sent out as Lieutenant Governor of the Eastern Province, and Queen Adelaide Province was handed back to the tribes. This was the last straw as far as the frontier farmers were concerned. With the hope of rich farms in the new province gone they streamed out of the colony to the north. 1836 was the great year of the Trek. Party after party crossed the Orange River and pressed on northwards to a rendezvous near the Wesleyan mission station of Thaba Nchu. They travelled in fairly small parties generally made up of close relatives. Some stopped by the wayside to graze their cattle on the borders of Moshesh's kingdom or in the neighbourhood of the Griquas, but the majority moved on northwards. A few parties went across the Vaal River to hunt and prospect the land.

Coming unexpectedly and unannounced, they were mistaken by the Ndebele regiments that Mzilikazi kept on patrol in the area for yet another of the hostile Griqua invasions that had twice almost destroyed the kingdom. The wagons were attacked and a number of families massacred, but others were alarmed in time. They gathered together under the leadership of Potgieter and beat off their attackers at the battle of Vegkop (October 1836). As they had lost all their cattle they were glad to retire to join their companions at Thaba Nchu. In January 1837 they felt strong enough to retaliate, and a Boer commando with support from the Griquas and the Rolong penetrated to Mzilikazi's capital at Mosega and launched a surprise attack. Large numbers of cattle were taken and the party returned in triumph.

The majority of the trekkers accepted Piet Retief as their leader and agreed that Natal should be the destination of the movement, but Potgieter and a number of his supporters were determined to resume the struggle with Mzilikazi. Thus while Retief rode into Natal to hold discussions with Dingaan, Potgieter launched another attack on the Ndebele. The advantage of surprise and superiority of arms gave the Boers another victory in seven days of fighting in the Marico valley. Mzilikazi, who had been attacked in the same year by Dingaan and was already thinking of finding a safer home, led his people northwards into modern Rhodesia, and Potgieter could claim a vast ill-defined area by right of conquest.

Dingaan received Retief's request that the Boers be allowed to settle in Natal with considerable alarm. He had long ago been warned by the Xhosa interpreter Jacob that once the white men were allowed to come they would arrive in ever increasing numbers until they seized the kingdom. Knowing the superior military value of fire-arms, he was afraid to offer a blank refusal,

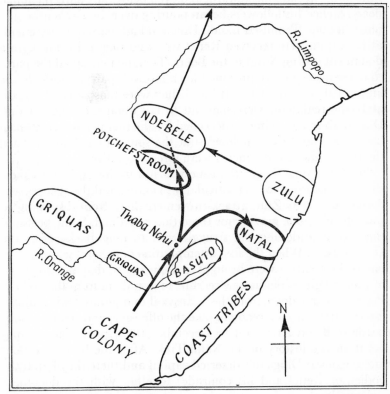

Fig. 21   Main lines of Boer migration among the Bantu peoples.

so he temporised by telling Retief that the Tlokwa chief, Sikonyela, had stolen some of the royal cattle; if the Boers would get these back he would consider letting them settle in Natal. Perhaps the wily Tlokwa chief would destroy the invaders or something else would happen to avert the threat. At all events there would be time to prepare. But instead of the situation improving it deteriorated. Retief tricked Sikonyela into trying on a pair of handcuffs, then held him to ransom for the cattle required by Dingaan. Two Zulu indunas who were present were impressed by the white man's evil magic, treachery and disregard for the authority of chiefs. At the same time the news of Mzilikazi's defeat and flight came to be known. Dingaan prepared to save himself and his people by a desperate blow. In December 1838 Retief and a party of his men rode down to claim his reward, and even before any agreement had been reached his followers began pouring over the Drakensberg to settle in their 'Promised Land'. Dingaan had massed his regiments at his capital. He received Retief well and placed his mark on a document ceding Natal to the Boers. Then he persuaded the party to enter his enclosure unarmed for a farewell party. Suddenly the king cried 'Kill the wizards!' and they were massacred. Immediately the regiments were sent out to fall upon the Boer wagons. Dingaan's scheme almost succeeded for the first parties were taken by surprise and overwhelmed, but the sound of gunfire alarmed the others and the regiments were forced to retire.

For some time longer the issue was still in doubt. The trekkers had suffered great losses particularly in cattle, and the ever present danger of a new Zulu attack prevented them from dispersing to provide adequate grazing for those that remained. Some began to think of abandoning the struggle and turning back across the Drakensberg. When the first attempt at a counter-attack ended in fiasco the trekkers were brought to the verge of despair. But news of their plight brought new recruits to join them from the colony. Pretorius came down from the Transvaal to organise their military forces. Soon they felt ready to take the offensive, and the victorious battle of Blood River (on 16 December 1838) proved a turning-point in the history of the Natal Trek. After the battle the Boer forces entered Dingaan's deserted capital and there they found the bodies of Retief and his comrades together with the document ceding Natal.

By this time the Cape government alarmed at news from the interior had sent a force to Port Natal. Faced with the news of the Boer victory and their possession of the charter, there was little they could do before sailing away again except to offer their good offices in arranging peace with the Zulu. Dingaan was anxious for peace for, although he still retained the bulk of his fighting forces, the Blood River campaign had demonstrated beyond doubt the superiority of Boer fighting methods. The Boers also were anxious for an end to the conflict so that they could break up their armed camps and graze their cattle at large. Nevertheless they made hard terms, and Dingaan (in a clause kept secret from the commander of the British force) was forced to cede a strip of territory on the Zulu side of the Tugela River and promise to withdraw his people farther north. This he attempted to do and sent his regiments to raid the Swazi to open a path for him. But military defeat, followed by the command to abandon their precious country, had placed intolerable strains on Zulu loyalties and one of Shaka's brothers, Mpande who had been considered incompetent and harmless, took the opportunity to make a bid for the throne. With a large group of followers he refused to follow Dingaan, fled across the Tugela and put himself under Boer protection. Steadily his forces increased until he felt ready to try conclusions with the Zulu king. Then, supported by a Boer column which marched separately, he advanced into Zululand. The two Zulu armies met at Magongo in February 1840 and in a bitter battle Mpande's followers were victorious. The Zulu fighting machine had turned inward on itself and the Boers who had not fired a shot were able to reap the fruits of victory. The struggle for Natal was over.

CONCLUSION

The Great Trek from one point of view was simply an acceleration of the process of white expansion under the pressure of land-hunger which had been going on from the earliest days of the Cape Colony. Even if it had not taken the form it did, this expansion would have continued since Boers were passing in increasing numbers into the southern part of the modern Orange Free State well before the Trek began. Others had continued pressing up the eastern coastal corridor, and before the outbreak of the 1835 war some had even penetrated beyond the Kei River. But the Trek was different from the gradual forward movement, not only in scale but also in motivation. The advancing settlers of earlier times had intended to take the frontiers with them but the Great Trek was a conscious movement of secession. The Boers left the colony determined to shake off British rule forever and to establish a community of their own to be governed on their own principles. They had many grievances, but supreme amongst them was their hatred for the principle of racial equality which the British, through the 50th Ordinance and the abolition of slavery, seemed to be forcing on them. In this sense the Trek was a continuation of the series of revolts against attempts to modify the internal race/class stratification of Cape society which began with the Graaff Reinet uprising of 1795.

The movement cannot however be explained in terms of developments within white society alone, for it was to a great extent a reaction to previous developments in the Bantu world. A glance at the map reveals the strategy of the movement. Held back from further advance along the line of highest rainfall by the heroic resistance of the Xhosa, the whites turned inland. Skirting the heavily populated territory of Moshesh, they poured into the relatively empty lands of Natal and the Transvaal where the wars of the previous years had opened the way, and where a single decisive battle would give them vast stretches of land unencumbered by a heavy population. The Great Trek was thus a stage in the drama of conflict and interaction between the races which is the central theme of South African history.

It marks a new era in the development of this story. Before the period of the Great Trek, Boer and Bantu had been in contact with one another only along the eastern Cape frontier. The problem had been marginal for both groups. But with the Trek they were brought face to face on a much more extensive basis. A vastly extended frontier of racial contact had been created, every section of which was destined to be the scene of conflict as the process of territorial expansion inherent in the structure of white society turned the newly settled areas into further growing points. This affected not only the external relations between the races but also the internal relations between racial groups in the white-dominated community. One of the bases of white racial attitudes was the sense of physical insecurity. The bitter fighting of the Great Trek period and its aftermath inevitably deepened this feeling very considerably.

Before the period of the Great Trek the labour force of the Cape community was mainly made up of slaves, Hottentots and Bushmen who intermarried with one another to form the Cape Coloured People. In the process the Hottentot language and culture fast disappeared and the labour force became culturally identical with the white ruling class. Even before the Trek, however, Bantu had begun to take the place of Hottentots as the labour force of the frontier districts, and after the great white migration the Bantu became the main element in the labour force (except in the old colony). The Bantu was much more firmly attached to his culture than the Hottentot; even on a white farm he continued to live his own life, speaking his own language and practising his ancient customs. Thus the cultural difference between master and servant remained sharp and clear, and this helps to explain the pattern of the subsequent development of racial attitudes in different parts of South Africa. In the Cape, where military conflict remained a border problem, the policy embodied in the 50th Ordinance won general, if not enthusiastic, acceptance everywhere, except in the frontier areas themselves. In the Boer republics, founded by a movement of revolt against legal equality and faced with an external and internal military problem, race attitudes were to be much stronger. But the same was true of Natal with its border troubles with the Zulu and its large Bantu working class, even when Englishmen replaced Boers as the dominant element in white society.

If the Great Trek added a new dimension to the problems of race relations in South Africa and sharpened the distinctions between peoples of different colour in most of the country, it only did so in so far as it brought them into closer relationships with one another. From this point of view the period of the great folk movements can be seen as an accelerated phase in the process by which originally separate peoples have been fused into a single community and a frontier struggle turned into a class struggle within a unified economic and political framework.

QUESTIONS FOR FURTHER STUDY AND DISCUSSION

1 Why did the British government fail to solve the problem of conflict on the eastern frontier of South Africa between 1806 and 1836?

2 How did Shaka transform the traditional Bantu political system in his Zulu kingdom?

3 What would you regard as the most important consequences of the Mfecane for South African history?

4 What were (a) the causes and (b) the consequences of the Great Trek?

5 Examine the role of the missionaries in South Africa in the nineteenth century.

SELECT BIBLIOGRAPHY

E. Walker, *A History of Southern Africa*, Longmans, 3rd edition, 1957.

W. M. Macmillan, *Bantu, Boer and Briton in South Africa*, O.U.P., revised and enlarged edition, 1963.

E. A. Ritter, *Shaka Zulu*, Longmans, 1955.

P. Becker, *Path of Blood: The Rise and Conquest of Mzilikazi*, Longmans, 1962.

L. Marquand, *The Story of South Africa*, Faber and Faber, 2nd edition, 1963.

E. Walker, *The Great Trek*, A. & C. Black, 4th edition, 1960.

G. Tylden, *The Rise of the Basuto*, Juta, Capetown, 1950.

23   South Africa from the Great Trek to Unification

J. D. OMER-COOPER

THE Great Trek had vastly increased the area that the whites occupied in South Africa, but the structure of the South African farming economy ensured that even this would not suffice for their needs. Throughout the period down to unification the process of white expansion continued and the Bantu were progressively deprived of their remaining lands. The other aspect of this process was the demand for labour by the white farmers. As the white frontiers advanced some Bantu were required for work on the white ranches; as the Bantu-occupied area shrank increasing numbers had to work in the white-dominated areas to support themselves. The forces of white demand both for land and labour thus tended to complement each other. The white frontiers continued to advance until the areas of the Bantu were reduced to a size incapable of supporting independent communities, but able to serve as labour reserves whose very existence helped to keep the price of labour low. Finally, European authority was established over the remaining areas of Bantu occupation and taxes were introduced designed to ensure a steady flow of labour into the white areas.

The Bantu fought back often with heroism and some success, but gradually, as they were integrated into the white South African economy, the form of the struggle began to change. Instead of fighting to preserve their independence and their lands they began to adopt the forms of white-dominated society. This was seen in the spread of the Ethiopian Movement that sought to form churches under African control, and the growth of Bantu political movements aimed at securing greater rights within South African society. Cutting across this development were the effects of mineral discoveries and the beginnings of an industrial revolution which was to transform South Africa from an agrarian society to an industrial one, and to shift the focus of racial struggle from the land to the towns; categories of employment replaced territorial borders as a source of conflict. The balkanisation of white South Africa resulting from the Great Trek and the vagaries of British policy further complicated the situation. The discovery of diamonds and the beginnings of the 'Scramble' for Africa inevitably and vitally influenced British policy.

The cataclysm of the Boer War and political unification brought the period to an end and contributed to a strengthening of the Boer sense of community—Afrikaner nationalism—dedicated to the preservation of the existing race/class stratification of society. Unification left the balance of power in the hands of this conservative force just at the time when economic development and non-white attitudes demanded flexibility and peaceful evolution away from racial division.

The Great Trek left the British government in a dilemma. As the emigrants were British subjects, Britain could not avoid responsibility for their activities in the interior. The Cape of Good Hope Punishment Act, passed on the eve of the Trek, made British subjects amenable to the Cape courts for crimes committed outside the colonial frontiers as far as the twenty-fifth degree of south latitude, and this seemed to imply the extension of British authority to all areas occupied by emigrants. But this would involve the heavy expense of administering a vast and economically unproductive area. Furthermore, what guarantee could there be that if sweeping annexations were made the Boers would not retreat still farther into the heart of the continent? On the other hand, to accept the *de facto* independence of the Boers involved several dangers. If they were to establish a viable port at Port Natal might this not lead to another European power gaining a foothold on the eastern coast of South Africa, thus endangering the route to India and subverting the whole purpose of Britain's presence at the Cape? Moreover, the Boers had established themselves west and north of a great block of Bantu peoples—the Basuto of Moshesh and the southern Nguni-speaking coastal tribes—who also had a border with the Cape colony. Any conflict between the Boers and these Bantu might start a chain reaction which would plunge the colonial frontier into turmoil. So long as the Cape could not control the neighbouring white communities the colonial government would be unable to dictate its own frontier policy, and would be involved in heavy military expenditure which it was anxious above all to avoid. The same problem arose with regard to Natal and the Transvaal. Both had borders with the Zulu kingdom and neither could move without affecting the other. Small wonder that in these circumstances British policy vacillated widely between annexation and a determination to leave the Boers alone—swings of policy arising from the developing situation in South Africa itself and changes of opinion in Britain—and resulted in Britain losing the power to control the general development of South African history.

Hardly had the Boers established themselves in Natal than their activities began to worry the Cape government. An adventurer named Smellekamp who claimed influence with the Dutch government was enthusiastically welcomed; the enormous herds of cattle demanded as reparations by the Boers after Mpande's defeat of Dingaan aroused the philanthropists; and soon the Natal republican government appeared to be losing control over its citizens and moving towards a conflict with its Bantu neighbours which would endanger the peace of the eastern frontier. The vast lands which came into the Natal republic were given away freely and with little control almost at once, and though very little land was effectively occupied by its nominal owners there was too little to satisfy the many claimants, and a similar mistake was made with regard to cattle. The reparations paid by the Zulu should have been ample to set up all the citizens, but some grabbed so much that others were left without.

As soon as the news of the defeat of Dingaan became known, the original Natal population which had been kept pent up to the south in the neighbourhood of the Pondo or forcibly incorporated in the Zulu kingdom, returned to their ancestral lands, now allocated as Boer farms, in a mass migration which created grave problems of security. The Republican government's only idea of solution lay in segregating the newly returned Natal populations in a suitable reserve.

Unable to coerce its own citizens to accept unpopular measures the Natal government was forced into an aggressive posture towards its neighbours. The Bhaca chief Ncapayi was attacked under the pretext that his men had stolen cattle, and a great booty of cattle was seized. The Natal government also proposed to take a large strip of territory between the Umzimkulu and Umzimvubu rivers, claimed by the Pondo ruler Faku, to use as a reserve for the newly returned Natal Bantu population. These developments finally stung the British Government into action in response to philanthropic feeling against the expropriation of Bantu lands and in alarm on politico-strategic grounds. The Boers' plans with regard to Pondoland promised to spread confusion along the coastal corridor to the Cape frontier. A small force, sent first to Faku's capital and then to Port Natal, became involved in fighting with the Boers; British honour and prestige were committed and there could be no withdrawal. The port passed into British hands and the Republican government gradually collapsed. In 1845 Natal was formally annexed.

Faced with the very government they had trekked to escape, a high proportion of the Boers in Natal crossed the Drakensberg on to the plateau. Englishmen replaced them but the new colony inherited the problems of the old republic. The settlers remained a tiny minority in a large Bantu population living under the shadow of the neighbouring Zulu kingdom. The English settlers developed racial attitudes as extreme as those of their Boer predecessors and were subject to frequent alarms and panics. In administering the Bantu population in Natal, they adopted a modified version of the policy of segregation *en masse* which had provoked the British intervention; the hope of finding a suitable area outside the limits of white settlement for 'surplus' Bantu haunted policy makers in Natal for many years.

On the interior plateau the Trek produced a confused situation in the area between the Orange and Vaal rivers where a considerable white population had grown up alongside the Griquas of Adam Kok and the Basuto of Moshesh. In the southern part of the area the majority were farmers who had migrated there before, or independently of, the Trek and they regarded themselves as British subjects. In the northern part the whites were Trek Boers who regarded themselves as part of the Natal republic. The two sections were mutually hostile, but they shared a common belief in white superiority and a determination not to submit to the authority of the Bantu and Griqua chiefs recognised by the British as sovereign rulers of the territory. Anxious to salve its conscience for the situation created by British subjects, the British government afforded the chiefs paper protection. Treaties were signed with Adam Kok and Moshesh recognising their authority. They were to keep order in their areas of jurisdiction and send white criminals back to the Cape to be dealt with under the Cape of Good Hope

Punishment Act. In return they were to receive a small subsidy. Moshesh's frontiers caused a problem even at this stage: the Rolong of Thaba Nchu, strongly supported by the Wesleyan missionaries, pressed for their territory to be left out of Moshesh's domains, and this difficulty was left unresolved, but elsewhere the treaty recognised most of his claims. These arrangements made by Governor Napier were no solution of the area's problems. They ignored the vital difficulty that large numbers of whites, who had

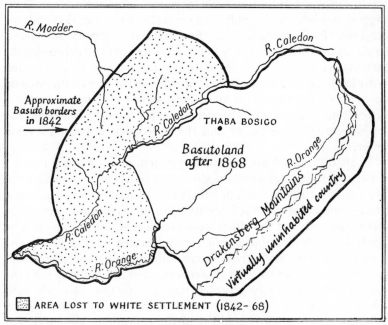

Fig. 22   The contraction of Basuto territory under white pressure.

no intention of submitting to non-white jurisdiction and who were too powerful for the chiefs to coerce, were settled in the area. When in January 1844 Adam Kok attempted to arrest a Boer the whites of Trans-Orangia flew to arms. The then Governor Maitland sent a force to the rescue of the Griqua chief and the Boers were easily dispersed at Zwartkopjes. It was clearly time for some workable system to be found.

In agreements drawn up with the major Trans-Orangian chiefs at Touwfontein, Maitland tried to achieve a solution that recognised that white settlers too powerful for the chiefs to control were settled on their territories, and attempted to solve the problem of jurisdiction while protecting the rights of the chiefs and their people. Each chief was asked to divide his territory into 'alienable' and 'inalienable' parts. The ultimate sovereignty of the indigenous rulers over both sections was confirmed, but they were to delegate the exercise of that sovereignty in the alienable areas to a British Resident. Within the alienable areas land could be leased to whites and half the rents would be paid to the chiefs while the rest would go towards the administrative expenses of the Resident. This ingenious scheme suffered from a central defect; Boer demands for land were far in excess of what the chiefs felt they could surrender, so the agreement would only work if the Resident could coerce the farmers when necessary to abandon farms they had occupied outside the agreed limits. But to provide the Resident with force on such a scale would involve expense far beyond the meagre returns of rents on white farms. Warden was appointed as Resident, but he had no effective power and the agreement remained a dead letter.

In 1846 the Stockenstroom treaty system on the eastern frontier broke down and yet another war broke out. The system had not been without its merits. The chiefs had proved very co-operative at first: stock theft declined and many of the cattle that were stolen were returned. But the chiefs were increasingly unable to exercise control over their subjects when trade, service for wages on white farms and missionary activities were undermining respect for the old order. The frontier authorities were often not in sympathy with the system and too readily accepted settlers' accounts of cattle theft when losses might have been due to wild animals or negligence. White scallywags further added to the confusion. Moreover, the insistence of the Cape authorities on treating the land between the Great Fish and the Keiskamma as colonial territory occupied by the Bantu on good behaviour increased the suspicions and frustrations of the frontier tribes. In March 1846 followers of a chief named Tola rescued a member of his family who had been arrested for stealing an axe and killed a Hottentot policeman. They then refused to surrender the murderers. Maitland sent a force across the border but it was ambushed at Burnshill and the Xhosa poured into the colony. The war of the Axe had begun. Fighting dragged on for more than a year but by December 1847 the tribes had been crushed.

In that month Sir Harry Smith arrived as Governor. He had been appointed not only as Governor at the Cape but as High Commissioner with responsibility for settling the affairs of the neighbouring territories. An impetuous and theatrical personality with some experience as a military commander on the eastern frontier in the war of 1834–5, he had complete confidence in his capacity to solve the problems of South Africa quickly. His first act was to apply a new remedy to the perennial eastern frontier problem and to annex the area between the Fish and the Kei as British Kaffraria. The tribesmen were to retain their land, but were to accept the position of British subjects and be governed by colonial law. Then Sir Harry set off to ride at high speed through Trans-Orangia and deal with the problems of Natal. A glance at the situation beyond the Orange convinced him that a radical solution was necessary. The proximity of whites, living without ordered government, schools or clergy, to independent African tribes could only mean continual instability which must affect the peace and security of the colony. He summoned the chiefs and representatives of the Boers to a hasty conference, then rode on to Natal where in February 1848 he decreed the annexation of the whole area between the Orange and Vaal rivers, including the lands of Adam Kok and Moshesh, as the Orange River Sovereignty. A strong section of the Boers objected violently to this arrangement and under Pretorius, the hero of the Zulu struggle, they turned Warden out of Bloemfontein. Smith reacted swiftly, a colonial force crossed the Orange and routed the Boers at Boomplaats (August 1848). Pretorius fled and Warden was reinstated.

Smith's annexation was too precipitate. It was undertaken without authorisation from England and was only reluctantly accepted in the belief that it would not constitute another drain on the exchequer. But if the purposes of the annexation were to be fulfilled, the representative of British authority needed the backing of effective force entailing considerable expenditure. Warden was left in the unenviable position of having to attempt a settlement of the mutually incompatible interests of Boer, Griqua and Bantu while dependent for the exercise of force on the goodwill of white farmers already alienated from the regime.

Moshesh was in an equally difficult position. He recognised from the first that the technical superiority of the whites meant that they would almost certainly be the victors in any prolonged struggle.

Hence his policy was to conciliate as far as possible without sacrificing the essential interests of his followers, an almost impossible undertaking in view of the land-grabbing propensities of the Boers. Hoping to use British protection as a shield against Boer expansionism, Moshesh welcomed the 1848 annexation. But British policy, if well intentioned, was too indecisive to take a firm stand against the white farmers. The difficulties of his diplomatic position were increased by the heterogeneous nature of his kingdom; a sacrifice which broke the tenuous links of loyalty holding it together would destroy everything he was fighting for. On the borders, the Rolong persisted in claiming independence and the Tlokwa awaited any sign of weakness to attack their old enemy. Moshesh needed all his genius for statecraft to save his people from being expropriated and dispersed.

The first problem facing the Orange River Sovereignty was to define the occupation limits of the different peoples. Warden, unable to coerce the Boers, inevitably defined the boundary between them and the Basuto so as to involve the minimum disturbance to Boer farmers. Moshesh was forced to accept the arrangement under protest, and Warden, conscious of Basuto resentment, felt it necessary to limit Basuto power as much as possible. He favoured the Rolong and the Tlokwa at the Basuto's expense and defined frontiers for these lesser tribes which cut off a good deal of what Moshesh regarded as his territory. Fighting soon broke out and Warden, determined to establish his authority, led a quite inadequate force into Basutoland. It was defeated at the first encounter and the sovereignty fell into chaos. Warden appealed for help to the Colony, but none could be spared for another war had broken out on the eastern frontier.

Sir Harry Smith's frontier settlement possessed the advantage of recognising Bantu land rights and attempting an administrative rather than a merely military solution to the problem of settler/Bantu contacts. But it was essentially an autocratic system imposed on a proud and independent people by force of arms. Smith's view of the relations between his government and the Bantu chiefs was exemplified in his dramatic attempt to impress them by loading a wagon with dynamite and blowing it up before their eyes. The application of colonial law to the newly annexed area was carried out with an unimaginative lack of appreciation of traditional Bantu law and custom. In October 1850 violence flared up and it was not until March 1852 that the rebellion was finally suppressed.

These two wars came at a crucial time in the development of British policy. The philanthropic movement had fallen into decline in the reaction which followed the achievement of emancipation. With the intellectual dominance of free-trade theories, colonies were believed to be a burden to be abandoned as soon as possible, and so the policy of granting self-government to white settler groups was enthusiastically advocated. In place of the fervour for protecting aboriginal peoples the cynical view gained ground that these peoples were bound to disappear in the course of historical evolution. South Africa seemed to supply evidence for a reversal of the previous policy of accepting responsibility for the activities of the trekkers and attempting to give some protection to the Bantu peoples. Britain was pouring forth blood and treasure on a perfectly worthless area which showed the futility of attempting to govern from a distance and the sentimentality of a concern for the aborigines. Philanthropy made the Bantu better fighters but worse savages. Opinion swung strongly in favour of abandoning the sovereignty and a commission was sent out to tidy up South African affairs.

Its first major step was to remove the threat of Transvaal interference in the affairs of the sovereignty by entering into the Sand River Convention with representatives of the Transvaal farmers. This reversed the previous policy of regarding all emigrant farmers as a British responsibility: Transvaal farmers were given their independence and a free hand in their relations with Bantu tribes north of the Vaal River. Indeed Britain openly sided with the Boers by promising that they would be allowed to buy gunpowder in the Cape and that this would be denied to the Bantu. This agreement cleared the way for a settlement in Trans-Orangia. Before taking a final decision on the fate of the sovereignty, however, the new Governor, Cathcart, felt that the problem of relations with Moshesh must be resolved and British honour redeemed.

Faced with an ultimatum demanding 10,000 head of cattle to be paid in three days, Moshesh, as usual, did his utmost to prevent war, but the fine demanded was far more than he could hope to collect in the time allowed. He sent 3,500 on the appointed day but Cathcart was not satisfied and marched into Basutoland. Like Warden, he underestimated the fighting ability of the Basuto. His force suffered a severe check and he pulled back to regroup. Moshesh then scored a brilliant diplomatic coup. Realising that the British would have the advantage in a prolonged war he offered Cathcart an easy way out. He sent a message saying that as the British had defeated his people and seized many cattle he hoped that they would be content and not punish him any more. Cathcart, who knew how unpopular further military expenditure would be, agreed. Moshesh had emerged victorious.

The decision to abandon the sovereignty then became irrevocable. It was unpopular both with many of the Boers who did not like the prospect of being left to deal with the Basuto single-handed, and with Moshesh himself who, though he had no reason to be pleased with the behaviour of the British, still regarded them as a protection against the Boers. Nevertheless the government was determined to withdraw. An assembly of Boer farmers willing to accept independence was collected and the Bloemfontein Convention signed. This agreement was along the same lines as the previous convention with the Transvaalers. So anxious was the government to disentangle itself from responsibilities in the sovereignty that it left border problems unresolved. Moshesh was given the clear impression that the war had abrogated previous agreements and that the question of frontiers was open to negotiation between him and the government of the Orange Free Republic *de novo*. The Free State authorities on the other hand believed that the Warden line still stood.

The Convention's policy was part of a general movement of opinion in favour of limiting colonial responsibilities as much as possible, abandoning areas like the Orange River Sovereignty where British interests were not too deeply involved, and devolving authority on local populations where this was possible.

Ever since the 1820 settlement there had been a growing demand for representative institutions at the Cape. Municipal councils were established as early as 1837, and in 1852 the Cape received an Order-in-Council establishing an elected Parliament. In both these representative institutions the attempt was made to preserve the principle of the 50th Ordinance: no racial bar and a franchise dependent on income. In the case of the Parliament, the economic qualification was deliberately set at a low level and arrangements were included so that goods received in lieu of wages could be counted in order to insure that at least some non-whites would qualify for the vote. In time considerable numbers of non-Europeans, particularly members of the Cape Coloured community, were registered as voters and were able to exercise some influence on policy. Nevertheless any income qualification naturally bore most heavily on the non-white peoples who were almost invariably the poorest members of society. The white voters were in a large majority, and whenever the balance of representation seemed to be shifting they altered the franchise regulations to protect their position.

The withdrawal of responsibility embodied in the Sand River and Bloemfontein Conventions confirmed the balkanisation of white South Africa which resulted from the Great Trek. It was not long before its inconveniences were felt. Sir George Grey who came out to South Africa in 1854 soon saw that a series of white states too weak to provide for the maintenance of law and order on their frontiers by normal methods would be incapable of following just and rational policies with regard to their non-European neighbours. They would be forced to try and maintain peace by a policy of terror, involving periodic wars with the neighbour tribes. At the same time different white states bordered the same mass of Bantu tribes and, so long as there was no co-ordination of policy, all the white states would be in a position of permanent insecurity. Lacking the means to provide for the education of their citizens, moreover, they could not produce leaders capable of taking an enlightened and objective view of race relations. South Africa appeared to him to be drifting into 'disorder and barbarism'.

His conviction of the dangers of continued division were strengthened by the outbreak of the first Free State/Basuto war. In spite of mutual suspicions, relations between the new Free State government had begun well. The first President had entertained Moshesh at a dinner in Bloemfontein and in return had been given a most hospitable reception on a state visit to Thaba Bosiu. But the rumour that the President had given Moshesh some gunpowder to make up for what was expended in firing salutes during his visit led to an uprising and he was forced to resign. The frontier problem between Free State farmers and the Basuto remained unsolved and in 1858 the Free State declared war. Their forces penetrated to the foot of Thaba Bosiu but, faced by the Basuto, they realised that it was impracticable to attempt an assault on the mountain. Learning that the Basuto were devastating their homes behind their backs, the farmers suddenly broke up the commando and rode home to protect their farms and families. President Boshoff was forced to beg Governor Grey to intervene and arbitrate for peace.

Moshesh, anxious to avoid an all-out war with white forces, accepted Grey's decisions even though they did not give the Basuto what he felt to be their right. With the population increasing rapidly in Basutoland and in the Orange Free State, it was obvious that, in the absence of a more general settlement, conflict would soon break out again. Grey sought to improve the situation by a federation of white states. The British government however was not prepared to see the policy it had just adopted completely reversed and Grey was recalled. Although he was subsequently sent back again it was on condition that his federation scheme should be abandoned.

Despite the British government's determination to cling to a policy of limitation of responsibility, its hand was soon forced. In 1863 the second Free State/Basuto war broke out. This time the Free State was much stronger: its population had increased and it was led by an able President, Jan Hendrik Brand. Moshesh, an old man, could no longer exercise complete control of affairs, and his sons were already jockeying for power with a view to the succession. The Basuto were also hampered by the operation of the gunpowder clause in the Bloemfontein Convention. The Boers failed to capture Thaba Bosiu but wore down Basuto resistance by a policy of systematically destroying crops and food stores. In 1866 Moshesh was forced to buy a breathing space by signing the treaty of Thaba Bosiu in which he ceded all the land occupied by the Boer commandos to the Orange Free State. This was only a truce. As soon as the commandos broke up the Basuto reoccupied their land and began planting their crops. Two Boer fathers who tried to take grants in the areas ceded under the treaty were murdered and the war began again.

Moshesh exerted all his influence to gain British protection, the only thing which could save his people from being broken up. He had powerful advocates, for philanthropic enthusiasm had recovered to some extent and the Boers committed a tactical blunder by expelling the French Missionaries from the stations which fell into their hands. Wodehouse, the governor at the Cape, realised that if the Boers succeeded in their demands the Basuto would be left with too little land to continue to exist as a united people. More-over, the Boers might be strong enough to defeat the Basuto but lacked the means to replace Moshesh's kingdom with an alternative form of law and order. The break-up of the Basuto state would be likely to involve the whole mass of tribes between the colony and Natal in chaos. Thus, while pretending to be neutral, Wode-house secretly encouraged Moshesh to hold out at Thabu Bosiu at all costs while he tried to gain permission to annex the country. At last he received qualified permission to take action and at once sent the Cape police into Basutoland to declare it annexed uncon-ditionally. He then faced the home government with the alternative of recognising his action or receiving his resignation. In the ensuing conference, Wodehouse succeeded in saving enough land for the Basuto to remain a united people but not enough for them to hope to be self-sufficient. Thereafter the produce of their land would have to be supplemented by wage labour amongst the whites.

The same position had already been reached on the eastern frontier. Sir George Grey, in a misguided belief in the value of direct contact between the races as a means of resolving racial tensions, introduced numbers of white farmers into British Kaffraria to create a pattern of mixed settlement. The move would undoubtedly have provoked another frontier war if the Xhosa, driven to desperation by the loss of their lands and the repeated failure of their forces in face of superior white firepower, had not given way to a mood of religious hysteria. A prophetess pro-claimed that if they slaughtered their cattle and destroyed their grain the sun would rise in the west and their ancestral heroes would return aided by a mighty wind to sweep the white man into the sea, when their slaughtered cattle and destroyed grain would be miraculously replaced several times over. The tribesmen feverishly complied and when the miracle failed to occur they were reduced to despair. Many died of starvation and thousands more were forced into the Colony to take service with the whites. Their military power was temporarily broken. The frontier tribes fought one last war for their lands and independence in 1877-8, but by that time they had already been largely reduced to a labour pool for white South Africa.

The British government had been forced to cross the Orange River once again and take action which amounted to a unilateral breach of the Bloemfontein Convention. Before long it took another step in the same direction. In 1867 the chance discovery of a diamond started South Africa's first mineral boom and there was a rush to stake out claims to diamond diggings. The diamondiferous areas fell within territory disputed between the Orange Free State, the Transvaal, the Griquas of Waterboer and two Tswana tribes. They would no doubt have fallen into the hands of the Free State and Transvaal if it had not been for a lawyer named Arnot, who spotted the legal confusion and saw the way to a fortune in acting as agent for Waterboer and the Griquas.

By this time the British government had begun to rethink its policy in South Africa. The arguments of Grey and the lesson of subsequent developments contributed to the belief that the Conventions had been a mistake. The white governments of South Africa should be brought together again within the British orbit without any expenditure on Britain's part: the most effective scheme seemed to involve giving the Cape responsible government and encouraging it to absorb the other white states into a federation which it would dominate. The developing situation at the diamond fields constituted a danger; if they were absorbed by the Free State and the Transvaal, the balance of white population in South Africa would be greatly altered and the inland states might not be prepared to join the Cape. Philanthropic pressures also urged the annexation of the diamond fields to save the Griquas from Boer slavery. While the question of jurisdiction remained unsettled the turbulent population at the diamond fields was a threat to law and order throughout South Africa. In view of these considerations, Governor Barkly was given permission to annex the lands of Waterboer provided the Cape Parliament agreed. The Cape Parliament however failed to give its permission in unambiguous terms and Barkly, feeling that something must be done quickly, annexed the diamond fields without more ado. The Cape Parliament then refused to agree to the annexation of Griqualand west to the Cape, and the British Government was left with yet another unwanted responsibility. In April 1872 the Responsible Government Bill was passed and in December Molteno became the first Prime Minister.

The development of the diamond fields marked the beginning of a fundamental change from a rural to an industrial society. It brought capital into the country on a previously unknown scale and this made possible the beginnings of railway building and other technical developments. It introduced large-scale capitalism. The development of the diamond mining called for labour on a large scale and the migrant labour system began to develop in its modern form. From all over South Africa, Bantu flocked to the diamond diggings to work. They left their families behind and returned home after they had saved up enough to purchase a few highly prized commodities, including guns. A huge trade in fire-arms took place at the diggings and, finding that the possibility of purchasing guns was the chief inducement to bring labour to the mines, the Griqualand West administration turned a deaf ear to protests from the Boer states against this traffic. Through the process of labour migration the remaining areas occupied by independent Bantu tribes were increasingly brought within the economic system of white-dominated South Africa. The processes of cultural change in Bantu society were greatly accelerated, and as men from many different tribes met at the diamond mines the development of a sense of common identity in face of the white ruling group was hastened.

The diamond fields afford the first example of a development that was to become much more important after the discovery of gold: the transference of the race/class structure of rural South African society to the organisation of industry. The Griqualand administration attempted at first to follow the principles of the 50th Ordinance. There was to be no racial bar to ownership and operation of diamond concessions. But the majority of white diggers strongly opposed this policy. They claimed it made the control of theft and illicit diamond dealing by Bantu mine workers practically impossible and encouraged lawlessness and immorality. In 1875 the system was abandoned and the right to own and operate a diamond concession became an exclusively white privilege. The principle that in industry, as on the land, ownership and management should be white while unskilled labour was exclusively non-white was taking shape.

The annexation of the diamond fields strengthened Britain's desire to see a federation of white states in South Africa. Such a federation appeared to offer an honourable way of resolving the question of ownership of the fields and freeing Britain from the burden of their administration. Since the Cape's revenues had greatly expanded with the income of customs charges on goods destined for the diamond workings such a federation seemed likely to be economically viable, and since the diamond fields were in British hands it would be likely to remain within the British orbit. In January 1874 when Disraeli took office as Prime Minister in England, an active colonial policy was promised and Carnarvon, the Colonial Secretary, with memories of success in bringing about federation in Canada, began to take steps to urge South Africa along the same path. To strengthen his hand in the expected negotiations he first sent Sir Garnet Wolseley to reform the Natal constitution in the direction of greater imperial control, and then sent a despatch to the High Commissioner in Cape Town suggesting a round table conference in South Africa to deal with matters of common interest, including the possibility of Confederation.

Conditions in South Africa were not altogether unpropitious for Carnarvon's initiative. The Cape was overwhelmingly the richest and most heavily populated of South African states, and the two Boer republics, landlocked and poverty stricken, might well be expected to agree to the surrender of their nominal independence to become members of a self-governing federation with all the economic advantages it would entail. What is more, the need for a co-ordinated policy towards the Bantu had become glaringly obvious with the development of diamond mining. On the other hand the difficulties in the way of Carnarvon's plans were very considerable. The Orange Free State had acquired a considerable distrust of British policy after the annexation of Basutoland and Griqualand West. President Brand was personally not opposed to the idea but he was not prepared to act against the wishes of his Volksraad. He felt that his state had been treated unjustly over the diamond fields and was not prepared to agree that compensation for this wrong should be linked to the question of joining a federation.

The Transvaal was far and away the poorest of South African states. In the aftermath of the Great Trek the dispersal of the white farmers had resulted in political subdivision. A constitution for a united Republic (Grondwet) was drawn up as early as 1857, but it was in 1858, after the failure of attempts to link the still divided Transvaal with the Orange Free State, that effective political union was achieved. The internal history of the country like that of South Africa generally had been the record of continuous expansion of the white farmers and progressive limitation of the land holdings of Bantu tribes. The Transvaal, however, contained much larger areas of African land holdings within its borders than other South African states, and its relations with neighbouring Bantu peoples were still far from stabilised. Partly for this reason, and partly on account of poverty, lack of education and contact with the outside world, its farmers were the most conservative of white South African communities. Cherishing the spirit of the Great Trek, they were totally opposed to the racial egalitarianism implicit in the Cape legal and constitutional system (if not in actual social life). Their President Burgers, elected after the failure of his predecessor to gain recognition for any Transvaal right in the diamond fields, would not have been opposed to the federal idea, but his thinking was far ahead of most of his fellow countrymen and his authority rested on slender foundations. When the confederation discussion came to a head he was away in Europe trying to raise money for a scheme to build a railway into his republic from Delagoa Bay.

The most formidable obstacle to the confederation scheme, however, was the Cape itself. In granting responsible government to the colony Britain had sacrificed the authority to dictate solutions in South Africa. Molteno was not at all in favour of the confederation idea and distrusted initiatives coming from Britain so soon after the colony had won self-government. He was horrified at the change of the Natal constitution. He felt that the Cape, with its revenues heavily committed to railway building, was in no position to share its limited resources with the other territories. The potential defence burdens were frightening, especially the thought of defending Natal against the Zulu. Federation might upset the delicate balance of political power in the Cape and revive agitation for a separate status for the Eastern Province which he had just succeeded in suppressing. The colony should be given a chance to settle down under responsible government before being pushed into new adventures. His government gave no support to the Colonial Secretary's suggestion, but popular feeling in favour of federation was quite considerable, and an agitation supported by the historian Froude, was almost successful in forcing Molteno's hand, when Carnarvon ruined the chances of the scheme by a tactical blunder. He suggested that as public discussion had done everything that a conference could in South Africa, the venue of the conference should be shifted to London. This gave all the main interested parties an opportunity to avoid participating and the scheme collapsed. Carnarvon, however, was not prepared to abandon the idea of confederation because of a minor check. He looked for some convenient lever to prise South Africa out of its stubborn conservatism. Fortune provided him with what appeared the perfect opportunity in the Transvaal.

The period of continued white expansion since the Great Trek had modified but not destroyed the pattern of Bantu South Africa created by the Mfecane. The Zulu, Swazi and Basuto nations still survived; the tribes of Bechuanaland were still free of European control and, in the Zoutpansberg area where the Pedi had once fought desperately with regiments of Mzilikazi, their chief Sekukuni had built up a considerable tribal empire. As white expansion continued, the nature of the struggle became more obvious to the various Bantu peoples and their determination to resist increased. They began to arm themselves with modern weapons bought at the diamond fields and the stage was set for a series of severe settler/Bantu wars.

In Zululand, militarily the most powerful and dreaded of the Bantu states, Cetewayo, who had succeeded Mpande after a bitter succession dispute, revived Shaka's military system in its entirety. He was anxious to remain on good relations with the British government of Natal and reluctantly accepted the restraint imposed on the use of his military machine by Shepstone the Natal Secretary for Native Affairs. But, though Cetewayo showed no inclination to aggression against the whites, the mere existence of his army was a cause of nightmares to the Natal farmers.

President Burgers of the Transvaal succeeded in raising considerable sums in Europe for his projected Delagoa Bay railway: materials were assembled but, in the absence of technical knowledge and careful planning, they remained rotting on the quay at Lourenco Marques. As security for the loan the President had pledged an area of land claimed by the republic but effectively controlled by Sekukuni. If the Transvaal was to fulfil its obligations it must assert its authority in this area. War with the Pedi broke out in 1876. The President was not popular; his outlook was far too liberal and his religious beliefs too heretical for most of the Transvaalers. When Sekukuni successfully defended himself in his mountain terrain, the farmers, seeing no immediate profit for themselves in the fighting, suddenly broke up their commando. Burgers was left with a bankrupt state; farmers refused to pay taxes; the Cape banks refused further credit. The Pedi were triumphant. There were rumours that Cetewayo was preparing to seize the opportunity to send his well-trained regiments into the republic to settle land disputes between the Boers and the Zulu once and for all. British subjects in the republic appealed for protection, and philanthropic opinion in Britain urged action to put an end to Boer mistreatment of the Bantu.

Carnarvon sent Shepstone to the Transvaal to see whether annexation could be amicably arranged. If the Transvaal were in British hands, he felt confederation would follow easily. Shepstone did not succeed in persuading the Volksraad to accept annexation, but several of its members told him privately that there was no alternative and he hoisted the British flag. Though there was no open opposition to the annexation at first, Sir Bartle Frere, who came out to South Africa to carry the confederation movement to a successful conclusion, found himself faced with unexpected difficulties. The annexation aroused Boer national feeling throughout the country against what seemed to them a callous act of aggression. The Orange Free State government would have nothing to do with confederation until a representative assembly of Transvaalers should have ratified the annexation; and the Cape became more suspicious of the idea than ever.

The original idea at the time of the Transvaal annexation was to summon a representative assembly and introduce self-government as soon as possible. But, in view of the Volksraad's attitude on the eve of the annexation, it was feared such an assembly might complicate matters by condemning Britain's actions outright, so it was delayed, with the result that the difficulties in the way of restoring representative government increased. The only way that the British government could have made itself acceptable to the Transvaalers was by a very generous financial policy. The Treasury was prepared to be generous with regard to the existing national debt but it was not prepared to see the Transvaal administration run at a permanent loss. This meant that representative government was out of the question and Britain must be prepared to face rising demands by the Transvaalers for the restoration of their independence. In these circumstances the British turned to the only remaining means of winning Bore goodwill. They must be gratified with land taken from the Bantu. In 1878 the struggle with Sekukuni was resumed and the British decided to use the military forces of one Bantu state against another. The Swazi were asked to lend their army for the campaign and with the help of their age-regiments the Pedi were completely defeated. Then as confederation still failed to materialise, Sir Bartle Frere turned his attention to the Zulu. So long as Cetewayo's age regiments remained active neither Natal nor the Transvaal could feel secure and the Cape would be chary of taking over British responsibilities for their defence. The Transvaal, moreover, had claims to a part of the Zulu country known as the Blood River territory. If Britain could break Zulu power, one of the most formidable obstacles to federation would be removed, the Transvaal farmers could be given valuable farming land and British policy, liberated from its association with pro-Bantu philanthropy, would win immense popularity. The object was to be attained under a cloak of legality. A judicial commission was set up to investigate the Blood River dispute. It was anticipated that it would decide in favour of the Transvaal and that Cetewayo would fight rather than surrender his peoples' land, so military preparations were set in hand for the expected campaign. But the judicial commission came to the opposite conclusion. The Transvaal's claim was found to be without legal foundation and Cetewayo was awarded even more than he had asked for.

The High Commissioner was in an absurd position. To carry out the award would drive the Transvaalers to despair and ruin all hopes of achieving federation under British auspices. Accordingly he took advantage of an incident in which British sovereignty had been infringed when some of Cetewayo's men had pursued two runaway wives of their king and murdered them on Natal soil. Cetewayo was sent an ultimatum demanding the abandonment of the regimental system and the complete break-up of the Zulu state organisation. As Cetewayo showed no inclination to conform, the troops marched into Zululand. The result was a fearful disaster for British arms. A whole regiment was caught unawares by the Zulu forces at Isandhlwana, with its ammunition sealed in boxes that could not be quickly opened, and massacred. Militarily, the defeat was soon retrieved. The defence of Rourke's Drift by a tiny but heroic garrison and Cetewayo's reluctance to engage in more than a defensive war spared Natal from Zulu invasion. Overwhelming

forces were assembled and marched on Cetewayo's capital. At the
battle of Ulundi, the Zulu army, relying on its traditional mass-
formation fighting in the face of modern weapons, was decisively
crushed. Cetewayo was taken as a prisoner to Cape Town. But the
political effects were more far-reaching. Britain had been severely
shaken and showed all the signs of loss of nerve.

Sir Bartle Frere was censured and, though not recalled, his
authority was divided: a Lieutenant-Governor was appointed for
South East Africa. After the great Zulu struggle, Britain drew back
from annexing the country and instead tried to keep it weak by
dividing it into thirteen chiefdoms. Her military prestige had
received a severe blow, and the Transvaal Boers were holding
open-air meetings to demand independence. Gladstone's Mid-
lothian campaign with its stirring remarks about the suppression
of Boer freedom gave them new heart, but once in office he found
that the problems of the Transvaal were not so simple as they had
previously appeared. There were, for instance, the Bantu to be
considered as well as the Boers. Driven to desperation by what
they regarded as British duplicity, the Boers rose in armed
rebellion. The small British garrison in Pretoria was penned up in
the town and a relief column badly shot up at Bronkhorstspruit.
Sir Pomeroy Colley hurried across the Drakensberg with reinforcements from Natal, but he was first checked at Laings Nek and then
severely defeated at Majuba where he lost his life. Even before
Majuba, however, Britain had decided to negotiate. Plagued by
an uneasy conscience about the whole annexation affair, Gladstone
capitulated. The Transvaal was to regain internal autonomy under
British suzerainty. Its foreign relations with other European powers
were, however, to remain under British control, and Britain was
also to have a say in native policy through a Resident in Pretoria.

The Pretoria Convention was hardly signed before the old
process of Boer expansion began again. The thirteen chiefdoms
failed to bring any kind of stability to Zululand and the attempt
was made to restore the unfortunate Cetewayo. During his
imprisonment, however, his opponents had been gathering
strength, and the chief was driven out of his kingdom, to die
shortly after as a refugee. A civil war then followed and one of the
contestants appealed for Boer support. Volunteers under Lukas
Mayer came gladly to his aid. They placed Dinizulu on the throne
but took about half of the remaining Zulu land in return. A

short-lived republic, the New Republic, was established there before it was absorbed in the Transvaal.

A similar process took place on the western frontiers of the republic. Armed white freebooters with the tacit support of the Transvaal intervened as volunteers in the disputes of the Tswana tribes. In return for military aid they demanded land concessions on which they established the two petty republics of Stellaland and Goshen. By this time, however, the international position had changed. The 'Scramble' for Africa was under way and the British government was forced to recognise German annexation of South West Africa. There was an obvious danger that the Germans would link up with the Transvaal, excluding British trade from the interior and threatening the whole strategic position of the Cape and the India route. A new convention was signed with the Transvaal in London under which the term suzerainty was to be dropped and nominal British control over Transvaal native policy abandoned in return for an agreement that the two little republics were outside the Transvaal boundaries. Negative agreements were not enough however, and the question of Stellaland and Goshen was settled in 1885 by the Warren expedition which also declared a British Protectorate over the tribes of modern Bechuanaland Protectorate.

In South Africa, one of the loudest advocates of action to seize the road into the interior before it should be closed to British trade was Cecil Rhodes. He had come out to South Africa for his health and drifted to the diamond fields where he discovered the diamond miners were in trouble. When they had been sifting earth in shallow excavations for the precious stones the system of small individual claims had been perfectly adequate, but as each miner dug deeper and deeper it became absurd. Wide areas were converted into deep honeycombs of excavations separated from one another by narrow walls of earth along the top of which they pushed wheelbarrows. Each miner naturally dug as close to the limits of his claim as possible, and the separating walls frequently fell burying workers in the pits and making access impossible. Water accumulated at the bottom of the diggings and in the absence of mechanical devices was very costly to remove. Rhodes saw that by consolidating diggings they could be worked far more economically. He began by buying up the claims of bankrupt owners, and as his profits increased he was able to buy up more and more. He had a rival in Barney Barnato who had come to the fields with no more capital than a few hundred cigars, and who also saw the economic advantages of amalgamation. Eventually the two men held almost all the diamond mines between them and a grim struggle for power developed. With the help of Beit and Rothschild, Rhodes was victorious and almost the whole diamond production of South Africa was brought together in De Beers Consolidated. Barney Barnato was a director but control was firmly in the hands of Rhodes. Rhodes's ambition was not confined to making money, however; to him money was a means and a symbol of success rather than an end in itself. He was a man who found satisfaction in building big: a born empire builder. His vision reached out to the whole of Africa, and indeed to the world itself, embracing the extension of British imperial authority from the Cape to Cairo which would be linked by a trans-Africa railway and telegraph. Africa so united under the British flag would be one element in an imperial federation, which, in alliance with the United States of America, would dominate the world for the peace and progress of humanity. He was to be the key figure in this gigantic plan, using his immense financial resources as a lever to move more short-sighted and conservative men. Fascinated by the scale of his ideas he had little concern for the morality of his means. Those who opposed his schemes were mere obstacles to be swept away; he was in too much of a hurry to afford nice scruples. For the African part of his programme with which he was most immediately concerned the South African white community seemed the natural base. He hoped to see Briton and Boer in a federated South Africa combining their forces for the great north-ward advance. For this reason and because he wanted to keep developments in his own hands, he was opposed to the idea of imperial expansion being directed from London.

In his scheme of things the African had little part. Rhodes was prepared to use the slogans of philanthropy when it paid, but normally he thought of Africans, as indeed he tended to do of all men, either as means for the attainment of his ends or as obstacles to be removed. His idea of a South African Federation seemed likely at first to be realised without difficulty for the Transvaal, though independent, remained poverty stricken. In 1885 it actually asked the Cape for a customs union, but the Cape politicians were too selfish and short-sighted to agree to sharing their customs revenue. The following year the chance was gone, for gold had been discovered at the Witwatersrand and the great gold rush was under way.

The development of gold-mining in the Transvaal revolutionised the balance of power in the sub-continent. The Transvaal suddenly became by far the richest of the white states and the other communities increasingly dependent on supplying goods to the Johannesburg market. If it had once seemed inevitable that the Cape would absorb the other states, it now seemed not improbable that this role would be filled by the Transvaal; especially as Boer national feeling inspired by the success of Transvaal rebellion was still a powerful force even in the Cape itself. Such a development would be a disaster for British policy. A rich and united South Africa outside the British orbit and possibly allied with Germany would undermine Britain's entire strategic position in the world; particularly in relation to the Indian empire.

In the Transvaal itself gold brought with it capitalists and mineworkers of every European nation, but predominantly from Britain. They formed a turbulent population quite out of sympathy with the rustic farmers who ruled the Republic. Kruger, the Transvaal President, was the very antithesis of Rhodes, the capitalist imperialist. He had taken part in the Great Trek as a child and had grown up a true Boer: he was honest, brave and God-fearing, according to the narrow tenets of the creed in which he had been reared. He took a high view of his duty and could not compromise on matters of principle affecting the hard-won independence of his people. He could not comprehend and deeply despised the sophisticated double-dealing of his English adversaries. On the other hand, he was ill-educated and quite out of touch with the development of thought in the world at large. Kruger was particularly ill-fitted to deal with a situation of revolutionary economic and social change. Now that the Transvaal had money in abundance, Kruger's policy was to ensure its continued political and economic independence by establishing an outlet to the sea. The long-planned railway line to Lourenço Marques was put in hand while he delayed the building of lines from the Cape and Natal until he was sure that the alternative route would materialise.

Against this background, Rhodes and his plans appeared to offer a perfect solution to the problems of British policy. He had already inserted a clause in the constitution of the De Beers Consolidated

Company to allow profits to be used for purposes other than diamond mining. Looking to the north his agents succeeded in 1887 in obtaining the Rudd mining concession from Lobengula, Mzilikazi's successor as King of the Ndebele, and this Rhodes was prepared to interpret very widely. He proposed to form a chartered company which would take possession of much of modern Rhodesia, the hinterland of the old Monomatapa, whence the Portuguese had exported gold and where it was expected that gold mines far richer than those of the Witwatersrand would be found. The Transvaal, surrounded by British territory and economically eclipsed by a dominant northern state, would then easily be persuaded to join a federation.

Mzilikazi after his flight from the Transvaal in 1837 had found a new home for his people in modern Matabeleland. There he had continued his career of conquests incorporating the defeated Shona peoples in his age-regiments and building up a Zulu-type kingdom which dominated the whole of modern Rhodesia, though its members occupied only Matabeleland. While he was in the Transvaal, Mzilikazi had met the pioneer missionary Moffat and felt affection for him. Even though he had suffered severely at the hands of the Boers, his desire to see his old friend was so strong that he gave permission for Boer hunters and other whites to enter his kingdom. Mzilikazi's hopes of seeing Moffat were fulfilled but they brought many troubles in their wake, for white men began infiltrating his kingdom and, as he grew old and incapacitated, he lost the power to control them. By the time of his death, whites were already beginning to intrigue with a view to establishing control over the Ndebele kingdom.

After the death of Mzilikazi, Shepstone attempted to gain control of the kingdom by encouraging the rumour that his horseboy was really the true heir. The plot failed and Lobengula succeeded in establishing himself on the throne. But he inherited a very difficult situation. He realised that white interest in his kingdom was increasing, and on the other hand he was aware of white military power and extremely anxious not to be involved in a conflict with it. His kingdom was organised on military lines but in accordance with methods which were out of date in an age which possessed the rapid-firing gun. Thus, unable to understand the implications of documents put before him by Rhodes's persuasive emissaries and attracted by a promise of large quantities of firearms, Lobengula put his mark to the fatal Rudd concession.

Impressed by the opportunity of enjoying the advantages of imperialism without the expense, the British government gave Rhodes his Charter and, to smooth his path, agreed also to allow the Transvaal to seize Swaziland in spite of the known opposition of the Queen Regent and her people. Britain however hastened to establish her sovereignty over remaining independent Bantu peoples along the coast wherever there was any likelihood of the Boers being able to establish a port.

In 1890 Rhodes's pioneer column set off for the Mashonaland area of modern Rhodeisia. Like the Boers trekker before them, the predominantly English settlers went in search of farms. It was an English Great Trek but supported by capitalism and part of Rhodes's wide-ranging imperial plans, and their establishment in Mashonaland simply extended the South African situation to the area of modern Rhodesia. Each member of the expedition was promised a farm of 3,000 acres as well as a number of mining claims, and no sooner were they established than they began taking over Bantu lands, forcing them to serve as labourers. Economically the settlement in Mashonaland proved disappointing since the expected rich goldfields were not discovered. It was difficult to see how the British South Africa Company was ever going to pay dividends to its shareholders, and, far from dominating the Transvaal, the new settlement seemed likely to be its economic satellite: especially as Rhodes failed in his plans to seize part of Mozambique to give his colony an independent outlet to the sea. Their first thought was to destroy the Ndebele kingdom and seize the rest of modern Rhodesia since it was believed that the gold reef ran through Lobengula's capital Bulawayo. Lobengula was caught in a tragic situation. He was desperately anxious to avoid any conflict with the whites but Rhodes was determined to get his kingdom. The militarist organisation of the Ndebele state made it impossible for him to forgo tribute-collecting raids on the Shona altogether, but however carefully he instructed his indunas to avoid any conflict with the whites it would always be possible to use these raids as a *casus belli*. In 1893 an Ndebele raid which approached the neighbourhood of Salisbury was made the pretext for war. The B.S.A. company's forces, with support of government troops in the Bechuanaland Protectorate, mowed down the

Ndebele regiments with machine guns and Lobengula fled to die a miserable refugee.

The Company then had extensive and excellent grazing land to satisfy its supporters, but gold had still not been found in the quantities that would be necessary if Rhodesia was to play the role which Rhodes had originally intended. Thus, though the company had secured treaties which gave it, or appeared to give it, controlling rights in what is now the state of Zambia, and Harry Johnson with a subsidy from Rhodes was establishing British authority in modern Malawi, the whole basis of Rhodes's scheme remained insecure while the Transvaal with its immense resources remained outside the orbit of British South Africa. Rhodes's personal power on the other hand was at its apogee. He had entered Cape politics in 1888 and had succeeded in winning over Hofmeyer, leader of the Afrikaner Bond (originally an expression of anti-British Boer nationalism), to his idea of a combination of English and Boer South Africans. With Bond support and the judicious use of his economic power, Rhodes became Prime Minister of the Cape in 1890. Combining this position with control over the largest diamond business in the world, a less important gold-mining concern in the Transvaal and the B.S.A. Company with its infant colony in Rhodesia, he was more than ever convinced of his ability to reorganise the world single-handed and more than ever impatient of irritating obstacles like Kruger with his dedication to Transvaal independence. Thus Rhodes turned his mind to the idea of achieving his object by a *coup*. He had a natural belief in the power of money, and Kruger's government seemed to him an anachronistic facade which would inevitably collapse if the mine-owners and their followers chose to overthrow it. The mine-owners had their grievances: Kruger, anxious to preserve the heritage of his people, was not prepared to give the uitlanders the vote until they had been resident in the Republic for a considerable period, and his economic policies mitigated against maximum profit for the mines. Generally, the cosmopolitan mining population was out of sympathy with a government of Dutch-speaking ultra-conservative farmers.

Rhodes's idea was to urge the mining population to open revolt. They would seize the Rand while Rhodes brought a mobile column across the border from a base in the Bechuanaland Protectorate. Once again this was a plan which would rid the

British government of its worries about South Africa without its having to pay. Chamberlain gave his consent and an elaborate conspiracy was hatched involving the High Commissioner at Cape Town and Flora Shaw, the African correspondent of *The Times*, who was to publish information about the uprising in such a way as to justify the conspirators. The plot ended in the fiasco of the Jameson Raid. The mine-owners when it came to the push were not really revolutionaries and tried to back out. Dr Jameson, in charge of the mobile column, went in to precipitate revolt instead of support an existing rebellion. Rhodes failed to realise that at the critical moment fighting ability would count more than any amount of money. The Maxim guns which had easily destroyed the close-packed Ndebele regiments were of little use against a force of highly skilled sharpshooters who knew every inch of the terrain and kept up a murderous fire from behind cover. The column was surrounded and forced to unconditional surrender before ever reaching Johannesburg. Rhodes lost his premiership of the Cape and almost his control of the B.S.A. Company. In Rhodesia the fiasco was followed by the Ndebele rebellion which was joined by the Shona to the distress of the colonists who had failed to realise that their rule was more odious to their Bantu subjects than the tyranny of Lobengula's regiments. Rhodes brought the Ndebele rebellion to an end by an act of personal heroism. He went into the Matoppos Mountains where the Ndebele were holding out and negotiated terms of peace.

The raid and its failure had made the clash of interests between Britain and the Transvaal insoluble except by force. The rearmament of the Transvaal and the Orange Free State with German arms, the incident of the Kaiser's Telegram[1] and the obvious determination of Kruger to establish independent relationships with European powers other than Britain meant that Britain must insist on acquiring virtually sovereign powers over the Republic. Kruger, on the other hand, would never make concessions that would bring about such a result. In 1899 Chamberlain and his fanatically imperialist High Commissioner, Milner, forced the Boer Republics into war.

The Great Boer War turned out to be far more serious and infinitely more expensive than the British authorities had anticipated. It started with a series of severe British defeats and, even after Roberts and Kitchener had restored the military position and occupied the capitals of the Boer republics, the commandos kept up a long drawn out guerilla war. To counteract this, Boer farms were burnt and the women and children collected in concentration camps. At last, weariness on both sides forced a compromise. The Peace of Vereeniging marked the Boers' surrender of independence, but the British were equally anxious for peace. They were prepared to obtain it at the cost of sacrificing their moral responsibilities, making the fatal concession that no non-white franchise would be granted in the ex-republics until they had been restored to responsible government. Vast sums in aid were also promised to restore the shattered country. Milner, who controlled the reconstruction programme, took the opportunity of British control of the whole sub-continent to try to strengthen imperial ties. He sought to introduce large numbers of English settlers, especially to the Transvaal, and to anglicise the Boers, but at the same time intended to keep firm control in imperial hands. Mass education for Boer children had begun in the concentration camps under idealistic English ladies who came out to work there. This 'public education' was carried on when the camps were broken up and numerous government schools for white children were opened. But Milner insisted that the medium of instruction must be English, making allowance for only the very minimum of instruction in the Dutch language. This roused the Boers to establish a movement for Christian National Education which founded a number of rival schools. Although these were not very successful, the movement had important political consequences. In the aftermath of the war the Boers were bitterly divided amongst themselves. Some had fought on to the end (the Bittereinders), others had surrendered when they felt the ultimate conclusion could not be in doubt (Handsoppers), and others had even joined the imperial forces against their countrymen (National Scouts). The Cape Boers who had for the most part kept out of the war were also not unnaturally unpopular with their cousins from the ex-republics. Now faced with what appeared a threat to their language and their very existence as a people the different sections drew together in a common political movement.

To achieve his plans, Milner had to get the Transvaal economy back into full operation as soon as possible and for this mine-labour was needed on a large scale, but, with extensive reconstruction work going on all over South Africa, sufficient Bantu labour could not be found. He therefore tried the experiment of introducing Chinese. This brought the mines back into full production in a very short time, but proved intensely unpopular with white South Africans who were frightened of these new and incalculable non-Europeans. It was even more unpopular in England, where the highly unsatisfactory labour conditions on the Rand gave the Liberals the rallying cry of Chinese slavery with which they defeated the government in 1905. The Liberal government hastened to undo the wrongs of its predecessor by introducing responsible government to the ex-republics without delay, thereby throwing away the chance of permanently influencing the development of South African society.

In the Transvaal a Boer party called Het Volk, led by Botha and Smuts, won the poll. In the Orange River Colony power passed into the hands of the Orangia Unie party, with Fischer as Prime Minister and Hertzog as his chief assistant. In the Cape the strongly pro-British Progressive administration headed by none other than Dr Jameson gave way to a government representing the Afrikaner Bond though led by Merriman. The way was open for South Africa to be united under Boer auspices. Already Selbourne, the High Commissioner who succeeded Milner, had prepared a memorandum in relation to railway affairs, pointing out the dire results of a return to political disunity, and members of Milner's original team of young administrators (Milner's Kindergarten) were advocating union. Thus when the main remaining pro-imperialist government disappeared with the fall of Dr Jameson, negotiations between Merriman and Botha began at once.

The South African National Convention which drew up a draft for union wrestled with a number of major problems. The will to unity was so strong that the idea of a federal system was easily swept aside in favour of a unitary constitution. The most vital issue was the nature of the franchise. The Cape delegates for the most part favoured the extension of the Cape franchise to the whole of the country, but the Transvaal was irrevocably opposed to any non-white franchise and wanted it removed from the Cape. In this the ex-republics were strongly supported by the English delegates from Natal who showed the strongest racial feelings. Ultimately a compromise was reached. The Cape was to retain its existing franchise, and this was to be protected by a clause so that it could not be changed without a two-thirds majority of both Houses of

Parliament sitting together. No non-white franchise was to be introduced in the ex-republics, however, and no non-European was to be eligible for election to the Union Parliament even if he stood for a Cape constituency. The agreement also contained arrangements which favoured the Transvaal against the Cape in the distribution of seats. A particularly important clause gave relatively higher representation to rural areas, the seat of die-hard Boer conservatism, than to the more cosmopolitan and liberal-minded urban areas.

Liberal whites at the Cape, including the Afrikaner Bond leader Hofmeyer himself, protested against the franchise arrangements. Schreiner formed an association to carry a petition against the constitution to London. The African Peoples organisation of the Cape Coloured community did likewise, and the occasion gave rise to the first nation-wide Bantu political organisation which also sent delegates overseas. But all these protests were unavailing. Britain as often before, after South African troubles, was in the mood to wash her hands of the sub-continent. The chance of securing a united South Africa within the British empire was too good to be missed and the draft constitution was accepted without substantial amendment.

CONCLUSION

The period between the Great Trek and 1910 was one of profoundly important changes. The long process of conflict for land between settlers and Bantu had resulted in the latter being confined to areas too small to support them. There could be no further great expansion of the areas of white occupation. The period of frontier struggles was over, and instead of white and Bantu existing as independent communities they had been brought together in a single economic system. The frontier wars had been replaced by a class struggle. This transition was accompanied by great cultural and economic changes affecting all sections of society. South Africa was launched on an industrial career and urbanisation of all races was proceeding apace. Amongst the Bantu the influence of education started by the missionaries was producing important effects. At the time of union there were actually more non-Europeans with an elementary education than whites. The migrant labour system, which drew Africans from every part of the Union and beyond its boundaries, into the economic net of the gold and diamond mines spread knowledge of industrial life to remote corners of the country and hastened cultural change. In these circumstances the African reaction to European dominance adjusted itself to the new order: instead of tribal wars and uprisings African resistance was adopting the language of the new society. This was exemplified in the great Ethiopian Movement which led to the establishment of innumerable break-away African churches before the end of the nineteenth century and represented acceptance of Christianity but rejection of white domination. The Zulu Bambata rebellion of 1906, the last major military struggle between whites and Bantu, combined the old element of tribal feeling with the new religious attitudes. Before the end of the nineteenth century, modern-type political organisations were being formed by the Bantu, even though they were small and highly localised at first. The short-lived South African Native National Conference formed to fight the franchise clauses in the constitution was the first ephemeral attempt at a national organisation. The African National Congress was formed two years after the union.

The true significance of the unification lies in the fact that it occurred at a time when the Boer War and its aftermath had greatly strengthened the forces of conservative Afrikaner nationalism, so that the spirit of the frontier was able to triumph over the more flexible outlook of the Cape. In accepting the franchise clauses of the constitution Britain finally consummated her failure to provide the South African community, for which she had so long held responsibility, with a legal and political framework to allow the social evolution demanded by economic change to proceed without revolutionary upheaval. South Africa was left in a constitutional straitjacket; the balance of power created by the franchise system has determined the pattern of South African history ever since.

A NOTE ON SOUTH WEST AFRICA

South West Africa is one of the most arid areas south of the Sahara. Only the northernmost parts of the territory near the border with modern Angola enjoy a moderate rainfall and can support a relatively dense population. In spite of the desert or semi-desert condition of most of the country, however, considerable areas can support cattle and sheep if their density per square mile is kept very low. Even the true Kalahari can provide grazing for a part of the year when the shallow pans still retain some of the rain-water.

At the beginning of the nineteenth century the territory was still mainly occupied by Hottentots belonging to a group known as Nama (Namaqua). Cattle-keepers, like all Hottentots, they were organised in loose clan-based tribes, with the tribe later known as the Rooi Nasie (Red Nation) enjoying a measure of paramountcy. Bushman hunting bands found a livelihood in areas unsuitable for cattle, and some of these areas sheltered a small group of people known as Berg-Damas who although Negroes had adopted the Bushman's way of life.

In the north of the territory the Bantu had already established themselves, and the areas bordering on modern Angola were settled by a population of typical Bantu-mixed farmers known as the Ambo (Ovambo). Farther south, the Herero, a Bantu people who relied solely on cattle, were advancing towards the vicinity of what is now Windhoek.

Soon after the beginning of the century groups of mixed white/Hottentot descent and pure Hottentots who had been influenced by white culture began to enter the area from the south in search of refuge from servitude on white farms and colour discrimination in the Colony. Some formed separate communities of their own like the Rehobothers, who founded a tiny republic with a constitution reminiscent of the Boer states; others settled with existing peoples.

The most colourful and important of these Orlams, as the Nama called them, was Jonker Afrikaner. His father, Jager Afrikaner, had been provoked into participating in the murder of his employer, a rascally frontier Boer, and had established an impregnable camp on an island in the Orange River. From this base he terrorised white and non-white alike before being converted by the missionary Moffat, pardoned and received in audience by the Governor in Cape Town. His son chafed under missionary restraint after his father's death and migrated to South West Africa, establishing himself near the frontiers of Herero settlement. He undertook a long series of campaigns against the Herero which were part robbery and part a struggle of Hottentot against Bantu. He brought a large part of the Herero under his paramountcy, using

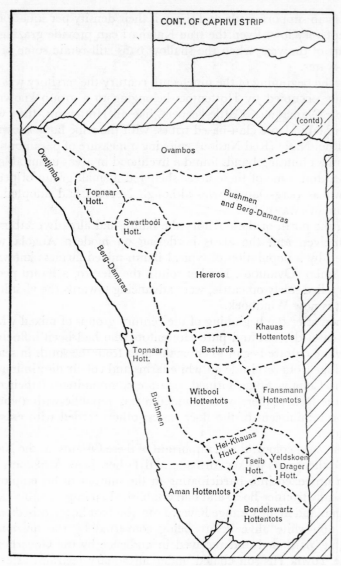

Fig. 23 (a)   South West Africa in 1890.

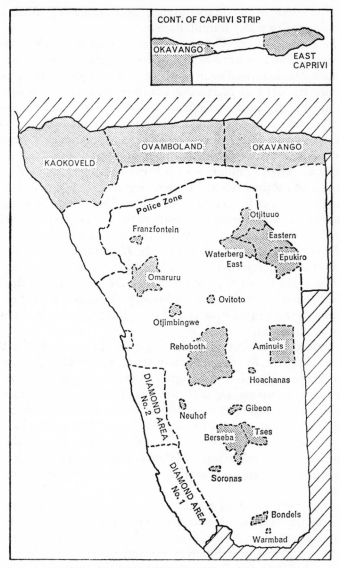

Fig. 23 (*b*) South West Africa at the present day.

their warriors as auxiliary troops, and subjecting their chief Kamaherero to many humiliations.

The coming of the Orlams was associated with other 'white' influences. The London Missionary Society, the Wesleyans and the Rhenish Missionaries began work with the tribes. Traders began to enter the area in increasing numbers and many missionaries combined trade with evangelism; traders created a ready market for captured cattle and provided in return the ammunition which kept Afrikaner's forces in the field. These developments served to alter the balance of power between Hottentot and Bantu. The Herero acquired familiarity with firearms from Afrikaner's campaigns, and missionaries and traders began to settle amongst them. After the death of Jonker Afrikaner (the elder) his son was unable to maintain the Hottentot paramountcy. The Herero, led by Kamaherero and assisted by white traders and missionaries, threw off the yoke and struck back against the Hottentots. Afrikaner's son was decisively defeated in 1864. Fighting continued, however, and in 1868 a Hottentot expedition looted the shop of a trader and robbed the Rhenish Missionary Society. A request for protection was sent to the king of Prussia and complaint was also made to the Cape government.

It looked for a time as if the Cape would annex South West Africa. Palgrave, as special commissioner for the Cape, succeeded in persuading the Herero to agree to treaties placing themselves under Cape protection, but the Cape Parliament refused to shoulder the expense that would be involved and nothing happened apart from the British annexation of Walvis Bay in 1878. In 1880 war between the Herero and the Hottentots broke out again, and Bismarck asked whether Britain could guarantee protection for German missionaries, but once again no action was taken.

In 1883 the German trader Lüderitz bought land at Angra Pequena Bay and the German government decided to press its claim to South West Africa. Britain and the Cape woke up too late. In 1884 a British warship was warned off from the bay by a German gunboat and Bismarck exploited the international situation to win British official recognition for his annexation of South West Africa.

The first concern of the Germans was to extend their control inland from the coast. The Herero were persuaded to sign a treaty, which they later repudiated, but the Hottentot tribe of Hendrik Witbooi refused to surrender their independence and even wrote to Kamaherero pressing for a common stand. German forces were then sent against the Witboois and they were forced to accept the treaty.

With the new government came traders and then settlers in small but increasing numbers. Relying on the support of their government, the German traders shamelessly fleeced the Herero and other peoples and gained possession of the greater part of their herds. As settlers began to stake out farms and ask for labour, the land of the Herero was progressively reduced. In 1904 they rose in an all-out rebellion and, until reinforcements arrived from Germany, the regime was in danger of collapse, but the Herero armed with rifles had nothing to match the quick-firing weapons of the Germans; in August 1904 they were decisively defeated in a desperate battle at Hamakari. A high proportion of the survivors became refugees roaming the desert, or sought shelter in the Bechuanaland Protectorate where a large part of the tribe still lives. The Germans attempted to crush the spirit of independence of the Herero and forced them to accept work on white farms; although they were an almost exclusively pastoral people, they were forbidden to own cattle.

The Herero revolt was hardly crushed when the Hottentots rose under the leadership of old Hendrik Witbooi, then in his eighties. He kept up a grim guerilla struggle for a year until he was killed in action. Leadership then passed to Jacob Marengo and the struggle was maintained for a further two years, but by 1907 all the tribes were forced to surrender.

In the First World War German South West Africa was seized by South African forces, and after the war South Africa succeeded in obtaining a League of Nations Mandate to administer the country. Under the auspices of the League, it might have been expected that the tribes would recover their land and freedom, but the appointment of South Africa as the administering power meant the extension to the new territory of the pattern already established in the rest of South Africa. The wide ranching lands of the Mandated Territory created the opportunity for yet another Trek of land-hungry farmers; governmental policy sought to keep white South African farmers on the land, even at the expense of heavy subsidies. Thus the tribes saw their territory shrink rather than

28

expand. Indeed the South African policy of restricting non-European land-owning to areas small enough to serve only as labour reserves was imported into South West Africa and used to keep the white farmers supplied with cheap labour. The South African system of social discrimination was extended to the area, and white supremacy insisted on. The proud republicans of Rehoboth were deprived of the vestiges of independence and movements of protest like that of the Bondelswarts in 1922 were ruthlessly crushed with modern weapons.

Under South African administration the territory was divided into two parts: a police zone, including the area occupied by white farmers, the mineral deposits and the remaining reserves of the Hereros and Hottentot groups, and the Ovamboland area. Non-European life in the police zone was strictly controlled in the interest of security, but the Ambo have been allowed a slightly greater measure of freedom. Their area has seen virtually no development and is treated strictly as a breeding ground for workers in South West Africa and South Africa itself.

The value of South West Africa to South Africa depends largely on its mineral resources. During the German period, diamonds were discovered and the Orange River mouth area has proved one of the richest and most easily exploited source of these precious stones in the world. Very little of the immense wealth derived from this activity is spent to help the indigenous peoples, however, and the demand for labour on the diamond fields is a further incentive to the policy of keeping the tribal reserves poor and small to ensure cheap labour.

In the years between the wars South Africa was subjected to repeated and increasingly pointed criticisms by the League of Nations Permanent Mandates Commission, but though this was embarrassing for South Africa's representatives it did not produce a significant change of policy.

The Second World War and the creation of the United Nations began a new stage in the history of the country. It has witnessed the struggle of the South West African peoples and their friends of all races to gain a hearing for their grievances and secure international action to redress them, and the South African government's attempts to fend off international pressures and absorb the territory completely. Neither side has so far completely succeeded in its objects. The peoples of South West Africa and their champions (notably the Rev. Michael Scott) have succeeded in winning international concern for the problems of the country but not in gaining effective international action to coerce South Africa to modify substantially its policies. The South African government has gone a long way towards incorporating South West Africa and has representatives of the South West African whites sitting in its Parliament, but has not been able to destroy the international status of the territory. The motion filed by Ethiopia and Liberia before the International Court of Justice seeking a ruling that South Africa has forfeited its mandate might bring about the international pressures for which South West Africa's peoples have so long looked in vain. Meanwhile many have lost confidence in international action. Their interest is concentrated on developing a strong local political organisation and, like non-European peoples everywhere in South Africa, they are being unwillingly forced to contemplate violence and sabotage as their last and only hope.

NOTE

1   Sent by Emperor William of Germany to President Kruger on 3 June 1896 congratulating him on his success in suppressing the Jameson Raid. This step created an acute crisis in Anglo-German relations.

QUESTIONS FOR FURTHER STUDY AND DISCUSSION

1 How would you explain the frequent border wars between white settlers and their Bantu neighbours in the period between the Great Trek and the unification of South Africa?

2 Examine the role of Moshesh in South African history.

3 Why did British policy in South Africa fluctuate between advance and retreat during the period between the Great Trek and unification?

4 In what ways did the discovery of diamonds and gold alter the historical situation in South Africa?

5 Compare the policy and attitudes of Cecil Rhodes with those of Paul Kruger.

6 What is meant by saying that in the constitution of the Union of South Africa the spirit of the frontier triumphed over that of the Cape?

7 Describe the different peoples of South West Africa in the nineteenth century.

8 Why has South West Africa been so frequently discussed at the United Nations?

SELECT BIBLIOGRAPHY

E. Walker, *A History of Southern Africa*, Longmans, 3rd edition, 1957.
C. W. de Kiewiet, *History of South Africa: Social and Economic*, O.U.P., 1941.
—— *British Colonial Policy and the South African Republics, 1848–72*, Longmans, 1929.
—— *The Imperial Factor in South African History*, C.U.P., 1937.
L. Marquand, *The Story of South Africa*, Faber & Faber, 2nd edition, 1963.
G. Tylden, *The Rise of the Basuto*, Juta, Cape Town, 1950.
S. J. Halford, *The Griquas of Griqualand*, Juta, Cape Town, 1949.
J. Van Der Peel, *The Jameson Raid*, O.U.P., 1951.
B. Williams, *Cecil Rhodes*, Constable, 1921.
L. M. Thompson, *The Unification of South Africa, 1902–10*, O.U.P., 1960.
Ruth First, *South West Africa*, Penguin Books, 1963.

24 Nationalism in South Africa

COLIN LEGUM

SOUTH AFRICA'S historical development has produced not one but three nationalist movements. They have their origins in centuries of conflict between the two white communities on the one hand—the Afrikaners (or Boers) and the English-speaking South Africans (the British)—and, on the other hand, between the two white groups and the Africans (the Bantu-speaking tribes). The conflict between 'Boer and Bantu' followed on the first European settlement in the Cape of Good Hope (now the Cape Province) in 1652. More than a century later the conflict between 'Boer and Briton' began with the British occupation of the Cape in 1795. While the British and the Boers fought intermittently against each other until the beginning of the twentieth century, at other times they combined with each other to fight against African tribes.

NOMENCLATURE

Boer is synonymous with Afrikaner. Its ordinary meaning in Dutch is farmer and the early Dutch settlers were mostly farmers on the frontiers. They were sturdy, independent-minded frontiersmen who were proud to be described as Boers to distinguish themselves from the officials of the Dutch East India Company which was responsible for opening up the Cape route to the east. The Boers later came to be known as Afrikaners (which means Africans) and their new language was called Afrikaans. There are today 1,800,000 Afrikaners. They are the largest white group in the Republic.

The British element regards itself as English-speaking South African, not as English or British. Their only loyalty is to South Africa, and although they speak English most know nothing about England. This was not always so. Before the Union of South Africa was created in 1910, the British in South Africa felt themselves to be British and maintained close ties with the mother country. But after 1910 they increasingly cut themselves off from Britain; they have come to accept a single loyalty to South Africa. There are almost 1,200,000 English-speaking South Africans.

The Bantu peoples, i.e. the Africans, include many tribes like the Zulu, Xhosa, Basuto, Bapedi. Bantu is not the name of any particular tribe; it applies to a large number of tribes with certain linguistic affinities which live in areas stretching from Eastern Nigeria in the west and Kenya in the east all the way down to the Cape Province. Bantu simply means the people. But its use as a political description is resented by Africans in the republic because the Afrikaners, who used to call them 'kaffirs', or more politely, 'natives', refuse as a matter of political principle to call them Africans and officially describe them as Bantu.

These three elements, Boer (Afrikaner), Briton (English-speaking South African) and African (Bantu), have been involved in a three-sided struggle for power over three centuries. Each side has tried either to dominate the other two or to avoid being dominated by the others, but, while Boer and British rivalries remained keen until the 1930s, the permanent feature of the relationship between the races in South Africa has been the desire of the two communities of European stock to maintain white supremacy over the Africans. This triangular struggle for power produced three types of nationalism: Afrikaner, African and South African.

The exclusive nature of Afrikaner nationalism and South African nationalism reflects their determination to maintain a political society based on white supremacy. The political, economic and social domination of the white minority over the black majority has been the *status quo* in South Africa ever since 1652. This action by the white communities produced as its reaction African nationalism.

To understand these modern nationalist movements it is necessary first to describe briefly the conditions which gave rise to them.

A WHITE ARISTOCRACY

The enduring reality of South Africa's modern historical development is the establishment and maintenance in South Africa of an aristocracy in which all whites—irrespective of origin, religion or accomplishment—are entitled to share fully, and from which all non-whites—irrespective of their accomplishments or qualifications—are virtually excluded. This pattern, as Chapter 21 has shown, evolved in the early decades of white settlement in the middle of the seventeenth century. It was the creation not of the Dutch East India Company but of the settlers themselves. Official and church policy tried hard at first to draw the social line, not between the races but between 'Christians and barbarians'. Van Riebeeck held this to be the proper distinction between 'civilised' and 'uncivilised' peoples. And, indeed, for two centuries the Dutch Reformed Church upheld the principles of the oneness of all Christians. 'The issue was not what a man's colour was, but whether he was a member of the Christian Church.' It was not until 1857 that the races were separated in the Dutch Reformed Church.

Racial co-mingling had reached the point within sixteen years of the founding of the colony where intimacy between whites and non-whites was denounced as a 'disgrace to the Netherlands and other Christian nations'. In 1685 intermarriage was forbidden officially between whites and freed slave-women. But although the early settlers were prepared, at first, to worship with non-whites and to cohabit with them, they were not prepared to work with them. Right from the start a caste system based on labour was erected. All hard work was regarded as 'kaffir work' and socially degrading.

This reluctance to do any hard work became 'a way of life', with taboos, religious and social sanctions to justify it. Within a single generation the foundations were laid of a society of masters and servants; of black servants and white masters; of superiors and inferiors; of people with inherent privileges and of others with inherent duties. Writing of the settlers in the eighteenth century General Janssens said 'they describe themselves as humans and Christians, and the Kaffirs and Hottentots as heathens; and by believing in this they permit themselves everything'. Whenever they needed more land they moved the frontier and took what they wanted. Soon it was observed that 'the common Europeans have become gentlemen, and they desire to be well attended upon . . .' By the end of the eighteenth century a young Dutch seaman could describe the outlines of a social system which is still what prevails today: 'From his youth onwards, accustomed to call for slaves, he (the Afrikaner) believes that he is elevated above all and may only be obeyed. . . .'

From 1836 when this master-servant society appeared to be threatened in the Cape by the British overlord—who had become permanently established in 1806—frontiersmen trekked into the interior to found new republics in the Orange Free State and the

Transvaal, and to establish settlements in Natal, Bechuanaland and beyond. One of the reasons set forth in Piet Retief's Manifesto of 1837 was that they 'should adopt such regulations as will maintain the proper relationships between master and servant'. Both the Boer republics wrote into their constitutions that citizens should consist of *all white citizens*. 'All masters, all farmers, all Gentlemen,' wrote the Rev. D. van der Hoff of the Transvaal Republicans in 1858.

Although this white aristocracy was founded by the Afrikaners, it was accepted and defended by the successive waves of immigrants into the Cape; by the French Huguenots (who merged with the Dutch settlers) at the end of the seventeenth century; by the British settlers in the early nineteenth century; and by the German immigrants in the second half of the nineteenth century. Whatever the bitter quarrels that divided them, once the tribes rose on the frontiers, the whites 'drew laager' together. This attitude was characteristically described by a delegation of Boers who called on Mr Joseph Chamberlain in 1903. 'It is necessary to make it plain to the natives that the war (the South African War) altered the relations between the two white races, but not between the White and Coloured population of the country.'

The 'aristocratic society' was originally adopted as the way of life of frontiersmen, but it was taken over and refashioned to meet the new circumstances of an urbanised society at the end of the nineteenth century when the discovery of gold and diamonds caused the onset of industrialisation. The Masters' and Servants' Act regulated these relationships; and it was buttressed by a wide range of complementary legislation. Not even the growth of an industrial working class of Europeans could weaken it. White workers even staged a full-scale revolt in 1922 to uphold what is still called the 'civilised labour policy'. There were good economic reasons compelling white workers to fight against 'cheap labour', but the result was to establish and entrench an economic colour bar as a corollary to the social colour bar. Thus it was not class but colour that determined the privileges of the white aristocracy. Seen in this perspective it is easy to understand why perhaps four-fifths of all whites in the Union, irrespective of whether they speak Afrikaans or English, or whether they are rich or poor, agree on the need to maintain their aristocracy. Professor P. V. Pistorius has summed up the crux of this conflict in modern political terms:

'The bare and unashamed fact is that the European needs the Native as a labourer, but that he is not prepared to allow him to cross the economic colour bar nor to give him political equality'.

This white aristocracy required for its way of life a plenitude of land; if this meant a scarcity for those outside the charmed circle, so much the better: landless peasants are essential to an expanding labour market. There is room for argument about how land was acquired in the first place; but there is no dispute about the outcome. Today the whites in South Africa own all but one-eighth of the land. Africans are not allowed to buy land except in native reserve areas which measure $17\frac{1}{2}$ million morgen ($12\cdot9$ per cent) of the Union's area. These are broken up into 264 separate units.

Except in the earliest years of frontier settlement the weight of development in South Africa has been against a vertical territorial demarcation between the races. The Great Trek (1836–8) finally wiped out all frontiers, and the steady absorption of land by the expanding white communities drove the Africans into smaller land units. The majority came to work on the white farms and in the white industries and towns. Two-thirds of all Africans live in and among the whites, where they are segregated residentially and socially. This is the traditional segregation pattern. The overall pattern is that of communities of whites encircled by vastly greater numbers of personal black servants and other workers. 'Always,' President Paul Kruger wrote, 'the new immigrant's first concern was to get Coloured labour.' That was so on the farms, and it was so when mining and industrialisation sucked millions of workers into the new towns.

The total effect of land policy and of the social and economic pressures has been to force non-whites into what are regarded as white areas. As a result these white areas have become steadily 'black'. The distribution of Africans at the last census was over four million in the Native Reserves, about five million in the so-called white rural areas and 3,500,000 in white urban areas.

SOUTH AFRICAN NATIONALISM

The English-speaking people of South Africa failed to produce their own distinctive nationalism. Instead, after union in 1910, the English-speaking community promoted the idea of merging all the whites into a single South African nation based on two languages (English and Afrikaans). An important section of Afrikaners identified themselves with this aspiration. They were led by men like General Louis Botha, the Commander-in-Chief of the Boer Forces in the South African War and the First Premier of the Union; Field-Marshal J. C. Smuts, who won renown not only as a Prime Minister but also as an imperial statesman and philosopher; and Mr Jan Hofmeyer, the leader of liberalism among the whites. The political outcome of this idea was the creation in 1934 of the United Party. It formed the government until 1948, and is now the official opposition in Parliament.

After South Africa became a republic in 1960, Afrikaner nationalism also adopted this aspiration of a single white nation, but under Afrikaner leadership.

The common feature of Afrikaner nationalism and South African nationalism is that both are *exclusive* nationalisms: they exclude certain groups from thei ideas of the nation. Thus Afrikaner nationalism excluded the Africans and, until lately, the English-speaking community; and South African nationalism excluded the Africans. African nationalism, on the other hand, has always been *inclusive* in that it aspired to include into a single nation all peoples, irrespective of their origins, who regard South Africa as their only homeland.

THE RISE OF AFRIKANER NATIONALISM

The most militant and the most effective of the nationalist movements in South Africa is that of the Afrikaners. Its two traditional 'enemies' are the British and the Africans. In the first phase of their nationalism the Boers not only rejected Dutch rule but Dutch culture as well. Their desire to become a distinctive national group led them to evolve a language of their own, Afrikaans, which, though rooted in Dutch, is a separate language with a literature of its own. The struggle for an independent language ('the taal') was a notable factor in creating national-consciousness in the last quarter of the nineteenth century. It provided Afrikaner nationalism with an important cultural weapon.

Right from the start the Boers saw themselves, and they still do, as 'God's chosen people' to bring 'civilisation' to 'the barbarians'. To fulfil this 'sacred mission' they feel themselves called to maintain their 'blood purity', their religion and their culture; otherwise they fear that because of their numerical smallness they would be 'drowned in the sea of barbarians'. They believe it necessary for the fulfilment of their 'higher purposes' in Africa that they must keep political control in the hands of 'white civilisation' by maintaining complete political and social segregation between whites and non-whites. Fortified by this belief in their 'divine duty' and armed with the Bible and the gun, the Boers felt themselves to be invincible. There was in Afrikaner nationalism 'a sense of having been called and chosen . . . a belief in a kind of supernatural or mystic creation of the Afrikaner nation'.[1]

Afrikaner nationalism took root in the Eastern Cape among the Boer frontiersmen. They were ruggedly individualistic, except when they felt themselves to be threatened by the Xhosa-speaking peoples on whose territory, as previous chapters have shown, they progressively encroached: then they combined for security. For three-quarters of a century from 1775 the frontiersmen fought nine wars with the Bantu tribes, which resulted in their continuous expansion into the interior. Their Great Trek out of the Cape (1836-9) produced a scattering of Afrikaners all over the interior, and led to the establishment of the two Boer republics, the Transvaal (whose most famous President was Paul Kruger) and the Orange Free State. The Great Trek and the formation of their own republics consolidated the Afrikaners' national-consciousness. But it also brought them greater dangers because the deeper they penetrated into the interior the more numerous their African 'enemy', and the less they could count on the support of the colonial power in the Cape. Their nationalism relied for its physical superiority not on numbers but on fire-power: even the famed spears of the Zulu armies (impis) were no match for their weapons.

Having subdued the Bantu tribes by war and enforced treaties, the emerging Afrikaner societies in the two Boer republics were still left to contend with their second 'enemy', the British.

The Boers' greatest desire in trekking away from the Cape was to 'throw off the British yoke' and to establish their own way of life, free from alien control. But the British empire had its own interests in the interior of South Africa. It was especially interested in the Kimberley diamond fields, the Witwatersrand goldfields, and in keeping the route open to the north. The harder the British pushed the Boers the more tenaciously they fought back. Their deadliest foe was the great financier, Cecil John Rhodes, who had great influence in London. This is why Afrikaner nationalism developed a special hatred for 'international finance' which, in its mythology, it caricatured as Hoggenheimer. When Rhodes's agent, Dr Jameson, led a raid into the Transvaal in 1897, Afrikaners in all parts of South Africa reacted in unison to demand justice for Kruger's Transvaal republic. This national-consciousness among the Boers in the Cape, Natal, the Orange Free State and the Transvaal showed for the first time that the Afrikaner nation had in fact come into existence. Its new-found sense of unity was promoted by the three-year South African War fought between Boer and Briton from 1899–1901.

But although this new nation was defeated militarily it was not conquered. The Afrikaner spirit remained alive in political, religious and cultural organisations. The Dutch Reformed Church was the 'Church of the Boer Nation'. The Society of True Afrikaners formed in 1875, and the Journal *Die Patriot* (The Patriot) founded in 1876, fanned the Afrikaners' sense of injustice and inspired them to be 'true to the volk' (the people). The Afrikaner Bond had been formed in the Cape in 1879: it was the forerunner of the Afrikaner Nationalist Party. The view the Afrikaners formed of their historic mission at that time is shown in an appeal to join the Bond issued in 1886.

> Just think from whom we Afrikaners are descended. We are largely descendants of poor refugees on account of their belief, from European countries, who earned their freedom in South Africa, at that stage still a wilderness, full of vermin and barbarous tribes. Just think how our forefathers fought and struggled to ensure their freedom and our freedom, and how many of them had to sacrifice their lives. They strove for their freedom in that desert region full of wild animals and barbarous races from Table Bay to Natal Bay, but all of no avail; they were driven out.

The British had been strongly divided over the South African War and a Liberal government decided in 1907 to restore freedom to the defeated Boer republics in order to create an independent unified state. Thus was born the Union of South Africa in 1910. But the Afrikaner nationalists were not to be thus easily conciliated. They saw the Union as a British 'creation', infused with British ideas, and dominated by people whose 'home country' was

Britain. Those of their numbers who had joined with the British to form the first Union government were denounced as 'traitors' to the Afrikaner people. The leader of this twentieth-century Afrikaner nationalist movement was General J. B. M. Hertzog. Its basic aim was to assert the will of the Afrikaners as supreme in the Union of South Africa. In 1912 Hertzog formed the Afrikaner National Party which finally won for Afrikanerdom complete political power on its programme of 'apartheid' in 1948. But, by then, Hertzog had abandoned the Afrikaner nationalists in favour of the movement for South African nationalism which he temporarily joined in 1934. His successors were Dr D. F. Malan, Mr J. G. Strijdom and Dr H. F. Verwoerd.

The reaction of Afrikaner nationalism to British attempts at domination showed signs of feelings of injustice and frustration. 'There was a feeling of inferiority, of having been insulted, of having been looked down upon, and of having had honour and dignity offended. There was also a sense of suppression and subjection that led to indignation and grievances.'[2]

Yet Afrikaner nationalism showed no awareness that Africans might react in exactly the same way to their attempts at domination as they had themselves reacted to the British. But this is precisely what happened. In the same year, 1912, that General Hertzog formed his Afrikaner National Party, Africans formed their Native National Congress (later renamed the African National Congress).

THE RISE OF AFRICAN NATIONALISM

Between the seventeenth and nineteenth centuries when Afrikaner nationalism was rising to its position of dominance, the Bantu tribes fought their battles separately. There was not attempt to create a 'Black Front' for common defence. The first leader to think in terms of such an alliance was Cetewayo of the royal household of Shaka who became King of the Zulus in 1873. Although the Zulu army had been defeated by the Boers at the battle of Blood River in 1838, its power was still unbroken. Cetewayo wanted to keep his army intact until his diplomacy could produce joint action by the tribal armies in the Boer republics and in Natal. But before his plans came to anything the British authorities in Natal launched a military campaign in 1879 to destroy the military strength of the Zulu state once and for all.

Cetewayo was taken prisoner and sent to England where he was lionised. Although he was later restored to his throne it was over a broken and divided kingdom. He died in 1884, but his ideas of forming a 'Black Front' lived on.

The pioneers of modern African nationalism came mainly from the generation of mission-educated men in Natal and, especially, in the Cape Province where, under the influence of British liberalism, education opportunities up to university standard were available for an elite group in the last quarter of the nineteenth century. In the Cape, too, the right to vote as equal citizens was granted to men of education irrespective of race in 1852. By the beginning of the present century there was a small but influential African elite, some of whom had taken their degrees in England and America.

The doyen of the Cape African intellectuals was John Tengo Jabavu, who held a university degree and owned his own paper *Imvo Zabantsundu* (African Opinion). A staunch Christian and supporter of the Cape liberals, he favoured the idea of white and black collaboration to achieve justice for his people.

Jabavu's ideas did not appeal to his contemporary Dr Pixley Ka I. Seme who was also strongly influenced by Cetewayo's ideas. Pixley Seme had worked his way up, with the help of missionaries, from herdsboy to barrister, with university training in both England and America. He liked to dress like a gentleman with top hat and striped trousers; but he was a fierce nationalist and a believer in the role of the chiefs in the fight for African political rights. His close collaborator was the Rev. John Llangalakhe Dube, heir to a Zulu chieftaincy, who had been educated in America. On his return home Dube established both a college and a newspaper in Natal. Neither Seme nor Dube, however, favoured black domination in place of white; they merely insisted on racial equality.

Bambata was a leader of a different order. A minor Zulu chief, he was the last of the tribal leaders to put his faith in violent resistance to white domination. His effort to defend his lands by rebellion in 1906 was crushed; but Bambata's example inspired some of the rising young nationalists.

The three paths to African freedom pointed by these leaders— co-operation with whites, black unity and violent resistance—have all had their supporters in the rise of African nationalism. But the strongest influence was that of the nationalists who believed in black-white co-operation.

Modern African nationalism grew out of the fear that the British decision to disengage from its colonial role in South Africa would result in the Africans being handed over—voiceless and without rights or protection—to the white minority. Africans heard with amazement the future foreseen for the Union of South Africa by the British High Commissioner, Lord Milner, in 1908: 'The ultimate end is a self-governing white community supported by well-treated and justly-governed black labour.' These anxieties mounted when—despite protests, petitions and delegations to London—the National Convention which was to draft a constitution for the new Union was confined to whites only. Their worst fears were quickly confirmed. For the sake of 'white unity' the Convention agreed that while the franchise for non-whites should remain in the Cape it would not apply to any of the three other provinces. One of the, first measures taken by the new Union Parliament was to introduce a Land Act (finally passed in 1913) which permanently froze the land Africans could buy for their own occupation to roughly one-eighth of the entire land area of the country. Thus the white aristocracy entrenched by law their physical possession of seven-eighths of South Africa.

If the exclusion of Africans from the National Convention was felt to be a betrayal, the enactment of the Land Act was the taste of its first bitter fruit. 'Awaking on Friday morning, June 20, 1913, the South African Native found himself, not actually a slave, but a pariah in the land of his birth.' So wrote Sol T. Plaatje, a largely self-educated African journalist and author of *Native Life in South Africa*. Plaatje, who was proficient in German, Dutch, English and several African languages and who had met Dr Du Bois and other Pan-Africanist leaders in Europe and America, was one of the African leaders who congregated in the Orange Free State capital, Bloemfontein, in January 1912 to form the South African Native Congress. (In 1935 it was renamed the African National Congress.) There were teachers, lawyers, clergymen, clerks, messengers and servants. Many were chiefs. Some wore frock coats and top hats. They opened the meeting with prayers and sang Nkosi Sikelel i-Afrika ('God Bless Africa') composed by a Xhosa musician, Enoch Sontonga. (It has since become the national anthem not only of black South Africans but of Africans throughout

Central and East Africa.) Pixley Seme, in the opening speech, declared:

> We have discovered that in the land of their birth, Africans are treated as hewers of wood and drawers of water. The white people of this country have formed what is known as the Union of South Africa—a Union in which we have no voice in the making of the laws and no part in the administration. We have called you, therefore, to this conference so that we can together find ways and means of forming *our* national union for the purpose of creating national unity and defending our rights and privileges.

The objectives of Congress were declared 'to encourage mutual understanding and to bring together into common action as one political people all tribes and clans of various tribes or races, and by means of combined effort and united political organisation to defend their freedom, rights and privileges'.

The issues on which Congress fought hardest in its earliest years were the right to the vote, the land question, the Pass Laws and the Masters' and Servants' Act. The Pass Laws control the free movement of African peoples. No adult African may move freely without a permit, 'the pass', and a certificate showing he has paid his taxes. Africans were compelled to carry with them at all times no fewer than nine passes. The Masters' and Servants' Act makes it a criminal offence for a servant to leave the employ of his master until his contract has expired.

EFFECTS OF INDUSTRIALISATION

Industrialisation, which at first came slowly upon South Africa, has in the last quarter century made it the most economically advanced country in the continent. At every stage of its development, Africans, though indispensable to its growth, were brought under increasing restraints. From its inception, the South African economy has rested on a system of migratory labour which has militated against Africans becoming a permanent part of the urban and industrial community. Its effect has been to encourage African males to leave their families in the impoverished reserves (the areas set aside for exclusive African occupation) while they go out to work for a period of years in the mines and factories, and on white farms. This system has affected African family life and contributed to the impoverishment of the reserves' agriculture.

The migratory labour system has for decades been reinforced by other restrictive measures which prevent Africans from benefiting as fully as other racial groups from the country's prosperous industrial life. The Mines and Works Act and the Native Building Workers Act restrict Africans from doing any kind of skilled work in 'white areas'. These segregation laws were all applied in different degrees long before apartheid became the accepted policy of the country in 1948.

In the 1860s there was almost no wage-earning class in the country. By 1910 there were, in the mining industry alone, 25,000 whites and 195,000 Africans. Within half a century, by 1960, there were 1,140,000 whites in industrial and commercial employment, 3,439,000 Africans and 6,674,000 Asians and Coloureds. Thus the Africans comprised sixty-five per cent of the total working population.

In 1960 the country's national income was over £2,135 million. The average income per head of population (white and non-white) was about £133 a year. This places it about halfway between the very rich and the very poor countries of the world.

The distribution of South Africa's wealth shows how political dominance can ensure economic dominance. In 1946–7 (shortly before the Afrikaner nationalists came to power) the average annual wage and salary for whites was £405·7; for Asians and Coloureds £167·3; and for Africans £100·2. In the first twelve years of Afrikaner rule (by 1960–1) the average annual income of whites had more than doubled to about £1,000, while African wages had risen to just under £185 per annum, and Asians and Coloureds to almost £295 per annum. The gap between white and African wages had, therefore, widened even farther. Although nearly two out of three workers in the South African economy are Africans, their rewards (on average) are below one-fifth of those received by whites, and much less than those of Asians and Coloureds.

AFRICAN NATIONALIST TACTICS

The methods used in the African nationalist struggle were in the main constitutional. They presented petitions, sent delegations to the authorities and made representations through the Native Representative Council, a purely advisory body set up in 1936 as a substitute for the African right to vote or to be represented in Parliament. Periodically they staged demonstrations and they gradually developed the techniques of non-violent passive resistance based on Gandhi's teachings.

None of these methods was successful. So far from achieving reforms, the laws became tougher as the years went by. These failures kept the African National Congress weak. They produced rival organisations such as the All African Convention which tried to adopt the method of boycott: total non-collaboration with the authorities and with white liberal organisations. Some Africans turned to the Communist Party, but this was no more successful and contributed to creating further divisions within the nationalist movement. One of the most successful nationalist movements was the Industrial and Commercial Workers Union formed in the late 1920s by a fiery Nyasaland worker in Johannesburg, Clements Kadalie, and a rebellious Zulu leader, A. W. G. Champion. But it, too, failed in the end. Its importance lay in the fact that it was the first nationalist organisation which tried to base itself on the urban African working class.

BACKGROUND TO APARTHEID

The reason why these African movements were so unsuccessful was largely due to economic weakness and the vulnerability of Africans to legal repression, backed by police and military force. Throughout this century the African societies in the towns and rural areas were continuously changing to adjust to the new conditions imposed by an authoritarian modernising state. Poverty and the break-up of family life were the chief concern of the peasants in the reserves; in the urban areas the growing proletariat and middle class were caught up in the exciting but painful experience of becoming townsmen. Those who managed to achieve some security and a stake in the economy were often reluctant to risk the little they had by joining in political action.

Despite the imposition of legal discrimination over virtually every aspect of African life, the situation had some positive features as well. Up to 1948 the segregation practices were unevenly applied, and the economic forces swept Africans into higher positions in commerce and industry notwithstanding the industrial colour bar. Progress in education was especially marked, although higher education was confined to a small proportion of Africans.

Down the years from 1912 the leadership of the African nationalists remained largely in the hands of the middle class: professors, teachers, lawyers, clerks, ministers. They were at the same time more sophisticated and more cautious in their choice of political weapons. Nevertheless, as African labour became more important with the growth of industrialisation and as larger numbers of Africans became educated and urbanised, there was a notable change in the mood of Africans about accepting their status as second-class citizens. So, even while the African nationalist organisations remained weak, the clamour of Africans to be given a voice in the country's affairs grew louder. With the sudden, rapid expansion of industry during the Second World War, Africans flooded into the towns, their labour was wanted and, under the exigencies of war, they were allowed to do work previously reserved for whites only. They demanded, and got, higher wages. They entered the trade unions. The white aristocracy suddenly awoke to the massive presence of Africans in its midst. They saw leaders who were often as well educated and sophisticated as themselves; and they heard them voice demands in terms of modern politics: Human Rights, The Atlantic Charter, Christian brotherhood, one-man-one-vote. The white aristocracy awoke to the fact that they were faced with a new challenge and new decisions: either to go forward to full economic integration and political democracy, or to retreat into a new and harsher struggle to defend white supremacy.

In the 1948 elections a minority of the white electorate won enough seats in Parliament to take South Africa along the second road. The first all-Afrikaner government took power with their new policy of apartheid.

THE NATURE OF APARTHEID

Apartheid can be quite simply defined as 'setting the races apart'. There is, of course, nothing intrinsically new about such a policy in South Africa: the idea of segregation, or separation, has been a feature of the country's policy throughout its modern existence. What makes apartheid different from previous policies is that it presents separation as an ideology; like all ideologies, it

had to be applied totally and rigidly, regardless of any consequences.

Although some advocates of apartheid believe that its aim
should be to divide the country gradually into completely separate
white and black territories, this is not official policy. Its aim is
restricted to creating Bantustans, or black states, in that one-eighth
part of the country, the reserves, retained for the exclusive use of
Africans. Africans, however, are still to be encouraged to come and
work in the so-called 'white part' of the country, but on the clear
understanding that they are to have no rights there. Under the
Bantu Laws Amendment Act, no African can claim the right to live
or work in the 'white areas', not even if he was born there or had
lived all or most of his life in a particular place.

The doctrine of apartheid proposed that Africans should be
allowed political and economic rights only in the Bantustans. (So
far, only one, the Transkei, has been established.) As far as seven-
eighths of the country is concerned Africans will be regarded as
'sojourners'.

The objectives and methods of apartheid are best illustrated by
the laws adopted since 1948, of which the following are typical.
The Population Registration Act introduced a rigid system of race
classification so that every person could be put into a separate
water-tight compartment. The Prohibition of Mixed Marriages
Act and the Immorality Amendment Act prohibited marriages or
sexual relations between members of different races. The Group
Areas Act provided for total residential segregation between the
different races. The Native Laws Amendment Act restricted
African visits to white areas in which they are not resident or
employed to up to seventy-two hours without a permit; thereafter
it is a criminal offence for them to be there at all, even if they
happen to be the wives or children of the person they are visiting.
It also empowered the authorities to remove any African who is
unemployed, 'idle, or undesirable' to one of the reserves. The
Natives (Urban Areas) Amendment Act gave the authorities
powers to order an African to leave an area if they considered his
presence to be detrimental to peace and order. The Industrial
Conciliation Act and the Native Labour (Settlement of Disputes)
Act prohibited 'mixed' trade unions, and prevented Africans from
operating trade unions on the same basis as whites. The Job
Reservation Act enabled the Minister of Labour to reserve any

category of work for a particular race; this has been used mainly to secure jobs for whites and, in the Cape, for Coloureds—always at the expense of Africans.

Although measures like these have brought economic and social hardship, few have been as bitterly resented as the Bantu Education Act and the Extension of University Education. When he introduced the first of these Acts, Dr Verwoerd said: Education must train and teach people in accordance with their opportunities in life, according to the sphere in which they live. Apart from establishing different curricula and standards for the education of whites and blacks, the Act limits the amount of money to be spent on African education by the state (there is no such limit on the amount available for white education); additional expenditure must be paid for by Africans themselves. A measurable result of this policy is that seven years after its enforcement there were only 716 African entrants for matriculation in 1960 (as against 547 in 1953) and of those only 17·9 per cent passed.

So far from extending academic education, the Extension of University Education Act in fact closed the doors of the Open Universities where non-whites had in the past been admitted with white students. In its place separate university colleges were established for Africans, Coloureds and Asians, under conditions different from what is usually associated with academic institutions.

Through such measures apartheid has tried to set apart the races at every point of contact except in employment, where contacts are strictly regulated by laws and regulations.

AFRICAN REACTIONS TO APARTHEID

The African nationalist movement failed utterly to stop the juggernaut of apartheid. In 1952 the African National Congress staged a Defiance Campaign in support of its demands for the repeal of the pass laws and other repressive laws. Volunteers of all races set out deliberately to contravene pass laws, apartheid regulations at railway stations and post offices, etc. By the end of the year over eight thousand volunteers had been arrested. The government made no concessions; instead it intensified the application of apartheid.

Notwithstanding the refusal of the authorities to respond to non-violent pressures and to pleas for peaceful negotiations, African nationalist leaders persisted in their traditional methods of passive resistance, petitions and entreaties for the first twelve years of the apartheid regime. During this time, however, violence began to mount on both sides. In many parts of the country Africans rioted and adopted other violent methods to ventilate their grievances despite their leaders' insistence on non-violence. Counter-action on the government side took the form of police and military repression, a large increase in the expenditure on arms and defence, the wholesale banning of militant leaders of all races, mass trials and the outlawing of nationalist and left-wing organisations.

The reasons why African nationalists and their allies had for so long opposed the use of violence were twofold. First, the Gandhian philosophy of non-violence as a method of waging a liberation struggle was an act of faith among many African leaders. Secondly, even those who did not share this philosophy felt that in any violent conflict the forces at the command of the state were so overwhelmingly strong that African resistance would be crushed and the struggle made even more bitter. Two events were to contribute to changing African nationalist tactics.

The first was the Sharpeville shootings in 1960; the second was the decision to make South Africa a republic in 1961, despite the opposition of a large section of the white community (led by the South African nationalists) and the overwhelming majority of Africans.

During the crucial decade from 1950–60, three leaders had emerged who symbolised the new spirit of African nationalism.

Albert Lutuli, the chief of a small Zulu clan, was elected President-General of the African National Congress in 1952. He was then fifty-four. He had been a teacher before becoming a chief. A staunch Christian and a devoted disciple of the idea of non-violence, the government deposed him from his chieftaincy because he had supported the Defiance Campaign. As leader of Congress he was tried for treason and acquitted; he was assaulted; and he was banned from living in his own home area. Nothing he says or writes may be published anywher e in South Africa. Nevertheless, Lutuli's influence grew rather than diminished in his own country. In 1961 he became the first African ever to win the Nobel Peace Prize, the most coveted award of its kind in the world.

Lutuli succeeded better than any African leader in making

himself 'the father of the nation'. Not only Africans, but influential whites (like the Liberal leader and author, Alan Paton) came to regard him as the best Prime Minister South Africa could choose.

Robert Mongaliso ('the wonderful') Sobukwe belongs to a younger generation of Africans. From his student days at Fort Hare College he showed himself to be a militant nationalist. Later, as a lecturer at the predominantly white University of Witwatersrand in Johannesburg he continued to play a leading role in the A.N.C.'s Youth Wing. But after the Defiance Campaign he became increasingly critical of what he regarded as a lack of militant leadership by the 'Old Guard'. He was especially critical of the close alliance between the A.N.C. and the white, Indian and Coloured congresses, as well as with the role of the Communists in the nationalist movement. In 1958 Sobukwe's Pan-Africanist Congress (P.A.C.) emerged from the A.N.C. as a separate movement dedicated to building an Africanist, socialist and non-racial nation. Sobukwe taught that in the immediate struggle for freedom each of the racial communities should organise on its own. (Later, however, the P.A.C. admitted white members to its ranks.) Even so, Sobukwe did not propose violent action but talked of mass action based on effective organisation.

Sobukwe's first call for 'mass action' came on 21 March 1960. Having torn up their passes, Sobukwe and his lieutenants marched in their bare feet to Johannesburg police headquarters, inviting arrest. At Sharpeville, an African township, thirty-five miles from Johannesburg, police opened fire on a large crowd, killing 69 and wounding 180 people. In Cape Town 50,000 tried to march on Parliament; troops were called out and a state of emergency was declared. Sobukwe was sent to prison for four years and subsequently banished indefinitely to Robben Island.

Nelson Rolihlala Mandela was the youngest of this trio of new leaders. He is member of the royal family of the Tembu, and defied his family to go to university at Fort Hare. With another student, Oliver Tambo, who later became his law partner and deputy to Lutuli, Mandela joined Sobukwe among the militants in the A.N.C. Youth Wing. When Lutuli was banned, Mandela took over active leadership of the A.N.C. Because he was wanted by the police he had to lead an underground life; his skill in evading arrest earned him the title of the 'Black Pimpernel'. In May 1961 he called for a nation-wide strike to coincide with South

Africa becoming a republic. But this was unsuccessful. A month later he and a few colleagues took the momentous decision that as violence was inevitable, it would be unrealistic and wrong for the African leaders to continue preaching peace and non-violence at a time when the government met peaceful demands with force. They decided to form *Umkonto We Sizwe* (The Spear of the Nation), an underground movement committed to sabotage and violence (but not against persons). Meanwhile P.A.C. and a group of white liberals had formed their own sabotage groups. Thus with the birth of the Republic of South Africa, the fulfilment of which marked the highest aspiration of Afrikaner nationalism, there ended a chapter in the history of the African nationalists' dedication to non-violent resistance.

When Mandela was finally arrested he was sent to Robben Island to serve a life sentence. Facing his judges, Mandela refused to deny any of the charges brought against him. His last words to them were:

> During my lifetime I have dedicated myself to this struggle of the African people. I have fought against white domination, and I have fought against black domination. I have cherished the ideal of a democratic and free society in which all persons live together in harmony and with equal opportunities. It is an ideal which I hope to live for and to achieve. But if needs be, it is an ideal for which I am prepared to die.

Different though their paths have been, there is little that separates Lutuli, Sobukwe and Mandela in their objectives. Sobukwe defines the purpose of African nationalism as:

> . . . government of the African, by the African, for the African, with everybody who owes his only loyalty to Africa and who is prepared to accept the democratic rule of an African majority, being regarded as an African. We guarantee no minority rights because we think in terms of individuals not groups.

Chief Lutuli has expressed the same idea more crisply:

> We all stand for non-racial democracy where colour is irrelevant.

But in South Africa today colour is still the most relevant factor in its politics and lies at the heart of the struggle between its conflicting nationalisms.

NOTES

1 F. A. van Jaarsveld, *The Awakening of Afrikaner Nationalism, 1868–1881,* Human & Rousseau, Cape Town, 1961.
2 F. A. van Jaarsveld, op. cit.

QUESTIONS FOR FURTHER STUDY AND DISCUSSION

1 Describe the reasons for the growth of Afrikaner nationalism.
2 What do you understand by the policy of apartheid?
3 African nationalism in South Africa chose a policy of non-violence for fifty years. Discuss the reasons for this.
4 Chief Albert Lutuli is the first African to have been awarded the Nobel Prize for Peace. Describe his role in South Africa's political life.
5 The age-old conflict between 'Boer, Briton and Bantu' has now resolved itself into a direct conflict between Afrikaner nationalism and African nationalism. Describe the dominant attitudes reflected in these two opposing types of nationalism.
6 South Africa is the most highly developed industrial society in the continent. Describe the positive and negative results of this development.

SELECT BIBLIOGRAPHY

M. Benson, *The African Patriots,* Faber & Faber, 1963.
—— *Chief Albert Lutuli of South Africa,* O.U.P., 1964.
C. and M. Legum, *South Africa: Crisis for the West,* Pall Mall, 1964.
P. van Rensburg, *Guilty Land,* Jonathan Cape, 1962.
J. Ngubane, *An African Explains Apartheid,* Praeger, New York, 1963.
W. H. Hutt, *The Economics of the Colour Bar,* O.U.P.
S. Pienaar and A. Sampson, *South Africa,* O.U.P., 1960.
I. B. Tabata, *Education for Barbarism in South Africa,* Pall Mall, 1960.
L. Marquand, *The Peoples and Policies of South Africa,* O.U.P., 3rd edition, 1962.
S. T. Plaatje, *Native Life in South Africa,* King, 3rd edition, 1916.
F. A. Van Jaarsveld, *The Awakening of Afrikaner Nationalism, 1868–1881,* Human & Rousseau, Cape Town, 1961.
E. Roux, *Time Longer than Rope,* University of Wisconsin Press, 2nd edition, 1964.
A. Lutuli, *Let My People Go,* Collins, 1962.
B. Modisane, *Blame Me on History,* Thames & Hudson, 1963.

25 The Omani Empire and its Impact on East African Societies

J. C. ANENE

THE east coast of Africa from very early times attracted the attention of merchant adventurers from southern Arabia and India. This was primarily due to a remarkable geographical phenomenon: every December the monsoon begins to blow from the north-east and continues with remarkable consistency till the end of February; from April to September the process is reversed and the monsoon blows from the south-west. Arab traders from the coast of Arabia could therefore sail eastwards to India, then cross the Indian Ocean to East Africa, and sail back after a few months' sojourn devoted to trading. The coast of East Africa witnessed therefore the comings and goings of merchants from Arabia and from western India. In continental Africa the Bantu had made their way to East Africa, to be followed by other linguistic groups called the Nilo-Hamites, the Galla and the Somali. No precise details are available concerning the early movements of peoples in East Africa, but there can be no doubt that Bantu Africans made their way to the coast, and that, through them, the trade of the hinterland flowed to the coast where Asians exchanged lances, hatchets, glass and so on for African ivory, tortoise-shell, rhinoceros-horn, gold and slaves.

It is not known when merchants from Arabia and India began to settle on the east coast of Africa. The immigrants learnt the language of the Africans, married local women and were increasingly absorbed by the people among whom they settled. In time commercial communities emerged. These were neither Arab nor African; they were a mingling of many peoples—Arab, Bantu, Indian and even Persian. The east coast of Africa came to be known as the land of the Zinj and the earliest available accounts of its people tell us that they were black or dark-skinned. The upheavals which followed the death of Muhammad in Arabia led to the flight to the coast of East Africa of many refugees from

Arabia. These refugees undoubtedly gave the settlements in East Africa an increasingly Muslim complexion, and many writers have therefore wrongly described the towns of East Africa as Arab colonies. Through inter-marriage and social amalgamation a distinct people known as the Swahili emerged, with a language that was basically Bantu though drawing many words from Arabic. The Swahili civilisation which developed was neither wholly African nor wholly Arab. It was a synthesis of the two.

The chief settlements which grew along the coast and its islands included Mogadishu, Pate, Lamu, Malindi, Kilifi, Mombasa, Pemba, Zanzibar, Mafia, Kilwa, Mozambique and Sofala. They became substantial towns, laid out in regular streets, and possessing impressive houses of stone with large windows, terraces, courtyards and gardens. There were also mosques, exquisitely decorated. When the Portuguese arrived towards the end of the fifteenth century they were astonished at the spectacle of flourishing trade, prosperity and a level of civilisation hardly inferior to that of Europe. Throughout the period of Zinj prosperity, southern Arabia was the great centre of the maritime trade which brought prosperity to all the countries west and east of the Indian Ocean. From here fleets of ships continued to sail down to the East African coast to carry on trade.

The Arab country most closely associated with the East African coast was Oman, which occupies the south-east corner of Arabia. The ruler of the country was given the title of Imām. The most important town was Muscat which became 'a tempting doorway to the life and wealth of the sea'. Men of Oman therefore played a very substantial part not only in the growth of the Indian Ocean trade but also in the foundation of the commercial settlements of East Africa. Their ruler was destined to transfer his court from Muscat to Zanzibar, but this did not occur till the nineteenth century. In the meantime the towns on the east coast of Africa remained separate states. Often there was inter-state strife for political and commercial supremacy, so they were not prepared for concerted effort in the defence of their independence when the Portuguese attacked them during the first decade of the sixteenth century. The Portuguese conquest proved a colossal disaster to the prosperity of the coast settlements. During the two hundred years of Portuguese domination the story was one of decline and poverty. The spirit of independence was not crushed, however, and the

Arab aristocracy in due course turned towards Oman for deliverance from the Portuguese yoke.

OMANI INFLUENCE

It was not until 1650 that the Omani themselves were able to eject the Portuguese from their capital Muscat and from the whole Arabian seaboard. Then, under the energetic Sultan bin Seif, they pursued the Portuguese into East Africa. But the news of Portuguese discomfiture at the hands of the Omani had at once rekindled the old feeling of independence all down the East African coast. Mombasa took the lead in appealing to Sultan bin Seif to rescue his fellow Muslims from the greedy grasp of the Portuguese. Omani attacks on Portuguese positions on the east coast shortly began and enjoyed varying success. Each town which admitted Omani ships or pirates was ferociously punished by the Portuguese, but the latter were a spent force. Near the close of the seventeenth century Oman made an immense effort which culminated in the capture of the most impregnable of the Portuguese forts, Fort Jesus in Mombasa. By 1730 Portuguese power north of Cape Delgado had collapsed. They left behind crumbling walls and dilapidated mosques where two hundred years before they had found beauty and wealth.

If the East African towns thought that the overthrow of Portugal meant the restitution of their former independence they were mistaken. Omani rulers began to claim the overlordship of all the East African coast towns and islands freed from Portuguese control. Governors were appointed by Omani rulers in the more important of the towns, but usually by selecting the heads of the leading local families, e.g. the Mazrui of Mombasa. As Oman was encompassed by long periods of civil strife, Omani rulers could do little to give reality to their claims of overlordship of East Africa, and the spirit of independence grew among the East African local rulers. The Mazrui governor of Mombasa formally repudiated the nominal allegiance to Oman. Most of the other towns did likewise. Towards the end of the eighteenth century all, except Zanzibar and Pemba, were independent.

In 1806 a young Arab of the Omani princely house emerged from the characteristic uncertainties and intrigues of Arab succession as the firm ruler of Oman. The achievement of unity and security at home was a prerequisite of overseas adventure. The new prince, Seyyid Said, now reasonably secure on the throne of Oman, began to revive Omani hereditary claims to overlordship of what they regarded as the 'Arab' towns of the East African coast. The coast towns were as much plagued with disputed successions as Oman and it was this political disease in Lamu and Pate which offered Said opportunities to intervene in their internal affairs. Backed by Omani troops, Said's *protégés* were installed as rulers. In the light of Omani energy and decisive action most of the towns, except Mombasa, formally acknowledged the suzerainty of Oman.

The Mazrui rulers of Mombasa knew that their obduracy would not be ignored indefinitely by the Omani ruler, so they attempted in 1824 to secure British protection. The attempt failed when the British government repudiated the Owen Protectorate, and the British flag was removed from Mombasa in 1826. The anger of the Omani ruler, Said, soon descended on Mombasa in the form of an ultimatum to submit and surrender Fort Jesus. The Mazrui temporised and in the meantime strengthened their defences. Towards the end of 1827 Said sailed with an expeditionary force for Mombasa and began the bombardment of Fort Jesus, but without effect. Said then tried diplomacy and, through a clever stratagem, secured the instalment of Omani forces in the fort. He thereafter sailed for Zanzibar to see for the first time the island that had remained consistently loyal to Oman. Then the news of a rebellion in Oman sent Said rushing back to his homeland.

In the meantime the Mombasa people subjected the Omani troops in Fort Jesus to a relentless siege. A second expedition from Oman, again under Said, opened negotiations with the Mazrui of Mombasa, but for the second time, in 1830, Said had to hurry home because of internal strife. It was becoming increasingly clear to Said that absence from Oman meant strife. His presence, and security at home, appeared inconsistent with a firm permanent hold on the East African coast. So he gradually made up his mind to stake his future in a new Omani dominion in East Africa, and the undisputed control of Mombasa was necessary. In 1835 a disputed succession to the throne of Mombasa played into his hands. On the death of Shaikh Salim, his sons and brothers split into different factions and, after a long period of deadlock, the Arabs and Swahili of Mombasa decided to invite Said of Oman to intervene. Intrigue and bribery were Said's weapons and these succeeded where military expeditions had failed. The rival contestants were banished and were never heard of again.

SAID AND ZANZIBAR

Shortly after, Said decided to transfer his throne to East Africa. There were obvious reasons for this bold decision. East Africa had undoubted physical advantages over the torrid heat and the dust and yellow sand of Oman. Said was probably tired of the interminable intrigues which characterised the internal politics of his country. The choice of Zanzibar as his new capital was brilliant. The island possessed a deep and spacious harbour and he set out to make it, together with the fertile maritime belt on the coast, the centre of a commercial activity which merited its description as the Omani empire of East Africa. A large number of Said's compatriots followed him to Zanzibar, many no doubt attracted like him by the commercial potentialities of the East African dominion. Said's ambition was to create an economic, not a territorial empire, in East Africa. This must be borne in mind in any attempt to appreciate the character of the new era of Arab rule inaugurated by Said.

Said laid the foundations for the systematic exploitation of the resources of the area; as Said himself reportedly confessed to a French visitor, he was nothing if not a merchant. He began with Zanzibar where, before his arrival, the inhabitants had a few palms and grain and the land was on the whole little used. Said forthwith began an experiment which was to produce dramatic results. He planted clove trees which produced the famous spice very much in demand in Europe and encouraged the Zanzibar landlords to follow his example. In a short time the prodigious yield of cloves guaranteed Zanzibar an export crop which came next to ivory and slaves in value.

Said also aimed at unifying the customs and other port duties throughout the Arab-controlled East African coast. Before Said's arrival each coast town had on the whole been a law unto itself; each followed its own devices with regard to custom charges and, in the resulting confusion, trade was retarded and all kinds of irregularities had developed. Now Said removed all obstacles which might restrain the free flow of trade. The only tax was a uniform five per cent import duty. Said's policy of facilitating the flow of trade included the introduction of a new currency. A large number of small copper coins were imported from India and put into circulation at the rate of 135 to the existing 'Maria Theresa dollars'.

Said recognised that his own people, the Arabs, were not skilled in finance. Indian financiers had been behind the many ramifications of the Indian Ocean trade and had proved their financial ability to the Omani rulers. It is not surprising therefore that Said hastened to invite many Indians to his new dominion. The Indians, known locally as the banyans, were despised by the Arabs, but Said took them into his confidence and employed their services in the financial affairs of the 'empire'. The key post of collector of customs was invariably held by an Indian. Said's policy was to farm out the customs revenue and let the Indians do their best to recoup themselves from the actual duties paid at the various towns. The Indians were responsible, too, for financing the systematic expansion of caravan activities which penetrated to all the interior regions of East Africa.

SAID AND THE HINTERLAND

To increase the volume of trade that flowed from the hinterland, i.e. ivory, slaves, gum copal, coconuts, copra and palm oil, Said was interested in extending and affording security to the whole system of inland trade. It is not known for certain to what extent the Arabs had, before Said's arrival, developed the caravan routes which became famous in the nineteenth century. Without substantial finance which the Indians alone could provide and in the disunity which characterised the political relations of the coast settlements, it is reasonable to assume that Arab penetration of the hinterland before Said's arrival must have been haphazard and modest. Certainly after 1840 there was a spectacular increase in Arab hinterland enterprise. More and bigger caravans were organised and opened new areas for exploitation; trading settlements were founded in the hinterland. The routes of these caravans can be divided into three groups: the first ran from Bagamoyo (opposite Zanzibar) to Tabora and thence to the lakes Tanganyika and Victoria; another group of routes radiated from Kilwa to Lake Nyasa and beyond to Katanga; lastly, the most northerly route ran from Tanga to Lake Victoria. The scarlet flag of Zanzibar carried before the caravans symbolised that they enjoyed the protection of Said. The authority and prestige of the Zanzibar ruler must have contributed a great deal to the sense of security with which the Arabs pushed deeper and deeper into the hinterland of East Africa.

The demand for slaves in the clove plantations begun by Said and the Arabs naturally was an important factor in the expansion of the slave trade in the nineteenth century. Slaves were of course

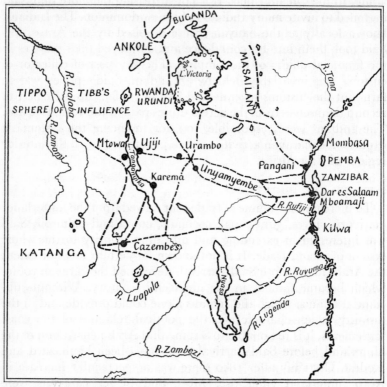

Fig. 24 The main caravan routes of East Africa in the nineteenth century.

still in great demand in Arabia. The European nations were beginning to turn their backs on the slave trade, but their countries needed the other things that East Africa could produce provided good markets could be guaranteed. There was growing demand in Europe and America for ivory, gums and vegetable oils. Said therefore recognised the wisdom of negotiating commercial treaties with the United States, France, Britain and Germany. Consuls from these countries took up residence in Zanzibar during the 1840s, and were no doubt interested in their own export trade in cotton, muskets, gunpowder, brass wire and beads to East Africa.

One important aspect of Arab penetration under Said was the establishment of Arab 'colonies' in the hinterland. These 'colonies' began as collecting centres for slaves, ivory and food for the caravans. A great deal therefore depended on the factors enumerated above, and, where the native Africans were well-organised, the goodwill of the indigenous African ruler was indispensable. For example, the establishment of the strategically placed 'colony' of Tabora was the result of a diplomatic exchange between the ruler of Zanzibar and the Nyamwezi ruler. So too were the settlements in the interlacustrine region west and south of Lake Victoria. A description of a typical trade caravan is given by Coupland in his *East Africa and Its Invaders*. The caravan wound its way in a single file along the narrow forest and jungle track. A native guide carrying the scarlet flag of Zanzibar was followed by a long straggling line of slaves, all carrying on their heads bundles of cloth, beads and coils of wire for trade in tusks, grain and so forth. At intervals along the slave line were a few Swahili with guns. Then the company of Arab merchants who commanded the expedition followed in the rear.

THE CHARACTER OF OMANI RULE

Said's ambition was to be a great middleman in a position to control the trade between East Africa and the rest of the world, and so territorial expansion was not an indispensable part of his plans. However he had to guarantee peace and security where they were vital for trade. The islands of Zanzibar and Pemba were firmly held by the Omani ruler. Even here Said's administration was a simple enough affair. The 'native' inhabitants managed their own affairs, except for a poll-tax which they paid to Said through their chief. The real business of government was concerned with the Arabs, the Indians, the half-castes and the plantation slaves. The administrative structure was the typical patriarchal absolutism of an Arab shaikh. There were no official advisers, no council of ministers; except for the governor and the 'customs master' there were no administrative officers. The business of collecting taxes was in unofficial hands, as Said usually farmed out the customs duties to a leading member of the Indian community. The judicial

30

system was equally simple. The Qur'ān was the recognised code and the Kadi presided over judicial proceedings. Said himself held durbars twice a day and any of his subjects could make a direct appeal to him.

As for the East African coast, there was no doubt that after the fall of Mombasa all the towns from Mogadishu to Lindi acknowledged Said's overlordship. In these places Said installed governors, sometimes an Arab from Zanzibar supported by a token force, sometimes a local man. The governors paid their feudal dues but were left very much to their own devices. Said's only concern was peace and the receipt of customs duties payable to him at every port. Along the coast of what is now Somalia, the towns came under the control of the militant inhabitants of the hinterland. The German missionary, Krapf, summarised the nature o Said's authority on the coast as follows: 'The Arabs and Africans submit to his (Said's) nominal pretensions as long as their own old arrangements are not too stringently interfered with. They receive the Sultan's governors and pay the dues which he levies from their ports; but beyond that Seyyid Said seems to have no hope of their further obedience and subjection.'

Indeed Said wished for no more than the kind of overlordship which guaranteed exclusive commercial and fiscal control and an ever-increasing flow of trade. His rule over the coast is best described as a peculiar kind of protectorate. As regards the hinterland tribes, the attitude of Said was not different from his attitude to the coast towns. Peace was the condition which did not prejudice trade. Even among the weaker tribes like the Nyika in the hinterland of Mombasa Said did not attempt territorial conquest, but ordered chastisement when trade was interfered with. In relations with well-organised African groups, Said relied on mutually satisfactory diplomatic relations in order to guarantee the security of the Arab caravans.

THE IMPACT ON THE AFRICANS

It is necessary to consider a few hinterland groups in order to show the extent of the Zanzibar-Arab influence which Said exercised through the caravans. The largest caravans set out from Zanzibar and were financed by the Indian *protégés* of the Sultan. The caravan leaders were Said's subjects, and it was the scarlet flag of Zanzibar that was held aloft as the caravans pushed their way through the territories of the hinterland inhabitants. With the flag went the name and prestige of the distant prince to whom the wealthy and well-armed caravans owed allegiance. All this could well have impressed weak and ill-organised Africans. With the aggressive or well-organised ones it was probably another matter.

In the north, above the Juba, the Arabs could not pretend to exercise any authority over the warlike Somali and Galla peoples who not only often raided the coast towns situated in their neighbourhood but made life insecure for Arab traders who tried to do business there. The caravans could not safely traverse their country. Any Arabs found were seized and carried off into slavery. In what is now Kenya there were tribes whom the Arabs did everything to avoid. The first were the Masai, who although not integrated into a united political entity were yet the terror of their neighbours. Their two preoccupations were cattle and warfare. Their domain lay between Lake Victoria and the sea and here they raided in all directions not for territory but for cattle. Krapf said of the Masai: 'They are dreaded as warriors, laying all waste with fire and sword so that the weaker tribes do not venture to resist them in the open field, but leave them in possession of their herds, and seek only to save themselves by the quickest possible flight.' The Masai were not interested in the slave or ivory trade. Arab caravans were wise to do everything to avoid crossing the path of a people engaged in periodic long-distance raids. The Nandi to the north of the Masai refused to have any dealings with the Arabs and were left alone.

The Kikuyu also were not constituted into a centralised kingdom. They were a very vigorous people and produced outstanding individuals who led them in wars with the Masai. Among the Kikuyu the Arabs from the coast invariably encountered a hostile reception, and the best they could achieve was trade with the people on the periphery of Kikuyu country. They made no attempt to penetrate Kikuyu country, much less impose Arab rule over it. The Arabs and Said never exercised any influence over the Masai, the Nandi and the Kikuyu.

The area of the Kilimanjaro mountain slopes was the home of the Chagga who had developed a fairly strong system of chieftainship. Even before the arrival of Said in Zanzibar, the Chagga had produced a remarkable chief in the person of Horombo who built defensive forts. Under him they could hold their own against the warlike Masai. In due course another indomitable Chagga leader known to Europeans as Mandara further consolidated their state. They took little interest in extensive trading, though they welcomed traders from the coast and would sell to them some captives from the many wars in which they were engaged. The Arab traders relied on the goodwill of the Chagga rulers to carry on their trading activities, but the security of the caravans depended on the good behaviour of the Arabs in Chagga country. So here there could be no question of Arab or Zanzibar authority.

Immediately to the west of Tanga lay the very powerful African kingdom of Usambara. What is known about this remarkable state is mostly due to the records of the missionary mentioned already, Krapf. The most notable of its rulers was King Kimweri born at the beginning of the nineteenth century. Gifted with both military and administrative acumen, Kimweri conquered in all directions and most effectively organised his dominion. The central government was controlled under him by a Prime Minister, a Commander-in-Chief and a Captain of the Bodyguard. The districts were taken care of by princes of the royal blood, although each prince was expected to co-operate with a representative of the central government. The subjects of Usambara called their king 'Lion of Heaven'. Over a kingdom such as this the Arab ruler of Zanzibar could assert no overlordship. As a matter of fact coast towns including Pangani paid tribute to the ruler of Usambara. The path up the river running from Pangani to the slopes of Kilimanjaro was an area of intense trading activity. The Usambara apparently had many captives from their wars of conquest which they were willing to sell to the Arabs, but the political dominance of the Usambara ruler was unquestioned. The powerful ruler Kimweri indeed appointed his own men along the coast, and their relations with the Zanzibar governor of Tanga must have been based on mutual respect and compromise.

The history of the Arab colony of Tabora throws a great deal of light on the kind of relationship which developed when the Arabs from the coast came into the territory of a comprehensively organised African state. Tabora was ideally situated to stimulate Arab exploitation of areas stretching towards lakes Tanganyika and Victoria and westwards to the Congo. But then the site of the town was owned by an African people known as the Nyamwezi.

These were a united and prosperous people who had for a long time produced leaders of outstanding stature. The earliest accounts of them show that they were excellent traders themselves and had dominated the trade routes leading westwards to Katanga. Thus, when the Arabs appeared, it seemed that conflict would develop from trade competition. The Arabs thought it expedient to negotiate and as a result were allowed to build Tabora which was to be exempt from all taxes on merchandise. It was of course possible for the Arabs in Tabora to throw their influence on the side of an African contender for the throne of Nyamwezi who appeared to be pliable at their hands. This kind of interference in local politics provoked a war in which a Nyamwezi chief, Munua Sera, brought great devastation to Arab trade. The next powerful ruler, Mirambo, nearly succeeded in wiping out the Arab colony of Tabora. The Arabs sought peace, which was finally concluded in 1876 and the original equilibrium restored. The Arabs learnt that it was extremely unwise to take part in local quarrels where Africans could rally behind a powerful chief.

In the area west of Lake Victoria and east of lakes Edward and Kivu Arab influence and pretentions were very negligible. Here were located remarkable interlacustrine Bantu kingdoms including Bunyoro, Toro, Buganda, Rwanda and Burundi. Smaller states immediately to the south-west of Lake Victoria included Buhaya and Buzinza. The Arabs had quickly realised the economic potentialities of the region. Slaves and ivory were abundant and there was great demand for cloth and guns. From Tabora the Arabs established themselves along the routes that led towards the Bantu kingdoms.

These powerful Bantu kingdoms welcomed the new traders, confident that the free flow of guns would play a major part in the inter-state conflicts which dominated their history during the nineteenth century. There is no evidence that the Arabs tried to exploit inter-state quarrels among the Bantu; thus their trade here did not degenerate into the raids, violence and rapine which marked Arab activities in areas where the Africans were not well organised and where they lived in small isolated communities. By the middle of the nineteenth century Buganda was well on its way to ascendancy. The Kabaka (king) was careful to ensure that the distribution of guns which the Arabs brought into the kingdom was based on equality and diplomatic etiquette. For instance, in 1869, a special

Buganda embassy was despatched to Zanzibar and trade relations between the Baganda and the Arabs were discussed and regularised. The Arabs supplied cloth and guns. The export items available in Buganda were provided by Baganda traders, so the Arabs did not have to raid for slaves and ivory or to guarantee their own security. The Baganda undoubtedly raided their neighbours for slaves, cattle and ivory, but the Arabs were expected to behave themselves as long as they were in Buganda. There is evidence that even in the smaller kingdoms the Arabs paid heavy tolls for the passage of their caravans.

Apart from the country behind Mombasa where the Arabs could completely dominate the weak and fragmented Nyika, there were two notable areas where Arab settlements, caravans and raids criss-crossed the life of the indigenous Africans. The coast between Bagamoyo and the Ruvuma River and the hinterland as far west as lakes Nyasa and Tanganyika have been described as the 'slave hunters' paradise'. The African groups encountered here, including the Yao, the Maravi, the Hehe and so on, were divided into small groups. They therefore fell an easy prey to Arab slave-raiding and devastation. The Arabs established settlements where they liked, dominated the life of the Africans and instigated petty war when they needed slaves and ivory. They could penetrate where they wished and their possession of firearms made them appear all-powerful to the Africans, who lived in isolated and disunited groups and were armed only with bows and arrows.

Another area where the indigenous political condition was confused and played into the hands of the Arabs was the Upper Congo territory to the west of Lake Tanganyika. Each village was independent of its neighbour. Worse still, the villages and their petty chiefs were often at war with one another. When the first bands of the more lawless type of Arabs moved into the area, the burning of villages and the seizure of people and ivory by force increasingly marked the character of Arab dominance. From this state of affairs emerged the career of an Arab half-caste called Tippo Tib who was born in Zanzibar about 1830. As a youth he had accompanied his father to Tabora, and later led his first expedition to Lake Tanganyika; subsequently he moved into the Upper Congo, where he came to the conclusion that the acquisition of items for the export trade could best be accomplished through the mechanism of political control. Tib established a formidable territorial empire in which he controlled petty African village chiefs, collected taxes and dominated both the trade and and politics of the region. It is not clear to what extent Arab adventurers like Tippo Tib acted as agents of the Sultan of Zanzibar. As long as trade flowed into Zanzibar from the interior, the Arabs of the interior were left very much to their own devices.

On the whole, therefore, it can be claimed that the Omani rule in East Africa was no more than a system of economic penetration with considerable political activity in a number of regions where African resistance was non-existent or negligible. The old proverb first spoken in Said's day that 'when one pipes in Zanzibar they dance on the lakes' grossly exaggerates the pervasiveness and effectiveness of Arab 'rule' in East Africa.

BRITISH INTERVENTION

When the ambition to found an East African 'dominion' first began to mature in the mind of Seyyid Said, he apparently had little to fear on the score of possible European intervention. The Portuguese were already a spent force and had been pushed to the south of the Ruvuma River. The French had enough to do importing slaves into their islands in the Indian Ocean. The British had no territorial ambitions at that time in East Africa. The unilateral decision of a naval captain to establish a British protectorate over Mombasa in 1824 was countermanded by the British government. The way had therefore been cleared for Said to transfer from Oman to Zanzibar and inaugurate the peculiar empire we have been discussing. A shadow which, whether Said suspected it or not, portended the future course of events lay across Said's path to ascendancy and wealth. This was the anti-slaving activities of the British government. For many reasons the British government was willing to deal patiently with the Omani Arab ruler. To the Arabs in East Africa and elsewhere slavery and the slave trade were indispensable institutions. The type of exploitation which the Arabs embarked on so formidably in East Africa was inconceivable without slavery and its corollary.

The British government on the whole was prepared to use persuasion rather than force. Persuasion implied a recognition of Said's overlordship of East Africa and, as long as this was so, the clever Arab was willing to humour the British. Thus in 1822 the famous Moresby Treaty was signed and the Arab ruler undertook to prohibit all external traffic in slaves in his 'dominions and dependencies'. It also provided for the appointment of a British agent at Zanzibar or on the African coast 'to watch the traffic'. Said was undoubtedly aware that he had to pay a price for British support and the security of his dominion in East Africa. The French, the Germans, the Americans had also begun to arrive. They were all interested in trade, not in territory, and Said must have found this out with great relief.

One thorn in Said's flesh was the British agent in Zanzibar with his perpetual complaints about the slaving activities of Said's subjects. Another was the missionaries and travellers who began to swarm into the hinterland and soon revealed in its stark reality the devastation perpetrated under the leadership of Zanzibar Arabs. The protestations of the missionary travellers swelled the growing volume of world opinion against the slave trade in the interior of Africa. Seyyid Said's skilful diplomacy sufficed to postpone the evil day for his preserve in East Africa. But he died in 1856 and his successors were to prove unequal to the task of maintaining his peculiar dominion.

The struggle for the throne of Zanzibar precipitated by the sons and brothers of Seyyid Said helped to undermine the very centre of Arab authority. If the British and the French had wished they could have set aside the Arab contestants and partitioned East Africa. Both powers preferred to guarantee the independence of Zanzibar. Another Sultan in 1870 relied on British help to secure his throne. At this time too the British government decided to take sterner measures against the slave trade. The new Arab ruler, Barghash, found the new British representative, Sir John Kirk, a harassing companion. Kirk was not prepared to trust the Arab's promises in regard to the suppression of the slave trade, although the Arab ruler for his part argued that to adopt the policy of abolition was tantamount to 'suicide'. However the British under pressure from missionary bodies had decided on a policy of dictation. If the Zanzibar ruler proved obdurate the British navy would blockade Zanzibar. In 1873 Barghash issued the following proclamation: 'Know that we have prohibited the transport of slaves by sea in all our harbours and have closed the markets for the sale of slaves throughout all our dominions. . . .' It should be borne in mind that in yielding to British pressure the Zanzibar ruler was choosing the lesser of two evils—evils from the stand-point of the integrity of his dominion. To abolish the slave trade was to undermine the whole economic system which the original founder of the East African empire had so effectively built up. The local Arab shaikhs on the coast, and probably the Arabs in the hinterland, had been willing enough to acknowledge the overlord-ship of Zanzibar as long as Zanzibar safeguarded the economic facilities which East Africa afforded. The most important of these facilities was trade. In this trade ivory and slaving were comple-mentary items in the absence of transport and currency. In any case the Zanzibar Sultan could rightly anticipate that a procla-mation abolishing the transport of slaves would from the start be a 'dead letter'. To please the British, thereby averting the blockade of Zanzibar and probably other untoward developments was the best way to preserve the 'empire' of Zanzibar.

When David Livingstone, the great missionary traveller, spoke of going back to East Africa 'to try to make an open path for commerce and Christianity', he was foreshadowing the events which would culminate in the destruction of the Arab hold on this region. The European travellers who went to East Africa for purely missionary work or in the interest of geographical knowledge were followed by others who were determined to serve the imperialist interests of their motherland. The new situation produced the curious spectacle of the representatives of European powers travel-ling in the interior and busily negotiating 'treaties' with African chiefs and headmen. The implications of these events were clear to the Arab ruler in Zanzibar. But German ambitions, methods and manners roused the anxieties not only of the Sultan but of Britain. German agents denied that the Sultan of Zanzibar had any authority along the East African coast, outside Zanzibar; his authority in the hinterland was even more inconceivable, argued the Germans. In any case, they declared, any overlord who could not check the 'anarchy and savagery' which ravaged the territory had no right to continue to rule.

The Sultan of Zanzibar who had in the meantime paid a visit to England fell back on his traditional friendship with the British government. He was quite prepared to accept a British Pro-tectorate as the only alternative to European partition, but the policy of friendship with Britain could not save the Zanzibar empire. By 1890 East Africa was partitioned between Britain and

Germany. Both powers in due course dealt with what they regarded as the 'open sore of the world'. The Arabs who operated in the region of the Upper Congo were crushed in the closing years of the nineteenth century by a series of military expeditions launched by the 'Congo Free State'. The Omani rulers lost their empire and were indeed lucky to retain Zanzibar though not as independent sovereigns. East Africa entered a new phase in its history under European, rather than Arab, dominance.

CONCLUSION

The question of the precise impact of the Omani empire on East African societies is one on which opinion is divided. The missionaries who scoured East and Central Africa during the nineteenth century had no doubt whatsoever in their minds that the presence of the Arab in East Africa had produced nothing but chaos. Arab activities were bound up with slaving and flooding the region with guns. The evils attendant on these instruments of destruction were blamed on the Arabs. The exploitation of East and Central Africa followed a path of brutalisation and chaos; depopulation following the devastation of villages, the slaughter or capture of their inhabitants and the ruin of their crops left its mark on East Africa. The loss of people in sale or in the agonising march to the coast staggers the imagination. Petty fights between villages and between states were no longer carried on for limited purposes. The Arabs in East and Central Africa had fastened on the Africans as parasites, draining from their blood the elements of normal civilising growth.

On the other hand, at least one European traveller called attention to the role of Arabs as agents of civilisation in the region. Adolphe Burdo who was a member of a Belgian east coast expedition wrote as follows: 'In the midst of savage Africa, if you come across fertile rice plantations, the cultivation of wheat, lemons and guavas, and splendid plantations of bananas, it is entirely due to the Arabs. The plain of Tabora is an excellent example; they have cleared this vast area . . . and turned it into a vegetable garden . . . where formerly there was only a desolate plain, the lair of a few savage bandits.'[1] Burdo concluded that the Arabs were the 'authors of good fortune and redemption' for the Bantu. Tabora might have been as Burdo described it. East and Central Africa was much more than Tabora. To what other areas did the

Arabs bring peace rather than disruption, confusion and chaos? Perhaps it was not for nothing that the Africans of Zanzibar at last rallied in 1964 to expel the last representative of the Omani rulers.

NOTE

1   Quoted Slade, *King Leopold's Congo*, p. 87, O.U.P., 1962.

QUESTIONS FOR FURTHER STUDY AND DISCUSSION

1 Account for the relative ease with which the Omani Arab ruler established an East African 'empire' in the nineteenth century.

2 Why were Arab activities in East and Central Africa bound to intensify the slave trade?

3 Consider the significance of either Seyyid Said or Tippo Tib.

4 Describe the difficulties of the successors of Seyyid Said in maintaining the Omani empire in East Africa.

SELECT BIBLIOGRAPHY

R. Coupland, *East Africa and its Invaders*, O.U.P., 1956.

—— *The Exploitation of East Africa, 1856–1890*, Faber & Faber, 1939.

R. Oliver and G. Mathew (eds.), *History of East Africa*, Vol. 1, O.U.P., 1964.

W. H. Ingrams, *Zanzibar, its History and its People*, H. F. & G. Witherby, 1931.

D. Livingstone, *Last Journals* (ed. Horace Waller), 2 vols., J. Murray, 1874.

H. M. Stanley, *Through the Dark Continent*, Harper & Bros., New York, 1906.

R. Oliver, *The Missionary Factor in East Africa*, Longmans, 1952.

F. D. Lugard, *The Rise of our East African Empire*, 2 vols., W. Blackwood & Sons, 1893.

26 The Missionary Factor in East Africa

J. R. GRAY

WHEN in 1856 Livingstone emerged at the mouth of the Zambezi, from a journey which was to change the whole impetus of the missionary penetration of Bantu Africa, only two groups of missionaries had begun to touch the outer fringes of East Africa. At Rabai, on a hill behind Mombasa, the Church Missionary Society had started work in 1844 under the leadership of Krapf, Rebmann and Erhardt. These enterprising German Lutherans explored the coast and nearby hinterland, and their eye-witness reports of the snow-capped mountains and the hearsay information of great inland seas led directly to the European exploration of the interior. But the openings which they had found among the Chagga and Shambaa remained unexploited for lack of reinforcements, and by 1856 Rebmann was left alone to maintain a weary vigil at Rabai until the 1870s. The other group consisted of some priests sent to the Sudan by the Vatican to staff the Vicariate of Central Africa, established in 1846. On paper the boundaries of this new division of the Catholic Church stretched across Africa from the interior of Senegal to the Red Sea and southwards somewhat indefinitely to Ptolemy's Mountains of the Moon, but the scene of its operations was the White Nile, where expeditions sent by Muhammad Ali, ruler of Egypt and conqueror of the Sudan, had discovered a navigable highway stretching from Khartoum one thousand miles into the centre of the Southern Sudan. Here, it seemed, was an unrivalled opportunity for European merchants and missionaries to bring commerce and Christianity to hitherto untouched peoples in the heart of Africa, and already in 1852 one of the priests was working among a small Luo tribe who were in tenuous trading contact with the great Bantu lacustrine kingdoms of Bunyoro and Buganda. But by the end of the 1850s the mission was withdrawn, decimated by disease and threatened by the robbery and violence into which the ivory trade had deteriorated, and for the rest of the century the missionary thrust from the north remained in abeyance. The evangelisation of the interior of East Africa had yet to begin.

Islam had been present on the East African coast for nearly a thousand years, but by the mid-nineteenth century it was only just beginning to penetrate into the interior along the newly opened Arab and Swahili trade routes. This vast area, however, was far from being a religious *tabula rasa*. Behind the varied pattern of clan and tribal gods the peoples of East Africa shared certain common values, for they lived in a spiritual universe. Man's health, success, fertility and security depended on spiritual influences; man was strengthened or weakened by the powers which impinged upon him, and the deepest preoccupation of the individual, the family and the tribe was to remain in an essential harmony with these forces of the universe. In this task the ancestors often played a leading role, and amongst the living they were assisted by a variety of ritual experts. Thus throughout East Africa, from the highly organised divine kingship systems of the lacustrine area to the nomadic Masai or simple agricultural homestead, the missionaries were confronted with a coherent way of life in which tribal beliefs were a vital part of daily life. It was this fact, more perhaps than any other, that explains the difficulties that the missionaries were to encounter; and their failure to appreciate the strength of traditional religion left a legacy of unsolved problems for the church in East Africa.

LIVINGSTONE

Livingstone returned to London in 1856 with a great geographical feat to his credit, and, even more important, with revolutionary ideas on the aims and methods of pioneer missionaries in tropical Africa. Fifteen years earlier he had started work on the missionary frontier in Bechuanaland, where the contrast between the tribes who had had close contact with mission influences and those who still remained untouched led him to a startling conclusion. He began to maintain that the indirect results of mission work or what would have been called its 'civilising' effects, the awakening of new needs and interests, were of far greater immediate significance to isolated tribes in the interior than the direct results of conversion and the saving of individual souls. Nearly all contemporary missionaries believed that they had the dual task of bringing to Africa Christianity and civilisation, i.e. legitimate commerce and the techniques of industrial Victorian England. This idea was of course the driving force behind the Niger expedition of 1841 and the theme was a common one in South African missionary literature. But, until Livingstone, it was assumed by missionaries that their 'civilising' role was merely a subsidiary by-product of their primary, evangelistic objective. For them a pioneer missionary was someone like Robert Moffat, Livingstone's father-in-law, who settled amongst the nearest unevangelised tribe and spent his life patiently building the foundations of a small Christian community. Livingstone reversed these priorities. Obsessed by the fate of the suffering heathen, and an eye-witness of the threat to the tribes in the interior from first the Boers' thrust from the south, and secondly, after his Zambezi journey, from the even greater menace of the slave raids from the East Coast, he proclaimed throughout Britain the urgent, immediate necessity of a rapid missionary occupation of the remote interior.

As a starting-point Livingstone persuaded the British Government to send him back in command of an official expedition to explore the navigable possibilities of the Zambezi, and two missionary societies agreed to co-operate. The London Missionary Society (L.M.S.), with whom Livingstone had worked in Bechuanaland, sent an expedition to Barotseland on the Upper Zambezi, and the Universities Mission to Central Africa (U.M.C.A.), founded as a direct result of Livingstone's lecture at Cambridge in 1857 and drawing its support from High-Church Anglicans in contrast to the Evangelical C.M.S., sent a group of missionaries headed by Bishop Mackenzie to start a mission in the Shire highlands, just south of Lake Nyasa. Yet all three initiatives ended in failure. The Zambezi proved wholly unsuitable for navigation, from the L.M.S. party a single survivor returned south through the Kalahari; and the U.M.C.A., broken by disease and threatened by slave raids, had to withdraw from the Shire highlands and started to work among freed slaves in Zanzibar.

Livingstone's vision of a dramatic occupation of East and Central Africa seemed completely discredited, and in 1866 he himself set out alone on his final journey. This time there were no spectacular geographical discoveries, yet these last seven years of wandering between Lakes Nyasa and Tanganyika and the upper reaches of the Congo took Livingstone to the heart of the slave trade, and his detailed reports of its extent and devastation led directly to British pressure on Zanzibar to sign an abolition treaty in 1873. His death among the swamps of Lake Bangweulu in the same year, the epic march by his African companions bearing his corpse to the coast and the state funeral in Westminster Abbey, awoke the mass interest and enthusiasm needed to support the series of audacious thrusts into the interior which he had advocated for so long in vain.

Livingstone's countrymen, the Scots, began the movement. By 1875 the Scottish Churches, supported by Glasgow industrialists, had launched a steamer on Lake Nyasa and founded mission stations in the Shire highlands and on the shore of the lake itself. At the same time the U.M.C.A. under Bishop Steere began to make its way back inland to Lake Nyasa. At Masasi, a hundred miles inland from Lindi, he founded a colony of freed slaves from the Makua and Nyanja tribes, and from there the mission gradually penetrated the powerful Yao and other peoples of the lakeside. Robert Arthington, an extraordinary figure who might have stepped straight out of one of Dickens' novels, provided the backing for the next ventures. A millionaire, who lived in solitary penury in one room of his large Yorkshire house, Arthington maintained an extensive correspondence with geographers and explorers, using his knowledge and his wealth to assist the hurried preaching of the Gospel throughout the world and thus, he believed, hasten the coming of the millennium. He was therefore wholly in sympathy with Livingstone's ideas, and in 1875 gave the L.M.S. £5,000 to place a steamer and start a mission on Lake Tanganyika, while two years later a similar gift to the Baptists at the mouth of the Congo started off the rapid missionary penetration of the vast Congo basin. Arthington may also have been involved in the last of these direct responses to Livingstone's challenge. In November 1875, after the publication of a letter from the explorer Stanley from the court of Kabaka Mutesa of Buganda appealing for Christian missionaries, the C.M.S. were given anonymously another £5,000 to start a mission in this key lacustrine kingdom. Thus within two years of Livingstone's death his vision was being actively translated into reality, at a time when other European interests in the interior of East Africa were still virtually non-existent.

LAVIGERIE

The response of Catholic Europe to these new openings was also largely determined by the intervention of one remarkable man. In 1866 Charles Lavigerie, an intensely able forty-one-year-old Bishop, full of ambition for the Church and in particular for those parts with which he was connected, in the midst of a brilliant ecclesiastical career turned down the offer of the see of Lyons, a sure stepping-stone to the Cardinalate, and chose instead to become Archbishop of Algiers. Once in Africa he created asylums and orphanages for Algerian Muslims, using his extensive contacts in Europe to support a new society, the Société de Notre-Dame d'Afrique, or the White Fathers, which he founded to help in this work and in the evangelisation of pagan Africa. In 1868, at his request, Pope Pius IX created him Apostolic Delegate of the Sahara and the Sudan, and the first White Fathers were sent south into the Sahara. They were killed by the Tuareg, and for a while Lavigerie waited, until, early in 1878, he laid before Propaganda Fide, the Congregation of Cardinals in Rome which directs Catholic missionary activity, a secret memoir which is one of the most decisive documents in the history of Christian expansion. Acutely recognising that the missionary occupation of the interior had been revolutionised by Livingstone, and sensing the forces stirring in Europe and the possibility of enlisting these powers in the task of opening up Africa, Lavigerie realised that the evangelisation of Africa now demanded not a slow, patient creep inwards from the periphery but a bold crusade into the interior. Disregarding therefore the whole weight of previous pioneer Catholic experience—the retreat from the Southern Sudan; the thorough, cautious advance of the Holy Ghost Fathers from their coastal station at Bagamoyo; and the White Fathers' hard-won experience in the Sahara—Lavigerie proposed the immediate division of the vast area of inner Equatorial Africa into four vicariates, all of which, he suggested, should be entrusted to a single guiding hand. At the same time he promised that the White Fathers could send fifty missionaries to occupy the area immediately. Only Lavigerie with his contacts, vision and energy could launch such a movement, and in February 1878 Pope Leo XIII entrusted the task to him and his society. Two months later the first expedition of White Fathers had sailed for Zanzibar to found stations at Tabora, in Buganda and around Lake Tanganyika.

THE BAGANDA

Buganda was to prove the test case for all these pioneer missions in the tribal interior of East Africa. On the coast, at the freed-slave settlements near Mombasa, Bagamoyo, and even at Masasi, the missions were faced with the problem of giving a new hope and coherence to people whose tribal life had been completely shattered. Here the European missionaries exercised temporal as well as spiritual power, and here they regulated every aspect of the life of their converts, constructing secure Christian havens which slowly succeeded in attracting some free outsiders to this extra-tribal existence. In Buganda the situation was entirely different. In this powerful, despotic state the European pioneers were at the mercy of Baganda political forces, and the growth of the churches depended primarily on the leadership of African Christians. Here then the focus lay from the start not so much on the missionary factor but on the reactions, response and initiative of Africans. The initial welcome given to the missionaries by the Kabaka Mutesa was undoubtedly political in motivation: threatened by the Egyptian expeditions pushing down from the Southern Sudan, Mutesa intended to use the missionaries as pawns in his diplomacy and as technological experts. Later he exercised consummate skill in playing off the White Fathers against the C.M.S., and both groups of missionaries against the Muslim traders from Zanzibar. The long theological disputations which he delightedly instigated at his court had then primarily a political purpose; but gradually they also acquired a profound religious significance for the Baganda. It is possible even that Mutesa himself was influenced by the new religious ideas. Before the missionaries arrived, probably as a result of bold criticisms from Zanzibari Muslims, the Kabaka had modified ritual practices and decreased sacrificial slaughters, while he himself told the missionaries that 'when Speke was here I was a heathen, but now I know better'. Later, having listened to the Gospel accounts of the life and teaching of Jesus Christ, he is reported to have murmured in genuine admiration, 'Isa—was there ever anyone like him?' While, however, it is unlikely that Mutesa himself ever seriously considered adopting Christianity, his apparent indecision and vacillation when faced with these rival

31

religious teachings opened the door for the missionaries to reach what was becoming by far the most significant sector of Baganda society.

The young pages of the Kabaka (four to five hundred in number), of the Queen Mother and of court officials, had for long enjoyed a privileged if precarious position, as service at the royal court was the recognised road to promotion. The opening of long-distance trade, with the introduction of the use of firearms and other skills readily acquired by these personal servants of the Kabaka, enormously increased the political and social significance of this group, with whom the missionaries, restricted by the Kabaka's orders to residence within the royal capital, were thrown most closely into contact. At first it was largely the acquisition of a new skill—reading—that attracted these impressionable young men to the missions, but when the Kabaka failed to give a lead in the religious disputations, the pages and other Baganda at the capital began to think and decide for themselves. Gradually the missionaries found themselves at the centre of new circles of allegiance remarkably similar to those enjoyed by chiefs in Baganda society, and the process of conversion was probably assisted by the fact that the new faith restored Katonda (the creator God) to the plane which it seems that He originally possessed in Baganda thought. After three or four years' work both Catholics and Anglicans had baptised a fair number of the Kabaka's pages together with a few prominent individuals, and it was these men who rapidly supplied the leadership of the Christian communities.

Their first major test came in November 1882 when the White Fathers, harassed by the uncertainties of Mutesa's attitude towards them and ordered by Lavigerie not to risk their lives unnecessarily, decided to withdraw temporarily from Buganda. Twenty-two-year-old Joseph Mukasa, Mutesa's most trusted personal page, took over the leadership of some 150 Catholic adherents among the pages and soldiers of the bodyguard. In particular he looked after those who served within the royal apartments; outside in the capital there were Andrea Kaggwa, master-drummer and head of the Kabaka's band, who during an outbreak of bubonic plague turned his homestead into a hospital for its victims, and Mathew Kasule, who as the Kabaka's gunsmith occupied a position of great military significance. Away from the capital Matthias Kalemba, the Mulumba, a prominent war-captain and trusted lieutenant of his county chief, fostered a Christian community and inspired them by his fearless and uncustomarily humble example. Some idea of the contagious zeal of these newly baptised Christians can be seen from the fact that when the White Fathers returned in July 1885, after Mutesa's death, they found eight hundred catechumens under active instruction. Simultaneously Baganda leaders of the Anglican Church were emerging, the heads of household 'clusters' of converts, and in 1886 twelve of these leaders, including Nikodemo Sebwato, a leading sub-chief from Buddu, were appointed as a church council.

At first it was hoped that the accession of Kabaka Mwanga would strengthen the churches: Joseph Mukasa was promoted to the responsible post of major-domo, and Andrea Kaggwa became the inseparable hunting and travelling companion of the young Kabaka. A bitter struggle for power, however, developed between these new young men and the older tribal chiefs headed by the Katikkiro or Prime Minister. In February 1885 the Christian leaders by offering the Kabaka the help of two thousand armed men were able momentarily to frustrate the Katikkiro, but when news of the German occupation of the Tanganyika coast reached Buganda, the tribal chiefs were able to play upon the Kabaka's fears that the missions represented the spearhead of European intervention. In October 1885 Joseph Mukasa was beheaded for protesting against the murder of the first Anglican Bishop, and in 1886 from fifty to one hundred Christians were martyred including Andrea Kaggwa and Matthias Kalemba, while other leaders including Sebwato and Apolo Kaggwa were severely beaten. The young churches went underground, but baptisms increased as did the power of the regiments of new men. For three years the fortunes of the Christians became linked with active rebellion, and a series of *coups d'état* ended with Mwanga finally owing his throne to the Christian regiments, with the Anglican Apolo Kaggwa as his Katikkiro and the other Christian leaders in the places of the great Baganda chiefs. The churches had become established in Buganda, but only by participating in a successful revolution.

Nowhere else in pre-colonial East Africa did the missions penetrate so intimately into tribal society. On Lake Tanganyika the L.M.S. missionaries, weakened by deaths and resignations, gradually relinquished the east coast route and concentrated their work to the south of the lake in what was to become Zambia. The White Fathers established a ring of stations based on the lake and developed these into well-disciplined Christian enclaves for freed-slaves, orphans and other refugees, but in this pioneer period the general experience of the missionaries was that, apart from Buganda, it was difficult if not impossible for an individual to become a Christian while remaining a full member of his tribal community.

ARAB OR EUROPEAN POWER?

During this early period a few of the pioneer missionaries had sometimes thought wistfully of the benefits which European imperial intervention might bring. The leader of the first Scottish missions suggested, albeit in vain, that a gunboat be placed on Lake Nyasa to intercept Arab slave dhows, and later, more successfully, the Scottish missionaries urged that a consul be appointed to protect the area against Portuguese expansion. In Buganda, exposure to the restrictions of Mutesa and the persecutions of Mwanga had turned the C.M.S. missionary, Mackay, into an active advocate of imperial intervention by December 1885. But this imperialistic trend remained relatively unimportant until suddenly in 1887-8 a series of Arab attacks, motivated partly perhaps by the Mahdist movement in the Sudan but principally in direct reaction to the German occupation of the Tanganyika coast in 1885, threatened the work of the missions throughout the interior. On Lake Nyasa a missionary was seized by the Yao, and Mlozi, an Arab trader, threatened to sweep the Scottish missionaries from their station at Bandawe. Farther north the work of the L.M.S. was interrupted by a Swahili trader, and the White Fathers were forced to abandon three stations. In 1888 their Bishop and a party of missionaries were arrested by Arabs at Tabora and narrowly escaped massacre. In Buganda the *coup d'état* of the same year was engineered by Arab traders. These developments then faced the missionaries with the question, in Mackay's words, of whether 'Arab or European power' was 'henceforth to prevail in Central Africa', and increasingly they threw all their weight behind the movement for European intervention. Lavigerie, now a Cardinal, became a powerful and outspoken imperialist, rallying support throughout Europe for a crusade against the Arab slave trade. The Scottish missions on Lake Nyasa became militant advocates for the establishment of a British protectorate, though, when it was found that Rhodes was paying the bill, they were careful to insist that the country came under Foreign Office rule rather than fall into the South African sphere of interest. In Buganda the C.M.S. played a leading role both in persuading the Baganda to accept British emissaries and also in influencing British public opinion in favour of imperial intervention.

Thus, for the missionaries, the threat of Arab conquest and the expansion of the slave trade were sufficient to justify the 'Partition' of East Africa, and the security and improved communications which European rule promised gave a further stimulus to the missionary occupation of the area. In Berlin a group of active imperialists launched a new missionary society which started work on the Tanganyika coast. A German congregation of Benedictine monks took over the area south of the Rufiji River, and both the White Fathers and the Holy Ghost Fathers opened recruiting centres in Germany in order to expand their work in German East Africa. Finally, two older German Protestant missionary societies, the first Berlin Missionary Society and the Moravians, both of whom had at first by no means welcomed the imperialist current, sent expeditions to the north of Lake Nyasa in 1891, and from this bridgehead started to penetrate northwards and eastwards. The missionary occupation of the interior of Kenya was a direct consequence of the building of the Uganda Railway which opened up the fertile Kikuyu highlands. By 1914 the C.M.S. and the Church of Scotland, the Holy Ghost Fathers and the Italian Consolata Fathers, the American-based Africa Inland Mission and parties of Quakers and American Adventists were all working in the interior.

The first experiences of these new missions were, however, almost identical with those of the early pioneers in the pre-colonial era. For at least a decade most of them found themselves virtually excluded from tribal society and had to be content with founding small communities of individuals who had broken away from their tribes. Only in Uganda was there an immediate marked contrast. The declaration of a British protectorate and the signing of the Uganda Agreement (1900) set the seal on the Christian revolution in Baganda. Baptism became a status symbol, and Buganda itself witnessed continuous and remarkable mass conversions, while Buganda teachers, warriors and pastors took the British flag and the Christian Gospel to the other tribes in the protectorate. As early as 1891 the Catholics were holding open-air catechisms attended by three thousand people, and the White Fathers reported that the Baganda arrived at the mission already knowing their prayers and catechism 'for they teach themselves with a really extraordinary zeal'. Among the Anglicans a revival produced 260 new African evangelists in one year. With their help the Church spread rapidly in Toro, Bunyoro and Ankole, and by the first decade of the twentieth century Baganda evangelists were working in the Southern Sudan. Canon Apolo Kivebulaya was an outstanding representative of these pioneers, working first in Toro, then in the Congo, and finally among the Pygmies of the forest. Elsewhere in East Africa the missions' break-through into tribal society on any extensive scale had generally to wait for the effects of colonial rule to be felt among the tribes. A decisive defeat such as the suppression of the Maji Maji rebellion (1905-7), or employment on European farms and plantations, or, more positively, the desire to master European techniques, were factors which increasingly exposed the limitations of tribal life and led to an opening for, in some areas, Islam and, in others, Christianity. As in Uganda however, it was the African catechists and evangelists, rather than the European missionaries, who formed the spearhead in this expansionary phase, while at a quite different level the development of colonial rule faced the missions with a new set of challenges.

CHALLENGES AND PROBLEMS

The first issue arose in Kenya where in 1919 the Governor authorised the use of what was virtually compulsory labour, not merely for public works but also on the private estates of European settlers. The Alliance of Protestant Missions in Kenya, established as a result of the Kikuyu conferences (1913-18), immediately opposed this move, and in London their protest was taken up by J. H. Oldham. Secretary of the newly formed International Missionary Council and one of the leading figures of the ecumenical movement, Oldham also rapidly became the protagonist of the rights of Africans against European settlers. In a series of detailed memoranda submitted to the Colonial Office he successfully established the principle that 'the chief wealth' of the East African territories was its indigenous population, and he was largely responsible for the official recognition in 1923 that in Kenya 'the interests of the African natives must be paramount'. In the same year, again mainly as the result of Oldham's initiative, the Colonial Office established an Advisory Committee on Native Education in Tropical Africa, which ensured increasing government financial support for the educational work of missions and reinforced the proposals of the Phelps-Stokes Commission (1922) to adapt missionary education to the needs of Africa. Thus was launched a movement which, as it steadily gained momentum (by 1938 Makerere College started on its first steps to become a college of the University of East Africa), inevitably held within itself the key to the ending of alien rule.

If, however, at the highest level the missions protected African rights and co-operated in the vital task of education, at the local village level only too often was the missionary identified with the attitudes and way of life of the settler or the administrator, and was seen as the protagonist of an alien culture, condemning polygamy and cherished tribal customs. For some Africans this meant that only in a complete separation from the mission churches could they reconcile the new faith with their African way of life. Among the Kikuyu, resentment at missionary condemnation of female circumcision merged with deep-rooted political grievances to support a determined fight for independent schools and the formation of tribal churches free from foreign control. In Uganda the roots of separatism were primarily religious. One of the leading Baganda chiefs, Joswa Kate Mugema, a close friend of the early martyrs, became convinced that recourse to medical assistance implied a lack of trust in God. For several years he practised his convictions privately, but finally broke with the Anglican Church in 1914 and launched a mass movement which by 1921 numbered 91,000 followers in Buganda alone. A few years later a much younger man, Reuben Spartas, an outstanding example of the new intellectual elite, after avid theological reading became dissatisfied with the Anglican position, and in 1929 formed a branch of the African Orthodox Church, which had been started in America by Marcus Garvey. Subsequently Spartas' search for theological truth led him to accept reunion with the Alexandrian Patriarch of the Greek Orthodox Church. Thus religious motives predominated in both these Baganda movements, but political aspects were also present. In Mugema's case there was a long-standing feud with the

Katikkiro, Apolo Kaggwa, and a profound rejection of the land settlement in the 1900 Uganda Agreement, and for Spartas there was the early desire to launch a cultural liberation movement of Pan-African significance. Yet at a deeper level the support given to these leaders illustrates the tensions to which the mass of Africans were exposed by the missionaries' message and the impact of the west.

For Africans who remained within the mission churches, the missionaries' increasing involvement with governments in education and technical services raised other problems in addition to these tensions. The first rudimentary village schools had grown quite simply out of the Christian's need for literacy. The village catechists and school-teachers worked as a team patiently initiating their charges into the life of the local Christian community. Rightly, in one sense, the Phelps-Stokes Commission judged them to be 'educationally futile'; but, as administrators and missionaries placed a new emphasis on efficiency, the school system, though successfully enabling a tiny minority of Christians to enter the competitive, bourgeois westernised world, ceased to serve the church at its local level. In a hitherto integrated society gaps between rich and poor, educated and semi-literate, increased, and the missionaries often lost contact with the mass of African Christians. Only very slowly was their place taken by an ordained African priesthood and ministry. Bishop Hirth opened the first seminary in Uganda in 1893 but it was twenty years before two of the students were raised to the Catholic priesthood, and, as Bishop Tucker's experience in formulating a constitution for the Anglican Church in Uganda demonstrated, other European missionaries in withdrawing upwards still sought to hold the leading strings. But by 1938 African clergy outnumbered Europeans in all Anglican dioceses in East Africa, other Protestant missions were following in their steps, and in 1939 the first African Roman Catholic Bishop in East Africa, Bishop Kiwanuka, took charge of the Diocese of Masaka with a staff of fifty-six African priests. With these developments the significance of the European missionary factor began to diminish, and increasingly the Christian impact on the development of East Africa depended on the African leaders and members of the churches.

QUESTIONS FOR FURTHER STUDY AND DISCUSSION

1 Consider the contributions made by Africans in the expansion of Christianity in East Africa.

2 To what extent, and for what reasons, did Christian missionaries in East Africa advocate imperial intervention?

SELECT BIBLIOGRAPHY

R. Oliver, *The Missionary Factor in East Africa*, Longmans, 1952.

C. P. Groves, *The Planting of Christianity in Africa*, Vols. 2 and 3, Lutterworth, 1948–54.

J. V. Taylor, *The Growth of the Church in Buganda*, S.C.M. Press, 1961.

J. P. Thoonen, *Black Martyrs*, Sheed & Ward, 1941.

F. B. Welbourn, *East African Rebels*, S.C.M. Press, 1961.

D. A. Low, *Religion and Society in Buganda, 1875–1900*, East African Studies, no. 1, Institute of Social Research, Kampala, 1953.

J. A. Rowe, 'The Purge of Christians at Mwanga's Court', *Journal of African History*, Vol. V, no. 1, 1964.

A. R. Tucker, *Eighteen Years in Uganda and East Africa*, 2 vols., E. Arnold, 1908.

T. J. Jones (ed.), *Education in East Africa* (Phelps-Stokes Report), 1925.

C. C. Wrigley, 'The Christian Revolution in Buganda', *Comparative Studies in Society and History*, Vol. 2, 1959–60.

A. Luck, *African Saint, The Story of Apolo Kivebulaya*, S.C.M. Press, 1963.

J. Trimingham, *Islam in East Africa*, O.U.P., 1964.

J. F. Faupel, *African Holocaust*, Geoffrey Chapman, 1962.

G. H. Wilson, *The History of the Universities' Mission to Central Africa*, Universities' Mission to Central Africa, 1936.

H. M. Smith, *Frank, Bishop of Zanzibar*, Macmillan, New York, 1926.

H. Gale, *Uganda and the Mill Hill Fathers*, Macmillan, 1959.

R. P. Ashe, *Chronicles of Uganda*, N.Y., A. D. F. Randolph & Co., 1895.

C. F. H. Battersby, *Pilkington of Uganda*, London, 1899.

E. C. Hore, *Tanganyika*, E. Stanford, 2nd edition, 1892.

R. M. Heanley, *A Memoir of Edward Steere*, G. Bell, 1888.

27 The Partition of East Africa

J. R. GRAY

THE opening moves in the 'Partition' of East Africa can be traced back to two events in Egypt in 1869. The opening of the Suez Canal in that year shortened the sea voyage from East Africa to Europe by two thousand miles, and at the same time placed Egypt and the Red Sea in the forefront of the strategic plans of the British rulers of India. East Africa no longer lay in a backwater but had been brought close to a major axis of world power. To the repercussions of this event we must return later; they are well known and have even perhaps been recently somewhat over-exaggerated; the other event of 1869, the decision of the Khedive Ismā'īl, ruler of Egypt, to launch an expedition under the command of Sir Samuel Baker up the White Nile to establish Egyptian rule at its source has remained relatively unnoticed. Yet at the time Baker's expedition had far-reaching repercussions in Britain: it revealed the possibilities of establishing an alien rule in the heart of Africa for the first time, and also stimulated a small group of humanitarians to take the first step towards a British intervention in the East African interior.

On a previous hunting trip up the White Nile, Baker had reached Lake Albert in 1864. The founder of a successful planta-tion in Ceylon, he was an early representative of those imperialists who felt that force was needed both to abolish the slave trade and to compel the African to cultivate new economic crops. His senti-ments were, indeed, to be echoed by King Leopold and many a white farmer in Kenya or Central Africa. 'Unless by a vigorous authority compelled to work, Africans,' he wrote, 'would quickly relapse into hopeless apathy and indolence . . . Negro would enslave Negro as before, should the paternal but strong arm be withdrawn.' In actual fact Baker, faced with the established pattern of hostilities in the Southern Sudan, managed to achieve virtually nothing, but the dramatic reports of his expedition obscured this failure from the eyes of contemporaries, who imbibed his views and studied his example. Rapturously *The Times* compared his task to that of the Spanish in Mexico or the English in India; military leaders listened enthusiastically to his account of the effects of rockets, light artillery and cavalry in African warfare; the Duke of Cambridge, with the Asante expedition in mind, declared that 'what had been done once could be done again'; and the Foreign Secretary congratulated Baker on his exploits, remarking that he knew 'nothing that is going on in the world just now so remarkable as the steady and rapid progress which we are making in opening-up Africa'.

Yet, whatever the significance of this changing attitude to Africa, British participation in the partition of East Africa was not primarily the result of a shift in public opinion, of a developing, popular belief in colonial expansion. More important, therefore, than Baker's positive example was the fact that the Egyptian thrust to the source of the Nile stimulated the first expressions of concrete British interest in the interior, and momentarily, though prophetically, challenged the established British policy in Zanzibar. Until the end of the 1880s, when Rhodes and Salisbury controlled the decisive stages of the scramble, British intervention in East and Central Africa was represented by a small group of anti-slavery enthusiasts, who hoped to establish Christianity and legitimate commerce in the interior. As early as October 1873 reports of Baker's expedition stimulated a distinguished humanitarian delegation to express forcibly to the Foreign Office their paternal, proprietary interest in 'the farther regions of the Nile', and two years later, at the very moment when the Church Missionary Society had decided to send missionaries to Buganda, a further intervention from Egypt forced the Foreign Office to define its attitude to imperial expansion in East Africa.

Disheartened by the difficulties of moving supplies and reinforcements up the long, interrupted navigation of the Nile, Gordon, Baker's successor, a brilliant eccentric young army officer who had already achieved fame in China, had suggested to the Khedive the need for a supporting penetration to the lacustrine area from the Indian Ocean. Ismā'īl had already envisaged such a move during Baker's expedition, and he immediately dispatched four Egyptian warships with troops, who overpowered the garrisons of the Sultan of Zanzibar at the mouth of the River Juba in November 1875. The Sultan, together with Sir John Kirk, the powerful British consul at Zanzibar, vigorously protested at this violation of his territory, and *The Times* stigmatised it as 'a wanton outrage'. Ismā'īl therefore recalled the expedition, turned to diplomacy, and requested the support of the British government for his attempt to obtain a port on the East African coast. The Foreign Office was thus presented with a genuine dilemma. On the one hand, as Ismā'īl pointed out, Egypt had spent large sums in attempting to suppress the slave trade on the Upper Nile, and Britain was anxious to buttress Egyptian authority in north-east Africa in order to prevent France or Italy from obtaining a foothold on the Red Sea coast. Against this was the fact, as Kirk argued, that support for Ismā'īl would involve the repudiation of the alliance with Zanzibar, the very basis of British policy in East Africa. For more than half a century Britain had supported the Omani rulers of Zanzibar and the coastal ports. Not only did Britain hope, by guaranteeing the independent sovereignty of the Sultan, as in the Anglo-French agreement of 1862, to prevent European powers from obtaining a foothold in East Africa, but also Sultan Barghash, as a result of considerable anti-slavery pressure, had agreed to a complete prohibition of the sea-borne slave trade as recently as 1873. Kirk's arguments proved decisive, Ismā'īl was overruled and the British position in Zanzibar was further strengthened.

Ismā'īl's intervention, however, sufficiently startled the British humanitarians into undertaking a direct, private initiative on the East African coast. The lead was taken by Sir William Mackinnon, a cautious Scottish Presbyterian, self-made head of the British India Steam Navigation Company, one of the first shipping companies to exploit the newly opened Suez Canal, which in 1872 had started a service to Zanzibar. Together with Sir Thomas Fowell Buxton, whose grandfather had been responsible for the Abolition Act and the 1841 Niger Expedition, Mackinnon started in 1876 to construct two roads inland to the lakes. In 1877 he opened negotiations with the Sultan for a concession to develop the mainland with a company modelled on the lines of the old East India Company. The British government, however, were not prepared at this stage to support Mackinnon by granting a charter for his projected company; indeed Lord Salisbury, the Conservative statesman who had just taken office as Foreign Secretary, took secret steps to impede the negotiations, apparently fearing that the scheme might involve the British government in unnecessary and expensive adventures on the mainland. Thus the early humanitarian initiative, sparked off by Ismā'īl's imperialism, ended in failure; plans for a company remained in abeyance; and, though neither Mackinnon nor the Foreign Office realised it, Salisbury's determination to remain unentangled at this stage with the affairs of East Africa had lost both Britain and Zanzibar a uniquely favourable opportunity for intervention which was never to recur. The long calm period of undisputed British influence, when Kirk and the navy utilised, yet upheld, the Sultan's authority, and the humanitarians tentatively planned to take up Livingstone's challenge on a basis of philanthropy plus five per cent, was soon to be shattered rudely by the sudden whirlwind of European rivalries and the introduction of *realpolitik*.

EUROPEAN REALPOLITIK

It was indeed the other event in Egypt in 1869, the opening of the Suez Canal, rather than Ismā'īl's lunge into Equatorial Africa, which led imperceptibly to British intervention in East Africa, and indirectly greatly facilitated Bismarck's creation of a German colonial empire. For it was European and world strategy which was to impinge so suddenly upon East Africa, and to make so sharp a break with previous developments in the area. Ever since Napoleon's Egyptian expedition, Britain and France had recognised that Egypt was the key to India and the Far East. Both these rivals agreed on a policy of defending Turkey against Russia, and both preferred to compete for influence at Constantinople and Cairo rather than assume direct responsibilities in the area. As in Zanzibar, the European powers hoped to achieve their political aims by manipulating the traditional rulers. The Canal immensely enhanced the strategic importance of Egypt, but its opening did not immediately involve a change in either British or French policy. Ismā'īl's debts, however, incurred both by his imperial adventures and by his attempts at modernisation—of which the Canal was but one example—led by 1879 to his bankruptcy, deposition and the institution of a system of financial control exercised by British and French agents on behalf of Egypt's creditors. Although neither power wished to extend their responsibilities, their interference aroused an Egyptian nationalist movement under Colonel Ahmad Urabi, who came into power as Minister of War in February 1882. Gladstone and his Liberal government were dragged by the French towards a policy of intervention, and then, left in the lurch by them at the last moment, the British went in alone, and defeated Urabi at the battle of al-Tal al-Kabīr in September 1882. The expedition was conceived by the Liberals as a temporary intervention, similar to the Ethiopian or Asante campaigns of 1868 and 1874; but with the success of the Mahdi's revolt in the Sudan, Britain gradually found herself ever more deeply involved, taking over the defence and administration of Egypt, and becoming responsible for the payment of its debt. By 1884, then, the occupation of Egypt had left Britain a hostage to the fury of frustrated French imperialists, and helplessly exposed to the calculations of Bismarck, who could demand British concessions elsewhere. The moment was ripe for Germany to act.

German firms had been trading with Zanzibar since 1844, and by the 1870s a fifth of Zanzibar's trade was in German hands. Theorists and some business men advocated imperial expansion, but Bismarck, Chancellor of a Germany which he had united under Prussian leadership, was far too shrewd a statesman to rush unprepared into colonial adventures in Africa or elsewhere. At home he was still faced in the 1870s with fierce political opposition, and in Europe he was confronted by France, bitterly obsessed with his victorious seizure of Alsace-Lorraine in 1870; thus his refusal in 1874 to accept an offer from the Sultan to place Zanzibar under German protection was merely one example, among many, of a policy of watchful abstention. By the early 1880s, however, the situation had changed. The foundation of the Kolonialverein in 1882 marked the alliance of German industrial and commercial interests to create 'a national impulse' towards the acquisition of colonies, and domestically Bismarck was no longer at odds with his naturally conservative allies. In France, Jules Ferry, with Bismarck's encouragement, led his countrymen to seek compensation in Africa for their lost provinces in Europe; while Britain, entangled in Egypt, found herself hopelessly isolated at the Berlin Conference (1884–5) where her hopes of excluding her rivals from the Congo basin received a disastrous setback. With so favourable a situation at home and abroad, Bismarck moved rapidly and decisively. In April 1884 he declared a protectorate over a German settlement in South West Africa, in July he annexed the Cameroons and Togoland, and in October he appointed a consul for East Africa as a preparation for his master-stroke there.

Before this fell, however, a quaint and somewhat ludicrous episode gave Britain yet one more opportunity to forestall him. In September, while the Foreign Office was smarting under this succession of reverses, a letter was received from Harry Johnston, a remarkable young explorer who had been sent by the Royal Geographical Society on a botanical expedition to Kilimanjaro. Johnston had been welcomed by Rindi (or Mandara), ruler of the small Chagga chiefdom of Moshi and an exceedingly able diplomat, who had built up his power against rival Chagga chiefs by exploiting a series of alliances, first with the neighbouring Warush tribe, then with Swahili traders, and finally by attempting to monopolise contacts with visiting Europeans. The welcome extended to Johnston was therefore merely a minor incident in Rindi's grand strategy, but it encouraged Johnston to write enthusiastically to Lord Edward Fitzmaurice, the Parliamentary Under-Secretary of State, suggesting that he should be authorised to conclude a treaty with Rindi, offering him British protection in return for permission to found a small colony of English planters. The country, Johnston wrote, was 'as large as Switzerland . . . eminently suited for European colonisation . . . within a few years it must be either English, French or German. . . . However I am on the spot, the first in the field, and able to make Kilimanjaro as completely English as Ceylon.' Fitzmaurice and his chief, Lord Granville, jumped at this opportunity to anticipate their European rivals, and ordered Kirk, still consul at Zanzibar, to cable his opinion of the scheme. Yet although Kirk realised that his system of maintaining British paramountcy in East Africa based on a supremacy of influence in Zanzibar, was already threatened by the imminent possibility of other European powers annexing key-points in the interior, he was reluctant to take the first step in such a scramble. At this critical juncture, therefore, he advised a policy of inaction. The opportunity passed, for three months later when the Foreign Office finally directed him to take the initiative in an amended plan of assisting the Sultan to negotiate treaties with the Chagga chiefs, Gladstone, ever an anti-annexationist, angrily vetoed the whole idea. 'Terribly have I been puzzled and perplexed,' he wrote to one of Granville's supporters, 'on finding a group of the soberest men among us to have concocted a scheme such as that touching the mountain country behind Zanzibar with an unrememberable name.'

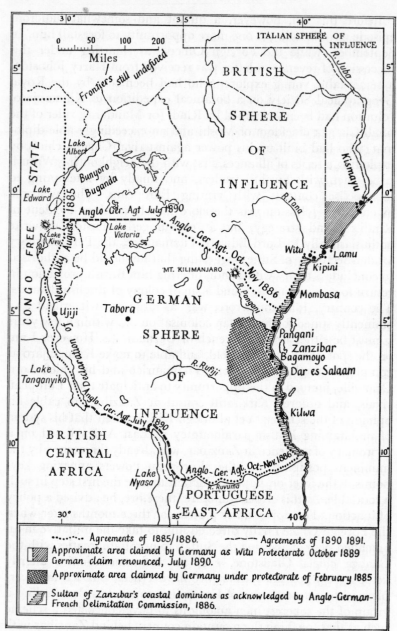

ITALIAN SPHERE OF INFLUENCE

BRITISH

SPHERE

OF

INFLUENCE

CONGO FREE STATE

Lake Albert

Bunyoro Buganda

1885

Lake Edward

Lake Kivu

Anglo-Ger. Agt. July 1890

Lake Victoria

Neutrality August

Declaration of

Anglo-Ger. Agt. Oct-Nov 1886

R. Tana

Witu Lamu
Kipini

'MT. KILIMANJARO

R. pangani

Mombasa

GERMAN

SPHERE

Ujiji Tabora

OF

Lake Tanganyika

Anglo-Ger. Agt July 1890

INFLUENCE

R. Rufiji

Pangani
Zanzibar
Bagamoyo
Dar es Salaam

Kilwa

BRITISH

CENTRAL

AFRICA

Lake Nyasa

Anglo-Ger. Agt. Oct-Nov 1886

R. Ruvuma

PORTUGUESE EAST AFRICA

30° 35° 40°

Frontiers still undefined

0   50   100   200
Miles

Kismayu

R. Juba

·········· Agreements of 1885/1886.   ———— Agreements of 1890 1891.
Approximate area claimed by Germany as Witu Protectorate October 1889
German claim renounced, July 1890.
Approximate area claimed by Germany under protectorate of February 1885
Sultan of Zanzibar's coastal dominions as acknowledged by Anglo-German-French Delimitation Commission, 1886.

Fig. 25 Partition of East Africa.

It was the last opportunity for Britain and Zanzibar to consolidate their unique position in East Africa, for on 10 November 1884 Karl Peters landed secretly on the Tanganyika coast. In ten days he secured treaties with twelve befuddled, minor chiefs in the interior, who, unaware of the full significance of their actions, granted away their sovereignty to the Gesellschaft fur Deutsche Kolonisation, a company formed by Peters and other extremist members of the Kolonialverein, with the aim of acquiring colonies for Germany by independent, direct action. By February 1885 Peters was back in Berlin with his treaties, and Bismarck soon issued a *schutzbrief* placing the territories claimed by the company under Imperial German protection and, as in the case of the British chartered companies, delegating administrative authority to the Company. The British, deeply committed in Egypt—Khartoum had fallen in January, with Gordon killed by the victorious Mahdists—and threatened with a war over Russian intrusion into Afghanistan, were in no position to oppose Bismarck. Gladstone even openly welcomed the arrival of Germany as a colonising power. Sultan Barghash of Zanzibar, abandoned by Britain and faced with a German naval squadron, was forced to recognise the German claims in the interior and to grant control of Dar es Salaam and the coastal customs. In October 1885 Germany, Britain and France set up a delimitation commission which agreed, over the Sultan's head, to limit Zanzibar's territory on the mainland to a ten-mile strip, and a year later the Anglo-German agreement of October 1886 calmly divided the immediate hinterland of these coastal areas into British and German spheres of influence. The first act in the partition of East Africa drew to a close.

By this time Lord Salisbury had replaced Gladstone as Prime Minister, and for the rest of the century British foreign policy was largely shaped by the ideas and objectives of this disenchanted aristocrat. Almost completely unconcerned with local African problems and opportunities, he calmly directed the 'partition', tenaciously defending Britain's strategical interests and jettisoning all else in the cause of European concord. In 1886 he was still quite uninterested in the interior of East Africa. Faced with a proposal to rescue Emin Pasha, leader of the beleaguered Egyptian garrison in Equatoria, Salisbury merely thought that the Germans should undertake this task, and in fact Karl Peters leapt at the chance of

32

intervening in the lacustrine area. The development of British interests in East Africa was, therefore, for the moment left to private enterprise; to Mackinnon and his British East Africa Association (later the Imperial British East Africa Company), which in May 1887 obtained a concession from the Sultan of Zanzibar granting full rights for fifty years over his mainland possessions in the British sphere. The next two years witnessed an intense rivalry between the British and German companies to establish claims in the interior. The Germans operating from their bases in Tanganyika and Witu threatened to reduce the British sphere to an insignificant triangle from its coastal baseline and exclude them from the fertile lacustrine area. At first Salisbury remained unmoved by this rivalry and refused in 1887 to grant a charter to Mackinnon's group; but by September 1888 he had completely changed his attitude, the charter was quickly granted, and Salisbury began to take decisive diplomatic measures to establish British paramountcy on the Upper Nile.

Salisbury's conversion was determined by Egyptian and not East African considerations. In March 1887 he still hoped that Britain could soon withdraw from Egypt and that the European powers would agree to guaranteed re-entry rights for Britain if necessary. The idea, however, was vetoed by France and Russia, and gradually, on two counts, Salisbury became convinced that the British occupation of Egypt would have to be permanent. There was, firstly, the strategic impossibility of defending the Dardanelles against the combined fleets of France and Russia, and as British influence declined in Constantinople the importance of holding Cairo, the other key to India, increased. Secondly, in Egypt itself the British, influenced by their imperial experience in India, were embarking on a long-term programme of authoritarian reform to protect the peasant, which could only be sustained by force, since it led them to detest the nationalist politicians. 'Once our troops go,' wrote Salisbury in June 1889, 'the Khedive will not last six months.' And once the occupation of Egypt was regarded as permanent, it became imperative to prevent the Nile waters, the life-blood of Egypt, from falling into hostile hands. Preparations for the re-conquest of the Sudan were begun, and Salisbury took over the diplomatic defence of Uganda.

While Salisbury's lack of interest in East Africa had changed in under two years, into a determination to win the Nile sources for

Britain, events were forcing Bismarck to become more accommodating. In France in 1885 Ferry was replaced by Clemenceau, committed to a continuing hostility to Germany, and in these circumstances, wrote Bismarck's son, 'Salisbury's friendship is worth more to us than the whole of East Africa'. Bismarck's reluctance to support Peters in his rivalry with the British was further strengthened by the fierce resistance which the Company's high-handed actions had provoked on the Tanganyika coast. By the end of 1888 the coastal peoples, led by Abushiri ibn Salim al-Harthi, a member of an old Arab family, were up in arms. Powerful tribes such as the Wahehe and the Yao helped Abushiri and the Germans were hemmed in to a few hastily constructed stockades. Bismarck was forced to intervene, sending an Imperial Commissioner, von Wissmann, at the head of an armed force, to take control, and only after two desperate encounters was Abushiri defeated, captured and hanged in December 1889. By the time, then, that Salisbury had reached his decision Germany was ready to negotiate. On 1 July 1890 an agreement was signed by which in return for the cessation of Heligoland, a barren yet strategic island off the German coast, Germany agreed to evacuate Witu and recognise Uganda as a British sphere of interest. Karl Peters protested bitterly that two kingdoms had been sacrificed 'for a bath-tub in the North sea', and the veteran explorer Stanley exclaimed that 'a new pair of trousers had been exchanged for an old trouser button', but, for both powers, European and global strategy counted far more than the mere acquisition of colonies.

THE AFRICAN SCENE

So far then the main lines of the partition of East Africa had been determined by the policies of two European statesmen, neither of whom was primarily interested in the peoples or potentialities of the area itself. In the last stage of the partition, however, the scene shifts decisively to Africa and in particular to Buganda. The 1890 agreement merely defined a British sphere of influence. It did not establish a British protectorate in Uganda, and it was unrecognised by other European powers, notably France and Belgium. Only effective occupation by treaty or conquest could render it permanent, and, although Salisbury was ready to defend strategic interests by diplomacy, he was still quite unprepared to thrust imperial adventures and responsibilities on a reluctant and hostile House of Commons. It remained therefore very much an open question whether Britain would establish her rule in the interior, and this question was largely determined by the course of events in Buganda and their repercussions in Britain.

By 1890 the situation in Buganda was explosive, and Mackinnon's Company found itself helplessly involved first in the internal struggle for power in Buganda and then in Buganda's rivalries with its neighbours. The whole story is indeed an outstanding illustration of the way in which the actual course of the European occupation of Tropical Africa was so often moulded by traditional African politics and manipulated to serve specific African objectives. Following the *coup d'état* of the Arab-led party in 1888, the exiled Kabaka, Mwanga, together with the Christian Baganda leaders who were campaigning for his reinstatement, appealed in 1889 to Jackson the leader of an Imperial British East Africa Company's caravan, and agreed to sign a treaty with the company. His message, however, was intercepted by Karl Peters, leading a rival German caravan, who hurried to Buganda in February 1890, where he found Mwanga and the Christians back in power, but still threatened by the Arabs and their allies who had withdrawn to Bunyoro; Peters immediately offered Mwanga an alternative treaty. No help had materialised from Jackson, and Mwanga was advised by the Catholic missionaries to accept Peters' offer. This brought to a head the rivalry between Catholic and Protestant Baganda, and the situation was further complicated when, a few days later, Peters, hearing of Jackson's approach, hurriedly withdrew. Jackson tried to force a stiff treaty on Mwanga, who with Catholic support refused to sign, so that when Lugard arrived in Buganda in December 1890 with orders to bring the country under Company rule, he was faced with an ominous situation in which the Protestants or 'Ingleza' had become identified with the Company's British flag, and the Catholics or 'Fransa' were united in a royalist suspicion of British rule. Behind both factions lurked the Muslims and Arabs in Bunyoro, and in May 1891 Lugard temporarily reunited the Christian Baganda to defeat the Muslims on the frontier of Bunyoro. He then cut west into Ankole and Toro to intercept Bunyoro's supply route to the south, thus initiating the conquest of Buganda's ancient rival. In Buganda itself tension developed rapidly and, in January 1892, Lugard, in order to maintain his position, was forced to assist the Ingleza by

issuing arms to them; subsequently intervening decisively with his
Maxim gun to defeat Mwanga and the Fransa chiefs. Henceforth
the British presence in Uganda was intimately dependent on its
alliance with the ruling faction in Buganda.

BRITISH EAST AFRICA

Meanwhile, in Britain Mackinnon's Company, faced with the
threat of bankruptcy, requested government assistance from
Salisbury in December 1890. Salisbury, however, failed in July 1891
to pass a scheme for a Uganda railway survey through the House
of Commons and the Company decided to withdraw. At this
critical juncture Bishop Tucker and C.M.S. supporters collected
£15,000 to enable Mackinnon to maintain Lugard in Uganda for
a further year. But this only postponed the need for a decision until
the autumn of 1892, by which time a Liberal government had
succeeded Salisbury. In opposition the Liberals, led by Gladstone
and Harcourt, had resolutely refused to sanction any assumption
of imperial responsibilities in the interior of East Africa, but, in
order to strengthen his cabinet, Gladstone appointed Lord
Rosebery as Foreign Secretary, a man who thoroughly accepted
Salisbury's estimation of the vital strategic importance of holding
Egypt and the sources of the Nile. It is unlikely, however, that by
themselves strategic needs would have overcome the deep-seated
reluctance. Even in Earl Rosebery's mind, reinforcing the strategic
consideration, was the fear of what would happen in Buganda if the
Company were not replaced by British authority. Lugard himself
reported that evacuation would 'inevitably result in a massacre of
Christians such as the history of this century cannot show', and in
September Rosebery, by threatening to resign and hence destroy
the Liberal government, persuaded the Cabinet to obviate the
danger of immediate evacuation by agreeing to authorise a delay
of three months. During this breathing space the missionaries,
chambers of commerce and humanitarians, with Lugard's support,
mobilised public opinion throughout Britain in favour of the
retention of Uganda. As a result, when in November the Cabinet,
on Rosebery's insistence, decided to send Gerald Portal as
Imperial Commissioner to report on the situation, Roseberry was
able to assure him privately 'that public sentiment here will expect
and support the maintenance of the British sphere of influence'.
From there it was but a short step to the declaration of a British

protectorate in 1894. Strategy, the missionaries and the power-conflict in Buganda had all contributed to this decisive rout of the Liberal, anti-imperialist forces, and British colonial rule in East Africa continued to be harnessed to the needs of Buganda. Mackinnon's company, lacking the mineral or commercial resources of a Rhodes or Goldie, had severely over-strained itself by striving to reach the lacustrine kingdoms. Undercapitalised and mismanaged, it had completely failed to gain the confidence of the tribes along the inland route. Portal reported that among the Kikuyu 'by refusing to pay for things, by raiding, looting, swashbuckling and shooting natives, the Company have turned the whole country against the white man'. It was an ominous prelude for a colonial regime which, preoccupied with the problem of making the Uganda Railway pay, was to rely on white settlement for the rapid development of Kenya.

'GERMAN' EAST AFRICA

In German East Africa the defeat of Abushiri and the change from company to imperial control laid the foundation for the expansion of colonial rule into the interior. Gradually an alliance developed between the Germans and the coastal peoples, similar in some respects to the British-Baganda relationship. Swahili was developed as a *lingua franca*, and Swahili clerks, interpreters and askari (soldiers or policemen) became the influential intermediaries between the administrators and the tribes. Some of the leading Arab traders in the interior welcomed the extension of German law and order, as did the large Sukuma tribe in the north. The fiercest opposition came in the southern half of the territory from the Yao and even more from the Wahehe. Under the leadership of Mkwawa, the Wahehe had established a hegemony over most of central-south Tanganyika. In 1888 Mkwawa sided with Abushiri and, after the latter's defeat, he continued to harrass the caravan trade, practically annihilating a German column in 1891. Three years later, the Governor captured and destroyed Mkwawa's central fort, but the chief escaped to conduct a brilliant and fierce guerilla war until July 1898, when, worn out and overwhelmed, he chose suicide rather than submission. The African response to the partition was not however by any means limited to pliant passive acceptance on the one hand or courageous, yet fruitless, opposition on the other. Many shrewd African diplomats successfully manipulated the incoming forces for their own traditional, tribal ends. Rindi, the Chagga chief who welcomed Harry Johnston in 1884, was an outstanding example of those who exploited diplomacy, successfully establishing close relations first with the missions and then with von Wissmann, using both for his own ends. With false information he poisoned the Germans' relationship with his much more powerful rival Sina of Kibosho, who was provoked into opposition and subsequently destroyed after a fiercely fought campaign in February 1891. By then, however, Rindi was an old man, and after his death, later that year, his methods were taken over and perfected by Marealle, head of a rival chiefdom, who in similar ways succeeded in twisting European rule to the advantage of his tribal section. Yet, in his last years, Rindi's diplomatic subtlety merely overlaid a more profound sorrow—a haunting awareness that sovereignty had passed to others, that the old freedom had died. As he faced the end he sang songs of death to his elders:

> Now I lament to you, you old ones,
> To you I lament sorrow and pain.
> Now help me to bewail sorrow.
> Now the distress is mine, woe clings to me
> But I forsee it will be yours.
> I leave my home, the pain will remain with you.

And when the elders asked, 'Why do you say this?' the old chief answered, 'I am now weary, the bull is ready to be slaughtered! But you will be tied down with pegs so that you cannot move as you wish.'

The partition imposed upon East Africa, as elsewhere, a series of arbitrary boundaries drawn to suit the convenience of strategists in Europe with little consideration for those people, like the Yao, Masai, Acholi and Somali, who suddenly found themselves cut in half. It left, therefore, particularly in the case of the Somali, a dangerous legacy to the African states of the future. The immediate impact of the partition, however, differed from area to area. At first the impact was felt most strongly west of Lake Victoria where the ancient kingdom of Bunyoro lost heavily to its rivals Toro and Buganda. East of the lake the 1890s witnessed the decline of Masai power, but this was not wholly due to the British intrusion or the imposition of a *Pax Britannica*, some of the causes being a series of disastrous epidemics, the deaths of several outstanding leaders and the increasing ability of the Nandi and other tribes to defend themselves against the Masai raids. Perhaps then, for the peoples of East Africa the greatest result of the partition was the improvement in communications which it brought. It was the railways rather than the new frontier posts which ushered in the twentieth century revolution, but it is at least arguable that without the one the other would not have come.

QUESTIONS FOR FURTHER STUDY AND DISCUSSION

1 'The Arab penetration of East Africa led inevitably to the Partition.' Discuss.

2 Compare the motives and methods of Bismarck and Salisbury in the partition of East Africa.

3 Account for the failure of the experiments of company rule in East Africa.

4 Why did Britain establish a Protectorate in Uganda?

5 Assess the significance for the partition of East Africa of the following: Mkwawa, Harry Johnston, Khedive Ismā'īl, Karl Peters, Seyyid Barghash, Kabarega, Leopold II, Emin Pasha.

SELECT BIBLIOGRAPHY

R. Robinson, J. Gallagher, *et. al.*, *Africa and the Victorians*, Macmillan, 1961.

R. Oliver and G. Mathew (eds.), *History of East Africa*, Vol. 1, O.U.P., 1964.

R. Coupland, *The Exploitation of East Africa, 1856–1890*, Faber & Faber, 1939.

M. F. Perham, *Lugard, Vol. 1, The Years of Adventure*, Collins, 1956.

R. Oliver, *Sir Harry Johnston and the Scramble for Africa*, Chatto & Windus, 1957.

K. M. Stahl, *History of the Chagga People of Kilimanjaro*, Mouton, 1964.

Cambridge History of the British Empire, Vol. 3, 1959.

K. Ingham, *A History of East Africa*, Longmans, 1962.

W. L. Langer, *The Diplomacy of Imperialism*, A. Knopf, New York, 1956.

C. Peters, *New Light on Dark Africa*, Ward, Lock & Co., 1891.

M. E. Townsend, *The Rise and Fall of Germany's Colonial Empire, 1884–1918*, Macmillan, New York, 1930.

P. L. McDermott, *British East Africa or I.B.E.A.*, Chapman & Hall, 1893.

D. A. Low, 'British Public Opinion and the Uganda Question, October to December, 1892', *Uganda Journal*, Vol. 18, 1954.

R. Oliver, 'Some Factors in the British Occupation of East Africa, 1884–1894', *Uganda Journal*, Vol. 15, 1951.

28 The Development of African Politics in the Plural Societies of East Africa

BETHWELL A. OGOT

WITH most records still closed to the historian, and in a chapter of this length, one can only provide a very general and simplified account of political change in East Africa. The colonial period of East Africa's political history may be divided into three main periods. During the first period (1886–1914), which may be called the 'protection era', the East African colonies were regarded as a source of national pride, and their usefulness assessed in terms of the international power struggle. Britain and Germany, the main imperialist powers in the region, considered their primary duty to be the protection of their respective 'spheres of influence' against possible external threats. The second period, the inter-war years (1918–39), is the 'trusteeship period', the era of 'indirect rule' and of the first movement for a closer union of East African territories. Though the need for a positive colonial policy was generally realised, Britain, as the imperial power now in charge of the whole of East Africa, assumed she had unlimited time in which to effect her welfare schemes. Hence gradualism became the official British policy. The third and last period (1945–62) may be referred to as the 'Uhuru period', when demands for self-government became persistent, and when a new factor, African nationalism, emerged. These three periods are distinguishable by successive shifts in emphasis, but they have two important factors in common: the traditional African society and the new colonial regime. The latter gradually but surely eroded the former, until today we have in East Africa, as in the rest of Africa south of the Sahara, what is in effect a cultural crisis

THE 'PROTECTION PERIOD': 1886–1914

Despite the extravagant political claims of the Sultan of Zanzibar, his rule was confined to the east coast. The interior of East

Africa was inhabited by different ethnic groups—Bantu, Nilotic, Sudanic and Nilo-Hamitic—most of whom had never heard of the Sultan. These societies had reached different stages of political development, ranging from the centralised interlacustrine kingdoms of western Uganda, Rwanda, Burundi and north-western Tanzania to the 'stateless societies' of the Dorobo of Kenya and the Sandawe of Tanzania.

Economically, on the other hand, East Africa gradually came to be regarded as one economic system between 1840 and 1890. This was due mainly to the activities of the Arab and Indian subjects of the Sultan who, during this time, penetrated to most parts of East Africa in search of slaves, gum copal and ivory. This may be regarded as the beginning of the East African Common Market. The economic prosperity of East Africa soon attracted foreign traders from America, Germany, France and Britain to Zanzibar, where they were welcomed by the Sultan. But Seyyid Said's policy of encouraging foreign traders to his land had its risks, for, as had happened in India and elsewhere, the flag was to follow trade.

In 1886, without consulting any African leaders, and in spite of a strong plea by the Sultan for time to consider the question, Britain and Germany each carved out a 'sphere of influence' from the East African mainland, leaving Zanzibar, Pemba, Mafia and a ten-mile strip of land along the coast to Barghash. The vague boundaries of these 'protectorates' were finally defined in 1890, when as a result of the Anglo-German treaty, the future Uganda, Kenya and Zanzibar, and the future Tanganyika and Ruanda-Urundi, were placed in the British and German spheres of influence respectively. Germany, with the help of 'the big stick', succeeded in buying off the Sultan's rights to the ten-mile-wide coastal strip along German East Africa, with the result that, unlike in Kenya, there was no coastal strip problem for the Tanganyika and British governments to solve before independence.

Political events forced Britain to declare a protectorate over Buganda in 1894 and, in the following year, over British East Africa, which after the First World War was renamed Kenya. Although Britain formally assumed responsibility for these territories, she did not have any positive policy for their development; and it was left to the local administrators to devise schemes to keep their territories viable.

In Uganda, Britain had originally proclaimed a protectorate

over Buganda only. But between 1894 and 1914 a successful effort was made to extend this protectorate to include non-Baganda, first by trying to create a Greater Buganda, especially in western Uganda, under the sway of the Kabaka and, when that failed, by using Baganda agents to establish British overrule in the northern and eastern provinces of Uganda. In July 1899 Sir Harry Johnston was appointed Special Commissioner for Uganda. His main task was to establish a system of administration for the whole protectorate. In 1900, he concluded an agreement with Baganda chiefs which, in effect, separated Buganda from the rest of Uganda. In the same year he signed a much simpler treaty with the Omukama of Toro, recognising his rule over the Bwamba, Bakonjo and Batoro; and in 1901 an agreement similar to the Toro one was concluded with Ankole. The major result of the reorganisation plans of Johnston was that four different types of administration were created which, with minor modifications, have survived to this day: (1) Buganda, a state within a state; (2) the treaty kingdoms, Toro and Ankole; (3) areas of direct rule such as Lango, Acholi, Teso, Bukedi; and (4) Bunyoro, which was the only conquered territory, today classified with the treaty kingdoms.

The attitudes of the British government toward Buganda at this time are important for a proper understanding of the subsequent politics of Uganda. The kingdom was treated, not as a subject state, but rather as a colonial partner of Britain. The Kiganda political system was indiscriminately introduced in almost all parts of Uganda; Baganda agents helped the British to pacify and to administer the country; and Baganda pastors followed in the footsteps of the agents, with Luganda Bibles under their arms. But soon after the First World War a sharp reaction set in. The non-Baganda opposed this 'unholy alliance' between Buganda and Britain. They were determined to resist Buganda 'imperialism' and to reassert their identities. So successful were they in their opposition to this misalliance that Buganda decided, with the paternal encouragement of Britain, to withdraw into her political cocoon, the 1900 Agreement, never to leave it again.

The second important decision made locally during this period had even more far-reaching results for the political development of Uganda. Sir Hesketh Bell, the Governor of Uganda, decided contrary to the opinion of some of his predecessors such as Lugard and Johnston, who favoured plantation agriculture, that Uganda should be developed by Africans and that European initiative and technical skill would be welcomed so long as they contributed to the main objective—peasant agriculture. European settlement on a large scale was therefore out of the question, and Uganda was thus spared the bitter land politics that have beset other territories such as Kenya, Rhodesia and South Africa.

In Kenya we find the same story at this time: a lack of any policy on the part of Whitehall on the one hand, and local initiative on the other hand. On the completion of the Uganda Railway in 1901, and after the transfer of the present Western Kenya from Uganda to the East Africa Protectorate in 1902, Sir Charles Eliot, Commissioner for the Protectorate from 1901 to 1904, came to the conclusion that if his territory were to make ends meet European settlement must be encouraged. The Commissioner was further convinced that the mere presence of civilised European islands in a sea of savagery would be of great importance socially to the country. The white settlements would be the leaven of the territory.

This single decision was to mould Kenya's future. White settlement came to be regarded as the backbone of Kenya's economy, and all efforts up to 1952 were directed toward developing the 'white highlands' at the expense of the African areas. Instead of developing his land, the African was encouraged or compelled through labour laws and hut tax to go and work on European farms. Special 'Native Reserves' were later created for the indigenous inhabitants; and according to a dispatch issued in 1908 by the Colonial Secretary, Lord Elgin, the Indians were to be excluded from the 'white highlands' as a matter of administrative convenience. This so-called 'Elgin Pledge' was at the root of the 'Indian Problem' which troubled Kenya in the early 1920s, for it was tantamount to an official condonement of racial discrimination.

Whatever economic benefits these reservations have produced— and much of the pioneering work in agriculture was done by the white settlers—the spectacle of large individual European estates, sometimes undeveloped, surrounded by overcrowded African reserves within which it was illegal to grow lucrative cash-crops such as coffee and tea, produced the bitter racial politics that culminated in the Mau Mau uprising in 1952.

Furthermore, the white settlers began to agitate for 'self-government now' as soon as they arrived. And as a result of their pressures Legislative and Executive Councils were established in Kenya as early as 1906. The settlers' demand for 'uhuru', coupled with the lack of any policy on the part of Britain, engendered fears among the non-Europeans which further polluted the already muddy political waters. Settler politics were, and up to 1953 continued to be, irresponsible and aggressive, consisting chiefly of threats, civil disobedience and insults. And as Sir Philip Mitchell, a former Governor of Kenya has said, settler politicians like Lord Delamere and Francis Scott, Col. E. Grogan and F. Cavendish-Bentinck, set the political pattern which was soon imitated by the Indian National Congress.[1] When, after 1945, the African nationalist emerged, he soon realised that if he was to survive politically in Kenya he had to adopt the shock-tactics of the settlers.

When we turn to the German 'sphere of influence' we find that much of the period was taken up with the establishment of German administration in the region. But unlike Kenyan and Ugandan Africans, the indigenous populations of Tanganyika offered a much greater and a more sustained resistance to German rule, which took the form of a series of rebellions such as the Abushiri revolt on the coast, the Wahehe war of 1894–8, and the bloodiest uprising of all—the Maji Maji rebellion of 1905–7. The basic cause of the last was similar to that of Mau Mau: the African's pride and dignity were hurt by an oppressive regime. The rebellion was suppressed ruthlessly by the Germans who adopted a 'scorched earth' policy. The south of Tanganyika especially was devastated: villages were destroyed, leaders hanged and crops destroyed causing famine. According to official estimates, which are bound to have been conservative, about 120,000 persons died.

Up to 1907 it may be correctly said that Germany ruled the territory with an iron rod. But as the Mau Mau was to do about a half-century later in Kenya, the Maji Maji uprising, together with the Herero revolt in South West Africa, which occurred almost at the same time, compelled the imperial authority to change its attitude towards the Africans. Also, the socialists in Germany, like the socialists in Britain during the Kenya Emergency, strongly criticised the government's colonial policy to the extent of forcing a General Election on the issue. And although they lost the election, the government could not ignore their views.

From 1907 onwards the Colonial Office, under the able direction of Dr Dernberg, adopted a rudimentary theory of 'trusteeship' which embodied Kant's maxim that everybody, including Africans, should be treated as an end and not as a means. Land which was callously acquired for white settlement prior to 1904, in spite of the Imperial Decree of 1895 which recognised the need to protect the interests of the Africans, was now to be exploited for the benefit of all. There was to be no Native Reserve, and the Africans were not forbidden to grow cash-crops such as coffee, cotton and sisal, introduced by the Germans into the country.

It is thus evident that by 1914 the stage was set, and the different protectorates had taken shape. Uganda was to be developed primarily as an African country, with the kingdom of Buganda occupying a special status in the protectorate; Kenya had become a 'white man's country', with all that this concept implies; and Germany's oppressive regime in German East Africa was to be used as an excuse in 1919 for transferring the territory, now renamed Tanganyika, to a more 'responsible' colonial power, Britain.

THE PERIOD OF TRUSTEESHIP: 1918–39

In the Treaty of Versailles, Germany had been condemned as unfit to rule over 'backward' races because of her past oppressive policies. Under Article 119 of the Treaty of Peace which Germany signed on 28 June 1919, she renounced in favour of the Principal Allied and Associated Powers all her rights over her overseas possessions, including the area formerly known as German East Africa, which was placed under British tutelage. The Tanganyikans were regarded as 'peoples not yet able to stand by themselves under the strenuous conditions of the modern world', and therefore their country was placed in the Class B of mandates.

Because of the mandatory terms under which Tanganyika was to be governed, and also because the mandatory powers such as Britain were determined, during the inter-war period, to demonstrate the superiority of their colonial regimes, Britain formulated the doctrine of trusteeship. This was the old Burkian idea that political power over subject peoples should be exercised ultimately for their benefit. The revised version of the trusteeship doctrine was formulated by Lord Lugard in his *Dual Mandate in Tropical Africa*, published in 1922. 'The tropics,' wrote Lugard, 'are the heritage of mankind, and neither on the one hand has the suzerain Power a right to their exclusive exploitation nor on the other hand have the races which inhabit them a right to deny their bounties to those who need them.' Nobody seriously questioned the moral right of colonial powers to exploit Africa for their benefit, until after 1945 when the African nationalists denied that any outside group or power had any right, moral or otherwise, to exploit Africa.

But although trusteeship became the official policy of Britain during the inter-war period the colonies were expected to be self-sufficient. It was therefore difficult for the local agents of the imperial government to formulate any 'five-year plans', especially when world depressions put the exporters of primary products completely at the mercy of world prices. The result was that few development programmes could be implemented.

In East Africa, therefore, more emphasis was laid on the protection of native interests than on development. The famous Devonshire White Paper issued in 1923 not only proclaimed the 'paramountcy of native interests' policy but also killed the settlers' hopes for self-government. But the origin of this paper had little to do with 'native interests'; rather, the original issue had been the status of Indians in Kenya. The Indians were protesting against their inferior status *vis-à-vis* the Europeans. By the 'Elgin Pledge' they had been excluded from the 'white highlands', and they were not represented in the Legislative Council until 1919 when they were given two representatives compared with eleven given to Europeans. To add insult to injury the Secretary of State for the Colonies, Lord Milner, decided to support racial segregation in the towns, despite the declaration by the standing joint committee of the Houses of Lords and Commons on Indian Affairs in 1921 that 'there is no justification in Kenya for assigning to British Indians a status inferior to any other class of His Majesty's subjects'. The Kenya settlers firmly maintained that the Indians should not have any political rights in the country; and some of the missionaries who detested the unchristian customs of the Indians besought God to save Kenya from the 'oriental menace'.

Whitehall was, however, reluctant to provoke settler opposition by upholding the general principle accepted by the joint committee, until the settlers themselves made the mistake of over-emphasising the importance of safeguarding native interests. Then the British government decided to issue the Devonshire White Paper, inappropriately called *Indians in Kenya*; inappropriately because the White Paper dealt chiefly with native policy and the doctrine of trusteeship, and failed miserably to answer the Indian case. True, the Indians were offered five seats in the Legislative Council, but these were to be elected on a communal roll. And, according to the White Paper, the interests of all minorities were to be protected. This meant protecting the 'white highlands' and the 'white' areas in the towns. The paper also declared that 'primarily Kenya is an African country', and yet some of the best farming lands in Kenya were to be reserved in perpetuity for white settlers.

As well as enunciating the 'paramountcy' principle, the White Paper also enunciated the principle of trusteeship for the whole of East Africa. 'As in the Uganda Protectorate, so in the Kenya Colony, the principle of trusteeship for the natives, no less than in the mandated territory of Tanganyika, is unassailable. This paramount duty of trusteeship will continue, as in the past, to be carried out under the Secretary of State for the Colonies by the agents of the Imperial Government, and by them alone.' In other words, the 'sacred trust' was not to be shared with the white settlers. And yet in all the East African territories the immigrant communities exercised through the territorial legislatures political influence disproportionate to their numbers. Imperial control, it is true, was maintained through the device of the official majority in the legislatures; but nevertheless the Africans, who throughout this period were encouraged to concentrate on native authority, found their lives and future greatly affected by laws passed by remote bodies in which they were not represented.

The inter-war period was also the age of 'indirect rule'. The principle of 'indirect rule' was evolved mainly by Lugard and his able pupil, Sir Donald Cameron, who later in 1926 introduced it in Tanganyika, as a political convenience which was defended on utilitarian grounds. But the principle soon acquired the status of a religious dogma. It was sincerely held by most people at this time that Western political institutions were unsuitable for Africans. Africa, they contended, should evolve her own native institutions. This argument, which was used mainly by non-Africans to justify the policy of 'indirect rule', is today being used by African politicians to defend a one-party system in Tanzania and Kenya and a federal system in Uganda.

Throughout this period, self-government was regarded by the

British government as a very distant goal. The duty of Britain was, therefore, not to prepare her dependent territories for self-government, but to devise an instrument which would enable her to discharge her sacred trust. And that instrument was 'indirect rule', which encouraged the development of tribal institutions. Buganda separatism received further stimulus, and the position of the other traditional rulers in Uganda was greatly enhanced. In Tanganyika, Cameron, who regarded 'indirect rule' as an indispensable aspect of British trusteeship, maintained however that parliamentary democracy was unsuitable for Africans. Instead he advocated tribal democracies which ultimately were to be combined to form a Central Legislature—for the tribal African. The educated African was later to be admitted to the exotic legislature which had been introduced in 1926 for the non-Africans. How these two legislatures were eventually to be integrated into one system, Cameron argued, was to be left to the genius of the Africans.

'Indirect rule' as a system of government was not applied to Kenya, where 'direct rule' through the District Commissioners and the government-appointed chiefs was the rule. But as a political philosophy it was applied to Kenya as much as to the other East African territories. The Africans were advised to concentrate on local governments which had been established in 1925. But the aggressive politics of the settlers, with their persistent demands for responsible government on the Southern Rhodesian pattern, soon led to demands by politically precocious Africans for representation in the legislature. Although the British government had rejected the settlers' demand for self-government in 1923 it had not substituted a new objective. And the non-Europeans feared that Britain might yield to settlers' pressure as she had done in 1909 in South Africa, and again in 1923 in Southern Rhodesia.

It was under such circumstances that Lord Lugard suggested, as a solution to the Kenya problem, that the 'white highlands' should be turned into a separate state and be given self-government, leaving the 'Native Reserves' to develop along traditional lines. But there were strong economic reasons against such apartheid, because European agriculture wholly depended on cheap African labour.

In all three East African territories during this period, supra-tribal associations were frowned upon by the colonial authorities,

33

and any agitation for more representative institutions by the 'mission boys' was regarded as subversive. Most of the Africans were politically inarticulate; and all the African pressure groups such as the Kikuyu Central Association and the Kavirondo Tax-payers and Welfare Association in Kenya, the Chagga Cultural Association in Tanganyika and the Bataka Union in Uganda—all formed to air grievances concerning specific issues such as land, taxation, forced labour, female circumcision and so on—were tribal in character.

The system of parallel institutions—Native Authority for the Africans and Central Legislatures vested with most of the power for the immigrant races—was bound to cause political instability ultimately. In fact the problem of unifying the two systems has not been completely solved. When 'indirect rule' was finally aban-doned after 1945, there still remained the question of welding the different tribes and races into nations, and there was very little time in which to achieve this. The development of any national loyalties having been discouraged for so long, the Africans after 1945 were expected to behave like long-established nations. It is a remarkable achievement on their part that a country like Tangan-yika which, up to 1954, was nothing but a congery of tribes and races, attained independence as one nation.

Before we leave this period, let us look briefly at the attempts that were made at this time to bring about a closer union of the East African territories. The movement was initiated in 1924 by the Colonial Secretary, Mr L. S. Amery, who in 1925 appointed Sir Edward Grigg (later Lord Altrincham) Governor of Kenya, charged with the duty of bringing about the federation. Fortu-nately for East Africa, Mr Amery appointed in the same year Sir Donald Cameron to be the Governor of Tanganyika. The latter was a firm believer in British trusteeship, and he stubbornly main-tained that Amery's plan was contrary to the obligation of Britain as a trustee. Several commissions were sent to East Africa to investigate the possibility of establishing such a union, followed by protracted discussions in London. But the only important develop-ment that stemmed from Amery's plan was the Governors' Conference, the predecessor of the East African Central Legis-lative Assembly, which was to be convened regularly from 1926 onwards.

Why was it thought necessary to federate the East African

territories? And why did the scheme fail? These are important questions, particularly at a time when plans for an East African Federation are quietly being shelved by African leaders. The motives of the Kenya and Tanganyika settlers, supported by Mr Amery, Sir Edward Grigg and a few Uganda Europeans, in promoting federation was to obtain by the back door what they had failed to achieve openly. They were not merely interested in creating a common market or an administrative union, although these were their professed aims. Their main objective was to create a settler-dominated, self-governing federation from the Limpopo to the Nile. If they had attained their goal they would have killed two birds with one stone: they would have obtained self-government and they would have destroyed the British trusteeship and the mandatory system in Tanganyika. They failed to achieve what the Central African settlers later achieved in 1953, the abdication of Britain.

Those who opposed the federation—the Africans and Asians, the Uganda and Tanganyika governments and the Permanent Mandates Commission—feared that such a federation would be dominated by Kenya, the Southern Rhodesia of East Africa, and this would inevitably have meant the extension of her racialist policies into other territories. The Tanganyikan Africans and Asians contended that European domination was incompatible with the terms of the mandate, which enjoined fair and equal treatment for all. And the Baganda reminded everybody that such a move would be contrary to the terms of the 1900 Agreement.

But the Second World War demonstrated the need for a central administrative body to co-ordinate the common services of the East African territories. And mainly through the efforts of Sir Philip Mitchell, the East Africa High Commission, an administrative union was established in 1947 with its headquarters in Nairobi.

In concluding this section, a passage from Arthur Gaitskell well summarises British colonial policy in East Africa during the inter-war years: 'A policy halting between the two alternatives of a trusteeship objective and a power objective may forfeit the strength of either. The right hand may defeat what the left hand is trying to do, and vice versa. To educate but not to associate is to alienate.'[2] The British taught the African many new ideas during this period but they failed completely to associate him with real power. The result was the alienation of the African.

UHURU PERIOD: 1945–62

After 1945 the colonial powers were faced with a revolutionary situation for which they were ill-prepared. Colonialism was regarded as outmoded; and Europe, demoralised by two world wars, found it difficult to justify the continuation of the 'Dual Mandate'. In East Africa the political scene was completely transformed. Urbanisation, money economy, new organisations such as trade unions, welfare societies and clubs, Christianity and Islam, contact with the outside world and the 'politics of inequality' practised by the immigrant races—all these factors and many more finally resulted in the emergence of African nationalism. Hitherto the political conflict in East Africa had mainly occurred between the ambitions of the white settlers and the ideals of the Colonial Office. From now on the battle was to be fought between the Colonial Office and the African nationalists. During the inter-war years Britain conceived her prime duty in East Africa to be that of protecting the interests of the natives. But in the post-Second World War period Britain's supreme responsibility in East Africa was to safeguard the interests of the minorities.

The goal of self-government had long been regarded as suitable for the white colonies of North America, Australia, New Zealand and South Africa. But it took another forty years before Britain accepted this objective as applicable to Asia and Africa. Despite the signing in August 1941 by Roosevelt and Churchill of the Atlantic Charter, which laid down, *inter alia*, the principle that all peoples had a right to choose the form of government under which they wish to live, many Europeans, including Churchill, were later shocked when the Asians and Africans demanded the right of self-determination. Britain, unlike France, Belgium, Holland and Portugal, accepted the inevitable. Dependent countries were to be prepared for self-government, and economic and social institutions were to be built in readiness for such a goal. The objective was no longer doubtful; the *pace* became the real issue.

In order to implement her new colonial policy, Britain realised that she had to abandon the old economic principle that every colony had to be financially self-supporting. From 1940 onwards a series of Colonial Development and Welfare Acts were passed by the British Parliament providing for the expenditure of large sums of money on development projects in the colonies.

In the plural societies of East and Central Africa this new policy meant that governments would eventually be in the hands of African majorities. The system of 'indirect rule' and parallel development was to be abandoned in favour of that of parliamentary democracy; and native authorities were to be replaced by responsible local government authorities.

Although the goal was clear in the case of Uganda which, everyone agreed, was to be developed as an African country, it was far from being definite in the case of Kenya and Tanganyika. Britain, in deference to the wishes of the white settlers, maintained that parliamentary democracy could not work in the plural societies of Kenya, Tanganyika and Central Africa, if civilised standards had to be kept. 'Multi-racialism' or 'partnership' was therefore evolved as the system of government suitable to these areas. This was an attempt on the part of Britain to reconcile the national aspirations of the Africans with the vested interests of the Europeans. 'Multi-racialism', which was based on Rhodes' dictum of 'equal rights for all civilised people', was completely rejected by the Africans who demanded equal rights for all human beings.

In Kenya the Europeans continued to demand self-government on the Southern Rhodesian pattern up to 1952. It was the Mau Mau outbreak which finally convinced the settlers and the British government that the Southern Rhodesian model could never work in Kenya. The Lyttelton Constitution, which came into force in April 1954, and which introduced a multi-racial form of government, split the white settlers into two rival factions for the first time. The United Country Party, led by Mr Michael Blundell, accepted the new constitution, while a group of die-hards, led by the late Group-Captain Briggs, formed the Federal Independence Party to oppose them. Briggs's party revived the idea first proposed by Lugard of dividing Kenya into autonomous regions, one of which was to be the 'white highlands'. It is interesting to note that the former opposition party, the Kenya African Democratic Union, advocated in 1962–3 a similar policy under the new name of 'regionalism'.

Both the Lyttelton Constitution and its successor, the Lennox-Boyd Constitution imposed in 1957, were successfully opposed by the first group of African elected members who rejected 'multi-racialism' as a political philosophy and who employed the shock tactics of European settlers. They demanded that the British government declare Kenya an African country, and the Macleod Constitution of 1960 went a long way towards meeting their demands. The Africans, according to the new constitution, were to have a majority in the Legislative Council. Moreover, the majority of the ministers in the new government were also to be Africans. The reactionary elements among the Europeans regarded this as a betrayal of their work in Kenya over a period of sixty years. They formed a new party, the Kenya Coalition, under Cavendish-Bentinck, in what proved to be a last-ditch rearguard action.

Among the Africans there also occurred important political developments. With independence in sight, the facade of unity that African politicians had hitherto maintained against the Colonial Office and its agents began to show cracks. Problems of tribalism and personal struggles for power eventually drove a rift into the wall of African nationalism resulting in the birth of two political parties: the Kenya African National Union (destined to be led by Kenyatta) and the Kenya African Democratic Union. The latter claimed to represent the so-called minority tribes. And at the 1962 Constitutional Conference, the main issue between these two parties was the question of safeguards: what is the best way of protecting minorities in an independent Kenya? After protracted negotiations Kenya achieved her independence in December 1963 with one of the most complicated constitutions in the world.

The story was much the same in Tanganyika, at least in the initial stages. Apart from the Tanganyika European Council which was formed in 1949 to fight for European domination, most Europeans seem to have accepted the policy of 'multi-racialism' as the only policy that could safeguard their interests. In 1956 the United Tanganyika Party was formed with official encouragement. It claimed to be both nationalist and multi-racial, and it was opposed to universal franchise. The multi-racial policies of this party were vigorously opposed in Tanganyika itself as well as at the United Nations by a rival party, the Tanganyika African National Union (TANU), which had been formed in 1954 under the leadership of Mwalimu Julius Nyerere. [3]

The Tanganyika government naturally sympathised more with the multi-racial policies of the UTP than with those of Nyerere, who was still regarded as a dangerous demagogue. It is interesting to read government and European criticisms of Nyerere's activities at this time and to contrast them with the eulogies of his statesmanship we are now so much accustomed to hearing from the same people. On the flimsy ground that Nyerere's political activities were 'prejudicial to the maintenance of peace, order and good government', several branches of TANU were closed, others were refused registration, and finally a ban was imposed on Nyerere himself, restricting him to certain areas.

But it would be incorrect to give the impression that African nationalists in Tanganyika underwent the same kind of political training as their brothers, say, in Kenya. European settlers of the reactionary type were lacking, and many were Greek, German and other non-British nationalities who could not justifiably demand 'the ancient right of English people to govern themselves wherever they may be'. Their solidarity was therefore imperfect. Furthermore, constant pressures from the Trusteeship Council compelled Britain to make concessions. And unlike Kenya and Uganda, tribalism was not a real issue in Tanganyika, with its 122 tribes, none of them large enough to dominate the rest.

In August 1960, in new elections, TANU won seventy out of seventy-one seats. And on 9 December 1961, Nyerere became the Prime Minister of an independent Tanganyika with most of the fears of minority races allayed. As the famous debate in October 1961 on proposals for citizenship legislation showed, Nyerere firmly believes that 'discrimination against human beings because of their colour' is wrong. Perhaps this is the best answer to South Africa and Southern Rhodesia, and the surest safeguard for the minorities.

In Uganda, on the other hand, the goal was never in doubt. The British government, as early as the 1920s, had accepted the point that Uganda would be developed as an African country. This policy was reiterated in a more explicit manner in 1952. Consequently the problems of 'multi-racialism' that beset both Kenya and Tanganyika in the 1950s were lacking in Uganda. The main problem there was the absence of a powerful nationalist movement that could both produce a charismatic leader, a father of the nation, as well as engender the nationalistic sentiments essential to the creation of a nation. The Uganda African Farmers' Union, founded by I. K. Musazi in 1948, was largely a Buganda movement directed against the 'exploiters'—ministers and chiefs. The Union's agitation (which was essentially tribal, although it later developed anti-imperialist sentiments when the protectorate government intervened) resulted in serious rioting in April 1949.

Nor did the Uganda National Congress, founded in 1952 by Musazi, Abu Mayanja and Joseph Kiwanuka, succeed in redirecting the attention of the masses toward nationalist objectives. The work of the Congress was made more difficult by the fact that Buganda separatism had reached such a stage that not even this Baganda-led party could integrate the kingdom with the rest of Uganda. This separation in turn made the non-Baganda suspicious of Baganda motives, and as a result the Congress remained ineffective outside Buganda.

It was therefore left to Sir Andrew Cohen, a dynamic Governor, to fight the nationalist battle for the Africans. Convinced that Uganda had to be developed as a unitary state and on the West African pattern, he proceeded to introduce constitutional reforms both at the local government level and at the centre that soon strengthened the hands of the nationalists. The success of this policy, coupled with Cohen's determination to create a unitary state, aroused the suspicion of the Baganda, who were afraid of losing their identity. The Kabaka of Buganda therefore refused to co-operate with Cohen. As a result, on 30 November 1953, the Governor withdrew recognition from the Kabaka. This move was a miscalculation which only served to unite the Baganda in their opposition to the Central government. The British government, however, capitulated; and on 17 October 1955 the Kabaka returned triumphantly to his kingdom. Sir Andrew Cohen, in order to placate the Baganda, concluded a new agreement with their leaders, which offered them what was tantamount to political autonomy. Buganda separatism reached its climax at the end of 1960 when she declared herself independent.

The two issues that remained to be settled at this time were the future of the traditional rulers and, closely allied to this, the form of government for an independent Uganda. To tackle these problems two political parties had emerged in the country: the Uganda People's Congress led by Milton Obote and the Democratic Party led by Benedicto Kiwanuka, with most of the Baganda remaining aloof from either party. At the Constitutional Conference in London in September 1961, a quasi-federal constitution safeguarding the position of the traditional rulers was worked out. And on 9 October 1962 Uganda achieved her independence with Mr Obote as Prime Minister. But although Buganda was brought back to the fold, her special status, first established in 1900, is still one of the most intractable post-independence problems facing the leaders of Uganda.

1963 was thus the 'uhuru year' for East Africa. But political independence is a means toward the achievement of a fuller and happier life than is possible in a colonial set-up. Many problems remain to be solved: the lack of capital for economic and social development; the dearth of skilled personnel; the evolution of appropriate political institutions; and the formulation of a creed which will give the new African societies meaning and direction once the force of nationalism is spent. All these problems, and many others, have to be approached realistically if independence is to be meaningful.

NOTES

1 P. Mitchell, *African Afterthoughts*, p. 100, Hutchinson, 1954.
2 A. Gaitskell, *Grezira*, p. 337, Faber & Faber, 1959.
3 Mwalimu is a Swahili word and means 'teacher'.

QUESTIONS FOR FURTHER STUDY AND DISCUSSION

1 Describe the traditional social institutions of any one East African people and show how they have been modified during the past century.

2 What do you consider to have been (*a*) the assets, and (*b*) the liabilities of German colonialism in East Africa?

3 What difference did the mandated/trust status of Tanganyika make to the historical development of the country?

4 Contrast the twentieth-century development of Kenya and Rhodesia.

5 Do you consider an East African Federation (*a*) desirable, (*b*) feasible? Give reasons for your view.

SELECT BIBLIOGRAPHY

G. Bennett, *Kenya—A Political History*, O.U.P., 1963.
B. T. G. Chidzero, *Tanganyika and International Trusteeship*, O.U.P., 1961.
D. A. Low and C. Pratt, *Buganda and British Overrule*, O.U.P., 1960.
T. J. Mboya, *Freedom and After*, André Deutsch, 1963.
J. G. Taylor, *The Political Development of Tanganyika*, O.U.P., 1963.

29 African Politics in Central Africa

A. J. WILLS

A GREAT deal has happened in Central Africa, as in the rest of the continent, during the past sixty or seventy years—the life-span of one man. If history tells us anything, it is that revolutionary events do not change men, or the societies in which they live, as completely as we often think they do. The strands go on. As the 'colonial period' in Africa recedes, the old patterns can be expected to reappear, altered but recognisable. Any survey of the development of modern politics must look back, however briefly, at the origins of present African societies in pre-colonial days.

THE PEOPLES OF CENTRAL AFRICA

The iron-age communities who were settled north and south of the Zambezi a hundred and fifty years ago were all Bantu-speaking, but their economies and political development varied widely. Their arrival in the region during the past thousand years had been in three waves. First were the early settlers from A.D. 500 to 1000. These included the Tonga of the Zambezi valley and the Nyasa lake shore, and the somewhat later the Shona of the southern plateau. Second were the largely matrilineal, non-cattle-owning groups from the Angola and Congo highlands. First of these were the Malawi tribes who settled along Lake Nyasa and, like the Cewa and Nsenga, in the country between the Shire and Luangwa rivers. Later in this wave came the great Luba dispersal (1550–1750) from the upper Congo tributaries, populating much of north-western Zambia, and including the Bemba, the Luapula Lunda, the Luvale and the Luyi or Lozi of the upper Zambezi plain. These movements were completed by 1800. In the nineteenth century there arrived the third wave of settlers, this time from the south. Warrior patrilineal cattle-owning tribes of Nguni stock, such as the Ngoni and Ndebele, and of Sotho stock such as the Kololo, having been turned back from their pastoral southward drift through South Africa, fought their way towards and beyond the Zambezi, winning dominant positions among the complex of more agricultural peoples already established there.

These peoples today make up the African populations of Malawi, Zambia and Rhodesia. It is possible to find common factors that unite them, but easier to point to the Zambezi valley, which divides the broad tableland of south-central Africa, as an historical frontier as well as a geophysical one.

In the first place the later tribes, those of the second wave, remained north of the river. Less influenced by contact with Bushman and early Hamitic inhabitants of the first centuries A.D., they remained more wholly Negro with Congolese affinities. Then the Arab influence, exerted here mainly through the slave trade (1860–90), was found north, but not south, of the Zambezi. The Lozi and the Ngoni remained aloof from slave-trading influence, but particularly in north-eastern Zambia and in Malawi, the Arab incursions after 1860 disrupted tribal life and traditional economy, and deprived hereditary chiefs of their authority. Again, for various reasons, early missionary activity was most widespread north of the river. Though the Moffats of the London Missionary Society worked for years among the Ndebele it was with little success; whereas in the north, against the background of Livingstone's work, the influence of Francois Coillard in Barotseland and Robert Laws among the Nyasa tribes, to mention only two, was profoundly important because it preceded the arrival of commercial interests and political control.

South of the Zambezi, on the other hand, lay the centre of a Shona-Rozwi 'divine kingdom' which had no counterpart in the north. Its roots lay far back in the early mingling of Bantu and Hamite and, though later undermined by Arab and Portuguese exploitation, it had flowered into the Zimbabwe culture with its elaborate kingship rituals, its use of skilled stone masonry for temple construction and defence works, its well-developed system of law. Broken up by civil war, and finally destroyed by Ngoni and Ndebele invasions in the nineteenth century, Zimbabwe stands in history as a monument to human progress in south-central Africa.

Finally, the country south of the Zambezi, being of more moderate climate because of its latitude and altitude, and being contiguous with white-settled South Africa, was from the outset of the colonial period much more under the influence of Europeans, who settled there in relatively large numbers in the first decades of the present century, and whose economic enterprise—farm and

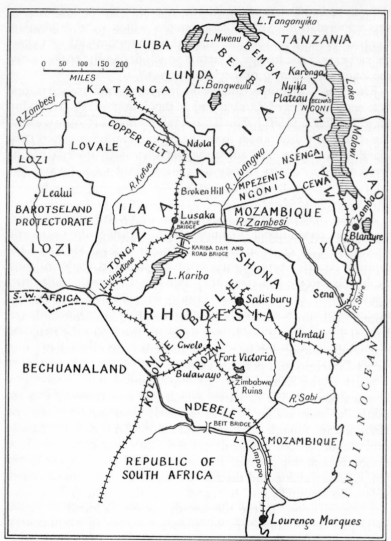

Fig. 26   Peoples of Central Africa.

mine and railway—were much more widely distributed than in the north.

In spite of these contrasts the colonial period, largely owing to the work of Cecil Rhodes, was to impose a partial unity on this region, of which the final manifestation has been the recent but short-lived Federation of the Rhodesias and Nyasaland. This unity was imposed from without, for reasons which were external to Central Africa. Now that the colonial period is drawing to a close, we can expect the historical factors which divide the region along the Zambezi valley to reassert themselves.

There are of course divisive factors that tend to separation between the tribes of Zambia and Malawi, north of the river; but these are less powerful than an overall community of origin: all the strongest tribes (apart from the Ngoni who have mixed their blood with the peoples among whom they have settled) having arrived in the country during the period of the second wave.

EXTERNAL INFLUENCES

Around 1875 the African population, which had only a generation before reeled under the impact of the Nguni-Sotho backwash, were having to cope anew with a double threat. First was the aspiring Arab empire-builder, with his insidious trade in guns, cloth and slaves, and soon after him the European trader and coloniser with his technical superiority in medicine, weapons and machines. The Arab impact, though outwardly more harmful than the 'civilising' influence of the European owing to its destruction of human life and order, was far less total in its effect. The slave trade, evil and essentially a negation of humanity, was, like other slave trades, a temporary factor in an expanding world trade. How long it might have lasted had not western, principally British, action intervened to destroy it is a matter for speculation. The far worse exploitation of the Congo by the Belgians was allowed to continue till 1912. But if we consider Arab trade and Arab influence as a whole we cannot deny a cultural influence, whose effect was far more partial and gradual than that of the white 'gods' from Europe.

The beneficial results of this influence, entirely obscured by the horrors of the slave trade, had only begun to reach parts of eastern Zambia and Malawi when the second threat to the traditional African way of life appeared in the form of the European coloniser and trader. Moffat's isolated missionary work had been proceeding in Matabeleland since 1861, but, north of the Zambezi, established mission stations did not begin their work till 1875 in Malawi country and 1885 in Barotseland. Close in their tracks came the concession seekers, towering among them Cecil Rhodes, who with the sometimes reluctant support of the British government gained in seven years (1888–95) by negotiation, purchase and war, control over the central region covered by the present states of Malawi, Zambia and Rhodesia.

It so happened that much of the region at this time was in a state of turmoil. The slave traders (Mambari in the west, Arab in the north-east, Yao and Portuguese in the east), profiting from the world boom in sugar, cloves and ivory, were spreading their depredations far and wide. In Malawi country, Mbelwa's, Chikusi's and Mpezeni's Ngoni, still in the second generation of settlement, were terrorising the tribes. Meanwhile the Ndebele, led by Lobengula since Mzilikazi's death in 1868, continued to raid round all points of the compass year by year.

Looking back over the space of more than half a century we can see that this widespread disorder was temporary, not endemic. We can see, moreover, that it was world factors, not local factors, which brought it about. European and Arab expansion, and world economic growth, were bringing inexorable pressure to bear on the internal politics of the African continent, well in advance of the first traders and administrators. None the less it seemed to the newcomers from Europe that Africa was essentially a land of war and barbarism. Believing themselves in the van of the inevitable march of progress they had no difficulty in justifying their political supremacy, bringing gifts of orderly administration, civilised communications and honourable trade.

AFRICANS AND 'THE SCRAMBLE'

African leaders varied in their appreciation of these gifts. Lewanika of Barotseland was outstanding in his welcome of teachers and technical instruction; but Lozi society already had a more complex economy than most, while Lewanika alone of the Central African chiefs visited Britain and saw for himself the best side at least of a modern industrial country. The Ndebele and Ngoni were less willing to accept the revolution in their way of life that the change from a tribal iron age to a developing industrial economy involved. It is not surprising that African rulers were more able to grasp the political implications of change than the social and economic consequences. To African chiefs the trader and the missionary appeared, not as harbingers of a new order, but as pieces in the game for political power. Lewanika first saw

Queen Victoria as an ally against Lobengula. Mpezeni, needing no such ally in his secure position among the western Malawi, scorned the need to associate with the white man. The Bemba factions in eastern Zambia used both Arab and Company support in their struggles for supremacy, but, having done so inevitably succumbed to company control when Arab power was destroyed.

In the last resort, the cause of the tribes was bound to be a lost one as the resort to arms by Lobengula and Mpezeni and the Yao showed. It was for diplomacy, without power behind it, to win what gains it could. Lewanika's treaties with Lochner in 1890 and with Coryndon in 1897 were triumphs of diplomacy. So would Lobengula's with Rudd have been had he not been outwitted and outmanoeuvred by Rhodes. By 1900 the Lozi alone retained some genuine political independence. For the rest the chiefs held only scraps of paper which, on signing, they had been able neither to read nor to understand.

The first Central African tribes to accept European settlement and, virtually, rule were the Shona group. Rhodes's pioneers hoisted their flag on the high plateau near the source of the Mazoe River on 12 September 1890, naming their camp Fort Salisbury. The name seemed well chosen, for it was Lord Salisbury's government at Westminster that had granted the Royal Charter to Rhodes's British South Africa Company. Rhodes, already Prime Minister of the Cape Colony and a millionaire, now possessed the right, as far as such a right existed, to establish political administration throughout the region as far north as Lake Tanganyika, provided that agreement with the chiefs could be obtained. By 1893 his relations with Lobengula, who regarded himself as overlord of Mashonaland, had deteriorated and broken down. The conquest of Matabeleland followed, with war in 1893 and suppression of a rebellion in 1896. Thus, apart from the Nyika, neighbours of the Shona to the east, Rhodes was not able to extend his company's authority much further till 1897.

In that year, however, Robert Coryndon signed the treaty with Lewanika at Lealui which made the Lozi allies of Queen Victoria, gave their own country protectorate status and authorised the Company to extend its activities right across the Kafue basin and as far north as the Congo/Zambezi watershed. It is certain that Lewanika had no right to make such concessions regarding vast areas beyond his own dominion, but the Company were satisfied—

as well they might be. Later they used this treaty further to give them mining rights in Lamba country—the fabulously rich copper belt along the Congo border—of which the Coryndon treaty made no mention at all.

Meanwhile, in the east, the years 1890–6 had been taken up with military operations against the slave traders, Yao and Arab, who were ravaging Malawi country. Here Rhodes was not directly concerned. The initiative had been that of the Scottish missionaries who, originally inspired by Livingstone's example, found their work was impossible in the prevailing chaos and appealed to the British government for aid. Spurred on by the threat of Portuguese advance up the lower Zambezi, which worried Rhodes as much as the churches or the Foreign Office, and encouraged by Rhodes's offer to provide funds, Lord Salisbury agreed in 1891 to the declaration of a protectorate in Nyasa and Luangwa country, to be called British Central Africa. The first Commissioner was Harry Johnston, who had already travelled in East Africa and had served the British authorities on the lower Niger. Armed with a small police force, Sikh and African, Johnston subdued the Yao and Ngoni chiefs, in five years of tough fighting (1891–6), and overthrew the incipient 'Arab' empire of slave traders, principally the Swahili chief, Mlozi, in 1895. Representatives of Johnston and Rhodes travelled widely in the country between Lake Nyasa and the Luapula, making treaties with local chiefs that had little legal validity but served to strengthen the diplomacy of the Foreign Office in London, faced with rivalry from Portugal, Germany and Belgium. The importance of these treaties should not be exaggerated, for the final arrangements were governed by the political situation in Europe rather than by events in Africa itself.

The years 1898–1900 saw the subjection and absorption within the Company's administration of Mpezeni's Ngoni, the Bemba in the north-east and Kazembe's Lunda on the Luapula. By Orders-in-Council of 1899 and 1900, administration and law courts were set up in North-Eastern and North-Western Rhodesia. The white administration in Mashonaland and Matabeleland rested on the Southern Rhodesia Order-in-Council of 1898, while the British Central Africa Protectorate, to be renamed Nyasaland in 1907, was given a court system and constitution in 1902. District headquarters were set up, a postal system established, the telegraph network completed, and the railway extended more or less to its present form, though the line to Lake Nyasa was not laid till 1916.

THE IMPLICATIONS OF DEVELOPMENT

The effects of these events were slow to appear, but none the less profound. The area covered was so vast that for years many Africans had but the slightest contact with the handful of administrators scattered across the plateau. But the passing of war, and of slave- and cattle-raiding, enabled many communities to revert to a more productive existence. The Bemba no longer needed to huddle in large stockaded villages, nor the Shona to camp in rocky outcrops for security. Traditional crafts were resumed, encouraged and extended by mission training schools, notably at the Livingstonia stations in Nyasa country.

More positive and widespread was the effect on economic life of the tax system, and of the demand for labour on railway, mine and farm. Whatever the idealism in the mind of the Victorian empirebuilder, Rhodes's settlers and shareholders intended to profit by their undertakings. Government had to pay for itself. Minerals, the dreamed-of gold, the new-found copper, had to be mined and marketed. This called for labour. The tax served the double purpose of compelling men to work for wages and of contributing to the revenue. Africans did not resent the tax, but proved stubbornly reluctant to work for longer than was necessary to earn it. The first decade of the century was taken up with bitter settler recriminations over the 'idleness' of the African, and with resort to questionable methods of inducing men to work. To the African the idea of working to a fixed schedule was quite new, while that of accumulating a stock of goods and property, which would enable him to profit from his undertakings and distinguish him from his neighbour was revolutionary. The iron-age economy had largely been a communal one—land, the basis of wealth, had not been individually owned; capital, apart from livestock which in the last resort could be claimed by the chief, was non-existent; and labour had been shared.

The tax, while it introduced Africans to the new system, did not yet make them a part of it. It did, however, have two direct and immediate effects. Politically it compelled all Africans to recognise and submit to a new authority higher than the chief, and to weld them into a supra-tribal community for which, within a few years,

34

they were willing to give their lives in war. Economically it drove many, especially from the poorer parts of the region, to travel long distances in search of employment. As early as 1904, more than 7,000 Africans a year were crossing the Zambezi, many going as far as the Witwatersrand where better money could be earned than in the scattered gold mines of Southern Rhodesia. Most of these Africans were Malawi, for Nyasa country, relatively thickly populated, offered little scope for paid work; the railway and plantations could absorb no more than a fraction of the potential labour force. Later, after 1930, the Northern Rhodesian Copperbelt attracted African migrant workers in increasing numbers, especially from Bemba country, but also from a much wider area.

The results of this migrant labour system were far-reaching. First, it weakened the rural labour force on which the whole African economy depended, and tended to disrupt the fabric of traditional society already being undermined in other ways. Second, it allowed the growth in the urban areas of rootless workers without family life or permanent commitment, a fact which delayed the establishment of proper facilities and prevented training in industrial skills. Lastly, it had political effects. Life in mining towns, association with men of varied background and observation of European wealth combined to create political discontent. This was evident in the urban areas themselves after 1945 when urban populations began to stabilise, but began much earlier in some rural areas, particularly Nyasaland, where the higher proportion of migrant workers had their homes. Malawi tribesmen, returning after two or three years away, learned to value their country with its small white population and freedom from the colour bar as a haven of security from the advancing white man's world.

Much of this lay in the future. There were, however, early indications of Malawi political awareness. The first Native Association was formed at Karonga in 1912; others flourished in the immediate post-war years. John Chilembwe's uprising in the Blantyre district in January 1915 was partly a protest against the exploitation of Africans, as he saw it, in service of a foreign cause, and partly an assertion of African leadership in defence of an African way of life. Much of the inspiration for this revolt, however, was derived from outside Malawi, Chilembwe himself having lived in the United States. It was early for African-inspired forward-looking movements to appear. Such isolated violence as occurred was rather backward-looking, resentful of the new order, seeking often by occult means to recover the illusory security of a passing age.

Apart from the obligation to pay tax and find work, the main effect of the new order upon Africans during the first three decades was felt through church and school. The missionary societies, almost sole providers of education, lacked funds and aimed principally at literacy and evangelism. Not until the Phelps-Stokes Commission published its report in 1925 did the educational horizon widen fully to girls' education, cultural subjects, agricultural and industrial training. Though governments at once responded to this report, the crippling economies imposed by the Depression prevented any real progress till the late 1930s, when the Second World War, in its turn, intervened. Not till after 1945 did education begin to become a serious factor in African development. None the less, school and church had provided Africans with their outlets for leadership in the first years of the occupation. Some of the leaders from the late 1940s onwards (such as Nkumbula, Kaunda and Sithole) had first served as teachers or pastors. Most had a mission school background. The younger generation of leaders on the other hand came up more often through trade unions and welfare societies in the new urban areas.

In the first three decades of the century, however, little was heard of the African voice. The great iron-age kingdoms that had ruled over the vast plateau for generations—some for centuries—receded into the background as regional communities, while white settlers and governments built roads and dams and bridges, extended mining operations (the big copper mines came into production after 1930 following a large-scale aerial survey), brought thousands of acres of tobacco and maize into cultivation and created modern townships, linking them with services by road, rail and air. Though in time they were to gain greatly from this laying down of the foundations of a modern industrial economy, Africans at first benefited little from the growing wealth. Wages remained at subsistence level, and the real incomes of the great majority remained static, sometimes even declined, during the first fifty years of European rule.

THE POLITICAL SUPERSTRUCTURE

Meanwhile developments in the political superstructure of Central Africa passed important stages which emphasised the division along the line of the Zambezi that we have already observed. In 1911 Nyasaland ceased to depend on Rhodes's annual grant of £10,000, and appeared finally to cast loose from its association with the Company territories. With its railway development held up by the delay in bridging the Zambezi at Sena until 1935, and its small white population (2,000 in 1939) consisting largely of missionaries and civil servants, Nyasaland pursued a separate existence, politically quiet and economically poor, the 'Cinderella', as some called it, of Central Africa.

More striking was the separation of Northern from Southern Rhodesia in 1923. The British South Africa Company in that year surrendered its administrative responsibilities and confined itself to commercial enterprise, mainly in the mining field. Southern Rhodesia, by the vote of three-fifths of its European electorate,[1] became a self-governing colony under the Crown, the Westminster Parliament exercising a tenuous oversight of native policy and retaining control of defence and foreign affairs. A sequel to the granting of independence to the South African colonies after 1908, this move was also a part of the post-war imperial policy towards the creation of a Commonwealth of independent Dominions. Northern Rhodesia, by contrast, became a Crown Colony under the direct administration of the Colonial Office. With its relatively small white population (3,600) neither able nor willing to manage their own affairs, the territory came beneath the canopy of the new trusteeship policy already emerging. Lord Lugard, the greatest of Britain's proconsuls in Africa, had outlined this in *Dual Mandate in Tropical Africa*, published in 1922. This book, which largely guided British colonial policy in Africa till 1945, countenanced the economic development of territories by their European communities, but aimed at the same time at the preservation and, where possible, the development of African institutions. Though Britain provided few funds to support it, the 'trusteeship' side of this policy, emphasised by the Passfield Memorandum of 1930 declaring the paramountcy of native interests, became increasingly plain to the Northern Rhodesian white settlers. From 1931 their pleas for amalgamation with Southern Rhodesia became insistent.

By this time, however, the political separation of the two Rhodesias was leading to divergent policies in the spheres of land, local government, industrial conditions and trade unions, all of which were closely related to African life.

In 1930 the European population of Southern Rhodesia, numbering about 50,000, owned over 31 million acres of land (about half the colony). The amount was still increasing year by year. Native reserves had been set aside in 1915, but many of them were far from the railway essential for the marketing of maize, and in any case they could no longer contain the growing population. Seeking to limit the amount of land open to European purchase, the Land Apportionment Act of 1930 divided the colony's land into three classes—European Land (49m. acres), Native Land, including Native Reserves and a new Native Purchase Area (29m. acres) and an Unassigned Area (18m. acres), which could be allotted to the European or African area as occasion required. This arrangement was outstandingly advantageous to the small white population, but there was little protest at the time. The Imperial government, faced with the Native Affairs Act of 1926, had already shown their reluctance to intervene on behalf of the Africans of the colony. The Africans themselves, still leaderless and largely inarticulate, were unable to judge their cause as a whole. In the 1940s, however, when people were moved from villages they had occupied for generations, on the grounds that they were 'squatting' on European land, the logic of the policy began to appear.

North of the Zambezi, land legislation took a different course. The amount of land originally purchased by white settlers was much less, being mainly confined to the railway belt. Native reserves were set aside in 1925, mainly with the aim of concentrating the population for administrative purposes. There matters were allowed to rest for the remainder of the trusteeship period. In 1947, compelled to deal with land policy by the implementation of a Ten Year Development Plan, the Imperial government confined Crown (which was virtually European) Land to 11 million acres—only six per cent of the territory. The 64 million acres of Native Reserves were confirmed, and the remaining 109 million acres were designated Native Trust Land, to be used only in the interest of the African population as a whole.

A similar policy crystallised in Nyasaland in 1950. Crown Land (known here as 'Public Land') was confined, after repurchase, to seven per cent of the Protectorate, half of it in the Shire highlands. The remaining ninety-three per cent was African Trust Land. There were, none the less, land grievances. With a population much more congested than in Northern Rhodesia, it was difficult to preserve even seven per cent of the land for European enterprise. Many Africans had come to live on this land in the disturbed years of resettlement after pacification, and resented being compelled to pay rent or suffer eviction under the 'tangata' system. This was a perpetual source of African grievance from Chilembwe's rising in 1915 to Wellington Chirwa's crusade against Federation in 1953.

What the Land Appointment Act had in fact done for Southern Rhodesia, and what the northern protectorate policies had not done, was to give legal and concrete form to racial segregation. White and black were to live apart in rural areas and in towns. 'Points of contact,' stated the Morris Carter Report on the land question, 'should be reduced until the native has advanced very much further on the paths of civilisation.' Instead of such a policy the needs of economic development should have called for co-operation and economic integration between the races. The Industrial Conciliation Act of 1934 further discouraged such integration by denying Africans the right to join trade unions or to form their own, or indeed to benefit from negotiation in trade disputes. The Maize Control Act differentiated between maize grown by the African and the European farmer, regardless of its quality. Much of this legislation was aimed to protect the white settlers, struggling in the trough of the trade depression, from African competition. They were dikes to defend what Godfrey Huggins, who became Prime Minister in 1933, described as a white island of civilisation in a sea of black barbarism. The dikes were reinforced by the pass laws of 1936 and 1937 compelling Africans to carry documents if they should set foot inside the European area, which they must do, indeed were encouraged to do, in search of work.

The protectorate governments in the north did not go so far along this road of urban and industrial segregation. Town workers more often had their families with them, and permanent urbanisation began sooner. Riots on the Copperbelt in 1935 and 1940, leading to some African deaths, were followed by commissions of enquiry which gave sympathetic hearing to African grievances and called for a start to African advancement in industry. The desperate need for copper during the war crisis 1939–45 led the government to permit an agreement between mining companies and white unions which blocked African advancement. But once the war was over African trade unions were formed, notably the Northern Rhodesia African Mineworkers' Union in 1948. African unions appeared at the same time in Nyasaland. The Southern Rhodesian government on the other hand continued to reject the idea of African unions, but allowed African workers to join white unions, much later, in 1960.

Local government policies also diverged. In Southern Rhodesia the chiefs, shorn of most of their responsibilities, survived as remnants of a passing age, while administrative and judicial responsibilities were mainly borne by the white officials of the Native Administration. Native Courts and Councils were started in 1937, but they were permissive only and did not become universal. The northern territories after 1929 started a policy of 'indirect rule' that was in line with Lugard's thesis, and Native Courts and Native Authorities, with financial as well as other responsibilities were instituted.

These (northern) local authorities were used not only for administering rural areas, but also as channels of information by which the colonial administrations sought to discover the opinions of the African population as a whole. This attempt to turn the framework of local government into a pyramid of representation suffered from two defects. In the fast-changing world of the 1940s and 1950s it was no longer axiomatic that the voice of the chief was the voice of the people. Hereditary authority tended to be conservative. Progressive elements found that there was little scope for their ideas in the chief's court, and therefore in the Provincial Councils and African Representative Council (1946). Not only did such a system provide for nominees rather than representatives, but it took no account of the urban populations of the railway line. The detribalised communities of Broken Hill and the copper towns could not be ruled by a Native Authority system. Yet, in Northern Rhodesia at least, it was here above all that an African political awareness would emerge. Indeed, from 1940 onwards Africans on the Copperbelt and in other mining towns were spontaneously forming their own Welfare Societies and Associations. It was these societies that were to form the core of the African political movement.

Nyasaland also was provided with a system of 'indirect rule', the Native Authorities again forming the base of a pyramid leading to the African Protectorate Council. Here, too, Africans formed their own societies alongside the official framework, but with important differences. The Native Associations were mostly formed in the rural areas of the Protectorate, and they started much earlier than the urban Welfare Associations of Northern Rhodesia—the first was formed at Karonga in 1912. This is accounted for by the greater density of the rural population and by the higher rate of labour migration from the Malawi villages which helped to create a more advanced state of political awareness. Native Associations concerned themselves with matters such as education, agriculture and the working of the migrant labour system. They remained on good terms with the chiefs, who after 1930 became Native Authorities. This easy relationship was another contrast with Northern Rhodesia, where friction between chiefs and the African Congress appeared in the 1950s. Such friction had its origin in the sharp division between urban and rural society in Northern Rhodesia. Nyasaland, without big mining centres, was free from such a division. Thus the Malawi chiefs were, throughout the late forties and fifties, in close accord with the Nyasaland African Congress. This goes far to account for the much greater cohesion of the Malawi movement against the Federation.

Late in the pre-Federation period African members appeared in the territorial legislatures of Northern Rhodesia and Nyasaland. As these members were nominated through the indirect rule pyramid, they were unimpressive as political leaders, and the development should rather be seen as an improvement on the former practice, still continued alongside, of nominating European members to represent African interests.

By contrast, African political activity was slow to appear in the Southern Rhodesian townships. Here the practice of temporary residence was more persistent. Many Southern Rhodesian Africans, besides, worked in the Union of South Africa, while a high proportion of the colony's urban employees were of non-Southern Rhodesian origin. Union influence helped to form the Rhodesian Bantu Voters' Association in 1922 for those few who qualified for the franchise, and the Rhodesian Native Association of about the same time. These combined to form the Bantu Congress in the thirties, which in turn became the African National Congress after the war. But these associations operated mostly on the territorial level and lacked grass-roots dynamism. It was not till 1957 that, roused by franchise and land legislation, a new and active African National Congress was formed.

FEDERATION

It was of course the question of federation, actively debated after 1948, that aroused Africans to political activity in the north and burst the bud of African nationalism. The idea of closer association was, however, older than this. We have seen the Northern Rhodesia settlers responding to the Passfield Memorandum with a stream of petitions for amalgamation. Against this trend was their territory's quick recovery from the trade depression and the world boom in copper, so that by 1940 Northern Rhodesia was riding on the crest of a wave that could carry it well away from any future dependence on the south. Colonel (later Sir) Stewart Gore-Browne, appointed the first member for African Interests in 1938, strongly argued the case for independent responsible government in the north. He was outnumbered by the amalgamationists led by Leopold Moore and, later, by Roy Welensky, while south of the Zambezi, Godfrey Huggins, an amalgamationist throughout, was well supported by many Southern Rhodesian settlers, who observed with some envy the expanding copper revenues of their northern neighbour. In 1939 a Commission of Enquiry led by Lord Bledisloe was despatched from London to report.

After three months in Central Africa, the Commission stated cautiously that while there were no objections to an immediate link-up between the two northern protectorates there were serious obstacles to their amalgamation with the south. Contrasts in native policy were emphasised, and African opposition north of the Zambezi was seen as 'a factor which cannot be ignored'. This opposition had been most loudly voiced by the Native Associations of Nyasaland.

By 1945 events were moving at a faster pace. While the majority of Africans continued to live under subsistence conditions in remote rural villages, urban concentrations were growing and a huge industry was building up on the Copperbelt. Many Africans had served in the armed forces overseas. They returned to find a growing political awareness and means for its expression. Development plans in agriculture and education were under way. Meanwhile in the world at large the tide of war had carried away much of the paternal gradualism that had survived from the imperial era. In Britain a Socialist government was swept to power in 1945, pledged to colonial development and the advance towards independence of native peoples. Negotiations began for the transfer of power in India.

This new wind did not blow among the white communities of East and Southern Africa. Rather were their ranks increased—at a rate in the Rhodesias of several thousand a year—with the arrival of immigrants from Europe, many of whom sought to escape the restrictions of the new order, following the hard economies of the war. Huggins' strongly British (*vis-à-vis* Afrikaner) United Party swept the board in the Southern Rhodesian election of 1948. In that year, not satisfied with the Central African Council set up in 1945, he and Welensky launched their successful campaign for Federation.

Three factors made possible this success. First was the need for hydro-electric power. This was undeniable, though the contention that the capital could only be raised if the territories were combined was questionable. Nyasaland did not stand to gain, while Northern Rhodesians would have preferred to dam the Kafue gorge thus making it possible to irrigate the Kafue plain. Second, events in South Africa aroused misgivings in London. Malan's Nationalist Party, committed to apartheid, won power in 1948, thus heralding the end of forty years of friendly British-South African relations. The security of the High Commission Territories now appeared in jeopardy. A strong British stance in Central Africa would restore the balance. Lastly there was a swing of opinion in Britain itself. Reacting to the surrender of India, a regretful right wing turned its gaze to the state of the empire elsewhere, envisaging federal dominions in East Africa, Central Africa, South East Africa and the Caribbean. A strong dominion astride the Zambezi would be a check to Malan, solve the problem of Nyasaland, a growing economic liability, and provide an anchor for British influence on the continent. These sentiments accompanied the political recovery of the right in Britain, culminating in the return of the Conservatives to power in 1951.

White leaders in the Rhodesias were not slow to make use of

these factors. At the same time they used the formula of 'federation' in place of amalgamation as one which would permit the native policies of the northern territories to continue under local control. This was their only genuine concession to the reality of African opposition. Though Africans were invited to all the conferences on federation except the vital first one, their minority voice would have carried no weight and they were reluctant to attend. Knowing that the early fifties were the latest time in which they could hope to override African opposition, European leaders gambled on the continuing apathy of the pre-war years. This refusal to recognise the facts was to doom the Federation; but because the African political movement was not fully organised, co-ordinated or countenanced abroad, the gamble was to succeed in 1953.

AFRICAN NATIONALISM

Indeed African opposition was hardly observable in Southern Rhodesia, but it was strident in Northern Rhodesia and even violent in Nyasaland. In the latter protectorate the Native Associations and Protectorate Council had been on friendly terms with the colonial administration till 1943. These calm waters had then been shattered by James Sangala, a former Native Association official, calling on Nyasaland Africans to 'fight for their freedom'. The Nyasaland African Congress, built on the Associations, was formed in 1944. Charles Matinga reminded the public of African land grievances and called for African majority representation on Legislative Council, Township Managements and Land Boards. The outburst took missions and government by surprise, but the next four years showed that this was no shallow-rooted movement. Malawi leaders were in constant communication with European progressives in Nyasaland and Dr Hastings Banda in London. War and travel for many had emphasised a growing awareness that much in African society needed defending in the face of European 'civilisation', and that Africa was a vast continent whose peoples had but to work together to win their hopes and aims.

Thus the Malawi leaders were seeing the very reverse of the vision of Huggins and Welensky, aspirants now to federation in Central Africa. In 1951 the N.A.C. leaders declared bluntly that their aims and those of Europeans in Central Africa were 'poles apart'. '. . . our goal is African self-government. . . . Theirs is the establishment of a Central African Dominion, in which they will have an imperium over the African people.' The Federal Constitution being worked out between 1949 and 1953 appeared to point in this direction. Against such a development the chiefs and political leaders of the protectorate spoke with one voice. 'Nyasaland knows,' wrote Chief Mwase, 'that if she agrees to Federation, then she has deprived herself of self-determination.' Congress leaders referred to discriminatory legislation in Southern Rhodesia, and stated unequivocally that 'what the people of Nyasaland desire is self-government within the British Commonwealth of Nations'.

In Northern Rhodesia the opposition to Federation was equally strong but less coherently expressed. The population was more widely dispersed and less easily reached by Congress propaganda. In the urban areas there was rivalry between Congress and Trade Unions. The Congress-inspired 'national strike' in April 1953 failed utterly owing to lack of Union support. Some of the chiefs also looked askance at Congress, though the Bemba paramount chief Chitimukulu openly sided with Congress on the Federation issue. On the whole there was more bewilderment and uncertainty in Northern Rhodesia than in Nyasaland, which enabled Henry Hopkinson, the Minister of State who visited Central Africa in August 1952, to make the sweeping statement that ninety per cent of the African population knew nothing about Federation, let alone understood it. This was the standpoint persistently held by European leaders throughout the coming decade; that opposition was not spontaneous, but inspired through intimidation by agents of Congress.

The Southern Rhodesian electorate, still almost entirely white, again with a three-fifths majority, voted by referendum in favour of Federation, and the Imperial Parliament authorised the Federal constitution in October 1953. Critics were answered, though not silenced, by certain entrenched clauses in the constitution including an African Affairs Board, and by the inauguration of a policy of 'partnership' between the European and African races. This ideal of 'partnership' was the aerial balloon which launched Federation in 1953. Its buoyancy did not endure. A compromise formula to bridge the gulf between the 'parallel development' policy in the South and the 'paramountcy' policy in the

North, it was held with conviction by few, and made negligible difference to public or private race relations after Federation was begun. The African political movement, having failed to prevent Federation, lost momentum for the next three years. In this time nothing was done to win its support, while it became plain that the northern territories stood to gain little economically or financially. Nyasaland's deficit was financed by the Federal government, but with the largest of the three populations she was allowed the least part (six per cent) of the loan capital for investment. Prices of consumer goods were raised by the adoption of the Southern Rhodesian customs pattern. At the same time the Northern Rhodesians viewed with suspicion the siting of the Federal capital at Salisbury, and the sharing of their own growing copper revenues with the South.

The watershed in the life of the Federation was crossed in 1956. In response to demands for adjustment of the franchise, Huggins (by now Lord Malvern and Federal Prime Minister) introduced the Federal Electoral Bill, which split the Common Voters' Roll, and the Constitution Amendment Bill which increased the size of the Federal Assembly but reduced effective African representation. The African Affairs Board objected to both Bills as differentiating measures and complained of interference with the constitution before the scheduled conference in 1960–2. Despite a storm in the House of Commons, to which the Bills were referred, these objections were overruled and the measures became law in 1957 and 1958. The Federal elections in July 1958 brought an overwhelming victory for the United Federal Party, led by Welensky since Malvern's retirement, and pledged to seek Dominion status at the conference in two years' time. Constitutional adjustments also took place in Southern Rhodesia, where Todd, shortly before his fall from office, introduced the dual voters' role, and in Northern Rhodesia. A change in Nyasaland was postponed owing to the disturbed condition of the Protectorate.

In all three territories, in fact, African nationalists had been roused to new militancy. In Southern Rhodesia, stung to action by the new franchise law and by the implications of the Land Husbandry Act designed to revolutionise African farming without providing adequate land from the European area, a new African National Congress was formed. Its leaders were Joshua Nkomo, a former Welfare Officer on the Rhodesia Railways, and George Nyandoro, a vigorous opponent of the new land laws. In Northern Rhodesia also a new party, the Zambia African National Congress, appeared. Its leaders, Kenneth Kaunda and Simon Kapwepwe, were critical of Nkumbula's leadership of the old Congress. Achieving a new co-operation with chiefs and trade unions, Kaunda insistently demanded secession from the Federation. Finally Dr Hastings Banda, who had been living in independent Ghana, returned to Nyasaland, after forty years' absence, at the invitation of African leaders. His three months' whirlwind campaign against Federation brought turmoil and violence throughout the protectorate, and Governor Sir Robert Armitage declared a state of emergency in March 1959, during which fifty-two Africans were killed and 1,300, including Banda and other leaders, were detained. The declaration of a state of emergency in Southern Rhodesia two days previously, and the use of Federal troops in Nyasaland, brought charges of collusion, but these were later refuted by the Devlin Commission.

The Africans had made their point. In London the new Conservative government elected in 1959 sent the Monckton Commission to Central Africa to prepare for the constitutional conference. Its report called for a radical change in Southern Rhodesia's policies and for the right of secession from the Federation of individual territories. Harold Macmillan, touring southern Africa in 1960, declared plainly that the Federation could not have independence until the northern territories had achieved self-government. Welensky and European leaders complained that Britain was surrendering to African violence, and bitterly denounced Colonial Secretary Iain Macleod for allowing Dr Banda to go free. It was of no avail. The conference was postponed until 1962 while new territorial constitutions were prepared, but the end of the Federation was in sight. Rapid social reform removing the colour bar partially in Southern Rhodesia and almost wholly in Northern Rhodesia—it did not exist in Nyasaland —and establishing non-racial conditions in the Federal Civil Service, could do nothing to stop the tide of African nationalism.

The bitterness of Welensky and the federalists was intense, but despite threats they did not resort to extreme measures. This was due less to a lack of spirit than to a sense of relief among Southern Rhodesians (who formed the majority of the Federal electorate) that their uneasy association with the 'black north' was about to be broken, leaving them free once more to conduct their own affairs. The Kariba dam, after all, was complete. Its giant turbines, situated on the southern side of the river, first revolved in 1961. After the elections of 1962 Sir Edgar Whitehead's United Federal Party government gave place to a right-wing Dominion Party administration led by Winston Field. Plans to repeal the Land Apportionment Act and relax the policy of segregation were abandoned. A new constitution gave Africans, for the first time, representation on the legislature, with fifteen seats in a Parliament of sixty; but the demand for universal suffrage from Nkomo's Zimbabwe African Peoples' Union was firmly rejected.

The goal of universal suffrage was reached in the northern territories in new constitutions which granted internal self-government for Nyasaland in January 1963 and for Northern Rhodesia in January 1964. The new African governments were led by Dr Hastings Banda and Dr Kenneth Kaunda. Indeed the 'wind of change' had been blowing a gale in Africa for three years. Following the independence of the Sudan in 1956 and of Ghana in 1957, a flood of newly independent states appeared in 1960, including several former French territories, Nigeria and the Congo. Tanganyika followed in 1961, Uganda in 1962 and Kenya in 1963. The tragedy of the Congo could not reverse this trend, though Sir Roy Welensky sought through alliance with Moise Tshombe to build an alliance between black and white right wings that might yet stave off defeat for the Federation.

These efforts were in vain. In 1964 the Central African Federation was dissolved. Malawi (July) and Zambia (October) became independent republics within the British Commonwealth, while Southern Rhodesian Europeans sailed away on their perilous attempt to steer between the Scylla of African democracy and the Charybdis of white dictatorship, their objective, unchanged through two generations, still Rhodes' dictum of equal rights for all 'civilised men'.

It has been maintained that the chief blunder of the European leaders was that by forcing Federation upon Africans against their wishes they brought forward those very African nationalist movements which it was their main intention to suppress. This view should be accepted with some reserve. The only militant nationalist movement to appear after the Federation was begun was that in

Southern Rhodesia; and this was the one movement that did not concern itself with Federation but rather with franchise and land. The African Congress parties north of the Zambezi were started in 1944 and 1945, before closer association was a really live issue. Unless it is realised that the African movements sprang from a continuously evolving political awareness, and a natural growth of desire for political expression, among a people who, despite Sir Roy Welensky's assertion to the contrary, are highly politically-minded, the history of Central Africa in this century cannot be understood. Because history has been 'made' by Europeans in the sense that, owing to political and economic supremacy, they have held the initiative for sixty years, it is too easy to credit them with responsibility for everything that has happened in the African field. This is as misleading as it is to ascribe African nationalism to the subversive machinations of a handful of ambitious and self-seeking agitators. Intimidation within and support from outside there have certainly been; but these are secondary factors and cannot obscure the broad growth of African social and political inspiration which, as John Adams said two centuries ago of the American revolution, lay in the hearts and minds of the people from the beginning.

NOTE

1 Africans were allowed to vote, but were in practice excluded by the property qualifications.

QUESTIONS FOR FURTHER STUDY AND DISCUSSION

1 Give a description of the peoples of Central Africa before the advent of European settlement.

2 Account for the different political development of Zambia and Rhodesia in the twentieth century.

3 Discuss the view that in Central Africa Malawi has been in the rearguard of economic development but in the advance guard of political development.

4 Do you consider that the Central African Federation was doomed to failure from its inception? Give reasons for your view.

5 What do you consider to have been the significant achievements of three of the following: Joshua Nkomo, Kenneth Kaunda, Hastings Banda, Sir Roy Welensky.

SELECT BIBLIOGRAPHY

L. H. Gann, *A History of Northern Rhodesia*, Chatto and Windus, 1963.
J. R. Gray, *The Two Nations*, Institute of Race Relations, O.U.P., 1960.
P. Mason, *The Birth of a Dilemma*, Institute of Race Relations, O.U.P., 1958.
B. Williams, *Cecil Rhodes*, Constable, new edition, 1938.
E. A. Walker, *A History of Southern Africa*, Longmans, 1957.
A. J. Wills, *An Introduction to the History of Central Africa*, O.U.P., 1964.

30 Pan-Africanism and Nationalism

COLIN LEGUM

PAN-AFRICANISM is the expression of a desire for African unity
It is at the same time an expression of a sense of unity between all
peoples whose ancestors originally came from Africa. As such it
assumes a common brotherhood of black peoples everywhere—in
Africa, North America, the West Indies. Indeed, the birth of the
idea of Pan-Africanism occurred in the New World, not in Africa.

The reason for Pan-Africanism having its roots outside Africa
itself are easy to understand. The descendants of the Negro slaves
in the New World felt they had been made 'homeless' by their
transfer to foreign countries and subjection to alien cultures. They
felt they did not 'belong' to the New World. They felt themselves
as the orphans of Africa—aliens and strangers in a world of white
people who were chiefly interested only in their labour on the
plantations and hardly at all in their personality as Men. Thus
they felt themselves 'black outcasts', robbed of their dignity as
human beings, and with no claim to being 'of equal value in the
sight of God'.

What distinguished them from other men was only one thing:
their colour. Because they were black they were regarded as
inferior. While many Negroes passively accepted their place as
'bottom dogs' in a white world, others did not. There were no
fewer than 240 slave risings in the United States alone, and an
unknown number in the West Indies. The most important was the
successful revolt in Haiti led by Touissant l'Ouverture between
1791–1803. These risings were the strivings of men to be free and
equal. These two ideas—'free' and 'equal'—were felt to be
inseparable: you could not have the one without the other. Even
those who did not rebel openly expressed their desire to be
'themselves' in their separate churches, in the preservation of their
old cultures, and especially in their songs, their poetry and their
music which reveal longings for their 'Paradise Lost' in Africa, for
a 'Black Heaven where all God's chillun have wings'. They speak,
too, of feelings of loneliness, of being deprived of their manhood

and of their happiness. Always they speak of suffering and of deliverance.

Many of the descendants of Negro slaves had only the haziest ideas about Africa. Few even knew which tribes or territories their ancestors had come from. Therefore, when they thought of Africa it was as one great country in which all black men lived together and were happy and free. This view of an Africa without frontiers or divisions probably inspired the idea of 'One United Africa'. Since all black people in the New World were bound together in 'a single society of inferiors', it is possible to understand the emotional sense of a single African nationhood.

With education there grew a new spirit. Negroes began to travel; some to Africa. They began to speak on platforms and to write in their own newspapers. Bishop Alexander Walters of the African Methodist Episcopal Zion Church and Dr Edward W. Blyden began to spread the idea of a 'common destiny' which Negroes of the New World shared with Africa. In 1881 Blyden, at the opening of the Liberian College, warned against the dangers of Africans losing their traditions and of becoming assimilated. 'The African must advance by methods of his own. . . . We must show that we are able to go alone, to carve our own way.' In 1902 Dr Blyden's kinsman, Edward Blyden, spoke for the first time of 'an African personality' to describe Majola Agbebi, a Yoruba who had established the first independent native African church in West Africa. Agbebi has a special place in the growth of the Pan-African movement. Not only did he embody the 'African personality' in the special sense of an African asserting his own identity and destiny, but he also provided a link between the New World and what was being looked for in the New Africa.

EARLY POLITICAL MOVEMENTS

The first organised political expression of Pan-Africanism occurred in London in 1900. The initiative was that of a Trinidad lawyer, H. Sylvester Williams, who convened the first Pan-African conference ever held. There were few representatives from Africa itself, but a number came from America and the West Indies. Most were students living in England. Among them was Dr William E. Burghardt Du Bois, an outstanding Negro scholar and writer, who was to become the 'father' and prophet of

Pan-Africanism. Speaking at the turn of the century Du Bois uttered his famous lines:

> The problem of the twentieth century is the problem of the colour line—the relation of the darker to the lighter races of men in Asia and Africa, in America and the islands of the sea.

Du Bois was born in the United States in 1868 and died in Ghana in 1963 at the ripe old age of ninety-five. In his lifetime he had seen the seeds of his ideas begin to bear fruit in Africa. He was one of the founders of the National Association for the Advancement of Coloured Peoples (NAACP) which has led the struggle for Negro civil rights in America. He was a prolific author of political works, poetry and novels, and edited the NAACP's journal *Crisis*. He was also a skilful politician. Under his leadership four Pan-African Congresses were held.

The first was held in Paris to coincide with the Peace Conference at the end of the First World War in 1919. At this conference he was greatly helped by a prominent Senegalese leader, M. Blaise-Diagne, who in his day was the outstanding spokesman for French-speaking Africans. There were only fifty-seven representatives at that famous meeting: 'Negroes in the trim uniform of American army officers . . . coloured men in frock coats or business suits, polished French Negroes who hold public offices, Senegalese who sit in the French Chamber of Deputies. . . .' These fifty-seven men spoke in the name of black people everywhere in proclaiming their demands for African rights. The second conference under Du Bois' leadership was spread over two sessions in 1921—the first in London and the second in Brussels. Its message was that 'the habit of democracy must be made to encircle the world'. The emphasis was on the importance of inter-racialism and justice. The third conference was held in 1923 in both London and Lisbon. Its manifesto made this striking demand: 'In fine, we ask in all the world *that black folk be treated as men*. We can see no other road to peace and progress.' Four years later, Du Bois presided over a conference in New York in 1927. After this, organised Pan-Africanism lapsed for almost twenty years when a new star arose on the Pan-African firmament, George Padmore.

In the meantime, however, a bitter conflict broke out in the Negro world in which leaders like Du Bois were challenged by a phenomenal leader, Marcus Garvey.

THE 'BACK TO AFRICA' MOVEMENT

Garvey (1887–1940) was a figure both romantic and ridiculous; but his influence was enormous. Of him Dr Kwame Nkrumah later wrote that he was personally more influenced by Garvey's ideas than by anything else in America. Garvey was a Jamaican; a rough, tough, colourful politician who loved crowds, uniforms, parades and high-sounding titles. He called his movement the Universal Negro Improvement Association, and he proclaimed himself 'Provisional President of a Racial Empire in Africa'. He was fiercely proud of being black, and he wore his colour like a shield into battle.

Garvey's disagreement with Du Bois was over the future of the Negroes outside Africa. While Du Bois believed that Negroes in the New World should fight to establish their rights in 'exile', Garvey insisted that their only future lay in a return to Africa. Although his 'Back to Africa' movement was not the first of its kind, it was the first and last time that the idea stirred millions of Negroes. He raised large sums of money to establish the Black Star Line which was to transport Negroes back 'home'. But his enterprise failed, and he died an almost neglected figure in London in 1940.

Bitter though the rivalry was between Garvey and Du Bois it was by no means sterile. Negroes were stirred to think seriously of their place in the world and of their relations with Africa. No less important was the fact that hundreds of students from Africa, who were going in increasing numbers to America and to Europe after 1900, found fertile ideas in the clash of debate. Students from South Africa, from Malawi (Nyasaland) and Kenya and West Africa, many of whom were later to become leaders in their own countries, picked up the seeds of Pan-Africanism in the New World and bore them home with their academic degrees. Among the earliest converts were leaders from South Africa and Nyasaland. Later came the West Africans—first Nigeria's Dr Nnamdi Azikiwe, the doyen of West Africa's Pan-Africanists, and later leaders like Ghana's Dr Kwame Nkrumah.

THE IDEA OF NÉGRITUDE

In the 1930s, too, a parallel movement was taking root in Paris among French-speaking African students there. But it expressed itself in literary forms rather than political. Its inspiration was

Légitime Défense, a literary journal started by French-speaking West Indians. This movement developed the idea of *négritude* which became identified with *Présence Africaine*. Its great theorists were the Martiniquan poets Ettienne Lero and Aimé Césaire (the real father of *négritude*). Its outstanding African contributor was Dr Léopold Senghor, who later became the first President of Senegal.

Négritude reflected the special conditions of the French-speaking Africans in the world of Frenchmen. Unlike the British or Belgians, the French believed in a colonial policy of cultural assimilation—sometimes mockingly described as turning Africans into 'Black Frenchmen'. This assimilation was limited to a small elite which, feeling itself smothered in alien clothes and ideas, revolted intellectually. They insisted on the need to strip away their French cultural wrappings in order to discover their own true black skins. This intellectual revolt against enforced assimilation and the 'search for the roots of African origins' is the essence of the 'philosophy of blackness', i.e. *négritude*.

In its first phase *négritude* stresses the essential unity of black people. This is its racist mood. In the second stage it stresses the unity of all humanity This is its anti-racist mood. But this unity must be achieved by true assimilation as between equals and on a voluntary basis, not through the enforced assimilation of 'cultural imperialism'. It is because of this intellectual process that *négritude* is described as 'anti-racist racism'. Although its ideas are quite different from those spawned in the New World and England, its results have been similar. Both movements have emphasised the sense of the oneness of all Africans, and demanded of them a common struggle to regain their dignity and independence.

TWO HISTORIC CONFERENCES

The Second World War (1939–45) was the great divide between the old world of imperialism and the new world of great powers and scores of new, small, independent states. Two important events came between the ending of the war and the opening of a new chapter in Pan-Africanism. The first was the Pan-African conference held in Manchester in 1945. The second was the first Bandung conference of Afro-Asian states in 1955 where the sense of unity of 'all the coloured peoples of the world' found common expression.

The ideas of Pan-Africanism, which had evolved slowly over the first half of this century, were finally expressed as a programme of principles at the 1945 Manchester conference. Here, for the first time in the history of Pan-Africanism, the leading participants were no longer the Negroes of the New World but Africans from 'the homeland'. They included many future leaders like President Nkrumah and President Kenyatta. Although President Azikiwe was himself prevented from attending the conference his ideas and encouragement were of great importance.

The leader who successfully bridged the gap between the 'two worlds' of black peoples was George Padmore. He was born in 1903 in Trinidad, the grandson of a slave, and the son of a distinguished botanist. After working for a time as a journalist he went to university in the United States at the age of twenty-one. There he became a communist and went to Moscow in 1930. For a time he worked as the most influential Negro in the cause of international communism. But in 1933 he became disillusioned with the Communist International because he felt they were exploiting Africans for their own purposes and not in the interest of Africans. He therefore decided to devote his life to the cause of African independence and the promotion of Pan-Africanism. He made his home in London where he formed the Committee of the International African Friends of Ethiopia. After Ghana's independence in 1957 he became Dr Nkrumah's adviser on African Affairs, and played a leading role in creating the first Pan-African organisations in Africa. He died suddenly in 1958. He wrote many books of which the most important is *Pan-Africanism or Communism?*

In 1958 Dr Nkrumah was the host to the first conference of independent African states. It was attended by all the fully independent African countries. Eight countries participated at that first Pan-African conference on Africa's own soil: Ghana, Egypt, the Sudan, Tunisia, Morocco, Libya, Liberia and Ethiopia. At the second conference of independent African states held in Addis Abeba in 1960 the numbers of members had risen to fifteen. And when, in 1963, the Organisation of African Unity was formed in Addis Abeba the numbers had risen to twenty-eight.

As can be seen from the list of those who attended the first Pan-African conference in Accra (and all subsequent conferences), the members were drawn from both sides of the Sahara. Although there are some leaders within the Pan-Africanist movement who believe that the search for African unity should be limited, in the first place, to black Africans only, this attitude has never been accepted by the majority of the Pan-African leaders. The Sahara, it is affirmed, is a bridge and not a barrier between African states.

PAN-AFRICANISM: A SUMMING UP

Pan-Africanism, as we have seen, had its roots in what people of African stock felt about themselves and their conditions. These feelings were expressed in songs and poems and hymns and spirituals; they tell of the attitudes of black people, and their aspirations. Gradually these emotional feelings, attitudes and aspirations formed themselves into *ideas* for social and political action. Thus Pan-Africanism evolved from being a movement of emotions and ideas into an organisation with policies of its own. This occurred at the turn of this century when Pan-Africanism emerged as a movement of intellectual protest.

This revolt of the intellectuals was largely confined to people of education who formed the elites of black societies in the New World, in Europe and in Africa. But it had no mass following. Therefore it had no strength as a political movement with roots among the peoples of Africa. The political mass movements of African independence were provided by nationalism.

Described in its simplest terms, nationalism expresses the idea of nationhood, but the strange thing is that although the world is full of nations, and of nations in the making, there is no exact way of defining a nation. One can recognise a nation where one exists, yet there is no satisfactory way of describing nations which can be universally applied.

One of the greatest nationalists of all times, the Italian Mazzini, said that God 'divided Humanity into distinct groups upon the face of our globe, and thus planted the seeds of nations'. A century later this same idea recurred when the Cameroon leader, Ruben Um Nyobe, said in 1952: 'Speaking as a Christian, the whole world recognises that God created a single Cameroon.' However, except in those cases where nations grew around a common language (the 'linguistic nation'), most nations emerged in the way they did largely because of accidents of history. Only an accident explains why the Walloons (the French-speaking community) are part of the Belgian nation and not of the French nation. The same applies to the Flemish community of Belgium whose language and culture is more akin to the Dutch nation. Nations are not pre-ordained in heaven, as Mazzini and Um

Nyobe suggested, but are the products of historical circumstances. This is especially true in Africa.

In the context of Africa, the nation emerges as a supra-tribal community, made up of a number of tribes which either by choice or by compulsion have been joined under a single political authority.

The Senegal leader, Dr Léopold Senghor, suggests as a definition that 'The Nation groups fatherlands in order to transcend them. . . . The Fatherland is the heritage handed down to us by our ancestors: a land, blood, a language or at least a dialect, mores, customs, folklore, art, in one word, a culture rooted in a native soil and expressed by a race'. Applying Senghor's terms to Nigeria, the fatherlands are the Fulani and Hausa country, the Yoruba country, the Ibo and Ibibio country, the Tiv country and so on. Just as the tribe is made up of many families, so the nation is made up of many tribes. In the family the highest loyalty is to the head of the family. In the tribe the highest loyalty is to the tribal authority of the chief or Oba or Emir, etc. In the supra-tribal state (the nation-state) the highest loyalty is to the national authority.

Sometimes these loyalties to family, tribe and nation conflict; this creates difficulties. But in the same way as the tribe demands that its interests must come before the family's, so the nation demands that its interests must come before the tribe's. The way nations are formed is determined by several factors: geographic continuity; established frontiers; dominant political or military forces; and sometimes, too, by economic interests. But different tribal communities seldom merge themselves to form a greater political unity without strong pressures. This might take the form of military conquest, or of political movements. The political forces which encourage, or enforce, the transformation of separate tribal societies into a single nation are those of nationalism.

Nationalism is a political force which promotes the 'idea' of a nation, and which mobilises mass support to make this idea a reality. Thus the 'idea' of a nation exists before the nation itself exists; the 'idea' is formed in the minds of political leaders operating within a particular territory. They fix the constituents of the nation they wish to form as being mainly those people living within the existing frontiers of the territory within which they operate.

In Africa these frontiers are usually those which were artificially created under colonial rule. Thus the people who, by the accident of colonial expansion, happen to find themselves in a particular territory become the constitutent elements of the new nation. Nationalism arose in Africa in response to African demands for independence and freedom from alien rule. This desire for independence was a unifying factor which often transcended tribal interests. It provided a common interest through which the masses could be mobilised irrespective of tribe.

Although African nationalism was born out of the struggle against colonialism, once having sparked off its ideas these could not simply be extinguished when independence was achieved. Besides, in Africa nationalism was not only a force with negative purposes—to destroy colonialism. At an early stage it developed positive aims to create strong, modern societies capable of transforming the lives of the people—economically, educationally and socially—to enable them to take their place as equals in the world community. It has developed as a modernising force which belongs as much to the twentieth-century age of technology and science as to the continent's cultural traditions. This gives it a dual aim: to 'leap the centuries' and to adapt African societies to modern needs, while at the same time promoting a cultural regeneration of African traditions and values.

But nations do not arise overnight. Before a nation can be recognised as an observable fact, not just as an ideal, it must possess a national character and a national spirit. To achieve this it is not necessary that people should lose their ethnic, religious or linguistic identities. In the case of Nigeria, men can still be Hausas, Ibos, Yorubas, Ijaws or Tivs; but they must feel themselves to be a part of a political society whose symbols (the flag, the head of state, the anthem, etc.) transcend those of the tribal or regional society to which individual Nigerians may belong. It is never easy, nor can the pace be forced unnaturally, to achieve a true sense of harmony between different societies, to establish common interests, and to establish a single loyalty to the symbols of the new supra-tribal authority—the state.

First, there is the 'idea of the nation'. Next, there is the political process of working towards the realisation of that 'idea' which is the period of the 'evolving nation'. This is the present state of almost all the new African states.

In this way nationalism plants and spreads the 'idea of the nation'. It then works to keep the idea alive while the seed has time to grow into a nation which (in the words of Léopold Senghor) 'forges a harmonious *ensemble* from its different provinces: a single country for a single people, animated by the same faith, and striving towards the same goal'.

The nationalists are the architects of the nation; but the contractor who does the actual building is the state. In the period of the struggle for independence the nationalist leaders seek to get control of the state, which has been in the hands of the colonial powers, in order to use it for the achievement of their own ideas and objectives. The state includes all the institutions needed by a nation: government and parliament, civil service, police and army, the judiciary, etc.

The state is not the government. The government is only the agent of the state. For while governments may come and go the state remains. And although it is legitimate to oppose the government of the day the state itself cannot be challenged; this is treason.

The state's physical limits are set by the frontiers within which its institutions exercise complete authority. The state's institutions are of crucial importance in the growth of the nation. Jean-Jacques Rousseau wrote: 'It is national institutions which form the genius, the character, the tastes and manners of a people which make it itself and not another people, which inspire it with that ardent patriotism which is based upon customs that cannot be uprooted. Therefore the process of nation-building requires the development of institutions which are in harmony with the habits and qualities of the different constituent elements of the evolving nation.'

The nation-state can be defined as the existence within clearly defined frontiers of people who share common institutions and a common destiny. Their destiny is to achieve a society with a character of its own which will make it distinctive and uniquely different from other societies within the world community. It greatly prizes the sovereignty of the state, that is, its complete right to decide all questions affecting its interests without dictation from outside.

The question that arises from this discussion of the ideas of Pan-Africanism and nationalism is whether these forces are likely to promote conflicting or mutual interests in Africa. For in the same way as nationalism demands a loyalty to the nation which overrides tribal and regional loyalties, so, too, Pan-Africanism demands a loyalty to Africa which overrides purely national loyalties. Africa is seen to be greater than any of its states, just as each state is greater than any of its separate tribal societies.

These interests are not necessarily in conflict with each other. Few nations in Africa are strong enough to be able to build strong states capable of promoting effective economic development, to defend themselves against external attack or, sometimes, even against internal attacks. Through co-operation between African states it is possible to achieve more than if each state were to act entirely on its own. Such co-operation might be developed on a regional basis and also on a wider continental basis.

On the other hand, it is possible to foresee that the majority wishes of a continental organisation—like the Organisation of African Unity—may not always suit the interests of all its members. Nationalism in Africa has been strongly influenced by the sense of a wider community of interests between all Africans. But with the achievement of independence some nationalist movements have shown tendencies towards concentrating mostly on their own country's affairs irrespective of the interests or wishes of others. It is possible, therefore, to describe some nationalist movements as being less strongly Pan-Africanist in outlook than others.

The Pan-Africanist leaders see the creation of the nation-state as only the first step towards creating a wider community of states based on the idea of a single African nationhood. Thus, Tanzania's President Julius Nyerere believes: 'The role of African nationalism is different—or should be different—from the nationalism of the past; that the African national state is an instrument for the unification of Africa and not for dividing Africa; that African nationalism is meaningless, is dangerous, is anachronistic, if it is not at the same time Pan-Africanism.' As against this view, many nationalist leaders see Pan-Africanism as being successful in independent Africa provided it does not weaken the position of individual nation-states. These attitudes contribute to the contemporary debate on Nationalism and Pan-Africanism.

QUESTIONS FOR FURTHER STUDY AND DISCUSSION

1 *Négritude* is both praised and criticised. What do you understand it to be, and give reasons for approving or disapproving of it.

2 Describe the ideas of the following three pioneers of Pan-Africanism: Marcus Garvey, Dr Du Bois, George Padmore.

3 Consider the relationship of nationalism and tribalism in the Pan-African movement.

SELECT BIBLIOGRAPHY

American Society of African Culture, *Pan-Africanism Reconsidered*, University of California Press, 1962.

C. Legum, *Pan-Africanism: A Short Political Guide*, Pall Mall, 1962.

N. Azikiwe, *The Future of Pan-Africanism*, Daily Times, Lagos, 1964.

G. Padmore, *Pan-Africanism or Communism?*, Dobson, 1956.

K. Nkrumah, *Africa Must Unite*, Heinemann, 1963.

W. E. B. Du Bois, *Soul of Black Folks*, A. C. McClurg & Co., Chicago, 1903.

—— *The World and Africa*, Viking, New York, 1947.

—— *Black Reconstruction*, Albert Saifer, Philadelphia, 1935.

T. Hodgkin, *Nationalism in Colonial Africa*, Muller, 1956.

L. Senghor, *Nationhood and the African Road to Socialism*, Présence Africaine, 1961.

M. Dia, *African Nations and World Solidarity*, Thames & Hudson, 1962.

M. Garvey, *Philosophy and Opinions*, 2 vols., Universal Publishing House, New York, 1926.

Index

Abbās II (Hilmi), Khedive, 176
Abbas, Ferhat, 200, 207, 211, 213
Abd al-Qādir, 295
Abd al-Salam, 296
Abdel Karim, 209
Abdullāhi, Khalīfa, 179
Abdullāhi, of Sokoto, 298, 300
Abeokuta, 112, 268; established, 263; Dahomean attacks on, 264, 266
Abidjan, 316
Abiodun, 259
Abonnema, 276, 278
Abora, 246, 248
Abrahams, Peter, 27
Abruquah, Joseph, 27
Accra, 328
Achebe, Chinua, 312
Achimota, 321
Adamanso, Asante victory at, 248
Adamawa, 283
Adams, John, 526
Adandozan, king of Dahomey, 260
Addis Abeba, 225, 227, 229, 232, 533
Adegun, Onikoyi, 261, 262
Adolo, Oba of Benin, 273
Adwa, Italian defeat, 127
African history, and purposes of school education, 1, 10–13; nature of, 1–2, 14; assets of, 2–3; challenges in teaching, 3–5; lacunae, 5–6; Western historians and, 6–8; teaching for School Certificate, 16–8; primary school teaching of, 18–19; pre-School Certificate teaching, 19–22; in transition from school to university, 22–5; methodology of teaching, 25–6; reading for, 26–7; oral work in study of, 27–9; written work in study of, 29–30; notes in study of, 30–3; essays on, 33–5
African National Congress, 427, 429, 432, 436, 437, 519
African Studies, as primary school subject, 19
Afrikaner, Jager, 411
Afrikaner, Jonker, 411, 414

Afrikaner Bond, 405
Afrikaner National Party, 427
Agaja, king of Dahomey, 257, 258
Agbebi, Majola, 529
Agbor, 272
Agonglo, king of Dahomey, 260
Agriculture, beginnings of, 48, 50, 52
Ahmadiyya, the, 161
Ahmad Urābi, Colonel (Arab Pasha), 116, 117
Ahmadu, Seku, 292, 301–3, 305
Ahmadu II, 302
Ahmadu III, 302–3, 304
Aja, the, 255, 256, 257
Akan peoples, origin of, 245
Akassa, 276
Akim, 80
Akitoye, 137, 138
Akran, chief of Portuguese Town, 137
Aksum, 71, 72, 87
Akwamu, 80
Al-Afghani, Djamal al-Din, 200
Alal al Fassi, 207
Albert, Lake, 84
Albuquerque, Tovar de, 289
Al-Daftardar, Muhammad Bey Khusraw, 167, 169, 170, 178
Algeria, 110, 152, 184–7, 314; economic pattern imposed by French, 145; settlers' attitude to race, 159; nationalist movement, 210–14; independence, 213, 214
Al-Hadirah group, 200
Al-hājj Muhammad, 291
Al-Hājj 'Umar, 237, 238, 240, 292, 302, 303–4, 305
Alibawa, the, 301
Alkalawa, Gobir capital, 293, 298, 299
Al-Kānemī, 299, 302, 303
Allada, 255, 256, 257
Al-Maghīlī, 297
Almohads, 89–90
Almoravids, 89, 90, 97
Al-Sharqāwi, Shaikh, 165
Amachree, King, 278

Shona, 511; arrival in Central Africa, 504; accept European settlement, 509

Shona-Rozwi kingdom, 505

Sierra Leone, 21, 63; slave trade, 100, 101, 108; becomes British colony, 110; elite in, 151, 152, 157; peoples of, 238–240; Britain's interest in, 242; a British protectorate, 242; colonial period begins, 308; constitutional advances, 323–4

Sifawa, 300

Sinnār, Fūnj Sultanate of, 167, 169

Slavery (and slave trade), in Forest Areas, 80; Portuguese and, 82, 98–100; 101–2, 289; in East Africa, 86, 105; institution of, 92–3; domestic, 93–5; voluntary, 93–4; Islam and, 94, 95–7, beginnings of trade, 95–6; Arabs and, 97–8; Dutch and, 101; British and, 100–101, 112; among the Wolof, 236–7; in Dahomey, 259–60; on Nigerian coast, 276; abolition, 276; in Congo, 285; in Angola, 289

Slessor, Mary, 312

Smelting, discovery of, 51

Smith, Adam, 308

So culture. See Sao

Sofala, 54, 55

Sofas, the, 242

Sokoto, 301, 302, 303; jihād, 293–9; and Bornu, 299–300

Sokoto, Sardauna of, 320

Somaliland, 113, 232

Songhay, mediaeval empire, 55, 291; copper importation, 66

Songye, the, 82

Soninke, the, 291, 301

South(ern) Africa, archaeological sites, 53–4; geographical region, 82–4, 338; Bantu in, 82–3; Hottentots in, 83; struggle between Bantu, Boers and British begins, 84; slave labour, 102; British-Boer rivalry, 127–8; Rhodes's ambitions, 128; role of missionaries, 142–3, 151; economic pattern imposed by settlers, 146; social effects of white man's activity, 146–7; displacement of Africans in services, 158; early history, 339–41; Bantu replace Bushmen and Hottentots, 341; Bantu culture, 342–6;

immigrants, 346–9; race relations, 349–355; modern history of, 379–417; nationalism in, 419–39. See also Union of South Africa

Southern Rhodesia, becomes self-governing colony, 514; European population, 515; Land Apportionment Act, 515; racial segregation, 516; African trade unions rejected, 517; belated African political activity, 518; support for federation, 519, 520, 521, 522; African nationalism roused, 523–4; state of emergency, 524; new constitution, 525. See also Rhodesia

Spain, and Morocco, 188

Spear, introduction of, 47

Speke, John, 106

Stanley, H. M., 116

Steel metallurgy, lack of knowledge of, 61

Stone Age, in Africa, 46–50

Stone-carving, 70

Stratification, as archaeological evidence, 42–4

Sudan, 160–1; decline of, 69; British conquest, 127; Mahdist revolt, 123, 125, 178–9; invaded by Muhammad Ali, 167, 169–70; Egyptian régime, 177–8; independence, 525

Sudan 'belt', microlithic industries, 47; early brass industries, 66, 67; decline of, 69; geographical region, 76–9; languages of, 78; trade routes, 78; effect of trade, 79; Islam and, 79

Suez Canal, 202, 203; Britain acquires Khedive's shares in, 114; Britain and, 117; France and, 117

Sullebawa, the, 294, 298, 301

Sunni 'Ali, 291

Susus, the, 239

Swahili culture, in East Africa, 86

Sweet potatoes, introduced to Africa, 52

Tabkin Kwotto, 297

Tafari Mekwennin. See Haile Sellassie I

Takedda, 66

Tanganyika, 145, 313; Germany and, 122–3; small African elite, 157; independence, 525

Tangier, 188

I Showcase for the display of African Art.

II Historical models made by the associate students of the Institute
of Education, Ibadan University, and based on R. E. Crookall,
Historical Model-making for African Schools, U.L.P., 1964.

III A scene from *Usuman dan Fodio*, a classroom play written and produced by postgraduate students of the Institute of Education, Ibadan University.

IV The cast of *Usuman dan Fodio*.

V An example of late Meroitic architecture showing Egyptian, Greek and Roman influences.

(*Photo:* Denis Williams)

VI Wrought-iron shrine figure said to have been made for the cult of Gu, god of iron and war. It is the largest piece of wrought-iron sculpture known from Africa and is 5 ft. 5 in. high.

VII Brass-smith's equipment, Northern Nigeria, showing grooved clay moulds, crucibles, file, punches and two cast brass bracelets.

(*Photo:* Denis Williams)

VIII Ibo bells, British Museum Collection.

(*Photo:* Denis Williams)

IX Yoruba sacred bronze, Nigeria.

(*Photo:* Frank Speed)

X Nok terracotta head, Nigeria.

(*Photo:* Frank Speed)

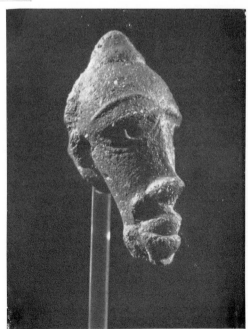

XI Palace of Amanishakete, Meroë, showing brick walls, pillars and remains of plaster dressing.

(*Photo:* Denis Williams)

XII Temple of Hatshepset, Der al-Bahri, Egypt.

XIII and XIV Monolith, Aksum, Ethiopia, about 70 ft. high, decorated in the likeness of a nine-storey building, dated beginning of the Christian era.

XV Rockhewn Church of St George, Lalibela, Ethiopia, shaped in a single piece, c. A.D. 1200.

XVI Castle of Iyasu the Great, Gonder, Ethiopia, A.D. 1700.

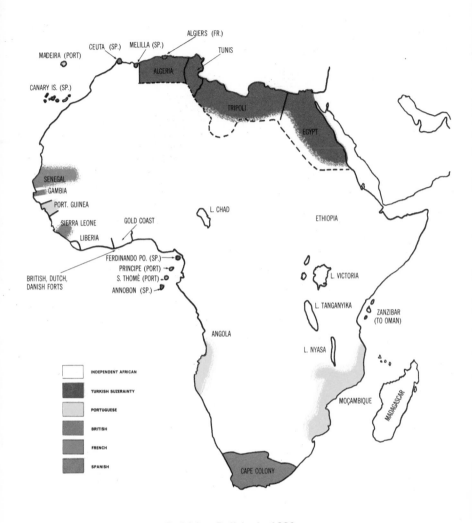

MADEIRA (PORT)

CANARY IS. (SP.)

CEUTA (SP.)   MELILLA (SP.)   ALGIERS (FR.)
                                  TUNIS
ALGERIA
TRIPOLI
EGYPT

SENEGAL
GAMBIA
PORT. GUINEA
SIERRA LEONE   GOLD COAST
LIBERIA

L. CHAD

ETHIOPIA

BRITISH, DUTCH,
DANISH FORTS

FERDINANDO PO. (SP.)
PRINCIPE (PORT)
S. THOMÉ (PORT)
ANNOBON (SP.)

L. VICTORIA

L. TANGANYIKA   ZANZIBAR
                (TO OMAN)

ANGOLA

L. NYASA

MOÇAMBIQUE

MADAGASCAR

INDEPENDENT AFRICAN

TURKISH SUZERAINTY

PORTUGUESE

BRITISH

FRENCH

SPANISH

CAPE COLONY

C Africa Political: 1830

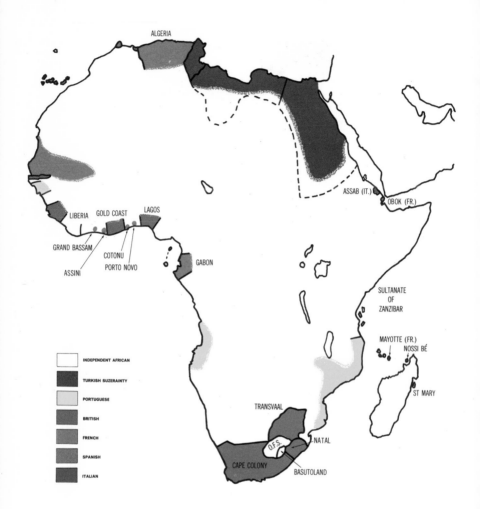

ALGERIA

LIBERIA GOLD COAST LAGOS

GRAND BASSAM

COTONU
ASSINI PORTO NOVO

GABON

ASSAB (IT.)
OBOK (FR.)

SULTANATE
OF
ZANZIBAR

MAYOTTE (FR.)
NOSSI BÉ

ST MARY

TRANSVAAL

NATAL
O.F.S.
CAPE COLONY BASUTOLAND

INDEPENDENT AFRICAN

TURKISH SUZERAINTY

PORTUGUESE

BRITISH

FRENCH

SPANISH

ITALIAN

D Africa Political: 1880

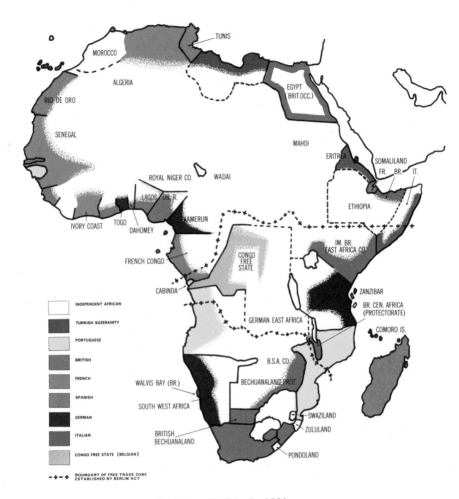

	INDEPENDENT AFRICAN
	TURKISH SUZERAINTY
	PORTUGUESE
	BRITISH
	FRENCH
	SPANISH
	GERMAN
	ITALIAN
	CONGO FREE STATE (BELGIAN)
⁻⁺⁻⁺⁻⁺	BOUNDARY OF FREE TRADE ZONE ESTABLISHED BY BERLIN ACT

Map labels:
TUNIS
MOROCCO
ALGERIA
RIO DE ORO
SENEGAL
EGYPT (BRIT.OCC.)
MAHDI
ERITREA
SOMALILAND FR. BR. IT.
ROYAL NIGER CO.
WADAI
LAGOS OIL R.
KAMERUN
ETHIOPIA
IVORY COAST
TOGO
DAHOMEY
FRENCH CONGO
CONGO FREE STATE
IM. BR. EAST AFRICA CO.
CABINDA
ZANZIBAR
BR. CEN. AFRICA (PROTECTORATE)
GERMAN EAST AFRICA
COMORO IS.
B.S.A. CO.
WALVIS BAY (BR.)
BECHUANALAND PROT.
SOUTH WEST AFRICA
SWAZILAND
ZULULAND
BRITISH BECHUANALAND
PONDOLAND

E Africa Political: 1891

SP. MOROCCO

CANARY IS.

IFNI

RIO DE ORO

LIBYA

GA.

P.GU.

S.LE.

LI.

GOLD COAST
TOGOLAND

SP. GUINEA

NIGERIA (NORTH)

(SOUTH)

FR.
EQUAT. AFRICA

ANGLO EGYPTIAN SUDAN
(CONDOMINIUM)

EMPIRE OF
ETHIOPIA

FR. EQ. AF.

BELGIAN CONGO

UGANDA

BRITISH
EAST AFRICA

NYASALAND

NORTH
RHODESIA

SOUTH
RHODESIA

BECHUANALAND

UNION OF
SOUTH AFRICA

SWAZILAND

BASUTOLAND
(BR. PROTECTORATES)

INDEPENDENT AFRICAN

PORTUGUESE

BRITISH

FRENCH

SPANISH

GERMAN

ITALIAN

CONGO FREE STATE (BELGIAN)

F Africa Political: 1914

TANGIER
(INTERNATIONAL)
SP. MOROCCO
IFNI
MOROCCO
TUNISIA
RIO DE ORO
ALGERIA
EGYPT
GAMBIA
FRENCH WEST AFRICA
PORT.
GUINEA
SIERRA LEONE
LIBERIA
GOLD COAST
TOGOLAND
CAMEROONS
FR.
EQUAT. AFRICA
SP. GUINEA
CABINDA
KENYA
TANGANYIKA
ZANZIBAR
SOUTH
WEST
AFRICA

INDEPENDENT AFRICAN
PORTUGUESE
BRITISH
BRITISH MANDATE
FRENCH
FRENCH MANDATE
SPANISH
ITALIAN
CONGO FREE STATE (BELGIAN)
BELGIAN MANDATE

G Africa Political: 1924

AFRICA 1965

U.S.S.R.

Caspian Sea

TEHRAN
IRAN

Black Sea

Sofia
BULGARIA
Tirana ALBANIA
ISTANBUL
ANKARA
TURKEY
YUGOSLAVIA

ITALY
ROME
NAPLES
Sardinia (It.)
Corsica (Fr.)

ATHENS
GREECE
Crete

Cyprus

Sicily

C. Bon
Tunis
Sfax
TUNISIA
March 1956
Tripoli
Benghazi

ALGERIA
July 1962

Algiers
Oran
Constantine
Bône

BARCELONA
MADRID
SPAIN
PORTUGAL
Lisbon
Gibraltar (Br.)
Tangier
Rabat
Fez
Casablanca
MOROCCO
Marrakesh March 1956

Madeira (Port.)

Canary Islands (Sp.)
Las Palmas

IFNI (Sp.)
El Aaiun

SPANISH SAHARA

Villa Cisneros
C. Blanc

MAURITANIA
Nov.1960
Nouakchott
Tidjikja

Str. of Gibraltar

Mediterranean Sea

Ghat

Ahaggar Mts
2973
Tamanrasset

LIBYA
Dec.1951

Tropic of Cancer

MALI
Sept.1960
Timbuktu
Bamako

Niger

Ouagadougou
Aug.1960
UPPER VOLTA

SENEGAL
St. Louis
C.Verde Aug.1960
Dakar
GAMBIA
Bathurst
PORT. GUINEA
Port Bissau
GUINEA
Oct.1958
Conakry
SIERRA LEONE
April 1961
Freetown
LIBERIA
July 1847
Monrovia

IVORY COAST
Aug.1960
Abidjan

GHANA
March 1957
Kumasi
Accra
Sekondi
Takoradi

TOGO April 1960
DAHOMEY Aug. 1960
GAMBIA Feb. 1965

Lomé
Porto Novo
DAHOMEY
TOGO

Niger

NIGER
Aug.1960

Agadès

Niamey

Kano
Kaduna
Maiduguri

NIGERIA
Oct.1960
Ibadan
Lagos
Benin
Enugu
Port Harcourt
Fernando Poo (Sp.)
Principe (Port.)
São Tomé (Port.)

Gulf of Guinea
Equator

CHAD
Aug.1960
L. Chad
Ft. Lamy
Shari

CAMEROON
Jan.1960
Douala
Yaoundé
RIO MUNI (Sp.)
Libreville

CENTRAL AFRICAN REPUBLIC
Aug.1960
Bangui
Ubangi
Congo
GABON Aug.1960

Stanleyville

SUDAN
Jan.1956
Khartoum
Omdurman
El Obeid
Nyala
Wau
White Nile
Blue Nile
Atbara

ETHIOPIA
Asmara
Addis Ababa
FR. SOM.
Djibouti

SOMALI REP.
July 1960
Hargeisa
C. Guardafui
Gulf of Aden
Aden (Br.)
SOUTH ARABIA FED.
Mogadishu

YEMEN
San'a

SAUDI ARABIA
Riyadh
Mecca
Medina
QATAR
Persian Gulf
Kuwait
Basra
Baghdad
IRAQ
Tigris
Euphrates
Damascus
SYRIA
Beirut
LEBANON
ISRAEL
Jerusalem
JORDAN
Amman
Port Said
Suez
Suez Can.
CAIRO
Pyramids
ALEXANDRIA

U.A.R.
EGYPT
March 1922
Aswân
Aswân Dam

Red Sea
Port Sudan

Nile

KENYA
UGANDA
Oct.1962
Kampala
Entebbe
L. Victoria
L. Albert
L. Rudolf
L. Kyoga
Nakuru

ATLANTIC OCEAN

SCALE
1:37
million

Ascension
(Br.)

O C E A N

St Helena
(Br.)

Tropic of Capricorn

Tristan da Cunha
(Br.)

CABINDA
(Port.)
Matadi
Léopoldville June 1960
Luanda
Lobito
Benguela
Walvis Bay
Windhoek

ANGOLA
(Port.)

SOUTH
WEST
AFRICA
(S.A.)

Cuanza
Cubango
Cuando
L. Ngami
Okavango

Cape Town
C. of Good Hope

C O N G O

Elisabethville
Jadotville
Ndola
ZAMBIA Oct.1964
Lusaka
Kariba Lake
Victoria Falls
Serowe
Gaberones
Kimberley
Bloemfontein
JOHANNESBURG

BECHUANALAND
(Br.)

REP. OF
SOUTH AFRICA
C. Agulhas

Port Elizabeth

East London

L. Mweru
L. Tanganyika
L. Bangweulu

TANZANIA
Dec.1961
Tabora
Dodoma
L. Nyasa

MALAWI
10/1964
Zambezi
Blantyre
Zomba

RHODESIA
Oct.1964
Bulawayo
Limpopo
Pretoria
Vaal

BASUTOLAND
(Br.)
Pietermaritzburg
Durban
SWAZILAND
(Br.)

MOZAMBIQUE
(Port.)
Mozambique
Beira
Lourenço Marques

Pemba
Zanzibar
Dar-es-Salaam

Comoro
Islands
(Fr.)

Aldabra Is.
(Br.)

MALAGASY REP.
(June 1960)
Tamatave
Tananarive

Mozambique Channel

I N D I A N

O C E A N

40°

20°

0°

20°

SCALE
0   500   1000   1500 Miles
0   500 1000 1500 2000 2500 Kms
Zenithal Equal Area Projection

H Africa Political: 1965
Independence dates are shown in red

©Thomas Nelson and Sons Ltd.(C100)

Pocket
inside

oil

ABYSSINIAN

HIGHLANDS

Kenya
Highlands

copper
✗

Libyan Desert

oil

S A H A R A

D E S E R T

oil

oil

oil

✗ phosphates

oil

tin columbite
✗

coal
✗

oil

phosphates
✗
✗
bauxite ✗
gold ✗
manganese

manganese

phosphates

iron
✗ iron

iron
✗

bauxite
✗
diamonds
✗

Tropic of Cancer

iron
✗

A   T   L   A   N   T   I   C

Equator

02